P9-DCW-841

Handbook of Child and Adolescent Sexual Problems

Series in Scientific Foundations of Clinical and Counseling Psychology
Eugene Walker, Series Editor

Robert G. Meyer, Practical Clinical Hypnosis: Techniques and Applications (1992)

John M. Reisman and Sheila Ribordy, Principles of Psychotherapy with Children, Second Edition (1993)

Vincent B. Van Hasselt and Michel Hersen, Handbook of Adolescent Psychopathology: A Guide to Diagnosis and Treatment (1995)

George A. Rekers, Handbook of Child and Adolescent Sexual Problems (1995)

Handbook of Child and Adolescent Sexual Problems

Edited by

George A. Rekers

LEXINGTON BOOKS
An Imprint of The Free Press
NEW YORK   LONDON   TORONTO   SYDNEY   TOKYO   SINGAPORE

Library of Congress Cataloging-in-Publication Data

Handbook of child and adolescent sexual problems / edited by George A.
  Rekers.
      p.   cm. — (Series in scientific foundations of clinical and
  counseling psychology)
      ISBN 0-02-926317-4
      1. Psycholosexual disorders in children—Handbooks, manuals, etc.
  2. Psychosexual disorders in adolescence—Handbooks, manuals, etc.
  3. Sexually abused children—Handbooks, manuals, etc.   4. Sexually
  abused teenagers—Handbooks, manuals, etc.   I. Rekers, George Allen.
  II. Series.
      [DNLM: 1. Sex Behavior—in infancy & childhood—handbooks.   2. Sex
  Behavior—in adolescense—handbooks.   3. Psychosexual Development—
  in infancy & childhood—handbooks.   4. Psychosexual Development—in
  adolescence—handbooks.   5. Child Abuse, Sexual—handbooks.   WM 34
  H2353   1995]
  RJ506.P72H36   1995
  618.92´8583—dc20
  DNLM/DLC
  for Library of Congress   94-40653
                                                                    CIP

Lexington Books
An Imprint of Macmillan, Inc.
866 Third Avenue, New York, N.Y. 10022

Maxwell Macmillan Canada, Inc.
1200 Eglinton Avenue East
Suite 200
Don Mills, Ontario, M3C 3N1

Macmillan, Inc. is part of the Maxwell Communication Group of Companies

Printed in the United States of America

printing number

1 2 3 4 5 6 7 8 9 10

Contents

Part 5   Problems of Sexual Behavior

Preface

This reference handbook provides the practitioner, for the first time, with a comprehensive summary of clinical procedures for the broad spectrum of both common and rare sexual problems seen in minors. Although there are excellent books on selected subsets of the more common childhood or adolescent sexual problems—for example, child sexual abuse, unwed adolescent pregnancy, sex education, or adolescent sex offenders—presently there is no other multidisciplinary handbook that covers all the sexual disorders comprehensively in one volume. This reference manual is designed to be at the fingertips of the busy, practicing child professional who needs up-to-date, state-of-the-art reviews of clinical procedures not only for these common childhood sexual problems, but also for the relatively rare disorders they encounter such as sexual asphyxias, eroticized repetitive hangings, specific fetishes, gender identity disorders, specific physical anomalies in sexual development, sexual adjustment problems of handicapped children and youth, juvenile prostitution, or risk-taking homosexual behavior.

These handbook chapters provide specific reviews of available diagnostic assessment and treatment procedures for individual sexual disorders in sufficient detail for direct, immediate application by child and adolescent clinicians. For general practitioners and nonclinicians also working with children and teenagers, I also asked the authors of the clinical practice–oriented chapters to equip the nonspecialist in sexual problems with information concerning effective screening of patients for potential referral for necessary treatment. For this reason, concerned parents, parent educators, and school teachers can also use this manual to help them identify children and teenagers with potential needs for professional help. Parents, educators, and clinicians will also find this handbook to be a detailed guide and reference book for the sex education of children and youth.

I would like to express my appreciation to the series editor, C. Eugene Walker, for providing the opportunity to develop this project; to Margaret N. Zusky, senior editor, and Tammy Fergus, assistant editor, at Lexington Books, for their essential contributions; and to Josephine Evans, for her word processing of portions of the handbook manuscript. I also wish to express my special thanks to the many authors of these handbook chapters. Because child and adolescent sexual problems are addressed by a variety of helping professionals, the chapters of this handbook were authored or coauthored by leading experts from the fields of clinical child psychology, medicine, clinical social work, psychiatric nursing, child psychiatry, pediatrics, pediatric nursing, psychoendocrinology, family life education, sex education, experimental psychology, and sociology. It is my hope that many child professionals in these and related fields will find this handbook useful in helping many children and adolescents to achieve sexual adjustment.

—George A. Rekers

Contributors

William B. Arndt, Jr., Ph.D., Psychologist. Professor of Psychology, University of Missouri, Kansas City

Christopher Bagley, Ph.D., Clinical Social Worker. Professor, Faculty of Social Work, University of Calgary, Alberta, Canada

John M.W. Bradford, M.B., ChB., FRCPC, Psychiatrist. Director of Forensic Service, and Director of Sexual Behaviours Clinic, Royal Ottawa Hospital, and Professor of Psychiatry, Faculty of Medicine, University of Ottawa, Ontario, Canada

Ann Wolbert Burgess, D.N.Sc., R.N., FAAN, Psychiatric Nurse Specialist. van Ameringen Professor and Division Chair, Psychiatric Mental Health Nursing, University of Pennsylvania School of Nursing

Rochelle L. Cherpak, Research Assistant, Psychoendocrinology. Division of Child and Adolescent Psychiatry, Children's Hospital of Buffalo

Steven P. Cuffe, M.D., Child and Adolescent Psychiatrist. Research Director, Abuse Recovery Center, and Assistant Professor of Neuropsychiatry and Behavioral Science, University of South Carolina School of Medicine

Donna Cook Culley, Ph.D., Forensic Clinical Child Psychologist. Chief Psychologist, South Carolina Department of Juvenile Justice, and Assistant Professor of Neuropsychiatry and Behavioral Science, University of South Carolina School of Medicine

Kim Dobson, M.D., Child and Adolescent Psychiatrist. Clinical Assistant Instructor in Psychiatry, Division of Child and Adolescent Psychiatry, School of Medicine, State University of New York at Buffalo

Kathleen Coulborn Faller, Ph.D., A.C.S.W., Clinical Social Worker. Professor, School of Social Work; Director, Family Assessment Clinic; and Co-director, Interdisciplinary Project on Child Abuse and Neglect, University of Michigan, Ann Arbor

Clyde H. Flanagan, Jr., M.D., FACP, Child and Adolescent Psychiatrist. Director of Psychoanalyic Training, and Clinical Professor of Neuropsychiatry and Behavioral Science, University of South Carolina School of Medicine

Sandra B. Frick-Helms, R.N., Ph.D., Pediatric Nurse and Registered Play Therapist-Supervisor. Associate Professor of Nursing, Director of Play Therapy and Community Education, and Adjunct Associate Professor of Neuropsychiatry and Behavioral Science, University of South Carolina College of Nursing and College of Medicine

Thomas Gratzer, M.D., Psychiatry Resident. Department of Psychiatry, University of Ottawa, Ontario, Canada

Carol R. Hartman, R.N., D.N.Sc., Psychiatric Nurse Specialist. Professor of Psychiatric Mental Health Nursing, Boston College School of Nursing

Mark D. Kilgus, M.D., Ph.D., Child and Adolescent Psychiatrist. Assistant Professor of Neuropsychiatry and Behavioral Science, University of South Carolina School of Medicine

Brett R. Kuhn, Ph.D., Clinical Child and Adolescent Psychologist. Assistant Professor of Pediatrics, Meyer Rehabilitation Institute, University of Nebraska Medical Center

Michael S. Lundy, M.D., M.S., Child and Adolescent Psychiatrist. Associate Professor of Neuropsychiatry and Behavioral Science, University of South Carolina School of Medicine

Tom Mazur, Psy.D., Pediatric Psychologist. Clinical Assistant Professor of Psychiatry and Pediatrics, School of Medicine, State University of New York at Buffalo, and Director of Psychoendocrinology, Division of Child and Adolescent Psychiatry, Children's Hospital of Buffalo

Gregory Motayne, M.D., Psychiatry Resident. Department of Psychiatry, University of Ottawa, Ontario, Canada

Patrick W. Nolten, Ph.D., School Psychologist. Department of Pediatrics, Meyer Rehabilitation Institute, University of Nebraska Medical Center

Anne Pawlak, M.D., Psychiatry Resident. Department of Psychiatry, University of Ottawa, Ontario, Canada

David L. Petty, Ph.D., Sociologist and Sex Educator. Professor of Sociology, Stephen F. Austin State University

George A. Rekers, Ph.D, FAClinP, Clinical Child and Adolescent Psychologist. Diplomate in Clinical Psychology, ABPP, and Professor of Neuropsychiatry and Behavioral Science, University of South Carolina School of Medicine

Walter R. Schumm, Ph.D., Family Life Educator. Professor of Human Development and Family Studies, Kansas State University

William J. Warzak, Ph.D., Clinical Child and Adolescent Psychologist. Associate Professor of Pediatrics, Meyer Rehabilitation Institute, University of Nebraska Medical Center

Part 1

Early Identification and Prevention of Sexual Problems

1

Early Detection and Treatment of Sexual Problems

An Introductory Overview

George A. Rekers

Professionals who work with children and adolescents face many opportunities to identify and treat a wide variety of sexual adjustment problems. The early detection of sexual problems in youth permits treatment interventions that can prevent the embarrassing and distressing sexual disorders of adulthood, many of which are much more difficult to treat in the adult years (Rekers, 1981a, 1992). But identifying children and adolescents at high risk for adulthood sexual disorders can be a difficult task for the clinician who does not specialize in sexual disorders. And yet, at the same time, the preventive treatment of child and adolescent sexual problems in the greater population requires that the nonspecialist in sexual disorders be equipped to recognize, treat, and/or refer young patients for appropriate interventions (Rekers, 1991a, 1991b; Rekers & Milner, 1979). This handbook is a response to the need for an up-to-date review of the psychological, family, social, and medical factors involved in the development and perpetuation of each sexual disorder; it is designed to equip busy practicing clinicians with the most accurate diagnostic methods and interventions for such disorders.

Clinical Issues Regarding Child and Adolescent Sexuality

Professionals are better able to take appropriate steps to assist children and adolescents when equipped with up-to-date reviews of scientific and clinical literature that address the questions they face in their professional practice:

• What is the basis for a definition of this specific sexual problem?

3

- What are the developmental norms to which this child's behavior can be compared?
- What are the childhood diagnostic indicators of a potentially developing adult sexual disorder?

Early Detection of Initial Symptoms of a Developing Sexual Problem

Not all forms of sexual variance in youth constitute sexual disorders per se, for example, the symptoms and sexual adjustment of child or adolescent victims of sexual assault. In other cases, the early development of a sexual deviation can involve one or more symptoms that do not yet cluster in a way to warrant a diagnosis of a sexual disorder, and yet it would serve the interests of the child and society to intervene before the problem becomes a fully developed disorder with its attendant psychological distress and/or social disruption (Rekers, 1978, 1981b). For these reasons, the accurate detection of child and adolescent sexual problems necessitating clinical attention is more complex and subtle than the diagnosis of a fully developed adulthood sexual disorder where the clinician matches adulthood manifestations of sexuality to established diagnostic criteria (American Psychiatric Association, 1994). In this context, it is generally helpful for a clinician to evaluate a given child or adolescent across the major dimensions of sex and gender (Rekers, 1991a):

- Physical sex
- Social assignment
- Gender identity
- Sex role identity
- Sexual arousal
- Gender role
- Sexual behavior

These dimensions of sex and gender are defined in Table 12–1 and the accompanying discussion in Chapter 12. Any incongruity across these dimensions of sex and gender can constitute a form of sexual deviance or variance that is a potential source of psychological and/or social conflict, even prior to the full development of a sexual disorder per se (Rekers, 1986; Rosen & Rekers, 1980).

Etiological Questions, Diagnostic Issues, and Assessment Pertaining to Sexuality

Professionals will encounter the questions of children, adolescents, parents, and child caretakers regarding what is sexually normal and what is sexually deviant (Rekers, 1985, 1988; Rekers & Swihart, 1984). For example, clinicians are asked about specific sexual behavior patterns, sexual identity issues, masculine and feminine role behaviors, boy–girl relations, and the adjustments to the various phases of pubertal development (Rekers, 1984, 1986, 1992; Schumm & Rekers, 1984). For this reason, I invited leading child research scholars and practicing clinicians to contribute chapters in their areas of expertise to present currently available methods for the accurate detection and assessment of sexual problems in children, and also to assist the clinician in answering parental questions regarding what is normal versus what is atypical in a particular child.

Parents often ask their child's clinician questions that boil down to these kinds of general inquiries:

- Is my child's sexual behavior pattern normal or abnormal?
- What does this atypical sexual behavior mean to my child?
- Is this sexual behavior just normal curiosity or is it a sign of a developing deviation?
- Is my child physically normal, or is the sexual problem caused by a genetic or other physical defect?
- Does my child need treatment for a potential sexual problem?
- What are the chances that my child will have a normal adult sex life?

To answer such questions requires that the clinician understand the scientific evidence concerning both the etiology of specific sexual conditions (e.g., Byne & Parsons, 1993; Rekers, 1992; Rekers, Crandall, Rosen, & Bentler, 1979) and how a sexual problem manifests itself at different ages and at different stages of its development. To acquire such knowledge, the clinician must have access to data collected on individuals over an extended period of time (Kendall, 1984). Of course, as children grow up, they must all make a number of developmental adjustments pertaining to their sexual status and maturation before and during puberty (Rekers, 1992). Child-helping professionals need to be prepared with knowledge of normal psychosexual development (e.g., Rekers, Amaro-Plotkin, & Low, 1977; Rekers, Sanders, Strauss, Rasbury, & Morey, 1989) and the various sexual disorders in order to reassure concerned parents about what may very well be normal phases of development (Rekers, 1992). On the other hand, these same professionals need to screen for different symptom patterns that would indicate the possible presence of a developing psychosexual disturbance. The sexual problems of adults are often the source of considerable emotional suffering, and a number of them are also very resistant to therapeutic change during the adulthood years. But many adult sexual problems have their precursors in the childhood and adolescent years—a time in life when therapeutic intervention holds substantial potential for the greatest lifetime change. Therefore, in many cases, the preferred approach is prevention: detecting symptoms of sexual adjustment problems early enough in childhood or adolescence to intervene in ways to prevent later adulthood sexual maladjustment (Rekers, 1991b).

For some childhood and adolescent sexual problems, some data exists in the professional literature to provide very specific answers to parental inquiries. The chapters in this book review such available research findings. However, for some sexual problems longitudinal research has not yet been conducted, and for yet other sexual problems assessment techniques differ depending upon the age of the person. Thus the data are difficult to compare even within the same individual over time. This handbook reports on the state of the art of knowledge on each specific child or adolescent sexual disorder, so that the clinician can accurately answer parental questions where definitive answers are known, and inform parents where scientific information is currently lacking.

Treatment Questions and Intervention Procedures for Sexual Problems

Once diagnostic assessment of their child has been completed, parents typically ask further questions (Ferguson & Rekers, 1979; Rekers, 1980) that boil down to these types of inquiries:

- What are the chances that my child will achieve a normal adult sexual adjustment *without* treatment now in childhood or adolescence?
- Is psychotherapy or some other treatment recommended?
- If so, what will be the treatment goals?
- What are the potential benefits of treatment for my child?
- What are the chances that my child will achieve a normal adult sexual adjustment *with* treatment now in childhood or adolescence?
- How will other children react to my child's sexual pattern?
- How will peer reaction affect my child's sexual adjustment?

The treatment chapters of this handbook were designed to assist the clinician not only in answering such parental questions, but also in formulating specific treatment plans. The currently available findings on empirical treatment outcome studies are presented, when available (e.g., Rekers, Kilgus, & Rosen, 1990), together with a discussion of professional and ethical issues involved in clinical decision making. When detailed treatment research is unavailable for a specific disorder, the current conventional treatment approaches by leading specialists in the field are presented in this handbook.

Overview of the Organization and Content of This Handbook

Part 1: Early Identification and Prevention of Sexual Problems

In addition to the present overview chapter, Part 1 contains two other introductory chapters that are designed to provide an orientation to diagnostic assessment methods for detecting childhood and adolescent sexual problems, and to present practical methods for meeting the needs for sex education in all children to prevent sexual maladjustment:

Chapter 2 was written by Donna Cook Culley, a clinical child and adolescent psychologist, and Clyde H. Flanagan, Jr., a child and adolescent psychiatrist and psychoanalyst. As psychodiagnostic specialists, they provide a review of issues and procedures involved in the "Assessment of Sexual Problems in Childhood and Adolescence." Culley and Flanagan realistically discuss the unique issues and particular difficulties faced by the clinician who (1) starts with a presenting problem of a sexual nature, (2) proceeds to assessing for a potential sexual problem, (3) interprets the assessment data, and (4) formulates a diagnosis, if any. Through use of case examples, they illustrate the contributions and limitations of clinical interview methods, selected psychological tests, and sexual anatomically correct dolls.

In Chapter 3, David L. Petty, a sex educator and sociologist, presents a very practical discussion of "Sex Education toward the Prevention of Sexual Problems." Petty presents a practical procedure for providing preventative sex education to all children and adolescents, regardless of the presence or absence of any potential sexual adjustment difficulty. Petty covers the physical and psychosexual development issues regarding sex education from early childhood through later childhood to adolescence, giving practical tips on how to share knowledge and values at each age without moralizing.

Part 2: Problems of Psychosexual Adjustment to Physical Development

As children physically develop from infancy through childhood to adolescence, they must make psychological adjustments to their sexual anatomy and the eventual stages of pubertal development. Part 2 explores the clinical issues that attend these adjustments to physical development by dividing the accompanying problems into three chapter topic areas.

"Psychologic Issues of Adjustment in Precocious, Normal, Delayed, and Incongruent Puberty" are covered in Chapter 4 by Tom Mazur, a clinical psychologist specializing in child and adolescent psychoendocrinology, and Rochelle L. Cherpak, his research assistant. With the aid of photographs and diagrams, this chapter informs the clinician about the adjustments that boys and girls must make to their sequence of sexual development whether they experience normal, precocious, or delayed pubertal timing. The authors provide helpful discussions of the problems of incongruent puberty, such as gynecomastia in boys and hirsutism in girls, and they also provide case management and treatment recommendations.

Focusing on another dimension of physical development, clinical psychologists William J. Warzak and Brett R. Kuhn teamed up with school psychologist Patrick W. Nolten to write Chapter 5 on the "Obstacles to the Sexual Adjustment of Children and Adolescents with Disabilities." This chapter gives special consideration to youth with visual and hearing deficits and to those with cognitive impairment resulting from developmental delays and traumatic head injuries. The chapter authors indicate the kinds of support these disabled youngsters need to prevent a poor sexual adjustment, and offer recommendations concerning reducing their risk for sexual exploitation.

Psychologist Tom Mazur and phsysician Kim Dobson have focused upon children born with defects to their anatomic sexual system in Chapter 6, entitled, "Psychologic Issues in Individuals with Genetic, Hormonal, and Anatomic Anomalies of the Sexual System: Review and Treatment Considerations." The anomalies covered include Turner's syndrome, Klinefelter's syndrome, 47XYY syndrome, and hermaphroditism/intersexuality/ambiguous genitalia, including androgen insensitivity syndrome and adrenogenital syndrome, hypospadias, cryptorchidism, micropenis, total agenesis of the penis, and congenital absence of the vagina. Mazur and Dobson review the specific medical and psychological care required by such children and adolescents, and the kind of education and support that their parents need.

Part 3: Problems Associated with Sexual Victimization

With five chapters, Part 3 is devoted to the various types of child and adolescent sexual abuse, the diagnostic assessment of abuse victims, and the indicated therapeutic interventions:

In Chapter 7, social worker Christopher Bagley theoretically explores the developmental disruptions associated with the phenomena of "Early Sexual Experience and Sexual Victimization of Children and Adolescents." Bagley reviews the findings of research studies to highlight a number of paradoxes and challenges posed for prevention, therapy, and research with sexually abused children.

The effects of "Child and Adolescent Sex Rings and Pornography" upon individual development are presented in Chapter 8, written by Ann Wolbert Burgess and Carol R. Hartman, professors of psychiatric mental health nursing. The specific types of sexual abuse experienced by these children and adolescents is described with case illustrations, and treatment recommendations are offered.

Next, Burgess and Hartman focus on "Adolescent Runaways and Juvenile Prostitution" in Chapter 9. By presenting case examples and by reviewing the findings of clinical research studies, Burgees and Hartman illustrate the psychodynamics and sexual problems involved in both male and female adolescents. Clinical assessment issues are discussed and appropriate interventions are described.

Kathleen Coulborn Faller, a clinical social worker, offers her expertise on "Assessment and Treatment Issues in Child Sexual Abuse" in Chapter 10. Offered here are discussions of indicators of sexual abuse in a child, specific assessment techniques, decision-making issues related to assessment questions, and issues surrounding abusefocused therapy.

This part concludes with Chapter 11 on "Treatment Intervention for Child Sexual Abuse," coauthored by child psychiatrist Steven P. Cuffe, and pediatric nurse Sandra B. Frick-Helms. After reviewing the findings of treatment outcome research, these clinicians describe the phases of treatment and offer a critique with their recommendations regarding family interventions, cognitive and behavioral interventions, social skills training, coping skills training, education, group therapy, play therapy, art therapy, individual psychotherapy, and medication.

Part 4: Problems of Gender Development and Sexual Orientation

The psychosexual dimensions of gender identity and gender role are related to the development of sexual orientation and adulthood sexual adjustment. For example, the *Diagnostic and Statistical Manual of Mental Disorders,* fourth edition (DSM-IV), reports, "By late adolescence or adulthood, about three-quarters of boys who had a childhood history of Gender Identity Disorder report a homosexual or bisexual orientation, but without concurrent Gender Identity Disorder" (American Psychiatric Association, 1994, p. 536). The first two chapters in Part 4 focus upon the childhood and adolescent conditions of gender identity disorder and transvestic behavior, while the final three chapters are devoted to the clinical presentation of the condition of homosexuality in children and adolescents:

In Chapter 12, George A. Rekers and Mark D. Kilgus discuss "Differential Diagnosis and Rationale for Treatment of Gender Identity Disorders and Transvestism." Based upon my clinical psychological assessment research with normal and atypical boys and girls, I collaborated with a child and adolescent psychiatrist, Mark Kilgus to write this review on the practical, clinical issues involved in determining whether a child's pattern of cross-gender characteristics and/or precursors to potential transvestic fetishism warrant a diagnosis and/or a specific treatment intervention.

In Chapter 13, I provide a specific presentation of "Assessment and Treatment Methods for Gender Identity Disorder and Transvestism." Based upon my clinical research spanning two decades (e.g., Rekers, 1981b, 1986; Rekers, Kilgus, & Rosen, 1990; Rekers & Lovaas, 1971, 1974; Rekers & Varni, 1977), I offer a description of specific assessment procedures that can be applied by child professionals, including clinical interview protocols for parents and children, validated parent report inventories, behavioral observation procedures for sex-typed play and gestures, useful psychological tests, assessment of athletic game skills, home and school observational methods, and indications for medical evaluation. Then general clinical management strategies and specific psychotherapeutic techniques are presented in sufficient detail for application by a child clinician.

I coauthored the next three chapters of Part 4 with Michael Lundy, a professor of child and adolescent psychiatry. In Chapter 14, we discuss the delicate, but clinically important topic of "Homosexuality: Development, Risks, Parental Values, and Controversies." Within the context of the life threatening public health epidemic of AIDS together with the health and psychological risks of early onset of sexual behavior, this chapter prepares child clinicians to deal thoroughly and sensitively with adolescents exhibiting high-risk sexual behavior patterns, in order to skillfully and ethically provide professional services that take into account the needs of the minor involved in high-risk sexual behavior, as well as appropriately attending to adolescent and parental values (Rekers, 1989).

Lundy and I next offer a practical discussion of the clinical assessment task and recommended individual and family interview approaches in Chapter 15, entitled "Homosexuality: Presentation, Evaluation, and Clinical Decision Making." Clinical case examples are presented to illustrate the complexity of the clinical decision-making process that is involved when children or adolescents present with homosexuality.

Finally, in Chapter 16, Lundy and I consider the clinically important topic, "Homosexuality in Adolescence: Interventions and Ethical Considerations." This review of the pertinent literature on adolescent homosexuality explores the various clinical intervention options facing the child clinician, providing ethical guidelines for promoting the "best interests of the child."

Part 5: Problems of Sexual Behavior

This final part addresses the problems of overt sexual behaviors that come to the attention of professionals serving children and adolescents.

Walter R. Schumm, a family life educator, provided Chapter 17 on "Non-marital Heterosexual Behavior." This thorough and lengthy review of the clinically relevant literature highlights the problems of unwed heterosexual behavior in minors (which parallel, in some respects, the problems of homosexual behavior that were reviewed in the immediately prior chapters). Schumm presents current research findings on both sexual attitudes and behavior, reporting findings on premarital sexual standards, onset of premarital sexual activity, premarital sexual activity, sexually transmitted diseases, acquaintance rape, unplanned pregnancies, abortion, and cohabitation.

Psychologist William B. Arndt, Jr., contributed Chapter 18 on "Deviant Sexual Behavior in Children and Adolescents." This chapter includes illustrative case examples and covers a variety of sexually deviant behaviors, including courtship disordered acts, sexual touching, fondling, sibling incest, arousal by objects, sexual asphyxia, anal masturbation, obscene phone calling, exhibitionism, fetishism, frotteurism, pedophilia, sexual masochism, sexual sadism, and voyeurism—many of which may be precursors to the potential development of one of the adulthood paraphilias listed in DSM-IV. Arndt reviews the interaction of such factors as masturbation fantasies, the dynamics of the development of the adolescent paraphilic lovemap, and overt deviant sexual behavior. He reviews assessment considerations and methods, as well as treatment goals and modalities for these sexual problems.

Chapter 19 on "Child and Adolescent Sex Offenders" was written by four physicians actively involved in a respected sexual behaviors clinic at the University of Ottawa: John M.W. Bradford, Gregory Motayne, Thomas Gratzer, and Anne Pawlak. This chapter thoroughly elaborates on the specific dynamics, clinical assessment, and treatment of the children and adolescents involved in overt sex offenses, which Arndt had introduced in the previous chapter. This chapter provides a current review of offense characteristics, victim characteristics, offender characteristics, psychological factors, and biological factors before specifying the details of assessment techniques employed for juvenile sexual offenders. The chapter concludes with a detailed review of treatment procedures for adolescent sex offenders.

Conclusion

This first comprehensive handbook on sexual problems of children and adolescents draws from the current state of the clinical literature on a broad spectrum of sexual presenting problems to provide clinical child professionals with practical expertise to apply in their day-to-day practice. The multidisciplinary nature of this volume reflects the spectrum of professionals who serve children and adolescents with sexual problems. While the reader will note some gaps in our current understanding of the dynamics, assessment, and treatment of some sexual problems, it is hoped that this handbook will not only assist child clinicians in serving the needs of their patients, but also prompt further clinical research to advance knowledge that will improve professional services to future children and teenagers.

References

American Psychiatric Association. (1994). *Diagnostic and statistical manual of mental disorders* (4th ed). Washington, DC: Author.

Byne, W., & Parsons, B. (1993). Human sexual orientation: The biologic theories reappraised. *Archives of General Psychiatry, 50,* 228–239.

Ferguson, L. M., & Rekers, G. A. (1979). Non-aversive intervention for public childhood masturbation. *Journal of Sex Research, 15*(3), 213–223.

Kendall, P. C. (1984). Behavioral assessment and methodology. In C. M. Franks, G. T. Wilson, P. C. Kendall, & J. P. Foreyt (Eds.), *Review of behavior therapy: Theory and practice* (pp. 44–71). New York: Guilford Press.

Rekers, G. A. (1978). Sexual problems. In B. B. Wolman (Ed.), *Handbook of treatment of mental disorders in childhood and adolescence* (pp. 268–296). Englewood Cliffs, NJ: Prentice-Hall.

Rekers, G. A. (1980). Therapies dealing with the child's sexual difficulties. In Jean Marc-Samson (Ed.), *Enfance et sexualité/Childhood and Sexuality* (pp. 525–538). Montreal and Paris: Les Editions Etudes Vivantes.

Rekers, G. A. (1981a). Childhood sexual identity disorders. *Medical Aspects of Human Sexuality, 15*(3), 141–142.

Rekers, G. A. (1981b). Psychosexual and gender problems. In E. J. Mash & L. G. Terdal (Eds.), *Behavioral assessment of childhood disorders* (pp. 483–526). New York: Guilford Press.

Rekers, G. A. (1984). Parental involvement with agencies serving adolescents in crisis: Adolescent sexuality and family well-being. In Hearings before the Subcommittee on Family and Human Services, Committee on Labor and Human Resources, United States Senate, on *Parental Involvement with Their Adolescents in Crisis.* Washington, DC: U. S. Government Printing Office.

Rekers, G. A. (1985). *Family building: Six qualities of a strong family.* Ventura, CA: Regal Books.

Rekers, G. A. (1986). Inadequate sex role differentiation in childhood: The family and gender identity disorders. *Journal of Family and Culture, 2*(3), 8–37.

Rekers, G. A. (1988). *Counseling families.* Waco, TX: Word Books.

Rekers, G. A. (1989). AIDS: Behavioral dimensions of medical care. *USC School of Medicine Report, 65,* 1272–1274.

Rekers, G. A. (1991a). Cross-sex behavior problems. In R. A. Hoekelman, S. Blatman, S. B. Friedman, N. M. Nelson, & H. M. Seidel (Eds.), *Primary pediatric care* (2d ed., pp. 691–693). St. Louis, MO: C. V. Mosby.

Rekers, G. A. (1991b). The need for a primary emphasis on prevention and for intervention research in community-based mental health services for children. In Hearings before the Select Committee on Children, Youth and Families, United States House of Representatives, on *Close to Home: Community-Based Mental Health Services for Children* (pp. 138–180). Washington, DC: U. S. Government Printing Office.

Rekers, G. A. (1992). Development of problems in puberty and sex roles in adolescence. In C. E. Walker & M. C. Roberts (Eds.), *Handbook of clinical child psychology* (2d ed., pp. 606–622). New York: John Wiley and Sons.

Rekers, G. A., Amaro-Plotkin, H., & Low, B. P. (1977). Sex-typed mannerisms in normal boys and girls as a function of sex and age. *Child Development, 48,* 275–278.

Rekers, G. A., Crandall, B. F., Rosen, A. C., & Bentler, P. M. (1979). Genetic and physical studies of male children with psychological gender disturbances. *Psychological Medicine, 9,* 373–375.

Rekers, G. A., Kilgus, M., & Rosen, A. C. (1990). Long-term effects of treatment for childhood gender disturbance. *Journal of Psychology and Human Sexuality,* 3(2), 121–153.

Rekers, G. A., & Lovaas, O. I. (1971). Experimental analysis of cross-sex behavior in male children. *Research Relating to Children, 28,* 68.

Rekers, G. A., & Lovaas, O. I. (1974). Behavioral treatment of deviant sex-role behaviors in a male child. *Journal of Applied Behavior Analysis, 7,* 173–190.

Rekers, G. A., & Milner, G. C. (1979). How to diagnose and manage childhood sexual disorders. *Behavioral Medicine,* 6(4), 18–21.

Rekers, G. A., Sanders, J. A., Strauss, C. C., Rasbury, W. C., & Morey, S. M. (1989). Differentiation of adolescent activity participation. *Journal of Genetic Psychology, 150*(3), 323–335.

Rekers, G. A., & Swihart, J. J. (1984). *Making up the difference: Help for single parents with teenagers.* Grand Rapids, MI: Baker Book House.

Rekers, G. A., & Varni, J. W. (1977). Self-monitoring and self-reinforcement processes in a pre-transsexual boy. *Behavior Research and Therapy, 15,* 177–180.

Rosen, A. C., & Rekers, G. A. (1980). Toward a taxonomic framework for variables of sex and gender. *Genetic Psychology Monographs, 102,* 191–218.

Schumm, W. R., & Rekers, G. A. (1984). Sex should occur only within marriage. In H. Feldman & A. Parrott (Eds.), *Human sexuality: Contemporary controversies* (pp. 105–124). Beverly Hills, CA: Sage.

2
Assessment of Sexual Problems in Childhood and Adolescence

Donna Cook Culley
Clyde H. Flanagan, Jr.

In order to conduct a high-quality assessment of sexual problems in children and adolescents, one must first be well versed in good general assessment principles. One such principle is that a comprehensive assessment integrates data collected from a variety of sources using a variety of techniques. For example, assessment should include not only the child but parents, siblings, caseworkers, and teachers. Information should be collected using a variety of assessment procedures such as clinical interviews, psychological testing, behavioral observations, and play (diagnostic) interviews. O'Donohue and Elliott (1991) recommend that assessment include evaluation of the child's environment, consistent with the behavioral approach; assessment of beliefs, attributions, and other cognitive factors, consistent with a cognitive approach; and assessment of the child's family functioning, consistent with a family systems approach. This holds true whether the sexual problem being assessed is one of abuse, gender identity disorder, sexual perpetration, or paraphilic behavior.

Another general consideration when conducting evaluations of sexual problems in children and adolescents is the potential forensic application of the assessment. Especially when working with children who have problems associated with sexual abuse or sexual perpetration, the possibility exists that your clinical evaluation may be subpoenaed for court purposes. Consequently, it is advised that one be vigilant to the liability risks involved in such cases. It is always best to clarify these issues up front, if possible, and establish whether the evaluation is primarily forensic or treatment-oriented.

However, there are times when one may not be able to predict the potential use of collected data. Therefore, it is important not to contaminate an evaluation with the use of suggestion that will bias the child's responses (Walker, 1990). The first interview is considered the most important, and can be spoiled if the child hears and incorporates erroneous information provided by the assessor (Goodman & Helgeson, 1988). Thus, it is recommended that the initial interview be general and nonspecific, with subsequent interviews moving to greater detail.

Be prepared for potential legal scrutiny of your work before it occurs. One should maintain careful records of the evaluation process, be able to defend the use of specific assessment procedures, form a diagnostic opinion, and develop a treatment plan based on the assessment (Walker, 1990).

Clinical Interviews

Clinical interviews are the most valuable evaluation tool available to the clinician. The nature of the interview will differ greatly depending on the specific sexual problem being assessed (i.e., abuse, perpetration, paraphilia). Thus, specific interview recommendations will be addressed at various points throughout this chapter. However, there are some general comments that are applicable to interviews regardless of referral problems. For example, it is recommended that multiple interviews be conducted including parent-alone interviews, parent and child interviews, and child-alone interviews.

Clinical interviews with the parents or guardians of the child are very important. These people are usually the best source for obtaining a description of the presenting problem, settings where it occurs, developmental sexual history, and behavioral observations. It is important to assess parental attitudes and overt reactions to the sexual behavior in question. In addition, adult, peer, and media (TV, books, magazines, videos, music, pornography) influences on the child's sexual behavior should be evaluated. Assessing the presence or absence of sex education—including the knowledge and values of the parents and the child/adolescent—will provide the clinician with valuable information. One may wish to conduct some interviews with the child and parents together to observe father–child and mother–child interactions and relationships.

A clinical interview with the child/adolescent alone should address awareness and level of insight into their sexual behavior, developmental sexual history, sexual arousal and behavior patterns, and history of social and sexual relations with male and female peers and adults.

Clinical interviews with the child should be tailored according to the specific nature of the sexual problem (i.e., abuse, paraphilia, perpetration); these are described in detail in subsequent sections of this chapter. However, in general, interview techniques will vary with age, intellectual functioning, and emotional functioning of the child/adolescent. The clinician must feel comfortable discussing sexual material that may be abusive, bizarre, or violent. The clinician should convey a level of comfort with the topic of sexuality in order to facilitate discussion of what may be very painful, embarrassing, or self-incriminating material. Typically, those being interviewed will take their cues from the evaluator, and if the clinician conveys feelings of discomfort, disgust, or rejection, the child/adolescent will know that it is not safe to self-disclose.

Psychological Testing

Psychological testing can be helpful in identifying both general emotional distress and specific symptomology associated with sexual problems. Instruments such as the Child Behavior Checklist (CBCL; Achenbach & Edelbrock, 1983) have been used to evaluate the presence of general emotional problems.

More specific assessment devices have been developed in recent years to address sexual issues directly. For example, the Sex Knowledge and Attitude Test for Adolescents (SKAT-A) was developed to assess adolescents' sexual knowledge, attitudes, and behaviors (Lief, Fullard, & Devlin, 1990). The Kirby Knowledge and Attitude Scale focuses on birth control, sexually transmitted diseases, physical development, relationships, sexual activity, pregnancy, marriage, and personal values (Kirby, 1984).

Instruments that measure behaviorally defined dissociative symptoms in sexually abused children have become popular given the association with post-traumatic stress disorder that has been made by some researchers and clinicians (Deblinger, McLeer, & Henry, 1990; Mallnosky-Rummell & Hoier, 1991). The Child Dissociative Checklist (CDCL; Putnam, 1988) and a six-item dissociation subscale of the CBCL (Achenback & Edelbrock, 1983) are examples of instruments being psychometrically evaluated for their usefulness in assessing sexually abused children.

The use of projective assessment can sometimes be helpful in understanding the child's perception of his/her world, but these techniques should only be utilized by individuals with proper clinical training in their administration and interpretation. However, the use of projectives is only a small part of a complete assessment. Some authors naively advocate that "the use of the Draw-a-Person or Kinetic Family drawing techniques provides the school counselor with a simple procedure that does not require extensive training in art, special equipment, or a clinical setting" (Riordan & Verdel, 1991, p. 120). This could not be further from the truth. These authors further suggest that "human figure drawings can be used in a informal way for general assessment of blatant indications of sexual abuse" (p. 117).

Hibbard, Roghmann, and Hoekelman (1987) stated emphatically that drawings cannot be used as a screening test for sexual abuse and that they should not be overinterpreted. They empirically studied the drawings of 52 sexually abused children and 52 matched nonabused children and found no statistically significant differences between the two groups. Genitalia were present in only 6 of the 104 children's drawings, with 10 percent of the abused group drawing genitalia and 2 percent of the nonabused group. Professionals should not be in the business of performing "informal assessments" of sexual abuse under any circumstances, much less by looking exclusively at the routine artwork of schoolchildren. To engage in such whimsical practice indicates a complete lack of appreciation for the severity of making an allegation of sexual abuse. The damage that can result to a child and his or her family is enormous even if the resulting "diagnosis" is a false positive.

Sexually anatomically correct dolls have been used in evaluations to assess whether or not abuse has occurred. Given the importance of this issue, a growing body of literature has developed to address the proper use of this technique (see Elliott, O'Donohue, & Nickerson, 1991; Mountain, Nicholson, Spencer, & Walker, 1984; Walker, 1988). Adequate treatment of this literature cannot be made here, but it should be noted that use of anatomically correct dolls requires proper training, standardized administration, and careful interpretation. Nonetheless, Boat and Everson (1988) found that child protection workers, law enforcement workers, mental health professionals, and physicians reported widespread use of the dolls in their evaluations of abuse; however, these users were, for the most part, inexperienced and untrained. When training did occur, it consisted of an occasional lecture or workshop. More research on the use of dolls is needed before this technique can be used with any degree of professional certainty. To date, studies indicate that sexually abused children may possibly engage in more sexualized play with dolls compared to nonabused children (Jampole & Weber, 1987; Sivan, Schor, Koeppl, & Noble, 1988). However, the utility of this technique is controversial and should not be used solely to decide whether or not abuse has occurred. While dolls should not be used for diagnostic or interpretive purposes, many advocate that proper use of dolls can help children communicate through demonstration and can be a useful adjunct to the interview process (Melton & Limber, 1989).

Often, the clinician conducting the evaluation is not the same individual who will be providing treatment. However, the evaluator should always be mindful of preparing the child or adolescent for therapy. The evaluation itself should be therapeutic to some degree, such that the child's dignity and self-worth are restored when concluding the assessment (Walker, 1990).

Assessment should be viewed as an ongoing process that does not end when treatment begins. Commonly, new information is revealed during the therapeutic process as a result of the child's increased rapport and comfort with the therapist. Given the sensitive nature of the material, one would expect that the most painful or embarrassing data would be discovered later in the process. An example of this is the assessment of adolescent sex offenders. Commonly, little information is disclosed during the initial interview. However, once therapy has begun and the adolescent progresses, additional sex offenses are frequently disclosed that were initially denied.

Problems of Adjustment to Physical Development

Children and adolescents often have problems adjusting to physical development whether a sexual disorder has been identified or not. During puberty an array of problems may arise in assessment and treatment such as behavioral problems, social difficulties, and poor self-concept. For example, research conducted with women diagnosed with Turner's syndrome (a genetic defect in which one X chromosome is either missing or damaged) suggests that these individuals experience immaturity, poor attention skills, and poor peer relationships (Sonis et al., 1983). These problems appear to be related to the onset of puberty (Perheentupa et al., 1974). Perheentupa et al. (1974) theorize that the girls who do not develop physically along with their peers exhibit socially withdrawn and immature behavior and fantasies.

However, adjustment to sexual development is not easy even when that development is normal. Problems surface in the areas of behavior, self-concept, social relationships, and family relationships for children and adolescents without sexual disorders. Research is being conducted that attempts to better understand the process of sexual development and the impact it has on the individual and society. The problems associated with adolescent sexual behavior have centered on unwanted teen pregnancy, sexually transmitted diseases, and most recently AIDS.

With a few exceptions, there has been little theoretical research on adolescent sexual behavior (Hayes, 1987). However, Benda and DiBlasio (1991) compared four theories of adolescent sexual exploration to address the variance in adolescent sexual behavior. Their data indicated that differential peer association is the major factor influencing adolescent sexual behavior, such that teens who perceive their best friends as sexually active have a greater frequency of intercourse than those who believe their friends are sexually inactive.

Most of the research in the area of adolescent sexuality has looked at factors that influence this behavior. A review of the recent literature (White & DeBlassie, 1992) addresses sexual behavior as it relates to delinquency, religion, and psychological needs. Elliott and Morse (1989) reported a significant increase in sexual intercourse in adolescents with a history of delinquency or drug use. They identified the typical sequence as delinquency, followed by drug use, and then sexual intercourse. In addition, they found that sexual intercourse was related to a general desire to engage in more risky behavior.

The role of religious participation was examined by Thornton and Camburn (1989). They found adolescents who attend church frequently and place value on the role of religion in their lives are less experienced sexually and have less permissive attitudes.

The importance of psychological and emotional needs as they relate to sexual expression cannot be overlooked. Adolescents may be seeking affection, trying to bolster their self-esteem, ease loneliness, confirm sexual identity, escape boredom, or vent anger (Hajcak & Garwood, 1988). Through conditioning, these sexual and nonsexual needs become paired. Hajcak and Garwood (1988) suggest that intervention would involve helping adolescents to learn to satisfy these needs independently of sexual behavior. In addition, Shaughnessy and Shakesby (1992) argue that emotional intimacy plays an important role in adolescent sexual intimacy. They recommend that emotional education be provided in addition to sex education.

Problems Associated with Sexual Victimization

The area of sexual abuse of children has received increased attention in the last 20 years (Okami, 1992). Much research has been generated and much has been learned with respect to the assessment and treatment of child sexual abuse. Freud in an historical 1896 publication proposed that the etiology of hysterical symptoms in adult women could be traced to incest. Memories retrieved under hypnosis indicated sexual abuse, most often by the father (Freud, 1962). Frenczi (1933) also contributed a major work connecting adult manifestation to the effects of childhood sexual abuse. Both of these major reports were received by peers with considerable condemnation and skepticism. Freud later changed his theory that all psychoneuroses were the consequence of childhood sexual abuse, active in hysteria, passive in obsessive–compulsive disorder. He could not accept evidence indicating that childhood sexual abuse was occurring with such frequency (Masson, 1984).

Problems associated with sexual victimization may manifest at any age and be acute, chronic, or delayed. Sometimes the meaning of the event is changed to a traumatic one by maturation and development. Some clinical examples are presented to illustrate this followed by discussion of pertinent research findings.

Case Report: Terry

Terry was 11 years old when he disclosed to his parents that his 16-year-old brother had been sexually abusing him since he was 9 years of age. This abuse included fellatio and receptive anal penetration. The older brother admitted to the sexual abuse of his brother. At that time, Terry manifested poor school performance, sleep problems, and no real motivation for school or any other activity. He could not sustain a task for any period of time. He was very delayed in social interaction. He had been suspended from school for sexually inappropriate speech and behavior with his female teacher and girls in his class. In psychotherapy Terry often made derisive remarks about himself and his therapist. He was extremely anxious and depressed. He did not feel safe in any relationship and was quite socially immature. Two years after reporting the abuse by his older brother, Terry sexually abused his 4-year-old brother.

Case Report: Juan

Juan, a 38-year-old very successful professional, sought help for depression after his wife of 11 years confessed to an affair with the husband of a close friend. During evaluation it became obvious that Juan had actively encouraged his wife to have the affair, in part as the result of his own guilt feelings over many affairs of his own. Furthermore, he had severe sexual conflicts and inhibitions. During intercourse his wife had to lie perfectly still or he would lose his erection. He frequently experienced premature ejaculation or orgasm without ejaculation. Only after some time in intensive psychotherapy was Juan able to relate details of sexual abuse by a sister 10 years older. This abuse began when he was 7 years old. She would undress and allow him to fondle her. He saw himself as a passive participant in this activity. When he experienced his first pubertal ejaculation during such sexual interaction with his sister, she terminated the sexual relationship. He was angry that she did so and experienced it as a rejection of his manhood. However, as a facade, Juan continued to remain emotionally a small, innocent child. The small child is not responsible and is allowed to be present with women while they undress, bathe, and otherwise gratify voyeuristic pleasures. To grow up and become an adult is to lose this innocent position. As with Peter Pan, Juan maintained "I don't want to grow up."

Case Report: Ted

Ted was 37 years old when he was first hospitalized for severe depression with suicidal impulses. Married for 16 years with one 15-year-old child, Ted and his wife had severe marital conflicts, which Ted related to sexual issues. In addition to compulsive masturbation, Ted reported a struggle for most of his married life with over exhibitionistic behavior, with frequent impulses to expose his genitals to unsuspecting women. For most of his married life, he frequented adult pornographic book and video stores where he engaged in sexual acts, mostly fellatio with other men. As early as he could recall, age 3 or earlier, Ted had been forced by his mother to engage in oral sex, licking her genitals and the semen from intercourse with his father, which she would force him to watch. He stated that father went along, due to mother's demands. Later during adolescent years he was seduced by the minister of the family church, engaging in fellatio and passive anal intercourse. This relationship was active for most of his high school years and ended when he graduated from high school and joined the military. Prior to his hospitalization, he reportedly stopped sexual activity outside of marriage due to fear of AIDS and guilt feelings. However, his wife was unable to meet his resultant sexual demands. In addition, he had married a woman who was quite sexually inhibited. This contributed to the marital dysfunction. The traumatic reenactment of the early childhood experience with his wife included olfactory hallucination of a bad odor from his wife's body.

Professionally, the field of child sexual abuse is still in its infancy (Konker, 1992). The limits of our knowledge and roles as clinicians must be noted up front. Despite our increased interest in and attention to the area of child sexual abuse, training for those engaged in investigating allegations of sexual abuse is sorely lacking (Robin, 1991). Consequently, the validity of such evaluations if often called into question. One of the major problems is that interviews are not approached in an objective, unbiased manner. Too often clinicians assume that the allegations of abuse are true and do not even entertain alternative hypotheses. Such preconceived beliefs greatly influence the result of the interview (Dent, 1982). Clinicians ask questions that are consistent with their own beliefs, interpret data in a way that matches their bias, and are less likely to explore other hypotheses.

Certain coercive techniques have been identified that may invalidate the assessment and should be avoided in clinical interviews (Robin, 1991). They include demands for the truth, providing rewards for correct answers, repetitive questioning, threats, and refusal to accept the child's answer. Subtle behavioral indicators such as facial expression, eye contact, and body posture can also indicate approval or disapproval by the examiner. In 1985 a National Summit Conference on Diagnosing Child Sexual Abuse was held in Los Angeles. This conference led to the founding of an interdisciplinary group, the American Professional Society on the Abuse of Children (APSAC; Corwin, 1992). Hopefully, increased standardization of evaluation techniques will be investigated by this group.

Assessing a victim of sexual abuse requires good clinical interviewing skills and knowledge of developmental norms. It is important to be objective and neither to predetermine the child's emotional state nor to suggest material. The clinician must carefully gauge the individual's level of embarrassment, guilt, fear, and anger about what has happened to him or her. In some instances establishing rapport is extremely important due to the violation of trust that these children and adolescents have suffered. In others, a false pseudointimacy and precocious maturity may be encountered. The assessment should progress at a pace comfortable for the victim and should respect his/her body space requirements, which may be extreme. Depending on the age of the child, the clinician may need to adapt his/her language to a level that the child understands or use the child's words for anatomy and behaviors.

Becker (1989) suggests that the clinician phrase interview questions in terms of "unwanted" acts since some victims may not view the event as rape or abuse, especially if the perpetrator was an acquaintance or relative. She also urges clinicians to learn as much about the abuse as possible, noting not only the duration and specific activities, but also how the victim feels about the behavior and what effect it has had on her or him.

The child's perception of his or her victimization is very important. For example, if penetration or other forms of injury have occurred, the child may see herself or himself as permanently ruined. This "damaged goods" self-perception may result in lower self-esteem and may discourage self-protection in the future, leading to increased risk for further abuse (Ryan, 1991). In addition, if the child experienced sexual arousal or pleasurable sensations, the child may report extreme confusion and guilt (Conte, 1988). The clinician should be sensitive to these issues during assessment and help normalize these feelings for the child. Abusers frequently use threats of physical harm to prevent disclosure of their abuse. In one study of 67 children sexually abused in day care centers, 98 percent were threatened (Kelley, 1992).

Be sure to collect sufficient data by interviewing all available family members. When interviewing parents and siblings, keep in mind that they too have been traumatized by the event, each in their own way. This trauma varies due to factors such as whether the abuse was incestuous, the result of stranger molestation, or perpetrated by an acquaintance. Parents often feel ultimately responsible for their child's abuse, even if they were not aware that it was occurring. It is important that the clinician not imply parental fault for not protecting the child (Ehrensaft, 1992).

Mothers and fathers may develop their own symptomology in response to the victimization of their child. Mothers may respond with fear and anxiety, become overly protective, and experience headaches, nightmares, and tearfulness. Fathers, on the other hand, may become more rageful, irritable, suffer from sleep difficulties and headaches (Ehrensaft, 1992). Marital difficulties in families of sexually abused children are not uncommon due to the stress that the family unit experiences. Siblings can become angry and fearful that the same traumatic event could happen to them, or it may indeed have already occurred. In assessing the parents of sexually abused children, a good clinician should be sensitive to the emotional reactions and needs of all family members.

The task of determining the validity of alleged sexual abuse is most difficult. The tendency to assume that all allegations of abuse are true is a temptation for many and the staunch belief of a few. However, if the report has not been substantiated, the objective interviewer must make no assumptions until all the information has been assembled. Faller (1988) reported that most abused children will be able to provide details about the abuse and that the most frequently made untrue statements are when children *deny* abuse that has occurred. There have occasionally been reported cases of intentional false reporting of sexual abuse. In their study of a large sample of child protection service cases, Everson and Boat (1989) concluded that approximately 2.5 percent of the cases were deliberately fabricated. Most of these fabricated charges were made by adolescents who were seeking changes in placement, retaliation against an adult, or attention.

Some researchers have attempted to identify symptoms of sexual abuse that can be applied to all or most victims, such as the child accommodation syndrome (Summit, 1983). However, as Ryan (1991) notes, sexual victimization does not occur in isolation from other life events, and thus the experience is affected by all that has occurred before and by all that follows. O'Donohoe and Elliott (1991) report that an important factor in the child's reaction to sexual abuse is the overall functioning of the child and the family prior to the abuse. They take into consideration factors such as preexisting coping skills, family problems, hyperactivity, and problem-solving skills. Thus, many factors can either mediate or exacerbate the child's psychological response to an abuse situation. In addition, Walker (1990) points out that the child's reaction can also be related to factors such as the amount of violence associated with the abuse, the child's relationship to the abuser, and the reaction of the child's support system.

Robin (1991) agrees that sexually abused children are a diverse group with some showing few or no symptoms of abuse and others displaying a variety of emotional and behavioral problems. While there are some symptoms such as enuresis, thumb sucking, depression, and anxiety that have been observed in sexually abused children, these "indicators" are also symptoms of other clinical disorders, and depending on the age of the child may be developmentally normal. Thus, the use of symptom checklists to diagnose sexual abuse is certainly an unreliable approach, especially when used by interviewers without knowledge of the sexual development of children. The most frequently cited behavioral indicators of abuse are precocious sexual behavior, seductive behavior, and advanced sexual knowledge given the child's age (Berliner, 1988; Faller, 1988). However, good normative developmental data for sexual behavior and knowledge does not exist (Okami, 1992). Thus, even well-trained clinicians must carefully evaluate and integrate all available data to discern whether the child is merely engaging in childhood sex play or whether these behaviors are an indication of sexual abuse.

There are some symptoms that are commonly associated with child sexual abuse, including cognitive disturbances (flashbacks, concentration difficulties, and recurrent memories of the events), depression, problems in interpersonal relationships, loss of interest in activities, sleep disturbance, anxiety, hypervigilance, irritability, and extreme startle response (Walker, 1990).

Since the child, regardless of age, may have experienced abuse when sensorimotor memories predominate (since word symbols are not available), the only means of expression are through the medium of symbols, such as actions through play or reinacted relationships. Therefore, interviews should occur in a setting with ample supplies of play materials. Evaluate the child for evidence of post-traumatic stress signs and symptoms in play, art work, dreams, and reenactment activities related to trauma. Unless some evidence of post-traumatic stress symptoms are present, other possibilities must be considered. Other possibilities include suggestion by others, falsehood, or more severe forms of induced cognitive distortions (Terr, 1986).

Symptoms that have been used to differentiate sexually abused children from those with no known history of abuse include:

1. Overinhibition or excessive expression of sexual drive
2. Inability to trust or be intimate with others
3. Victimizing others in the same way that victimization occurred
4. Depression, with feelings of despair and hopelessness about the future
5. A general lack of confidence in one's judgment and pervasive sense of ineffectiveness in dealing with one's surroundings
6. A belief of having been permanently damaged and forever unattractive in physical appearance
7. Overinhibition of anger or excessive expression of anger
8. Physically self-destructive acts, such as self-mutilation
9. Inappropriate minimization of injuries
10. Exaggerated sense of responsibility for the victimization experience (Corwin, 1992)

The child's reaction to sexual abuse may depend in part on his/her gender. Often, victims of sexual abuse are assumed to be female, but research has demonstrated that a large percentage of young children are molested are male. For male victims abused by males, the issue of homosexuality exists. It can assume the form of questioning one's own sexual preferences and orientation, or can result in homophobia (Ryan, 1991). Males are socialized to externalize negative experiences, as opposed to females who are more inclined to internalize experiences. Consequently, the reactions to sexual abuse can manifest very differently in male victims. Male victims may be more inclined to express anger as opposed to sadness, distrust as opposed to anxiety, and aggression toward others, as opposed to suicidal behavior.

As illustrated in the cases of Juan and Ted described above, symptoms of incest or child molestation may endure for years and affect the victim into adulthood. Long-term responses to child sexual abuse may include fear, anxiety, depression, impaired social functioning, sleep disturbances, sexual dysfunctions, substance abuse, eating disorders, and relationships difficulties (Becker, 1989; Finkelhor, 1986; Ryan, 1991). Sexual dysfunctions in adulthood can take the form of hypersexuality, hyposexuality, or fetishes (Ryan, 1991). Examples of sexual excesses include promiscuity, sexual addictions, compulsive masturbation, or deviant arousal patterns. Clinically diagnostic sexual disorders may include inhibited desire or arousal, impotence, or sexual aversions. Fetishes for particular items or cross-dressing may also result from childhood sexual abuse.

Atypical Sexual Behavior Problems

Deviancy may mean different things to different people. Generically, it refers to any quality, conduct, appearance, behavior, belief, or thought that significantly diverges from a standard or norm and can be determined by laws, customs, or society (Steele & Ryan, 1991).

Sexual deviancy may mean different things to different people, but Wincze (1989) categorizes a variety of atypical behaviors according to whether or not there is a victim and whether the behavior is paraphilic or nonparaphilic. For example, paraphilias that do not involve a victim include transvestism and fetishism. Examples of paraphilias that do involve a victim may include pedophilia, voyeurism, and exhibitionism. Nonparaphilic behaviors that involve a victim include child sexual abuse by on older child, rape, and incest. Thus "sexual deviancy" spans a wide array of behaviors, some that are not harmful to others, but can be distressing to the individual, and some that inflict severe injury to victims. In either case, individuals with deviant sexual behaviors usually do not present for assessment and treatment voluntarily. Individuals who engage in victimless paraphilias often enter therapy only when forced to do so by a significant figure in their life (i.e., a spouse who discovers them cross-dressing). Those engaged in assaultive behaviors are usually seen for evaluation only after they have been caught by law enforcement agencies and ordered to receive treatment by the court.

Clinicians involved in evaluation of atypical sexual behavior problems should be prepared to hear and discuss very graphic descriptions of unconventional practices. Thus it is important to know one's own limitations in dealing with this population. Even if the behavior evokes feeling of disgust, amusement, shock, or anger, it is important that the clinician not express these feelings overtly to the client (Winzce, 1989). Even subtle expressions of feelings should be concealed so as not to isolate the client, damage rapport, or impede self-disclosure. Given these conditions, not all clinicians are well suited to work with these clients. It is best to make a referral if one does not feel competent and comfortable in dealing with male clients who, for example, sexually victimize women or who dress in women's clothing.

In order to provide assessment and treatment, it is important to understand how sexually deviant behaviors develop. Steele and Ryan (1991) note that sexual urges are inborn, but sexual expression is learned, or, as in the clinical case of Ted, a reenactment of traumatic sexual abuse. They hypothesize that deviant sexual behaviors are the result of early childhood experiences. Winzce (1989) argues that when children experience atypical behaviors or fantasies that are coupled with sexual arousal and orgasm, the atypical behavior is reinforced and strengthened. Given the diversity and complexity of deviant sexual behavior, it is often difficult to identify the interactions of various factors.

One of the most difficult and most important deviant sexual populations to assess and treat is adolescent sexual offenders. The assessment and treatment of adolescent sexual offenders has been an area of growing interest and concern in recent years. Research indicates that 20–30 percent of rapes and 30–50 percent of child sexual abuse are the result of adolescent perpetrators, who, as illustrated in the clinical case of Terry, have been abused themselves (Gilby, Wolf, Goldberg, 1989). Research has also shown that most adult perpetrators began victimizing others during their adolescent years (Abel, Mittelman, & Becker, 1985; Brecher, 1978; Groth & Birnbaum, 1979). This continued pattern of offending behavior into adulthood underscores the importance of providing treatment as early in the development of the offender as possible to prevent future victims. For too long adolescent sexual offenses were seen as a "boys will be boys" event. However, data suggests that adolescent sexual offenses need to be taken seriously and should not be treated as sexual experimentation (Becker, Kaplan, Cunningham-Rathner, & Kavoussi, 1986). Attention has even recently turned to the alarming problem of young children sexually victimizing other children (Cantwell, 1988; Johnson, 1988).

The assessment of child and adolescent sex offenders is a very specific and complicated process if done correctly. (Details will be addressed in subsequent chapters that focus on this topic.) During this assessment the clinician must be prepared to deal skillfully with issues such as denial, minimization, projection, and rationalization. Offenders usually have a variety of cognitive distortions that allow them to perpetrate and avoid taking responsibility for their actions. Often this is a frustration for the clinician, but if seen as part of the clinical presentation it can be incorporated into treatment planning.

When assessing risk for future offending, the evaluation should address several variables such as honesty, self-disclosure, cooperation with the interview process, amount of violence in the offenses, frequency of offenses, progress of sexual aggression, number of victims, precipitating factors, social relationships, and past victimization (Ross & Loss, 1991). Obviously, this is a very time-consuming process and is typically conducted over the course of several sessions. Collecting collateral information from police reports, victims statements, and juvenile court records is vital. This data should be reviewed carefully prior to the evaluation.

In addition to the clinical interview, the penile plethysmograph is another method of assessment used with sex offenders. A penile strain gauge is used to measure the sexual arousal of an individual as he is exposed to visual or auditory stimulation. This technique has been used in conjunction with psychological tests to identify males who are attracted to children, have fetishes, or are aroused by violence. In addition, it has been used as a component of treatment to evaluate progress. However, the validity of this procedure has been questioned. Some reports indicate that individuals can affect the results of the test by intentionally thinking of material other than that being presented (Kendall, 1984). Consequently, this method of assessment should be used cautiously and should not be the sole measure of treatment outcome.

Summary

This chapter has provided some introductory comments regarding assessment of child and adolescent sexual problems. There are many difficulties in conducting these assessments, interpreting the results, and making a diagnosis. The problems that face clinicians include the need for more research on developmental norms, the need for longitudinal studies that follow child disorders into adulthood, and the need for standardized assessment techniques. Despite these limitations, it is important to provide sexual evaluations. The identification and treatment of child/adolescent sexual problems may prevent the development of adulthood sexual problems. Thus clinicians and researchers must continue to work in the relatively new field of child and adolescent sexual problems.

References

Abel, G. G., Mittelman, M., & Becker, J. V. (1985). Sex offenders: Results of assessment and recommendations for treatment. In H. H. Ben-Aron, S. I. Hucker, & C. D. Webster (Eds.), *Clinical criminology: Assessment and treatment of criminal behavior.* Washington, DC: M&M Graphics.

Achenbach, T. M., & Edelbrock, C. S. (1983). *Manual for the Child Behavior Checklist and Revised Child Behavior Profile.* Burlington: Department of Psychiatry, University of Vermont.

Becker, J. V. (1989). Impact of sexual abuse on sexual functioning. In S. R. Leiblum & R. C. Rosen (Eds.), *Principles and practice of sex therapy: Update for the 1990's*. New York: Guilford Press.

Becker, J. V., Kaplan, M. S., Cunningham-Rathner, J., & Kavoussi, R. (1986). Characteristics of adolescent incest sexual perpetrators: Preliminary findings. *Journal of Family Violence, 1*(1), 85–96.

Benda, B. B., & DiBlasio, F. A. (1991). Comparison of four theories of adolescent sexual exploration. *Deviant Behavior: An Interdisciplinary Journal, 12*, 235–257.

Berliner, L. (1988). Debate forum: Resolved: Child sex abuse is overdiagnosed: Negative. *Journal of the American Academy of Child and Adolescent Psychiatry, 28*, 792–793.

Boat, B., & Everson, M. (1988). Use of anatomically correct dolls among professionals in sexual abuse evaluations. *Child Abuse and Neglect, 12*, 171–179.

Brecher, E. (1978). *Treatment programs for the sex offenders*. Washington, DC: U. S. Department of Justice.

Cantwell, H. (1988). Child sexual abuse: Very young perpetrators. *Child Abuse and Neglect, 12*, 579–582.

Conte, J. (1988 October). *The effects of sexual abuse on the child victim and its treatment*. Paper presented at the Fourth National Symposium on Child Sexual Abuse, Huntsville, AL.

Corwin, D. L. (1992). Sexually abused children's symptoms and disorders of extreme stress not otherwise specified: Does this proposed psychiatric diagnosis fit? In A. Burgess (Ed.), *Child trauma: Issues and research* (pp. 87–115). New York: Garland.

Deblinger, E., McLeer, S. V., & Henry, D. (1990). Cognitive behavioral treatment for sexually abused children suffering post-traumatic stress: Preliminary findings. *Journal of the American Academy of Child and Adolescent Psychiatry, 29*, 747–752.

Dent, H. R. (1982). The effects of interviewing strategies on the results of interviews with child witnesses. In A. T. Trankell (Ed.), *Reconstructing the past* (pp. 93–113). Deventer, The Netherlands: Kluwer.

Ehrensaft, D. (1992). Preschool child sex abuse: The aftermath of the Presidio case. *American Journal of Orthopsychiatry, 62*(2), 234–243.

Elliott, D. S., & Morse, B. J. (1989). Delinquency and drug use as risk factors in teenage sexual activity. *Youth and Society, 21*(1), 32–57.

Elliott, A. N., O'Donohoe, W., & Nickerson, M. (1991). *The use of sexually anatomically correct dolls in the assessment of sexually abused children*. Manuscript submitted for publication.

Everson, M., & Boat, B. (1989). False allegation of sexual abuse by children and adolescents. *Journal of the American Academy of Child and Adolescent Psychiatry, 28*(2), 230–235.

Faller, K. (1988). Criteria for judging the credibility of children's statements about their sexual abuse. *Child Welfare, 67*(5), 389–401.

Finkelhor, D. (1986). *Sourcebook on child sex abuse*. Beverly Hills, CA: Sage.

Frenczi, S. (1933). Confusion of tongues between adults and the child: The language of tenderness and passion. In M. Balent (Ed.) and E. Mosbacher

(Trans.), *Final contribution to the problems and methods of pscyhoanalysis* (pp. 156–167). London: Maresfield Reprints.

Freud, S. (1962). The etiology of hysteria. In J. Strackey (Ed. & Trans.), *The standard edition of the complete psychological works of Sigmund Freud* (Vol. 2, pp. 253–305). London: Hogarth Press.

Gilby, R., Wolf, L., & Goldberg, B. (1989). Mentally retarded adolescent sex offenders: A survey and pilot study. *Canadian Journal of Psychiatry, 34*, 542–548.

Goodman, G. S., & Helgeson, V. S. (1988). Children as witnesses: What do they remember? In L.E.A. Walker (Ed.), *Handbook on sexual abuse of children* (pp. 109–136). New York: Springer.

Groth, A. N., & Birnbaum, H. J. (1979). *Men who rape: The psychology of the offender*. New York: Plenum Press.

Hajcak, F., & Garwood, P. (1988). What parents can do to prevent pseudo-hypersexuality in adolescents. *Family Therapy, 15*(2), 99–105.

Hayes, C. D. (Ed.). (1987). *Risking the future: Adolescent sexuality, pregnancy, and childbearing*. Washington, DC: National Academy Press.

Hibbard, R. A., Roghmann, K., & Hoekelman, R. (1987). Genitalia in children's drawings: An association with sexual abuse. *Pediatrics, 79*(1), 129–137.

Jampole, L., & Weber, M. K. (1987). An assessment of the behavior of sexually abused and nonsexually abused children with anatomically correct dolls. *Child Abuse and Neglect, 11*, 187–192.

Johnson, T. C. (1988). Child perpetrators—children who molest other children: Preliminary findings. *Child Abuse and Neglect, 12*, 219–229.

Kelley, S. (1992). Stress responses of children and parents to sexual abuse and ritualistic abuse in day care centers. In A. Burgess (Ed.), *Child trauma: Issues and research* (pp. 231–257). New York: Garland.

Kendall, P. C. (1984). Behavioral assessment and methodology. In C. M. Franks, G. T. Wilson, P. C. Kendall, & J. P. Foreyt (Eds.), *Review of behavior therapy: Theory and practice* (pp. 44–71). New York: Guilford Press.

Kirby, D. (1984). *Sexuality education: A handbook for the evaluation of programs*. Santa Cruz, CA: Network Publications.

Konker, C. (1992). Rethinking child sexual abuse: An anthropological perspective. *American Journal of Orthopsychiatry, 62*(1), 147–153.

Lief, H. I., Fullard, W., & Devlin, S. J. (1990). A new measure of adolescent sexuality: SKAT-A. *Journal of Sex Education and Therapy, 16*(2), 79–91.

Malinosky-Rummell, R. R., & Hoier, T. S. (1991). Dissociation in children: A validation study of measures of dissociation in community and sexually abused children. *Behavioral Assessment, 13*, 342–357.

Masson, J. M. (1984). *The assault on truth: Freud's suppression of the seduction theory*. New York: Penguin.

McCauley, E., Ito, J., & Kay, T. (1986). Psychosocial functioning in girls with Turner's syndrome and short stature: Social skills, behavior problems, and self-concept. *Journal of the American Academy of Child Psychiatry, 25*(1), 105–112.

Melton, G., & Limber, S. (1989). Psychologists' involvement in cases of child maltreatment. *American Psychologist, 44*(9), 1225–1233.

Mountain, H., Nicholson, M., Spencer, C., & Walker, L. (1984). *Incest: Colorado State Department of Social Services revitalization training.* Denver, CO: Nicholson, Spencer, & Associates.

O'Donohoe, W., & Elliott, A. N. (1991). A model for the clinical assessment of the sexually abused child. *Behavioral Assessment, 13*, 325–339.

Okami, P. (1992). Adversaria: Child perpetrators of sexual abuse: The emergence of a problematic deviant category. *Journal of Sex Research, 29*(1), 109–130.

Perheentupa, J., Lenko, H. L., Nevalainen, I., Nittymaki, M., Soderholm, A., & Taipale, V. (1974). Hormone therapy in Turner's syndrome: Growth and psychological aspects. *Growth, Development, and Endocrinology, 5*, 121–127.

Putnam, F. W. (1988). *Child Dissociative Checklist (Version 22).* Unpublished manuscript, National Institute of Mental Health, Washington, DC.

Riordan, R. J., & Verdel, A. C. (1991). Evidence of sexual abuse in children's art products. *School Counselor, 39*, 116–121.

Robin, M. (1991). Beyond validation interviews: An assessment approach to evaluating sexual abuse allegations. *Child and Youth Services, 15*, 93–113.

Ross, J., & Loss, P. (1991). Assessment of the juvenile sex offender. In G. D. Ryan & S. L. Lane (Eds.), *Juvenile sexual offending: Causes, consequences, and correction.* Lexington, MA: Lexington Books.

Ryan, G. D. (1991). Consequences for the victim of sexual abuse. In G. D. Ryan & S. L. Lane (Eds.), *Juvenile sexual offending: Causes, consequences, and correction* (pp. 163–174). Lexington, MA: Lexington Books.

Shaughnessy, M. F., & Shakesby, P. (1992). Adolescent sexual and emotional intimacy. *Adolescence, 27*, 475–480.

Sivan, A., Schor, D., Koeppl, G., & Noble, L. (1988). Interaction of normal children with anatomical dolls. *Child Abuse and Neglect, 12*, 295–304.

Sonis, W. A., Levine-Ross, J., Blue, J., Cutler, G. B., Loriaux, P. L., & Klein, R. P. (1983 May). Hyperactivity and Turner's syndrome. Paper presented at the American Academy of Child Psychiatry Annual Meeting, San Francisco.

Steele, B., & Ryan, G. (1991). Deviancy: Development gone wrong. In G. D. Ryan & S. L. Lane (Eds.), *Juvenile sexual offending: Causes, consequences, and correction* (pp. 83–102). Lexington, MA: Lexington Books.

Summit, R. C. (1983). The child sexual abuse accommodation syndrome. *Child Abuse and Neglect, 7*, 177–193.

Terr, L. (1986). The child psychiatrist and the child witness: Traveling companions by necessity if not by design. *Journal of the American Academy of Child Psychiatrist, 25*, 462–472.

Thornton, A., & Camburn, D. (1989). Religious participation and adolescent sexual behavior and attitudes. *Journal of Marriage and the Family, 51*, 641–652.

Walker, L.E.A. (1988). *Handbook on sexual abuse of children.* New York: Springer.

Walker L.E.A. (1990). Psychological assessment of sexually abused children for legal evaluation and expert witness testimony. *Professional Psychology: Research and Practice, 21*(5), 344–353.

White, S. D., & DeBlassie, R. R. (1992). Adolescent sexual behavior. *Adolescence, 27*, 185–191.

Wincze, J. P. (1989). Assessment and treatment of atypical sexual behavior. In S. R. Leiblum & R. C. Rosen (Eds.), *Principles and practice of sex therapy: Update for the 1990's* (pp. 382–404). New York: Guilford Press.

3
Sex Education toward the
Prevention of Sexual Problems

David L. Petty

rom birth to death, from cradle to grave, humans are sexual beings; we are multidimensional creatures, and one of our dimensions is sexuality. Because sexuality is an important dimension of our humanity, it is worthy of our attention. Sex (sexuality) education is a lifelong process during which information is taken in, processed, and manifested in diverse behavioral patterns.

U.S. society is experiencing a multitude of problems associated with our sexual behavior. While it is not within the scope of this chapter to document these problems, suffice it to say that poor education in human sexuality has contributed significantly to the problems of unintentional pregnancies and sexually transmitted diseases. Conversely, many people believe that planned sexuality education lessens or eliminates these problems.

The purpose of this chapter is to present information that addresses and stresses the importance of knowledge, attitudes, and values as they combine to form a basic format for sexuality education for parents, caretakers, teachers, clinicians, and other adult professionals who may have occasion to deal with preadults in meaningful ways.

Information and suggestions will be presented first in terms of the chronological periods from infancy through the teen years. Within each period, both physical and psychosocial sexual development will be presented, as well as corresponding issues and suggestions for those wishing to provide educational information. Following this part of the chapter, I will discuss several issues that seem especially critical in our society today regarding their relevance to sexuality education.

At the heart of this chapter are two ideals: one I have borrowed from another author; the other I have developed myself as a guide for adults who care about children and what their sexuality potential might be under ideal circumstances.

Ideals, I think, should be lofty goals, goals not easily reached but worth the effort of striving to achieve. In fact, I believe that the higher we rise toward trying to achieve a lofty goal, the more successful we will be at every point along the way.

Frank Cox (1981) described the ideal family as "one that allows all children to grow up in the most healthful manner possible." He added that this definition implies that:

> (1) children are wanted by both partners, (2) the partners are healthy enough physically and psychologically to supply love and security to children, (3) family economics are such that children can be properly nourished and kept physically healthy, and (4) the family can supply their children with sufficient educational opportunity to learn the skills necessary to survive and enjoy success within the culture. (1981, p. 291)

With many others, I share the belief that parents ought to be the sex educators of their children. All things being equal, two parents should be able to do that job better than one; intact families should be more functional than fractured families; happy families should be better for all members than families that are unhappy because of serious conflicts. Such a list could continue indefinitely, but the point is that such statements represent ideals. Quality, caring education in human sexuality is a vital step toward the goal of attaining our ideals regarding sexual conduct.

The other expression of an ideal is my belief that a happy, healthy sex life is possible for all humans, though few have attained it. To attain such an ideal, we all need help. This help, I think, should begin in the individual's family and end with the individual's spouse. Between these, a host of caring persons (educators, clinicians, counselors, and others) might provide helpful insight along the way.

A happy, healthy sex life is hardly attainable without education in sexual knowledge, attitudes, and values, as well as genuine concern on the part of the educators and others with whom the individual interacts intimately. Such an ideal is almost a figment of our imagination, for there are so few role models whom we may observe or who will share their success with the rest of us.

One helpful sex education approach with children is to use a geographical analogy to explain the ideal of a happy, healthy sex life. The analogy can be explained like this: We are at "Nowsville," and we desire to go to "Happy Town." Instead of driving them by car, we must engage in sexual intercourse to get to "Happy Town." Is it possible and if so, how, to orchestrate sexual activity so that each experience gets us closer to that ideal destination? Since we cannot orchestrate it alone, who can help us and who cares enough to share with us their road map?

When persons become sexually active, many other "destinations" are possible. Unfortunately, judging from what we see and hear around our society, all of these other places are more probable destinations than "Happy Town." Four other notable destinations are:

- "Oops City"—inhabited by individuals who either became unintentionally pregnant or who unintentionally impregnated another.
- "STD Acres"—inhabited by individuals who have contracted a sexually transmitted disease through sexual contact with an infected partner.
- "Guiltland"—inhabited by persons who, after engaging in sexual intercourse, feel guilty.
- "Nonfulfillment Burg"—inhabited by individuals who expected sexual intercourse to be wonderful only to find it a painfully shallow and nonfulfilling experience.

U.S. citizens who are residing at these locations now or who travel to them periodically represent the multitude of problems stemming from irresponsible sexual behavior. If "Happy Town" is an ideal and a possible destination for us, surely we need a clear road map shared with us by individuals who have already arrived there and who earnestly care that we get there too. To that end, this chapter is addressed.

Physical/Psychosexual Development

Physical Development

Early Childhood. I have made the somewhat arbitrary decision to define this period of development as the years from birth through age 5. It is certainly true that human infants know nothing of society's sexual customs and values; but their exploratory sexual behavior begins almost immediately after birth, and adult reaction to their behaviors constitute the beginnings of their sexuality education.

Sol Gordon (1975) was correct, then, in his insistence that parents (or other caregivers) quickly become the sex educators of their children—whether they like it or not and even whether they realize it or not. Wayne Anderson (1971) has also argued that sex education begins at birth, for the child is constantly observing what is going on around him/her.

According to Hyde (1986, p. 295), "The capacity of the human body to show a sexual response is present from birth": boy babies have been born with erections, and vaginal lubrication has been found in baby girls within 24 hours after birth.

By age 2 or 2½, most children become aware of their gender. After about age 3 there is a marked increase in activity and interest in general, including sexual interest and activity (Hyde, 1986).

Sexual exploration of one's own genitals is common in infancy. Because such behavior recurs over time, some believe that the infant may in fact receive a sense of pleasure from it. Sometimes, though, adults interpret such behavior as fondling or even masturbation; depending on their attitudes, they may discourage such behavior as though it could be potentially harmful.

How parents respond to exploratory behavior will set the stage for later sexual values (Kelly, 1990). For example, if the parent repeatedly moves the infant's hand away from her vulva or his penis, over time the child may infer the message that the vulva or the penis is "bad" and not to be touched indiscriminately. Thus an innocent, natural phase of sexual exploration can be transformed into lasting negative consequences for the child (Kelly, 1990).

Following infancy, as the child's circle of friends and playmates expands, it is common for children to explore the genitals of their playmates. Games such as "playing doctor," "show and compare," and the like, are typical. These games are thought to be much more related to curiosity than to sexuality (Hyde, 1986; Bruess & Greenberg, 1988; Kelly, 1990).

Instructions regarding urination and defecation are given to children when their parents train them about these natural processes. Gordon (1975) advises that accidents related to these natural functions be played down. Associating the ideas of "bad" or "dirty" with any processes involving the genitals and the anus may produce negativism later. He also counsels using the correct anatomical terms rather than using cute terms that may be misunderstood by others later on.

Nudity in the home is a concern for many parents. Most children, I think, extend their interest and curiosity beyond self-exploration and "playing doctor." While many parents will sometimes bathe children (same and opposite sex) together and casually explain genital sameness (or difference), allowing children to see themselves or other adults nude is often a much different matter. Opinions seem somewhat polarized. In sorting through the pro and con arguments regarding nudity in the home, I have reached these conclusions: First, it is healthy for the young child to see both parents nude. At such times the parent(s) can casually explain several things, for example, why Mom has breasts but young daughter does not; why Dad's penis is larger than young son's; why both Mom and Dad have pubic hair; how daughter will grow up to look similar to Mom; how son will grow up to look similar to Dad; and so on. Second, it provides a good opportunity for each parent (or both together) to explain their feelings about modesty and privacy—two important lessons for children to learn.

Thus, I offer these suggestions:

1. If parents view their bodies as acceptable and to be respected, such attitudes should be instilled within their children.

2. If a child chances upon a nude parent, parental reaction is critical in giving a message to the child. If the parent screams or lunges for a gar-

ment or towel, the child may conclude that he/she has witnessed something evil or frightening (Strong & DeVault, 1988). It is possible to convey our concern for privacy without reacting in a way that might create fear or guilt in our children.

3. Most children will develop a sense of modesty as they grow older (Gordon, 1975; Strong & DeVault, 1988), and nudity should not be a problem. More importantly, children will feel good about themselves and their body image.

Later Childhood. Children between the ages of 6 and 10 continue to be interested in many things related to human sexuality. Instead of repressing their sexual feelings, as suggested by Freud's notion of sexual latency, children in later childhood maintain an active interest in such things as sexual pictures, sexual words, sexual stories told by friends, even sexual jokes (Gordon, 1975).

Instead of following Freud's concept of latency in which children are supposed to be more interested in friends of the same sex, far more children begin to develop heterosocial attachments. In fact, they appear to step through a sequence of events that paves the way to adolescent heterosexuality: romantic attachments are followed by feelings of "love" and then by arranging a "date" (Kelly, 1990).

After age 8, children commonly hear about sexual intercourse for the first time. They appear to react with a combination of disbelief and shock; it is particularly difficult for them to imagine their parents doing such a thing (Hyde, 1986).

Also after age 8, there is some separating of the sexes. Hyde uses the term "homosocial" to explain this normal part of sexual development; the homosocial stage of development is "a general form of social groupings in which males play and associate with other males and females play and associate with other females; that is, the genders are separate from each other" (1986, p. 302).

In prepubescence, some heterosocial parties and group dating emerge. Boys, who are often shorter in physical stature than girls, have more trouble adjusting to expected behavior. Boys, who want to roughhouse, and girls, who want to dance, can make for some comical parties. All in all, preadolescents tend to be sexually conservative (Hyde, 1986).

Adolescence. Strong and DeVault (1988, p. 232) define adolescence as "the psychological state occurring during puberty." Kelly (1990, p. 167) regards adolescence as the "period of emotional, social and physical transition from childhood to adulthood." Puberty is that "time of life when reproductive capacity develops and secondary sex characteristics begin to appear" (Kelly, 1990, p. 166).

The important thing for sex educators to know is that puberty stimulates a surge of sexual interest. A combination of factors converge to create heightened sensitivity, including rises in the levels of sex hormones, a developing awareness of bodily changes, and increased cultural emphases on sex (Kelly, 1990).

In adolescence a person's sexuality is publically recognized but is not permitted expression: masturbation and sexual intercourse are discouraged for girls and, though not entirely discouraged for boys, they certainly are not encouraged. While this discouragement does not entirely prevent these expressions, it can be a source of guilt and conflict. Our society seems to dangle sex before adolescents' faces on the one hand, and to censure them for partaking of it on the other (Strong & DeVault, 1988).

Physical Changes

For young adolescents, their bodies are a source of interest, wonder, and bewilderment. The fact that body development surges ahead of feelings, experiences, and maturity is a major factor in the dilemma of adolescence.

Statistics reveal that the range of ages for menarche, the onset of menstruation, is 9 to 17; the average range is age 12 to 13. While boys may already have experienced orgasm, with pubescent changes comes the ability to produce semen so that ejaculation now accompanies orgasm. Strong and DeVault (1988, p. 234) note that "Kinsey called first ejaculation the most important psychosexual event in male adolescence." Whether or not we agree with Kinsey, it is imperative to begin instructing our girls and boys about menarche and nocturnal emissions (wet dreams) *before they occur* (Gordon, 1975).

Often, parents may find their adolescents manifesting inordinate concerns about penis size or breast size and shape. While these concerns represent sensitive areas for discussion, knowledgeable parents and counselors can allay adolescent fears. For example, boys can be informed that the most notable variability in penis size is in the flaccid (nonerect) state. Of course, it is in this state in which most discrete observations (in restrooms and showers) are made. Girls, on the other hand, can be reassured that there is considerable diversity in women's breast size and shape, that a female's two breasts may be slightly different in size, and especially that little, if any, of this is significantly related to their sexual appeal or functioning.

Children learn a great deal about sexuality from their parents. Most of what they learn comes from observing their parents' behavior. As Strong and Devault (1988, p. 235) rightly note, "The silence that surrounds sexuality in most families and in most communities carries its own important messages. It communicates that some of the most important dimensions of life are secretive, off limits, bad to talk or think about." A commonly held fear that helps explain this parental silence is their notion that their children (especially their daughters) will become sexually active if they have too much information. However, there are no studies that support such a relationship (Gordon, 1975; Strong & DeVault, 1988).

Adolescents receive an overabundance of misinformation about sex from each other. This reality is one of the unfortunate results of parents not providing them with the necessary information they need. When children, and particularly adolescents, become desperate for information to help them make sense of the enormous changes they are experiencing, they typically turn to their peers, who are usually equally uninformed. When they are pressured to conform to the message that "everybody is doing it" (i.e., having sex), and they give in to the message, their experiences are commonly less than satisfying. Many adolescents are convinced, often mistakenly, that their friends are more knowledgeable and experienced regarding sexual matters; thus, they fear their initial real encounter. And, indeed, that first encounter may be quite dysfunctional. For example, a hurried sexual encounter typically results in a boy's premature ejaculation, which often becomes a recurring sexual dysfunction (Masters et al., 1982).

Issues in Sexuality Education

Sharing Knowledge/Demanding Accuracy

The core of any sexuality education program or emphasis is the knowledge (or facts) of the subject matter. Science and its attendant methodology insist on factual information. Humans need accurate information to best conduct life's affairs.

Because of the magnitude of the social problems associated with irresponsible sexual behavior, accurate information is essential to any hope of resolving these problems and preventing future problems. Reinisch and Beasley (1993, p. 157) tell us that "from the moment your child is born, you tell him about sexuality. . . . It is a good idea, then, to give your child accurate information about sex as they [*sic*] grow up, before misinformation is absorbed or invented."

Parents often ask these questions: "What do my kids need to know?" "How much information should I give my child?" "Do I know enough to instruct my child?" Each of these questions expresses parental concern, and certainly that concern is legitimate.

Persons need to know enough about their sexuality, sexual behavior, and related attitudes and values to make their sexual choices and experiences as healthy and pleasurable as possible. Put differently, they need to know how to get to "Happy Town."

Basically, I feel that we are talking about the physiological aspects of our sexuality, about statistical indicators of sexual behavior in our society, and about some sort of evaluation of these behaviors based on one's value system. As pointed out elsewhere, this information should be geared to the child's age, maturity, and inquisitiveness; and it should be provided on an ongoing and cumulative basis (Bernstein, 1977).

In their early childhood, children should become acquainted with the description, functions, and appropriate name(s) of their own genitals. I think it wise to acknowledge the body's natural functions (e.g., urination, defecation, menstruation, nocturnal emission, and so on), but also to observe the necessary societal controls on each for the benefit of the society as a whole. Also, we should deemphasize the negativity commonly associated with these functions (Anderson, 1971; Gordon, 1975).

While many families develop and perpetuate clever names for the genitals and natural processes, we would do better to use correct anatomical terms (Gordon, 1975). However, it would be helpful also to acknowledge others' use of slang terminology, which our children will surely hear, while gently explaining that we think these terms are inappropriate and that we choose not to use them. The point is that the child will know what *all* these terms mean, which ones we feel are best, and why we feel they are best.

The normal changes associated with puberty (menarche for girls and nocturnal emissions for boys) can be most unsettling to the child—particularly if she/he is unprepared for these events. Any parent (and preferably both) should be able to explain the onset of menstruation for a prepubescent girl and orgasm/ejaculation for the prepubescent boy. Which is better: instructing a child that with the coming of puberty she/he will become capable of reproduction and of enjoying her/his sexuality or neglecting this instruction so that puberty comes unawares to the child? Gordon has described the latter course of inaction:

> Sex can introduce confusion and overwhelming feelings to an adolescent who has no perspective with which to understand them. The excitement and apprehension accompanying first or early sexual experiences, coupled with the fact that the settings for these experiences are usually cars and other distracting situations, make for what are usually unsatisfactory or guilt-ridden encounters. As a result, many young people prematurely diagnose themselves as inadequate, impotent, frigid, . . . or whatever. (1975, p. 165)

In addition to the information just mentioned, our children need to know about the reproductive process. Explaining menarche to children (boys need to know about it too), provides an excellent opportunity to discuss menstruation, ovulation, sexual intercourse, conception, and pregnancy. Such a discussion ultimately necessitates wedding the facts of the biological process to the subtleties of social dating along with the ways two people become sexually involved. All children, whether or not they ask, should be told how a man's sperm cells get into a woman and reach her ovum. In all likelihood, parents will want to provide that information over an extended period of time; this process is far too complex to be adequately explained at one time.

Most parents probably will want their children to know about both conception control and birth control measures. Conception control involves the methods that prevent fertilization of the ovum by the sperm, while birth control is a broader term that includes both conception control and methods that induce abortion after conception. I have argued elsewhere that unintended pregnancies result from irresponsible sexual behavior. Since most people understand that humans often wish to engage in coitus without the intention of conception, they must know the most reliable methods of preventing pregnancy. Knowledgeable parents will undoubtedly want to instruct their children regarding contraceptives. If not, they might choose to ask a professional (medical doctor, family planning specialist, or the like) to provide this instruction. Three emphases should be part of any such instruction: (1) types of contraceptives and percentage risk of conception based on published data, (2) possible side effects associated with using particular contraceptive devices, and (3) complete instructions on effective use of the devices.

Parents and professionals alike will want to evaluate personally the importance of providing information on birth control (i.e., any control measure utilized once conception has occurred). Primarily, I am speaking of abortion. This is a most sensitive issue exacerbated by the lack of consensus generated in our society regarding the morality of the practice.

The general practice of abortion is so common in our society that every child deserves to be thoroughly aware of your (the sex educator's) views. Additionally, I feel that you should be prepared to defend your views based on any pertinent, factual information and your own values. Personally, I claim no measure of objectivity regarding the issue of abortion. Nevertheless, I firmly believe that the best, most responsible behavior is to take steps to keep from becoming unintentionally pregnant (or to unintentionally impregnate another). If we can help our children at this point, we will save them from a personal struggle with a grievous issue.

Sharing Values without Moralizing

Eunice K. Shriver (1977) recalled visiting a center for teenage girls where their teacher asked what they wanted to discuss: How to care for infants? The physiology of childbirth? Family planning? They appeared disinterested in all of these topics. Then the teacher asked if they would like to discuss how to say "No" to a boyfriend's proposal to have sex without losing his love. All hands quickly shot up! Shriver concluded that whatever sexuality education is provided, it should contain a moral as well as a biological dimension. Our children want us to teach them something to believe.

The method of teaching sometimes may be as important as the content of the message. Shriver (1977) points out that in teaching values, we do not have to be heavy-handed, rigid, or moralistic. Instead, we can discuss what it means to love and care for one another; we can emphasize trust, loyalty, selflessness, and character.

Jensen and Robbins (1975), in pointing out some common mistakes made by parents when discussing sex with their teenagers, believe that a chief problem is our urge to moralize. While it is indeed important to share our values with our children, we must stifle the tendency to use such rigid admonitions as "I don't want you to . . .," or "You must. . . ." Because they are free creatures, our children realize (or soon will) that they really do not have to do anything we say.

Former U.S. secretary of education William J. Bennett (1987, p. 120) believes that "sex education is about character and the formation of character. A sex-education course in which issues of right and wrong do not occupy center stage is an evasion and an irresponsibility." In that same vein, James DiGiacomo said,

> They [adolescents] need to formulate for themselves a set of standards, a sexual morality, not imposed from above and accepted uncritically, but based on their own values and felt needs, on their best and most generous instincts. But they cannot do it alone or without help from wise and caring adults who can share their world of ideas and concerns and lead them through the thickets of propaganda and half truths that surround them. This is what real sex education is all about, not the threats of puritanical zealots nor the well-meaning but shoddy tactics of the promoters of contraception (1987, p. 128)

Accentuating the Positive/Downplaying the Negative

Beginning with the premises that humans are sexual creatures and that our sexuality is an important dimension of our humanity, sexuality education will be more effective when expressed positively and less effective when expressed negatively. One may wonder how it is possible to be positive when the society seems almost overwhelmed by the negative results of irresponsible sexual behavior. I would simply remind us that "Happy Town" is a happy place, and we can get there if we choose the right route. Again, parental responsibility is critically important in accentuating the positive while downplaying the negative.

When a human infant comes into the world, it will be cared for by two parents who planned for it, wanted it, and are prepared to care for it. As Fishel (1993, p. 152) notes, "Babies come into the world with a 'skin hunger' as basic as their need for food. From the moment of birth, a baby needs to be touched, gazed at, and held. Cuddling your baby helps him thrive and helps build a bond that provides the base for later attachments."

As growing babies explore their genitals, our reactions help them begin to recognize themselves as sexual beings. As they become toddlers, they become more aware of their own bodies, and their natural curiosity leads to a greater awareness of others' bodies (same and opposite sex). Our comfort with nudity should assist them in developing gender identity, a sense of being a girl or a boy.

As toddlers become preschoolers, they usually develop a sense of privacy—for themselves as well as for others. Hopefully, they also become comfortable with asking their parents questions (Fishel, 1993).

School-age children hunger for information, and it can be provided at their level (Bernstein, 1977) in a positive, matter-of-fact way. Interestingly, as Fishel (1993, p. 153) notes, "This is also a time when children begin to bond with friends and to value their peer relationships as much as they value their family connections."

If parents want to help their children on the roller-coaster ride that begins with the onset of puberty, they should focus on the notion that the adolescent "has achieved another landmark in development rather than emphasizing the new burdens that accompany this change" (Fishel, 1993, p. 155).

In my course, "Sociology of Sex Education for Children," I ask my students to write about their perspectives on sex. I expect them to create a brief document that combines the presentation of sexuality facts (knowledge) with sexual morality (values). Several years ago a female student projected herself into the future in describing what she would say to her daughter-to-be: she called her paper "Introducing My Adolescent Daughter to the Adventures and Perils of Sex":

> You began to experience puberty, with slight physical changes a couple of years ago. Your straight little girl body began the *wonderful* transformation of changing into a woman. Your breasts started to grow, becoming knobby little bumps and your arms, legs and hips began to develop into female curves.
>
> At that time, we discussed your approaching menarche and some of the major characteristics that would affect you. As part of the preparation for the *exciting* occasion, we made a trip to school and from the homemaking teacher, we selected some brochures that had drawings showing how menstruation occurred. Finally, we went to the store and purchased a sanitary belt and napkins to put aside for your use when the *momentous occasion* arrived (emphases mine).

I remember thinking, "How fortunate such a daughter would be to have a mother who would paint such a beautifully positive picture of these inevitable changes accompanying puberty!" What a contrast to mothers who call menarche the beginning of a curse, a time of pain or discomfort, or something equally negative. And, what a stark contrast to the mother who sent the writer Charlie Shedd (1968, p. 125) a postcard with this message:

Sir:

... The government ought to protect us from people like you. But there is so much evil in Washington I don't suppose they will do anything. I don't want my daughter to know the awful things that go on today between all those juvenile delinquents. Don't worry about my Elizabeth. When she gets married, I will tell her all about her organs and what she is in for, and that will be soon enough.

Yours truly,

Communicating Comfort/Becoming Open to Questions

Medora and Wilson (1992, p. 24) note that some parents are scared of making mistakes. . . . Others may feel insecure and incompetent about telling it 'right.'" Gordon (1975, p. 23) wisely remarks, "As parents, we need to be more comfortable about our own sexuality before we undertake [guiding] our children's." Pamela Wilson put it this way:

> When you teach your child the names of various body parts, what message does your facial expression give? Do you smile when you name the eyes and nose but look nervous when you label the penis or vagina? Even if you are conveying a positive message verbally, your ambivalent or negative feeling about sexual parts of the body can come through. Your positive verbal and nonverbal messages let your child know that his body—including the genitals—is a source of pleasure throughout life. (Quoted in Fishel, 1993, p. 152)

Why are so many people uncomfortable with the subject of sex? Perhaps a chief reason is that so many of us were deprived of knowledge in our formative years. We, who are poor sex educators as parents, had parents who also were poor sex educators. Perhaps another reason is that some of the negative views of sex associated with Puritanism and Victorianism are still pervasive in our society. Whatever the reason(s) for our discomfort, unless we work to correct these attitudes, our ignorance about and discomfort with sexuality matters will perpetuate the problems for our children (Jensen & Robbins, 1975).

Parental anxiety regarding the discussion of sexual topics with their children will be exacerbated if they have not begun discussion early in the child's life. Some parents wait, erroneously believing that unless the child asks a question about sex, she/he has no interest in the topic and no need to know. To this notion, Art Linkletter (1976, p. 16) has pointed out: "The more introverted, shy ones [kids] may never ask, 'Where did I come from?' or 'How did you make me?' They prefer the method of deductive reasoning to direct interrogation."

If you begin discussions of sex (or any other topics) with your children early in their lives and if you display a comfortable, positive attitude to them, the chances are good that they will come to you with their questions. When your children are young, short, simple answers and explanations should suffice. As Bernstein (1977) has suggested, your responses should be geared to their level of understanding.

As your children grow older and mature, your responses should naturally become more sophisticated. Adolescents may pose real challenges as they struggle with the sexual pressure of their physiological changes and the social pressure created by their peers (Schumm & Rekers, 1984). Kathleen Fury (1980) advises that if our children want to discuss sexual concerns, we should try to listen *without* panic and *with* love. In this process, we may disagree with their stated sexual standards, but we should never withhold our affection or respect.

Distinguishing between "Making Love" and "Having Sex"

The term "making love" is widely used in our society as a reference to "having sex," that is, engaging in sexual intercourse. But how many people are really "making love" when they are engaging in sexual intercourse? How important is it to you that having sex be an expression of love? How important is love in making one's sexual expressions the most enjoyable experiences they can be? As a parental or professional sex educator, how important is it to you to include some instructions about love?

What is love? Is it an emotion, a sensitivity, a yearning, an action? Certainly the term has been discussed, written about, ridiculed, maligned, and used for a myriad of motives to justify human behavior. In the final analysis, how can a caring parent do complete justice to describing sexual behavior without including love in its context?

In my discussions with college students through the years on the topic of love, I have found the following expressions most helpful: though not a scholarly treatise, this contrast of love and infatuation by Ann Landers is potentially helpful for adult sex educator and teenager alike:

> Infatuation is instant desire. It's one set of glands calling to another.
> Love is friendship that has caught fire. It takes root and grows—one day at a time.
> Infatuation is marked by a feeling of insecurity. You are excited and eager, but not genuinely happy. . . .
> Love is the quiet understanding and mature acceptance of imperfection. It is real. It gives you strength and grows beyond you—to bolster your beloved. . . .
> Infatuation might lead you to do things you'll regret later, but love never will.
> Love lifts you up. It makes you look up. It makes you think up. It makes you a better person than you were before. (1977, p. 3E)

James McCary has helped me think of love as a dynamic process that can promote growth and maturity for individuals. As he remarks, "Mature love, the interaction between two emotionally mature individuals whose relationship is based on individual creativity, mutual esteem, and erotic fulfillment (O'Neill & O'Neill, 1972), grows as the relationship unfolds, and is not diminished by aging, physical infirmity, loss of looks, or changing situations" (1975, p. 135). I have experienced these things in my own marriage of more than 34 years, and it has been very good!

The concept of romantic love in our society is worthy of our consideration. Our children will undoubtedly hear some of the clichés associated with romantic love, and we should be able to help with their interpretations. We are told that "Love is blind," that someone is "head over heels in love," that a couple "fell in love at first sight." Such terms beg for explanations, for it is also commonly believed that romantic love is the proper prelude for marriage. McCary (1975) tells us that romantic love satisfies the ego, that it tends to idealize the loved one rather than to see her/him realistically, but that it *can* provide a basis for mature love. Adults, who have experienced some of these several expressions of romantic love, are advised to share their experiences with their children to at least help with the latters' developing expectations.

Finally, I have been impressed with at least three Greek terms rendered as "love" in the English: *eros, phileo*, and *agape*. Briefly, these have been expressed as carnal (sensual, physical) love, brotherly (affectionate, friendly) love, and spiritual (selfless) love, respectively. My wife and I have realized some erotic expressions in our love relationships, and we have attributed these to the physical attraction that comes from our human nature—a nature not greatly unlike that of other animals. However, we also have found that *agape* love helps each of us put the desires and feelings of the other as at least equal to our own and sometimes beyond our own. We have found that this consideration of the wants of the other as greater than our own wants has helped us develop a selflessness that has contributed to a maturing love.

My wife and I have tried to model these rich expressions of love to our sons. Even so, I recommend that before our children begin pairing off and dating, we share some explicit guidelines regarding caring and loving.

Dealing with Masturbation

Part of the ambivalence and complexity associated with human sexuality in this society is the lack of consensus displayed regarding numerous important topics. For example, there is little agreement on the nature, incidence, and effects of masturbation. Because masturbation is a concern for children and adults alike, it is worthy of consideration here.

Masturbation, according to Hyde (1986, p. 13), is the "self-stimulation of the genitals to produce sexual arousal," and according to Shedd (1968, p. 70), the "self-production of an orgasm by exciting the genital organs." Whether or not an orgasm is produced, the rubbing of one's genitals is apparently pleasurable to most individuals from infancy onward.

In the past, attitudes toward masturbation were largely negative and some people predicted dire consequences for those who practiced it. For those who practiced it to excess (usually subjectively measured), masturbation was thought to be particularly dangerous. Children, young or old, caught in the act might be told:

- It will cause pimples to erupt on your face.
- It will cause hair to grow on the palms of your hands.
- It will cause warts to grow on your body.
- It will lead to your insanity.

No scientific studies have ever corroborated any such phenomena, yet I wonder how many youngsters have developed significant guilt complexes from well-meaning adults who warned them of these and other dangers?

Most writers argue that masturbation is essentially a universal phenomenon. If so, it must be correct to say that the outlandish effects reported and believed by many in our society are just that: outlandish. Moreover, this revelation should bear great significance: it should relieve our anxieties, and it should reduce (even eliminate) our tendencies to perpetuate such myths.

What do children and teenagers need to know about masturbation? What information should concerned parents share about masturbation? What counsel can professionals provide as they deal with parents and children who are struggling with a perceived problem regarding masturbation? Several positives and at least one negative seems pertinent to consider.

Kelly (1990) describes masturbation as a healthy outlet for sexual tension, as a normal expression of one's sexuality. Bruess and Greenberg (1988) view masturbation as a normal part of growth and development. Calderone and Johnson (1981, p. 26) suggest that masturbation by a child is a "rehearsal for mature sex." Charlie Shedd (1968, pp. 70, 73) calls masturbation a "gift of God" and "preferable to teenage intercourse."

Shedd, however, also sounds a note of caution. He warns that masturbation may become compulsive-obsessive. Defining compulsion as a "feeling of being irresistibly driven to the performance" and obsession as "persistent preoccupation with an idea" (1968, p. 71), Shedd warns that we must not let masturbation control us. To be managed by masturbation (or anything else) is to go backward rather than forward.

Parents and professionals need to know that, though this form of autoerotic behavior is common, not all children will be inclined to masturbate. As we instruct children and parents about this topic, we should not insist that all children will masturbate, but we should also make it clear that for those who find it pleasurable to rub or caress their genitals, there is no reason to feel guilty about such activity, and that when done it should be done in private. When a child's masturbation becomes repetitively public, clinical intervention becomes necessary (Ferguson and Rekers, 1979).

Confronting the Issue of Abstinence versus Contraception

Dating from the 1960s, two models for family life education have developed: the earlier, nondirective model, and the later (since the advent of AIDS) directive model.

The nondirective model focuses on three emphases:

1. Transmitting information (knowledge) about sexuality to the student
2. Teaching decision-making skills
3. Promoting self-esteem

As Whitehead and McGraw (1991, p. 4) remark concerning this model, "The primary goal is said to be the enhancement of the student's ability to make sexual choices that will be in his or her best interest."

The directive model gained its impetus from the passage of the Adolescent Family Life Act in 1981, and its emphases are based on two assumptions: first, that "abstinence from pre-marital sexual involvement is a positive and normal lifestyle for adolescents," and second, "that parent and family involvement is the most important single factor in good outcomes for children and youth" (Whitehead & McGraw, 1991, p. 4).

According to Whitehead and McGraw (1991, p. 10), "In the non-directive model, abstinence is presented as an option that is 100% safe, but information on the risks, benefits, and methods of birth control are considered absolutely necessary in order for a family life education program to be truly 'comprehensive.'|" In the directive model, the message is that abstinence from premarital sexual activity is "a distinctly positive and normal lifestyle for children and youth" (Whitehead & McGraw, 1991, p. 10).

The foci of these two models clearly show the sharp fracture in our society considering sexual education and the truth that values are indeed important considerations in issues of human sexuality. Thus, I feel that this discussion is primary for parent and professional alike in ultimately determining how they will approach sexuality education.

The question that appears to underlie this whole furor is, "What are we trying to prevent?" Most would agree that the major preventive goals are the unintended and unwanted pregnancies of unmarried teenagers and the proliferation of sexually transmitted diseases. Beyond these, other answers that have been given are individual-specific or group-specific, depending on one's values.

Addressing the major preventive concerns, one should ask, "What is the most effective way to prevent unintended, unwanted pregnancies?" All groups recognize that abstinence is the only 100 percent safe method. And while all informed persons realize that AIDS and other STDs may be transmitted other than through sexual contact, these diseases are still aptly named: they are sexually transmitted diseases. Thus abstinence from sexual intercourse would be the most effective preventive for STDs as well as unintended pregnancies.

The next question, I think, is this: "How realistic is it to think that sexually active adolescents and adolescents who are contemplating sexual activity would seriously consider education calling for abstinence?" Most of my college students ridicule such a suggestion. They, like others in our society, say "Everybody's doing it." Out of this mind-set, of course, the nondirective model for sexuality education has emerged—beginning in the 1960s and 1970s (Whitehead & McGraw, 1991).

Two other questions now seem appropriate. First, "Have we tried, on a large-scale basis, to teach sexual responsibility from the perspective of directed abstinence?" This means, do we really have data to allow an informed answer to the previous question (i.e., would sexually active adolescents seriously consider education calling for abstinence?)? Second, "How effective has the nondirective model been in preventing unintended and unwanted pregnancies and epidemic STDs?" The answer to the first question above is debatable, yet I think we must give it serious consideration. The data on teen pregnancies and STDs make the answer to the second question painfully obvious.

Have we capitulated to the insistent sexual activity of our youth on the assumptions that knowledge, decision-making skills, and promotion of their self-esteem would eliminate or reduce pregnancies and STDs? Have we, in telling them about abstinence as a safe option along with educating them about using contraceptives and even dispensing condoms, believed that they would be responsible and mature enough to effect the intended preventive measures?

Before concluding this section, I wish to make a few personal observations about the nondirective and directive models. First, I believe that the three major emphases stressed in the nondirective model are well stated; education programs, as well as parental and professional helpers, would do well to increase accurate information for our youth, to teach decision-making skills, and to help our youth feel good about themselves. Beyond these appropriate goals, we must provide informed, realistic alternatives for their decision making and help them to determine what those best decisions are and why. Without our help, they cannot know that a place called "Happy Town" exists, much less learn how to get there. As they learn how to travel successfully to "Happy Town," I'm convinced that their self-esteem will be greatly enhanced.

The first assumption of the directed-abstinence model is that abstinence from premarital sexual intercourse is both positive and normal as an adolescent life-style. I would support use of the term "positive" in the sense that abstinence would effectively reduce unintended, unwanted pregnancies and STD proliferation. The other term, "normal," however, presents a problem. Normal, as a form of "norm," which means expected behavior, has an ideal and a real dimension. Proponents of the directed-abstinence model could argue, from an ideal perspective, that premarital abstinence should be the norm. However, opponents could argue, from a real perspective (based on what most people say they do), that premarital abstinence is not normal. Indeed, the data, based on reported behavior, support that latter contention.

To resolve this dilemma, we are back to the admission that values must be addressed. Can we as a society say with any confidence what is good or bad, right or wrong, better or worse? Is it time to take a courageous stand, in light of the obvious fact that too many of our youth are making wrong choices? Can we say to them, in light of our own experience, "This is better for you because . . ." or "Let me [us] help you aim for this goal and reach it!"

Conclusions

Being a sexuality educator is not an easy task, but making a determined effort to do the job well is worth every difficulty we may encounter along the way. To conclude this chapter, I wish to share these final thoughts and suggestions.

In their chapter entitled "Planned Sex Education Programs," Calderone and Johnson (1981, p. 210) list six values that they believe should undergird sexuality facts:

> 1. *Information.* "Correct information is better than ignorance or the wrong information; it makes responsible action possible."
> 2. *Responsibility.* "An action, sexual or otherwise, taken in the light of all its possible consequences, good or bad, present and future, can be called responsible."
> 3. *Control.* "Sex is power; . . . it must be controlled by the individual for good purpose."
> 4. *Consideration.* "The welfare and needs . . . of oneself, of others involved, and of society, must be considered in whatever a person does."
> 5. *Each Individual.* "The infinite value of others is worthy of our most caring and loving consideration."
> 6. *Communication.* "It is good to have opportunities . . . to make our feelings known and to learn the feelings of others through discussion and conversation."

Medora and Wilson (1992) have provided 15 suggestions to teachers, family life educators, and other professionals who work with children. The following seven are especially pertinent (see their article for the complete list):

> 1. "Start sexuality education early in the child's life and make it continuous because sexuality is not a separate aspect but an integral component of a person's total life (Chilman, 1990)."
> 2. "Present correct and developmentally appropriate information and ideas without embarrassment. These things should be done within the framework of family values."
> 3. "Parents and teachers could use information from books as a basis to become more knowledgeable and comfortable about one's own and one's child's sexuality. This can sometimes be accomplished when parents and children read a book together."
> 4. "Do not wait for questions from the child; instead, use teachable moments that arise naturally and spontaneously in day-to-day living."
> 5. "Use simple and correct terminology when parts of the body, including genitals, are discussed."
> 6. "Share personal judgments and insights concerning sexuality issues as well as the values that motivate these."
> 7. "Teach children that they have the right to say no. Children should be taught that they have the right to decline being touched, whether it be by another child or by an adult (Scott-Lowe, 1985)." (1992, pp. 26–27)

My encouragement of sexuality education, first within the family and later complemented by other social institutions—notably education and religion—is to hopefully replace our reactive mode with a preventive mode for dealing with the problems of irresponsible sexual behavior. If we can prevent the irresponsible behavior, we will not have to react to the problems caused by that behavior. To effect such a preventive mode, I believe that a positive approach (i.e., the road map to "Happy Town") is a better emphasis than a negative approach (i.e., the "gloom and doom" associated with "Oops City" and "STD Acres").

References

Anderson, W. J. (1971). *How to explain sex to children.* Minneapolis, MN: T. S. Denison and Company.

Bennett, W. J. (1987, February 14). Sex and the education of our children. *America*, pp. 120–125.

Bernstein, A. C. (1977). How children learn about sex and birth. In E. Powers & M. Lees (Eds.), *Encounter with family realities* (pp. 10–20). St. Paul, MN: West Publishing Company.

Bruess, C. E., & Greenberg, J. S. (1988). *Sexuality education: Theory and practice* (2d ed.). New York: Macmillan.

Calderone, M. S., & Johnson, E. (1981). *The family book about sexuality*. New York: Harper and Row.

Carro, G. (1979, August). "What parents need to know about a child's sexuality." *Ladies' Home Journal*, pp. 30

Clabes, J. (1993, May 4). Teens and sex: Parents need to give guidance. *Daily Sentinel*, (Nacogdoches) p. 8A

Cox, F. D. (1981). *Human intimacy: Marriage, the family, and its meaning*, (2d ed.). St. Paul, MN: West Publishing Company.

DiGiacomo, J. J. (1987 February 14). All you need is love. *America*, pp. 126–129.

Ferguson, L. M., & Rekers, G. A., (1979) Non-aversive intervention for public childhood masturbation. *Journal of Sex Research, 15*(3), 213–223.

Fishel, E. (1993). Raising sexually healthy children. In *Human sexuality,—Annual editions, 93/94* (pp. 152–156). Guilford, CT: Dushkin Publishing Group.

Fury, K. (1980, June). The troubling truth about teen-agers and sex. *Reader's Digest*, pp. 153–156

Gordon, S. (1975). *Let's make sex a household word: A guide for parents and children*. New York: John Day Company.

Gordon, S. (1984, December). Viewpoint: Sex education: moral vs. moralistic. *Sexual Medicine Today*, p. 38

Hacker, S. S. (1993). The transition from the old norm to the new. In *Human sexuality—Annual editions 93/94* (pp. 24–31). Guilford, CT: Dushkin Publishing Group.

Hyde, J. S. (1986). *Understanding human sexuality* (3d ed.). New York: McGraw-Hill.

Jensen, G. D., & Robbins, M. (1975, July). Ten reasons why sex talks with adolescents go wrong. *Human Sexuality*, pp. 7–23.

Kavesh, L. (1983, July 27). Teen-agers' magazines trying to set readers straight on sex. *Dallas Morning News*, p. 4E.

Kelly, G. F. (1990). *Sexuality today: The human perspective* (2d ed.). Guilford, CT: Dushkin Publishing Group.

Krupa, L. (1982, January). Educating children about sex. *Family Journal*, pp. 34–37.

Landers, A. (1977, June 15). One more time, folks, and that's it. *Corpus Christi Caller*, p. 3E

Linkletter, A. (1976, October). Kids and sex. *Plain Truth*, pp. 16–17, 44

Masters, W. H., et al. (1982). *Human sexuality*. Boston: Little, Brown and Company.

McCary, J. L. (1975). *Freedom and growth in marriage*. Santa Barbara, CA: Hamilton Publishing Company.

Medora, N. P., & Wilson, S. (1992). Sexuality education for young children: The role of parents. *Day Care and Early Education*, Vol. 19, pp. 24–27

O'Neill, N., & O'Neill, J. G. (1972). *Open marriage: A new lifestyle for couples*. New York: M. Evans and Company.

Peterson, L. (1987). *Adolescent abstinence: A guide for family planning professionals*. Seattle, WA: Center for Health Training.

Reinisch, J. M., & Beasley, R. (1993). Sensuality and kids: Straight answers to parents' sensitive questions. In *Human sexuality—Annual edition 93/94* (pp. 157–159). Guilford CT: Dushkin Publishing Group.

Safran, C. (1984, February). Speaking of sex. *Parents*, pp. 66–70, 149.

Shedd, C. W. (1968). *The stork is dead*. New York: Pillar Books.

Shriver, E. K. (1977, November). Teen-age sexuality: There *is* a moral dimension. *Washington Star*, pp. 153–154.

Schumm, W. R., & Rekers, G. A. (1984). Sex should occur only within marriage. In H. Feldman & A. Parrot, *Human sexuality: Contemporary controversies*, pp. 105–124, Beverly Hills, CA: Sage Publications.

Strong, B., & Devault, C. (1988). *Understanding our sexuality* (2d ed.). St. Paul, MN: West Publishing Company.

Whitehead, M., & McGraw, O. (1991). *Foundations for family life education: A guidebook for professionals and parents*. Arlington, VA: Educational Guidance Institute.

Yates, A. (1986). Discussing sex with adolescent patients. *Physician's Guide to Sexual Counseling, 20*, 150–155.

Part 2

Problems of Psychosexual Adjustment to Physical Development

4

Psychologic Issues of Adjustment in Precocious, Normal, Delayed, and Incongruent Puberty

Tom Mazur
Rochelle L. Cherpak

This chapter provides an overview of the normal timing of puberty and its sequence of events, in males and females. Emphasis is given to individuals whose puberty is either precocious or delayed or is not congruent with their gender identity/role. Adolescent gynecomastia in boys and hirsutism in girls constitute examples of incongruent puberty. Psychologic issues are discussed which accompany normal puberty and abnormal puberty. Finally, treatment recommendations are given.

Puberty is the awakening of the hypothalamic–pituitary–gonadal axis in males and females. Its somatic effects are development of secondary sexual characteristics, maturation of reproductive organs, a growth spurt, and ultimately the achievement of adult height. Why puberty starts when it does and what causes puberty to begin remain unknown. This chapter does not describe the specific neuroendocrinological events leading up to and including puberty. For this information, the reader is referred elsewhere (Styne, 1991; Underwood & Van Wyk, 1985).

Normal Pubertal Processes

Males

Pubertal onset for European and North American boys ranges approximately between 12 and 16 years (see Figure 4–1). This is on average approximately 2 years later than pubertal onset for girls. In boys, the onset of puberty is usually signaled by enlargement of the testes, and, as Figure 4–1 shows, can start as early as age 9.5 or as late as age 13.5. Figure 4–1 also shows the range of onset for height spurt and penile growth. Once a pubertal "event" has occurred, the sequence through puberty, although still variable, is less so than its time of onset. For example, the height spurt usually begins 1 year after the initial testicular enlargement and obtains its peak height velocity 1 year after that when the penis is growing maximally and pubic hair growth is at Stage 3 or 4 (Stages 3 and 4 refer to a system of rating some aspects of pubertal development originated by J. M. Tanner, M.D., of England). There are five stages for genital growth ("G. Rating" in Figure 4–1) which includes growth of the penis, testes, and scrotum which is the result of testosterone secreted by the testes. Pubic hair growth is the result of adrenal androgen. Onset of pubic hair is referred to as "adrenarche" if it is definitely known that the androgen that promotes this growth comes from the adrenal glands. If the source of pubic hair is not definitely known, it is called "pubarche" (There is no Stage 1 shown in Figure 4–1 for "G. Rating" or pubic hair growth because Stage 1 is the prepubertal stage). Figures 4–2 and 4–3 illustrate Tanner Stages 2 through 5 (adult stage), for genital and pubic hair growth, respectively. For a detailed description of these stages, see Tanner (1978).

Boys also experience a number of other physical changes. Axillary and facial hair, although highly variable, appear later in puberty, with axil-

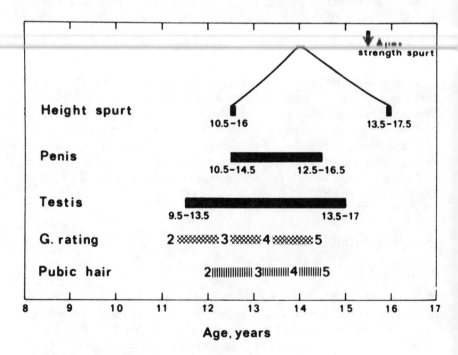

Figure 4–1. Sequence of pubertal events in boys.

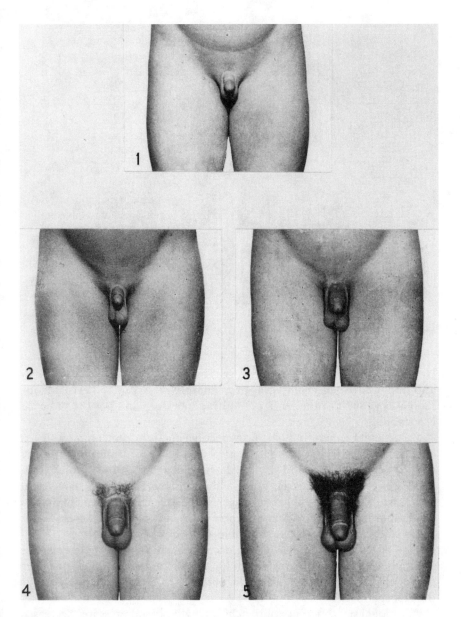

Figure 4–2. Tanner staging for genital growth in boys. Tanner Stage 1 is prepubertal.

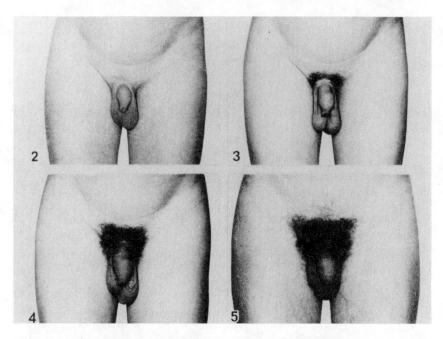

Figure 4–3. Tanner staging for pubic hair growth in boys.

~~lary hair starting approximately 2 years after Tanner Stage 2 pubic hair~~
and facial hair beginning at approximately 14.5 years. Testosterone
increases growth of the larynx, resulting in a deepening of the pubertal
boy's voice.

Breast enlargement in boys, or gynecomastia, is not uncommon. It has
been estimated to occur in between 49 and 70 percent of pubertal boys
(Biro, Lucky, Huster, & Morrison, 1990; Gallagher, 1968; Nydick, Bustos, Dale, & Rawson, 1961). It is usually transient, lasting less than 1 year
and is associated with pubic hair Stages 3 and 4. Such development may be
bilateral or unilateral and vary in degree from mild to severe. Severe breast
enlargement, however, is not reversible and requires surgery.

First ejaculation (spermache) can occur in early midpuberty because the
seminal vesicles, the prostrate gland, and the bulbourethral glands have
grown and developed along with the penis, testes, and scrotum. Mean age
for first spermache is 14.

Additional sex differentiation includes higher blood pressure, decreased
heart rate, increased lung size, and an increase in strength of skeletal mus-
cles for males. These changes usually occur during the growth spurt in
height which is the result of the synergistic action of testosterone, growth
hormone, and thyroid hormone (Styne, 1991).

Females

Based on data from North American and European girls, the average age of female pubertal onset is 11 years, but can range anywhere from 9 to 13 years (see Figure 4–4). The first sign of puberty is breast development (thelarche), more specifically referred to as breast budding. Thelarche, the result of estrogen release from the ovaries, is followed by the appearance of pubic hair, called "pubarche" or "adrenarche." Figure 4–4, shows the order of pubertal events.

Figure 4–5 illustrates the five stages of breast development. Stage 1 is the prepubertal breast and Stage 2 is breast budding where the breast and papilla are elevated and the diameter of the areola increase. It should be noted that some females may skip Stage 4, or stop at Stage 4, never developing to Stage 5. In addition to breast development, and the growth of pubic hair, puberty in females includes the growth of the vagina, clitoris, uterus, and labia. Figure 4–6 illustrates the four pubertal stages of pubic hair growth.

In females, the adolescent growth spurt occurs approximately 2 years earlier than males. Girls usually begin their growth spurt close to the onset of puberty about the age of 9.5 and finish growing at the age of 14.5; however, like all other pubertal events, this is variable. In their year of most rapid lin-

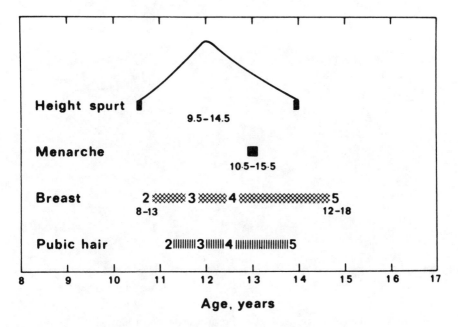

Figure 4–4. Sequence of pubertal events in girls.

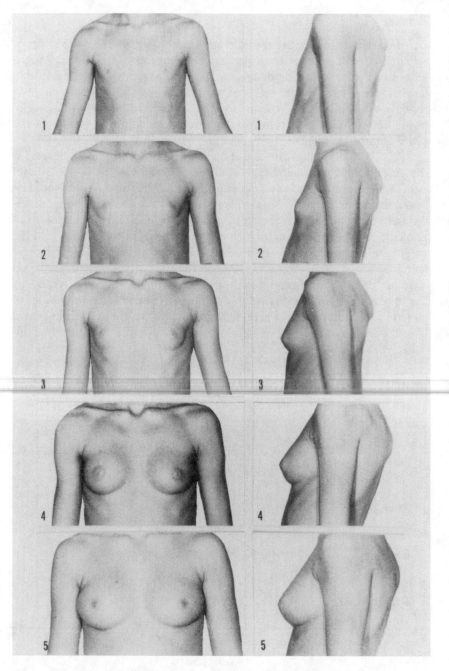

Figure 4–5. Tanner staging for female breast development.

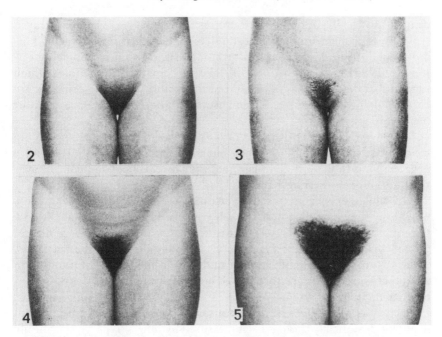

Figure 4–6. Tanner staging for pubic hair growth in females.

ear growth, boys grow 7–12cm in height, while girls grow 6–11cm in their corresponding year of greatest growth velocity. The difference in final adult height between the sexes is due to the later 2 years that boys have to grow. Like boys, growth spurt in girls includes muscle and skeletal changes as well, but not necessarily at equal rates. Another dimorphic characteristic of female growth spurt is the widening of the hips as well as the pelvic outlet.

Onset of menses (menarche) occurs within 2 years of the onset of breast development and at a point when the growth rate is decelerating. The average onset of menarche has been calculated to be between 12 and 13 years. Despite the fact that menarche is the last event of pubertal development, it does not necessarily signify reproductive maturation. Girls' first menses are usually very irregular and approximately 90 percent of all 12–14 year-old girls have anovular menses. Therefore, there is a period of partial sterility anywhere from 12 to 18 months after first menstrual cycle. It is important to note, however, that this does not occur for all females.

Response to Normal Pubertal Development

Puberty induces psychological responses in the individual adolescent, in his or her parents, in his or her peers, and in other adults, including clinicians. Historically, adolescent responses to puberty have been portrayed typically as problematic. It has been referred to as the time of "raging hormones and turmoil." Recent studies summarized by Offer and Schonert-Reichl (1992) have questioned this claim. They mention studies which suggest that the responses to puberty of the majority of adolescents are not abnormal and that the transition through puberty takes place without major difficulty.

Larson and Lampman-Petraitis (1989) showed that adolescents were no more moody than preadolescents, but older adolescents reported more negative moods. Parents complain that they lose contact and control over their adolescents. Seiffge-Krenke (1987) reported that at approximately age 15 adolescents begin to share personal matters with their peers where previously they would confide in their parents. Little is known about how parents respond to puberty. Yet it is known that most adolescents feel uncomfortable talking about puberty and sexuality with their parents. More research is needed to further understand the effects of puberty on parent–child relationships (Brooks-Gunn & Reiter, 1990; Offer & Schonert-Reichl, 1992; Petersen, 1988).

Teenagers themselves have responses to their own pubertal development, but historically this has been measured by others' reports, specifically the reports of parents and clinicians. Such indirect assessment has led to the belief that adolescents experience their puberty as negative and disruptive. But it has not been established that adolescents themselves would report their experiences in the same way.

Brooks-Gunn and Reiter (1990) report that adolescent girls reveal that puberty is not exclusively a negative experience; for most, however, the experience created ambivalence. For instance, the occurrence of menarche has been portrayed as a horrific experience for girls, when in actuality, upon being asked, most girls do not report it as it being a traumatic experience they cannot cope with. Anne Frank, although never asked, said as much in her diary when she wrote this description (reported by Brumberg, 1993) of her reaction to her menstruation: "Each time I have a period—and that has only been three times—I have the feeling that in spite of all pain, unpleasantness, and nastiness, I have a sweet secret, and that is why, although it is nothing but a nuisance to me in a way, I always long for the time that I shall feel that secret within me again."

Little is know about how boys interpret their puberty. In a small study (Gaddis & Brooks-Gunn, 1985) of midadolescent boys, the results indicated that positive emotional reactions to first ejaculations were stronger than negative ones, although some boys were frightened by it.

While we know very little about how adolescents interpret their own or others' puberty, we do have information on the behavioral effects of the timing of puberty. Brooks-Gunn and Reiter (1990) summarize this information. It is posited that girls who are "early maturers" and boys who are "late maturers" are at risk for adjustment problems such as poorer body image and lower self-esteem. Owing to the salience of secondary sexual characteristics (e.g., breasts), the early maturing girl can feel self-conscious and easily embarrassed. On the other hand, late maturing boys may feel self-conscious for exactly the opposite reason: they lack secondary sexual characteristics and therefore stand out. Both boys and girls who are early maturers may engage in sexual intercourse earlier than late maturers, but actual hormonal status does not seem to be associated with the psychosexual milestone of dating and behaviors associated with it. Results of an investigation of 7th and 8th grade boys (Halpern, Udry, Campbell, & Suchindran, 1993) suggest that change in pubertal development is related to the onset of sexual activity because of its social stimulus value, not solely because of changing hormone levels. And whatever differences exist between early and late maturing teenagers disappear as they become older.

What we do not know are the effects of pubertal timing on the parent–child relationship, which reinforces what has been already mentioned about the paucity of data on parental response to puberty.

In summary, the majority of adolescents appear to transit through puberty with little or no difficulty. The traditional view of adolescence as a period of "storm and stress" perhaps due to raging hormones is based upon clinical investigations of disturbed adolescents receiving some type of mental health service. Also, puberty does not define adolescence. They are not synonymous. Puberty is a subset of adolescence defined by specific neuroendocrinological and somatic events. So described, it has a clear beginning and end. Adolescence, on the other hand, cannot be that clearly delineated. It refers to a time of transition, which in addition to puberty, includes other cognitive, psychosocial, and psychosexual domains.

Adolescence is now being viewed and explained from a position of multifactorialism implicating both biology and the environment. Viewed in this manner, adolescence is conceptualized as more of a time of processing all these variables in contrast to the traditional view of adolescence as a time of passing through stages. This approach is currently being used to understand both normal adolescent development (Petersen, 1988) and adolescents at risk (Jessor, 1993).

If the distinction between puberty and adolescence is kept in mind alongside the new "process" approach, then unhealthy adolescent behavior (i.e., smoking, drinking, drugs, at-risk sexual behavior), serious psychiatric disorders (i.e., depression, anorexia, conduct disorders), and teen suicide will be viewed within a context that takes into account the hormones of puberty along with factors like family dynamics, parenting skills, cognition, socioeconomic status, education, media influences, and peer group relations.

Abnormal Pubertal Development: Precocious Puberty

There are children whose puberty falls outside the normal range because the onset of their pubertal development is either significantly early or delayed. Also, some children experience pubertal changes that are incongruent with their gender identity. The former consists of precocious and delayed puberty. Adolescent gynecomastia in boys and hirsutism in girls constitute the latter group.

Girls

In girls, true precocious puberty refers to the stimulation of the hypothalamic–pituitary–gonadal axis prior to age 8. When this activation results in accelerated somatic growth, secondary sexual characteristics and fertility, it is referred to as "central precocious puberty." The etiology varies, but the most common cause of central precocious puberty in girls is idiopathic, that is, unknown. Incomplete puberty occurs when only one or two characteristics (e.g., thelarche, adrenarche) appear before age 8. Regardless of cause or completeness, the abnormally early time of onset is the defining characteristic.

Behavioral data on the psychological effects of precocious puberty have come mainly from single case reports, small group reports, or girls with idiopathic precocious puberty (IPP). There are very few studies employing of matched controls using standardized instruments. Despite these caveats, these studies provide knowledge about (1) the psychosocial and psychosexual development of these girls, (2) the presence or absence of psychopathology, and (3) school achievement.

Hampson and Money (1955) reported detailed case histories on three girls (CA = 8, 6, 9) selected from 11 studied cases because they represented the "extremes and the middle" in terms of psychologic functioning and maturity. One child (IQ = 133) was exceptionally mature for her age; the second child, and the only one not to have menses, was behind her peers psychosocially and educationally. Her IQ was 83. The third girl was of average intelligence (IQ = 105) and despite starting her menses at age 7 was no different from her age-mates in her behavior and interests.

Solyom, Austad, Sherick, & Bacon (1980) performed a routine outpatient psychiatric evaluation on girls with either precocious thelarche, adrenarche, or IPP and their mothers in a pediatric endocrine clinic. They found no severe psychopathology in any of the precocious conditions but did suggest that somatic changes and parental reactions to such changes may pose problems for these girls developmentally. The IPP girls as a group seemed to have fared best. They appeared to have coped more successfully than any of the girls with precocious breast development alone or with only early pubic and/or axillary hair. The authors explain this finding by suggesting that the message communicated to the IPP child by both parents and physician is "Your body works OK; it is like your mother's body."

A group of 33 girls aged 6 to 11 years ($X = 8.1$) was studied by Sonis, et al. (1985) using the Child Behavior Checklist (CBCL) completed by the parents of these girls. Sixty-seven percent had IPP. The remaining 33 percent had known endocrine etiologies for their precocious development (e.g., hypothalamic hamartoma, McCune-Albright syndrome). When parental reports were compared with the sample used to standardize the CBCL, the results indicated a higher than expected prevalence of behavior problems and poorer social competencies for these girls. The authors did not suggest that these girls had psychiatric problems, but did indicate that they were experiencing adjustment difficulties secondary to their early puberty.

Sonis et al. (1986) also reported on 77 children (22 boys, 55 girls) aged 4 to 11 years ($X = 6.8$ years) with precocious puberty of varying etiologies. These 77 children were recruited from across the county to participate in a protocol using luteinizing hormone-releasing hormone analogue (LHRHa). The purpose of this study was to examine the relationship between brain lesions, height, and sex steroid exposure and behavior disturbance as measured by the CBCL. The authors wanted in addition to explore the hypothesis advanced by Money & Walker (1971) that early exposure to sex steroids affects behavior. Results indicated that children with precocious puberty were at risk for behavioral problems regardless of etiology and that children with precocious puberty resulting from brain lesions were no worse than children with IPP or with other causes for their early development. Sonis et al. (1986) speculated that the risk for behavioral difficulties may be mediated by perception of self, and by others, as well as sex hormones.

The most rigorous studies to date of IPP girls are those of Ehrhardt et al. (1984) and Ehrhardt & Meyer-Bahlburg (1986). Sixteen adolescent girls with a history of IPP were compared with closely pair-matched adolescent controls of comparable pubertal status and normal pubertal history. All subjects ($X = 17.5$ years) underwent a 2-day evaluation consisting of numerous psychologic and psychiatric assessment procedures of acceptable psychometric properties. Ehrhart and colleagues found no difference between the groups in the number of subjects having definite psychiatric diagnoses.

Differences, however, were noted between the IPP girls and the control group in two areas. First was that of menstrual distress symptoms. In both premenstrual and intermenstrual phases, IPP girls reported considerably increased psychosomatic symptomatology. Parents of IPP girls rated somatic complaints higher than parents of the controls, thus corroborating their daughters' reports. It was only during actual menstruation that the symptomatology for the control subjects approached that of the proband subjects. Ehrhardt & Meyer-Bahlburg (1984) suggested a possible increased psychologic sensitivity to hormonal changes to explain menstrual distress symptoms.

A second difference was the tendency for parents of IPP girls to report increased behavior problems on the CBCL when compared to parents' reports of the control children. Three possible explanations were given. First, IPP leads to earlier onset of social maturation, resulting in conflict over dependence versus independence. Second, IPP leads to greater psychologic stress. The third explanation, highly remote according to the researchers, is that both IPP and behavior problems represent subtle impairment of brain function.

Psychosexual development in girls with precocious puberty was first investigated by Money & Walker (1971). Fifteen girls were followed for a median period of 9.3 years (range: 1.4 to 18.1 years). At last interview, their mean age was approximately 17 years, with a range of 10.3 to 25.2 years. Money and Walker found that despite the readiness of their bodies for sexual response, these girls seldom experienced the imagery of erotic stimulation or sexual arousal. Childhood sex play was reported, but was consistent with chronologic age, not somatic age. Masturbation occurred (three cases) and the authors speculate that the age for onset might have been slightly early in these cases. Six girls reported having casual boyfriends, four reported having serious boyfriends, and five admitted to having premarital intercourse. Three were married. One had had three pregnancies at ages 12, 13, and 14. With the exception of the individual who first became pregnant at age 12, all the reported behaviors occurred at the age-appropriate period and in the expected developmental sequence. Money and Walker (1971) state that pregnancy in IPP girls is not as common as suggested by Reuben and Manning (1922, 1923) and concluded that psychosexual behavior in IPP girls follows chronologic age, not physique age. Overt sexual behavior requires appropriate experience and knowledge. The sexual behavior of IPP girls does not differ from that of normal children of the same age.

In the only matched-comparison study of IPP girls to date, Meyer-Bahlburg et al. (1985) found evidence to suggest that the timing of puberty has modest influence on female psychosexual development. The subjects were 16 IPP females with a history of IPP who at the time of evaluation were 13 to 20 years old ($X = 17.5$ years). They were compared with 16 controls with a normal pubertal history. The controls were matched on sex, race, age, SES, and menarcheal status. These subjects were the same ones reported on by Ehrhardt and colleagues (1984, 1986).

All IPP girls and controls had experienced crushes, dated, developed romantic relationships with boys, gone steady, and fallen in love. There were no differences between groups for the time of first crush and first date. However, IPP subjects reported having their first boyfriend ($X = 12.8$ years) and first steady relationship ($X = 15.5$) approximately a year earlier than the controls, and they also reported an earlier onset (5.5 years earlier) of masturbation. This latter finding recalls the three cases of Money and

Walker reported in 1971. Based on these data, the authors concluded that the onset of some psychosexual milestones (e.g., holding hands, kissing, petting, etc.) is modestly accelerated by precocious puberty. However, they also point out that the earlier onset of these milestones still occurred within the normal range of adolescent behavior and was not, by any means, as extremely advanced as the physical development of the IPP girls. No evidence of higher rates of current sexual activity in IPP girls was found when compared with controls. There was no difference in sexual orientation between the groups; all were heterosexual.

Boys

IPP occurs less frequently in boys than in girls. Penny (1982) reported that 65 percent of boys with sexual precocity (222/348) have a serious organic disorder, in contrast to girls in whom the incidence of organic disorder is 20 percent. Boys may show signs of complete or incomplete sexual development for various reasons. However, unlike girls, in whom the majority of central precocious puberty is idiopathic, boys with precocious puberty usually have more serious organic disorders. Precocious puberty in boys can also occur in cases of untreated or poorly controlled congenital adrenal hyperplasia (CAH), a defect in the adrenal cortex (see Chapter 6).

The first detailed psychological case study of a boy with IPP was by Money and Hampson (1955). This boy was 6 ½ years of age with a height-age of a boy 12 years old. His external genitalia were of adult size. An X-ray of his wrist, which gives one an estimate of bone maturation and potential for future growth, suggested a bone age of 15, indicating that he had reached his adult height. No medications had been given to him since the age of 2, at which time estrogen had been prescribed for a brief period in an effort to retard virilization. The methods of investigation included psychological testing and interviews.

As expected, there was incongruity between his physical appearance and his chronological age. He appeared to be a boy about 14 years old whose speech and conduct were that of someone much younger. This incongruity had its effect socially. He had friends his own age, and on occasion he played house with younger children. However, he preferred to play with older boys who grew inpatient with him because his skills were not up to their level.

A second study by Money and Alexander (1969) reviewed 18 cases of boys with precocious puberty. Four of these boys had the diagnosis of IPP; the remaining 14 boys had precocious puberty secondary to CAH. Money and Alexander concluded that, as with IPP girls, general psychological maturation of boys with precocious puberty parallels their chronologic and/or social age rather than their physique age. Difficulties were present stemming from the size, height, and age discrepancy. Money and Walker

(1971) reported that adults, parents included, and other children thought and expected these precocious boys to act older than their actual ages. Teasing also occurred and focused on height and size. There was also the problem of being accepted by children of the same age into their play groups. Finally, there was the readjustment in teenage years when most of the precocious boys' contemporaries not only caught up to them in pubertal development but also surpassed them in height and physique. They now had to learn how not to be the tallest (and perhaps how to be the shortest) in their group.

Money and Alexander (1969) reported no major psychiatric problems in their sample of 18 boys but there are case reports (Lebedinskaia, Rotinian, & Nemirovskaia, 1970; Mouridsen, 1991; Rosenberg, Crowner, Thomas, & Gourash, 1992) of psychosis or autistic behavior in children with IPP. These case reports not withstanding, it is safe to say that psychosis or serious psychopathology is not the rule in children with precocious puberty.

Psychosexual development of IPP boys, as with IPP girls, reflects their chronologic or social age and their experience and knowledge of sex. None of the boys investigated by Money and Alexander experienced infatuation or falling in love before the age of 12. Sex play was age-appropriate. Masturbation was reported by several boys before the age of 10, and sexual imagery, in all but two boys, was normal and reflected their actual age and current exposure to sex (e.g., television love scenes). The two cases of abnormal fantasies did not reoccur after proper sex information was given to both and following one of the boy's removal from a severely dysfunctional household. There are no reports using control or comparison groups of boys with precocious puberty.

Psychologic Management of Precocious Puberty

Boys and girls with precocious puberty are out of step with their peers in several ways. They are taller and look older. Their parents have concerns about sexual acting out and their ultimate height as adults (Mouridsen & Larsen, 1992). Sexual maturation is advanced, as is the onset of menses for girls. Consequently, such children may be at risk for behavioral difficulties because there is a discrepancy between their chronologic and their physique age.

A simple line drawing of three silhouettes (see Figure 4–7) can aid children and their parents in understanding this discrepancy and its behavioral consequences. Each silhouette represents three ages: (1) chronologic age, (2) psychosocial age, and (3) physique or height age. In most children, all three ages are so close that one silhouette could represent all three ages. However, in a child with precocious puberty, the ages become disparate because of secondary sexual characteristics and tall stature; one's height age is taller than one's chronologic age. Consequently, people expect the IPP child to act in accordance with their perception of age based on

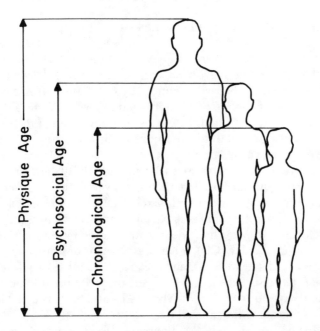

Figure 4–7. Silhouettes represent three ages that are disparate in a child with precocious puberty. Physique or height age is taller than chronological age. Consequently, others perceive the child as older and expect older behavior (psychosocial age).

stature. As a result, adults—parents and teachers included—and other children will automatically expect the child to act older than his/her actual age. Becoming aware of this expectation based on height age, parents and child can learn strategies to counter it (e.g., "I look older than my age. I want to be treated my real age.").

Teasing that focuses on height, size, and sexual characteristics can often result. Social isolation, partial or complete, also can occur. The counselor can help the parents and children to manage these issues. The child with precocious puberty and his/her parents can be embarrassed about somatic changes and need psychological support to help prevent creation of a negative or uncomfortable feeling about these changes.

Another possible behavioral effect is a sensitivity to mood changes, especially for IPP girls, around menses. Regardless of whether these changes are hormonally induced, the result of parent expectation, or both, parents need to be aware of this possibility and how best to cope with it and how to help their child. Handling menses especially during school is an issue that needs to be addressed. The counselor can be helpful here by discussing this and the disorder with school authorities.

Abnormal Pubertal Development: Delayed Puberty

Delayed puberty is the converse of precocious puberty. Here the onset of the hypothalamic–pituitary–gonadal axis is significantly delayed. Delayed puberty is somewhat arbitrarily defined. By convention, it is the onset of puberty in girls after the age of 12 or 13, and in boys after the age of 14 or 15. The onset is approximately 2 standard deviations (SDs) from the expected start of pubertal development in girls and boys respectively, which means approximately 3 percent of children are delayed in the onset of secondary sexual characteristics (Rosenfield, 1990). Boys are referred more frequently with this problem than girls even though delayed puberty occurs with equal frequency in both sexes (Gallagher, 1968). The suggested reason for this referral bias is parental and social pressures on the underdeveloped boy. Most individuals with delayed puberty are diagnosed with constitutional delay (CD), a harmless variant of normal growth. No pathology is associated with CD, and the prognosis for sexual development and normal stature is excellent. However, there are pathologic causes of delayed puberty, not the least of which are eating disorders. These and other causes must be differentiated from CD.

Psychologic research on delayed puberty has neither been as extensive nor as systematic as the behavioral investigations of precocious puberty. Some of the reports insufficiently describe their subjects, their endocrine diagnoses are mixed, and few or no details of methodology are provided. Consequently, one must be cautious in interpreting results.

Girls

Galatzer, Rosenblith, & Laron (1978) reported on 22 girls with "retarded sexual development with or without growth retardation." These girls showed no signs of initial puberty (e.g., breast buds) by age 13, and the heights of those with growth retardation ranged between 2 and greater than 4 SDs below the mean for chronologic age.

Eighteen (82 percent) of these girls reported many similar social problems and self-concerns as CD boys. They mentioned (1) avoiding approach of boys, (2) avoiding heterosexual social activities, (3) avoiding activities (e.g., beach with friends) where they might be expected to reveal in public the lack of breast development, (4) being called "girl" by peers and adults, and (5) having younger friends. Severe psychopathology was apparently absent, as it was not mentioned by the authors. Academically, 13 of the girls (59 percent) had difficulties related to school. Nine of these had an average IQ (90 to 110), and four had below-average IQ scores (less than 90). A structured self-concept questionnaire, the Tennessee Self-Concept Scale (TSCS), was administered to these girls as well as to 37 boys with sexual retardation. Results, which are not delineated by sex, suggest that these teenagers have low self-esteem. A three-way analysis of variance between sex, sexual development, and growth suggests that lack of sexual development was a more serious problem than height. However, this conclusion is questionable, because it assumes all the teenagers had growth retardation, and this is not clear. This group was mixed. Some were short and some were not. Certainly the questions raised in this article regarding the degree of influence of the lack of secondary sexual characteristics and short stature is an important one. Unfortunately, it is not answered by this report.

Boys

In Galatzer's study, 37 boys were grouped with the 22 girls and studied. Thirty out of 37 boys (with no initial signs of puberty before age 14) expressed concerns regarding social interaction and themselves. Like the girls already mentioned, they avoided social activities and interaction with the opposite sex. They worried about their gender identity, the size of their sex organs, and their lack of secondary sexual characteristics.

Academically, 24 of the boys (65 percent) experienced school-related problems. Two had IQ scores above 110, 17 had average IQ scores (90 to 110), and 5 had IQs below 90. Once again, caution is needed in explaining the results because the diagnoses of these boys are not clear.

A longitudinal report by Lewis, Money, & Bobrow (1977) on 12 boys with CD divided them into two groups. The first group ($N = 5$) had onset of puberty later than age 15, a bone age retarded by at least 2 years, and a mean height at follow-up of 67 inches (range: 63 to 72). The mean age at last follow-up was 24 years (mdn = 22 years) with a range between 18 and 35 years. The second group ($N = 7$) had onset of puberty during the second half of their 15th year, no retarded bone age, and a mean height at follow-up of 72 inches (range 67 to 76). The mean age at last follow-up was 24 years with a range between 16.1 and 29.8 years.

Hormonal treatment of some type was initiated in both groups. For all five boys in Group 1, the age of onset of treatment ranged from 15.5 years to 17.5 years. In Group 2, five out of seven were treated, and for them the range of treatment onset was 15 to 16 years. Academically, boys in both groups did well. There was only one underachiever (in Group 1). Many were in college or had already graduated from college.

Behaviorally, the majority of boys in both groups manifested signs of tantrums, depression, anxiety, and concerns about their height and the size of their genitals. There were two boys, one in each group, who demonstrated no behavioral problems by history.

Psychosexually, the five patients in Group 1 (showing prolonged pubertal delay) did not fare well. Only two married and were considered to have had adequate social and dating histories. For this group, there are no reports of masturbation or erotic thoughts before hormone therapy. After therapy, four out of five reported such behaviors.

The results were mixed with Group 2, the late-normal pubertal individuals. Two of the five who received hormone therapy married. Of the remaining three, two did not date or lead active social lives. The third reported romantic relationships. None of the five dated prior to treatment. Reasons given for not dating were (1) height (too short), (2) teasing, and (3) lack of self-confidence. Only one of the two untreated boys had a girlfriend by age 15; the other said he liked girls but played with boys 1 to 2 years younger than himself. Others also reported younger playmates.

Delayed Puberty: Psychologic Management

Teenagers with delayed puberty face a similar dilemma as children with precocious puberty but for the opposite reason. Instead of their bodies running ahead, they are running behind. They are "running behind" precisely at the time their friends are acquiring new social skills involving same-sex peers and members of the opposite sex. Psychologic evaluation can be beneficial in determining how severe the delayed adolescents' psychosocial and psychological development is and how much stress the individual is experiencing. Such assessment can help in determining whether or not hormone treatment would be beneficial. Rosenfeld, Northcroft, & Hintz (1982), in a randomized study, demonstrated the usefulness of testosterone treatment in eight boys with CD.

In cases where hormone therapy is initiated, teenagers and their parents still need guidance and support until such time as they feel it unnecessary to receive additional support. Some teens will be short in stature compared to peers because they have yet to experience their growth spurt. Consequently, they are at risk for being teased and infantilized; that is, being treated younger than they are because of the discrepancy between their physique and birthday age (Lee & Rosenfeld, 1987).

The same line drawing (Figure 4–7) used with IPP children can be used to help short-stature adolescents with delayed puberty to understand this discrepancy. In this case the labels of chronologic age and physique age need to be reversed, thus indicating that short stature makes one appear younger than chronologic age. Consequently, the adolescent and parents will need to be aware of how this can effect the perception and expectation of others.

Pubertal Disorders of Congruence

Precocious puberty and delayed puberty are disorders of pubertal timing, not of congruence. Disorders of congruence of pubertal development refer to conditions in which pubertal development is incongruent with the individual's genetic sex, gonadal sex, and gender identity. In hirsutism and gynecomastia, it is the discordance or incongruence of somatic development with psychosexual development that is believed to create emotional stress.

Hirsutism

Hirsutism is a disorder in genetic females characterized by excessive body hair in a distinctly male pattern. In extreme cases, a female presents with hair on her cheeks, chin, upper lip, breasts, abdomen, and interior thighs. There may also be clitoral enlargement, secondary amenorrhea, and obesity.

For years, physicians have noted in clinical reports the emotional impact of hirsutism on their patients. Money & Clopper (1974) suggest that the psychological problems for hirsute teenage girls parallel those of a boy with gynecomastia. The hirsute girl's primary concern is restoration of a female appearance. Hirsutism makes her feel a sense of shame and freakishness; anxiety can be associated with this condition (Rabinowitz, Cohen, & Le Roith, 1983). She may withdraw socially. Dating and romance may be disrupted. Ehrhardt and Meyer-Bahlburg (1975) echo this description in their review of the literature, but neither their report nor Money & Clopper's provides actual data on hirsute teenagers. The few scientific reports—none solely on teenagers—reinforce clinical observations. But none present rigorously obtained quantitative behavioral data. Some present only psychodynamic interpretations extracted from projective techniques such as the Rorschach and the Draw-A-Person tests.

Shah (1957) interviewed 34 hirsute women (15 to 41 years of age) regarding their reasons for visiting a doctor. In order of frequency, their reasons were (1) fear, theirs or a relative's, that their hirsutism would jeopardize their chance to marry, (2) fears they were changing sex, (3) husbands dislike of them since the hirsutism, and (4) wanting to know if knowledge about their condition would prevent a similar problem in their prepubertal daughters. Zerssen & Meyer (1960) studied 15 women in Germany with idiopathic hirsutism. Based on projective test data (Rorschach), they concluded that sexual identification and interpersonal contact were impaired in all 15 women; work proficiency was not impaired. Perrault, Werblowsky, & Rose (1983) asked six hirsute women, ages 20 to 32, to perform a series of five drawings. They concluded these women suffered disturbances of sexual identity, interpersonal conflict, and social isolation and suggested that the psychologic effects of hirsutism on women were underestimated.

Hirsutism is an endocrinologically complex phenomenon. Its etiology varies, and other problems such as obesity and menstrual irregularity are often associated with it. Consequently, psychologic effects often cannot be attributed solely to excessive hair growth. However, the clinical observations reported above suggest that psychologic treatment, coupled with medical intervention when indicated, focus on helping the person adjust to and cope with the effects of hirsutism while maintaining a positive sense of self and body image. Evaluation of sexuality, especially the component involving gender identity and sense of femininity, is important since hirsutism may challenge these aspects of psychosexual development.

Gynecomastia

Gynecomastia is the development of breasts in boys. It varies in degree of severity from minimal to breast tissue growth of approximately the amount found in an adolescent girl. The mild degree is usually transient; the more severe forms are irreversible and require surgery. Breast development may be bilateral or unilateral and is associated with liver disease, tumors of the hypothalamic–pituitary–gonadal axis, endocrinologic or cytogenetic anomalies (e.g., Klinefelter's and Reifenstein syndromes), or excessive marijuana use (Braunstein, 1993). However, physiologic or idiopathic gynecomastia is the most common diagnosis in adolescent boys and occurs quite frequently in this group.

Regardless of cause, common sense suggests that gynecomastia in adolescents, even if transient, may be a source of concern to the developing adolescent. Schonfeld (1961) reported that adolescents construe their gynecomastia as discordant with their self-image. Fisher and Fornari (1990) reported two case studies of boys with eating disorders associated with breast development.

Money and Lewis (1982) reported on 10 boys with idiopathic adolescent gynecomastia (IAG) and 8 boys treated for CAH. The purpose of the study was to compare these groups with respect to behavioral conformity with the male stereotype and heterosexual/homosexual status. The investigators wanted to see if differences occurred between groups and whether those differences might be associated with a difference in their hormonal status at puberty. All 10 were recommended for reduction mammoplasty; 7 had surgery. The 3 IAG boys who questioned their male status and did not have surgery were homosexual/bisexual in orientation, cross-dressed as children, and did not participate in male stereotypic sports. The remaining 7 IAG subjects could not be distinguished from the 8 CAH boys in terms of conformity to male stereotypic life-styles. Because the 3 homosexual youths had a prepubertal history of incongruity between anatomic sex and gender role (cross-dressing), Money and Lewis concluded that gynecomastia is not a sufficient cause to explain homosexuality in these cases.

Severe breast development that requires surgical intervention is also an assault on a developing boy's sexuality, especially his gender identity.

Money & Lewis (1982) found that whereas the CAH group was benignly teased about their short stature, the IAG group was traumatically teased about their breasts ("Are you half boy, half girl?" "I heard you got your titties cut off."). Seventy percent of IAG boys showed a history of social isolation. While the above study had only 10 IAG boys in it, psychologists need to be aware of and sensitive to these issues, first by evaluating the teenager for any signs of gender doubts and social isolation, and then providing needed support and guidance.

Psychologic Management: Common Issues

The above recommendations for psychologic treatment were specific to the syndrome discussed. There are also issues common to all these disorders that need to be incorporated into the psychologic management plan.

Medical evaluation is required in all cases. Medical intervention may be required depending upon many factors such as pubertal status, age of onset, and severity of condition. Such interventions include medroxyprogesterone acetate used for decades to treat IPP, and now the newer gonadotrophin releasing hormone (GNRH) agonists such as leuprolide which appears to be making the former drug obsolete (Wheeler, 1991). Testosterone enanthate is used to treat boys with pubertal delay (Richman & Kirsch, 1988; Rosenfeld, Northcroft, & Hintz, 1982; Rosenfield, 1990). Surgery is necessary in idiopathic gynecomastia that is severe and does not regress (Braunstein, 1993). Hirsutism is treated with various endocrine agents depending upon the needs of the patient and etiology (Ehrmann & Rosenfield, 1990; Hatch, Rosenfield, Kim, & Treadway, 1981). Part of all psychologic management is to make sure the parties involved have a good understanding of the medical intervention and the need for it.

A second commonality is the need for both parents and teenager to be properly and adequately informed about the nature of the pubertal disorder. Such education can alleviate unnecessary stress. For example, it has been shown that even in cases of innocent thelarche and adrenarche, parents have fears of their child having serious diseases. In our clinic, a trained psychoendocrine staff member meets with the family to discuss their initial fears, translate medical jargon, and in the process explain to them the nature of the specific disorder in terms they can comprehend. They are encouraged to ask questions and are told that we can become the liaison between physician and family if necessary. For those patients with precocious pubertal development, a pamphlet (Mazur & Voorhess, unpublished) is given to the parents. This pamphlet explains both normal and precocious puberty and has a glossary of medical terms. This pamphlet has proved beneficial for patients with other pubertal disorders because of the lack of knowledge of normal pubertal development that many parents and teens have. If normal pubertal development is not clearly understood, pubertal disorders are virtually incomprehensible. Figures 4–1 through 4–6 are helpful in illustrating the various stages of pubertal events.

Sex education is also essential as these disorders involve sexual development of the child and adolescent. Today, many parents are still ill-prepared to discuss this topic with their children and often feel uncomfortable at even the thought of doing so. As one mother whose daughter was diagnosed with central precocious puberty at 6 years of age said: "How do I tell her about this stuff [breasts, menses] at 6? I did not know how I was going to tell her about female things even when she became a teenager!" Sex education can be given over time and graded to the child's age, level of understanding, and interest. A number of books (Calderone & Johnson, 1981; Mayle, 1973, 1975; Waxman, 1976) and videos (Mayle, 1985, 1986; Nilsson, 1986) can be used to help impart sex education material to children and their parents. Also, the sex education story found in the book *Sex Errors of the Body* (Money, 1968) has been useful.

Final Remarks

Methodological limitations inherent in the research findings reviewed in this chapter make it necessary to view the results with caution. However, they can prove helpful to clinicians if they are viewed as potential issues requiring further evaluation and assessment.

Clinicians can provide beneficial psychologic support by focusing on issues common to all of these conditions, as well as to the issues specific to each syndrome.

Acknowledgements

Figures 4–1 through 4–6 reprinted with the permission of J. M. Tanner.

David E. Sandberg, Marian Goodman, and Pat Michael critically read this manuscript and offered suggestions. Mrs. Lucy Wargo and Mrs. Laurie Cameron provided library assistance. Ms. Tammy Masterman helped prepare and typed the final draft. The Children's Growth Foundation of Western New York supports the work of the Psychoendocrine Program. Without their continued support to obtain money from the local United Way and Variety Club, Tent #7 psychological services would not be available to the children and their families described in this chapter.

References

Biro, F. M., Lucky, A. W., Huster, G. A., Morrison, J. A. (1990). Hormonal studies and physical maturation in adolescent gynecomastia. *Journal of Pediatrics, 116,* 450–455.

Braunstein, G. D. (1993). Gynecomastia. *New England Journal of Medicine, 328,* 490–495.

Brooks-Gunn, J., & Reiter, E. O. (1990). The role of pubertal processes in the early adolescent transition. In S. S. Feldman & G. R. Elliott (Eds.), *At the threshold: The developing adolescent* (pp. 16–53). Cambridge, MA: Harvard University Press. 1990.

Brumberg, J. J. (1993). "Something happens to girls": Menarche and the emergence of the modern American hygienic imperative. *Journal of the History of Sexuality, 4,* 99–127.

Calderone, M., & Johnson, E. (1981). *The family book about sexuality.* New York: Bantam Books.

Ehrhardt, A. A., & Meyer-Bahlburg, H. F. L. (1975). Psychological correlates of abnormal pubertal development. *Clinics in Endocrinology and Metabolism, 4,* 207–222.

Ehrhardt, A. A., & Meyer-Bahlburg, H. F. L. (1986). Idiopathic precocious puberty in girls: Long-term effects on adolescent behavior. *Acta Endocrinologica, 279* (Supp.), 247–253.

Ehrhardt, A. A., Meyer-Bahlburg, H. F. L., Bell, J. J., Cohen, S. F., Healy, J. M., Stiel, R., Feldman, J. F., Morishima, A., & New, M. I. (1984). Idiopathic precocious puberty in girls: Psychiatric follow-up in adolescence. *Journal of the American Academy of Child Psychiatry, 23,* 23–33.

Ehrmann, D. A., & Rosenfield, R. L. (1990). An endocrinologic approach to the patient with hirsutism. *Journal of Clinical Endocrinology and Metabolism, 71,* 1–7.

Fisher, M., & Fornari, V. (1990). Gynecomastia as a precipitant of eating disorders in adolescent males. *International Journal of Eating Disorders, 9,* 115–119.

Gaddis, A., & Brooks-Gunn, J. (1985). The male experience of pubertal change. *Journal of Youth and Adolescence, 14,* 61–69.

Galatzer, A., Rosenbith, E., & Laron, Z. (1978). Psychological and rehabilitation aspects of short stature and delayed puberty. In L. Gedda & P. Parisi (Eds.), *Auxology: Human growth in health and disorder. Proceedings of Second Symposium* (Vol. 13, p. 303–311). London: Academic Press.

Gallagher, J. R. Adolescents and their disorders. (1968). In R. Cooks (Ed.), *The biologic basis of pediatric practice.* pp. 1670–1685 New York: McGraw-Hill.

Halpern, C. T., Udry, R., Campbell, B., & Suchindran, C. (1993). Testosterone and pubertal development as predictors of sexual activity: A panel analysis of adolescent males. *Psychosomatic Medicine, 55,* 436–447.

Hampson, J. G., & Money, J. (1955). Idiopathic sexual precocity in the female. *Psychosomatic Medicine, 18,* 16–35.

Hatch, R., Rosenfield, R. L., Kim, M. H., & Tredway, D. (1981). Hirsutism: Implications, etiology, and management. *American Journal of Obstetrics and Gynecology, 140,* 815–830.

Jessor, R. (1993). Successful adolescent development among youth in high-risk settings. *American Psychologist, 48,* 117–126.

Larson, R., & Lampman-Petraitis, C. (1989). Daily emotional states as reported by children and adolescents. *Child Development, 60,* 1250–1260.

Lebedinskaia, K. S., Rotinian, N. S., & Nemirovskaia, S. V. (1970). Role of accelerated sex maturation in the clinical picture of psychoses in children. *Nevropatol-Psikhiatr, 70,* 1517.

Lee, P. D., & Rosenfeld, R. G. (1987). Psychosocial correlates of short stature and delayed puberty. *Pediatric Clinics of North America, 34,* 851–863.

Lewis, V. G., Money, J., & Bobrow, N. A. (1977). Idiopathic pubertal delay beyond age fifteen: Psychologic study of twelve boys. *Adolescence, 12,* 1–11.

Mayle, P. (1975). *What's happening to me?* Secaucus, NJ: Lyle Stuart.

Mayle, P. (1986). *What's happening to me?* (Video). Los Angeles: LCA, New World Video.

Mayle, P. (1973). *Where did I come from?* Secaucus, NJ: Lyle Stuart.

Mayle, P. (1985). *Where did I come from?* (Video). Los Angeles: LCA, New World Video.

Mazur, T. & Voorhess, M. L. *Precocious puberty: A phamplet for parents* (unpublished).

Meyer-Bahlburg, H. F. L., Ehrhardt, A. A., Bell, J. J., Cohen, S. F., Healey, J. M., Feldman, J. F., Merishima, A., Baker, S. W., New, M. I. (1985). Idiopathic precocious puberty in girls: Psychosexual development. *Journal of Youth and Adolescence, 14,* 339–353.

Money, J. *Sex Errors of the Body: Dilemmas, Education, Counseling* (1968). Baltimore: Johns Hopkins University Press.

Money, J., & Alexander, D. (1969). Psychosexual development and absence of homosexuality in males with precocious puberty: Review of 18 cases. *Journal of Nervous and Mental Disease, 148,* 111–123.

Money, J., & Clopper, R. R., Jr. (1974). Psychosocial and psychosexual aspects of errors of pubertal onset and development. *Human Biology, 46,* 173–181.

Money, J., & Hampson, J. G. (1955). Idiopathic sexual precocity in the male. *Psychosomatic Medicine, 18,* 1–15.

Money, J., & Lewis, V. (1982). Homosexual/heterosexual status in boys at puberty: Idiopathic adolescent gynecomastia and congenital virilizing adrenocorticism compared. *Psychoneuro-endocrinology, 7,* 339–346.

Money, J. & Walker, P. A. (1971). Psychosexual development, maternalism, non-promiscuity and body image in 15 females with precocious puberty. *Archives of Sexual Behavior, 1,* 45–60.

Mouridsen, S. E. (1991). Pervasive developmental disorder and idiopathic precocious puberty in a 5-year-old girl [letter]. *Journal of Autism and Development Disorders, 19,* 351–353.

Mouridsen, S. E., & Larsen, F. W. (1992). Psychological aspects of precocious puberty: An overview. *Acta Paedosychiatrica, 55,* 45–49.

Nilsson, L. (1986). *The miracle of life* (Video). New York: Crown.

Nydick, M., Bustos, J., Dale, J. H., & Rawson, R. W. (1961). Gynecomastia in adolescent boys. *Journal of the American Medical Association, 178,* 449–454.

Offer, D., & Schonert-Reichl, K. A. (1992). Debunking the myths of adolescence:

Findings from recent research. *Journal of the American Academy of Child and Adolescent Psychiatry, 31,* 1003–1014.

Penny, R. (1982). Disorders of the testes. In S. A. Kaplan (Ed.), *Clinical pediatric and adolescent endocrinology* (pp. 300–326). Philadelphia: W. B. Saunders.

Perrault, L., Werblowsky, J. H., & Rose, L. I. (1983). Psychological effects of hirsutism: Analysis of drawing by hirsute females. *Arts in Psychotherapy, 10,* 157–165.

Petersen, A. C. (1988). Adolescent development. *Annual Review of Psychology, 39,* 583–607.

Rabinowitz, S., Cohen, R., & Le Roith, D. (1983). Anxiety and hirsutism. *Psychological Reports, 53,* 827–830.

Reuben, M. S., & Manning, G. R. (1922). Precocious puberty. *Archives of Pediatrics, 39,* 769–785.

Reuben, M. S., & Manning, G. R. (1923). Precocious puberty (continued). *Archives of Pediatrics, 40,* 27–44.

Richman, R. A., & Kirsch, L. R. (1988). Testosterone treatment in adolescent boys with constitutional delay in growth and development. *New England Journal of Medicine, 319,* 1563–1567.

Rosenberg, D. R., Crowner, S., Thomas, C., & Gourash, L. (1992). Psychosis and idiopathic precocious puberty in two 7-year-old boys. *Child Psychiatry and Human Development, 22,* 287–292.

Rosenfeld, R. G., Northcroft, G. B., & Hintz, R. L. (1982). A prospective, randomized study of testosterone treatment of constitutional delay of growth and development in male adolescents. *Pediatrics, 69,* 681–687.

Rosenfield, R. L. (1990). Diagnosis and management of delayed puberty. *Journal of Clinical Endocrinology and Metabolism, 70,* 559–562.

Schonfeld, W. A. (1961). Gynecomastia in adolescence: Personality effects. *Archives of General Psychiatry, 5,* 46–54.

Seiffge-Krenke, I., (1987). Disclosure behavior in adolescence. In A. Spitznagel (Ed.), *Recent developments in psychology* pp. 128–135. Berlin: Springer.

Shah, P. N. (1957). Human body hair: A quantitative study. *American Journal of Obstetrics and Gynecology, 73,* 1255–1265.

Solyom, A. E., Austad, C. C., Sherick, I., & Bacon, G. E. (1980). Precocious sexual development in girls: The emotional impact on the child and her parents. *Journal of Pediatric Psychology, 5,* 385–393.

Sonis, W. A., Comite, F., Blue, J., Pescovitz, O. H., Rahn, C. W., Hench, K. D., Cutler, G. B., Jr., Loriaux, D. L., & Klein, R. P. (1985). Behavior problems and social competence in girls with true precocious puberty. *Journal of Pediatrics, 106,* 156–160.

Sonis, W. A., Comite, F., Pescovitz, O. H., Hench, R. N., Rahn, C. W., Cutler, G. B., Loriaux, D. L., & Klein, R. P. (1986). Biobehavioral aspects of precocious puberty. *Journal of American Academy of Child Psychiatry, 25,* 674–679.

Styne, D. M. (Ed.). (1991). Puberty and its disorders. *Endocrinology and Metabolism Clinics of North America, 20,* 1–245.

Tanner, J. M. (1978). *Foetus into man: Physical growth from conception to maturity.* Cambridge, MA: Harvard University Press.

Underwood, L. E., & Van Wyk, J. J. (1985). Normal and aberrant growth. In J. D.

Wilson & D. W. Foster (Eds.), *Textbook of endocrinology* (7th ed., pp. 155–205). Philadelphia: W. B. Saunders.

Waxman, S. (1976). *What is a girl? What is a boy?* Culver City, CA: Peace Press.

Wheeler, M. D. (1991). Physical changes of puberty. *Endocrinology and Metabolism Clinics of North America, 20,* 1–14.

Zerssen, D. V., & Meyer, A. E. (1960). Psychologische Untersuchungen frauen mit Sogenanntem idiopathischem hirutiemus. *Journal of Psychosomatic Research, 4,* 206–235.

5

Obstacles to the Sexual Adjustment of Children and Adolescents with Disabilities

William J. Warzak
Brett R. Kuhn
Patrick W. Nolten

I n addressing issues related to the sexual adjustment of youth with disabilities we make the assumption that the development of an individual's sexuality is a basic part of the human experience and that expressions of sexuality can be life-enhancing and should be made available to all (Bernstein, 1985; Kaeser, 1992). An individual's disability may shape or limit the ultimate repertoire of his or her sexual expression but the right to sexual expression is no less basic. Societal concerns regarding an individual's ability to cope with his or her sexuality and a desire to protect those who might be vulnerable to sexual exploitation should not diminish their rights to sexual expression (Baugh, 1984; Bernstein, 1985; Crooks & Baur, 1990; Keller & Buchanan, 1984; Tharinger, Horton, & Millea, 1990).

Satisfactory sexual expression in adulthood rests upon a foundation of sexual adjustment established in childhood and adolescence. The present chapter will focus on the difficulties experienced by youth known to be at risk for poor sexual adjustment, due in part to limitations imposed by their disabilities. We will report common concerns and note issues likely to affect some individuals more than others because of specific disabilities. In particular, the obstacles to sexual adjustment encountered by adolescents who are developmentally disabled, have sensory impairment, or have acquired cognitive deficits (i.e., traumatic brain injury) will be emphasized. We will discuss the increased risk for sexual abuse among members of

The authors gratefully acknowledge the critical comments and other assistance of Sandra Houser, Christine T. Majors, Sonya Nixon, and Steven D. Sherrets in preparing this manuscript.

these groups and present suggestions to prevent these occurrences and foster overall sexual adjustment.

Sexual Adjustment

Adaptation to emerging sexuality is among the most difficult of developmental tasks. Increased growth and energy, emotional lability, and the development of secondary sexual characteristics create a difficult period of adjustment for adolescents, particularly if they are unprepared to deal with these changes (Rekers, 1992; Shendell, 1992a). Youth with disabilities often have special needs and require support in adjusting to sexuality, yet they are often among the least informed about these matters (Kempton, 1988; McNab, 1978). Lack of information, ignorance, and misconceptions are often more detrimental to sexual adjustment than are purported psychological obstacles to adjustment arising from disability (Cole, 1988; Cornelius, Chipouras, Makas, & Daniels, 1982).

Society has historically denied the expression of sexuality by those with disabilities and has also perpetuated a state of dependency and paternalism regarding these individuals. Information regarding sex and sexual functioning was considered unnecessary for those who are disabled and was often deliberately withheld from them (Crooks & Baur, 1990; Peuschel & Scola, 1988). People with developmental disabilities, in particular, have been disadvantaged in this regard, although these concerns apply equally to many disabling conditions (Brantlinger, 1988; Keller & Buchanan, 1984; Kempton & Kahn, 1991; Linsenmeyer & Perkash, 1991). The normalization movement of the 1960s prompted an increased awareness that individuals with disabilities should have the right to experience sexuality as do others in society (Brantlinger, 1988; Daniels, Cornelius, Makas, & Chipouras, 1981; Kempton & Kahn, 1991). Many individuals with disabilities, however, require assistance in their sexual adjustment to achieve this goal.

Sexual adjustment connotes an accommodation to the various aspects of personal functioning which result in the expression of maleness or femaleness and gender identity (Brown, 1992b; Cole, 1981). While a discussion of gender identity is beyond the scope of this chapter, we recognize its importance to the final expression of an individual's sexuality and its influence on sexual adjustment. Many factors including the individual's sociocultural context, the psychosocial meaning of social sex assignment, and the biological aspects of physical sex status affect gender identity and sexual adjustment (Rekers, 1981). Sexual adjustment also may be profoundly altered by disability. Knowing during which stage of development an injury was experienced is important to assess an individual's sexual adjustment. For example, a congenital disability will be integrated into ongoing sexual development and maturation and sexual adjustment itself will be shaped by the experience of disability. A disabling injury that occurs in childhood or adolescence may disrupt long-held beliefs and expectations regarding maleness and femaleness. Exposure to information and experiences that shape behavior may be curtailed (Cole, 1988; Knight, 1989). An individual's comparisons to his or her premorbid self may be especially difficult and disruptive to adjustment (Crooks & Baur, 1990; Kempton, 1988).

Obstacles to Adjustment.

The health education needs of students with disabilities are similar to those of regular education students, but the problems associated with adolescence may be more complicated (Adams, 1981). The development of youth with disabilities does not generally differ from that of other adolescents, although variations occur, occasionally from hormonal changes associated with chronic illness or traumatic brain injury (Blendonohy & Philip, 1991; Maxwell et al., 1990). They experience sexual development and an interest in sexual matters at approximately the same chronological age as other adolescents, although some delays have been noted for those with severe to profound developmental deficits. However, youth with disabilities run the risk of delayed psychosocial development, often reflecting missed learning opportunities and impaired acquisition of information and skills relating to the development of interpersonal social relationships and sexual behavior (Baugh, 1984; Cole, 1981; Tharinger, Horton, & Millea, 1990; Williams, 1987).

The availability of relevant information is affected by circumstances as varied as limited mobility to a lack of appropriate materials for individuals with sensory deficits. Parents and providers may deprive their children of information critical to their sexual adjustment by failing to anticipate issues related to sexual maturation and sexual functioning (Baugh, 1984; Dodge, 1979; Neff, 1983). Some parents may be reluctant to provide information to their children for fear of nurturing sexual independence and exposing their children to the risks attendant to sexual activity, such as sexual exploitation, STDs, or parenthood (Manikam & Hensarling, 1990; Peuschel & Scola, 1988). In addition, adolescents with cognitive and developmental disabilities may lack essential communication skills necessary to initiate inquiries regarding sexuality or to respond to discussions initiated by parents and providers. Cognitive deficits and limited communication skills also limit understanding of community standards and the consequences of sexual behavior (Freeman, Goetz, Richards, & Groenveld, 1991; Giami, 1987; Williams, 1983).

Particular disabilities directly hinder the educational process, interfering with the detection of subtle social cues such as facial expressions or voice intonation, which provide information relevant to socially acceptable and unacceptable sexual behavior (Schuster, 1986; Warzak, Evans, & Ford, 1992; Warzak & Kilburn, 1990). In addition, the individual's ability to monitor his or her own behavior may be limited, increasing the likelihood that others will misread unintentional cues emitted by the individual with disabilities. For example, those with visual impairments are deprived of opportunities to view their own body and that of the opposite sex (Cornelius et al., 1982). They have limited opportunities to tactilely explore a body of the opposite sex in a fashion analogous to the visual exploration of sighted children.

Sexual adjustment usually develops within an interpersonal context and is influenced by the behavior of others. Indeed, much of adolescent development occurs within a context where the influence of peers is pivotal. Those with a pleasing physical appearance, appropriate social behavior, and intelligence are more likely to be accepted by their peers than individuals with characteristics that tend to set them apart or stigmatize them (Schor, 1987; Yarris, 1992). Individuals with significant impairment often become socially isolated and may be deprived of a social environment within which appropriate sexual development and sexual adjustment may take place. Because of limited opportunities to observe the social-sexual behavior of others, their attempts to engage in interpersonal sexual behavior may be awkward, ineffective, or inappropriate (Baugh, 1984; Cole, 1981).

The sexual adjustment of adolescents with developmental and cognitive deficits is frequently ignored until inappropriate public sexual behavior forces others to attend to this aspect of development. Poor judgment and impulse control, more common among those with developmental delays and traumatic brain injury, may contribute to inappropriate sexual behavior, such as public masturbation or inappropriate touching (Larkin, 1992; Warzak & Kilburn, 1990; Zencius, Wesolowski, Burke, & Hough, 1990). Overly affectionate or inadvertently seductive behavior may also result, in part, from efforts by caregivers to foster adaptive and compliant social behavior (Williams, 1983).

The special needs of these children and adolescents often require them to spend considerable time in special education or rehabilitation settings. Many staff are unprepared or unwilling to present issues related to sexual adjustment. Surveys indicate that some staff believe that individuals with disabilities will have little or no opportunity to engage in interpersonal sexual behavior and require no preparation for this eventuality (Howard, 1992; Malloy & Herold, 1988). Others may be under pressure to avoid situations that might offend parents or result in controversy for that facility. Unless staff are thoroughly supported administratively, they may fear repercussions for broaching sensitive and potentially charged subject matter (Brown, 1992b). These factors may result in support of only the lowest level of innocuous interpersonal sexual behavior, with staff more inclined to limit rather than to expand efforts to assist sexual adjustment (Knight, 1989; Manikam & Hensarling, 1990).

Sexual Abuse

Vulnerability to Sexual Abuse

"Child sexual abuse" is a broad term that encompasses an array of sexual contacts between a child and another person, wherein the contact is designed for the gratification of the offender. Perpetrators are not restricted to adults. Children and adolescents may also be abusive. Nor is abuse limited to physical touch. Abuse can include other exploitative behavior such as being tricked into exposing one's genitals or into looking at the genitals of another person (Cole, 1986; Finkelhor & Korbin, 1988).

Youth with disabilities confront obstacles in their sexual adjustment that put them at risk for sexual exploitation by others. For those who have been abused, covarying issues of guilt and shame and their impact on self-esteem and self-worth can be detrimental to adjustment and further contribute to vulnerability. A history of sexual abuse may increase the risk of poor sexual adjustment; and conversely, poor sexual adjustment may increase an individual's risk for sexual abuse.

Incidence of Abuse

The exact incidence of abuse among children and adolescents with disabilities is difficult to estimate. A recent review concluded that 5 percent of all sexually abused children exhibited some form of intellectual impairment, while 3 percent had physical or sensory deficits. These rates are higher than the 1 to 3 percent prevalence of disability in the general population (Sobsey & Varnhagen, 1991). The incidence of sexual abuse may be highest among persons with developmental disabilities (Anderson, 1982; Crossmaker, 1991; Sobsey & Varnhagen, 1991). Estimates of abuse in this population have ranged from 2 percent (Jaudes & Diamond, 1985) to 96 percent (Brookhouser, Sullivan, Scanlon, & Garbarino, 1986), with persons exhibiting mild impairment evidencing higher rates of abuse than those more severely impaired (Chamberlain, Rauh, Passer, McGrath, & Burket, 1984).

Risk Factors

Risk factors for sexual abuse include the specific characteristics of the perpetrator and victim, environmental or situational factors, and cultural influences. Finkelhor (1984) has developed a theoretical model that incorporates these factors and posits four basic preconditions for child sexual abuse: (1) motivation to abuse, (2) overcoming internal (societal) inhibitions, (3) overcoming external (situational) inhibitions, and (4) overcoming the child's resistance. A closer look at this model can alert professionals to the dangers children and adolescents with disabilities experience with regard to sexual abuse, and highlights aspects of sexuality to be addressed in order to avoid exploitation and facilitate adjustment.

1. *Motivation to abuse.* The motivation to abuse typically arises when an adult obtains satisfaction from relating sexually to children, is sexually aroused by children, or is unable to fulfill sexual and emotional needs in adult relationships (Finkelhor, 1984). There are no data to suggest that pedophiles are more or less attracted to youth with disabilities over and above their greater vulnerability, although it has been suggested that some pedophiles may be attracted to the childlike behaviors of adolescents with developmental delays (Schor, 1987).

2. *Overcoming internal (societal) inhibitions.* Societal perceptions and negative attitudes toward persons with disabilities may contribute to sexual abuse (Cole, 1988; Sobsey & Mansell, 1990; Sobsey & Varnhagen, 1991) by reducing internal inhibitions to abuse (Sobsey & Doe, 1991) or making it easier to intellectualize the abuse (Schor, 1987). Rates of abuse have been found to be higher in cultures that devalue people with disabilities than in cultures in which such individuals are not devalued (Justice & Justice, 1990).

3. *Overcoming external (situational) inhibitions.* Youth with developmental disabilities often have fewer situational safeguards to protect them from exploitation (Schor, 1987). They live more isolated lives and are less likely to live with their natural parents. Many are exposed to multiple caregivers, which in and of itself increases the risk for abuse because many offenders come in contact with their victims through specialized services (Ammerman, Van Hasselt, Hersen, McGonigle, & Lubestsky, 1989; Blatt & Brown, 1986; Brown, 1992a; Sobsey & Doe, 1991).

4. *Overcoming the child's resistance.* Sexual offenders identify vulnerable children through behavioral clues that suggest a child is unlikely to report, is "needy," or is very trusting of adults (Conte, Wolf, & Smith, 1989). The sexual naïveté and social immaturity common to youth with developmental disabilities may make it difficult for them to distinguish appropriate from exploitative touch (Knight, 1989; Krajicek, 1982a; Sobsey & Varnhagen, 1991; Tharinger, Horton, & Millea, 1990). Those who lose a sense of personal boundaries because they are frequently examined by the medical community are similarly vulnerable (Cole, 1988; Morgan, 1987).

Adolescents with disabilities are at additional risk for abuse due to the particular characteristics of their disabilities. Many of those who are abused do not possess sufficient communication skills to report or identify an abuser, while others lack the strength or mobility to resist coercive sexual contact (Ammerman et al., 1989; Crossmaker, 1991; Sobsey & Varnhagen, 1991; Tharinger, Horton, & Millea, 1990). Persons with visual or auditory impairments may not see or hear cues that might otherwise warn them of dangerous situations; others may be aware of these cues but their disability prevents them from leaving threatening situations independently (Freeman, Goetz, Richards, & Groenveld, 1991). Still others may be unaware of inadvertent cues their behavior may provide to those with whom they interact. Dressing and privacy issues must be addressed with those whose impairment limits their ability to directly assess the appropriateness of their presentation to others (Kempton, 1988). An overemphasis on compliance and respect for authority, without appropriate discrimination or assertion skills, also places individuals with disabilities at increased risk for exploitation (Anderson, 1982; Crossmaker, 1991; Sobsey & Varnhagen, 1991; Tharinger, Horton, & Millea, 1990), although there are no empirical data implicating compliance as a risk factor for sexual abuse. Finally, reports of abuse by individuals with more severe disabilities may be discounted by those who believe severe disability precludes eligibility for the sexual attention of others (Cole, 1988).

Assessing Abuse

Identifying victims of sexual abuse poses a major difficulty for professionals who work with youth with disabilities (Baladerian, 1991). Cases of sexual abuse are identified primarily through victim disclosure or investigation of signs and symptoms that suggest sexual abuse (Tharinger, Horton, & Millea, 1990). However, many children with multihandicapping conditions or more severe forms of mental retardation are unable to verbalize episodes of abuse (Morgan, 1987). Tools used to evaluate nonverbal but developmentally unimpaired children who have been sexually abused (e.g., anatomically detailed dolls) have not been validated for persons with developmental delays (Elvik, Berkowitz, Nicholas, Lipman, & Inkelis, 1990). Therefore, providers must rely on behavioral observations to detect sexual abuse in this population.

Unfortunately, the base rate of many symptoms of sexual abuse is higher in populations with disabilities, sometimes as a function of disability itself. Inappropriate sexual behavior such as compulsive masturbation, rarely seen in unimpaired populations, is more common in persons with developmental and cognitive disabilities (Johnson & Johnson, 1982; Krajicek, 1982b), making it more difficult to determine if the behavior is indicative of abuse. The increased rate of psychiatric and behavior disorders among persons with developmental disabilities further complicates one's ability to implicate sexual abuse as contributory to these behaviors (Lewis & MacLean, 1982; Rutter, Tizard, & Whitmore, 1980). Because there is no single behavior or "syndrome" to implicate sexual abuse, those having day-to-day contact with children and adolescents at risk need to be especially attuned to changes in a child's behavior that may signify distress and prompt further investigation.

Sequelae of abuse vary as a function of child variables (e.g., intellectual ability, prior adjustment, coping skills), and abuse variables (e.g., force, frequency, duration, relationship to the perpetrator). There is some indication that the sequelae of abuse may be more severe among those with developmental delays (Varley, 1984), although this view is not universal (Cruz, Price-Williams, & Andron, 1988). With the exception of sexualized behavior and post-traumatic stress disorder (PTSD), short-term effects of sexual abuse are similar to what one sees in clinically referred populations in general (e.g., anxiety, fears, nightmares, withdrawn behavior, somatic complaints, aggression, and school problems) (Beitchman, Zucker, Hood, daCosta, & Akman, 1991; Kendall-Tackett, Williams, & Finkelhor, 1993; Mansell, Sobsey, & Calder, 1992). Sexualized behavior can include sexualized play with dolls, inserting objects into the anus or vagina, excessive or public masturbation, seductive behavior, requesting sexual stimulation from adults or other children, and age-inappropriate sexual knowledge (Beitchman et al., 1991). Sexualized behavior is not diagnostic in itself, as nonabused and physically abused children may also exhibit certain types of sexualized behavior (Deblinger, McLeer, Atkins, Ralphe, & Foa, 1989; Schroeder & Gordon, 1991).

Many symptoms are developmentally specific and do not appear across all age groups. For example, in preschoolers one might see nightmares and inappropriate sexualized behavior, while with adolescents depression, withdrawal, truancy or substance abuse are more likely (Kendall-Tackett, Williams, & Finkelhor, 1993). It has been estimated that anywhere between 21 to 49 percent of sexual abuse victims appear or are ostensibly asymptomatic, perhaps as a function of the relative severity of the abuse, lack of sensitive measures, or because the victim effectively suppresses symptoms that may become manifest later in time. It is also possible that some children experience abuse without ever exhibiting significant symptomology (Kendall-Tackett, Williams, & Finkelhor, 1993). The higher base rate of these behaviors among children with disabilities and the varied presentations of abuse may be confusing to inexperienced providers. Professional committees, such as the Suspected Child Abuse and Neglect Team (Baladerian, 1991), constitute a community resource to investigate child abuse. These teams meet on a regular basis to make informed decisions regarding the identification and reporting of abuse based on the pooled expertise of members.

Addressing Abuse

Studies have shown that between 45 and 54 percent of victims with disability have difficulty finding suitable treatment services; even when found, many services fail to provide any accommodation to special needs. Individuals with more significant cognitive impairment typically have very few appropriate services tailored for them (Mansell, Sobsey, & Calder, 1992; Sobsey & Doe, 1991). Interventions based on verbal or introspective abilities are often inappropriate for those with limited cognitive and communicative abilities (Sullivan, Scanlon, Brookhauser, Schulte, & Knutson, 1992; Tharinger, Horton, & Millea, 1990). Modeling (Szymanski & Jansen, 1980) and role-playing (Monfils, 1985) exemplify successful alternatives. Augmentative communication, such as American Sign Language and other systems employing visual, tactile, or kinesthetic stimuli, may facilitate communication between providers and victims of abuse who are disabled (Spackman, Grigel, & McFarlane, 1988).

There has been only one treatment outcome study in recent years that assessed the effectiveness of therapy with sexually abused children with a disability. In that study, 72 sexually abused children at a residential school for the deaf received a broad-based psychotherapeutic intervention. When compared to an untreated control group, those children receiving therapy had significantly fewer post treatment behavior problems, as measured by the Child Behavior Checklist, than children not receiving therapy (Sullivan et al., 1992).

Unfortunately, few professionals are adequately trained to provide therapeutic services to individuals with disabilities. Even medical providers are often unfamiliar with the particulars of various disabilities (Cole, 1988). Professionals working in this area are required to possess expertise in not just one, but several specialty areas including disability, sexuality, and abuse (Baladerian, 1991). Professionals with competency in one of these areas might consider consulting with other experts or forming cotherapy relationships with other professionals before providing treatment. In addition, basic staff training regarding sexuality and the steps required to assist in the sexual adjustment of children and adolescents is essential to the development of a context that supports sexual adjustment. Finally, family members, caregivers, and staff are also significantly affected by abuse and may require access to mental health services. Fortunately, as this area receives more attention in the literature, additional resources and clinical services are becoming increasingly available (Baladerian, 1991; Cohen & Warren, 1990).

Facilitating Adjustment

Education

Along with normalization and community integration comes a responsibility to educate youth about sexuality and sexual functioning, to assist them in developing safe and responsible behavior, and to promote sexual adjustment (Baugh, 1984). It has been suggested that school personnel should deal with these issues proactively as is often done for regular education students (Adams, 1981). Early efforts tended to focus on hygiene and warnings about the potential risks associated with sexual behavior, serving more to control students than to instruct them (Daniels, Cornelius, Makas, & Chipouras, 1981). However, curricula for students with disabilities, particularly those with developmental delays, have begun to evolve and the Council on Sexuality and the Mentally Retarded has developed guidelines to be used in creating effective sexual education curricula (Kempton & Kahn, 1991).

The need for sex education is suggested by an increase in teenage pregnancy and births among girls with developmental disabilities (Rowitz, 1988). Most children with developmental delays or sensory impairments have some awareness of coitus and pregnancy, but many lack adequate information about contraception, sexually transmitted diseases (STDs), or strategies to avoid sexual exploitation and abuse (Brantlinger, 1985). Females with disabilities are at a particular disadvantage when it comes to the availability of appropriate information regarding these issues (Cole, 1988). Learning difficulties, uninformed peers, and limited opportunities to observe unimpaired peers are common obstacles that interfere with acquiring information about these issues. Alternative sources of information, such as television, may provide a distorted view of social sexual behavior and complicate rather than facilitate sexual adjustment (Crossmaker, 1991; Kempton, 1988; Krajicek, 1982a; Schuster, 1986). Curricula should address pregnancy prevention and prevention of STDs, especially as many methods of birth control do not provide protection against STDs. Essential health and hygiene skills, such as menstrual hygiene training, comprise basic curriculum elements, particularly among those with developmental delays (Epps, Prescott, & Horner, 1990; Epps, Stern, & Horner, 1990). Issues related to community values and morés should be included as appropriate.

Sex education programs must be tailored to accommodate individual limitations, including general developmental level and cognitive, sensory, and social skills deficits. Contraceptive methods requiring planning and judgment may not be suitable for individuals whose cognitive processes are very immediate and concrete. Other techniques may require manual dexterity incompatible with particular disabilities (Williams, 1993). An assessment of individual needs also includes an evaluation of existing sexual information and current behavioral repertoire. Failure to adequately evaluate individual needs may result in discrepancies between problems targeted for intervention and those actually experienced by those receiving services. Such discrepancies may limit the efficiency and effectiveness of intervention (Michaelis, Warzak, Stanek, & Van Riper, 1992). Education must also include an awareness that the threat of molestation is not restricted to strangers. The greatest danger may come from individuals known to the victim, often within the context of gradual but escalating physical contact (Cole, 1988).

Several approaches to working with individuals with disabilities have evolved in recent years. Curricula that focus on individuals with developmental disabilities have received the most attention. For example, the PLIS-SIT approach generates programs that provide *P*ermission, *L*imited *I*nformation, *S*pecific *S*uggestions, and *I*ntensive *T*reatment to address specific sexuality issues (Keller & Buchanan, 1984). The intensity of the intervention varies to meet the needs of the individual. Similarly, the Developmental Skills–Based Approach is an intensive individualized therapy involving (1) an assessment of individual needs and capacities, (2) facilitation of knowledge and skills for sex adjustment, and (3) implementation of a plan developed by the participant and teacher (Keller & Buchanan, 1984).

Programs such as the Life Horizons curricula (Kempton, 1988) accommodate those with sensory deficits and those with developmental disabilities, in part through extensive use of slides and visual aids. The Life Horizons curriculum addresses people across varied levels of functioning. Different modules inform participants about the physiological, psychological, and social aspects of sexuality. Materials may be presented across weeks or months, allowing for the repeated presentations and overlearning often required by those with developmental delays or head injuries. Other programs emphasize the nature of relationships, including concepts of personal space, social distance, and appropriate social-sexual behavior. For example, the Circles curriculum (Champagne & Walker-Hirsch, 1982) provides a concrete and systematic approach to presenting factual information as well as helping students with developmental delays learn correct social-sexual behavior and prevention of abuse and STDs.

Social Skills Training

Youth with disabilities often lack access to unimpaired peers, thereby limiting their social repertoires and the ability to establish social relationships (Yarris, 1992). Having a limited or inappropriate social repertoire can severely impede the development of relationships and adversely affect adjustment. Defective social behavior may be the result of multiple cognitive and behavioral factors including anxiety, inappropriate learning history, or simple lack of social skill (Curran, 1977; Michelson, Sugai, Wood, & Kazdin, 1983). Social skills training has been used to remediate skill deficits with many different populations including those with disabilities (Yarris, 1992). A training package consisting of a rationale, modeling, behavioral rehearsal, feedback, and reinforcement has been successful in shaping a variety of effective social behavior (cf. Kelly, 1982).

Of particular relevance are programs that focus on teaching assertive behavior to individuals who have difficulty recognizing situations appropriate to initiating sexual behavior, refusing unwanted sexual behavior, or requesting safe sex behavior from an appropriate and willing partner (Duggan-Ali, 1992; Howard, 1985a, 1985b; Sobsey & Doe, 1991; Warzak & Page, 1990). Learning the assertive skills required to report abusive episodes is also a concern (Kolko, 1988). Most assertiveness training programs in this area have focused on unimpaired populations and have emphasized information, communication skills, and contraceptive issues (Burke, 1987; Committee on Adolescence, 1987; Flaherty, Marecek, Olsen, & Wilcove, 1983; Schinke, 1984; Shendell, 1992b). These programs have met with very limited success (Dawson, 1986; Melton, 1988). Few programs have been geared toward working with individuals with disabilities and few have specifically targeted sexual refusal skills. Yet unlike other contraceptive strategies, refusal skills are portable and require no advanced planning once learned, suggesting their potential benefit for these populations.

Warzak and Page (1990) extrapolated refusal skills technology from the addictive behavior literature and applied it to sexually active adolescents with disabilities, with some success. Individual needs assessments were conducted and behavioral deficits were identified. Specific contexts in which problematic sexual behavior occurred were also assessed (cf. Warzak, Grow, Poler, & Walburn, submitted for publication), an important consideration given the situational specificity of assertiveness (Eisler, Hersen, Miller, & Blanchard, 1975). However, the behavioral components of refusal were not empirically cross-validated. In fact, there are no studies that have cross-validated the behavioral components of sexual refusal skills for any population. This may be a critical omission because the affective component of sexual behavior and sexual refusal is undoubtedly greater than the affective component involved in refusing cigarettes or alcohol. Typical components of refusal behavior as exemplified by the addictive behavior literature, such as eye contact, verbal communication, and the like, may be ineffective or may even aggravate unwanted sexual situations. More work is needed in this area before effective strategies can be confidently developed for sexual refusal with any population, including youth with disabilities.

Special Considerations

Many issues related to facilitating sexual adjustment are specific to particular populations. Among adolescents with hearing impairments, limited communication skills and the resulting lack of information comprise significant barriers to sexual adjustment. The inaccessibility of information on sexuality affects both sexual knowledge and sexual attitudes of individuals with hearing impairments (Cornelius et al., 1982). When addressing issues of sexuality with hearing-impaired students, several recommendations are relevant, including increasing contact with hearing peers, helping parents learn manual communication to facilitate discussion of sexuality issues, increasing interaction among deaf students at residential schools, providing specialized training in sexuality and disability for those who work with deaf individuals, and increasing awareness and sensitivity regarding sexual implications of deafness (Baugh, 1984; Cornelius et al., 1982).

Adolescents who are congenitally visually impaired are unable to see the many shapes of the human body in various stages of dress and undress. Cultural factors may inhibit them from gaining this information by touch, contributing to a lack of basic sexual information (Cornelius et al., 1982; Scholl, 1974). There is some controversy regarding the best means to provide sex education to youth who are visually impaired. It has been suggested that current social taboos against physical contact be reevaluated to permit children to explore their parents' genitalia through tactile interaction (Schuster, 1986), although others have suggested that extraordinary measures are not necessary for blind children to develop a healthy sexual self-concept and satisfactory sexual adjustment (Daugherty, 1988). Several recommendations have been formulated to address issues of sexuality with the visually impaired, including the development of audio and tactile resources, increased interaction between males and females within residential settings, and the implementation of sexual education curricula within classroom and daily life settings (Cornelius et al., 1982).

Consideration must be made of the special needs of individuals who are cognitively impaired by virtue of developmental delays or traumatic brain injury. Deficits related to impaired attention, retention, and recall, language delays, and limited ability to deal effectively with abstract concepts are common among these populations (Warzak, Evans, & Ford, 1992; Warzak & Kilburn, 1990). Concrete and dichotomous thinking, poor concept of future time, and difficulty understanding how today's behavior may contribute to disease many years later also contribute to maladaptive decision making (Daugherty, 1988; Hingson, 1987; Passer, Rauh, Chamberlain, McGrath, & Burket, 1984). Simple language, audiovisual materials, and repetition are needed to promote retention and retrieval of sex education facts. Structured settings with few distractions may be required. Behavioral strategies that promote attention to materials and compliance with procedures may be helpful in maintaining student cooperation and promoting safe and responsible behavior (Warzak & Kilburn, 1990).

Recommendations and Future Directions

Children and adolescents with disabilities confront many obstacles to sexual adjustment. Not the least of these has been the historic denial of issues related to the sexual functioning and adjustment of youth with disabilities by parents and providers who believed that these individuals would not or should not be sexually active (Bernstein, 1985; Crooks & Baur, 1990; Keller & Buchanan, 1984). Fortunately, recent years have witnessed a better understanding of the special needs of these children and efforts to assist in their sexual adjustment are increasing (Brantlinger, 1988; Daniels et al., 1981; Kempton & Kahn, 1991).

Youth with disabilities are neither a unidimensional nor a homogeneous population. No single approach will satisfactorily accommodate everyone (Knight, 1989; Manikam & Hensarling, 1990). Issues ranging from the level and type of disability to the cultural heritage of participants may affect strategies and procedures developed to promote sexual adjustment (Schwartzbaum, 1992). Given that there is no single societally approved standard of sexual behavior (Kempton, 1988), it is imperative that providers also obtain input from parents and community advisers prior to program implementation. Parents and providers must agree on a common set of programmatic goals that focus on the sexual adjustment of these individuals.

Programs should serve the whole person, with self-acceptance and self-esteem being essential goals of any program attempting to promote satisfactory sexual adjustment and the prevention of sexual exploitation (Finkelhor, 1984). Programs should be broad-based and not limited to issues related to anatomy, hygiene, and sexual functioning. Many assertive skills are relevant, both to refuse unwanted sexual activity and to report it when it occurs. Skills related to initiating social relationships and appropriate levels of interpersonal sexual behavior are crucial to sexual adjustment. Local standards of appropriate and inappropriate behavior also must be communicated, including community moral and ethical concerns.

In-service training at schools, residential facilities, and day programs can help parents and staff develop an awareness of the issues related to the sexual adjustment of those in their care. Caregivers must recognize that children with disabilities often enter puberty without the same level of information, experience, and social skills common to their unimpaired siblings and peers (Smith, 1983). They should be aware of the cognitive, physical, and developmental limitations that present barriers to the sexual adjustment of these children and render them vulnerable to exploitation.

Finally, there is a dearth of empirical work regarding the efficacy of many training and treatment programs. Much of the literature is characterized by program descriptions, opinion pieces, and editorials regarding the sexual adjustment of youth with disabilities. Programs that have been evaluated, most commonly in the abuse literature, too often measure effectiveness in terms of acquisition of information or improvement in role-play performance. Pre–post measures, control groups, and long-term follow-up data are typically not reported (Kolko, 1988). Little is known about the relationship between sex education and adjustment and relevant outcome variables such as initiation of appropriate social-sexual behaviors, successful refusal of unwanted sexual activity, or incidents of abuse. The influence of teaching contexts (e.g., school or residential), methods and types of treatment (e.g., didactic or role-play), and participant variables (e.g., age, sex, history) on program outcome remains unknown (Kolko, 1988).

The social acceptability of programs related to sexual adjustment, including the interest of students and staff in participating in them, has not been evaluated. Programs that lack interested participants and dedicated staff are bound to be ineffective. If we are truly committed to the sexual adjustment of youth with disabilities we must obtain the coordinated efforts of parents, providers, and researchers, as well as the active participation of those children and adolescents who stand to benefit from these efforts.

It is acknowledged that there are many different kinds and degrees of disability, each with potentially unique challenges to sexual adjustment for children and adolescents. Few empirical resources are available to assist the practicing clinician who confronts these many challenges while assisting children and adolescents with disabilities. The scope of this chapter has also been limited by the sparse empirical research literature in this area. We hope that this review will be instrumental in challenging clinical investigators to pursue applied research in this area of study.

References

Adams, R. (1981). Sexuality and the handicapped. *Journal of School Health, 51,* 622.

Ammerman, R. T., Van Hasselt, V. B., Hersen, M., McGonigle, J. J., & Lubestsky, M. J. (1989). Abuse and neglect in psychiatrically hospitalized multihandicapped children. *Child Abuse and Neglect, 13,* 335–343.

Anderson, C. (1982). *Teaching people with mental retardation about sexual abuse prevention.* Santa Cruz, CA: Network Publications.

Baladerian, N. J. (1991). Sexual abuse of people with developmental disabilities. *Sexuality and Disability, 9,* 323–335.

Baugh, R. (1984). Sexuality education for the visually and hearing impaired child in the regular classroom. *Journal of School Health, 54*(10), 407–409.

Beitchman, J. H., Zucker, K. J., Hood, J. E., daCosta, G. A., & Akman, D. (1991). A review of the short-term effects of child sexual abuse. *Child Abuse and Neglect, 15,* 537–556.

Bernstein, N. (1985). Sexuality in mentally retarded adolescents. *Medical Aspects of Human Sexuality, 19*(11), 50–61.

Blatt, E. R., & Brown, S. W. (1986). Environmental influences on incidents of alleged child abuse and neglect in New York state psychiatric facilities: Toward an etiology of institutional child maltreatment. *Child Abuse and Neglect, 10,* 171–180.

Blendonohy, P., & Philip, P. (1991). Precocious puberty in children after traumatic brain injury. *Brain Injury, 5*(1), 63–68.

Brantlinger, E. A. (1985). Mildly mentally retarded secondary students' information about and attitudes toward sexuality and sexuality education. *Education and Training of the Mentally Retarded, 20,* 99–108.

Brantlinger, E. A. (1988). Teacher's perceptions of the parenting abilities of their secondary students with mild mental retardation. *RASE: Remedial and Special Education, 9,* 31–43.

Brookhouser, P. E., Sullivan, P., Scanlon, J. M., & Garbarino, J. (1986). Identifying the sexually abused deaf child: The ontorolaryngologist's role. *Laryngoscope, 96,* 152–158.

Brown, H. (1992a). Abuse of adults with learning difficulties. *Nursing Standard, 6,* 18–19.

Brown, H. (1992b). Sexual issues for people with learning difficulties. *Nursing Standard, 7*(12), 54–55.

Burke, P. J. (1987). Adolescents' motivation for sexual activity and pregnancy prevention. *Pediatric Nursing, 10,* 161–171.

Chamberlain, A., Rauh, J., Passer, A., McGrath, M., & Burket, R. (1984). Issues in fertility control for mentally retarded female adolescents: 1. Sexual activity, sexual abuse, and contraception. *Pediatrics, 73*(4), 445–450.

Champagne, M. P., & Walker-Hirsch, L. W. (1982). Circles: A self-organization system for teaching appropriate social/sexual behavior to mentally retarded/ developmentally disabled persons. *Sexuality and Disability, 5,* 172–177.

Cohen, S., & Warren, R. D. (1990). The intersection of disability and child abuse in England and the United States. *Child Welfare, 69,* 253–262.

Cole, S. (1981). Disability/ability: The importance of sexual health in adolescence. Issues and concerns of the professional. *SIECUS Report, 9*(5–6), 3–4.

Cole, S. (1986). Facing the challenges of sexual abuse in persons with disabilities. *Sexuality and Disability, 7*(3–4), 367–375.

Cole, S. (1988). Women, sexuality, and disabilities. *Women and Therapy, 7,* 277–294.

Committee on Adolescence. (1987). Role of the pediatrician in management of sexually transmitted diseases in children and adolescents. *Pediatrics, 79*(3), 454–456.

Conte, J. R., Wolf, S., & Smith, T. (1989). What sexual offenders tell us about prevention strategies. *Child Abuse and Neglect, 13,* 293–301.

Cornelius, M., Chipouras, S., Makas, E., & Daniels, S. (1982). Sexuality and visual impairment: A review of the literature. *Who cares? A handbook on sex education and counseling services for disabled people* (2nd ed.) pp. 137–147. Baltimore: University Park Press.

Crooks, R., & Baur, K. (1990). *Our sexuality.* New York: Benjamin\Cummings.

Crossmaker, M. (1991). Behind locked doors: Institutional sexual abuse. *Sexuality and Disability, 9,* 201–219.

Cruz, V. K., Price-Williams, D., & Andron, L. (1988). Developmentally disabled women who were molested as children. *Social Casework: The Journal of Contemporary Social Work, 69,* 411–419.

Curran, J. P. (1977). Skills training as an approach to the treatment of heterosexual-social anxiety: A review. *Psychological Bulletin, 84*(1), 140–157.

Daniels, S., Cornelius, M., Makas, E., & Chipouras, S. (1981). Sexuality and disability: The need for services. *Annual Review of Rehabilitation, 2,* 83–112.

Daugherty, W. D. (1988). Implications of acquired immunodeficiency syndrome for professionals in the field of visual impairments and blindness. *Education of the Visually Handicapped, 20*(3), 95–108.

Dawson, D. A. (1986). The effects of sex education on adolescent behavior. *Family Planning Perspectives, 18*(4), 162–170.

Deblinger, E., McLeer, S. V., Atkins, M. S., Ralphe, D., & Foa, E. (1989). Post-traumatic stress in sexually abused, physically abused, and nonabused children. *Child Abuse and Neglect, 13*, 403–408.

Dodge, R. (1979). Sexuality and the blind disabled. *Sexuality and Disability, 2*, 201–205.

Duggan-Ali, D. (1992). Social skills and assertiveness training integrated into high school sexuality education curriculum. In I. G. Fodor (Ed.), *Adolescent assertiveness and social skills training* pp. 219–233. New York: Springer.

Eisler, R. M., Hersen, M., Miller, P. M., & Blanchard, E. B. (1975). Situational determinants of assertive behavior. *Journal of Consulting and Clinical Psychology, 43*, 330–340.

Elvik, S. L., Berkowitz, C. D., Nicholas, E., Lipman, J. L., & Inkelis, S. H. (1990). Sexual abuse in the developmentally disabled: Dilemmas of diagnosis. *Child Abuse and Neglect, 14*, 497–502.

Epps, S., Prescott, A., & Horner, R. (1990). Social acceptability of menstrual-care training methods for young women with developmental disabilities. *Education and Training in Mental Retardation, 25*(1), 33–44.

Epps, S., Stern, R., & Horner, R. (1990). Comparison of simulation training on self and using a doll for teaching generalized menstrual care to women with severe mental retardation. *Research in Developmental Disabilities, 11*, 37–66.

Finkelhor, D. (1984). *Child sexual abuse: New theory and research*. New York: Free Press.

Finkelhor, D., & Korbin, J. (1988). Child abuse as an international issue. *Child Abuse and Neglect, 12*, 3–23.

Flaherty, E. W., Marecek, J., Olsen, K., & Wilcove, G. (1983). Preventing adolescent pregnancy: An interpersonal problem-solving approach. *Innovations in Prevention, 2*, 49–64.

Freeman, R., Goetz, E., Richards, D., & Groenveld, M. (1991). Defiers of negative prediction: A 14-year follow-up study of legally blind children. *Journal of Visual Impairment and Blindness, 85*(9), 365–370.

Giami, A. (1987). Coping with the sexuality of the disabled: A comparison of the physically disabled and the mentally retarded. *International Journal of Rehabilitation Research, 10*(1), 41–48.

Hingson, S. L. (1987). Acquired immunodeficiency syndrome and adolescents: Knowledge, beliefs, attitudes, and behaviors. *Pediatrics, 79*, 825–828.

Howard, M. (1985a). How the family physician can help young teenagers postpone sexual involvement. *Medical Aspects of Human Sexuality, 19*, 76–87.

Howard, M. (1985b). Postponing sexual involvement among adolescents: An alternative approach to prevention of sexually transmitted diseases. *Journal of Adolescent Health Care, 6*, 271–277.

Howard, R. (1992). Discomfort with sexual programming. *Headlines, 3*, 9.

Jaudes, P. K., & Diamond, L. J. (1985). The handicapped child and child abuse. *Child Abuse and Neglect, 9*, 341–347.

Johnson, D. M., & Johnson, W. R. (1982). Sexuality and the mentally retarded adolescent. *Pediatric Annals, 2,* 847–853.

Justice, B., & Justice, R. (1990). *The abusing family* (Rev. ed.). New York: Plenum.

Kaeser, F. (1992). Can people with severe mental retardation consent to mutual sex? *Sexuality and Disability, 10,* 33–42.

Keller, S., & Buchanan, D. C. (1984). Sexuality and disability: An overview. *Rehabilitation Digest, 15,* 3–7.

Kelly, J. (1982). *Social skills training.* New York: Springer.

Kempton, W. (1988). *Sex education for persons with disabilities that hinder learning: A teacher's guide.* Santa Monica, CA: Stanfield.

Kempton, W., & Kahn, E. (1991). Sexuality and people with intellectual disabilities: A historical perspective. *Sexuality and Disability, 9*(2), 93–111.

Kendall-Tackett, K., Williams, L., & Finkelhor, D. (1993). Impact of sexual abuse on children: A review and synthesis of recent empirical studies. *Psychological Bulletin, 113,* 164–180.

Knight, S. E. (1989). Sexual concerns of the physically disabled. In B. W. Heller, L. M. Flohr, & L. S. Zegans (Eds.), *Psychosocial interventions with physically disabled persons* (pp. 183–199). New Brunswick, NJ: Rutgers University Press.

Kolko, D. J. (1988). Educational programs to promote awareness and prevention of child sexual victimization: A review and methodological critique. *Clinical Psychology Review, 8,* 195–209.

Krajicek, M. (1982a). Developmental disability and human sexuality. *Symposium on Sexuality and Nursing Practice, 17*(3), 377–386.

Krajicek, M. J. (1982b). Sexuality and the developmentally disabled. In H. M. Wallace, R. F. Biehl, A. C. Oglesby, & L. T. Taft (Eds.), *Handicapped children and youth: A comprehensive community and clinical approach* (pp. 223–228). New York: Human Sciences Press.

Larkin, M. (1992). Reacting to patients with sexual problems. *Headlines, 3,* 2–8.

Lewis, M., & MacLean, W. (1982). Issues in treating emotional disorders. In J. L. Matson & R. P. Barrett (Eds.), *Psychopathology in the mentally retarded* (pp. 1–36). New York: Grune & Stratton.

Linsenmeyer, T., & Perkash, I. (1991). Infertility in men with spinal cord injury. *Archives of Physical and Medical Rehabilitation, 72,* 747–754.

Malloy, G., & Herold, E. (1988). Factors related to sexual counseling of physically disabled adults. *Journal of Sex Research, 24,* 220–227.

Manikam, R., & Hensarling, D. S. (1990). Sexual behavior. In J. L. Matson (Ed.), *Handbook of behavior modification with the mentally retarded* (pp. 503–521). New York: Plenum.

Mansell, S., Sobsey, D., & Calder, P. (1992). Sexual abuse treatment for persons with developmental disabilities. *Professional Psychology: Research and Practice, 23,* 404–409.

Maxwell, M. B., Karacostas, D., Ellenbogen, R. G., Brzezinski, A., Zervas, N. T., & Black, P. M. (1990). Precocious puberty following head injury. *Journal of Neurosurgery, 73,* 123–129.

McNab, W. L. (1978). The sexual needs of the handicapped. *Journal of School Health, 48,* 301–306.

Melton, G. B. (1988). Adolescents and prevention of AIDS. *Professional Psychology: Research and Practice, 19*(4), 403–408.

Michaelis, C., Warzak, W. J., Stanek, K., & Van Riper, C. L. (1992). Parental and professional perceptions of problems associated with long-term pediatric home tube feeding. *Journal of the American Dietetic Association, 92*(10), 1235–1238.

Michelson, L., Sugai, D. P., Wood, R. P., & Kazdin, A. E. (1983). *Social skills assessment and training with children.* New York: Plenum.

Monfils, M. (1985). Theme-centered group work with the mentally retarded. *Social Casework: The Journal of Contemporary Social Work, 66*(3), 177–184.

Morgan, S. R. (1987). *Abuse and neglect of handicapped children.* Boston: Little, Brown and Company.

Neff, J. (1983). Sexual well-being: A goal for young blind women. *Journal of Visual Impairment and Blindness, 77,* 296–297.

Passer, A., Rauh, J., Chamberlain, A., McGrath, M., & Burket, R. (1984). Issues in fertility control for mentally retarded female adolescents: 2. Parental attitudes toward sterilization. *Pediatrics, 73*(4), 451–454.

Peuschel, S. M., & Scola, P. S. (1988). Parents' perception of social and sexual functions in adolescents with Down's syndrome. *Journal of Mental Deficiency, 32,* 215–220.

Rekers, G. A. (1981). Psychosexual and gender problems. In E. J. Terdal & L. G. Mash (Eds.), *Behavioral assessment of childhood disorders* pp. 483–526. New York: Guilford Press.

Rekers, G. A. (1992). Development of problems of puberty and sex roles in adolescence. In C. G. Walker & M. C. Roberts (Eds.), *Handbook of clinical child psychology* (2nd ed., pp. 607–622). New York: John Wiley & Sons.

Rowitz, L. (1988). The forgotten ones: Adolescence and mental retardation. *Mental Retardation, 26,* 115–117.

Rutter, M., Tizard, J., & Whitmore, K. (1980). *Education, health, and behavior.* New York: Wiley.

Schinke, S. P. (1984). Preventing teenage pregnancy. In M. Hersen, R. M. Eisler, & P. M. Miller (Eds.), *Progress in behavior modification* (pp. 31–64). Orlando, FL: Academic Press.

Scholl, G. (1974). The psychosocial effects of blindness: Implications for program planning in sex education. *New Outlook, 68,* 201–209.

Schor, D. P. (1987). Sex and sexual abuse in developmentally disabled adolescents. *Seminars in Adolescent Medicine, 3,* 1–7.

Schroeder, C. S., & Gordon, B. N. (1991). *Assessment and treatment of childhood problems* (p. 239). New York: Guilford Press.

Schuster, C. S. (1986). Sex education of the visually impaired child. *Journal of Visual Impairment and Blindness, 80,* 675–680.

Schwartzbaum, R. C. (1992). Social skills training: Ethical issues and guidelines. In I. G. Fodor (Ed.), *Adolescent assertiveness and social skills training* pp. 67–81. New York: Springer.

Shendell, M. B. (1992a). Adolescent development and social skills training: A multifaceted perspective. In I. G. Fodor (Ed.), *Adolescent assertiveness and social skills training* pp. 28–42. New York: Springer.

Shendell, M. B. (1992b). Communication training for adolescent girls in a junior high school setting: Learning to take risks in self-expression. In I. G. Fodor (Ed.), *Adolescent assertiveness and social skills training* pp 205–218. New York: Springer.

Smith, S. (1983). The link between sexual maturation and "adolescent grieving" in parents of the dependent disabled. *Sexuality and Disability, 6*(3–4), 150–154.

Sobsey, D., & Doe, T. (1991). Patterns of sexual abuse and assault. *Sexuality and Disability, 3*, 243–259.

Sobsey, D., & Mansell, S. (1990). The prevention of sexual abuse of people with developmental disabilities. *Developmental Disabilities Bulletin, 18*(2), 51–66.

Sobsey, D., & Varnhagen, C. (1991). Sexual abuse and exploitation of disabled individuals. In C. R. Bagley & R. J. Thomlinson (Eds.), *Child sexual abuse: Critical perspectives on prevention, intervention, and treatment* (pp. 203–218). Toronto: Wall and Emerson.

Spackman, R., Grigel, M., & McFarlane, C. (1988). Individual counseling and therapy for the mentally handicapped. *Alberta Psychology, 19*(5), 14–18.

Sullivan, P., Scanlon, J., Brookhauser, P., Schulte, L., & Knutson, J. (1992). The effects of psychotherapy on behavior problems of sexually abused deaf children. *Child Abuse and Neglect, 16*(2), 297–307.

Szymanski, L. S., & Jansen, P. E. (1980). Assessment of sexuality and sexual vulnerability of retarded persons. In L. S. Szymanski & P. E. Tanguay (Eds.), *Emotional disorders of mentally retarded persons: Assessment, treatment and consultation* (pp. 195–214). Baltimore: University Park Press.

Tharinger, D., Horton, C. B., & Millea, S. (1990). Sexual abuse and exploitation of children and adults with mental retardation and other handicaps. *Child Abuse and Neglect, 14*, 301–312.

Varley, C. K. (1984). Schizophreniform psychoses in mentally retarded girls following sexual assault. *American Journal of Psychiatry, 141*, 593–595.

Warzak, W. J., Evans, J., & Ford, L. (1992). Working with the traumatically brain injured patient. Implications for rehabilitation. *Journal of Comprehensive Mental Health Care, 2*, 115–130.

Warzak, W. J., Grow, C., Poler, M., & Walburn, J. N. (submitted for publication). Identifying situations which place adolescents at risk for unwanted sexual activity.

Warzak, W. J., & Kilburn, J. (1990). Behavioral approaches to activities of daily living. In D. E. Tupper & K. D. Cicerone (Eds.), *The neuropsychology of everyday life: Vol. 1. Assessment and basic competencies* (pp. 285–305). New York: Martinus Nijhoff.

Warzak, W. J., & Page, T. (1990). Teaching refusal skills to sexually active adolescents. *Journal of Behavior Therapy and Experimental Psychiatry, 21*, 133–140.

Williams, C. (1993). Expert evidence in cases of child abuse. *Archives of Disease in Childhood, 68*(5), 712–714.

Williams, D. N. (1987). Becoming a woman: The girl who is mentally retarded. *Pediatric Nursing, 13*, 89–93.

Williams, J. K. (1983). Reproductive decisions: Adolescents with Down's syndrome. *Pediatric Nursing, 9*, 43.

Yarris, S. (1992). Assessment of social skills of physically disabled adolescents. In I. G. Fodor (Ed.), *Adolescent assertiveness and social skills training* pp 183–200. New York: Springer.

Zencius, A., Wesolowski, M., Burke, W., & Hough, S. (1990). Managing hypersexual disorders in brain-injured clients. *Brain Injury, 4*(2), 175–181.

6
Psychologic Issues in Individuals with Genetic, Hormonal, and Anatomic Anomalies of the Sexual System
Review and Treatment Considerations

Tom Mazur
Kim Dobson

Human beings do not come into the world with their psychosexual status completely finished and differentiated. Such status must await postnatal events that interact with those prenatal variables (e.g., genes, hormones, brain development) present in utero. In essence, psychosexual differentiation is a continuation of the embryonic development of sex which includes, among other systems, the differentiation of the reproductive system. For various reasons errors sometimes occur in this differentiation and an infant is born with a defect of the sexual system. This chapter addresses genetic, hormonal, and anatomic anomalies of the reproductive organs, as well as the psychological effects associated with these defects. Also discussed are the medical and psychological treatments for these individuals and their families.

Turner's Syndrome: 45X and Variants

In 1938 Henry Turner reported seven phenotypic females who exhibited sexual infantilism, short stature, increased carrying of the elbow (cubitus valgus), and congenital webbed neck. Since that time Turner's syndrome (TS), as it has become known, was discovered to be a spectrum of abnormalities that result from absence, partial or complete, of the second chromosome. A number of variants have been described, including deletions of the short arm of the X chromosome, various deletions of portions of the X chromosome, and various mosaics. Such chromosomal abnormalities can arise through several mechanisms.

The gonads of the TS female are often absent or not fully developed. Exploratory surgery often reveals small dysgenetic ovaries or a fibrous streak that will not produce eggs or female sex hormones. Therefore these girls will have delayed or absent pubertal development, will have primary and secondary amenorrhoea, and are typically sterile.

These females exhibit various somatic anomalies. Typical stigmata and physical findings include (1) short stature; (2) congenital webbed neck; (3) low hair-line; (4) abnormal facies micrognathia (small jaws), low-set malformed ears, middle ear problems; (5) shield chest, immature nipples; (6) congenital heart defects including coarctation of the aorta and valvular (aortic) stenosis; (7) urinary tract anomalies including double kidney and double ureter; (8) pigmented nevi (moles); (9) cubitus valgus; (10) dysplasia of fingernails; (11) swelling of the hands and feet at birth; (12) absent sexual development.

The frequency of TS is approximately 1 out of 2,500 female births. Approximately 98–99 percent of pregnancies with TS abort spontaneously and approximately 10 percent of fetuses from pregnancies that have spontaneously aborted have TS (Hall, Sybert, Williamson, Fisher, & Reed, 1982).

Cognitive, psychiatric, psychosexual, and psychosocial behaviors of TS have been examined over the years. Polani (1960) suggested that a high prevalence of mental retardation in TS patients was the result of sampling bias. More recent study has shown mental retardation in those individuals with TS is almost always associated with the presence of additional chromosomal abnormality in addition to the abnormal or absent X chromosome (Hall et al., 1982). Global and verbal intellectual abilities of TS individuals fall into the normal range (Shaffer, 1962). However, they often exhibit specific cognitive deficits. Many exhibit deficient skills in perceptual motor organization and visual–spatial perception in addition to impairments in memory and significant underachievement in arithmetic, numerical ability, mental calculation, geometry, and reasoning (Rovet, 1993).

Psychiatric disturbances have been reported in patients with TS, including schizophrenia (Sabbath, 1961), bipolar affective disorder (Hoffenberg & Jackson, 1957), and anorexia nervosa (Dougherty, Rockwell, Sutton, & Ellinwood, 1983; Forssman, Melbin, & Walinder, 1970; Kron, Katz, Gorzynki, Gorzynski, & Weiner, 1977). Early observations of TS patients did not confirm an increased rate of psychopathology. Nielsen, Nyborg, and Dahl (1977) and Money and Mittenthal (1970) found TS patients to be unusually stable as opposed to emotionally labile, anxious, and restless. Money and Mittenthal refer to this stableness as "inertia of emotional arousal." However, McCauley, Sybert, and Ehrhardt (1986) in a study of TS women aged 12–48 years found a subgroup (22 percent) reporting major psychiatric difficulties (major depression, anxiety) and exhibiting a considerably impaired sense of self-esteem.

Though an increased risk of frank psychopathology appears inconclusive, TS associated with psychopathology may be due to chance since depression and the like occurs with high frequency in general. Data on the psychosocial function of both TS children and adults are more clear. Recent study of girls with TS versus normal controls utilizing the Child Behavior Checklist (CBCL) revealed that TS patients have poor peer relations, immaturity, and decreased attentional skills (Sonis et al., 1983). McCauley, Ito, and Kay (1986) found that TS girls aged 9–17 compared to a control group of girls with short stature had fewer friends, had more difficulty understanding social clues, and needed more structure to socialize. Downey, Ehrhardt, Gruen, Bell, and Morishima (1989) comparing TS women to controls— their siblings and women with constitutional short stature—found that TS adults were less likely to have positive symptoms such as acting-out behavior, suicide, and substance or alcohol abuse. However they also seemed to be less emotionally reactive, a finding reminiscent of Money and Mittenthal's (1970) observation. TS women were also found to lack intimate relationships, have fewer social supports, and avoid novel experiences.

TS girls are more stereotypically feminine than constitutional short stature controls (Downey, Ehrhardt, Morishima, Bell, & Gruen, 1987). They reported more parenting rehearsal, less tomboyishness, and less expressions of aggression. However, in the area of social relationships, TS girls and women report limited heterosexual contact (Nielsen, Nyborg, & Dahl, 1977; Downey et al., 1989). This lowered frequency of dating may be secondary to decreased self-esteem arising from concerns about short stature and other stigmata. It may also be secondary to delayed pubertal development and altered hormonal balance. It is consistent with psychological findings of avoidance of novel experiences and lack of intimacy with both friends and lovers (Downey et al., 1989).

Lifetime prevalence of marriage is unknown. Overall marital adjustment is also unknown. There is no physical reason for increased risk of sexual dysfunction beyond vaginal dryness in the absence of estrogen replacement.

Most TS patients are infertile. The literature contains reports of at least 11 pregnancies in women with 45X karyotype and greater than 100 pregnancies in women with mosaicism (Singh, Hara, Foster, & Grimes, 1980). Miscarriages, stillbirths, and malformations are common. Risk of spontaneous abortion is about 50 percent (Singh et al., 1980).

TS patients generally present to the pediatrician (1) as neonates with swelling of hands or feet or congenital webbed neck, (2) for short stature, and (3) for failure of pubertal development with primary or secondary amenorrhea. Diagnostic testing previously utilized the buccal smear to rule out the TS diagnosis. However, this technique led to misdiagnosis in individuals with an isochrome X or in mosaics. Banded chromosome studies are now recommended. Ultrasound examination of the heart, kidneys, and pelvis is recommended as part of the medical workup.

Most girls with TS will not develop secondary sex characteristics, and will not initiate or maintain regular menses without exogenous hormone replacement. Approximately 10 percent of nonmosaic TS women and 20 percent of mosaics will have spontaneous menses (usually irregular and ceasing prematurely) and may not require medication to initiate puberty (Hall et al., 1982).

Recently, human growth hormone has been successful in increasing the adult height of some TS girls (Rongen-Westerlaken et al., 1992; Rosenfeld et al., 1992).

Additional medical treatment may include removal of streaked gonads in early childhood of individuals with 45X/46XY karyotype to avoid the risk of neoplasia. Gonadoblastoma occurs almost exclusively in persons mosaic for a Y chromosome. Cosmetic surgery for correction of congenital neck webbing is often attempted in later childhood. However, these individuals are prone to keloid scaring that could greatly diminish any cosmetic enhancement of the surgery itself.

Amniocentesis should be offered to all pregnant women with TS. Fertility counseling is a necessity. TS patients should be informed of their need for exogenous hormones to go through puberty and of the likelihood that they will probably be unable to conceive children.

Psychologic management consists of providing information about the medical diagnosis, treatment options, and both the medical and behavioral consequences. Such information needs to be provided to the parents upon diagnosis with continued follow-up sessions as requested by them or as part of medical visits. Information is given to the child over time, should be geared to her age and level of understanding, and should build on previous information given to her.

A second aspect of psychologic management is assessment and evaluation of overall behavioral and cognitive development. Cognitive or educational assessment is especially important in view of the fact that girls with TS may have certain cognitive weaknesses as outlined above. Ideally, all girls with TS should be tested for such deficits upon diagnosis. If cognitive disabilities are discovered, this information needs to be communicated to the appropriate school authorities so they can provide special help to the child. In addition to this information, school personnel will benefit from general information on TS. Finally, TS individuals and their families can benefit from meeting other persons with the same diagnosis. To quote one individual with TS: "To know and to talk to another who has had similar experiences is immeasurably helpful. It softens the pain of feeling like a stranger in one's land. I know my confidence and self-esteem have increased in direct proportion to the strength and number of friendships I have made with other TS women" (Tesch, 1989, p. 187).

There is a national organization headquartered in Minnesota for TS individuals and their families. It publishes a newsletter, holds a national meeting, and provides updates on current medical and psychologic knowledge and opportunities to be put in touch with other families. The address is: Turner's Syndrome Society of the United States, 768–214 Twelve Oaks Center, 15500 Wayzata Blvd, Wayzata, Minnesota 55391.

Klinefelter's Syndrome: 47XXY and Variants

In 1942 Harry Klinefelter and associates described nine men with infertility, small testes, gynecomastia (breast development), and various endocrinologic, urinary findings. In 1959 Jacobs and Strong (cited in Hughes & Griffith, 1984) reported an extra chromosome in Klinefelter's syndrome males. Klinefelter's syndrome (KS) is now understood to be a spectrum of phenotypic anomalies resulting from a sex chromosome constitution of two or more X chromosomes and at least one Y chromosome (Mandoki, Summer, Hoffman, & Riconda, 1991).

Mosaicism and polysomic X variants of KS are present in 10–20 percent of patients (Schwartz & Root, 1991). A common mosaic pattern is 46,XY/47XXY. Other well-studied variants include 48XXYY, 48XXXY, and 49XXXXY. Stigmata and cognitive function findings can differ in KS variants.

The frequency of KS is approximately 1 in 500 to 1 in 1000 live male births, two-thirds of which are 47XXY (Hamertor, Canning, Ray, & Smith, 1975). KS results from meiotic nondisjunction. It has been suggested that there is an increased risk for 47XXY live birth with advanced maternal age (Carothers & Filippi, 1988).

The common clinical findings of KS can include small penis, cryptorchidism, somatic/skeletal anomalies, tall stature, eunuchoid habitus, small testes, gynecomastia, infertility, delayed puberty, increased gonadotropins, skin problems, learning disabilities, behavior disorders, and in some polysomic variants mental retardation. Short stature is found in the 49XXXXY variant.

The behavioral effects of KS have also been well examined since the discovery of the syndrome. The effects include cognitive, psychosexual, psychosocial, and psychiatric pathology. The diagnosis of KS is not a predictor of IQ. Early studies implied a risk of mental retardation in addition to a risk of psychopathology (Fossman & Hambert, 1963; Maclean, Court Brown, Jacobs, Mantle, & Strong, 1968; Maclean & Mitchel, 1962; Nielsen, 1970). But these early studies were based on clinical or institutionalized populations. These findings are questionable because of the high degrees of selection bias inherent in these settings. More recent studies involving KS patients identified through consecutive screening of newborns and other less-biased populations have yielded less disturbing results. Studies reveal intellectual function within the average range (Nielsen, Sorensen, & Sorensen, 1982; Walzer et al., 1986). Lower IQ scores have been found on verbal scales with preservation of performance scale scores (Graham, Bashir, Stark, Silbert, & Walzer, 1988; Nielsen, Sillesen, Sorensen, & Sorensen, 1979; Pennington, Bender, Puck, Salbenblatt, & Robinson, 1982; Ratcliffe, Murray, & Teaque, 1986; Stewart et al., 1982).

Speech and language delay is common in KS. Expressive language is more impaired that receptive language (Walzer, Bashir, & Silbert, 1990). Difficulties can be detected as young as 2 years of age (Walzer, Graham, Bashir, & Silbert, 1982) and can continue into adulthood (Thielgarrd, 1984).

Poor school performance is also common in the KS individual. In spite of average intellectual function, reading and spelling skills can be poor. These reading and spelling difficulties may be related to their expressive language deficiencies. Ratcliffe and colleagues (1982) and Graham and associates (1988) found general educational problems in a majority of XXY boys in comparison to matched controls.

XXY males have been described as quiet, introverted, timid or passive, and having an inadequate personality (Becker, 1972; Money, 1968; Nielsen et al., 1979; Stewart et al., 1982). Low testosterone has been suggested as a partial explanation for these personality features. Various studies have found that XXY adolescents rate themselves and are rated by observers as apprehensive and insecure in groups (Bancroft, Axworthy, & Ratcliffe, 1982; Thielgarrd, 1984). Using measures such as the High School Personality Questionnaire and spontaneous reports from parents, Bancroft, Axworthy, & Ratcliffe have concluded that XXY adolescents are more passive, more dependent, more nervous, and less assertive than controls. Peer group relationships appear to deteriorate in the teen years. This deterioration may have its origins in changes in physical appearance during that maturational stage and shyness coupled with expressive language difficulties. An exaggerated tall thin gangly appearance, gynecomastia, small penis, and small testes could lead to insecurity and low self-esteem (Bancroft, Axworthy, & Ratcliffe, 1982).

Fire-setting behavior has been reported in four KS individuals, two of whom had a 47,XXY karyotype. This same report (Miller & Sulkes, 1988) indicated that in three of the four cases there was no evidence of fire-setting behavior following testosterone therapy. General behavior of these KS individuals also improved as a result of testosterone therapy.

In terms of psychosexual development, XXY males, compared to matched controls, report lower masculinity scores as measured by the Thematic Apperception Test (Thielgarrd, 1984). However, masculine interests and activities were rated no differently than the matched control group for boys or adolescents. No difference was found in feminine interests and activities (e.g., play-acting, fantasy games) between XXY boys and controls. XXY adolescents demonstrated lower scores on masculine scales of the Bem Sex Role Inventory. However their scores were also lower on neutral and feminine scales when compared with controls. XXY males reported decreased interest in females, less dating, and more limited sexual experiences than controls (Ratcliffe et al., 1982).

Approximately 59 percent of XXY males in a 20-year-long follow-up study were married or involved in a long-standing heterosexual relationship (Nielsen & Pelsen, 1987). All nonmosaic 47XXY males are infertile secondary to azoospermia (lack of sperm production). Some mosaics are fertile.

KS is often not identified in the preadolescent or even the adolescent male. Before puberty, small penile length, small testes (below 2 ml volume), decreased upper/lower body ratio, hypospadias, and cryptorchidism are the physical characteristics that would warrant a karyotype.

Testosterone treatment is recommended because of its beneficial effect on concentration, school performance, fatigue, and osteoporosis (Nielsen & Pelsen, 1987; Nielsen, Pelsen, & Sorensen, 1988). Neilson and colleagues' studies were with adult men treated an average of 3.6 years and with a mean age of 25.5 years at time of follow-up. No change in cognitive function was noted or expected. Schwartz and Root (1991) have suggested beginning testosterone therapy at age 11–12 years with the goal of gradually inducing virilization. There is no assurance that testosterone therapy will prevent or treat gynecomastia. However, hormone therapy may normalize puberty to some extent and have an ameliorating effect on behavioral problems as well as improving self-esteem.

Testosterone therapy has been reported to be beneficial in cases of mentally retarded individuals with KS (Johnson, Myhre, Ruvalcaba, Thuline, & Kelly, 1970). Five individuals with varying degrees of retardation were given testosterone. It not only improved their physical appearance but also their behavior, which became more goal-directed. Their assertiveness increased as well as their sex drive.

KS individuals are at risk for behavioral difficulties, school problems (especially related language expression and comprehension), low sex drive, impotence in later life if not treated hormonally, and feelings of inadequacy (especially about the lack of secondary sexual characteristics). Consequently, the role of the psychologist is to make the family aware of the risks and to evaluate the child for these difficulties. Educational and IQ testing should be done once the diagnosis is made. If deficits are found, remediation should be attempted. Ways to help the child cope with these difficulties need to be addressed with school personnel. Psychologic assessment should include evaluation of the KS child's personality and friendships. If the child appears to be shy and passive, then this behavior needs to be addressed. The psychologic evaluation should also include the individual's psychosexual status. Questions of whether or not the child has any doubts about his gender identity\role need to be explored in light of the above information. Also, sexual arousal and penile erection capability needs to be assessed because testosterone therapy may help these functions.

Testosterone treatment has been shown to promote better overall psychologic and sexual functioning. A psychologic evaluation can help the physician determine when to start treatment. A psychologist can also help monitor behavior once an individual is on hormone treatment. Such monitoring can be helpful because some physicians are hesitant to either start hormone therapy or continue it if there is a history of acting-out behavior. However, it can be the case that continued therapy, so monitored, can help individuals transit through difficult periods to more psychologically beneficial ones.

Finally, the KS individual and family can benefit by being fully educated about the condition. Once diagnosed, the person will need to be informed about all of the above information in a manner which the person and family can absorb. The parents need to know about the 7 percent risk of recurrence of KS in subsequent children versus the 3–4 percent baseline risk of any birth defect (Graham et al., 1988). While there is presently no national organization for KS individuals and their families, there is a newsletter, *The Even Exchange*. It is published in California and can be obtained for a nominal fee ($10.00) by writing: KS and Associates, P.O. Box 119, Roseville, California 95678–0119.

47XYY

The XYY syndrome is often subtle with subclinical features. Some would argue that its symptoms are too vague to constitute a syndrome. These individuals are phenotypically male. The small number of children randomly screened and discovered at birth yield few to no physical, intellectual, or behavioral characteristics when studied prospectively. There is a pattern of variable abnormalities that can be found in 47XYY patients. The frequency of XYY live births is approximately 1:975 (Hook, 1973).

XYY infants may be long at birth but growth is accelerated through middle childhood. The XYY male may have large teeth, a prominent forehead, facial asymmetry, and long ears. Skeletal findings may include increased length versus breadth and mild pectus excavatum. Occasional cryptorchidism, small penis, small testes, and EKG abnormalities are found as well. These males are prone to severe cystic acne during adolescence, can demonstrate poor coordination, and may have poorly developed pectoral and girdle musculature. There are no well-established endocrinologic findings (Jones, 1988).

As in other cases of sex chromosome abnormalities, original investigations for XYY syndrome took place with clinical or institutionalized populations and revealed increased risks for criminality and mental retardation due to selection bias. Later prospective studies of the cognitive development of these boys revealed significantly lower mean full scale IQ scores versus those for controls. However, mean scores are in the average range (Nielsen, Sorensen, & Sorensen, 1982; Nielsen et al., 1986; Walzer, Bashir, & Silbert, 1990). XYY boys were noted to have more diversity of communication deficits. Deficits were found in receptive and expressive language, as well as in fluency (Walzer, Bashir, & Silbert, 1990).

Though the rate at which XYY males are found in mental hospital or prison settings is approximately 24 times their rate of birth, studies show this may not be related to aggression (Zeuthen, Hansen, Christensen, & Nielson, 1975). Utilizing a multidisciplinary approach, Thielgarrd (1983) concluded that XYY males did not differ impressively in terms of violence and criminality from XXY controls or XY controls matched for IQ.

When compared to prisoners of 46XY karyotype in the same institution, XYY individuals were found to have younger mean age of first arrest (13 years opposed to 18 years). The XYY individuals had fewer convictions for violent crime, 9 percent, versus 22 percent for XY controls (Price & Whatmore, 1967). In 1976, Witkin and colleagues also found no statistical increase in personal violence. It is suggested that these individuals are impulsive and get in trouble with the law because of difficulties in gratification delay rather than violent crime. Their crimes are more against property than against people (Money, 1993).

Boys with a XYY chromosome constitution demonstrate higher levels of motor activity and distractibility when compared to XY and XXY controls (Walzer, Bashir, & Silbert, 1990). Multiple studies reveal these boys have more school difficulties, with poor performance based on impulsive behavior problems (Nielsen, Christensen, Fredrich, Zeuthen, & Ostergaard, 1973; Money, Gaskin, & Hull, 1970; Zeuthen et al., 1975). As a group, the XYY males may be at risk for behavioral disabilities, though not every XYY individual manifests behavioral difficulties (Money, Gaskin, & Hull, 1970; Walzer, Gerald, & Shah, 1978).

In terms of psychosexual behavior, impulsivity is again noted, with case reports of bisexuality, child incest, pedophilia, exhibitionism, transvestism, and voyeurism (Baker, Jelfer, Richardson, & Clark, 1970; Daly, 1969; Money, Gaskin, & Hull, 1970; Money, 1975a). However, these cases are limited to a select population of XYY males.

Marriage and fertility rates are unknown. There is no physiologic reason to suspect decreased fertility.

Hermaphroditism/Intersexuality/Ambiguous Genitalia

Professionals use the above three terms interchangeably to refer to the birth of an infant in which the external genitalia appear unfinished to such a degree that the sex of announcement and rearing becomes an issue. Such a situation is unusual because most infants are announced as "Its a boy!" or "Its a girl!" based upon the external sex organs' complete formation without defect. It is also a medical emergency when such a baby is born because it is important to assign sex as soon as possible.

Hermaphroditism is classically defined by the nature of the gonads. Based upon this classification scheme, there are three types of hermaphroditism: true, male, and female. The latter two are sometimes referred to as "pseudohermaphroditism." True hermaphroditism is the presence in one individual of both ovarian and testicular tissue. Such tissue can occur separately, that is, an ovary can form on one side and a testis on the other. The tissues can also appear together, forming an ovotestis. The genetic sex is most often 46,XX. Female hermaphroditism is the presence of ovaries in an individual with ambiguity of the internal and/or external reproductive structures. The genetic sex is most usually 46,XX. Male hermaphroditism is the presence of testes in an individual, usually 46,XY, with ambiguous sex organs. There is a fourth situation that is not accounted for by this classification system. This is the situation where an individual has undifferentiated gonads such as individuals with TS.

While the problem, traditionally speaking, in hermaphroditism, is that of ambiguity of the external sex organs, this is not always the case. For example, individuals with complete forms of androgen insensitivity (discussed below) do not present with ambiguous-looking external genitalia. A second example is that of an infant born with a perfectly formed penis and testes descended into a completely formed scrotum, but possessing a uterus internally.

There are different subtypes of male and female hermaphroditism based on known etiology. It is not the aim of this section to describe each one in detail in terms of endocrinopathology or psychology. The reader is referred to other sources for details on etiology (Griffin & Wilson, 1980; Imperato-McGinely, Petersen, Gautier, & Sturla, 1979; Josso, 1981; Naftolin & Butz, 1981; Wilson & Foster, 1992) and on psychosocial and psychosexual development (Ehrhardt & Meyer-Bahlburg, 1981; Ehrhardt & Money, 1967; Money & Ehrhardt, 1972; Rubin, Reinisch, & Haskett, 1981) not covered here. There is also a recent clinical case book by Money (1991) providing detailed biographies of individuals with various types of hermaphroditism.

Differentiation of Sexual System

Regardless of type of hermaphroditism, ambiguity of the external sex organs leaves everyone confused as to the sex of the baby. To understand this confusion, it is necessary to have a basic understanding of normal differentiation of the reproductive system.

Differentiation and development occurs in a certain sequence. First in the sequence is genetic sex, which is determined by which chromosome, X or Y, from the male is supplied to the X chromosome from the female. Chromosomal pattern helps direct the next step in the sequence, differentiation of the internal reproductive structures (see Figure 6–1), by directing differentiation of the undifferentiated gonad. The typical pattern is for the gonad to become

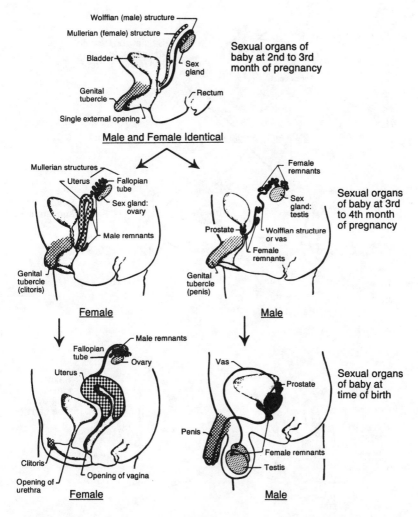

Figure 6–1. Three stages in the differentiation of the internal sexual system, internal and external. Note the early parallelism of the mullerian and wolffian ducts with ultimate vestigation of one and the development of the other.

a testis if the genetic makeup is XY, and for it to become an ovary if the genetic sex is XX. The gonad is, therefore, sexually bipotential. Once the gonad is differentiated, the internal reproductive structures develop. Just as the gonad has the potential to develop into either an ovary or a testis or in some cases an ovotestis, the human fetus has the potential to develop either female or male internal sex organs. However, in contrast to the ovaries or testes, which differentiate and develop from one structure (gonad), there are two structures, the mullerian and the wolffian, from which the female and male internal structures develop, respectively (Figure 6–1).

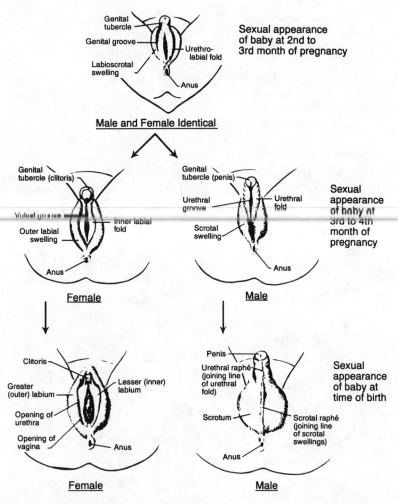

Figure 6–2. Three stages in the differentiation of the external genital organs. The male and female organs have the same beginnings and are homologous with one another.

If the gonad becomes a testis, it secretes two hormones. One hormone, testosterone, signals the wolffian, or male, structures to develop into seminal vesicles, vas deferens, and epididymis. The other hormone, antimullerian substance, tells the female or mullerian ducts to regress and become vestigial structures. If the gonad becomes an ovary, it secretes no hormones in utero to our knowledge. The absence of any hormones permits the development of female internal structures and the regression of male ones.

Following creation of the internal structures is the differentiation and development of the external sex organs, the third and final step in the sequence of the reproductive system in utero. In contrast to the internal sex organ differentiation and, like gonadal differentiation, the external genitalia come from one structure (see Figure 6–2). This structure is masculinized by testosterone from the testes. The genital tubercle differentiates into a penis; the skin that would become the head of the clitoris and labia minora in the female wraps around the penis to cover it and also forms the foreskin. The labioscrotal swellings fuse to form the scrotum. If no testosterone is present, as is the case when ovaries are present, then the genital tubercle becomes a clitoris; the skin that would wrap around the penis becomes the clitoral hood and labia minora.

Given how the sexual reproductive system differentiates and develops, it becomes clear why an infant born with a defect to the external genitalia is cause for concern and confusion about sex. The study of individuals born with such defects have added to our understanding of the theory of gender identity\role (Money & Ehrhardt, 1972). This theory is sequential and multifactorial, involving the interaction of both prenatal and postnatal variables (see Figure 6–3). Two of the better known and researched types of hermaphroditism, one male, the other female, are now briefly discussed.

Androgen Insensitivity

Androgen insensitivity (AI), previously referred to as testicular feminization syndrome, is one type of male hermaphroditism. The frequency of occurrence is unknown, but it can occur in complete and incomplete forms. In the complete form, the individual's entire body is unable to utilize testosterone. As a consequence, XY individuals with undescended testes are born with female-appearing external genitalia and are announced as girls. They are reared as girls and parents and others respond to them as such. At puberty, they fail to develop pubic hair and other body hair that is androgen-dependent, and they also fail to menstruate because no female internal reproductive structures are present due to the presence, in utero, of antimullerian substance. It is usually at the time of puberty that the diagnosis of AI is made. Occasionally, the diagnosis is made in childhood because the undescended testes attempt to descend, resulting in what appears to be bilateral hernias. On even rarer occasions, the diagnosis is made shortly

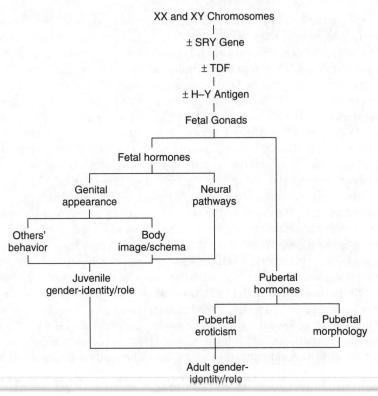

Figure 6–3. Diagram to illustrate the sequential and interactional components of gender identity/role (expanded version).

after birth because the parents and physician are expecting a "boy" as a result of an amniocentesis test indicating XY chromosomes. Once the diagnosis is made, closer inspection of the vagina reveals a blind vaginal pouch. If the diagnosis is not made until puberty, these girls have a feminizing puberty, with the exception of menses, because the hormones from the testes aid in the development of a female body shape and breasts; thus the origin of the term "testicular feminization."

Girls with the androgen insensitivity syndrome develop a female gender identity/role. They have the conviction of themselves as females and clinical investigations have documented that they prefer playing with stereotypic female toys such as dolls to stereotypic male toys such as guns. They also want to be married and raise a family. Their sexual thoughts and fantasies are heterosexual in nature (Lewis & Money, 1983; Masica, Ehrhardt, & Money, 1971; Money & Ehrhardt, 1972; Money, Ehrhardt & Masica, 1968).

Medical Management. Sex of announcement and rearing should always be female because the fundamental rule of sex assignment is never to assign a male sex of rearing to an infant where there is no possibility that the phallic structure will grow to a size adequate to function as a sexual organ in intercourse. Due to the nature of AI, the phallic structure will not grow to be an adequate-sized penis.

If the diagnosis is made before puberty, the testes are removed because of the increasing risk of cancer with age, especially after the second decade of life (Saenger, 1984). For this same reason, the gonads are removed even when the diagnosis is made at puberty. However, in the former case, hormones will need to be initiated at the time of puberty to promote breast development and female body shape. In the latter case, such puberty has already occurred. In both cases, once hormone therapy has begun it needs to be continued to ensure moistness of the vaginal walls and skin, and to prevent osteoporosis. Vaginal surgery or a dilation technique will be needed to create a vagina of adequate depth for intercourse. When this is done depends upon the age of the individual, her emotional maturity to undergo the procedure and to assist in her own care, and her motivation for the procedure.

Psychologic Management. The first task of psychologic management is to explain to the parents the nature of the condition and how it came about (Money, 1975b). Helpful here are the use of Figures 6–1 and 6–2 which outline the development and differentiation of the internal and external sexual reproductive system. With such an explanation, it is relatively easy to take this situation (i.e., birth defect of the sex organs) out of the realm of freakishness because it becomes clear that with the body's insensitivity to testosterone the natural course of development produces female external genitalia. A second task is to explain that an individual's gender identity, that is, one's subjective conviction of one's gender, is not determined by sex chromosomes or gonads but is the product of many factors, prenatal and postnatal, that interact in a sequential manner. The diagram (see Figure 6–3) showing an expanded version of the theory of gender identity/role development (Money & Ehrhardt, 1972) along with an explanation, helps calm parents' fears that their child is "really a boy" because of the chromosomes and gonads.

Siblings, grandparents, and other adults will need to be given some information. How much and when depends on the need to know. The individual herself will need to know why she must take hormones, needs vaginal construction, and cannot become pregnant. Individuals with AI or other forms of male hermaphroditism can learn about their condition, including their chromosomal status, in a nontraumatic manner over time. For example, one young woman with the diagnosis of male hermaphroditism of unknown etiology, when hearing her XY status, reacted without severe shock or trauma. She commented that she had difficulty relating to this information. She was asked to explain:

"I've been raised as a female, and my perception of myself is female. So relating to it is difficult. I mean, if I was a male, I could relate to it. But as far as I'm concerned, I'm female. Even though my genes say otherwise. So, meaning I couldn't relate to it since it was alien because I consider myself female and not male." (Quattrin, Aronica, & Mazur, 1990, p. 706)

This young lady learned about her diagnosis and what it meant for her both medically and behaviorally in graduated steps. This learning process started when she was a young child and she would come to the endocrine clinic for her yearly evaluation. Tied to this visit was a psychoendocrine visit where the psychologist would review with her and her parents what transpired with the endocrinologist. The psychologist would use this visit as a platform from which to add new knowledge and review this knowledge with her and her parents. She was also involved in the timing of estrogen therapy to give her breasts. When the time came to inform her of her chromosomal status, the process was straightforward because of her knowledge base, her relationship with the professionals providing her care, and her own background in science, which gave her an additional framework within which to understand this information.

For those individuals without such a background and who need a frame of reference within which to begin to understand that their chromosomes are discordant with their gender identity, one approach is to talk, first, about various known chromosomal patterns in human beings (Mazur, 1983). Talk about 46,XX (males and females); 46,XY (males and females); and other variants such as 45,X(TS), 47,XXY(KS), and 47XYY. Such information provides a person with a broader framework within which to understand that gender identity is determined by multiple factors.

Adrenogenital Syndrome

The androgen insensitivity syndrome is an example of male hermaphroditism. The adrenogenital syndrome (AS), also referred to as congenital virilizing adrenal hyperplasia (CVAH) or simply congenital adrenal hyperplasia (CAH), is an example of female hermaphroditism when diagnosed in 46,XX individuals. This disorder is autosomal recessive. The most common enzymatic deficiency observed in CAH is 21 hydroxylase. Estimated incidence of CAH due to this deficiency is 1:5,000 in Switzerland and 1:11,000 to 1:40,000 in the United States (New & Levine, 1981). The defect occurs in the adrenal cortex and results in the production of androstenedione instead of cortisol, and, in some cases, loss of the salt-retaining hormone aldosterone. The presence of adrostendione masculinizes, in varying degree, the external sex organs of the genetic female fetus. In some cases only clitoral hypertrophy will occur (Saenger, 1984); in other cases, there is clitoromegaly, with partial fusion of the genital swellings giving the appearance of a bifid labioscrotum and only one external opening. In the most severe degree of masculinization the result is a fully formed penis and an empty scrotum. There are on record 46,XX individuals with severe virilization of the external genitalia who were announced and reared as males. The gender identity role of these individuals is male (Money & Daléry, 1976) and their romantic and sexual fantasies are heterosexual, that is to say, directed toward females. Medically, these men required virilizing hormone regulation, testicular prosthetic implants, and surgical removal of female internal reproductive structures (present because no antimullarian hormone was secreted because the gonads were ovaries). If they also had salt loss, they were given appropriate hormone-replacement therapy. The existence of 46,XX men, like that of 46,XY females, provide evidence that gender identity\role is not solely determined by chromosomes or gonads.

The outcome of individuals with varying degrees of masculinization reared as females is different. Before the discovery of cortisone therapy, 46,XX females with CVAH were chronically virilized, yet they developed a female gender identity consistent with their sex of rearing (Ehrhardt, Evers, & Money, 1968). In terms of gender-role behavior, they identified themselves as tomboys throughout childhood. Ehrhardt, Evers, and Money (1968) also found that in the 23 cases they studied, 30 percent had homoerotic imagery, and 18 percent had additional homoerotic experience. Two married prior to feminization with cortisone therapy, and 11 after such treatment. Five women had at least one pregnancy, but the majority rated career as preferential over full-time mother and homemaker.

Since this study, there have been a number of studies (Dittmann, Kappes, & Kappes, 1992; Money, Schwartz, & Lewis, 1984) involving CVAH girls who received both hormone treatment and surgery (feminization of genitals) in infancy or prior to their first birthday. Results of these studies indicate a female gender identity, a tomboy label in childhood with increased energy expenditure and rough-and-tumble play, decreased interest in dolls and infant-care rehearsal play and increased interest in stereotypic male play toys (i.e., cars, trucks). It was also found, as in the Ehrhardt, Evers, and Money (1968) study, that these girls preferred career to marriage and family and that they had a delayed onset of dating experience when compared to others their age without CVAH.

Studies (Dittmann, Kappes, & Kappes, 1992; Money, Schwartz, & Lewis, 1984) of erotosexual function in CVAH females have suggested greater than chance occurrences of homosexuality and bisexuality. Dittmann and colleagues interviewed 34 CAH females plus 14 control sisters regarding their psychosexual development and sexual orientation. They found that fewer of the CAH women had experienced heterosexual love relationships when compared to their sisters. They also discovered that 20 percent of the CAH individuals and none of the sisters wished for or had had homosexual relationships. Based on these results, which corroborate earlier reports (Ehrhardt, Evers, & Money, 1968; Money, Schwartz, & Lewis, 1984), CAH females are both delayed in reaching psychosexual milestones (e.g., onset of dating, first crush) and have an increased chance of bisexual\homosexual fantasies and experience.

Money, Lewis, and Schwartz (1984) studied 30 adult AS women who had been treated early in life. Thirty-seven percent (11) rated themselves as bisexual or homosexual. Only 7 percent of the control or comparison groups so labeled themselves. The comparison groups consisted of 15 women with androgen insensitivity syndrome and 12 women with Rokitansky syndrome (discussed below). These authors also compared their results to Kinsey's 1953 sample which found that 15 percent of women experienced homoerotic arousal by imagery by age 20 and 10 percent had actual homosexual experience. Seventeen percent of the CVAH sample reported homosexual contact. The explanation given for these findings is the masculinizing effects of prenatal and/or postnatal testosterone on the developing brain in interaction with other developmental variables (Money, 1993).

Marriage rates are usually not reported. One study (Mulaikal, Migeon, & Rock, 1987) reported pregnancy in CVAH females. Pregnancy is extremely rare in women with the salt-losing variant of CVAH, but less so in the non-salt-losing type. In this study both groups were maintained on cortisol therapy.

Psychologic Management. In cases of AS where there is not a question of sex assignment, psychologic management focuses primarily on issues of medical management, capacity for normal sexual functioning, and fertility (Baker, 1981). These families can also benefit from an understanding of how their daughter's genitals developed the way that they did. Figures 6–1 and 6–2, as well as Figure 6–3, can be helpful in this regard.

However, for families where there was initially a question of sex of announcement, or where sex was first announced as male then changed to female (not uncommon in cases of AS), it is imperative that the parents understand sexual differentiation and gender identity\role development. These families in particular need to be prepared for all aspects of psychosexual behavior including various forms of sexual orientation and the possibility of atypical gender-role behavior in their daughters. They need to be reassured that it is not unexpected and that it does not mean, as one mother said, "She's turning into a boy and the doctors were wrong." Once again, the general rule of gradual education of the family, child, and sibs applies in cases of CAH as it does in other cases of hermaphroditism.

Hypospadias

Hypospadias refers to the placement of the urethral meatus on the underside of the penis. It can occur anywhere from the glans (first degree) to the juncture of the penile shaft and scrotum (penile–scrotal hypospadias). It is a very common congenital defect occurring in 1 in 250 live male births (Leung, Baird, & MacGillivray, 1985). Inadequate fetal testosterone is thought to be the etiology of this and other forms of incomplete or urethral development (see Hughes & Griffith, 1984). Surgical intervention is required, and in the less severe degrees of hypospadias can be performed as early as 1 year of age. Surgery must be delayed in the more severe conditions and may require more than one surgery.

Berg and colleagues (Berg, Svensson, & Aström, 1981; Berg, Berg, & Svensson, 1982) reported on the social and sexual adjustment and mental health status of 34 adults operated on in childhood for hypospadias. These men were compared to 36 who had no history of hypospadias. Most of the hypospadiac males had a satisfactory sexual life but were less active than controls. There was no difference in the age of first ejaculation but the age of first intercourse was later than that of the controls. Even patients with a less-than-perfect surgical result were reported to have a satisfactory sexual life. Social adjustment was similar in the two groups, but the authors note that the hypospadiac men might show some psychological differences based on job selection. Hypospadiac males tended to be in less competitive jobs.

While it appeared that both groups adjusted well in childhood and adulthood, the retrospective reports of the hypospadiac men indicated more problems. They reported being shy, timid, and isolated as youngsters. Enuresis was also reported as a problem. Berg and his colleagues assessed the hypospadiac males to be at risk in social relationships and recommended psychologic guidance and counseling for boys with hypospadias and their parents. This recommendation was again made in a later paper (Berg & Berg, 1983), when these authors, using a series of projective techniques and an attitude survey, concluded that more of the hypospadiac men were insecure in their gender identity and tended to take more feminine than masculine roles.

Sandberg, Meyer-Bahlburg, Aranoff, Sconzo, and Hensle (1989) conducted a postal survey in an attempt to gain further knowledge about the psychosocial and psychosexual development of boys with hypospadias. Sixty-nine parents of boys, ages 6 to 10, with varying degrees of hypospadias repair, completed the CBCL, Child Behavior and Attitude Questionnaire, and Impact-on-Family Scale.

Results of this study suggest that hypospadias, corrected in childhood, is not associated with significant psychopathology, even for those with more severe defects. Based upon the CBCL reports, there are mild increases in problem behaviors, a finding consistent with Berg's work suggesting more behavior problems and poor social adjustment for hypospadias than a matched control group. However, the total problems reported were markedly below those of a group referred for mental health problems. While boys with hypospadias did evidence an increase in the frequency of gender-atypical behavior when compared to nonclinical subjects, the majority did not seem to exhibit a clinically significant degree of gender disturbance. Furthermore, hypospadias did not seem to have a negative impact on the family. The authors' overall conclusion was that the adjustment of boys with hypospadias was good. They recommended referral for mental health services only for selected individuals in whom biological and psychosocial factors interact in such a way as to place the hypospadiac child at risk for adjustment problems. Sandberg and colleagues also caution about extrapolating beyond the age of their subject, and suggest that perhaps older subjects (e.g., teenagers) undergo changes and challenges that may predispose them to psychological problems that may warrant clinical attention.

In conclusion, it appears that the only psychologic intervention for a boy with hypospadias and his family is psychoeducation. Explain to them the nature of the defect and what will be done to correct it.

Cryptorchidism

Cryptorchidism refers to a condition in which the testis or testes remain intraabdominal in their position. Approximately 5 percent of live male births will exhibit this condition, but the testes of most of them will descend in the first year of life. If the testicle cannot be manipulated manually into the scrotum after the first year, the condition is diagnosed. Surgical correction is recommended to avoid the problems of neoplastic conversion and infertility (see Hughes & Griffith, 1984).

A study by Raboch, Mellan, and Starka (1977) of adult cryptorchids and sexual development was conducted with both unilateral and bilateral cryptorchids. It was found that serum testosterone levels for these groups and controls were about the same until age 13 years. After age 13 the serum levels of individuals with both testicles descended averaged significantly higher. Based on responses to the Heterosexual Development of the Male questionnaire, adult cryptorchids were found to be retarded in heterosexual development compared to fertile and potent males. Bilateral cryptorchids more so than the unilateral. Responses to the Sexual Activity of the Male questionnaire revealed the sexual activity of unilateral cryptorchids was lower than that of the controls; the bilateral cryptorchid group scored the lowest of the three groups.

Marriage rates in the general cryptorchid population are unknown. However, fertility prospects for children post orchiopexy (correction) is proposed as good (Gilhooly, Meyers, & Lattimer, 1984).

Micropenis

A micropenis is a penis that is perfectly formed, usually with the urethral meatus at the tip, but is greater than 2 SDs below the mean length for age and pubertal status. Length of the flaccid penis is not measured but rather the length of the fully stretched penis, because this is purported to be close to the erectile length. The technique for measuring the penis plus criteria for determining the presence of a micropenis have been published (Lee et al., 1980).

Micropenis is a clinical sign and not a syndrome. It can occur in many conditions and syndromes (e.g. Klinefelter's and Riefenstein's) or it may occur alone (Danish, Lee, Mazur, Arnheim, & Migeon, 1980; Lee, Danish, Mazur, & Migeon, 1980; Lee et al., 1980).

In the newborn, the corpora of the penis may be pencil-thin and erectile capability may or may not be present. The penis may be retracted or pendulous, depending upon the length of the penis. A micropenis in a newborn is a measured length, stretched, of 1.9cm or less. Both testes may or may not be in a perfectly formed scrotum and the chromosomes are usually 46,XY, although, as already mentioned, some 47,XXY individuals can have a micropenis.

The problem clinically for professionals when a baby is observed to have a micropenis is whether or not the child will be able to stand to urinate and whether the penis will be long enough to be used successfully in sexual intercourse. Some professionals believe that a child with a micropenis is best served if reassigned at birth as a female and reared as such with eventual hormonal and surgical intervention to induce a feminizing puberty and to create a vagina, respectively. There are others who support the position that the child should be reared as a male, with the treatment of choice testosterone therapy as needed to help keep the penis in the normal range. Burnstein, Grumbach, and Kaplan (1979) recommend using low-dose testosterone as a test to determine whether or not the micropenis will grow significantly before deciding sex of assignment. Others (Lee et al., 1980) agree that no response to testosterone is predictive of an inadequate response at puberty but question whether a positive response predicts adequate response at puberty and a penile length in the normal range in adulthood. Money, Lehne, and Pierre-Jerome (1984) present data on eight cases of micropenis boys reared male where prior treatment with testosterone provided no size advantage over those without treatment. These authors suggest that counseling and guidance focusing on sex education and on creating an open and nonjudgmental atmosphere about sexuality and function is beneficial to individuals, children, teens, and adults coping with a micropenis.

van Seters and Slob (1988) reported on three individuals with micropenis. Two of the three were 46,XX individuals reared as males. Their diagnosis was CAH. As adults, their penis length was 3cm at age 36 and 7cm at age 21, respectively. The third individual was 46,XY whose penis was 3.5cm at age 45. Cases 1 and 3 reported that intromission was not possible. However, all three were married and rated their sexual lives as good. These authors concluded that these three individuals, despite little or no medical and psychologic support, were fortunate in being able to obtain a mutually satisfying heterosexual life despite micropenis. They also recommended against any type of surgery to the penis in an attempt to make it longer. This study, like the one by Money and Daléry (1977), involved CAH individuals. Reilly and Woodhouse (1989) interviewed 20 out of a possible 50 individuals with a micropenis. The diagnoses varied and included idiopathic micropenis, male hermaphroditism, hypogonadotropic hypogonadism, and mixed gonad dysgenesis. All but one had been given human chorionic gonadotropin, testosterone, or cortisone during childhood. They were divided into pre- and postpubertal groups. Only one individual (prepubertal group) had a stretched penis above the 10 percent percentile, and the authors were not sure that for the postpubertal group hormone treatment made any difference in final adult penile length. All individuals developed a male gender identity, but for some there were concerns about their genitals and shyness in their behavior. Six of the 12 postpubertal individuals recalled teasing by peers and fear of voiding in public. Nine of 12 reported heterosexual intercourse. All claimed satisfactory intercourse for themselves and their partners (not interviewed); two reported difficulty maintaining penetration and needed to utilize nonpenetrating techniques in their love making.

Reilly and Woodhouse (1989) found that the strongest influence for all their subjects was parental attitude. Supportive parents who explained the problem and did not hide it produced confident individuals. Parents who emphasized the abnormalities, or who refused to discuss them with the child and at times told the child to hide the problem, produced anxious and shy children. Based upon their results, it was concluded that individuals with a micropenis develop and differentiate a male gender role. This finding is consistent with other studies. Reilly and Woodhouse also conclude that a micropenis alone "should not dictate a female gender reassignment in infancy." What is needed is a prospective study to help answer this question.

Until further study is conducted, some children with a micropenis will be reared male and some will be reared female. Psychologic support needs to include open and straightforward discussion about the problems, first with the parents and then with the child. It is also imperative that sex education be given so that these children have the optimum chance of developing a healthy and satisfying sexual life as adults. There is one case report (Money & Mazur, 1977) of a boy with a micropenis wearing a prosthetic penis especially made for him so he could stand to urinate. He did wear it for a while and reported satisfaction with it. It was hypothesized that wearing such a device, even part-time, early in life would allow for the possibility that it could become incorporated into his body image (much like eyeglasses), thus reducing the resistance to using such a device in his love making as an adult. Unfortunately, no information is available on this child as an adult since he was lost to follow-up.

Total Agenesis of the Penis

Not far removed from micropenis is the rare condition of total agenesis of the penis in 46,XY newborns. The infant has a fully formed scrotum and usually both testes are descended, but there is no penile corpora and the urethral opening can be found on the rim of the anus. This condition requires that the infant be announced and reared as a female. Medical management includes induction of a feminizing puberty via hormones at the age-appropriate time, surgical construction of a vagina, and, if possible, repositioning of the urinary opening.

Psychologic management includes education of the parents so that they understand the nature of the condition and why sex of rearing as a female is the only viable choice. There is at present no surgical procedure to create a functional natural-appearing penis. The child herself needs to be gradually informed of the condition and the consequences (infertility, hormonal therapy, and surgery). The same method of counseling, education, and support given to children with various forms of hermaphroditism can be followed.

There are no long-term reports on the psychosexual and psychosocial development of children with total agenesis, but clinical observation indicate development of a female gender identity.

Congenital Absence of the Vagina

Congenital absence of the vagina was first described by Mayer in 1829, then by Küster in 1910, and by Rokitansky in 1938. A constellation of associated anomalies was described by Hauser et al. (1961). The Mayer-Rokitansky-Küster syndrome consists of (1) congenital absence of the vagina, (2) uterus that varies from totally absent to immaturely formed to normal, (3) 46XX karyotype, (4) female levels of testosterone, (5) normal ovarian function, (6) normal breast development and body contours, (7) frequent renal and/or skeletal anomalies (Miller, Willson, & Collins, 1945; Bryan, Nigro, Counseller, 1949; Neinstein & Castle, 1983). The incidence is approximately 1 in 4,000–5,000 births. The etiology is a malformation in the development of the muellerian ducts. This disorder is the second leading cause of primary amenorrhea (Ross & VardeWele, 1974).

These girls generally present for the problem of primary amenorrhea and therefore are not diagnosed until puberty. Gynecologic investigation of primary amenorrhea is often delayed until age 16 years. This condition is differentiated from androgen insensitivity (AI) based on karyotype (46XY in AI) and testosterone levels (normal male in AI). Pelvic ultrasound is utilized to visualize the presence or absence of uterus and its condition. Laparoscopy is also helpful in complete visualization of internal anatomic structures.

Treatment can be either surgical or nonsurgical. The nonsurgical technique involves the use of a bicycle stool and a successively increasing series of vaginal dilators (Ingram, 1981). Nonsurgical techniques are best used when there is a vaginal dimple. If there is no dimple, then surgery is recommended (Rock & Jones, 1989).

In a study by David, Carmil, Bar-David, and Serr (1975) 14 patients with this condition were noted to express "shock" and "confusion" upon learning the diagnosis. Though it was reported they questioned their femininity, no direct examination of gender identity, role, or orientation was conducted. They all appeared to consider themselves female consistent with sex of rearing. Their choice of mate was unanimously male. Most reported decreased self-esteem, some anxiety, depression, and anger (Kaplan, 1968). Sexual exploration after creation of a vagina is not uncommon.

Anticipatory guidance is required in the treatment of these individuals. The timing of the interventions (both medical and psychological) is important. The medical and surgical intervention require emotional maturity to ensure compliance. Therapy should not be postponed until after frustrated attempts at intercourse have failed.

Conclusion

Psychosexual theory postulates that adult psychosexual status is the final result of a complex process beginning in utero with embryonic differentiation of many systems, not the least of which is the sexual and reproductive system (Money, 1986). Just as the reproductive system is sexually dimorphic, so too is behavioral and psychic development.

Children born with defects to their anatomic sexual system are at risk for sexual difficulties during all stages of development: childhood, adolescence, and adulthood. They and their families need both good medical and psychological care. Psychologic care must address (1) the nature of the condition, and how it came to be, (2) consequences of the condition, medically and behaviorally, (3) sex education that includes all aspects of psychosexual development and differentiation, including present knowledge about the effects of the medical condition on gender identity, role, and sexual orientation, and (4) ways to cope with these effects. Parents need to be supported and educated to be open, honest, and encouraging with their children, especially in the area of sex. Such openness increases the chances of developing a child confident in himself or herself despite a defect to his or her sexual system. To not provide such psychologic support enhances the chances that even more insult will be done to the psychosexual system, and in the end to the person.

Acknowledgments

Figures 6–1, 6–2, and 6–3 reprinted with the permission of J. Money. Mrs. Lucy Wargo and Mrs. Laurie Cameron provided library assistance. Ms. Tammy Masterman and Mr. Bill Tallmadge helped prepare and type the final draft. The Children's Growth Foundation of Western New York supports the work of the Psychoendocrine Program. Without their continued support to obtain money from the local United Way and Variety Club, Tent #7 psychological services would not be available to the children and their families described in this chapter.

References

Baker, F., Jelfer, M., Richardson, C. E., & Clark, G. R. (1970). Chromosome errors in men with Klinefelters and XYY chromosome pattern. *Journal of the American Medical Association, 214,* 869–878.

Baker, S. W. (1981). Psychologic management of intersex children. In N. Josso (Ed.), *The intersex child* (pp. 261–269). New York: S. Karger.

Bancroft, J., Axworthy, D., & Ratcliffe, S. (1982). The personality and psychosexual development of boys with 47XXY chromosome constitution. *Journal of Child Psychology and Psychiatry, 23,* 169–180.

Becker, K. L. (1972). Clinical and therapeutic experiences with Klinefelters syndrome. *Fertility and Sterility, 23,* 548–578.

Berg, R., & Berg, G. (1983). Penile malformation, gender identity and sexual orientation. *Acta Psychiatrica Scandinavica, 68,* 154–166.

Berg, R., Berg, G., & Svensson, J. (1982). Penile malformation and mental health: A controlled psychiatric study of men operated for hypospadias in childhood. *Acta Psychiatrica Scandinavica, 66,* 398–416.

Berg, R., Svensson, J., & Aström, G. (1981). Social and sexual adjustment of men operated for hypospadias during childhood: A controlled study. *Journal of Urology, 125,* 313–317.

Bryan, A. L., Nigro, J. A., & Counseller, V. S. (1949). One hundred cases of congenital absence of the vagina. *Surgical Gynecological Obstetrics, 88,* 79–86.

Burnstein, S., Grumback, M. M., & Kaplan, S. L. (1979). Early determination of androgen-responsiveness is important in the management of microphallus. *Lancet, 2,* 983–986.

Carothers, A. D., & Filippi, G. (1988). Klinefelters syndrome in Sardinia and Scotland: Comparative studies of parental age and other aetiological factors in 47XXY. *Human Genetics, 81,* 71–75.

Daly, R. F. (1969). Mental illness and patterns of behavior in 10 XYY males. *Journal of Nervous and Mental Disease, 144,* 318–327.

Danish, R. K., Lee, P. A., Mazur, T., Amrhein, J. A., & Migeon, C. J. (1980). Micropenis: 2. Hypogonadotropic hypogonadism. *Johns Hopkins Medical Journal, 146,* 177–184.

David, A., Carmil, D., Bar-David, E., & Serr, D. M. (1975). Congenital absence of the vagina: Clinical and psychologic aspects. *Obstetrics and Gynecology, 46,* 407–409.

Dittmann, R. W., Kappes, M. E., & Kappes, M. H. (1992). Sexual behavior in adolescent and adult females with congenital adrenal hyperplasia. *Psychoneuroendocrinology, 17,* 151–170.

Dougherty, G. G., Jr., Rockwell, W. J. K., Sutton, G., & Ellinwood, E. H., Jr. (1983). Anorexia in treated gonadal dysgenesis: Case report and review. *Journal of Clinical Psychiatry, 44,* 219–221.

Downey, J., Ehrhardt, A. A., Gruen, R., Bell, J. J., & Morishima, A. (1989). Psychopathology and social functioning in women with Turner's syndrome. *Journal of Nervous and Mental Disease, 177,* 191–201.

Downey, J., Ehrhardt, A. A., Morishima, A., Bell, J. J., & Gruen, R. (1987). Gender role development in two clinical syndromes: Turner's Syndrome versus constitutional short stature. *Journal of the American Academy of Child and Adolescent Psychiatry, 26,* 566–573.

Ehrhardt, A. A., Evers, D. K., & Money, J. (1968). Influence of androgen and some aspects of sexually dimorphic behavior in women with late treated adrenogenital syndrome. *Johns Hopkins Medical Journal, 1231,* 115–122.

Ehrhardt, A. A., & Meyer-Bahlburg, H. F. L. (1981). Effects of prenatal sex hormones on gender related behavior. *Science, 211, 1312–1318.*

Ehrhardt, A. A., & Money, J. (1967). Progestin induced hermaphroditism, IQ and psychosexuality in a study of 10 girls. *Journal of Sex Research, 3,* 83–100.

Forssman, H., & Hambert, G. (1963). Incidence of Klinefelters syndrome among mental patients. *Lancet, 1,* 1327.

Forssman, H., Melbin, G., & Walinder, J. (1970). Concurrence of Turner's syndrome and anorexia nervosa. *British Journal of Psychiatry, 116,* 221–223.

Gilhooly, P. E., Meyers, F., & Lattimer, J. K. (1984). Fertility prospects for children with cryptorchidism. *American Journal of Diseases of Children, 138,* 940–943.

Graham, J. M., Bashir, A. S., Stark, R. E., Silbert, A., & Walzer, S. (1988). Oral and written language abilities of XXY boys implications for anticipatory guidance. *Pediatrics, 81,* 795–806.

Griffin, I., & Wilson, J. D. (1980). The syndromes of androgen resistance. *New England Journal of Medicine, 302,* 198.

Hall, J. G., Sybert, V. P., Williamson, R. A., Fisher, N. L., & Reed, S. D. (1982). Turner's syndrome. *Western Journal of Medicine, 137,* 23–44.

Hamertor, I., Canning, L., Ray, N., & Smith, S. (1975). A cytogenetic survey of 14,069 newborn infants: Incidence of chromosome abnormalities. *Clinical Genetics, 8,* 223–243.

Hauser, G. A., Keller, M., Koller, T., et al. (1961). Das Rokitansky-Kuster syndrome: Uterus bipartitus solidus rudimentarius cum Vagina solida. *Gynaecologia, 151,* 111–112.

Hoffenberg, R., & Jackson, W. P. (1957). Gonadal dysgenesis: Modern concepts. *British Medical Journal, 2*, 1457–1462.

Hook, E. B. (1973). Behavioral implications of the human XYY genotype. *Science, 179*, 139–150.

Hughes, J. G., & Griffith, J. F. (1984). *Synopsis of pediatrics* (6th ed.). St. Louis: C. V. Mosby.

Imperato-McGinley, J., Peterson, R. E., Gautier, T., & Sturla, E. (1979). Androgens and the evolution of male gender identity among male pseudohermaphrodites with 5α reductase deficiency. *New England Journal of Medicine, 300*, 1233–1237.

Ingram, J. (1981). The bicycle seat stool in treatment of vaginal agenesis and stenosis: A preliminary report. *American Journal of Obstetrics and Gynecology, 140*, 867–871.

Johnson, H. R., Myhre, S. A., Ruvalcaba, R. H. A., Thuline, H. C., & Kelly, V. C. (1970). Effects of testosterone on body image and behavior in Klinefelter's syndrome: A pilot study. *Developmental Medical Child Neurology, 12*, 454–460.

Jones, K. L. (Ed.). (1988). *Smiths: Recognizable patterns of human malformation.* Philadelphia: W. B. Saunders.

Josso, N. (Ed.). (1981). *The intersex child.* New York: S. Karger.

Kaplan, E. A. (1968). Congenital absence of the vagina: Psychiatric aspects of diagnosis and management. *New York State Journal of Medicine, 68*, 1937–1941.

Klinefelter, H. F., Reitenstein, E. C., & Albright, F. (1942). Syndrome characterized by gynecomastia, aspermatogenesis without aleydigism and increased excretion of follicle stimulating hormone. *Journal of Clinical Endocrine Metabolism, 2*, 615–627.

Kron, L., Katz, J. L., Gorzynski, G., & Weiner, H. (1977). Anorexia nervosa and gonadal dysgenesis: Further evidence of a relationship. *Archives of General Psychiatry, 34*, 332–335.

Küster, H. (1910). Uterus bipartitus solidus rudimentarius cum Vagina. *Z Geburtshilfe Perinatol, 67*, 692–718.

Lee, P. A., Danish, R. K., Mazur, T., & Migeon, C. J. (1980). Micropenis: 3. Primary hypogonadism, partial androgen insensitivity syndrome and idiopathic disorders. *Johns Hopkins Medical Journal, 147*, 175–181.

Lee, P. A., Mazur, T., Danish, R., Amrhein, J., Blizzard, R. M., Money, J., & Migeon, C. J. (1980). Micropenis: 1. Criteria, etiologies and classification. *Johns Hopkins Medical Journal, 146*, 156–163.

Leung, T. J., Baird, P. A., & MacGillivray, B. (1985). Hypospadias in British Columbia. *American Journal of Medical Genetics, 21*, 39–48.

Lewis, V. G., & Money, J. (1983). Gender identity\role: G-I/R Part A: XY (androgen-insensitivity) syndrome and XX (Rokitansky) syndrome of vaginal atresia compared. In L. Dennerstein & G. Burrows (Eds.), *Handbook of psychosomatic obstetric and gynaecology* p. 51–60. Amsterdam: Elsevier Biomedical Press.

Maclean, N., & Mitchell, J. M. (1962). A survey of sex chromosome abnormalities among 4514 mental defectives. *Lancet, 1*, 293–296.

Maclean, N., Court, Brown, W. M., Jacobs, P. A., Mantle, D. J., & Strong, J. A. (1968). A survey of sex chromatin anomalies in mental hospital patients. *Journal of Medical Genetics, 5*, 165–172.

Mandoki, M. W., Summer, G. S., Hoffman, R. P., & Riconda, D. L. (1991). A reviewed Klinefelter's syndrome in children and adolescents. *Journal of the American Academy of Child and Adolescent Psychiatry, 30,* 167–172.

Masica, D. N., Ehrhardt, A. A., & Money, J. (1971). Fetal feminization and female gender identity in the testicular feminizing syndrome of androgen insensitivity. *Archives of Sexual Behavior, 1,* 131–142.

Mayer, C. A. J. (1829). Über Verdoppelungen des Uterus und ihre Arten: Nebst Bemerkungen über Hasenscharte und Wolfsrachen. *Journal Chir Augenheilkd, 13,* 525–564.

Mazur, T. (1983) Ambiguous genitalia: Detection and counseling. *Pediatric Nursing, 9,* 417–431.

McCauley, E., Ito, J., & Kay, T. (1986). Psychosocial functioning in girls with Turner's syndrome and short stature: Social skills, behavior problems and self-concept. *Journal of the American Academy of Child and Adolescent Psychiatry, 25,* 105–112.

McCauley, E., Sybert, V. P., & Ehrhardt, A. A. (1986). Psychosocial adjustment of adult women with Turner's syndrome. *Clinical Genetics, 29,* 284–290.

Miller, N. F., Willson, J. P., & Collins, J. (1945). The surgical correction of congenital absence of the vagina. *American Journal of Obstetrical Gynecology, 50,* 735–747.

Miller, M. E., & Sulkes, S. (1988). Fire-setting behavior in individuals with Klinefelter's syndrome. *Pediatrics, 82,* 115–116.

Money, J. (1968). *Sex Errors of the Body: Dilemmas, Education, Counseling* Baltimore: John Hopkins University Press.

Money J. (1975a). Human behavior cytogenetics: Review of psychopathology of 3 syndromes: 47XXY, 47XYY and 45X. *Journal of Sex Research, 1,* 181–200.

Money, J. (1975b). Psychologic counseling: Hermaphroditism. In L. I. Gardner (ed.), *Endocrine and Genetic Diseases of Childhood and Adolescence, 2nd ed.* Philadelphia, PA: W. B. Saunders Co., 609–618.

Money, J. (1986). *Venuses penuses: Sexology, sexosophy, and exigency theory.* Buffalo, NY: Prometheus Books.

Money, J. (1991). *Biographies of gender and hermaphroditism in paired comparisons* (Clinical supplement to *The handbook of sexology*). New York: Elsevier.

Money, J. (1993). *The Adam principle: Genes, genitals, hormones, and gender: Selected readings in sexology.* Buffalo, NY: Prometheus Books.

Money, J., & Daléry, J. (1976). Iatrogenic homosexuality: Gender identity in seven 46XX chromosomal females with hyperadrenocortical hermaphroditism with a penis. Three reared as boys, four reared as girls. *Journal of Homosexuality, 1,* 357–371.

Money, J., & Ehrhardt, A. A. (1972). *Man and woman, boy and girl: The differentiation and dimorphism of gender identity from conception to maturity.* Baltimore: Johns Hopkins University Press.

Money, J., Ehrhardt, A. A., & Masica, D. N. (1968). Fetal feminization induced by androgen insensitivity in the testicular feminizing syndrome. Effect on marriage and maternalism. *Johns Hopkins Medical Journal, 123,* 105–114.

Money, J., Gaskin, R., & Hull, H. (1970). Impulse, aggression and sexuality in the XYY syndrome. *St. John's Law Review, 44,* 220–235.

Money, J., Lehne, G. H., & Pierre-Jerome, F. (1984) Micropenis: Adult follow-up and comparison of size against new norms. *Journal of Sex and Marital Therapy, 10,* 105–116.

Money, J., & Matthews, D. (1982). Prenatal exposure to virilizing progestins: An adult follow-up study of twelve women. *Archives of Sexual Behavior, 2,* 73–83.

Money, J., & Mazur, T. (1977). Microphallus. The successful use of a prosthetic phallus in a 9-year-old boy, *Journal of Sexual and Marital Therapy, 3,* 187–196.

Money, J., & Mittenthal, S. M. (1970) Lack of personality pathology in Turner's syndrome: Relations to cytogenetics; hormones and physique. *Behavioral Genetics, 1,* 43–56.

Money, J., Schwartz, M., & Lewis, V. (1984) Adult erotosexual status and fetal hormonal masculinization and demasculinization in 46XX congenital virilizing hyperplasia and 46XY androgen insensitivity compared. *Psychoneuroendocrinology, 9,* 405–414.

Mulaikal, R. M., Migeon, C. J., & Rock, J. A. (1987) Fertility rates in female patients with congenital adrenal hyperplasia due to 21 hydroxylase deficiency. *New England Journal of Medicine, 316,* 178–182.

Naftolin, F., & Butz, E. (Eds). (1981). Sexual dimorphism. *Science, 211.*

Neinstein, L. S., & Castle, G. C. (1983). Congenital absence of the vagina. *American Journal of Disabled Children, 137,* 669–671.

New, M. I., & Levine, L. S. (1981). Adrenal hyperplasia in intersex states. In N. Josso (Ed.), *The intersex child.* (pp. 51–56). New York: S. Karger.

Nielsen, J. (1970). Criminality among patients with Klinfelters syndrome. *British Journal of Psychiatry, 117,* 365–369.

Nielsen, J., Christensen, K. R., Fredrich, U., Zeuthen, E., & Ostergaard, O. (1973). Childhood of males with XYY syndrome. *Journal of Autism and Childhood Schizophrenia, 2,* 5–26.

Nielsen, J., Nyborg, H., & Dahll, G. (1977). Turner's Syndrome: A psychiatric-psychological study of 45 women with Turner's Syndrome compared with their sisters and women with normal karyotypes, growth retardation and primary amenorrhea. *Acta Jutlandica XLV Medicine.*

Nielsen, J., & Pelsen, B. (1987). Follow-up 20 years later of 34 Klinefelter males with karyotype 47XXY and 16 hypogonadal males with karyotype 46XY. *Human Genetics, 77,* 188–192.

Nielsen, J., Pelsen, B., & Sorensen, K. (1988). Follow-up of 30 Klinefelters males treated with testosterone. *Clinical Genetics, 33,* 262–269.

Nielsen, J., Sorensen, A. M., & Sorensen, K. (1982). Follow-up until age 7 to 11 of 25 unselected children with sex chromosome abnormalities. *Birth Defects: Original Article Series, 18*(4), 61–97.

Nielsen, J., Sillesen, I., Sorensen, A. M., & Sorensen, K. (1979). Follow-up until age 4 to 8 of 25 unselected children with sex chromosome abnormalities compared with sibs and controls. *Birth Defects: Original Article Series, 15*(1), 15–73.

Nielsen, J., Wohlert, M., Faaborg-Andersen, J., Hansen, K. B., Huidman, C., Krag-Olsen, B., Mouluad, I., & Videbech, P. (1986). Chromosome examination of 20,222 newborn children and results of a 7.5 year study. *Birth Defects: Original Article Series, 22*(3), 209–219.

Pennington, B. F., Bender, B., Puck, M., Salbenblatt, J., & Robinson, A. (1982). Learning disabilities in children with sex chromosome anomalies. *Child Development, 53,* 1182–1192.

Polani, P. E. (1960). Chromosomal factors in certain types of educational subnormality. In P. W. Bowman & H. B. Mantner (Eds.), *Mental retardation: Proceedings of the First International Conference*, (pp. 421–438). New York: Grune & Stratton.

Price, W. H., & Whatmore, P. B. (1967). Behavior disorders and pattern of crime among XYY males identified at a maximum security hospital. *British Medical Journal, 1*, 533–536.

Quattrin, T., Aronica, S., & Mazur, T. (1990). Management of male pseudohermaphroditism: A case report spanning twenty-one years. *Journal of Pediatric Psychology, 15*, 699–709.

Raboch, J., Mellan, J., & Starka, L. (1977). Adult cryptorchids: Sexual development and activity. *Archives of Sexual Behavior, 6*, 413–419.

Ratcliffe, S. G., Bancroft, J., Axworthy, D., & McLaren, W. (1982). Klinefelter's syndrome in adolescence. *Archives of Diseases in Childhood, 57*, 6–12.

Ratcliffe, S. G., Murray, L., & Teaque, P. (1986). Edinburgh study of growth and development of children with sex chromosome abnormalities. *Birth Defects: Original Article Series, 22*(3), 73–118.

Reilly, J. M., & Woodhouse, C. R. J. (1989). Small penis and the male sex role. *Journal of Urology, 142*, 569–571.

Rock, J. A., & Jones, H. W., Jr. (1989). Construction of the neovagina for patients with a flat perineum. *American Journal of Obstetrics and Gynecology, 160*, 845–851.

Rokitansky, C. (1938). Über die sogenannten Verdoppelungen des Uterus. *Med Jahrbüch Kaiser König Österreich Staat, 26*, 39–77.

Rongen-Westerlaken, C., Wit, J. M., De Muinick Keizer-Schrama, S. M. P. F., Otten, B. J., Oostdijk, W., Delemarre-van der Waal, H. A., Gons, M. H., But, A., & Van den Brande, J. L. (1992). Growth hormone treatment in Turner's syndrome accelerates growth and skeletal maturation. *European Journal of Pediatrics, 151*, 477–481.

Rosenfeld, R. G., Frane, J., Attie, K. M., Brassel, J.0, Burstein, S., Cara, J. F., Chernausek, S., Gotlin, R. W., Kuntze, J., Lippe, B. M., Mahoney, P. C., Moore, W. V., Saenger, P., & Johanson, A. J. (1992). Six year results of a randomized prospective trial of human growth hormone and oxandrolone in Turner's syndrome. *Journal of Pediatrics, 121*, 49–55.

Ross, G. T., & VardeWele, R. C. (1974). The ovaries. In R. D. Williams (Ed.), *Textbook of Endocrinology*. (pp. 368–422). Philadelphia: W. B. Saunders.

Rovet, J. F. (1993). The psychoeducational characteristics of children with Turner's syndrome. *Journal of Learning Disabilities, 26*, 333–341.

Rubin, R. T., Reinisch, J. M., & Haskett, R. (1981). Postnatal gonadal steriod effect on human sexually dimorphic behavior: A paradigm of hormone-environment interaction. *Science, 211*, 1318–1324.

Sabbath, J. C. (1961). Psychiatric observations in adolescent girls lacking ovarian functions. *Psychosomatic Medicine, 23*, 224–231.

Saenger, P. (1984). Abnormal sex differentiation. *Journal of Pediatrics*, 104, 1–17.

Sandberg, D. E., Meyer-Bahlburg, H. F. L., Aranoff, G. S., Sconzo, J. M., & Hensle, T. W. (1989). Boys with hypospadias: A survey of behavioral difficulties. *Journal of Pediatric Psychology, 14*, 491–514.

Schwartz, M. D., & Root, A. W. (1991). The Klinefelter syndrome of testicular dysgenesis. *Endocrinology and Metabolism of North America, 20*, 133–163.

Shaffer, J. W. (1962). A specific cognitive deficit observed in gonadal aplasia. *Journal of Clinical Psychology, 18*, 403–406.

Singh, D. N., Hara, S., Foster, H. W., & Grimes, E. M. (1980). Reproductive performance in women with sex chromosome mosaicism. *Obstetrics and Gynecology, 55*, 608–611.

Sonis, W. A., Levine-Ross, J., Blue, J., Cutler, C. B., Loriaux, P. L., & Klein, R. P. (1983). *Hyperactivity of Turner's syndrome.* Paper presented at the October meeting of the American Academy of Child Psychiatry, San Francisco.

Stewart, D. A., Bailey, J. D., Netley, E. T., Rovet, J., Park, E., Cripps, M., & Curtis, J. A. (1982). Growth and development of children with X and Y chromosome aneuploidy in infancy to pubertal age: The Toronto study. *Birth Defects: Original Article Series 18*(4), 99–154.

Tesch, L. G. (1989). Turner syndrome: A personal perspective. *Adolescent and Pediatric Gynecology, 2*, 186–188.

Thielgarrd, A. (1984). A psychological study of the personalities of XYY and XXY men. *Acta Psychiatrica Scandinavica, 315*, 1–33.

Thielgarrd, A. (1983). Aggression and the XYY personality. *International Journal of Law and Psychiatry, 6*, 413–421.

Turner, H. H. (1938). A syndrome of infantilism, congenital webbed neck and cubitus valgus. *Endocrinology, 23*, 566–574.

van Seters, A. P., & Slob, A. K. (1988). Mutually gratifying heterosexual relationship with micropenis of husband. *Journal of Sex and Marital Therapy, 14*, 98–107.

Walzer, S., Bashir, A. S., Graham, J. M., Silbert, A. R., Lange, N. T., DeNapoli, M. F., & Richmond, J. B. (1986). Behavioral development of boys with chromosome aneuploidy: Impact of reactive style on educational intervention for learning deficits. *Birth Defects: Original Article Series, 22*(3), (1–21).

Walzer, S., Bashir, A. S., & Silbert, A. R. (1990). Cognitive and behavioral factors in the learning disabilities of 47XXY and 47XYY boys. *Birth Defects: Original Article Series, 26*(4), 45–58.

Walzer, S., Gerald, P., & Shah, S. (1978). The XYY genotype. *Annual Review of Medicine, 29*, 563–670.

Walzer, S., Graham, J. M., Bashir, A. S., & Silbert, A. R. (1982). Preliminary observations on language and learning in XXY boys. *Birth Defects: Original Article Series, 18*(4), 185–192.

Wilson, J. D., & Foster, D. W. (Eds.). (1992). *Williams textbook of endocrinology* (8th ed.). Philadelphia: W. B. Saunders.

Witkin, H. A., Medricks, S. A., Schulsinger, F., Bakkestrone, E., Christiansen, K. O., Goodenough, D. R., Hirshhorn, K., Lundsteen, C., Owen, D. R., Phillips, J., Rubin, D. B., & Stocking, M. (1976). Criminality in XYY and XXY men. *Science, 193*, 547–555.

Zeuthen, E., Hansen, M., Christensen, A. L., & Nielsen, J. (1975). A psychiatric-psychological study of XYY males found in the general male population. *Acta Psychiatrica Scandandinavica, 51*, 3–18.

Part 3

Problems Associated with Sexual Victimization

7
Early Sexual Experience and Sexual Victimization of Children and Adolescents

Christopher Bagley

> The world experienced (otherwise called the "field of consciousness") comes at all times with our body as its center of vision, center of action, center of interest. Where the body is, is "here"; when the body acts is "now"; what the body touches is "this"; all other things are "there" and "then" and "that." These words of emphasized position imply a systematization of things with reference to a focus of action and interest which lies in the body. . . . The body is the storm center, the origin of coordinates, the constant place of stress in all that experience-train. Everything circles round it, and is felt from its point of view. The word "I," then, is primarily a noun of position, just like "this" and "here."
>
> William James, 1890, pp. 154–155

It is the thesis of this chapter that prolonged and intrusive sexual abuse imposed on the physically immature body and the developmentally immature psyche of a child frequently creates an adolescent who cannot find adequate solutions to the dilemmas of identity development defined by Erikson (1980). As a result, the adolescent is extremely vulnerable to stress, and may develop in severe form a number of the psychological disorders (e.g., suicidal ideas and behavior, depression, eating disorders, alienation from school and peers, sexual problems, acting-out behaviors, and substance abuse) that have an increasing prevalence among adolescents (Olmstead, O'Malley, & Bentler, 1991; Garrison, McKeown, Valois, & Vincent, 1993).

The body of the sexually abused child has been violated and his or her integrity has been stolen. The victims of prolonged sexual abuse often have profound problems in finding a sense of self in which bodily consciousness, feelings, and emotions are fully integrated. Instead, the victim's body is feared, loathed, and punished in a variety of ways, eating disorders, sexual

135

problems, self-mutilation and suicidal behavior, somatic symptoms, somatic and free-floating anxiety, impaired self-esteem, and profound, long-term depression have all been identified as common, long-term sequels of long-term, within-family sexual abuse (Bagley & King, 1990).

Sexual Victimization

There are powerful normative arguments against the practice of incest since it undermines the patterns of care and socialization of vulnerable individuals, and indeed undermines the whole basis of the nuclear family system, which depends on new marital partners being recruited from other, unrelated families (Bagley, 1969). The paradox of motives implied by "incestuous abuse" that is not "incest" may be solved by regarding the sexual misuse and humiliation of children as a form of socialization in which young females learn to accept, without complaint, the role of lifelong subordination to and service of men. If this supposition is true, then the sexual exploitation of male children by adult males is phenomenologically different from the sexual abuse of female children. (Unfortunately there is much less research available on male victims of abuse, but this review will include studies of male victims where available.)

The changing role of the father in North American society implies that he is moving toward a role defined more by nurturance and mutual bonding, and away from a role defined by the values of traditional patriarchy (Chenais, 1981). A study by Parker and Parker (1986) provides insight into these changing values. This study compared men found guilty of sexual assaulting their biological daughters with nonassaultive controls who had daughters of the same age. The men who incestuously abused their children were significantly more likely than the controls to have been separated from their child for most of her first five years of life, for various reasons, including job-related absences. Fathers who were present in these crucial developmental years were likely to share in the intimate care of their child, including feeding, bathing, dressing, and the like. Such interactions proved to be a powerful inhibitor of any sexual interest in their child, perhaps because such close and tender interaction provides some hormonal or biological inhibition against sexual interest. It is also true that men prepared to enter into nurturing roles are much less likely to express sexual dominance and exploitation of their daughters.

Finkelhor (1979) was the first scholar to use the technique of adult recall to estimate the prevalence of child sexual abuse. Finkelhor's questionnaire, which asked about *all* kinds of sexual relationship in which the child had engaged, from earliest memory until late teens, was completed by a large sample of college students. This research and its replications (e.g., Sorrenti-Little, Bagley, & Robertson, 1986; Kilpatrick, 1992) generated a huge amount of data, since about 60 percent of children and adolescents have had some kind of sexual contact with a peer, an older child, or an adult.

I have argued (Bagley & King, 1990) that the child is immature in both a physical and a psychological sense. This immaturity means that *any* sexual relationship may do great harm to the child's developing psychosexual identity. At least a quarter of all children (i.e., those under age 17) who engage in a long-term sexual relationship with someone of any age who imposes that relationship by force or threat will suffer long-term psychological harm as a result (Bagley, 1991a; Bagley & King, 1990; Bagley, Rodberg, Wellings, Moosa-Mitha, & Young, 1993). In some 10 percent of cases the harm will be profound and result in long-lasting psychiatric disability. Since it is difficult to know at the outset of a sexual relationship who will be harmed and who will not be harmed, *any* sexual relationship imposed by an older upon a younger person is ipso facto wrong. Employing this idea of psychological harm, we used Finkelhor's questionnaire and found that those sexual relationships that were achieved through the use of coercion, threat, or manipulation (typically, by a person in authority over the child) were indeed strongly correlated with long-term negative mental health profiles (Sorrenti-Little, Bagley, & Robertson, 1986).

We also found (like other researchers) that many sexual relationships into which the child entered *voluntarily* with an older person who had no authoritarian control over the child had benign psychological outcomes. Indeed, as Kilpatrick (1992) has shown in her American work, age differences between the child and the other participant in the sexual relationship are *not* by themselves statistically significant predictors of long-term psychosexual impairment. However, no researcher has established with any certainty how to predict long-term outcomes (Kilpatrick, 1992). For these reasons alone, we argue that *any* sexual relationship between an adult and a child should be deterred by legal process.

In seeking to define child sexual abuse and to identify psychological sequels of such events, we have developed a different definition than that used by Finkelhor (1979). In our usage, child sexual abuse occurs when the child (i.e., someone under the age of 17) experiences an *unwanted* sexual contact with another person, of any age (Bagley, 1989a, 1991a). "Sexual contact" is defined as any unwanted physical contact by the other person upon the child's breast, genital, or anal areas, and/or any unwanted contact by the child with the sexual parts of the other person's body. All contacts, in this conservative definition, are made on the unclothed sexual areas of the body of the child and/or the assailant. These definitions have the advantage of adding a phenomenological element to the measurement of child sexual abuse, as well as a humanist dimension in that we are fundamentally concerned with how the victim (rather than any other person) perceives and interprets the sexual activity. Another advantage of questions enquiring about "unwanted" sexual activities is that they are much simpler to ask than those in other measures (e.g., Finkelhor, 1979), and can easily be adapted for use by clinical and lay workers screening for prior abuse in various child populations (Bagley, 1992c).

The conservative estimates of sexual abuse that result from asking only about unwanted, physical-contact sexual activity also implies a greater efficiency in identifying individuals who have been psychologically traumatized by the abuse.

Issues in the Prevalence of Child Sexual Abuse: Long-Term versus Single-Event Abuse

Recent epidemiological studies of community samples of young adults (1,500 men and women aged 18 to 27) have shown the importance of the distinction between single-event and multiple-event sexual abuse in childhood (Bagley, 1991c; Bagley et al., 1993). While the amount of single-event sexual abuse before age 17 in these samples was higher in women (32 percent in females vs. 15.6 percent in males) the amount of multiple-event abuse (i.e., continuing for more than a day, and sometimes for several years) was similar (6.8 percent in females vs. 6.9 percent in males).

While a single event of traumatic sexual abuse (e.g., a brutal rape) can create profound problems for long-term adjustment, evidence indicates that the large majority of never-repeated unwanted sexual acts imposed on children (both male and female) do not cause any long-term psychological harm that continues into adulthood (Bagley & King, 1990). Consider the following case:

> Ann, a 10-year-girl was assaulted by a 15-year-old cousin, who tried to insert his fingers into her vagina, and ordered her to fellate him. Ann escaped, running immediately to her mother to tell her of the incident. Ann was a normal child before the assault, had good relationships with her parents, and had good self-esteem. Ann's parents acted immediately to prevent any repetition of the abuse, and comforted their child. Ann's parents sought psychological assessment for their daughter, which rapidly established that she remained psychologically normal, without need for prolonged therapy. At follow-up five years later Ann's emotional and cognitive profiles were essentially normal. Ann had good ego strength prior to the assault; her excellent self-esteem, based on a warm and trusting relationship with both parents, had enabled her to seek help immediately. This same ego strength, reinforced by the calm and sympathetic reaction of her significant others, enabled her to overcome any trauma created by the incident. (Case from series reported by Bagley & Ramsay, 1986).

Contrast Ann's situation with that of Bonnie, sexually assaulted for the first time by her stepfather when she was 10:

Bonnie's biological father left the family when she was 5, and mother remarried when Bonnie was 8. According to school reports, Bonnie lacked confidence in social relationships. Her stepfather manipulated his authority, forcing Bonnie to keep silent about the abuse. He told her that she was wicked and dirty, and no one would believe her if she told others about the assault. By the age of 12 Bonnie had to endure vaginal and anal intercourse at least weekly. She ran from home, and by the age of 14 was a juvenile prostitute. She had devastated self-esteem, regular drug use, and a recent history of suicide attempts. (Case from series reported by Bagley & Young, 1987).

The crucial difference between these two cases at the onset of the abuse was the contrast between them in terms of ego strength, warm and trusting relationship with parents, and self-esteem prior to the abuse. Bonnie had poor self-esteem at the onset of the abuse, and this impaired her ability to seek help from others, or to resist the threats of her stepfather. Feelings of guilt, loneliness, and terror were imposed on an already vulnerable child who was then deeply traumatized by the continued assaults.

This case illustrates the probability, identified by several researchers, that long-term sexual abuse of female children is most likely to occur in dysfunctional families, and will often involve victims whose mental health has been impaired by psychological abuse and neglect, and oftentimes physical abuse or harsh punishment as well. Studies that identify a range of types of child abuse point to the fact that the combination of physical abuse, sexual abuse, and emotional abuse or neglect is particularly likely to be associated with long-term impairment of mental health (Bagley & King, 1990).

Clinical Identification of Victims of Child Sexual Abuse

Adult recall studies have been valuable in giving us some estimates of the prevalence of child sexual abuse (CSA), and the long-term damage it may impose on the victim. This knowledge has had a political impact. The much greater awareness of the problem of CSA has resulted in the development of methods of screening for victims (e.g., by presentations in schools) and the development of specialized teams for the protection, assessment, and treatment of victims (Bagley & King, 1990). The adult recall studies of prevalence have enabled us to show historical trends in abuse rates: these appeared to be steady throughout the century until the early 1950s—for example, women aged 30 to 39 recalled about the same amount of CSA in their childhoods as did women aged 60 to 69. However, women born after 1950 report much higher rates of CSA (Bagley, 1990). This was the time when divorce rates began to increase, and also the time when the expression of adult sexuality became less inhibited.

The adult recall studies suggest that many women were put at risk of CSA when their biological fathers separated from the family because of divorce and new adults males entered the family setting. These adults were not inhibited or deterred by the taboo on incest. The epidemiological data suggest that about 10 percent of stepfathers or cohabitees imposed sexual assault on female children in these "reconstituted" families. The recall studies show, too, that these victims were rarely able to tell adults about the ongoing abuse. With increasing awareness of the impact of child sexual abuse in the 1970s and 1980s, many victims (both past and current) were identified. These victims presented child protection and child and adolescent therapy programs with challenges in terms of both the procedures and the professional personnel required to provide support and treatment.

For a while in the early 1980s "worst case" scenarios often occurred, with an abused adolescent being removed from home when abuse was revealed. The victim was then placed in an emergency youth shelter, along with runaways and delinquents. No treatment for the CSA was available, and the girl would drift through a series of group and foster homes into the life of the street, and eventually into drug abuse and prostitution (Bagley, 1985; Bagley & Young, 1987; Bagley, Borrows, & Yoworski, 1990a).

The quality of professional practice in child protection across North America is uneven, particularly in rural areas. Most major cities now have integrated protection and treatment programs, with established protocols for school personnel to help them in recognizing and referring suspected cases of CSA (Thomlison & Bagley, 1991). Aspects of treatment programs are discussed below.

The Effects of Child Sexual Abuse: Clinical Studies

The child who comes to a treatment agency following child sexual abuse is atypical of the population of abused children. The abuse will have been discovered (sometimes because the child asked for help from a professional, often a teacher); but we know (from adult recall studies) that only a minority of abused children reach even this first stage. The abuse will have been verified by the child protection team, and some decision will have been made about the child's future. Ideally, when the abuser lives in the child's household, that person should leave, but when the alleged abuser is hostile and denies the abuse, legal options are limited. The large majority of men who are convicted of sexual assault upon a child plead guilty (Stephens, Grinnell, Thomlison, & Krysik, 1991): paradoxically, it is the hostile, arrogant, or psychopathic abuser who is most likely to escape prosecution.

Sexual abuse of a child can have paradoxical effects. The child may at first feel flattered, excited, and physically aroused. But the combination of sexual excitement simultaneously with shame and guilt often has powerfully negative influences upon psychosexual development, especially if the child is required to deceive her mother about the abuse, and has to collude with her father or stepfather in this wicked deceit. While Freud recanted his thesis that many of his female patients had been sexually abused in childhood, the psychic devastation wrought by child sexual abuse is compatible with Freud's theory of the incest taboo and the emotional chaos that could result in individuals who violate this taboo (e.g., Stekel, 1926). Psychoanalysts have been fascinated by cases in which fathers imposed a sexual relationship on their daughters and have presented several hundred case reports in the technical literature (reviewed in Bagley, 1969). The preponderance of this evidence indicates that if the sexual relationship is imposed in adolescence, crucial identity tasks for the child are disrupted, and latent Oedipal desires flood consciousness, with a sequel in profound degrees of guilt, anxiety, and depression. While there may have been a high degree of selection in such case reports, they do offer a theoretical model of why incestuous abuse (particularly that involving a father and daughter) are so damaging to the child's ego, in comparison with sexual abuse involving individuals who are unrelated. The post-Freudian, psychodynamic view of the psychological damage imposed by incestuous abuse is succinctly outlined by Levine (1990) and Wasserman and Rosenfeld (1992).

Child Sexual Abuse and the Violation of Self-Systems

In the young child self-esteem is often fragmented, with pride and confidence in one area coexisting with doubts and uncertainty over other achievements or relationships. However, by the age of 7 the child's self-esteem (evaluations of self characteristics) and self-concept (understanding of the roles and role performance required in interaction with significant others) begin to crystallize, as the child enters the fourth stage of identity building ("industry vs. inferiority," in Erikson's [1980] schema). The self-concept of the child becomes increasingly global, incorporating both knowledge of the roles to be performed and evaluations of the quality of action in those roles involving interaction between self and others. In this symbolic interaction framework the child absorbs (and sometimes rejects) the image of himself or herself created by others.

Adolescence is a crucial stage in this process of self-appraisal and self-understanding, when the young person incorporates many more roles into an ego framework and evaluates role performance in more comprehensive and complex ways. The ideal process is for a "diffused identity" (Erikson, 1980) to be formed by midadolescence. Within this identity structure the individual holds a model of the nature of key roles required (in respect to parents, kin, peers, school, and society at large); how those roles should be performed in terms of mastery and satisfaction (the beginning of what

Maslow [1973] calls "self-actualization"); and how self-confidence in role performance (i.e., optimizing self-esteem) can be achieved. Important evidence from longitudinal studies indicates that identity and global self-esteem measured in the first years of junior high school can predict many of the problems that will occur in later adolescence, including scholastic failure and school dropout; deliberate self-harm; use of drugs, alcohol, and tobacco; delinquency and runaway behavior; and teenage pregnancies (Kaplan, 1980).

It follows that if child abuse (physical, emotional, and/or sexual) impairs self-esteem and identity development, then the child will be at special risk for the development of various kinds of deviant and problem behaviors in adolescence and adulthood. Unfortunately, the evidence indicates that child abuse (and especially prolonged sexual abuse combined with physical and emotional abuse) is powerfully detrimental to the development of adequate levels of self-esteem and secure identity that can buffer the child against new stressors, or prevent a drift into various forms of self-defeating or deviant behavior.

Diminished self-esteem in CSA victims is a commonly observed short- and long-term sequel of abuse, especially if that abuse has continued for weeks, months, or even years (Bukowski, 1992). The evidence is fairly consistent in suggesting that the duration of the abuse (particularly abuse beginning in latency and extending into adolescence), the degree of physical imposition on the child (usually, penetration of the child's body), and the combination of sexual abuse with attachment and bonding failures, emotional abuse and neglect, and physical abuse are all associated in combination or interaction with diminished self-esteem in the child victim (Morrow & Sorell, 1989; Briere & Runtz, 1990; Jackson, Calhoun, Amick, Maddever, & Habif, 1990; Bifulco, Brown, & Adler, 1991; Hunter, 1991; Mannarino, Cohen, Smith, & Moore-Motilly, 1991; Alexander, 1992; Kilpatrick, 1992; Kendall-Tackett, Williams, & Finkelhor, 1993; Wyott, Guthric, & Notgrass, 1992; Brewin, Andrews, & Gotlieb, 1993). There is also evidence of impaired ego development in CSA survivors (Jennings & Armsworth, 1992), and of dissociation or splitting of self-characteristics (Cole & Putnam, 1992).

However, the thesis that impairment of self-esteem and ego strength, in turn leading to greatly increased problems of identity development in CSA victims, as a core process in the vulnerability of survivors, has found less universal support (Kendall-Tackett, Williams, & Finkelhor, 1991). Nevertheless, it is my argument in this chapter that prolonged CSA often impairs identity formation to the extent that the victim is vulnerable in many areas of development, including body image (e.g., as manifested in bulimia, anorexia, and induced obesity); presentation of the sexual self (e.g., as an unattractive asexual person or as a person who degrades the sexual self through promiscuity); as a person who enters helplessly into degrading relationships; and as a person who symbolically degrades the self through self-mutilation, deliberate self-harm, and drug and alcohol abuse. The evidence for these findings is gathered together by Bagley and Young (1990) and Bagley and King (1990).

Why does incestuous abuse impair self-esteem and identity development to such a profound degree in so many victims of such abuse? There are several complementary explanations. Continued guilt and fear and the disruption of the normal role obligations and expectations associated with the assaults mean that the child has many more identity tasks to perform than a normal adolescent, and also has a much more complex and fractured self-concept and lower self-esteem. The abuse takes away from the child the satisfaction at knowing that there is progress, humanity, and cooperation in most human relationships. As Gelinas (1983) puts it:

> Former victims show a profound impairment of self-esteem. The family relational imbalances have taught them that they literally have no rights, particularly to needs of their own; nothing is owned by them, inherently or because of their contributions, and they are allowed no claim to needs, reciprocity or even acknowledgment. With such fundamentally impaired self-esteem, incest victims tend to be extremely passive, to the point of paralysis. (p. 322)

Stigmatization, self-blame, and chronically impaired self-esteem often occur together in abuse survivors of both sexes. Chronic post-traumatic stress may also occur, with abundant amounts of free-floating and somatic anxiety, nightmares and sleep terrors, flashbacks of trauma, and dissociation of personality (Briere, 1989). Young (1992) conceptualizes these common psychological sequels to sexual abuse as "problems of embodiment," a kind of self-loathing for the body that has betrayed its owner. In identity terms, the adolescent and his or her developing body (which incorporates the sexual vision of the self) are profoundly dissociated. Chronic depression and suicidal ideation can also occur as a direct result of the sexual abuse, or as an outcome of the combination of poor self-esteem and lack of ego buffering in the face of new stressors.

In an experimental study of young women identified in a community mental health study, Bagley and Young (1990) studied a group of 149 women who had experienced prolonged sexual abuse as children. Such a history was associated with elevated scores on measures of depression and impaired self-esteem. Biographic reconstruction indicated that for the majority of the former abuse victims impaired self-esteem had become a chronic personality trait, while intermittent depression occurred as a reaction to stress. Experimental research demonstrated that group therapy, cocounseling, and structured social support for women who had been abused and had poor self-esteem—but who were not currently depressed—

was successful in enhancing self-esteem. Wait-list controls did not show any improvement in self-esteem. The longitudinal aspect of the study also supported our model of the genesis of depression in abuse survivors: poor self-esteem combined with various social stressors in the absence of social support led to a statistically significant increase in signs of depression. In the epigraph at the beginning of this chapter I quoted the seminal work of William James (1890) on the crucial importance of a person's body as the center and the essence of personal functioning. Prolonged sexual abuse can create a fundamental division between the child and her or his body, in a way that makes satisfactory achievement of the Eriksonian tasks of self-integration very difficult. Similarly, the stages of development described by Maslow (which are parallel to or similar to the Eriksonian stages; Young & Bagley, 1982) are difficult to achieve. Maslow (1973) argues that violation of an early developmental need—the need for safety and security—makes it difficult for a child to master later stages of development, including identity integration and self-esteem maintenance. The child who is sexually abused in her or his home is betrayed: home should be a place of safety and trust, not of fear, terror, and violation. Such violation of basic needs can lead to distorted patterns of development, including in extreme cases dissociated and multiple personality (Putnam, 1989).

Dissociative Personality Traits and Multiple Personality: Special Types of Ego Fragmentation

Although cases of multiple personality have been described in the psychiatric literature since the turn of the century, it is only in the past 15 years that we have begun to understand both how prevalent this distortion of personality development is and what are its fundamental causes (Putnam, 1989; Ross, 1989).

Some children who experience intolerable trauma (prolonged physical pain, physical abuse, sexual abuse, or combinations of these traumas) before the age of 6 may dissociate that part of themselves (in mind and body) that endures the pain and violent intrusion. This is an ego-protective strategy in that the child is able to create several alter egos who both endure the pain and comfort and protect the child. However, by the onset of the latency period, these alter egos enter into hidden areas of the child's psyche, sometimes emerging to dominate the ego in ways that direct the child into unanticipated behavioral paths. In these dissociated states the child or adolescent may injure himself, herself, or others, engage in delinquent behaviors, or flee from customary surroundings.

There is a psychological continuum between normal dissociation (e.g., being unaware of one's immediate surroundings while driving a car) through dissociative abnormalities (e.g., rapid and contradictory changes of behavior; inability to remember hours or days of one's recent existence; blocking out childhood memories covering a period of years; feeling possessed by another person, or hearing directive voices; episodes of bizarre or disturbed behavior observed by others, but not remembered by the child; and half-remembered terrifying dreams and frequent nightmares) to complex multiple personalities in which the alter egos exercise complete domination over the personality for short or long periods (Ross, 1985).

In a review of child welfare and adolescent treatment files in Canada and Britain, we found that 15 percent of those with a history of sexual abuse before age 6 manifested five or more dissociative symptoms (Bagley et al., 1993). These adolescents were much more likely than others to have histories of sexual abuse continuing into the latency period, multiple sexual and physical abuse occurring in disorganized families, and emotional abuse or neglect by mentally ill or alcoholic parents. The children with several indicators of dissociative personality style had high scores on Bernstein and Putnam's (1986) Dissociative Experiences Scale, and exhibited significantly more physical symptoms (frequent and severe headaches and abdominal symptoms), more eating disorders, more self-mutilation and suicide attempts, more delinquency, and more sexual and physical assaults on younger children. Some 75 percent of the adolescents with several dissociative signs had histories of sexual abuse continuing (or commencing) after the age of 6.

These findings are important for those who conduct adult recall studies of community populations (e.g., Bagley, 1991a) in order to discover the prevalence and long-term psychological sequels of sexual abuse. An unknown proportion of those interviewed will have many symptoms of adverse mental health, but cannot recall the events of sexual abuse that caused these problems. Because of this, the adult recall studies reviewed by Bagley (1992a) will underestimate both the actual prevalence of CSA and the psychological problems that are the long-term sequels of CSA. There is a conservative bias working against finding statistically significant correlates of CSA. Because of this bias, those findings that actually are significant (e.g., the finding of increased rates of depression, anxiety, impaired self-esteem, and suicidal thoughts and behavior in CSA populations) are especially important.

Child Sexual Abuse Histories in Special Populations: Runaways, Prostitutes, Street People, Prison and Mental Hospital Inmates

Adult recall studies indicate that about 6 percent of children of both sexes have endured prolonged and unwanted sexual relations imposed upon them by an older person. At least half of these individuals (about 3 percent of the population sampled) will suffer long-term impairment of mental health as a result of these experiences. In addition, some child victims of a brutal rape that is not repeated will nevertheless suffer from post-traumatic stress; however, the psychological outcomes of the rape victims are rather different from those experienced by victims of long-term, incestuous abuse (Briere, 1989). I must emphasize once again that these estimates of prevalence, and of psychological harm, are conservative ones.

One effect of incestuous abuse is rebellion by the child against family rules and values (which she rightly sees as hypocritical and meaningless when the arbiter of justice is also her sexual oppressor). Although she is psychologically incapable of denouncing her oppressor, nevertheless she acts with anger and despair at her fate. Often the victim is blamed for this disturbed behavior, and the system (the disciplinary procedures of school, juvenile court, and group homes) confirms the negative label imposed on her. She is likely to rebel against these sanctions, and the label then becomes self-confirming (Zingaro, 1987). Special studies of juvenile prostitutes, street kids, delinquents, drug users, adolescent psychiatric inpatients, as well as adult mental hospital patients, adult prisoners, and homeless adults, all indicate greatly elevated rates of prolonged, within-family abuse (Bagley & King, 1990; Bagley, Burrows, & Yoworski, 1990a; Thomlison & Bagley, 1991).

In a comparison of juvenile prostitutes in America and Canada it was found that at least two-thirds had suffered prolonged incestuous abuse in childhood (Silbert & Pines, 1983; Bagley & Young, 1987). Biographical analysis indicated a common sequence of events: the boy or girl rebelled against both the sexual abuse and the authority of the abuser; either ran away from home or was thrown out by the family; and on the streets the struggle for survival involved various delinquencies, including drug pushing and drug use. Absorption into prostitution often followed; in Canada, the *average* age of entry into prostitution is 15.5 years (Bagley, 1985; Bagley & Young, 1987). Thus about half of all Canadian prostitutes began hooking before the age of 16. Adolescent males, too, are drawn into the web of prostitution, and often they pair with an adolescent female prostitute, supporting each other emotionally and financially (Bagley, Burrows, & Yaworski, 1991a). Society holds a negative view of the pimp, but often he is simply a male victim of sexual abuse who is trying to survive on the street.

Young people in child welfare caseloads and in residential care institutions often have histories of child sexual abuse. Frequently, however, these children and adolescents were processed for reasons other than their earlier sexual abuse. Often, they were sent to residential care and treatment centers because of their acting-out behavior, runaway status, or delinquency. It is clear, too, from our extensive case-file reviews that professionals in the past only atypically understood the significance of child sexual abuse, and often failed to check or record this information. It is crucial that all child welfare workers and child care professionals in their assessments ask standard questions about histories of unwanted sexual contacts, as well as questions that try to establish the temporal sequence of disturbed behaviors that may be sequels of that abuse. It is technically quite simple to screen for such abuse (Bagley, 1990). It is crucial that frontline workers have the training and skills to undertake initial counseling and assessment prior to referring CSA victims for fuller psychological assessments, which can identify which kind of treatment program would be most effective. It is also crucial that social service delivery systems should actually have a range of treatment options available. While in the short run it is expensive to provide such specialized treatment, in the long run such interventions can be hugely cost-effective in preventing the drift of CSA victims into street life, crime, chronic drug and alcohol abuse, and mental illness.

Another problem in using adult recall studies to estimate the prevalence of CSA is that because suicidal ideas and behavior are known sequels of sexual abuse, those most severely damaged by abuse might well have killed themselves, and therefore do not show up as victims in prevalence studies using conventional epidemiological methods. Indeed, there is some evidence that adolescents and young adults who complete suicide may have been victims of a type of sexual abuse that co-occurs with family disorganization, as well as with physical and emotional abuse and neglect. This evidence comes from a review of several thousand files of the Alberta medical examiner which identified a type of completed suicide in which childhood abuse and neglect was a precursor (Bagley, 1989b). Furthermore, it is this type of suicide that has accounted for the increase in youth suicide, particular among males (Bagley, 1992b). While it is difficult to know whether prior abuse was a direct precursor of suicide, this finding is consonant with community surveys indicating that sexually abused males have a greatly increased prevalence of suicidal ideas and behavior and of depressive thinking (Bagley et al., 1993). Prior physical and sexual abuse and neglect are also precursors of "careless death," including alcohol-related, reckless behavior in adolescents and young adults (Bagley, Wood, and Khumar, 1990).

Who Are the Abusers? How Shall We Treat Them?

Knowledge about the status and motivation of sexual offenders against children and of how they may be treated, deterred, and perhaps reintegrated into society and family is imperfect. However, there are three clear research findings: the large majority of those who sexually exploit male and female children (probably in excess of 95 percent) are males; at least 80 percent of those who assault children are known to the child, although only one-fifth of males and around one-third of females will have been assaulted by someone in their immediate family; and one-third of sexual offenders are themselves adolescents. The motivation to use children sexually often develops in adolescence, which is also a crucial time for intervention and treatment (Bagley, 1992a).

Rush (1980) and Chenais (1981) stress in their historical accounts that adult males have rarely been deterred from sexually exploiting children simply because those children are physically immature or in a state of vulnerable dependency. Only the incest taboo itself has deterred closely related adult males from sexually exploiting children from the age of puberty through to middle adolescence. Children have in the past been protected from the sexuality of others principally because they were the property of a protective nuclear family and extended kindred. The price of this protection, however, was submission to the male-dominated ideal that the virgin adolescent could be given to (and perhaps traded with) another cooperative kin group.

The past 40 years in North America and northern Europe have seen an unprecedented rise in divorce rates and single parenthood. This means that many of the men introduced into these families are biologically unrelated to the children for whom they become the father figure. The incest taboo does not deter them, and some of these men seem to regard these female children as sexual extensions of their mother, to be used sexually when the whim occurs. The abuse perpetrated by these men seems almost casual in nature, without thought for the often fearful consequences that the children suffer. Several researchers have found that sexual abuse by nonbiological father figures is the most serious in terms of length of occurrence, frequency, and intrusiveness (involving repeated penetrations of the child's body). As Young (1992) observes:

> There is growing evidence that the most serious long-term effects result from highly intrusive sexual abuse such as oral, anal, or vaginal penetration; abuse that is violent, forceful, or sadistic in nature; abuse that continues over many years; and from intrafamilial abuse, particularly when the perpetrator is a parent, step-parent, or parent figure. (p. 89)

There is also evidence that some pedophiles (men with a fixation on children as sex objects or with a desire to achieve sexual relations with a child in preference to any other kind of sexual relationship) seek out single mothers as marriage partners with the intention of gaining sexual access to the children in that family (Bagley & King, 1990).

Studies of pedophile motivation (reviewed in Bagley et al., 1993) indicate that pedophiles can usually present themselves as "normal" when presented with the psychological tests [e.g., Rorschach, Minnesota Multiphasic Personality Inventory (MMPI)] customarily used in assessment. Moreover, such men may be manipulative liars. This makes inferences about causal factors in the developmental history of the offender difficult to assess. However, some sexually abusive males can be diagnosed after extensive observation and testing as manifesting "sadistic personality disorder" (Spitzer, Feister, Gay, & Pfohl, 1991). Such individuals frequently have histories of multiple abuse (sexual, physical, and emotional) in their own childhoods.

A rather paradoxical subgroup of offenders against children do not have a pedophiliac fixation and are easier to detect, assess, and treat. These are the so-called regressed individuals who for a variety of reasons have increasing difficulty in maintaining adequate psychosexual relationships with age peers and therefore turn to children for both emotional affection and sexual outlet. These men usually feel great distress at their behavior and are often relieved when their actions are discovered. While often these men will have imposed great psychological distress on the child, nevertheless, if their remorse is genuine and the child and the nonoffending spouse so wish, they can be reintegrated into their family after comprehensive and prolonged therapy (using either the humanist model or an adapted family therapy model, discussed below).

Almost certainly there are different types of offenders who need to be deterred and treated in different ways. All practitioners seem to be in agreement that the psychopathic individual, contemptuous of the sufferings of his child victims and cunning in his methods of sexual access and concealment, is a person who is difficult both to apprehend and to treat (Woody, McLellan, Luborsky, & O'Brien, 1985). Indeed, the majority of men who plead guilty to sexual offenses against children (and who receive terms ranging from probation to lengthy imprisonment) are the regressed type of offender who would be unlikely to reoffend, even without specific treatment (Bagley & King, 1990). There is also a type of sexual assault against children and adolescents that is simply casual and sexist in nature, and is usually imposed on the child by relatives other than a parent or a family friend. This type of abuse, although frequent, does not often come to the attention of those providing clinical treatment of victims or those processing offenders. Indeed, clinical sources, although often used to provide information on victim and offender profiles, will be overweighted by cases of incestuous abuse, particularly abuse that seems to have done a great deal of psychological harm to the victim.

In an attempt to avoid the pitfalls of generalizing from the biased data sources available from treatment agencies, we studied the motivation to sexually assault children in a random community sample of 750 men aged 18 to 27 living in a large Canadian city (Bagley et al., 1993). Respondents were assured anonymity through the use of a computerized response system. They completed a number of validated mental health instruments, a questionnaire on their own unwanted childhood sexual experiences, and a measure of their current sexual interests in and/or activities with children in various age and sex categories.

Fifty-two of these young men had experienced multiple, unwanted sexual contacts; 34 of these victims of sexual assault had experienced anal penetration; and all had experienced genital fondling or fellatio. These adult survivors had significantly poorer mental health than the 65 individuals who reported experiencing only a single assault, and those who recalled no unwanted sexual contact before their 17th birthday. The measure of prolonged sexual abuse was highly correlated with current sexual interests and activities involving minors, both male and female. However, the *majority* of the sexual abuse victims did not declare any sexual interest or activities involving minors: 41 percent of the prolonged abuse victims had pedophile interests, compared with 2 percent of the nonvictims. Regression analyses showed that combinations of physical and sexual abuse, emotional neglect or rejection within the boy's family, current poor mental health (particularly depression, low self-esteem, anxiety, dissociative personality traits, posttraumatic stress indicators, and suicidal ideas and behavior), and emotional attachment to the abuser were all independent, statistically significant predictors of pedophile interest. Combining these various indicators in a discriminant analysis successfully identified two-thirds of the young men with serious sexual interest in minors.

While this community survey suggests that only about 3 percent of the adult male population living in stable conditions (i.e., excluding institutionalized individuals, highly mobile people, and street dwellers) have strong motivations to involve children in sexuality, the fixated pedophile can nevertheless be of considerable danger in the community. For example, Weinrott and Saylor (1991, p. 291) found in a study of convicted sexual offenders that these 77 men "admitted to over 8,000 sexual contacts with 959 children. The number ranged from 1 to 200, with a median of 7." Identification and intervention with even a few actual or potential offenders at an early stage might prevent literally hundreds of children from suffering sexual assault.

Much more research needs to be undertaken on various ways of identifying and treating male victims of abuse and males who have entered the victim-to-abuser cycle.

Preventing Child Sexual Abuse

Primary prevention involves various strategies, including giving children the knowledge, skills, and psychological strengths to recognize sexual exploitation, to resist it, and to seek immediate help from a responsible adult. Research indicates that about one-quarter of children who are approached by an abuser who is know to them (usually, as a family member) are not able to resist such approaches, and are unable to get any immediate help from an adult (Bagley & King, 1990; Bagley, 1991; Bagley et al., 1993). Special educational programs can be very helpful in this regard.

Recent experience indicates that when children and adolescents are given adequate knowledge and skills concerning sexual abuse, approaches by children to their teachers about recent and current sexual abuse increase significantly (Bagley, 1992c; Bagley & King, 1990).

One of the paradoxes of prevention programs (e.g., the "Good Touch–Bad Touch" program extensively promulgated by the Canadian government; see Bagley & Thomlison, 1991) is that it purports to give children knowledge and skills about unwanted touching (the "bad" touch) that will help them to resist sexually exploitive approaches. Logically, however, if we ask children to reject "bad touches," they should have the right to resist all kinds of physical brutality and corporal punishment too. But as Strauss, Gelles, and Smith (1990) have amply demonstrated:

> Over 97% of American children experience physical punishment. . . . [S]uch widespread use of ordinary physical punishment is one of the factors accounting for the high rate of child abuse and wife beating. . . . Victimization in the family starts in infancy and, for half of all American children, continues until they leave home. Moreover, for one out of seven children the violence is severe enough to be classified as child abuse. (p. 421)

In our view (elaborated in Bagley & King, 1990), the sexual exploitation of children and adolescents can be properly prevented only when society itself is to some degree healed, when the large majority of families are both caring of children and nonviolent toward them. Epidemiological studies in Britain, Canada, and the United States have shown that families in which a child is sexually abused are overrepresented by families practicing haphazard or systematic violence against a child, and by families who emotionally abuse or neglect their children. Children who have been cowed by physical punishments, whose self-confidence is sapped by emotional rejection or neglect, have few ego resources left and quite easily fall prey to the sexually abusive adult, both inside and outside of their families. For males, emotional attachment to the male abuser also puts the adolescent at risk for entering the victim-to-abuser cycle of sexual violence.

Since so many sexual abusers escape detection, the imposition of punitive sentences as a declaration of public morality is likely to have a paradoxical impact. If the offender has the clear expectation of a long jail term if convicted, he is likely to lie convincingly or to cover his tracks in ways that will make criminal conviction difficult. In the worst case, when the penalty for child rape may be as severe as that for murder, a rapist may kill his child victim in order to prevent her or his testimony in a trial.

The most successful kind of criminal justice program (outlined in Bagley & King, 1990) seems to be one in which the sexual offender knows that if he cooperates with those who treat the victim, he will receive a light or suspended sentence. In Canada, jurisdictions that have such a policy have seen an increase in the number of men who plead guilty when charged with sexual assault on a child. Paradoxically, this puts up the rate of convictions for child sexual assault, leading some to argue that deterrent sentences really are necessary. This view ignores the fact that offenders making court appearances are still the tip of the iceberg. Another strategy is to appeal to potential abusers through public service messages, advising them of the great harm wrought by sexual involvement with a child.

All of these strategies will be ineffective with the fixated pedophile who also has a sadistic or sociopathic personality style (Spitzer et al., 1991; Feister & Gay, 1991). Such men lie unscrupulously, and also fabricate social and sexual histories (e.g., of abuse in their own childhood) in order to win sympathy from prosecutors, jurists, and therapists. For such individuals there is no real alternative to lengthy terms of imprisonment, not for any deterrent purpose but to keep these dangerous individuals out of the communities in which they do so much harm. Both chemical and physical castration has had limited effect, since the motivation to sexually assault for many sexual offenders lies in the psyche rather than in the hormonal system. The offender unable to gain erection can still do considerable harm while making sexual assault on a child.

Secondary prevention involves the prompt, humane, and efficient treatment of child sex abuse victims, once discovered. Primary prevention activities such as school programs on sexual abuse prevention also form a beginning stage of secondary prevention, when current victims seek help from a teacher. It is crucial for teachers to have a well-prepared protocol for handling such reports, with early involvement by child protection and law enforcement agencies. Child protection workers dealing with abuse allegations need to have special skills (including those required for cooperative work with the police personnel with whom they will simultaneously investigate the abuse allegation). They also need an adequate network of referral sources for medical examination, psychological assessment, and support for the child who must give evidence in court. Ideally, when within-family abuse is suspected, the suspected offender should leave the home. Removing the child from the home might prompt a "blaming the victim" reaction. Indeed, when child sexual abuse is seen by the community as a heinous offense, the child herself may become morally tainted by her victim status, and can be rejected along with the offender.

Several well-developed models for the investigation and treatment of child and adolescent sexual abuse victims have emerged (O'Donohue & Elliott, 1992). These programs have different approaches, but common elements:

1. The primary focus must be on the recovery of self-esteem and mental health of the CSA victim, rather than on the welfare of adults, or of the family as a unit.

2. Individual therapy must begin with the victim, endeavoring to remove the sense of guilt and shame that has accompanied the abuse and its revelation, addressing as well symptoms of post-traumatic stress. This is an essential first step in rebuilding self-esteem. If the offender agrees, he can assist this healing with an admission of his own responsibility for the assaults, together with an assurance to the victim that none of what happened was her fault.

Probably a range of counseling models and methods can work in the process of restoring the victim's self-respect; indeed, the commitment, warmth, and empathy of the counselor may be more important than the model of therapy used. Group therapy for victims can follow or coincide with individual therapy. Parallel groups of mothers are also valuable, as well as specific dyadic therapy, particularly that involving mother and daughter. Offenders can also be treated in groups by the agency treating the victim and her mother. This model, incorporating elements of the humanistic approach described by Giarretto (1982) is elaborated in Bagley and King (1990).

It is important that conventional family therapy should *not* be used in families in which a child has been sexually abused. Blaming a mythical "family system" for abuse inevitably involves blaming the victim, and will only depress her fragile feelings of self-worth yet further. However, a modified form of the family therapy approach has been developed by Larson and Maddock (1986) which avoids victim blaming. Careful screening (described by Babins-Wagner, 1991) can admit the offender into family therapy groups after individual assessment and counseling if it is established that he is not a fixated, pedophile offender, and he also is clearly remorseful in ways that can help to heal both the victim and her family.

A number of other potentially valuable approaches to therapy of the child and adolescent victim have been described (Friedrich, 1990; James, 1989; Kilpatrick, 1992; Mandell & Damon, 1989; Meiselman, 1990; Trepper & Barrett, 1989). What is much needed now is research on the optimization and evaluation of these various programs and investigation of the ways in which different programs and kinds of therapy can be tailored to fit the individual needs of the victim (Downing, Jenkins, & Fisher, 1988; O'Donohue & Elliott, 1992; Walker, 1992).

Another challenge to therapists is treatment of the male victim who in adolescence has begun a pattern of sexual offenses against others (Bolton, Morris, & MacEachron, 1989; Mezey & King, 1992; Ryan & Lane, 1991).

The complexities and potential success of an integrated approach to the treatment of child sexual abuse is illustrated by the following composite case, based on research and evaluation studies in Canada:

Joan was 12 years old when she complained to a teacher about her stepfather's sexual abuse. Two events precipitated this revelation: a presentation to her elementary school on sexual abuse by the local sexual assault center; and her father's recently expressed sexual interest in her 10-year-old sister. The teacher consulted a guidance counselor, who reassured Joan that she had done the right thing. In line with agreed protocols between the school board and social services, a specialized child protection worker arranged for Joan to be seen by a pediatric gynaecologist at the children's hospital. This forensic evidence was later produced in court. Similar procedures were used in the case of Sharon, the 10-year-old sister, and statements were taken from both girls by a detective who specialized in cases of abuse. Mother was disbelieving at first, but faced with the evidence from both her girls soon began to offer them support. Stepfather denied the abuse. Mother and the girls left the home, to stay with mother's sister. Stepfather was charged, but continued to deny the assaults. Joan was seen by a counselor specializing in integrated therapy for abuse victims. Joan was depressed, had suicidal thoughts, and an eating disorder. Sharon, her younger sister, had no obvious psychological symptoms. After reassurance, mother joined a mother's group, and the younger daughter entered group therapy also. Joan entered another group later, when her immediate psychiatric crisis was resolved. Both Sharon and Joan were supported by a family court clinic which introduced them to the procedures used by the court, and reduced their anxiety about having to give evidence. In court they were allowed to give evidence from behind a screen. The stepfather was convicted, and received a four-year jail term. At the time of sentence it was revealed that the man had a prior conviction for sexual assault of minors. Mother immediately began divorce proceedings, and moved back to the family home, which the stepfather was required to leave as a condition of bail. Sharon continued to receive individual therapy for a year because of continuing mental health problems. At follow-up two years later both girls had good mental health, recovered self-esteem, and were making good progress in school.

This case represents a "best case" scenario—even though the father denied responsibility, the mutually corroborating evidence from the two girls as well as forensic evidence was sufficient to enable a conviction. The abused girls had good therapy and support during the crucial stages preceding the trial, as well as long-term therapy. Mother, too, was supportive of her daughters.

It is still true, however, that "worst case" scenarios exist, in which the abused child is blamed for making false accusations, is labeled and scapegoated, receives no help from counseling or social service agencies, runs from home, becomes involved in drug subcultures, and spends time in a youth detention center. Services for sexually abused, runaway youth are not well developed, nor are foster parents well trained to cope with a behaviorally disturbed or sexually acting out teenager who has received no specific treatment for abuse (Raychaba, 1991). Sexualized behavior is one of the sequels of sexual abuse of children (Friedrich, 1993), and unprepared foster parents and child care staff may be involved in further sexual assaults on a disturbed child whose sexualized behaviors seem to invite them.

Mother's Role and the Feminist Perspective

The role of the mother in supporting her daughter after within-family abuse has been discovered. Revelation of the abuse presents the mother with a mental health crisis, when she realizes that a man she loved and trusted has deceived her, and abused her daughter. In a study of mothers of sexually-abused children referred to child protection workers, we found the less than 10 percent had any suspicions or knowledge of the abuse (Bagley & King, 1990). This estimate agrees with that of other researchers (Johnston, 1992).

Mothers in families where a child had been abused had some unique features (in comparison with control families): at least half of the mothers with a sexually abused daughter had themselves suffered prolonged sexual abuse in childhood. (More research is needed to clarify the dynamics involved in the low percentage of mothers with sexually-abused daughters who had any suspicions or knowledge of the abuse, when at least half of those mothers themselves had been sexually abused; while one might expect previously abused mothers to be more aware or vigilant to potential abuse of their daughters, they may, in fact, cope with suspicious signs of abuse with the psychological defenses of denial, suppression, or repression because of associated negative emotions that are elicited for them.) Two-thirds had escaped from families marked by neglect and abuse by marrying while still in their teens; one-fifth married when they were aged 16 or less. Divorce and remarriage rates were high, but some of the men who married young teenagers went on to sexually molest their daughters; it is probable that these men had pedophile impulses manifested in marrying a young girl, and then in assaulting her daughters later. One-half of the women escaped first marriages marked by domination and physical abuse only to enter relationships with seemingly similar men: in these new relationships the stepfather or cohabitee puts the daughters (and sons) of the woman at considerable risk of sexual abuse. Many of these women had entered a cycle of "learned helplessness," drifting hopelessly from one abusive relationship to the next, unable to provide a psychological climate in which children could appeal to their mother for protection. Nevertheless, these women rarely had any inkling about what was actually happening. Revelation of the abuse came as a profound shock, and many women began to relive the trauma of their own childhood abuse. Mental health interventions are crucially important for women at this stage, first as individual therapy and then in the form of mother's groups which provide mutual support and shared insights. Many of these women recover self-esteem and enter a phase of self-actualization in which they regroup their lives and escape exploitation in family, work, and social relationships (Bagley & Young, 1990).

The feminist perspective on child sexual abuse, which was so valuable in demonstrating the extent of child sexual abuse and the damage it imposed on victims, is also a relevant voice in providing mothers of victims with new strengths (Adams, Trachtenberg, & Fisher, 1992). Feminist social and group work can support women while they learn to become psychologically independent of men following the breakup of a first marriage. Even today, the normative pattern is for a divorced woman to relatively quickly enter a relationship with another male, sometimes with very negative consequences for her children. These consequences include a variety of forms of physical and emotional abuse: families in which a stepfather "adopts" the children of his new partner have high rates of disruption involving an acting-out child (Bagley & Young, 1993).

Conclusions: The Paradoxes of Child Sexual Abuse

I have referred frequently in this chapter to paradoxes, outcomes or events that seem contradictory but yet have logic in demonstrating the complexity of child sexual abuse, and the challenges offered to research, prevention, and therapy. By way of conclusion I offer the following paradoxes:

1. Child sexual abuse has existed at all times in recorded history, and yet its extent and potentially negative impact on the children and adolescents involved has only been fully recognized in the past two decades.

2. Recent research has established that about half of those children (i.e., those under the age of 17) who have a sexual relationship with an older person do not appear to suffer any long-term harm as a result. According to Kilpatrick (1992),

> Questions regarding the confusion of mores with actual harm done are raised by the finding that older partners are not found to be a significant factor in correlations with later adult functioning. This finding challenges the linear assumption that all children are victimized by any type of sexual experience with a person who is 5 or more years older than them. One must guard against making assumptions that have no empirical bases and against buttressing existing mores that may be actually harmful to children and adolescents. (p. 121)

Nevertheless *unwanted* sexual acts do cause severe long-term psychological harm to a substantial minority of children. Paradoxically, when a child enters into a sexual relationship with an adult "willingly" (despite difficulties for the child in giving informed consent to such a relationship), no significant long-term impact on mental health can usually be detected (Kilpatrick, 1992). I argue, nevertheless that adult sexual contact with children is morally wrong (as well as being in many cases illegal) because no one can predict at the outset whether or not any particular child will in the long run suffer psychological harm through the relationship. These potential risks for the child are far too grave for society to be tolerant about adult sexual involvement with children.

3. It is paradoxical that what many researchers and clinicians describe as "incest" is not in fact incest in a legal or sociological sense. The incest taboo does to a large extent protect adolescents from being forced to have sexual intercourse with close relatives. However, incestuous abuse that stops short of heterosexual intercourse is quite common, especially that involving a stepfather or relatives outside of the nuclear family. While at least 5 percent of both male and female children experience prolonged sexual assaults by an adult or older person, less than 1 percent of all children are victims of incest, as defined by criminal law. We offer an alternative definition, "incestuous abuse," to cover a wide spectrum of sexual assaults on children by a variety of relatives of family members, including stepfathers.

4. Freud has been rightly blamed for distorting his original findings of incestuous assault on children as a common precursor of adult neurosis. Nevertheless, analysts working within the Freudian tradition have provided valuable insight into why incestuous abuse can be so damaging for a child's psychosexual development. Ego psychologists who draw some inspiration from Freud, but who have significantly modified his paradigm, offer a valuable model for therapists: failure to achieve a level of self-esteem that is adequate for coping with various stressors and the development of an identity that incorporates consciously or unconsciously the impact of past trauma combine to prevent adequate solution of identity tasks at various stages of child and adolescent development.

5. Paradoxically, a single act of rape perpetrated upon a child may be less traumatic than a more gradual seduction imposed by an older person. Often the child will receive support from both her family and professionals after a single assault that the child is able to report to an adult. But the subtle and secret seduction of a child often imposes a psychologically corrupting burden that can gravely impair the young person's psychosocial development.

6. It is cruel paradox that those children least able to cope with the burden of sexual seduction are those most vulnerable to its effects. Children with good self-esteem, a trusting and confident relationship with an adult, and well-developed ego strengths are likely to report any attempted or achieved sexual assault immediately. However, a child whose ego development has been undermined by loss of a parent, problematic attachments

to adults, and depressed self-esteem because of emotional and physical abuse or neglect is particularly vulnerable, and is rarely able to prevent or report continuing sexual assaults. Unwanted, imposed sexual acts (particularly incestuous abuse) are likely to be gravely harmful to the child's identity development.

We need to have better information on both vulnerability and resilience of children faced by acute stress of the kind that sexual abuse may impose (cf. Kolko, 1992). While my own ideas on preexisting self-esteem and subsequent identity development as important factors predicting psychosocial outcomes for abused children are supported by evidence from various Canadian studies (Bagley, 1991a), replications and extensions of this thesis in other cultures (the United States, Europe, and Asia) are important (cf. Kendall-Tackett, Williams, & Finkelhor, 1993).

7. Just as there are subtypes of victim reaction, so there are subtypes of men who sexually offend against children. It is an ironic paradox that the determined and manipulative pedophile can both find access to children and through psychological wiles escape detection or prosecution, while the regressed offender, in his pathetic retreat into the psychosexual relationships of childhood, is the type of offender most likely to plead guilty when detected, and also the individual most likely to receive jail time. Another paradox of offending is that harsh sentences that reflect an attempt at deterrence, or a sense of community outrage, rarely have their intended effect and may actually discourage the cooperation of abusers with those offering therapy to the child.

8. One group is defined by paradox: males having been victims of sexual abuse themselves become, in adolescence and adulthood, sexual abusers, sometimes with a pedophile fixation on young children. A variety of factors may explain this reality: trying to gain mastery over the earlier abuse by repeating it, but in a controlling manner; socially learned behavior, reinforced by sexual stimuli; and attachment to the abuser, in youth whose own families provided imperfect emotional attachments.

9. Some prevention programs aim to give children knowledge about "bad touching" and ways in which such touching may be avoided or reported. Yet when the large majority of North American households impose physical pain on children as a means of control and socialization, prevention programs are unlikely to be fully effective until *all* bad touching is ended, including the beating, punching, kicking, caning, and strapping of children by adult "caretakers."

10. Even though we now have the skills, knowledge, and experience to offer successful therapy programs for children and their families following sexual abuse, the number of current and former victims who need help in childhood, adolescence, and young adulthood greatly exceed the resources of social service and counseling agencies. A child "protected" after sexual

abuse may drift through foster homes and youth facilities without receiving adequate help, even when the professional knowledge to offer such help has been developed.

11. Some youth act out in seemingly antisocial ways following sexual abuse: they are often blamed, processed, and incarcerated for such behavior, without the root causes being addressed. Blaming the victim may satisfy society's moral outrage, but in such condemnation there is no justice, and no healing.

References

Adams, J., Trachtenberg, S., & Fisher, J. (1992). Feminist views of child sexual abuse. In W. O'Donohue and J. Geer (Eds.), *The sexual abuse of children: Theory and research* (pp. 359–396). Hillsdale, NJ: Erlbaum.

Alexander, P. (1992). Application of attachment theory to the study of child sexual abuse. *Journal of Consulting and Clinical Psychology, 60,* 185–197.

Allen, C. (1980). *Daddy's girl: A very personal memoir.* Toronto: McLelland and Stewart.

Armstrong, L. (1978). *Kiss Daddy goodnight.* New York: Pocket Books.

Babins-Wagner, R. (1991). Development and evaluation of a family systems approach to the treatment of child sexual abuse. *Journal of Child and Youth Care, 10,* 103–128.

Bagley, C. (1969). Incest behavior and incest taboo. *Social Problems, 16,* 505–519.

Bagley, C. (1985). Child sexual abuse and juvenile prostitution. *Canadian Journal of Public Health, 76,* 65–66.

Bagley, C. (1989a). Prevalence and correlates of unwanted sexual acts in childhood. *Canadian Journal of Public Health, 80,* 295–296.

Bagley, C. (1989b). Profiles of youthful suicide: Disrupted development and current stressors. *Psychological Reports, 65,* 234.

Bagley, C. (1990). Development of a measure of unwanted sexual abuse; Validity of a measure of child sexual abuse; Is the prevalence of child sexual abuse increasing? *Psychological Reports, 66,* 401–402, 449–450, 1037–1038.

Bagley, C. (1991a). Psychological sequels of child sexual abuse: Canadian and European studies. *Annals of Sex Research, 4,* 23–48.

Bagley, C. (1991b). Mental health and the sexual abuse of children and adolescents. In J. Veevers (Ed.), *Community and change in marriage and the family* (pp. 314–325). Toronto: Holt.

Bagley, C. (1991c). The prevalence and mental health sequels of child sexual abuse in a community sample of women aged 19 to 27. *Canadian Journal of Community Mental Health, 10,* 103–116.

Bagley, C. (1992a). Characteristics of 60 children and adolescents with a history of sexual assault against others: Evidence from a comparative study. *Journal of Forensic Psychiatry, 3,* 299–311.

Bagley, C. (1992b). Changing profiles of a typology of youth suicide in Canada. *Canadian Journal of Public Health, 83,* 169–170.

Bagley, C. (1992c). Development of an adolescent stress scale for use by school counsellors: Construct validity in terms of depression, self-esteem and suicidal ideation. *School Psychology International, 13,* 31–49.

Bagley, C., Burrows, B., & Yaworski, C. (1990). Street kids and adolescent prostitution: A challenge for legal and social services. In N. Bala, J. Hornick, and R. Vogl (Eds.), *Canadian child welfare law: Children, families and the state* (pp. 109–131). Toronto: Thompson.

Bagley, C., & King, K. (1990). *Child sexual abuse: The search for healing.* London: Tavistock-Routledge.

Bagley, C., & McDonald, M. (1984). Adult mental health sequels of child sexual abuse, physical abuse and neglect in maternally separated children. *Canadian Journal of Community Mental Health, 3,* 15–26.

Bagley, C., & Ramsay, R. (1986). Sexual abuse in childhood: Psychological outcomes and implications for social work practice. *Journal of Social Work and Human Sexuality, 4,* 33–47.

Bagley, C., Rodberg, G., Wellings, D., Moosa-Mitha, M., & Young, L. (1993). *Physical and sexual child abuse and the development of dissociative personality traits: Canadian and British evidence from adolescent child welfare and child care populations.* Unpublished manuscript. Calgary, Alberta, Canada: University of Calgary.

Bagley, C., & Thomlison, R. (1991). *Child sexual abuse: Critical perspectives on prevention, intervention, and treatment.* Toronto: Wall and Emerson.

Bagley, C., & Thurston, W. (1989). *Preventing child sexual abuse: Key research.* (University of Calgary Rehabilitation and Health Monographs, no. 18). Calgary, Canada: University of Calgary Press.

Bagley, C., Wood, M., & Khumar, H. (1990). Suicide and careless death in an aboriginal population. *Canadian Journal of Community Mental Health, 29,* 127–142.

Bagley, C., Wood, M., & Young, L. (1993). Victim to abuser: Mental health and behavioral sequels of child sexual abuse in a community survey of young adult males. *Child Abuse and Neglect,* in press.

Bagley, C., & Young, L. (1987). Juvenile prostitution and child child sexual abuse: A controlled study. *Canadian Journal of Community Mental Health, 6,* 5–26.

Bagley, C., & Young, L. (1990). Depression, self-esteem and suicidal behavior as sequels of sexual abuse in childhood: Research and therapy. In M. Rothery and G. Cameron (Eds.), *Child maltreatment: Expanding our concepts of helping* (pp. 183–219). Hillsdale, NJ: Erlbaum.

Bagley, C., & Young, L. (1993). *Transracial and international adoptions: A mental health perspective.* Aldershot, UK: Ashgate.

Bernstein, E., & Putnam, F. (1986). Development, reliability and validity of a dissociation scale. *Journal of Nervous and mental Diseases, 174,* 727–735.

Bifulco, A., Brown, G., & Adler, Z. (1991). Early sexual abuse and clinical depression in adult life. *British Journal of Psychiatry, 159,* 115–122.

Bixler, R. (1992). Do we/should we behave like animals? In W. O'Donohue & J. Geer (Eds.), *The sexual abuse of children: Theory and research* (pp. 81–107). Hillsdale, NJ: Erlbaum.

Bolton, F., Morris, L., & MacEachron, A. (1989). *Males at risk: The other side of child sexual abuse.* Newbury Park, CA: Sage.

Brady, K. (1979). *Father's days: A true story of incest.* New York: Dell.

Brewin, C., Andrews, B., & Gotlieb, I. (1993). *Psychological Bulletin, 113,* 82–98.

Briere, J. (1989). *Therapy for adults molested as children: Beyond survival.* New York: Springer.

Briere, J., & Runtz, M. (1990). Differential adult symptomatology associated with three types of child abuse histories. *Child Abuse and Neglect, 14,* 357–363.

Bukowski, W. (1992). Sexual abuse and maladjustment considered from the perspective of normal development processes. In W. O'Donohue & J. Geer, *The sexual abuse of children: Theory and research* (pp. 261–282). Hillsdale, NJ: Erlbaum.

Chenais, J. (1981). *Hîstoîre de vîolence dans l'ouest.* Paris: University of Paris Press. (in French)

Cole, P., & Putnam, F. (1992). Effect of incest on self and social functioning: A developmental psychopathology perspective. *Journal of Consulting and Clinical Psychology, 60,* 174–180.

Downing, J., Jenkins, S., & Fisher, G. (1988). A comparison of psychodynamic and reinforcement treatment with sexually abused children. *Elementary School Guidance and Counselling, 22,* 291–298.

Erikson, E. (1980), *Identity and the life cycle.* New York: Norton.

Feister, S., & Gay, M. (1991). Sadistic personality disorder: Review of data and recommendations for DSM-IV. *Journal of Personality Disorders, 5,* 376–385.

Finkelhor, D. (1979). *Sexually victimized children.* New York: Free Press.

Fox, R. (1980). *The red lamp of incest.* London: Hutchison.

Friedrich, W. (1990). *Psychotherapy for sexually abused children and their families.* New York: Norton.

Friedrich, W. (1993). Sexual victimization and sexual behavior in children. *Child Abuse and Neglect, 17,* 59–66,

Garrison, C., McKeown, R., Valois, R., & Vincent, M. (1993). Aggression, substance use, and suicidal behaviors in high school students. *American Journal of Public Health, 83,* 179–184.

Giarretto, H. (1982). *Integrated treatment of child sexual abuse: A treatment and training manual.* Palo Alto, CA: Science and Behavior Books.

Hunter, J. (1991). A comparison of the psychosocial maladjustment of adult males and females sexually molested as children. *Journal of Interpersonal Violence, 6,* 205–217.

Jackson, J., Calhoun, K., Amick, A., Maddever, H., & Habif, V. (1990). Young adult women who report childhood intrafamilial sexual abuse: Subsequent adjustment. *Archives of Sexual Behavior, 19,* 211–221.

James, B. (1989). *Treating traumatized children: New insights and creative interventions.* Lexington, MA: Lexington Books.

James, W. (1890). Selections from *The Principles of Psychology.* In H. Thayer (Ed.), *Pragmatism: The classic writings* (pp. 135–179). New York: New American Library.

Jennings, A., & Armsworth, M. (1992). Ego development in women with histories of sexual abuse. *Child Abuse and Neglect, 16,* 553–565.

Johnston, J. (1992). *Mothers of incest survivors.* Bloomington: University of Indiana Press.

Kaplan, H. (1980). *Deviant behavior in defense of self.* New York: Academic Press.

Kendall-Tackett, K., Williams, L., & Finkelhor, D. (1993). Impact of sexual abuse on children: A review and synthesis of recent empirical studies. *Psychological Bulletin, 113,* 164–180.

Kilpatrick, A. (1992). *Long-range effects of child and adolescent sexual experiences: Myths, mores and menaces.* Hillsdale, NJ: Erlbaum.

Kolko, D. (1992). Characteristics of child victims of physical violence: Research findings and clinical implications. *Journal of Interpersonal Violence, 7,* 244–276.

Larson, N., & Maddock, J. (1986). Structural and functional variables in incest family systems. In T. Trepper & M. Barrett (Eds.), *Assessment and treatment of intrafamilial sexual abuse* (pp. 104–128). New York: Haworth Press.

Levine, H. (1990). *Adult analysis of child sexual abuse.* Hillsdale, NJ: Analytic Press.

Mandell, J., & Damon, L. (1989). *Group treatment for sexually abused children.* New York: Guildford Press.

Mannarino, A., Cohen, J., Smith, J., & Moore-Motily, S. (1991). Six- and twelve-month follow-up of sexually abused girls. *Journal of Interpersonal Violence, 6,* 494–511.

Maslow, A. (1973). *Dominance, self-esteem and self-actualization.* California: Brooks-Cole.

Meiselman, K. (1990). *Resolving the trauma of incest.* San Francisco: Jossey-Bass.

Mezey, G., & King, M. (1992). *Male victims of sexual assault.* New York: Oxford University Press.

Morrow, G., & Sorell, G. (1989). Factors affecting self-esteem, depression, and negative behaviors in sexually abused female adolescents. *Journal of Marriage and the Family, 51, 677–686.*

O'Donohue, W., & Elliott, A. (1992). Treatment of the sexually abused child: A review. *Journal of Clinical Psychology, 21,* 218–228.

Olmstead, R., O'Malley, P., & Bentler, P. (1991). Longitudinal assessment of the relationship between self-esteem, fatalism, loneliness, and substance abuse. *Journal of Social Behavior and Personality, 6,* 749–770.

Parker, H., & Parker, S. (1985). Father-daughter sexual abuse. *American Journal of Orthopsychiatry, 56,* 531–549.

Putnam, F. (1989). *Diagnosis and treatment of multiple personality disorder.* New York: Guilford Press.

Putnam, F. (1993). Dissociative disorders in children: Behavioral profiles and problems. *Child Abuse and Neglect, 17,* 39–45.

Raychaba, N. (1991). We get a life sentence: Young people in care speak out on child sexual abuse. *Journal of Child and Youth Care, Fall Volume,* 129–139.

Renovoize, J. (1982). *Incest: A family pattern.* London: Routledge.

Ross, C. (1985). DSM-III: Problems in diagnosing partial forms of multiple personality disorder. *Proceedings of the Royal Society of Medicine, 78,* 933–936.

Ross, C. (1989). *Multiple personality disorder: Diagnosis, clinical features, and treatment.* New York: Wiley.

Rush, F. (1980). *The best kept secret: Sexual abuse of children.* New York: McGraw-Hill.

Russell, D. (1986). *The secret trauma: Incest in the loves of girls and women.* New York: Basic Books.

Ryan, G., & Lane, S. (1991). *Juvenile sexual offending: Causes, consequences and corrections*. Lexington, MA: Lexington Books.

Silbert, M., & Pines, A. (1983). Early sexual exploitation as an influence on prostitution. *Social Work, 28*, 285–289.

Sorrenti-Little, L., Bagley C., & Robertson, S. (1986). An operational definition of the long-term harmfulness of sexual relations with peers and adults by young children. *Canadian Children, 9*, 46–57.

Spitzer, R., Feister, S., Gay, M., & Pfohl, B. (1991). Results of a survey of forensic psychiatrists on the validity of the sadistic personality diagnosis. *American Journal of Psychiatry, 148*, 875–879.

Stekel, W. (1926). *Peculiarities of behaviour* (2 vols.). London: Williams and Norgate.

Stephens, M., Grinnell, R., Thomlison, B., & Krysik, J. (1991). Child sexual abuse and police disposition: A Canadian study. *Journal of Child and Youth Care, Fall Volume*, 53–65.

Straus, M., Gelles, R., & Smith, C. (1990). *Physical violence in American families: Risk factors and adaptations to violence in 8,145 families*. New Brunswick, NJ: Transaction Press.

Thomlison, B., & Bagley, C. (Eds.) (1990) *Child sexual abuse: Expanding the research base on program and treatment outcomes*. Calgary, Canada: University of Calgary Press.

Trepper, T., & Barrett, M. (1989). *Systemic treatment of incest: A therapeutic handbook*. New York: Brunner/Mazel.

Vander May, B. (1992). Theories of incest. In W. O'Donohue & J. Geer (Eds.), *The sexual abuse of children: Theory and research* (pp. 204–260). Hillsdale, NJ: Erlbaum.

Walker, L. (1992). Helping heal violated children's trauma. *Contemporary Psychology, 37*, 46–48.

Wasserman, S., & Rosenfeld, A. (1992). An overview of the history of child sexual abuse and Sigmund Freud's contribution. In W. O'Donohue & J. Geer (Eds.), *The sexual abuse of children: Theory and research* (pp. 38–48). Hillsdale, NJ: Erlbaum.

Weinrott, M., & Saylor, M. (1991). Self-report of crimes committed by sex offenders. *Journal of Interpersonal Violence, 6*, 286–300.

Wells, M. (1990). *Canada's law on sexual abuse*. Ottawa: Department of Justice, Government of Canada.

Woody, G., McLellan, A., Luborsky, L., & O'Brien, C. (1985). Sociopathy and psychotherapy outcome. *Archives of General Psychiatry, 42*, 1081–1086.

Wyatt, G., Guthrie, D., & Notgrass, C. (1992). Differential effects of women's child sexual abuse and subsequent sexual revictimization. *Journal of Consulting and Clinical Psychology, 60*, 167–173.

Young, L. (1992). Sexual abuse and the problem of embodiment. *Child Abuse and Neglect, 16*, 89–100.

Young, L., & Bagley, C. (1982). Self-esteem, self-concept and the development of identity: Theoretical overview. In G. Verma (Ed.), *Self-concept, achievement and multicultural education* (pp. 41–59). London: Macmillan.

Zingaro, L. (1987). Working with street kids. *Journal of Child and Youth Care, 3*, 63–70.

8
Child and Adolescent Sex Rings and Pornography

Ann Wolbert Burgess
Carol R. Hartman

T he number of reported cases of child sexual abuse is increasing. This increase prompts questions as to whether it is due to better reporting by victims, to a more responsive criminal justice system, or to increase sexual deviance in U.S. society. For clinicians, however, the fact remains that skills are needed for the assessment, diagnosis, and treatment of child victims of sexual abuse. This chapter will outline the research and clinical findings to date on the phenomena of child and adolescent sex rings and the use of pornography. This chapter will define these terms, provide case examples, and suggest assessment and treatment interventions.

Child Sex Rings

The study of the sexual victimization of children has focused primarily on incest or family-member (intra familial) abuse of female children. Recently, reports have indicated a growing number of abusers who are outside the family (extra familial) and who abuse both males and female children. Furthermore, reports from the United States (Burgess, Hartman, McCausland, & Powers, 1984), the United Kingdom (Wild & Wynne, 1986), and the Netherlands (Jonker & Jonker-Bakker, 1991) emphasize the need for health professionals and law enforcement agencies to increase their efforts concerning sex ring cases involving multiple victims of the same offender.

"Sex ring crime" is a term describing sexual victimization in which there are one or more adult offenders and several children who are aware of each other's participation. There are three different types of child sex rings. The *solo sex ring* involves one, or occasionally two, adult perpetrators and multiple children (Burgess, Groth, & McCausland, 1981). No exchange of photographs nor any sexual activities with other adults takes

164

place. By contrast, a *syndicated ring* involves multiple adult perpetrators, multiple child victims, and a wide range of item exchanges, including child pornography and sexual activities. At a level between these two types of rings is the *transition ring*, in which the children and the pornography involving them are exchanged between adults, and in which money often changes hands (Burgess, 1984). These three types of rings will be described in some detail in this chapter with case illustrations.

Child pornography can be defined as any film, video, or print medium depicting sexually explicit conduct involving a child. Simply stated, child pornography is photographs or films depicting children being sexually molested. Sexually explicit conduct includes sexual intercourse, bestiality, masturbation, sadomasochistic abuse, and lewd exhibition of the genitals or pubic area. The child or children visually represented in child pornography have not reached the age of consent (Lanning, 1984).

Solo Sex Rings

Solo sex rings are characterized by the involvement of multiple children in sexual activities with one adult, usually male, who recruits the victims into his illicit activities by legitimate means. This offender can be assessed by his methods for gaining access to and sexual entraping children, establishing control of the children, and maintaining the isolation and secrecy of the sexual activities, as well as by the particulars of ring activities. The events surrounding disclosure of the ring and the victims' physical and psychological symptoms are also important elements of the ring. Victims can be both male and female, and their ages can range from infancy to adolescence. The distinguishing factor of solo sex rings is the age preference of the offender. Victims are typically found in nursery schools, babysitting and daycare services, youth groups and camps.

Case Examples

Case 1. A 26-year-old single male, employed by a local YMCA as an accountant and sports coach, became sexually involved with three boys, ages 8 to 9. His sexual activity continued for over a year, during which time he recruited many other boys. The ring was exposed after he selected two brothers for activity. One brother told the other brother about the activity; together they told their mother; and she informed the police. Although the boys were in this sports program for over a year, they claimed only one incident of sexual contact.

Case 2. An 18-year-old single male, employed as a sports coach by a YMCA in a city 25 miles from the offender in Case 1, became sexually involved with five boys ages 8 to 9. The sexual activity continued for more than 5 years until a new male roommate of the offender discovered video-tapes of nude boys and reported his discovery to law enforcement officials.

Dynamics of Child Sexual Abuse

In brief, sexual encounters between adults and children usually fall into a predictable pattern, involving access to and sexual entrapment of the child by the adult, subsequent efforts to isolate and maintain the secrecy of the sexual activities, and ultimate disclosure of the victimization which includes short- and long-term outcomes and impacts for the child and his family. In outlining these phases with the cases under consideration, one notes the consistency in the patterns and phases.

Access and Entrapment Stage. The sexual abuse of a child is a consciously planned and premeditated behavior. The adult is usually someone known both to the child and to the parents who has ready access to the child. The offender stands in a relationship of dominance to the child. Ambivalence as a component of the decision-making process is a characteristic of the young person's emotional life, and the offender trades on this ambivalence. The adult's desire for domination of the child is aimed at breaking the internal resistance of the subordinate child. After gaining access to the child, the adult engages the child in the illicit activity through the power and authority that adulthood conveys to the child, as well as by misrepresenting moral standards.

In the case examples, the adult was an authority figure vis-à-vis his position as sports director with a local youth group. The families were supportive of their sons being involved in YMCA sports programs because of the Y's reputation for promoting the positive development of young males. While in their roles as sports directors, both offenders became acquainted with the young boys and almost immediately began paying special attention to specific boys at the YMCA itself, during the activities at the YMCA's summer day camp, and when they were invited (singly or in groups) to the abusers' homes.

Isolation Stage. When an offender is successful in abusing his victim, he must conceal his deviant behavior from others. More often than not, he will try to pledge the victim to secrecy in several ways. Secrecy strengthens the adult's power and control over the child and perpetuates the sexual activity. Clinicians must understand that the child usually tries to keep the secret; indeed, some children never tell anyone about their sexual abuse. There are many reasons why the abuse is kept secret. The child may fear people will not believe his reports of such behavior; may fear that people will blame him for the activity; may fear there will be punishment for disclosure; may fear that the adult will carry out his threats; or may even want to protect the abuser.

In the case examples, sex education was the ploy used by the coaches. They programmed the boys they targeted for abuse to believe that they needed to be educated about sex and that the kind of activity they prompted was naturally practiced between men and their students. Magazines depicting heterosexual acts were shown to the boys to normalize the activity. The boys did not tell about the abuser's acts because of loyalty to their coach and their belief that they were very special to this adult. Most of the boys were unaware of each other's involvement with the same adult.

Sexual Activities. A wide range of sexual behaviors may occur between the adult and child as the result of a combination of psychological pressure and/or physical force. There may be a slow progression of advancing sexual acts perpetrated with the characteristics of sexual seduction or the acts may be forceful and sudden to the child.

In the case examples, youths described sexual acts including kissing, fondling, mutual masturbation, and oral and anal sex. Nude photographs and videos were taken of the youths without their knowledge. The boys were also shown sexually oriented materials with heterosexual content and female-to-female sex and pornographic videos.

Encapsulation Stage. As part of the isolation stage, the child is trapped in the sexual activity; he must participate yet also must be silent. Much of the psychological injury derived from the exploitation can be linked back to the manner of entrapment, the length of time of encapsulation, and the nature of the sexual activity. Children are confused over the use of power and authority, with resulting disorganizing impact on their thinking. As the abuse continues, their belief about sex between adults and children shifts from "This is wrong" to "This is right." Some think they can intervene and stop. The child often tries to protest the activity and begins to reenact and repeat the abuse, first to himself and then to others. This resistance is normal and usually present if one looks carefully for it. However, there is also a component of arousal disharmony, and because of the traumatic confusion associated with learning the behavior, the behavior is often reenacted.

Disclosure Stage. There are usually two ways child sexual abuse is discovered: accidental disclosure and purposeful disclosure. In accidental disclosure, a third party may observe symptoms of abuse in the child. In purposeful disclosure, a child consciously decides to tell the parent or an outsider about the abuse. With disclosure, the social meaning of the abuse becomes known, that is, the child must deal with the reactions of people (i.e., parents, friends, authorities) who now know about the abuse. It becomes important now that people believe the child, understand the confusion and fear that permeates the child's abuse experience, and take protective action on behalf of the child.

In Case 1, disclosure occurred when one boy told his mother about the abuse and the police were called. In Case 2, a new roommate of the offender found videotapes of the offender with nude boys and notified the police. After the offenders' arrests, some of the boys continued to deny their involvement with them until their photographs and videotapes surfaced. Others minimized the amount of sexual contact they had had with the offender. Denial is a major defense noted in male youths.

Psychological Injury Imposed on Children by Sexual Abuse

Psychological injury results from the control nature of the dynamics of the sex rings. The repetitive secret nature of the sexual abuse requires the victim to psychologically compartmentalize (encapsulate) the event, that is, to keep it separate from the rest of his or her life. Through this process the coping mechanism of dissociation is derived ("I thought of other things while he was doing it."). Inherent in the dissociation mechanism is cognitive confusion. At some level, the child knows that the sexual activity is wrong because it has to be kept secret. Thus, he does not let the outside world know about it. Social ties are broken. Commitment and social ties to values lose their color and dominance.

Further along in the dissociation phase the mechanism of splitting comes into play. Disruption is evidenced through the inhibition of normal developmental stages and the splitting of parental relationships. The abused child exhibits a strong lack of trust in people, and normal attachment or nonsexual bonding to people is weak or missing. To attach in a social way requires a degree of trust and faith, but this component of normal development has been shattered and destroyed for abused youths. Rather than developing a normal trusting social bond with others, the abused child develops a bond to the perpetrator and their shared sexual activities. Abused children are trapped by the abusing relationship.

Abused youths are typically unable to exert any action to protect themselves and to prevent or stop their own exploitation. Self-protection is inhibited and adult protection nonexistent. Because this inhibition cuts the abused children off from self-assertive behaviors, their aggressive drive is compromised and displaced in its direction. Thus, the abused children manifest anger and aggression in symbolic and/or inappropriate behaviors.

Impact on Victims

In the case examples, several issues impacted on the youths' lives.

There was betrayal of a trusted relationship. The boys were programmed by their sports coach to be overly attached to him. The youths were at a critical developmental period and thus vulnerable to an adult male who showed them attention. The coach gave the boys what appeared to them to be love and attention, meeting the narcissistic wish of a child to be the center of attention. In return, in exchange for being taught about sex and for being made to feel special, the coach demanded secrecy about their activities.

Symptoms that developed as a result of sexual abuse included intrusive thoughts and phobic/avoidance behavior. Moreover, the youths became unusually quiet, confused, less active, and less energetic. High-risk behaviors, depression, moodiness, and preoccupation were noted. Other symptoms included difficulty sleeping (trouble falling asleep, sleeping restlessly, or increased sleeping), nightmares, and startling easily.

Following disclosure, the abused boys exhibited difficulty listening, not hearing people clearly, and trouble concentrating and paying attention. Some of the youths skipped school, ran away from home, started fights, forced others to have sex with them, hurt animals on purpose, hurt other people deliberately, intentionally damaged things not their own, set fires, lied, stole, and robbed. Sexual problems surfaced. Some of the boys questioned their sexual identity.

A brief synopsis of the 8 boys' response to the trauma provides a perspective on the variance of response. Follow-up was conducted 7 years after disclosure on Case 1 and 3 years later in Case 2.

Victims of Case 1

Adam. Adam, age 16, reported being sexually abused over a month's time 7 years earlier while he attended local YMCA activities including a day summer camp. In addition, he went on overnight camping trips with the offender. The abuse occurred the summer between 3rd and 4th grade when Adam was 9. His mother remembers Adam saying he did not want to go out with the coach and noted that she would make excuses for why he could not go. The police called the mother at work to tell her they were arresting the coach and that they had found videos of Adam nude. The mother reported that when she talked to Adam, he "turned white."

The mother was concerned because Adam was very quiet and did not talk much. His grades were so low that he was unable to qualify for varsity sports. Symptoms noted by the mother included moodiness, day dreaming, lack of concentration, and getting angry very quickly. He was drinking alcohol. His self-esteem had been affected.

The mother did not think that Adam was performing to his potential. She said that he had no goals and had lost all his ambition. He did want to work that summer and had made plans to drive up north to work for an uncle. The mother said that Adam's pattern was to avoid confrontations, that is, to run away from and not work out any problems. She was concerned that if his grades kept deteriorating and his motivation continued to drop, he would not finish high school.

On testing, Adam's propensity for avoidant defenses came out in the personality traits of suspiciousness and mistrust. He lacked the belief that he could relate to and rely on other people, and this lack undermined his learning both in the formal sense and in the emotional interpersonal sense. His problems are further compounded by his confused sense of who he is. He tries to manage with overdeveloped thoughts and responses to control confusion and extreme mood shifts and interpersonal conflict.

Bob. Bob, age 16, was sexually abused over a period of time when he was 9 and 10. Bob participated in swimming and soccer at the local YMCA. During that time, the soccer coach pressured him to view sexually oriented materials, and then fondled and molested his genitals both with his hand and with a vibrator. He photographed Bob removing his clothes and showering. He also attempted oral sex with Bob.

Bob's propensity for avoidant defenses were revealed in by his drawings of partial figures and in various personality traits. For example, he did not have a secure sense of who he was; he felt victimized and yearned for a strong person to show him what to do. Bob admitted that he did not like talking about the abuse he suffered, and also admitted that it never left his mind. Part of him thinks he needs counseling, but another part does not want it. He does not trust people or feel good about himself. He failed the 7th grade the year the offender was apprehended.

Carl. Carl, age 17, and Bob's brother, was sexually abused over a short time period. Carl was at the YMCA for several years while the soccer coach was also there. Records and interview indicated that the offender involved Carl in a series of sexual acts, including manual masturbation, masturbation with a vibrator, pressuring him to play strip poker, recording sexual acts on a video recorder, watching Carl undress and take a shower, encouraging him to perform oral sex, and viewing pornographic films with him.

Carl was isolated socially, not dating, and not achieving academically in school. He realized that the abuse had affected him in that he is short-tempered with family and friends and that he was not reaching his full potential. The abuse was very much on his mind, despite his attempts to avoid thinking of it.

Carl's propensity for avoidant defenses were revealed by his isolation from people and his concerns about blowing up and being irritated by people. There was some sense of anger and depression and he used a belligerent stand-offish style that kept people at a distance and uneasy about dealing with him.

Victims of Case 2

Dan. Dan, age 14, was sexually abused starting around age 8 for an extended time period. He was coerced into performing masturbation, oral sex, and anal sex with the perpetrator. Dan talked about how much he trusted the coach, and noted that the coach was very important to him after his own father had left the household. The coach would explain to him that what they were involved in was normal, and he convinced Dan that what he wanted to do with Dan is what friends do to one another. Dan later realized he had been photographed nude at different times by a hidden video camera.

Dan's mother noted that Dan was withdrawn and moody. She thought he felt guilty for letting the sexual interactions happen. She found out a lot of the details at trial. The brothers had not discussed their abuse by the Coach in any detail. Dan complained of loneliness but seemed to like to be alone. He felt guilty, secretive, self-conscious, and shy. He suffered mood swings, was too concerned with neatness, and seemed sad all the time.

The mother said that after she and her husband separated, the home atmosphere improved. It was around this time that the coach came into the picture. She thought the coach was the "best thing." In fact, he became part of the family. He was her confidant and best male friend. He attended her father's funeral. The mother volunteered her belief that the coach was not gay because he had girlfriends, one of whom lived with him. The mother said she almost had a nervous breakdown when the news of the abuse was disclosed. She began therapy. She thought the boys would blame her for what had happened to them.

Dan had a post-traumatic stress disorder in partial remission. Interviews revealed that his ability to trust others and to assess people in a realistic way had been compromised. As a result, Dan, in a variety of settings, felt exploited by people, and taken advantage of. Conversely, he sometimes sought out help but then pushed the help-giver away. This behavior undermined his ability to connect with people for purposes of learning and positive self-development. He tried to manage his world through rigid expectations regarding himself and others. This was also his way to control his inner and external world and reality. This method left him isolated in his relationships and only able to view the world from his own perspective.

Earl. Earl, age 16, and Dan's brother, was sexually abused when he was 8 and 9 years old. Earl attended YMCA activities over a 4 to 5 year period during the school year, and also attended the YMCA summer day camp. His sexual activities began with the coach pressuring Earl to watch a pornographic video and to masturbate while doing so. These instructions were presented under the guise of learning about sexuality. The coach videotaped Earl with a hidden camera while he was masturbating.

Earl's parents added some information regarding the perpetrator. Earl often spent the night sleeping over at the coach's house. When Case 1 was reported in the newspaper, the mother talked to the coach about it. He reassured her that their YMCA had no such problems. The parents also used the coach as a babysitter.

The mother was concerned about Earl's level of anger now, especially his "hair-trigger rage." Recently at a school soccer game, another boy had made a remark about Earl's mother and Earl grabbed the boy by the hair and punched his face with uncontrollable rage. The game then had to be suspended. The mother reported that Earl sometimes deliberately tried to hurt people and that he had often come home drunk. She felt that his current girlfriend, with whom Earl was sexually active, had helped him. Earl's grades fluctuated and he had to attend summer school.

The mother stated that Earl was moody and isolated himself in his room. She described him as argumentative; boastful; obsessed with his girlfriend; restless; cruel; easily jealous; fearful of dogs; accident-prone; impulsive; and a loner. She complained that he physically attacks people; does poor school work; exhibits compulsions (constant showering); clowns too much; sleeps too little; is stubborn and hot-tempered; too concerned with cleanliness; and has trouble sleeping.

The avoidant and aggressive defenses Earl employed, noted on personality assessment, come about because the trauma and intimidation he experienced had impacted on his basic capacities to regulate emotion. Earl did not feel competent in interpersonal situations. He vasilated between feeling put upon and misunderstood and feeling irritable and angry toward others. He tended to handle his anger and aggression in a passive manner that appeared at times as stubbornness. The amount of internal confusion and anxiety he dealt with tended to interfere with his ability to do things rapidly and in an organized fashion. At times, this pattern was judged by others to be deliberate and hostile. This set up relationships where even when people tried to help Earl, they found it difficult because he was so moody and suspicious. Because of these repetitive and disappointing encounters, Earl tended to avoid people or he exploded and fought with them. Then he felt that he was being unfairly treated.

Fred. Fred, age 17, was sexually and physically abused over a 4 to 5 year period starting when he was 8 years old. Fred revealed that molestation began at YMCA summer day camp when the coach took away his underwear and refused to return it. Overt sexual activities began with the coach teaching him about "life," that is, how boys develop sexually. Sex acts between Fred and his coach included mutual masturbation and oral sex. He was shown pornographic videos involving male–female intercourse with some female–female sex. Fred remembers the coach taking pictures of him in the nude and making Fred take pictures of the coach in the nude.

Fred tried to tell his parents about this sexual abuse, but the coach was a family friend who would come for dinner and would even travel with the family on trips. The coach physically beat Fred and threatened to kill him if he told about their activities. The coach also made Fred feel like the sex was Fred's fault. The abuse ended when Fred was around 13 or 14 because the coach became more interested in younger boys.

Fred's parents reported the following symptoms: he could not concentrate, could not get his mind off certain thoughts, did not eat well, ate too much sugar, felt worthless or inferior, suffered from headaches and stomachaches, did poor school work, was self-conscious and easily embarrassed, had sleep difficulties, stared blankly, and thought he was treated unfairly. The also complained that he was stubborn, sullen, irritable, and sulky. He used obscene language, talked about killing himself, was often truant, was depressed, had no self-esteem, was self-destructive, and was apathetic about his future.

Psychological testing indicated a very disturbed and troubled young man who continued to show high levels of psychological pain and distress in spite of the psychotherapy and support he had received to date.

Fred, in describing the impact the abuse had on his current life, stated that it had interfered with every aspect of his life, most specifically his thinking and ability to concentrate. He continually thought of the abuse he suffered and alternated between severe depression and wanting to resume his life. He was unable to function at school or at work.

Fred was clearly suffering from post-traumatic stress disorder, in its chronic phase, and also exhibited attention deficit disorder. In addition, Fred had serious deficits in his information processing of the trauma. He was caught in a vicious cycle of despair and fantasy, and could not find his way out. He had fallen far behind in terms of school, friends, and family. Residential treatment at a facility that specializes in sexual trauma was recommended for him.

Greg. Greg, age 17, was sexually abused starting around age 10; the abuse went on for several years. The acts included masturbation, oral sex, and anal penetration. Greg had to perform these acts on the abuser and the abuser performed them on him. He also viewed sexually oriented materials and pornographic films. Like many other boys, he was videotaped in the nude by a hidden camera.

Greg had some organized memories of the abuse. However, he had shut down emotionally. His behavior strongly supported an avoidant response pattern. The lack of endorsement of symptoms forewarns that as Greg pursues the resolution of these abusive memories, he will have to struggle with intense emotional expressions. He did indicate in his self-report his fear over his ability to manage and control the emotion of anger.

When asked how the experience affected him, Greg stated, "It happened and I forgot about it. I never think about it." Greg did reveal his distress through his sense of preoccupation with disturbing thoughts, confusion about who and what he is, concern about the future, and a deep sense of feeling overwhelmed at times and lacking the ability to manage his own assertive and aggressive impulses. Greg was managing his distress by an avoidant pattern and could remain in this state for some time provided he was not challenged by an overwhelming emotional event. A subsequent event could be positive or negative. He has managed to wall off the intensity of emotions associated with prolonged sexual abuse through biopsychological operations that render him numb to emotional reactions. This reaction limits his capacity to grow and develop both as an individual and as a partner in intimate relationships. This highly defensive posture restricts his ability to set constructive goals to move him into the future.

Greg was in a state of restricted emotional response that is characteristic of unresolved trauma. His prognosis for a full responsive life was compromised. He is more confused about himself and his life today than he has ever been. The inability to project himself into the future suggests that if his life proceeds the way it has been going, he will be subjected to a depressive mood state.

Hugh. Hugh, age 19, and Greg's brother, was sexually abused beginning when he was 9 or 10; the abuse lasted several years. The abuser fondled, masturbated, and performed oral sex on Hugh, and Hugh had to reciprocate. The abuser attempted to normalize these activities by saying, "All kids do it." He also would say, "This is very personal; don't talk to anyone about it." At times, the activities were carried out with another boy present in the room.

Hugh was diagnosed with post-traumatic stress disorder with avoidant defenses. When asked how the abuse affected him, Hugh said, "It affected me negatively. I am skeptical of people and do not trust them. I can only do things my way now. I had trouble with the law; I stole baseball cards in the 10th grade. The coach hated me to collect cards—said it was stupid to spend money on cards. He stopped molesting me when I got bigger than him. He had younger boys. I got a DWI when I found out he was arrested. I heard it from my mother. She kept asking if he did anything to me and I kept saying no." Hugh indicated that the abuse was ongoing, long, and involved physical abuse.

Hugh presented as anxious with high levels of hypervigilence; he was scared for no apparent reason, he had difficulty leaving the house, and he had psychosomatic pains in his back. After graduating from high school, he took time off because he did not know what direction to take in his life. He felt disconnected from his life; he had a poor sense of himself; and he felt limited in his ability to control his anger.

His parents reported that he slept a lot, swears, was irritable and moody, appeared underactive, and was involved in using alcohol. He was noncommunicative, and in his last two years of high school he failed several courses.

This profile fits in with his basic distrust of people. He feels passive or ineffective in his ability to assert himself with others. He found it hard to utilize criticism; he felt guilty and wrong about himself.

Treatment Recommendations

Some of the general treatment goals for these youths include the following:

- Attachment to a caring, therapeutic figure who is experienced in dealing with child and adolescent trauma. This attachment will reduce the potential of the youth acting out in a self- or other-directed manner.

- Assessment of thought processes. It is critical to find out what is on the youth's mind. For example, how entitled versus disregarded did he feel in his family? Does he believe his family are uncaring? These are the premises laid down by the offender. He has been supported in transgressions by the offender. Are these thought still present?

- Assessment of sexual thoughts and fantasies. Areas to be explored include the following: How does sex get negotiated between the youth and another person? What fantasies excite him or are associated with masturbation? Does he have any fetishes? Look for themes of forcing or humiliation or degregation. Look too for the association of sex with aggressive acts involving knives or other weapons, or, conversely, masochistic courting of sex involving pain.

- Linking of the abuse to symptoms. The sexually abusive experience needs to be linked with current symptoms. People can have a conscious awareness of upsetting events but be totally incapable of connecting them to ongoing symptomatic behavior. The symptoms include dysregulation of emotion, attachment, appetite, sex, and the like. The anger and rage results from the violation, the exploitation, and the compromising that took place during the abusive relationship.

- Exploration of sexual identity issues. Does the youth, have comfort being male? Identify his sexual interest? Deal with points of confusion with polymorphus sexual interests that emerge, for example, sex with animals. Explore the youth's behavior and interest in this area.

Transition Sex Rings

In transition sex rings, multiple adults are involved sexually with the children, and the victims are usually adolescents. The children are tested out for eventual roles as prostitutes and thus are at great risk of advancing to the next level of sex ring, the syndicated ring.

It is speculated that children enter transition sex rings by one of several routes. Some children may be initiated into solo sex rings by the type of pedophile who has a sexual interest in and preference for children under age 13. These types of pedophiles, who lose sexual interest in the child as he or she approaches puberty, may try, through an underground network, to move the vulnerable child into sexual activity with those types of pedophiles with sexual preferences for pubescent youth. The children may already be incest victims who have run away from home and who need a peer group for identity and economic support, or they may be abused children who come from families in which parental bonding has been absent and multiple forms of neglect and abuse are present. Finally, some victims are missing children who have been kidnapped and forced into prostitution.

It is difficult to identify this type of ring because its boundaries are undefined and because the child may be propelled quite quickly from the ring itself into prostitution. Typically, adults in these transition rings do not interact sexually with each other, but instead share parallel sexual interests and involvement with adolescents, who exchange sex with adults for money as well as for attention or material goods.

A case example from the National Center on Missing and Exploited Children (NCMEC) Deceased Child Project illustrates the transition ring.

This case was originally called into the center by the police as an unidentified, white, deceased, 16-year-old juvenile girl. The victim had been badly beaten about the face and visible birthmarks on her body had been removed. Her hands had been severed from her body and deposited 70 miles away.

This child's morgue photograph was refined by the NCMEC's age-progression specialist, utilizing specialized computer techniques. This enhanced photograph was sent to law enforcement agencies to be used in a poster to be distributed locally. The photograph was also shown on national television. The victim was finally identified as a child in foster care who had disappeared at Christmas while enroute by bus back to her youth home after a visit with a former foster family.

A careful investigation determined that the victim had been "befriended" by a black male pimp who convinced her to accompany him to another state. What specifically happened to the child is unclear. The theory is that the pimp involved her in prostitution. The child either saw something, or discovered something that put the pimp in jeopardy, and so the pimp decided to kill her. According to the investigator, a common practice in the field of prostitution is for a pimp to tattoo a prostitute's hand in order to keep track of his "employees." That may have been the reason that the child's hands had been cut off and disposed of in another location.

Syndicated Sex Rings

Syndicated sex rings are well-structured organizations involving the recruitment of children, the production of pornography, the delivery of direct sexual services, and the establishment of an extensive network of customers. The solo ring or the transition ring may, depending on various factors, constitute different stages in the evolution of a syndicated child sex ring, or it may represent only a loosely organized association of adults exploiting small groups of children. The age of victims that might be involved in a syndicated ring generally ranges from 11 to 16. The victims may be transported across state lines.

Child and adolescent victims of transition and syndicated sex rings are generally involved in prostitution. Clinical considerations and treatment is covered in the next chapter.

Case Example of a Syndicated Ring Offender

Samuel Johnson's preoccupation with both males and females in bondage cannot be linked to any single event. However, it seems that following a divorce from his first wife he began purchasing pictures of people engaged in bondage activities. Later Johnson met Jason Stone and together they began taking pictures of children posed in bondage positions. This activity continued for nearly 20 years until both were arrested on charges ranging from assault and battery with a dangerous weapon to committing unnatural acts with a child.

Samuel Johnson grew up with his parents and one brother in Detroit. His parents were happily married, even though his father traveled a great deal on business and was usually only home with the family on weekends. Johnson graduated from high school and joined the U.S. Army, where he trained as a pilot. He left the military after serving in the Korean War, but later returned to active duty and was honorably discharged after serving a total of 20 years. Following his service in the military, Johnson worked as an electronics technician for a defense industry, but was often laid off in times of economic recession. He eventually found steady employment at a telephone company.

Johnson married twice. He has four children from his first marriage, which ended in divorce, and two children from his second marriage. Johnson married Stone's ex-wife and is currently separated from her. Johnson attributed both marital separations to a "dissatisfactory sexual life."

The men's sexual and pornographic exploitation of children was discovered when Johnson's daughter looked through a window at his residence and saw her father taking pictures of a boy who was tied-up. The girl told her mother, who was already separated from Johnson, and Mrs. Johnson reported the activity to the police. Upon executing a search warrant at the residence, police confiscated 15,000 slides and photographs depicting bondage, primarily with young girls, but also including pictures of both male and female children spanning a wide age range; correspondence indicating that bondage photographs had been exchanged with other bondage devotees; dangerous weapons, including a loaded .38 caliber semiautomatic handgun; various sexual devices; catalogues and forms for ordering sexually oriented correspondence; sexually explicit publications; and notebooks and a diary detailing sexual activity involving bondage.

On one occasion Johnson invited a 13-year-old boy to his home, "incapacitated" the child with rum, took him to the cellar, tied the boy up with ropes attached to pulleys on the ceiling, placed a copper ring with turnbuckle knobs on the child's penis, and took photographs of the scene. On another occasion, Johnson tied the same 13-year-old boy to a rack and Stone took pictures while Johnson held a whip and stood over the boy.

Another boy, aged 14, visited Johnson's home on several occasions during which he was given beer and shown obscene photographs of nude women and young children engaged in sex. In addition, Johnson brandished the .38 caliber gun and a knife and threatened, "You'd better not tell anybody or you'll be in serious trouble."

The following significant life events and behaviors of Samuel Johnson were obtained from interviews with the subject, records of professionals analyzing the subject, and criminal justice system reports. Johnson had an early and consistent exposure to pornography. He used it prior to and during his sex crimes against children. He tried to use pornography to relieve the impulse to commit an offense. The overall influence of pornography on his life was high.

Johnson stated emphatically that his victims' involvement was entirely voluntary and that no actual pain was ever inflicted on them. He also stated that expressions of pain were feigned for the purposes of the photographs. Obviously, the idea of pain was sexually arousing for him and he used the photographs as a vehicle for feeding his own sadomasochistic fantasy life. Johnson used a partner in creating the pornography, and interstate trafficking was suspected but police were unsuccessful in obtaining evidence.

Clinical Considerations

Assessment. With sex ring victims and pornography, there should be a general assessment for child abuse and a specific assessment on the sex ring organization and its operation.

The acronym TRIADS stands for the child abuse assessment areas of *t*ypes of abuse, *r*ole relationship of victim to offender, *i*ntensity of abuse, *a*utonomic response of the child, *d*uration of the abuse, and *s*tyle of offender (Burgess, Hartman, & Kelley, 1990).

Assessment of the sex ring should focus first on disclosure. Disclosure plays a role in strategies used to establish rapport with a child who has been in a sex ring. When the disclosure has come from a member of the sex ring, the child's response can be relief or defensive anger. Loyalties are built up between children and the adult members of a sex ring, and the adults also use various types of coercion to force child compliance with the rules of the ring. Often pictures of the children involved in sex acts are used to blackmail them into staying loyal to the ring. This becomes a particularly forceful mechanism if the child has been encouraged in any way to perpetrate against another child in the ring. Knowledge of the complexity of ring life is important to the person making the initial assessment in that a reluctance to detail what went on or a denial of the stress and symptomatology may operate because of the child's relationship and status within the ring.

Questions about disclosure include the follow:

1. How was the offender caught or identified?
2. What are your thoughts and feelings about him?

3. How did you first meet him?

4. Can you tell me what happened to you?

Impact of Abuse on the Child Victim. Information regarding the impact on the child victim comes not only from the child but from parental observations. Evaluating the impact on the child can follow a combination of standard assessment strategies and symptom measurements, as well as attention to specific behaviors and symptoms associated with trauma.

The symptoms include general anxiety symptoms relating to such basic life processes as appetite and eating, stomachaches, alterations in aggression, increased fighting and irritability, moodiness, and excessive risk-taking. There may be blunting or numbing symptoms marked by withdrawal from usual activities, spacing out, trouble concentrating, refusal to do school work, and either excessive sleep or avoidance of sleep.

There are a series of symptoms that are more trauma-specific. The most dramatic is the reexperiencing of the traumatic events. This can come via flashbacks, either stimulated by external cues that are reminders of the event or by internal cues. Other symptoms are ruminative preoccupation with sex ring experiences and guilt. Reenactment is less clear to the child as related to sex ring activities, but often involves sexualized and aggressive behavior toward other children or restructuring situations in which the child is victimized by others. In younger children, there can be repetitive and obsessive play that resembles events in the sex ring.

Sexual problems generally present themselves in terms of hypersexual activity and preoccupation with sex, or with hyposexual interest accompanied by avoidance, disgust, and denial of sexuality. Therefore, sexual acting out is viewed from the perspective of the reenactment of the trauma or through excessive learning of deviant sexual arousal. Assessment is made as to the confusion of the emergent sexuality that has been pushed more rapidly in the development of the youth because of the sexual exposure and abuse. In the pattern of fear, disgust, and inhibition of sexuality, we note a linking of the abuse and fear to merging sexuality.

In addition, an assessment has to be made of the social context in which the child now finds himself involved. Is he going to school? Is he maintaining relationships with friends? Is he restricted from making contact with certain children? Is the child ostracized by classmates because of public knowledge of his involvement in the sex ring? Social isolation has to be evaluated: Is it coming from the inside, that is, is the child avoiding other people, or from the outside, that is, are his peers and adults rejecting him?

Other more specific information regarding the sex ring activities themselves usually comes forth as fragments and as intermittent presentations. It is useful when there is adequate rapport between the clinician and the child to initially ask the child what he remembers happening to him while attending the activities organized by the perpetrator. At this point, the clinician hopes to gain markers concerning the structure, process, and key types of events of the abuse. This is not a time for dealing with the memories in emotional and perceptual detail. Rather, it is the time to gather the initial what, when, and where of information. Later, when the child begins to deal in therapy with the abusive activities, the clinician can create a framework for the child, thereby making the process of self-disclosure less invasive and more under the child's control.

Diagnosis. The most frequent diagnosis is post-traumatic stress disorder.

Treatment. A multimodal approach outlines recommended treatment modalities.

1. Two types of *individual counseling* are recommended: supportive counseling and trauma counseling. Supportive counseling is intended to build personal resources that help the child to develop the ability to relax and moderate stress as well as to deal with safety and protection issues. The child needs psychoeducational information regarding his own emotions. Trauma work should begin when the youth has mastery of his own internal distress, and should focus on processing the memories of abuse.

2. *Group counseling* should be instituted to assist the youth in developing skills to learn to trust and to interact effectively with his peers. This modality may run concurrently with individual counseling.

3. In addition, the youth needs *family therapy* with his parents. The family members need to work on dealing with the stress they have experienced and on strengthening communication within the family.

4. *Private tutoring* is critical for strengthening the youth's ability to concentrate, to think, and to learn. Because the child has lost trust in authority figures, he may have difficulties with his teachers. Private tutoring will be less threatening and will help to build confidence and help with schooling.

5. *Social interventions* are important. The youth needs to be able to elect recreational activities to develop self-esteem and mastery skills.

6. *Crisis intervention* is essential for unanticipated stressful events that may occur over time.

7. *Monitoring* is necessary for both physical and psychological concerns. This modality includes scheduled meetings to review and evaluate the youth's recovery.

8. *Vocational testing and education* is necessary to ensure that life goals and career become a focus. This, in turn, will expand self-esteem.

These modalities need to be available when anticipated key issues (sexual identity, dating, partnerships, parenting, career decisions) will arise. While monitoring activities occur, crisis therapy should be available for unanticipated stress events. This multidimensional treatment package should be in force until all developmental milestones have been completed, including, but not limited to, graduation from high school, graduation from college or a trade apprenticeship, and career implementation.

Parental Concerns

Two major concerns of parents whose children are victims of sex rings are whether the child should testify and sex education issues.

Child Testifying. A descriptive study of parents of testifying children from daycare sex ring cases (Burgess et al., 1990) found that parents are highly symptomatic and present strong evidence of experiencing chronic posttraumatic stress disorder. Another study found that reported stress is higher in fathers than in mothers with regard to symptoms, intrusive thinking, and avoidant behaviors (Kelley, 1992). Also, the parents of testifying children have more stressful life events following disclosure of the abuse and the court experience, suggesting that cumulative stress could serve to heighten anxiety.

For parents of sexually abused children, entry into the judicial system not only resurrects the trauma that surfaced at the time of abuse disclosure, but now introduces the parent to a process that raises more anxiety rather than bringing closure to a stressful situation.

What are the factors that account for this strong response in parents over time? First, the length of time that knowledge of their child's abuse is consciously operant may be one factor influencing the chronic stress. In the Burgess et al. (1990) study, the mean age of the child when the abuse began was 2.7 for the nontestifying group and 3.0 for the testifying group; the average length of duration of the abuse was 15 months. The mean age of the child at time of testifying was 6.8. Coping with the length of time between disclosure of the abuse and final court action is particularly difficult for those parents whose child is involved in testifying, for these parents are subjected to the review of the case and other activities that constantly resurrect in their mind the whole event, and they also must endure periods of time when their child is overtly distressed by his part in the legal process. During this time parents have to deal with their own distress and the symptoms of their child (Kelley, 1990) and attempt to return to a precrisis level of activity.

To gain a greater appreciation of the nature of the parents' response to their child testifying, Burgess et al. (1990) tallied responses to the following questions. "Before the trial, what did you fear most about your child testifying? Did this happen?" Parents' thoughts that did *not* happen were as follows:

- I thought that my daughter would go back to the way she was after the school was closed.
- I thought that she would just cry and wouldn't talk.
- I thought that the controversy created would filter down to her and that she would fall apart.
- I thought that she would be bullied by the defense attorney and made to feel stupid and inadequate.
- I was afraid that seeing those people again, confronting them, and talking about what happened would start her worrying about the threats coming true.
- I thought that he would feel more guilty about what happened.
- I thought that the defense attorney would harass and frighten her.
- I thought she wouldn't be able to say anything at all. I thought she might have a seizure.
- I thought that there might be acts of violence or vengeance against our family.

The fears of these parents can be classified into two groups: (1) fears that focus on the child being frightened, disqualified, or pressured in some manner that could precipitate acute symptoms and behaviors, and (2) concerns focused on the community response to the family, in particular that there would be a type of retaliation or revenge.

Statements made by parents that they reported *did* happen include:

- I thought that he would be badgered by the prosecutor.
- I thought that she would cry and not answer the questions asked by the defense lawyer, and that the defense lawyer would try to confuse her.
- I thought facing the defendants would make her regress.

These examples indicated that several parents experienced their worst fears after their child testified. Such an experience challenges parents as to their decision to permit their child to testify and requires that they cope with their doubts concerning their decision and of the retraumatizing trial experience. That parents were able to identify their fears about their child testifying suggest that this anticipatory anxiety can be a self-reinforcing process that sustains high levels of symptomatology. It may be that this same anticipatory anxiety is operant in the nontestifying parents but has not been compounded by the additional experience of the trial. Further research will be needed to explore and sort out this hypothesis.

What motivates parents to permit their child to testify? In 4 of the 17 cases in Burgess et al. (1990), the parents stated they left the decision up to the child. In the majority of cases, however, the decision was made by the parents after consultation with the prosecutor and/or the child's therapist. The analysis of motivation revealed parents' primary motive was to create safety for their child. Eighty percent of the parents whose child testified emphasized their motive as safety for their child as well as for other children. Safety was defined in terms of the child feeling safe by knowing that the perpetrator was "locked up" and that the child would be believed and protected during testifying.

Would parents do it over again? Burgess et al. (1991) asked the question, "Looking back, do you think the decision to have your child testify was the right one?" The majority of parents (N = 12) indicated that they thought they had made the right decision.

The fact that parents whose child testified reported more stressful life events than those whose child did not testify raises the question of source of psychological distress. Is the reporting of more stressful life events a function of the stress response itself? That is, are parents more sensitive to life events and do they recollect them as more stressful because they are presently under stress, or is this a visitation of more noxious life events. The prior interpretation may be warranted, especially considering that parents in both groups manifested psychological distress, and further that fathers were significantly more distressed than mothers. This suggests that the trauma has not been resolved and that for parents that agree to allow their children to testify there is every indication that the process activates and prolongs the traumatic recognition of their child's abuse in two ways. First, the trial demands a sorting and recounting of details of the child's abuse, and second, the trial itself, even with verdicts of guilty, is inconclusive (Montan et al., 1988).

The alternate interpretation of cumulative negative life events suggests that parental distress over child sexual abuse may be mediated by interim stress due to death in the family, separation, or reduction in income. These three factors certainly have to be taken into account when examining response of parents to their child testifying. The decrease of family income was associated in the descriptive data with mothers withdrawing from the work role for a period of time until safe childcare was secured. This withdrawal from the work role, the trauma of the sexual abuse, and the burden of their child testifying further interact with marital harmony and become a stressor that may, in fact, explain separation.

The Burgess et al. (1990) study revealed the impact on parents who decided to permit their child to testify and it also uncovers the high distress level of the fathers. The fathers are confronted with trying to manage the mother–child dyad, sustain the economic stability of the family, and manage their own response to the sexual abuse. The nature of the symptoms and reactions and the high intrusive imagery scales suggest that there is a strong visual component to how these men process information regarding the sexual abuse of their child and the role of their child in the justice system. This suggests a self-traumatizing mechanism operative in the fathers as well as the mothers. We have no consistent information on the structure of ideation in the fathers and its association either to past trauma in their life, anticipated trauma, or, for that matter, fearful identification with sexually aggressive acts in themselves. Since these children were abused in daycare settings where some of the perpetrators were females, there is little information on how parents deal with the realization that sexual and ritualistic abuse was initiated as well as condoned by female as well as male perpetrators.

The need of trauma-specific interventions for parents for their own adjustment to their child's trauma is strongly suggested by these findings. The therapeutic issues of how men process and deal with sexual abuse has only been eluded to in the clinical literature with regard to spouses and boyfriends of rape victims (Holmstrom & Burgess, 1979). There have been minimal efforts to provide support groups for males whose spouse or girlfriend has been raped. One finding in child trauma work is that fathers are not involved in the therapy of their children (Zimmerman et al., 1987).

Parents whose child testifies are carrying the double burden of resolving their own stress surrounding the abuse of their child and the stressful aspects of a court trial. This dilemma involves complex decision making to permit their child to testify as well as the monitoring of behaviors regarding stress and anxiety prior to trial, during trial, and after trial. At the same time, parents must pursue what efforts they have established to assist their child in resolving the impact of the abuse.

This awareness of the complex dimensions of parenting deserves attention in the overall framework of the justice system. That more parents of testifying children received counseling than nontestifying parents (82.3 percent vs. 61.2 percent) and still had high distress levels suggests the need to study further the nature of trauma therapy and the consideration of additional life events.

Sex Education. One of the more difficult issues confronting parents, particularly those whose young children are abused in nursery schools or other types of settings, is to confront the fact that their child is now aware of and at some level involved in sexual activity that is beyond their years. This is very painful to parents. Therefore, the issue of sex education under these circumstances is often fraught with conflict. A careful evaluation needs to be made before a working arrangement is established between the parents and the professional who is working with them to help the child modify and relate to his or her level of sexual awareness.

The aim of sex education should be to help the child feel that his or her sexual feelings are his or her own, that they are not bad or dirty, and that sexual curiosity is best handled through asking the parents questions. Children need to know that they will face no punishment or retaliation for their sexual interests and curiosities. They also need to be taught that how they behave toward other children and other adults in terms of sex requires restrictions. Sexual behavior is not to be freely engaged in or forced on others, nor is it to be forced on them. From these outcomes, there are basic types of information that children need at different ages regarding anatomy, the physiology of reproduction, and knowledge of sexually transmitted diseases. There is also the need at different ages to model for children the role of sex and sexual conduct in various relationships.

Parents need to avoid misinformation and punitive responses to their child. Resources for parents include the therapist they are working with and books on sex education.

Areas of sexual identity need to be covered by the therapist. Parents will be concerned as well as the child as to the meaning they attribute to the sexual abuse and their future sexual identity.

References

Burgess, A. W. (Ed.) (1984). *Child pornography*. New York: Lexington Books.

Burgess, A. W., Groth, A. N., & McCausland, M. P. (1981). Child sex initiation rings. *American Journal of Orthpsychiatry, 51*, 110–119.

Burgess, A. W., Hartman, C. R., & Kelley, S. J. (1990). Assessing child abuse: The TRIADS checklist. *Journal of Psychosocial Nursing, 28*(4), 1–6.

Burgess, A. W., Hartman, C. R., & Kelley, S. J. (1991). Parental response to child sexual abuse trials involving day care settings. *Journal of Traumatic Stress, 3*(3), 395–405.

Burgess, A. W., Hartman, C. R., Kelley, S. J., Grant, C. A., & Gray, E. B. (1990). Parental response to child sexual abuse trials involving day care settings. *Journal of Traumatic Stress, 3*(3), 401–404.

Burgess, A. W., Hartman, C. R., McCausland, M. P., & Powers, P. A. (1984). Response patterns in children and adolescents exploited through sex rings and pornography. *American Journal of Psychiatry, 141*(5), 656–662.

Herman, J. L. (1981). *Father-daughter incest*. Cambridge, MA: Harvard University Press.

Holmstrom, L. L., & Burgess, A. W. (1979). Rape: The husband's and boyfriend's initial reactions. *Family Coordinator, 28*(3), 321–330.

Jonker, F., & Jonker-Bakker, P. (1991). Experiences with ritualistic child sexual abuse: A case study from the Netherlands. *Child Abuse and Neglect, 15*(3), 191–196.

Kelley, S. J. (1989). Stress responses of children to sexual abuse and ritualistic abuse in day care setting. *Journal of Interpersonal Violence, 4*(4), 501–512.

Kelley, S. J. (1990). Parental response to sexual abuse and ritualistic abuse in day care settings. *Nursing Research, 39*(1), 25–29.

Lanning, K. V. (1984). Collectors. In A. W. Burgess (Ed.), *Child Pornography and Sex Rings*. New York: Lexington Book,: Macmillan Inc., p. 83.

Montan, C., Burgess, A. W., Garant, C. A., & Hartman, C. R. (1989). The case of two trials: Father–son incest. *Journal of Family Violence, 4*(1), 95–103.

Wild, N. J., & Wynne, J. M. (1986). Child sex rings. *British Medical Journal, 293*, 183–185.

Zimmerman, M. L., Wolbert, W. A., Burgess, A. W. & Hartman, C. R. (1987). Art and group work: Interventions for multiple victims of child molestation, *Archives of Psychiatric Nursing, 1(1)*, 40–46.

9
Adolescent Runaways and Juvenile Prostitution

Ann Wolbert Burgess
Carol R. Hartman

Adolescent runaways and juvenile prostitution are two serious social problems confronting our society in the 1990s. They meet the criteria for serious problems because they involve thousands of young people; many of these children suffer injuries, sustain emotional distress, or die prematurely; and they are primary, for they interact with other social problems (Garbarino, 1989). This chapter reports on clinical research studies on these two social problems and makes recommendations for clinicians working with these troubled populations.

Adolescent Runaways

Critical perspectives on social institutions, observe Fine and Rosenberg (1983), are often best obtained from exiles, that is, the persons who leave those institutions. This is perhaps why exiles' views are frequently disparaged as deviant and in some cases are conspicuously silenced. Runaways and the homeless, like high-school dropouts, fit this pattern very well. Many of these adolescent males and females have been pushed out of the home; some have opted to leave; all are regarded as failures. Labeling runaways as "bad," "wayward," "delinquent," or "helpless" shifts attention away from the social institution of the family or the foster home from which the youth flees.

We will use the colloquial term "runaway" throughout this chapter, but we recognize and want our readers to recognize that many of these youths have been kicked out, forced out, or never allowed into the spotlight in the family. Despite many runaways' critical perspectives on family life, they are frequently portrayed as "losers." In our culture, adolescent runaways who are also homeless are a group who challenge the dominant belief that allegiance to family values leads to school and work success, which in turn results in employment and income guarantees.

We will argue that this image delegitimizes the runaways' critique of families and the promise of achievement, and preserves the legitimacy of family as a social harmonizer. The critic is functionally silenced and maintains his or her exile, feeling "different" and "alienated" not only from his or her family but also from his or her childhood peers. They are forced, in a sense, to reconstruct their family on the street.

Before we continue, we do not wish to romanticize adolescents who run away from home. Clearly, some do feel bereft of hope, and others may not be able to stay in the home due to threats to the family. But neither can we neglect evidence that suggests a more radical potential within many of these youths. Their critical voices are rarely heard; they do not feel important in their family; they are not valued as a family member; and social institutions (foster homes, group homes, detention homes) tend to hold an equally dismal perception of the runaway seeking shelter.

Central to the analysis of adolescent runaways is the question of whether the "runaway" problem is one of individual differences and inadequacies or one of family structure. One position maintains that incapable adolescents seek their own level and drop out because of individual inadequacies. Another position holds families responsible for failing to integrate their child into the family system due to family conflict. A third position suggests runaways are the consequence of youth maltreatment usually carried out by parents or caretakers.

What happens to adolescents who run away? Do they, as often prophesied, end up on welfare, collect unemployment, and populate our prisons at disproportionate rates? If not, what does become of them? In either case, do these outcomes result because these youths lack personal strengths or because the structure of their home environments has eroded?

The Toronto Site

Motivated by the continued debate about the nature and consequences of running away, we received permission to conduct a study of adolescents seeking shelter at Toronto's Under 21, a Canadian Covenant House that provides temporary emergency shelter to runaways. Adolescents spend an average of three nights at the shelter. Staff counselors specially trained in the objectives and protocol for the study recruited adolescents who consented to participate.

Canadian Runaways

What emerged from the demographic data on the original 149 runaways follows. Of that number, 63 percent were males and 37 percent were females. Their ages ranged from 15 to 20 years with a mean of 17.9 years. The majority were white (81 percent) with blacks accounting for 9 percent and runaways of other racial groups (e.g., Native Indian) making up the remaining 10 percent. At the time of running, 90 runaways (62.5 percent) had been living with their families and 54 (37.2 percent) ran away from institutional settings and/or foster homes.

There was a strong history of abuse reported by the runaways: 40 percent reported that they had been attacked or raped; 73 percent reported being physically beaten, with 43 percent ranking physical abuse as the primary reason for running; 51 percent reported having been offered money for sex; 36 percent reported being forced to have sex; 31 percent reported having been sexually molested; and 19 percent reported being forced to witness sexual activity against their will (e.g., through viewing pornographic materials). Verbal abuse was reported by 51 percent of the runaways as a very important reason for running. However, the most important reason for running, reported by 54 percent of the youths, was an unhappy life.

Runaways reported first leaving home at ages ranging from 4 years to 19 years, 23.8 percent ran as a preteen; 36.4 percent ran as an early adolescent (ages 13–15), and 39.8 percent ran as a late adolescent (ages 16–19). Of the 34 preteen runaways, 85 percent reported physical abuse compared to 69 percent who left as an early adolescent and 70 percent who left as an older adolescent. The finding that preteen runaways are more likely to report physical abuse holds for both males and females. In terms of incidence of sexual abuse, 59 percent of the preteen runners reported sexual abuse compared to 55 percent of the early adolescents and 44 percent of the older adolescents. The relationship between report of sexual abuse and the age at which the youth first left home is stronger for females than males. Preteens and females who first left home between 13 and 15 years were much more likely to report sexual abuse than females who first left home as an older adolescent ($p = .05$).

Runaways reported leaving home from 1 to 110 times; almost half (46 percent) have left home more than three times.

Of the 110 runaways who estimated their family/household income, 41 percent reported incomes higher than most people, 39 percent reported incomes about the same as others, and 20 percent reported incomes lower than most people. The percentage reporting "higher than most people" (41 percent) is consistent with the finding that 45 percent of the runaways' families are supported by both mother's and father's salaries or wages. Thirty-two percent are supported by fathers only, 15 percent by mothers only, and 7 percent by general relief.

In terms of family structure, 69 percent of runaways reported a divorce or breakup in the family and 45 percent reported that one or both parents had remarried after divorce.

The majority of runaways (69 percent) claimed that religion is of no or limited importance in family life. This claim is consistent with the finding that 50 percent of runaways claim no personal religious affiliation and 35 percent claim no major family religious affiliation.

The majority (77 percent) of runaways reported having had trouble with either school officials or employers. Sixty-one percent had been suspended or expelled from school. Despite their problems in school, 87 percent of the runaways said there was a time in their lives when they thought they could make it in school.

In terms of family relationships, almost all (94 percent) runaways reported having had a serious argument with one or both parents and 88 percent reported serious arguments in the family. About one-third (32 percent) reported that someone in their family had to go to court or had been arrested for a serious violation.

The profile derived from the demographic data suggests that a runner emerges from a family that has some economic concerns but is more accurately characterized as a broken home, high in conflict, with parents arguing. The runaways gave a variety of reasons for their running, ranking family life intolerable and replete with physical, sexual and verbal abuse. In turn, the youths also reported their family's dissatisfaction with them. The runners also describe a difficult history of adjustment in school, adjustment to authority figures, and adjustment to religion.

We began our study with a question: Why do urban adolescents run away from home? Running away has been described as a response to abuse. On the surface this statement makes sense. The complexity of the statement resides in the fact that those who are abused and run frequently return home only to run away again. This strikes a poignant cord in attempting to describe patterns of running and what factors in the child and social environment support the running phenomena. Thus, we have to ask a parallel but equally compelling question: Why do they return home? The repetitious behavior directs a model that considers how a child is attached to an abusive environment. The model derived from studying the pathways for running suggests that a cognitive style of runaways, which emerges out of the context of their family life, acts as a mediating factor in the cyclic running phenomena.

The pathways in the model represent the alternatives youths have for running. In the four pathways identified in this study, the youth can run to or from the family, the institution, the street, and the shelter. The *family* represents the youth's family of origin (intact or separated) or the reconstituted family. The *street* represents the open environment that is unprotective, enticing, and exploitative; it includes subways, abandoned buildings, and other living arrangements. *Institutions* are pseudohome facilities such as foster or group homes; they may include legal or health facilities such as juvenile hall, mental institutions, correctional facilities, or jail. The *shelter* is a protective, temporary arrangement that provides food, a bed, and some form of companionship; shelter may be provided by a friend, a church group, or another human service organization.

The primary launching base for running for this sample was home (63 percent); a secondary launching base was an institution or group home (37 percent). The cyclic patterns of running include (1) family to street to shelter to family; (2) street to institution, shelter to street; or (3) family to institution, shelter, or family. There can be variations on this cycling.

There are two outcomes to running. The positive outcome includes social adaptation such as work, school, or family. Some runaways are able to break out of the cycle and and manage to work sporadically (about one-third of the sample). Some of the runaways reported on their reproductive history: 23 percent of the males said they had fathered a child and 30 percent of the females reported having been pregnant. The negative outcome, however, is the more dominant pattern. Once on the street, the outcome can be prostitution, criminal activity, drug addiction, or death by suicide, drug overdose, or being murdered.

This model of pathways and cycles of runaway youths highlights how little stands between the runaway and such negative life outcomes as delinquent behavior, substance abuse, and prostitution. For a runaway caught in the cycle, the bottom line is survival. Work is not a frequent accomplishment. Shelters are sought out, but can only provide temporary assistance. The street and the shelter become mediating factors for the youth and the family or other institutions. None of these environments are free from potential abuse and stress. The societal options are problematic in themselves; what operates in the youth that does not lead to self-sufficiency and a safe productive life is equally important in contributing to his or her repetitious running away.

The primary premise of the runaway model is that the internal beliefs of the youths regarding themselves and the expectations of their parents and others plays a critical role in the cyclic phenomena. The beliefs that other people, such as family members or caretakers, control events and that these events are therefore unpredictable reveals a seriously confused perception of others, of oneself, and of what can be expected in life. It is this cognitive confusion that plays a major role in the thinking patterns of runaway youths. Neither they nor their family can be held accountable for unpredictable events, yet somehow all "should" be responsible, yet they are ineffective and unable to right their confusing interpersonal relationships.

The expectations that things "should" be different links the youth back to the family. This works for the parents as well as for the youth. The youth believes that the parent "should" change and that he or she "should" be able to change also. It is suspected that exploration of the reason for "unhappy life" and the content of the "verbal abuse" would detail interpersonal experiences within the family in which there is great confusion with regard to what each member expects of themselves and others. While a belief that things "can change" is essential for productive living, a belief that things "should change" without sensing one's own and others' reasonable capacities for change can only result in repeated disappointment. When no change occurs, there is a repetition of nonproductive behaviors and cycles of running.

That the youth will return home or return to another unsatisfactory launching site can be expected because there is little basis for generating alternatives in the minds of these youths. One could also speculate that time away from a painful, confusing environment might be followed after a time by forgetting or disbelieving or questioning whether it was "that bad."

The runaways were highly symptomatic. They presented many symptoms of depression, anxiety, self-criticism, somatization, low energy, and self-destructive thinking. In addition, they reported physical and verbal fights among peers and confusion about their sexual identity. At the same time they reported that peers admire them and think well of them; that they believe themselves to be pleasant appearing; and that they feel happy yet alienated and isolated in personal contacts. These findings support our notions that patterns of expectations of this youthful population tend to be inconsistent and not very operable for successful living on their own. In essence, they vacillate from feeling good about themselves to feeling terrible. They have little tolerance for the frustration associated with learning, and their ability to evaluate their performance and correct behaviors to achieve possible goals is distorted. Needless to say, drugs and alcohol have a significant role in their activities. They report little pleasure in their lives or in their lives at home.

Family life is reported to be highly stressful. At home these children are given little support or attention. The child is not allowed to express feelings in an open way and the family atmosphere is laced with hostility and anger. The youth has not been encouraged to stand up for his or her own rights or to handle life problems. Home life is often characterized by a high emphasis on competition. The family is inflexible in its rules. It is important to note that it is not one factor alone, but a combination of factors that is detrimental to runaway youths.

It is assumed that high levels of parental expectations, particularly expectations that the youths are not able to meet, are delivered within a context of abuse. While a child may early recognize that the parents are wrong, because of his or her dependency and desires to love and be loved by the parents, he or she tends either to strive to meet the expectations, or in the face of failing to rebel. Eventually this kind of alternating behavior becomes the focus of the family. The child is blamed for his or her behavior, gets into more trouble, and is identified as a troublemaker. The child's stress increases and the child leaves home. In those situations where the child fails to recognize abuse, the child begins to believe that she or he is hurting the family and that the other family members would be better off without her or him. For those older adolescents who are asked to leave, their inability to function is usually tied in with asocial behavior, drug use, and sexual behaviors.

The gender differences in blame patterns (with men internalizing blame and women externalizing blame) suggest a differential response to sexual abuse by runaway males and females, implying a difference in the type of abuse, methods of psychologically controlling the victims, and family dynamics that support confusing and unreasonable expectations of runaways.

While the data collected cannot establish a causal link between this structure of thinking and sexual abuse, it supports clinical studies (Herman, 1981; Burgess et al., 1984) that suggest that control measures via the blame mechanism used by adults to sexually exploit children impact strongly on the child's thinking and reasoning. We mean by "control measures" that the child keeps the abuse secret, feels compelled to continue in the abusive relationship, and does not act against the abuser. This occurs because the abuser selects strategies that can control a particular child. The child's sense that he or she is being exploited and abused is disqualified by the adult. Control is maintained at some level by the adult convincing the child that he or she is responsible. Even though at another level the youth may not assume responsibility for the abuse, the self-destructive patterns of behavior manifested in actions such as running, being sexually indiscriminant, and using drugs reveals the child's disregard for the self.

We speculate that the majority of sexually abused female runaways were victims of intrafamily sexual abuse, and that the sexually abused runaway male was victimized external to the family. There is evidence that boys' experience in sex rings (Burgess et al., 1984), where they are in part held hostage in sexually abusive relationships with adults by committing predatory acts on peers, hold themselves more accountable for participating in the sexual activity. When they become the victimizer, they assume the power and control (i.e., they are able to change the roles). Girls who experience sexual entrapment in the family often respond by running—that is, they do not hold themselves responsible, they blame others, but they see abuse as unpredictable and uncontrollable. The sense of a capacity for personal change fits with existing gender differences in the socialization of males around power and control. Men blaming themselves are focused on issues of personal control as well as control of their environment. They may act out their sexual exploitation; they may hide it; they may try to reduce self-blame through fantasies of sexual power and prowess.

In summary, there is no modification of expectations or development of reasonable self-control for the runaway; instead, the youth becomes polarized between unattainable expectations and nothing. He or she becomes cognitively confused and is unable to gain perspective on himself or herself and the social world. Sexual and physical abuse compound the confusion of an unhappy, verbally abusive, and intolerable family life. The outcome is the cycling phenomena and continued victimization via prostitution, criminal activity, or death. Only a few runaways break out of the cycle and find a socially adaptive life-style.

Assessment and Interventions for Runaways

Assessment. Key questions to ask runaways should focus on their beliefs about running. The following questions are recommended:

1. What has gone on at home that contributes to your running away? (Ask for details of events, interactions, and relationships. If the youth says "Nagging," try to elicit examples. Examine responses for blame, derogatory name calling, and so on. Carefully interview for physical as well as verbal and sexual force.)

2. Given "event, relationship, and the like," how much control does the other or yourself have over this? How predictable is this type of behavior (yours/others); who's responsible (blame); how changeable are these behaviors/events by you/others?

3. What would have to be different for you to want to stay home? Have things even been this way in your home? If so, when? What made it change?

4. What would you need to make this happen?

5. What would other people need to make this happen?

6. How possible are these changes?

7. What do you want most for yourself?

8. What do you think you need first to get what you want?

9. If you were in my place, what is the most important thing to be said/done for a youth in your place?

10. On a scale of 0 to 10 with 10 being highest, how useful/safe is it for your return home? How safe/useful is it for you on the streets compared to home?

Interventions. Our levels of intervention are determined by the runaway's time away from home. At *Level 1*, the early runner who has been away from home less than a month has the strongest potential for working toward returning home. Careful assessment needs to be made concerning the youth's safety in the home, particularly if the youth is female and thus at high risk of having been both physically and sexually abused. A determination needs to be made of the reason for the youth's running away, the youth's choice of a stable environment, and the view of the family of the runaway.

At *Level 2*, the multiple runner who has been away from home one month to one year is not only at high risk for being physically abused in the home, but of having abuse occur while on the streets. In addition to Level 1 assessment, these runaways need to be assessed for general physical and sexual health, drug and alcohol use, and their own predatory criminal behavior while on the streets or in an institutional setting.

At *Level 3*, the serial runner who has been away from home for over one year is dealing with the compounded issue of homelessness. These youths are generally older and without satisfactory work experience; social expectations for the youth to be in the family home are therefore lower. In addition to Level 1 and Level 2 assessments, this youth needs to be stabilized in a safe environment; mobilized around existing skills, if any, for work; helped to decrease the tremendous tension and anxiety he or she feels; be detoxified (for drug and alcohol abuse); and assessed for potential aggression, especially for dangerousness to self as well as to others.

With this backdrop of levels of intervention, we offer suggestions about establishing contact with these youths. In general, the longer runaways have been away from home, the more self-demoralizing experiences they have had. Such experiences impinge on their ability to trust and to feel calm, connected, and committed to both people and places. The clinician needs to understand their heightened anxiety levels and their hypervigilance and impulsivity. They are oriented only to the present, and they defend against any reflection on their past. When the youth reveals abusive experiences, clinicians need to remember that this disclosure carries with it the resurrection of reactions to the trauma. This may activate a crisis reaction, which requires additional care and monitoring. A youth may even attempt to run away from the helping environment, such as the shelter, because of the intensity of his or her feelings about recounting the abuse. Emergency measures to protect the youth, measures that may go beyond the usual definition of service to the child, should be taken at this point.

Rapport is most readily established and maintained when runaways are responded to in a manner that gives them a sense of control, something they do not experience in their lives. Allowing the youth to feel in control of the interview imparts the feeling that he or she can make decisions and choose what will happen.

No matter how gently and skillfully directed, questions have great potential for arousing defensiveness in the youth. It is important to have a base to which both clinician and runaway can return in order to clarify why the question elicited a negative reaction. Because many runaways are inclined to blame themselves, they may interpret a question as suggesting that their views are not accurate. However, good rapport with the youth allows the practitioner to explore what the question means to the youth. Stressing that the intention of questions is to facilitate clarification is often useful in dealing with defensive reactions.

Cockiness is often used as a defense mechanism by the runaway and is perhaps best addressed by the clinician joining the self-aggrandizement, rather than by confronting the youth. Humor is another way of dealing with the runaway. These young people do not wish to experience additional painful arousal, and humor may serve to lessen the painful recounting of past experiences.

Finding out the runaways' reasons for running away reveals their perceptions of dilemmas at home. Physical and sexual abuse are often not easily acknowledged by the runaway, nor do runaways always realize that they have been or are being sexually or physically victimized. This is particularly true of adolescents. Consequently, asking for details on what transpired and how often, how the runaway dealt with abuse in the past, and what the youths consider as contributory factors helps clinicians to sift through and identify options as well as to establish risk factors remaining in the home.

Clinicians need to determine why a youth has run for several reasons. First, it must be determined whether a youngster is running from an unsafe environment. The issue of safety may not be uppermost in the minds of the youth. Instead, the youth may translate the safety issue into such issues as blame, fairness, expectations, demands, loyalty, and alienation.

Once a safe environment is provided for the runaway, clinicians can begin to address deeper problems and therapeutically deal with the thinking patterns and cognitive confusion of the runaway. Family work will be critical for those runaways who are able to return to a home that is safe. Group work with peer support is particularly useful in institutional settings that are known to be safe environments. Gradually, some youths can resume basic education and vocational goals.

It is important for clinicians to keep several general points in mind when interviewing runaways. First, one single interview will not provide all the information clinicians need. It may take many sessions to elicit the necessary responses. Second, clinicians need to keep an open mind and to avoid taking sides. Extreme judgmental attitudes often prevail in the life experiences of these youths; judgments from the clinician will only harm rapport and shut down effective communication.

Helping runaway youth presents the clinician with many challenges. The understanding of the cognitive confusion and the determination of a level of intervention designed to correct distortions are based on what the youth does or does not tell the clinician. From this understanding decisions can be made both by the youth and the helper, with the goal being to stabilize the runaway and mobilize resources aimed for positive life achievements.

Juvenile Prostitution

A primary method of procuring a juvenile is befriending or the use of feigned friendship and love. Oftentimes the prospective pimp will identify and fulfill an unmet need of the target youth. A combination of seduction and terrorism appears to be the most common approach used by pimps to recruit girls into prostitution. In these situations pimps will typically frequent areas where juveniles are apt to congregate, such as shopping malls, video game arcades, bus stations, and the like, and target isolated young girls.

A pimp's initial conversation with a girl is essentially an information-gathering mission where he attempts to identify her vulnerabilities. He is friendly or flirtatious, depending on which approach he believes she will respond to. During this initial conversation he encourages her to tell him information about herself that he will subsequently use to seduce her. Is she a runaway? Why? Is she window shopping, perhaps looking at clothing that she cannot afford? Is she a truant, tired of the restrictions of school and her parent's rules? Does she perceive herself as gawky, unattractive, unpopular? The pimp then uses the information that she so naively provides him to tailor his recruitment strategy—or rap—to meet what he perceives her needs to be. If she is a runaway, he will offer her food and shelter and vaguely hint at the possibility of a good job. Are her parents too strict? He will commiserate with her, perhaps tell her that she is too smart and too mature to have all of those restrictions. Is she lonely, or does she consider herself undesirable? Then he will fawn over her. Pimps then use a combination of flattery and charm, and the promise of money, protection, companionship, and intimacy to con or "sweet-talk" a young girl into prostitution.

Case Example: Lana

Family Background. Although an only child, Lana had many cousins and other relatives. Her father owned his own store and her mother worked in the store with him. She grew up in an urban area and her family's economic status was comfortable. During high school she used alcohol and some drugs.

According to Lana, her father beat her from age 3 until age 16, when he died. She remembers over-the-knee spankings and him telling her that she was an incorrigible little girl. At age 12 he began to spank her in front of her relatives and would actually gather relatives to watch her being bare-bottom strapped for periods as long as 20 to 30 minutes. This went on weekly. She claims that no one else in the extended family was so beaten. She believes that she was a bad girl and deserved everything she got. She described her relationship with her father as one where she constantly tried to please him but she seemed to always get in trouble with him. She felt that she always got in his way. Her relationship with her mother, on the other hand, was described as extremely good and currently remains good.

Recruitment. She was 14 when she first heard about prostitution and describes being introduced to it several years later by a man she met who was on furlough from prison. She was down and out and didn't have any money. This man introduced her to a pimp. The pimp convinced her to try prostitution because it guaranteed her money that she needed. Her first trick was straight intercourse. She felt guilty afterward but was willing to try again. She began prostituting regularly after the first trick. She turned tricks an average of 8 to 10 hours a day.

Prostitution History. There was a heavy escalation of drug use after she began her life as a prostitute. She did not stay with her first pimp very long. Lana met a woman, a madam who ran a brothel specializing in sadomasochism (S&M), at one of the sex parties that her pimp took her to. Lana was recruited by this woman and went to work in her brothel. The madam's customers usually spent the whole evening at her brothel. The madam threw many parties and Lana would be used in these parties. She soon learned that many of the tricks were prisoners who were in a furlough program.

The madam was a white Irish woman in her fifties who had two children, a son and daughter who attended universities. She had a variety of legitimate business enterprises as well as the prostitution ring. She lived in a well-to-do suburb.

The Abusive Relationship. Lana had a sexual relationship with the madam, who whipped and spanked her. Lana considered this a love relationship and strongly emphasized in her report that the madam punished her because she cared for her. She believed the madam loved her in a "perverted way as a daughter." She felt watched over and was supplied with an adequate amount of money.

Lana described herself as bisexual, stating that her experience with lesbianism grew out of prostitution. She said she enjoyed being treated roughly; if a john treated her roughly she enjoyed it. She had to perform all kinds of sex acts, as well as S&M.

Health Implications. Lana had contracted venereal diseases several times. She has no children and has never been pregnant. She said some of the S&M scenes were so rough that they probably had an emotional effect on her.

Mode of Exit. She left prostitution because of the AIDS epidemic and because people were encouraging her to leave. She owes this encouragement to the Paul and Lisa program. She was given support and direction for employment. She currently is working full-time at a supermarket. She is supporting herself and her mother and living in the family home.

She reported that she is looking for a man to marry. She wants to find someone she could trust enough to have an intimate relationship. She wonders, however, if men want an intimate relationship.

She recommends support groups for people leaving prostitution. Many of the women in prostitution do not believe there is anything else they can do in life. Many have children, and that is the reason they give for sticking with prostitution. If they had other job opportunities, emphasizes Lana, and some therapy, they would be able to leave prostitution.

Her future wish is to have enough money to take care of herself and her mother into old age; to be happy and to be able to do some traveling; and to find someone to settle down with that would love her, take care of her, and like her mother.

Discussion. There are several important points to the profile of Lana. First is the dual life she led and how this paralleled that of her madam. Lana does not believe that any of her friends knew she was a prostitute. After entering the world of prostitution, she outwardly lived the same kind of life and saw the same friends as before becoming a prostitute. She claimed that no one suspected that she had a hidden life. She was like the madam, who was a prostitute as well as having a visible legitimate life to the world and to her family. She had the legitimate business, the proper home, and children who went to the proper schools. The other half of her life was prostituting and having the "perverted daughter." This dual life represents her positive connection to the world as well as the negative.

Second, we can interpret Lana's prostitution as a behavioral reenactment of the trauma she suffered at the hands of her father. The prostitution and especially the beatings and other S&M activities she participated in reinforced her bad self-image that originated with her relationship with her father. This bad self-image was sustained and turned into something to be proud of through prostitution—that is, she was well-paid, singled out for attention by the madam, and made to feel special. All this behavior protected her from having to deal with inner rage toward her father. It was not surprising to note in the interview her irritation, anger, and resentment at the questions and the interview process. This anger wards off and defends her against memories that could trigger total recollection of the beatings her father gave her, and the acknowledgment of the pain and humiliation she suffered at his hands, as well as awareness of the eroticized aggression he subjected her to.

Third, the system of prostitution described by Lana was an organized ring with a customer base of men in a prison furlough program. There was considerable drug usage. Some of the networking was through word of mouth and some through advertising in magazines for men looking for women. That her customers were prisoners enabled the madam to exert more control over them. The madam could turn them in for violation of furlough conditions.

Pimps

It is instructive to hear from pimps themselves how they view their entry into pimping and their strategies for procuring and maintaining the prostitute. As part of a U.S. Department of Justice grant, a group of six pimps were interviewed (National Center for Missing and Exploited Children, 1992). Four agreed to be interviewed, provided they were paid. The negotiation for the interview is at the heart of what the pimp prizes as his skill. It is hustling and conning. For example, one pimp would not continue the interview unless he was paid additional money. He then attempted to strike a deal with the interviewer, offering to bring in another pimp if he was paid a finders fee. One pimp demanded more money and when the interviewer firmly said no, the pimp offered to bring in another pimp provided he got half of what was paid to the other pimp. Money and the con are the payoff in the conscious mind of the pimp.

The amount of money paid per interview was $50. The interviews extended over a 2 to 3 hour period. This amount is not unreasonable but what is found in the value system of the pimp is that some money is better than no money, and no matter what you do, you always get something for it. As one pimp said, "Ten dollars is better than no dollars, so every bit counts."

In essence the value system of the pimp is supported by the premise that "anyone can be bought." The pimp is willing to sell for the lowest price as well as the highest price. But he will sell to get a price.

Pimp Profile. The pimp profiles are based on interviews with pimps, how they present themselves, and how their methods of conducting their business contribute to profile characteristics noted in their interviews. First, the childhood environment is critical. The interview subjects learned how to pimp early. These pimps either learned it in the family or the neighborhood. They saw other people pimping and thought: This is the thing to do to be smart. Pimping gave them a sense of self. Second, there was a tendency in this group of pimps to be undereducated. Some of the pimps were functionally illiterate, that is, they could not read. Third, the pimps were socially inept. Their ability to hold their own in a social setting or social conversation was nonexistent. Fourth, pimps have a love–hate relationship with their prostitute(s) based on their dependence on a female. Pimps live off of women; they have no legitimate job.

While pimps present a variety of perspectives, they go to great lengths to deny or separate themselves from the role of exploiter or enslaver. They also attempt to separate themselves from the youthful nature of the girls they involve in prostitution, as well as from any violence they may use to control these girls and women.

The clinician needs understand the common tactics of power and control that pimps use to keep women and girls trapped in prostitution; otherwise, the clinician will not be able to create effective interventions for the women and girls that are exploited by pimps.

All pimps use a repertoire of tactics to control their women and keep them trapped in prostitution. These tactics include:

Isolation: He controls where she goes, who she sees, and what she does. He may move her to different cities or states and in some cases kidnap or hold her against her will.

Emotional Abuse: Pimps typically verbally abuse their women, calling them vile name such as "bitch", "slut", or "ho". The pimp turns women into a commodity and repeatedly tells them that they are only good for one thing.

Economic Abuse: The pimp typically takes most or all of a woman's money. He makes her ask permission to buy even the basic necessities she needs. If he fails in stopping her from leaving him, he will steal her possessions to ensure she leaves destitute.

Threats and Intimidation: A pimp will deliberately instill fear in a woman. He will make (and often carry out) threats against her, other prostitutes, even her children and family members.

Minimizing/Denial: A pimp will provide his woman with a set of positive or neutralizing definitions of prostitution to mask the abusive nature of their relationship. He will tell her she is smarter than other women who "give it away for free," that prostitution is "a job like any other job," or that all women are prostitutes: "Some do it for cash, others for dinner and a movie."

Sexual Abuse: The pimp compels his woman to engage in unwanted sexual activity with him or other men.

Using Male Privilege: The pimp treats his woman as his property and sells her to other men.

Unlike juvenile prostitutes, pimps do not reveal a clear history of childhood abuse. Their family histories often indicate that pimping and prostitution were family occupations. Or they were neglected and went to the streets and hustled. They were free to do anything they wanted to do, with no limits or discipline.

Pimp Case Example: Al and Joe. Al is a 41-year-old white divorced male convicted of conspiracy to commit murder. He and his 39-year-old brother Joe were convicted together and have served 13 years of a 15-year sentence.

The two brothers were raised in an unstable middle-class home environment with an older sister and a younger brother. Their father had had childhood polio that left him crippled. His sons believe this handicap led him to the heavy use of alcohol. His drinking caused problems at work and he was unable to hold a steady job. The boys' mother worked as a private-duty nurse. Al and Joe were raised by their paternal grandparents with their parents living separately from them. The parents would visit on occasion, with the boys having most of their contact with their father.

While the father was frequently drunk, the mother had bouts of depression and would make suicide attempts. The brothers witnessed arguments between their parents and the paternal grandfather, and the grandfather sometimes beat the boys' parents. The brothers attended military school for two years at ages 10 and 12. Their sister became pregnant at age 15, ran away from home, and never returned to the family. The brothers described their grandfather as the disciplinarian who was strict, fair, and dependable. His death when Al was 18 was a major loss for both brothers. Joe admitted to drinking heavily as a teenager. Al denied drug or alcohol use.

Al began purse snatching as a teenager. Before he was 16, he had graduated to assault with a deadly weapon and car theft. At age 16, Al and another teenager robbed a grocery store and spent a year at a reformatory. In his year in the reformatory he listened to the older inmates talk about criminal activity. Al reported "two important lessons" he learned in the reformatory. First, he was the youngest in the institution and when inmates made sexual advances to him, he made the decision to fight and claims he was not bothered any more. Second, he was schooled in the reformatory that organized crime would be the way to make money.

After the reformatory, Al claimed he did try to get into legitimate business but without an education the best job he could get was washing cars. He reflected that when he was released, his buddies were still 17 years old and "acting like kids." Also, his former interests and his new criminal interests were not the same.

Al joined with his brother Joe after his time in reform school to do some construction work and house painting. Al smashed his finger while working and was put on state compensation. That gave him money and time off. He claims he drifted into fencing stolen property because he could make in one day what he had made in one week working construction. Then Al started up some other businesses, including illegal gambling games.

Al decided in reform school that he wanted to make a lot of money as fast as possible. He renewed a friendship with a high school girlfriend who had been in reform school for truancy and incorrigibility. He claims she suggested they go into the prostitution business. She had a "trick book" compiled from names of customers who had patronized a house of prostitution where she had worked. Al estimated the cost of a good trick book in the 1960s–1970s to be around $10,000.

Another girl joined the team and Joe began pimping the two girls. The three were arrested. Police raided the apartments the girls used and discovered carefully documented trick books containing names of well-known people, among them a prominent criminal lawyer, a socially active architect, a common pleas judge, businessmen, and professional athletes. While in jail, the girls met another prostitute who referred them to a lawyer who defended many prostitutes. The trio pleaded guilty to misdemeanor charges and their sentences were suspended. They then moved their business to another section of the city.

Over a five-year period from 1968 to 1973, Al estimated working hundreds of girls. He claimed that he had a good reputation because the girls were protected and they would go periodically for a health checkup. Apartments were used on both the east and west side of town.

In their roles running their gambling enterprises the brothers met many pimps and prostitutes. This furthered their education and they decided to expand their prostitution business. They procured the names of potential customers and purchased many apartments throughout the city. These apartments were used to house their prostitutes, and some of them were used as brothels. Some of these brothels were managed with the assistance of madams. Al drove elaborately decorated and equipped limousines. He also dressed in a flashy manner: blue, purple, and green suits with patent-leather shoes to match. He bought horses and a boat. He was open about his work. Although still only in their 20s, the brothers had built up a network of contacts, from bartenders to doctors, who referred clients to them.

Prostitution was not only a means of making money, it was also an opportunity to associate with underworld characters the brothers admired. Al liked his role as a "gangster" and wanted to be the no. 1 procurer in town.

The brothers worked hard. Along with their thriving prostitution business, they developed other legitimate interests, particularly in various real estate ventures, and lumped them together under one holding company. Joe's business card identified him as an "investment broker." The brothers bought beauty shops because that gave them access to more women.

When Al and Joe were finally arrested for interstate prostitution, law enforcement agents located ledgers that revealed the brothers had earned $250,000 during the previous five years from prostitution alone.

Al and Joe discussed how they worked as pimps and differentiated levels of the prostitution business. To them, the lowest level was streetwalking. It was a high-risk form of prostitution because streetwalkers were very vulnerable to law enforcement. The "merchandise" tended to be young, that is, children and young teenagers, thus raising problems of violating statutory laws regarding sex with children. Streetwalkers also caused problems because they tended to be drug users. These factors were viewed by Al and Joe as the type of risk issues that they wished to avoid. They also alluded to the fact that controlling streetwalkers often involved threats and violence and to obtain recruits into such prostitution activities required seduction and time.

The more lucrative and less risk-laden form of prostitution relied on a trick book and/or the use of such fronts as escort services. Here, at this level, there was a complex network of procurers of prostitutes. Some of the prostitutes were directly solicited by Al and Joe and were under their direct command, while others were contracted for from outlying providers of prostitutes. This level often involved contacts made by johns who would arrange to meet girls at various places. There were also designated locations where johns could always go to obtain the services of a prostitute.

Al and Joe described the prostitutes they most frequently worked with as coming from a variety of backgrounds. One group they defined as the "housewife prostitute." These were women who freelanced. They would come in from the suburbs one or two nights a week. Their aim was to obtain money. Al and Joe claimed they were bored and wanted some excitement. They viewed these women as most desirable candidates and gave them preferential assignments. The more expensive services tend to be provided by attractive women who are dressed specifically to appeal to an upper-middle-class clientele or to those johns who could afford to pay high prices. Price was also set by level of deviancy and perversion. The provision of young children, bondage, and sadomasochistic sex are at the expensive end of the price range in prostitution.

The first thing Al and Joe emphasize is that these girls are dependent and they want to be dependent. The job of the pimp is to find out exactly what these young girls want and to use their wants to control them and hold them in a relationship.

They describe how the first step is to befriend the girl and not even to suggest that she prostitute herself. During this period of time, the pimp provides care and attention. For example, if the girl is a runaway the pimp will find shelter for her, sometimes taking her back to his own place. Sometimes he may turn her over to a madam who understands how to enhance the dependency of the young person. Often the extension of friendship and specialness creates an emotional bond toward the pimp. The girl comes to believe that the pimp thinks she is special. Somewhere at the juncture of this established dependency, a move is made to initiate the girl and define her as a prostitute. This can be done by the pimp first engaging the girl in sex himself and then later forcing or coercing the girl into having sex with another person.

Sometimes the pimp may in fact deliver the girl to another pimp who now claims she is a prostitute and gains control through beating her and informing her she is now committed and sold to him and that he owns her. Then the girl is turned out to the streets to work.

Pimps and prostitutes watch for the young and vulnerable. They are patient and try to read the individual just like a cat watches a bird or mouse. They will evaluate what the person needs, and create a dependency, and then move on that dependency. They will make small talk and find out if they are runaways and then provide shelter. If the runaway uses drugs, they will supply them. Transients or street people including runaways are motivated to enter prostitution to get money, food, clothing, shelter, and drugs.

Pimps use street girls for lengthy hours daily because they know their time on the streets is limited to six months or a few years. The girls burn out or take off after a while.

Pimps can place legitimate advertisements in newspapers, for example, offering interviews for a secretarial position. When a likely target comes to the interview, the pimp informs her that nothing is available or that someone else got the job. Then the pimp might try to date her. With continued contact, the pimp works on the woman's weakness and tries to find out what the woman is looking for. If it is money, he might note that a secretary is only going to make $125 a week, and then point out that another girl is making $1,000 a week. Sometimes pimps place ads for "dancers," "models," or "escort services."

Pimps establish their territory. The territory could be a bar, a corner on a street, or a truck stop. The street pimp gets his strength by maintaining his domain and keeping other pimps, prostitutes, or madams from coming into his area. Violence is a danger on the street. It happens to runaways going to a high-crime area (drugs, porn, strip bars). The pimp or prostitute will actually victimize the runaway if he or she feels the girl is cutting into his or her territory. Or as often is the case, they will "rescue" the girl or act as her "protector," thus fostering dependence.

The name of the game is hustling. The pimps and prostitutes hustle the regular individuals and each other. They call them "players." Players try to outplay each other. They try to steal each other's women.

Interventions

The intricacies of the systems of prostitution reveal that its substance is built upon myths. Any approach to providing assistance or eliminating the ravages of this public health disorder can only be partial until the condoning sources change regarding the demand for prostitution and regarding the tolerance toward those willing to reap the profits by exploiting impoverished juveniles of both sexes. By "impoverished," we mean those juveniles who by and large lack a caring nurturing environment.

Recognizing that our efforts in the most immediate sense are initiated long after the fire has started, three levels of addressing the potential victims are described. Level 1 is case finding for the high-risk juvenile before entering prostitution. The best time for this to occur is before pubescence and when the child is initially abused and neglected. Level 2 is when the youth enters the life of prostitution and is first picked up by authorities. A rigorous controlled environment and mandated intervention is required at this level. Level 3 is for the streetwise youth. Programs such as the Paul and Lisa Program in Westbrook, CT, are critical for this kind of youth, just as programs such as WHISPER (Women Hurt in Systems of Prostitution Engaged in Revolt) are critical for adult women (National Center for Missing and Exploited Children, 1992).

At every level of intervention there has to be comprehensive health assessment and evaluation. Of particular concern are the sexually transmitted diseases and HIV exposure and transmission. All evidence indicates that extensive substance abuse and a history of multiple sexual partners intensifies the risk of contracting sexually transmitted diseases and HIV infection. Of particular concern are children of prostitutes because they can not only be exposed to these diseases before and after birth, but they are at risk for sexual exploitation by other people in the mother's network.

Level 1: Identify High-Risk Children and Block Their Transition into Prostitution. The first step is to recognize what is the basis of the juvenile's sexual behavior. To view prostitution behaviorally is to understand that sexual behavior is not always in the service of sexual gratification. Often it serves the purposes of contact for comfort, rebellion, earning money, and surviving. Our attitudes toward these children and their highly sexualized behavior can be critical to saving them. We should not interpret the sexual behaviors as if they are enjoying the activity; we must instead see it as a defense and an adaptation to more threatening circumstances. Behind the immediate threatening circumstances there is often a history of physical and sexual abuse in the family, parental neglect, parental violence, and abdication of parental roles and responsibilities through the abuse of drugs and alcohol.

Most of the prostitutes interviewed had their primary life conditions made known to official agencies prior to transition into prostitution. Because so many of these youths were sexually and physically abused in their homes, their response to agencies and settings such as school is often distant, defiant, and aloof. This behavior prompts negative reactions from caretakers and often results in misreading the true life conditions of these children.

They are often returned to their troubled families and to the abuse they suffered there without any agent's effort to help them. This early failure to recognize the roots of the child's distress reinforces the "legitimacy" of an exploitive environment.

Strategies to be considered include:

1. *Legal representation for the juvenile.* The juvenile should be provided with a guardian who will assume responsibility for protecting the rights of the juvenile. The presence of a guardian allows family-life evaluation procedures to be carried out in a thorough, comprehensive manner. With this model, parents would have to avail themselves of services that deal with substance abuse and violent behaviors. If substantial abuse is identified, legal steps then need to be taken against the perpetrator.

2. *Education programs aimed at identifying juveniles at risk.* Programs held in the community at churches and schools should outline the risk factors and symptoms. A mandatory prostitution prevention curricu-

lum in the junior and senior high schools, one that attacks myths about prostitution (not sexuality), helps youths to identify recruitment tactics by pimps and johns, and teaches boys that it is inappropriate to coerce sexual compliance through payment.

3. *Education of all people who deal with youths.* Such people should be taught to recognize the signs of abuse and early entry into prostitution.

4. *Community education about the myths of prostitution,* and careful reevaluation of community laws regarding prostitution.

5. *Education about the employment practices of pimps.* Who is monitoring them?

Level 2: Transition Stage into Prostitution. This is when the juvenile first hits the street. The youths that get into prostitution go where there is a demand for their services (e.g., the bus stations, the truck stops, the pimp bars, the bogus modeling agencies). Pimps are known; they are identified by the police.

Services need to be available. There needs to be safe havens for juveniles. They need access to legal, health, and medical services. They need education as to their rights and what recourse they have when their parents are abusive. They need psychoeducation regarding the impact of trauma and what options are there for them to address their behaviors.

Young males, especially those between 14 and 19, who are on the streets need some sort of intervention that identifies pimping as abusive. A good intervention point here are street work projects that deal with homeless youth, storefront churches, food shelves, and so on. We keep trying to patch up the girls but allow the young predators to flourish until it's (almost) too late for them to make changes.

Level 3: Juveniles Who Have Adapted a Street Life-style. There are two types of prostitutes to identify at this level. The first is the streetwise youth who has been prostituting for some time. The second is the older female prostitute who has children or who through ill health and impoverishment needs assistance and protection to get out.

The role of drug programs is crucial at all levels. Staff need to be educated that prostitution is a problem in and of itself that may or may not be compounded by drug abuse. Another critical task is to work with foster-care programs to train perspective foster parents how to deal with the myriad of problems that arise in providing a home for such children.

Outreach programs are needed for street juveniles so that when they try to escape prostitution they have a route to travel. One of the frontlines of helping these juveniles involves protecting those who come in through *emergency* rooms for abuse, beatings, and substance abuse.

References

Burgess, A. W., Hartman, C. R., McCausland, M. P., & Powers, P. A. (1984). Response patterns in children and adolescents exploited through sex rings and pornography. *American Journal of Psychiatry, 141*(5), 656–662.

Burgess, A. W., Hartman, C. R., Wolbert, W. A., & Grant, C. A. (1987). Child molestation: Assessment of impact. *American Journal of Psychiatric Nursing, 1*(1), 33–39.

Conte, J. R. (1984). Progress in treating the sexual abuse of children. *Social Work, 258–263.*

Fine, M., & Rosenberg, P. (1983). Dropping out of high school: The ideology of school and work. *Journal of Education, 165, 257–272.*

Garbarino, J. (1989). Troubled youths, troubled families: The dynamics of adolescent maltreatment. In V. Carlson & D. Cicchette (Eds.), *Research and theoretical advances on the topic of child maltreatment*. Cambridge, England: Cambridge University Press.

Groth, A. N. (1979). Sexual trauma in the life histories of rapists and child molesters. *Victimology, 4*(1), 10–16.

Herman, J. L. (1981). *Father-daughter incest*. Cambridge, MA: Harvard University Press.

Janus, M. D. (1984). Youth prostitution. In A. Burgess (Ed.), *Child pornography and sex rings* pp. 127–146. Lexington, MA: Lexington Books.

Manis, J. (1974). Addressing the seriousness of social problems. *Social Problems, 22, 1–5.*

National Center for Missing & Exploited Children. (1992). *Female juvenile prostitution. Problems and responses.* Arlington, VA: Author.

Reich, J. W., & Gutierres, S. E. (1979). Escape/aggression incidence in sexual abused juvenile delinquents. *Criminal Justice and Behavior, 6, 239–243.*

10

Assessment and Treatment Issues in Child Sexual Abuse

Kathleen Coulborn Faller

The seriousness of the problem of child sexual abuse is measured by indices of prevalence and incidence rates. Research findings on *prevalence*, the number of people sexually victimized during childhood, vary because of variations in research methodology (Finkelhor, Peters, & Wyatt, 1986). However, the best estimates are that approximately one in three girls (Saunders et al., 1991; Saunders, Villeponteaux, Lipovsky, Kilpatrick, & Veronen, 1992) and one in six boys (Finkelhor, Hotaling, Lewis, & Smith, 1990) experience this trauma.

Incidence is reflected in national statistics collected since 1976 on reports of abuse and neglect to child protection agencies. In 1992 almost three million cases of child maltreatment were reported. The number and proportion of these that include sexual abuse have increased steadily since 1976, when 6,000 cases were 3 percent of reports, to the present day. Now child sexual abuse represents close to 15 percent of reports and approximately 400,000 cases (American Association for Protecting Children, 1988; McCurdy & Daro, 1993). Moreover, although the climate related to disclosure of sexual abuse is improving, research suggests most cases are not reported (Russell, 1986).

These findings provide a powerful argument for all mental health and health care professionals to have knowledge of assessment and treatment of sexual abuse.

Health and mental health providers play a range of roles in child sexual abuse cases. For example, they may note indicators of sexual abuse in a child. In such a circumstance, they become *reporters* to mandated child protection agencies. Although the decision to report suspected sexual abuse should not be taken lightly, in every state health and mental health professionals are required by law to make such reports; they can be subjected to legal penalties for failure to report; and they have legal protections if they report suspected abuse. Child protective services workers are responsible for investigating these cases. Reporters need not be absolutely certain of sexual abuse before making a report; they merely need to have "reasonable cause to suspect" abuse.

Health and mental health professionals may be asked to perform a range of *assessment* tasks. *Medical assessments*, which are undertaken by physicians and nurses, are beyond the scope of this chapter, but are nevertheless an important component in the overall assessment process. In fact, the medical examination has taken on an increasingly important role as advances have been made in medical diagnosis of sexual abuse (Bays & Chadwick, 1993). All cases of suspected sexual abuse should have medical exams, but these should be performed by health care providers with specialized training in sexual abuse exams.

Professionals may be asked to conduct *mental health assessments* of children suspected of sexual abuse. As described later, a variety of assessment questions may be posed. However, a somewhat unique question for mental health professionals, but one frequently asked, is whether sexual abuse actually occurred. The expertise needed to answer this question involves skills generally not taught during graduate training. Consequently, the emphasis in this chapter will be on describing these techniques.

One of the most important roles for mental health and health care providers is as *therapists* and healers. Virtually all abuse victims need some treatment, and some may require ongoing periodic treatment as they cope with life crises and developmental issues related to sexuality. Moreover, often the victim's family also needs therapy, in both extrafamilial and intrafamilial abuse cases. Offenders need treatment, too, but clinicians should not provide such treatment unless they have appropriate training and supervision. Moreover, offender therapists need to be integrated into the therapeutic and case-management network providing services in the case (Salter, 1988).

Finally, health and mental health professionals are increasingly being called as *witnesses* in child sexual abuse court cases. Because of its adversarial nature, most clinicians find the legal arena an alien environment, one for which they have received little professional preparation—either practical or psychological. Moreover, since they can be subpoenaed, they are not always willing participants in the court process. When working on sexual abuse cases, clinicians would do well to anticipate the possibilities of being called to testify and of having their case records scrutinized during an adversarial process. Care should be taken to follow accepted clinical practice and to carefully document all interventions and their rationale (Faller, 1990b).

The goal of this chapter is to provide information to assist health and mental health providers in their various roles in sexual abuse cases. With regard to assessment, this chapter will cover psychosocial indicators of sexual abuse, questions mental health professionals need to address, assessment techniques, and decision-making guidelines. With regard to treatment, the integration of child treatment into case management, the role of disclosure in treatment, affective and behavioral treatment issues, and future protection will be covered.

Assessment

Higher and Lower Probability Indicators of Child Sexual Abuse

Indicators of child sexual abuse can be categorized as medical or psychosocial. In both categories, there are higher and lower probability indicators. Since this chapter's focus is on the mental health aspects of childhood sexual problems, only psychosocial indicators will be covered. A differentiation will be made between sexual indicators, which are higher probability, and nonsexual behavioral indicators of stress, which are lower probability.

Higher probability indicators include (1) an explicit statement describing sexual abuse, (2) sexual knowledge beyond that expected for the child's developmental stage, (3) sexualized behavior, (4) sexual promiscuity during early adolescence, (5) adolescent prostitution, and (6) excessive masturbation. Although all of these are "red flags" for sexual abuse, they are not conclusive; instead, they signal the need for further exploration to understand the etiology of the behaviors or statements.

Lower probability indicators are so designated because they may be indicative of sexual abuse, but are just as likely to be signs of other trauma, for example, other types of maltreatment, family discord, trauma originating outside the family, and even natural disasters. Examples are bowel and bladder problems, sleep problems, eating problems, problems in interpersonal relationships, school difficulties, running away, substance abuse, suicidal thoughts and behavior, stealing, cruelty to animals, and fire setting.

Often the child presents with a combination of sexual and nonsexual symptoms, which taken together should result in a high index of suspicion. For example, a typical presentation for an adolescent girl who has endured chronic sexual abuse includes promiscuity, running away, substance abuse, and suicide attempts. Similarly, boys with histories of sexual aggression, enuresis, fire setting, and cruelty to animals have a very high probability signs of sexual abuse.

Issues to Be Addressed in Assessment

The issues clinicians may be asked to address can be conceptualized as five questions. Each will be briefly discussed.

Did Sexual Abuse Occur? This is often a threshold question that must be answered before other ones can be addressed. In many instances, child protection workers and law enforcement officers make initial judgments about the allegation's veracity, but mental health evaluators are also asked to address it. State-of-the-art techniques for data gathering and decision making will be described below. However, in some legal arenas mental health opinions regarding the veracity of children's disclosures and conclusions regarding whether sexual abuse occurred will not be allowed (Myers, 1992).

What Are the Characteristics of the Sexual Abuse? Characteristics include who the offender is, the types of sexual activity, age of onset, frequency, duration, last incident, use of force, and use of threats.

What Is the Impact of Sexual Abuse on the Child? Sexual abuse can vary in its impact from minimal to pervasive. The characteristics of the sexual abuse play a role in its effect. So does the child's perception of the abuse, the child's age, and the responses of others to the abuse and/or its disclosure. Although important information is gathered from the child, input from those close to the child is also usually needed. The evaluator investigates impact on both emotional functioning and behavior, specifically on the child's ability to trust (relationships with adults and peers), on mood (depressed, angry, fearful), on everyday functioning (sleep, eating, bowel and bladder functioning, school performance), and on other behaviors (e.g., sexual acting-out, aggression, incorrigibility).

What Is the Child's Overall Functioning? Other professionals, for example, child protection workers, are usually not prepared to assess overall functioning, a task mental health professionals are trained to perform. Sexual abuse will have an impact on functioning, and often it is hard to separate the effect of sexual abuse from the child's customary level of functioning. Children who have received good nurturing and who have experienced few traumas will usually be better able to cope with sexual abuse. However, its initial impact in such children may appear greater, precisely because abuse is such an unusual and unanticipated experience.

What Sort of Intervention Is Needed? Intervention involves both treatment and case management. The latter includes such issues as whether the child needs to be placed, whether the offender should be criminally prosecuted, and whether parental rights should eventually be terminated. Intervention recommendations and planning must integrate the actions of others—child protection workers, law enforcement personnel, prosecutors, and court staff, as well as other treatment providers. Sexual abuse cases are best handled in a multidisciplinary, collaborative manner (Bross, Krugman, Lenherr, Rosenberg, & Schmidt, 1988).

How to Conduct an Assessment

Five aspects of the assessment process will be discussed: (1) recording, (2) structure of the evaluation, (3) questioning techniques, (4) use of media, and (5) psychological testing.

Recording the Assessment. Unlike other types of evaluations, sexual abuse assessments rely on precise records of children's statements and behaviors. Various forms of record keeping can be employed, including note taking, audio-taping and videotaping. However, videotaping is best because it provides the most complete record and may reduce the number of interviews the child must undergo. Nevertheless, videotaping is not without drawbacks, the most problematic being that such tapes may be used to impeach the child, who may be somewhat inconsistent within the interview or in different interviews, and that they may be used to challenge the evaluator's assessment techniques. Evaluators should be willing to explain the rationale for their methodology, but the existence of a videotape may result in the case's focus shifting from what the child said to how the information was elicited.

Structuring the Assessment.
Who Should Be Seen? In addressing the likelihood of sexual abuse, one key question is: Who does the mental health professional interview? This issue had been the subject of debate and careful consideration. There is general consensus that the child interview is the central component of the assessment (American Professional Society on the Abuse of Children, 1990; Conte, Sorenson, Fogarty, & Dalla Rosa, 1991). Others, such as parents, may provide important ancillary information, but the evaluator must realize that these others may have vested interests in either confirming or disconfirming the child's information (Faller, 1984, 1988).

Similarly, it is inappropriate to weigh the child's account against the offender's to determine whose is more persuasive (Summit, 1983). Children rarely benefit from making a false allegation of sexual abuse and usually suffer for disclosure of true sexual abuse. On the other hand, actual offenders face serious penalties if the child's account is believed and may go to considerable lengths to convince the evaluator that the child is mistaken, lying, fantasizing, or crazy (Faller, 1988). Nevertheless, there will be a few cases in which the offender or others offer an alternative explanation for the accusation that indicate sexual abuse probably did not occur.

There has also been debate about the utility of interviewing the child with the alleged offender, a practice used to assess attachment in other types of child maltreatment and employed in divorce cases where questions of custody and visitation arise. This procedure is not used by most sexual abuse experts to evaluate whether a child has been sexually abused (Conte et al., 1991), and its ethical and practical drawbacks have been documented (Faller, Froning, & Lipovsky, 1991).

Similarly, the victim will be the best source of information regarding the extent of sexual abuse, its impact, and overall functioning, but others close to the child may also provide useful input. To make an intervention plan that goes beyond victim treatment issues, information from others beside the victim is needed.

How Many Interviews? There is no hard and fast rule about number of interviews needed. However, this issue has been the subject of professional concern and debate. Some researchers (Sorenson & Snow, 1991) have found most children need several interviews in order to make a full disclosure. On the other hand, professionals have asserted that too many interviews will result in programming and leave children wondering if they are believed (American Academy of Child and Adolescent Psychiatry, 1990).

Some cases and assessment circumstances will lend themselves to a single, fairly long session, for example, when child safety is an issue, or the family has to come from a long distance away. Others will be better handled in a series of shorter interviews, for instance, when children are young, have short attention spans, have been severely traumatized, or are very reluctant to disclose.

The number of interviews also depends upon assessment goals. If the evaluator has only been asked whether the child has been sexually abused, one interview may be sufficient. However, more are usually needed if the goals include assessing the extent of sexual abuse, its impact, and the victim's overall functioning.

How to Approach the Issue of Sexual Abuse. Evaluators approach sexual abuse as they would any sensitive topic. They first build a relationship with the child so that a degree of trust is established. The clinician and child can "get to know one another" by the evaluator explaining who he or she is and why the child is there, in a way the child can comprehend. The clinician also asks about typical aspects of the child's life, such as school, friends, interests, and some aspects of family, before dealing with the issue of possible sexual abuse. The general discussion can also be used to assess the child's overall functioning, competency, and developmental level, in part so that the evaluator has some idea how best to ask about sexual abuse (Faller, 1988).

Activities, such as dollhouse play with young children, coloring in a coloring book, drawing, or board games, can be used in several ways in an assessment. They can be used as an icebreaker and assessment medium at the beginning of the session. They can be used as a tension reducer, either during discussion of sexual abuse or as a breaktime activity when the child becomes too stressed. Finally, they can be used at the end of the interview as a kind of reward for hard work and a return to more normal activity.

It is advisable to progress from positive and/or neutral material to material that is more difficult and related to possible sexual abuse. As I suggested in the previous paragraph, the evaluator should be sensitive to the child's stress level and structure the evaluation to avoid retraumatization.

In the next section, questioning techniques and use of media will be described as separate activities, but usually they are employed together. In fact, media are never used without accompanying questions. The evaluator should expect to asknumerous questions and use a variety of media and approaches to elicit necessary information, whether confirming or disconfirming. Young children have difficulty with free recall and require appropriate questions to trigger their memories. Children of all ages may be reluctant to discuss sexual abuse and can be assisted by having several opportunities to reveal their experiences. Finally, because in many cases the goal of assessment is not only to understand who did what, but to uncover details of the sexual abuse, its context, the reactions of others in the child's life, and the impact of the abuse on the child, extended interviewing is usually needed.

Questioning Techniques during Assessment. Analogue research (studies of children's memory and suggestibility that use naturally occurring or staged events containing some characteristics of sexual abuse) with young children indicates that children usually do not provide information about sensitive topics when asked open-ended questions. They require direct questions to disclose this material; direct questions elicit very few false positives. Moreover, children are generally resistant to being led when asked a few suggestive questions (Saywitz, Goodman, Nicholas, & Moan, 1989). However, if they are interrogated by an authority figure (Clark-Stewart, Thompson, & Lapore, 1989) or repeatedly interviewed using leading questions, they are suggestible (Ceci, 1992; Doris, 1991).

The questioning strategy shown in Table 10–1 takes into account the analogue research findings and suggests a more conservative posture than the research warrants (Faller, 1990a, 1990b).

The questions represent a continuum from most to least open-ended, and evaluators should have greater confidence in responses the more open-ended

Table 10–1
Assessment Interview Questioning Strategy

Question Type	Example
1. General questions	1. Tell me all about daycare. 2. Why did you come to see me?
2. Focused questions	1. Is there anything Uncle Joe does that you don't like? 2. Did your peepee ever get hurt? 3. What happens when Johnny baby-sits? 4. Did you talk to your teacher about something Daddy did?
3. Multiple-choice questions	1. Do those bad things happen in the daytime or nighttime? 2. Did your daddy use his hand, his foot, his penis, or something else?
4. Yes-No questions	1. Was Uncle Joe the one who hurt your peepee? 2. Did John ever touch your vagina?
5. Leading questions	1. Isn't it true that your uncle molested you, not your father? 2. Your mother licked your penis, didn't she?

the question. They are advised to begin with open-ended questions and only resort to more close-ended ones when the former fail to elicit information. However, with the exception of leading questions, when faced with the choice between getting no information and asking a more close-ended question, the question should be asked. Once information is revealed, the evaluator should move back up the continuum to more open-ended questions.

As the research suggests, children, especially young ones, are not likely to provide information about sexual abuse in response to *general* questions. The next level, *focused* questions, will probably be more productive. The examples given in the table illustrate four types of focused questions: (1) those that are directed to the person who might have abused the child, (2) those directed to the body parts, (3) those directed to the circumstance of the abuse, and (4) those directed to the circumstance of initial disclosure (Faller, 1990).

The child may either not respond or may reply "I don't remember" to a focused question, leading to a decision to use a *multiple-choice* question. For example, suppose the child has said that her peepee got hurt when visiting grandma. The evaluator first asks a body part–focused question, "Who was it that hurt your peepee?" The child doesn't answer. The evaluator then might ask, "Was it your grandpa, your grandma, or someone else?" It is important not to pose a multiple-choice question that does not include a correct choice, hence the inclusion of "someone else" in the example. In addition, some advise limiting multiple-choice questions to the context of the abuse, that is, to *where* and *when* it happened, and avoiding their use when asking about *who* did it and *what* happened.

Yes-No questions are differentiated from focused questions in that they include both the person who may have committed the abuse and the type of abuse. Despite research findings suggesting that many children will not disclose without Yes-No questions, they should be used sparingly. There are concerns that a child might respond "Yes" because she or he doesn't know the answer or understand the question, or to please the interviewer (Faller, 1990b).

Leading questions are ones in which the desired response is clear from the question and should not be used in an evaluation for possible sexual abuse.

The evaluator asks questions not only about what happened (including details) and who did it, but when it started, how often it happened, how the offender got the child involved, who else might have known about it, any threats the offender might have used to prevent disclosure, where the abuse took place, how the child feels about what happened, what the child thinks should happen to the offender, whether the child knows if the offender abused anyone else, and whether anyone else has ever done something sexual with the child. The child's developmental level and functioning will govern the extent of questioning. Although questions should be asked about the abuse's impact, impact may be better understood from the child's nonverbal than verbal communication.

Use of Media during Assessment. Child sexual abuse evaluations present particular challenges because of the sensitive nature of the substantive material and the need for detailed information. As a consequence, specialized techniques have evolved for use in these assessments. These media can also be invaluable in abuse-focused therapy, to be described below. Four media will be discussed here: (1) anatomical dolls, (2) anatomical drawings, (3) free drawings, and (4) writing assignments.

Anatomical Dolls. Despite the controversy surrounding anatomical dolls, research indicates they do not elicit sexualized responses from sexually naive children. However, they do trigger sexualized responses in sexually knowledgeable children—which makes them useful in sexual abuse evaluations (Everson & Boat, 1990, 1994; Sivan, Schor, Koeppi, & Nobel, 1988). Moreover, among sexual abuse experts, they are the most widely used medium (Conte et al., 1991).

However, the dolls are not a diagnostic test; that is, responses to anatomical dolls alone do not determine whether children have been sexually abused. Many sexually victimized children will not engage in sexual behavior play with the dolls (August & Foreman, 1989; Cohen, 1991; White, Strom, Santilli, & Halpin, 1986), and children can learn about sex from experiences other than sexual abuse and may display such knowledge with anatomical dolls (Everson & Boat, 1990). Such sexual behavior play with dolls raises concern about sexual abuse and should result in questions about the source of the child's sexual knowledge.

There is no standard method for using anatomical dolls. Everson and Boat (1994) reviewed 20 guidelines for their use and found six functions endorsed. The four most common will be described.

If the evaluator elicits some information from questioning, for example, by asking a focused question about the suspected offender, the anatomical dolls can function as a *demonstration aid*. Used in this way, they can serve to facilitate disclosure, to clarify disclosure, or to corroborate disclosure. In the first instance, the child may be having difficulty talking about what happened and so the evaluator asks the child if it might be easier to show than to tell, and then together they choose appropriate dolls. In the second instance, the child may give a vague description of a sexual act, for example "Daddy humped me." The evaluator might then ask the child to show "humping" with appropriate dolls. In the third instance, the child has usually given a coherent statement, for example, "Mr. Jones put his peenie in my mouth." The evaluator asks for a demonstration with anatomical dolls, perhaps to guard against the possibility of a coached verbal response or merely to be able to document in the report that the child both described and showed the sexual act.

When the dolls are used as a demonstration aid, the evaluator asks questions to elicit explicit detail and to explore for advanced sexual knowledge. The following sorts of questions could be asked: "What did that feel like?" "Do you know whether the penis was sticking up or sort of hanging down?" "Did anything come out of the end of the penis?" "What did the stuff look like?" "What did it taste like?" "Do you remember how far in the penis went?"

If children are reluctant to demonstrate with the dolls, it is appropriate to ask them to indicate on the dolls which body parts were involved, and then see if the children will demonstrate the acts. If a child won't point to the body parts, evaluators may, themselves, point to parts, but it important to include (nonsexual) parts probably not involved, to avoid leading the child.

When the evaluator asks focused questions about body parts, anatomical dolls may be used as an *anatomical model*. In using the dolls as an anatomical model, four dolls—adults and children of both genders—are normally presented. The child undresses or is assisted in undressing the dolls. The evaluator then asks the child to identify both nonsexual and sexual body parts. Some clinicians ask the child to specify the functions of body parts. The child's names for body parts are used by the evaluator in future reference. The child is then asked focused questions about the relevant private parts, which include questions about potential victim and offender private parts. Illustrative questions include: "Did you ever see a pecker?" "Whose did you see?" "What was he doing when you saw it?" "Did anything not so good ever happen to your peepee?" "Did anyone ever hurt your front private spot?" "Did anyone ever want you to do something to that part of their body?" If affirming information is elicited, the interviewer asks the child to demonstrate, and then the function of the dolls shifts from an *anatomical model* to a *demonstration aid*.

Two other functions for the dolls, which usually occur concurrently, are as a *memory stimulus* and as a *diagnostic screen*. When the dolls are used for these functions, the evaluator allows free-play time during and after the dolls are undressed, makes note of the child's reactions and statements, and then asks questions. For example, suppose the child became distressed by the naked adult male doll. The evaluator might ask why the doll upset the child, or whether the doll made the child think of something upsetting.

Anatomical Drawings. Anatomical drawings (Groth & Stevenson, 1990) are less widely used than dolls (Conte et al., 1991), but have some of their advantages. Drawings come in five developmental stages, both genders, and both Caucasian and African-American. The clinician and child choose the appropriate drawings to be used. These are copies made from originals in Groth and Stevenson's book.

Anatomical drawings can serve all the functions of anatomical dolls, except it is more difficult, but not impossible, for children to demonstrate sexual acts with drawings. Therefore, children usually point to relevant body parts and describe the activity. In addition, the drawings are inscribed. The evaluator has the child mark on the drawings the body parts involved in sexual activity. The child or the evaluator writes down the child's verbal statements; it is useful to write down the evaluator's questions as well. It is important to date and put identifying information on drawings. They become part of the case record and may be entered as such or as an exhibit in litigation.

Free Drawings. Traditional free drawing tasks, such as Draw a Person and the Kinetic Family Drawing, are useful for evaluating overall functioning of sexual abuse victims, but less helpful for assessing the likelihood or impact of sexual abuse. Research on drawings of sexually abused children finds that they rather infrequently include indicators of their victimization, for example, genitalia (Friedrich, 1993; Burgess & Hartman, 1993).

However, drawings more specifically related to sexual abuse may be of assistance both in deciding whether sexual abuse occurred and in assessing its impact. The child might be asked to draw the alleged offender, the place where the abuse occurred, the abuse itself, or any instrument used to abuse the child. In all instances, the interviewer asks questions about the drawing to clarify information about the abuse and its context. In addition, to assess its impact, the child can be asked how he or she felt or what he or she thought at that time and what he or she is feeling or thinking now. As with anatomical drawings, the child's verbalizations and questions to elicit them can be written on the drawing. The picture should be appropriately identified and become part of the case record.

Writing Assignments. Older children may find writing a medium that facilitates abuse disclosure and an easier way to express affect than talking. Although writing assignments are usually given between sessions, there will be children who, during a session, prefer to write words or phrases on a piece of paper instead of answering questions verbally. Assignments for between sessions can include writing in a diary or writing about the abuse and/or feelings about it. The child might be asked to write just one paragraph, or a letter, that might be addressed to the offender, the clinician, or the mother. Sometimes, asking the child to write about feelings in general will provide material that can be productively pursued in session.

As with other productions, victims' written work should be labeled appropriately and preserved as part of the case record.

Psychological Testing during Assessment. Because most psychological tests are not specific to sexual abuse, testing is primarily useful in assessing the child's developmental level and overall functioning. However, test results may also assist the evaluator in assessing competency and the impact of sexual abuse.

There are some tests that are more useful in sexual abuse. The Achenbach Child Behavior Checklist (CBCL; Achenbach & Edelbrock, 1983), with versions for children ages 2 to 16, has been employed extensively in research on maltreated children and to a lesser extent in clinical work. Although research demonstrates differences in scores between sexually abused children and normal comparison groups, the former generally do not differ from other clinical populations, and the nature of differences vary by study (Kendall-Tackett, 1992). In addition, the CBCL has only one subscale specific to sexual abuse, the Sexual Problems subscale.

Two tests have been developed specifically for abused children. The Child Sexual Behavior Inventory (CSBI; Friedrich, 1990) consists of 36 items and has been found to reliably discriminate levels of sexual behavior between sexually abused children from 2 to 12 years old and children without such histories. However, not all sexually abused children exhibit sexualized behavior. Both the CBCL and the CSBI are completed by a caretaker, although the CBCL also has teacher and child versions.

The Trauma Symptom Checklist for Children (TSC-C; Briere & Runtz, 1989) is a 54-item instrument that assesses for the impact of sexual, physical, and psychological abuse in several areas and is completed by the child. Its target population is children 8 to 18, and it is presently undergoing validation.

Decision Making

Evaluators must form conclusions about the questions they have been asked to address. This is often a more difficult task than data gathering. Two protocols, one for deciding the likelihood of sexual abuse and a second for assessing its severity and impact, will be provided here, since these are the areas of assessment that are most unique to sexual abuse. These will be presented with brief comments, since many items are self-explanatory or were previously discussed. The evaluator completes the protocol form by writing in specifics.

Guidelines for Forming an Opinion about the Likelihood of Sexual Abuse. The evaluator examines findings from the child interview(s) and from corroborating sources.

Child Interview Data

1. Description or demonstration of sexual abuse, such as:
   a. Explicit acts _____
   b. A child's perspective _____
   c. Advanced sexual knowledge _____
   d. Identity of offender _____
   e. Frequency/duration _____
2. Description of the context, such as:
   a. Where _____

b. When _____

c. Inducements _____

d. Clothing worn/taken off _____

e. Whereabouts of other people _____

f. Threats regarding disclosure _____

g. Child's emotional state _____

h. Prior disclosure_____

3. Emotional state during disclosure, such as:

a. Reluctance to disclose _____

b. Other (e.g., fear, anger, depression, disgust, shame, sexual arousal)

_____

Corroboration

1. Offender admission/confession _____

2. Other victims_____

3. Witnesses _____

4. Medical evidence _____

5. Police evidence _____

6. Child statements in other contexts _____

The Sexual Abuse. Obviously advanced sexual knowledge and descriptions from a child's perspective will be most relevant to young children. There will be cases where it appears the child has been abused, but the offender's identity is unknown or uncertain.

Context. The amount of information gathered will depend upon the number of contextual questions asked and the child's age. Young children, because of their language limitations, will not be able to provide much contextual information. In asking *when* questions, it is important to use relevant reference points, such as "before school or after school?" or "when you lived in the green house or afterward?" Be aware that if the abuse happened more than once, it may have happened in several places. Ask about additional places, and make such questioning clear in the report.

Emotional State during Disclosure. Most children are reluctant to disclose, but willingness to talk does not mean the account is untrue and in some cases can be understood from case specifics. Children may experience a range of emotions during disclosure; all should be documented. However, flat affect does not mean the allegation is false and may be explained by victim or case characteristics.

Corroboration. The overwhelming majority of offenders do not confess. However, sometimes they indirectly provide supporting information, for example, by saying they may have forgotten doing it; they were drunk at the time; or the child couldn't have made the abuse up. Since multiple victims are the rule rather than the exception for most offenders, all children to whom he or she had access should be assessed. Very occasionally there are witnesses other than additional victims; however, sometimes they are accomplices or offenders themselves. Medical evidence is only present in a minority of cases; its likelihood depends upon the offense, the victim's age, and how quickly a medical exam was conducted. Sometimes law enforcement officials conducts crime-scene investigations, especially in multivictim, extrafamilial cases, that yield physical evidence, such as pornography or bed sheets with semen or blood stains. However, the fact that an offender passes or fails a police polygraph should not be given weight, unless he fails it and then provides a confession (Cross & Saxe, 1992).

There is no strict quantum of evidence that is required for the evaluator to form an opinion. However, false allegations are uncommon (Jones & McGraw, 1987). Jones and McGraw (1987) have suggested that there is a continuum of certainty, but with virtually no case falling at the extreme ends of the continuum, 100 percent certain that sexual abuse did happen or 100 percent certain that it did not. Since the evaluator was not there, circumstances will be rare when he or she can be absolutely certain the child was sexually abused as described. Likewise, (1) because sexual abuse is generally a private activity, (2) many victims do not disclose, and (3) most offenders deny, the absence of supportive evidence does not mean that no sexual abuse occurred.

If the notion of forming an opinion based on probability rather than certainty is troubling, it is helpful to remember than even in the legal arena, 100 percent certainty is not required. For a court to take temporary jurisdiction of a child suspected of sexual abuse, "preponderance of the evidence," or 51 percent probability, is required. Even for a criminal conviction, the standard is 95 percent probability, "beyond a reasonable doubt."

Guidelines for Assessing Severity and Impact of Sexual Abuse. Four general areas are evaluated to determine severity and impact.

Abuse characteristics
1. Type of sexual activity _____
2. Offender–victim relationship _____
3. Number of offenders _____
4. Age at onset_____
5. Frequency/duration _____
6. Use of bribes/force/threats _____
7. Presence of other types of maltreatment _____

Child's emotional reaction to abuse

1. Impact on trust _____
2. Perception of responsibility _____
3. Impact on sense of self/self-esteem _____
4. Impact on mood _____

Child's behavioral reaction to abuse

1. Sexualized behavior, such as:
   a. Sexual aggression _____
   b. Sexual activities with peers _____
   c. Sexual activities with older persons _____
   d. Sex with animals_____
   e. Sexual behavior with self and objects_____
   f. Adolescent prostitution _____
2. Habit disorders, such as:
   a. Sleep problems _____
   b. Toileting problems _____
   c. Eating problems _____
   d. Phobias _____
3. Relationship problems, such as:
   a. Poor peer relationships _____
   b. Won't mind caretakers_____
4. School problems, such as:
   a. Inability to concentrate _____
   b. Drop in school performance _____
   c. School refusal _____
5. Acting-out behavior, such as:
   a. Aggression toward younger children _____
   b. Cruelty to animals _____
   c. Tantrums _____
   d. Running away_____
6. Antisocial behavior, such as:
   a. Stealing_____
   b. Lying _____
   c. Criminal activity _____

7. Self-destructive behavior, such as:
   a. Substance abuse_____
   b. Suicidal behavior _____
   c. Self-injury _____

Reaction of others
   1. Nonoffending caretaker(s)_____
   2. Offender _____
   3. Extender family_____
   4. Peers_____
   5. Professionals _____

Abuse Characteristics. As a rule, the more intrusive the sexual activity, the earlier the onset; the more extensive the abuse, the more traumatic the effect. Proximate relationships, such as father–daughter, are thought to be more harmful than more distant relationships, although when the child holds the offender in high esteem, as in the case of a priest, the impact can be severe. Multiple perpetrators and the presence of other abuse make the experience more damaging. The type of inducement has a complex impact. When force or threats are used, children are more likely to be fearful and anxious. When bribery is employed, children may feel responsible for the abuse.

Child's Emotional Reaction. Children's emotional reaction is usually reflected in behavioral reactions. It is very common for victims to feel in some way responsible for their abuse and/or for the consequences of disclosure. Typical mood disturbances are depression, anger, and anxiety/fear.

Child's Behavioral Reaction. There are parallels between the earlier described psychosocial indicators of sexual abuse and behavioral reactions; signs of abuse are often its effects on functioning. The evaluator should attempt to determine whether the symptoms preceded sexual abuse or appeared after onset. However, in cases of long-standing sexual abuse, this issue is less relevant. In addition, some symptoms develop because of the consequences of disclosure.

Reactions of Others. Persons close to the child may have a variety of reactions. They may believe or disbelieve. They may blame the offender or the victim. They may provide the victim support or abandon the victim. They may pursue the victim's best interest or not. Crucial to ameliorating the impact of sexual abuse is the support of the nonoffending parent(s). Offender admission is also very beneficial to the victim. Sometimes families mobilize themselves and their support systems against the victim, which is devastating. Professionals must be ever mindful of the victim's needs and the impact of their actions on the victim, to avoid iatrogenic effects of intervention.

Treatment Issues

The discussion of treatment will cover contextual considerations and abuse-focused therapy.

Context Considerations

Victim therapy in relation to other therapeutic interventions and case management decisions will be considered in this section.

The Victim's Treatment Is the Context of Therapy for Others. The discussion of treatment will be victim-focused, but children, especially young ones, are treated in the context of their families or caretakers. In cases of intrafamilial sexual abuse, the usual practice is to initially separate the family. Ideally, offenders leave the home. However, the victim should be removed if the mother is not supporting the victim. When the goal is family reunification, the treatment plan typically entails individual treatment for victim(s), mother, and offender, followed by dyadic work, and then family therapy. Family members are usually concurrently involved in group therapy. Family reunification is predicated on treatment progress and is part of the treatment process.

When the abuse is extrafamilial or the child is in placement, caretakers still need to be involved in treatment. In nonfamily offender cases, parents often have significant reactions, including guilt, which require treatment. They can also assist in the victim's healing. In addition, caretakers need to be involved in child management strategies to address the victim's behavioral reactions to abuse.

Treatment in Relationship to Case Management. Case management decisions, such as child placement, criminal prosecution, and termination of parental rights, create additional issues for therapy that cannot be ignored. Often traditional victim treatment must be put on hold while children's feelings and behavioral reactions to these decisions, which affect them dramatically, but about which they usually have little say, are addressed.

In addition, when children are separated from their families, visitation can have a significant effect on the child and treatment. The child may want or not want visits or want them with some family members but not with others. Visits may be beneficial or not for the child, depending on the case. Visits or the lack thereof can impact victim functioning and can affect placement stability. However, agency policies in large part determine visitation patterns, and therapists may need to become advocates for appropriate visitation.

Finally, if the victim must testify in court, this markedly alters the course of therapy. The research on the impact of testifying suggests that as a rule it is not beneficial for children (Runyon, Everson, Edelsohn, Hunter, &

Coulter, 1988; Whitcomb et al., 1992). A pending court case usually means that the child cannot reach closure on issues in treatment. Impending testimony often results in exacerbation of symptoms, and hearings may be repeatedly postponed, so that victims must prepare to testify several times before they actually take the stand. For some children, the positive aspects of testimony are a chance to have her or his day in court, and if prosecution is successful, a feeling of being vindicated and believed. Therapists need to support children through court testimony and work through the experience in treatment.

Abuse-Focused Therapy

The term "abuse-focused therapy" is a reminder to both the therapist and the client of the issue to be addressed in treatment (Berliner, Conte, & Lipovsky, 1991). Four aspects of such treatment will be covered: (1) disclosure as a context for therapy, (2) emotional reactions requiring treatment; (3) behavioral reactions requiring treatment; and (4) future protection.

Using Disclosure as a Context for Treatment. For forensic reasons, the roles of evaluator and therapist are often separated. However, this division is not in the child's or the clinician's best interest. It may impede therapy because the child is reluctant to develop a new therapeutic relationship. Moreover, the therapist may mistakenly conclude that she or he need not discuss what happened, but only address its effects. This error reinforces the secrecy that surrounds abuse and the victim's fear of dealing with it.

Maximum therapeutic benefit is derived from addressing the victim's feelings as she or he describes the abuse experience. Moreover, it is more therapeutic to address the child's behavioral sequelae in the context of their etiology, rather than as merely the child's behavior problem, which can be victim-blaming.

The pacing of this work is much slower than assessment work and is introspective. The therapist probes for feelings and offers interpretations of the child's verbal and nonverbal communication or lack thereof. Similarly, during the child's account of abuse, the clinician makes connections between the victimization experience and current behavioral difficulties, for example, sexual aggression.

Emotional Reactions that Require Treatment. Sexual abuse affects children's feelings about themselves and the world. The most common of these feelings are (1) ability to trust adults, (2) sense of self and self-esteem, (3) guilt, and (4) anger (one effect on mood). Each will be defined and useful treatment approaches outlined.

Trust. A societal goal is for children to rely on adults to provide them with nurturance, protection, and guidance. Sexual abuse experiences teach children that adults exploit, harm, and manipulate. The proximity of the relationship and the extent of other, appropriate adult relationships will determine how pervasive the undermining of trust is.

Treatment entails experiences for the child with trustworthy adults. First and foremost is the therapist, who develops a healing relationship with the child, in which she or he keeps promises, is honest, is therapeutically nurturing, helps the child with her or his trauma, and does not abandon the child. The therapist also fosters other trustworthy adult relationships for the child, for example, by involving Big Brothers, by working with foster parents, and by helping parents change so they are trustworthy (Faller, 1988).

Sense of Self and Self-Esteem. Sgroi (1982) used the term "damaged goods syndrome" to refer to this problem. Victims suffer a loss of body and psychological integrity. For some boys (and their families), concerns about sexual identity develop.

Perhaps the most effective treatment approach is to foster situations in which children experience themselves as more than just sexual abuse victims. The therapist might arrange for the child to join the Scouts, tutor or care for younger children, or become involved in afterschool activities. Group therapy experiences in which the child can help others also serve this purpose. Especially efficacious are situations that allow the child to develop body control and feelings of mastery, for instance, through self-defense classes.

Guilt and Responsibility. Children often feel responsible for the sexual abuse, for its continuance, and for the consequences of disclosure, such as family breakup, unanticipated family expenses, placement in foster care, and incarceration of the offender. These feelings derive in considerable part from the offender's manipulations. The therapist can constantly remind the child that the offender sexually abused her or him, not the reverse, and that the offender knew it was wrong and that is why he or she told the child not to tell. However, probably more effective are affirming experiences in victim group therapy and what the offender does, in terms of taking responsibility for the sexual abuse and absolving the child of blame (Mayer, 1985).

Anger. A sense of outrage is an appropriate reaction to sexual abuse. Therefore, the therapist will frequently want to encourage this feeling. Being angry at the offender can mediate guilt feelings. Nevertheless, some victims, especially boys, act out their anger by harming others and engaging in acts that get them into trouble. The task in such situations is to help the child develop insight into the causes and effects of his acting out and to get the child to channel anger in appropriate but effective ways, for example, at the offender.

Behaviors that Require Treatment. A fairly complete list of behavioral sequelae of sexual abuse appears in the assessment guidelines itemized on pages 222 to 224. Treatment of most of them is not unique to abuse-focused therapy. The unique issue is *sexualized behavior*, a very troubling and stigmatizing reaction to sexual abuse. A multimodal approach that focuses primarily on sexual behaviors with others will be briefly described.

Intervention requires the cooperation of the child's caretaker. When sexualized behavior is a problem, the caretaker must be sure that the child has adequate supervision so he or she has no more opportunities for sexual acting out. The therapist also helps the adult develop strategies for involving the child in activities that are interesting and incompatible with sexual behavior.

The clinician may work with the child to help him or her become more introspective about the sexual behavior, specifically helping her or him to become aware of its impact on children who are the target of abuse and more sensitive to the feelings that precipitate sexual acting out. An excellent workbook with exercises addressing these issues is *When Children Molest Children* (Cunningham & MacFarlane, 1991). Victim empathy can also be enhanced by having the child recall her or his feelings when victimized and by reenactments with anatomical dolls of her or his acts against others.

Behavioral interventions, relying on both operant and respondent paradigms, may be of use. Using the caretaker, the therapist may work out a tangible reward system for absence of sexual acting out. For example, a child might earn stars, stickers, or baseball cards for "sex-free days." Teaching the child to monitor arousal, for example, by recording every time he or she has sexual feelings on a 3" × 5" card, can have the effect of thought stopping. Alternatively, an individualized thought-stopping strategy can be developed. For example, a 9-year-old boy decided he would clap himself on the forehead when he "felt the urge." Covert sensitization can also be effective (Friedrich, 1990).

Early and effective intervention is of utmost importance. Increasingly, professionals are becoming aware that abuse-reactive children can progress from being victims to becoming adolescent and adult offenders.

Future Protection. Sexually abused children are generally vulnerable to revictimization, and intrafamilial victims whose families are reunited may be at risk from their former abuser. With young children, future protection begins with educating them about appropriate and inappropriate touch. With all children, the therapist helps them develop a strategy to deal with future situations of risk. Children are taught to recognize grooming strategies or sexual invitations by older persons, to avoid these situations, and to tell someone if they occur.

In intrafamilial cases, reunification is usually predicated on a family plan, to be implemented by the nonoffending parent and acknowledged by the offender, specifying what will happen if the offender tries to or does reoffend. Usually this involves dissolving the marriage. However, therapists often find it advisable to have an additional plan for the child, which may entail telling a supportive relative, the therapist, a teacher, or the child protection worker (Faller, 1988).

Conclusion

Assessment and treatment of the sexually abused child poses significant challenges for health and mental health care providers. This chapter has provided an overview of the key aspects of these processes. However, this is a complex and developing field of practice. Although the guidance in this chapter should provide beginning competence, professionals wishing to specialize in sexual abuse should seek additional information about specific issues noted in this chapter and should be alert for developing knowledge in the field.

References

Achenbach, T., & Edelbrock, C. (1983). *The child behavior checklist manual*. Burlington: University of Vermont.

American Academy of Child and Adolescent Psychiatry (AACAP). (1990). *Guidelines for the evaluation of child and adolescent sexual abuse*. (Available from AACAP, 3615 Wisconsin Ave., N.W., Washington DC 20016.)

American Association for Protecting Children. (1988). *Highlights of official child neglect and abuse reporting*. Denver: American Humane Association.

American Professional Society on the Abuse of Children (APSAC). (1990). *Guidelines for the psychosocial evaluation of suspected sexual abuse in young children*. Chicago: Author.

August, R., & Foreman, B. (1989). A comparison of sexually abused and nonsexually abused children's behavioral responses to anatomically correct dolls. *Child Psychiatry and Human Development, 20*(1), 39–47.

Bays, J., & Chadwick, D. (1993). Medical diagnosis of the sexually abused child. *Child Abuse and Neglect, 17*(1), 91–110.

Berliner, L., Conte, J., & Lipovsky, J. (1992 June). *Abuse focused therapy*. Institute given at the Annual Conference of the American Professional Society on the Abuse of Children: Responding to Child Maltreatment, San Diego, CA.

Briere, J., & Runtz, M. (1989). The Trauma Symptom Checklist: Early data on a new scale. *Journal of Interpersonal Violence, 4*, 151–163.

Bross, D., Krugman, R., Lenherr, M., Rosenberg, D., & Schmidt, B. (1988). *The new child protection team handbook*. New York: Garland.

Burgess, A., & Hartman, C. (1993). Children's drawings. *Child Abuse and Neglect, 17*(1), 161–168.

Ceci, S. (1992, August). *Pre-school children's suggestibility*. Paper presented at the American Psychological Association Annual Meeting, Los Angeles.

Clark-Stewart, A., Thompson, W., & Lapore, S. (1989, April). *Manipulating chil-*

dren's interpretations through interrogation. Paper presented at the Society for Research on Child Development, Kansas City.

Cohen, D. (1991). Anatomical doll play of preschoolers referred for sexual abuse and those not referred. *Child Abuse and Neglect, 15*(4), 455–465.

Conte, J., Sorenson, E., Fogarty, L., & Dalla Rosa, J. (1991). Evaluating children's reports of sexual abuse: Results of a survey of professionals. *American Journal of Orthopsychiatry, 61*(3), 428–437.

Cross, T., & Saxe, L. (1992). A critique of the validity of polygraph testing in child sexual abuse cases. *Journal of Child Sexual Abuse, 1*(4), 19–33.

Cunningham, C., & MacFarlane, K. (1991). *When children molest children.* Orwell, VT: Safer Society Press.

Doris, J. (Ed.). (1991). *The suggestibility of children's recollections.* Washington, DC: American Psychological Association.

Everson, M., & Boat, B. (1990). Sexualized doll play among young children: Implications for the use of anatomical dolls in sexual abuse evaluations. *Journal of the American Academy of Child and Adolescent Psychiatry, 29*(5), 736–742.

Everson, M., & Boat, B. (1994). Putting the anatomical doll controversy in perspective: An examination of the major uses and criticisms of the dolls in sexual abuse evaluations. *Child Abuse and Neglect.*

Faller, K. C. (1984). Is the child victim of sexual abuse telling the truth? *Child Abuse and Neglect, 8,* 473–481.

Faller, K. C. (1988). *Child sexual abuse: An interdisciplinary manual for diagnosis, case management, and treatment.* New York: Columbia University Press.

Faller, K. C. (1990a, Spring). Types of questions for children alleged to have been sexually abused. *APSAC Advisor,* pp. 3–5.

Faller, K. C. (1990b). *Understanding child sexual maltreatment.* Newbury Park, CA.: Sage.

Faller, K. C. (1993). *Child sexual abuse: Intervention and treatment issues.* Washington, DC: Department of Health and Human Services.

Faller, K. C., Froning, M., & Lipovsky, J. (1991). The parent–child interview: Use in evaluating child allegations of sexual abuse by a parent. *American Journal of Orthopsychiatry, 61*(4), 552–557.

Finkelhor, D., Hotaling, G., Lewis, I., & Smith, C. (1990). Sexual abuse in a national survey of adult men and women: Prevalence, characteristics, and risk factors. *Child Abuse and Neglect, 14,* 19–28.

Finkelhor, D., Peters, S., & Wyatt, G. (1986). Prevalence. In D. Finkelhor & associates, *Sourcebook on child sexual abuse* pp 15–59. Newbury Park, CA: Sage.

Friedrich, W. (1990a). *The Child Sexual Behavior Inventory (Version 2).* Rochester, MN: Mayo Clinic.

Friedrich, W. (1990b). *Psychotherapy with sexually abused children and their families.* New York: W.W. Norton and Company.

Friedrich, W. (1993). Sexual victimization and sexual behavior in children. *Child Abuse and Neglect, 17*(1), 59–66.

Groth, N., & Stevenson, J. (1990). *Anatomical drawings.* Dunedin, FL: Forensic Mental Health Associates.

Jones, D., & McGraw, M. (1987). Reliable and fictitious accounts of sexual abuse to children. *Journal of Interpersonal Violence, 2*(1), 27–45.

Kendall-Tackett, K. (1992). *Comparative studies on the effects of sexual abuse.*

(Available from the author at Department of Sociology, Wellesley College, Wellesley, MA.)

Mayer, A. (1985). *Incest.* Holmes Beach, FL: Learning Press.

McCurdy, K., & Daro, D. (1993). *Current trends in child abuse reporting and fatalities: Results of the 1992 annual fifty state survey.* Chicago: National Committee for the Prevention of Child Abuse.

Myers, J. (1992). *Legal issues in child abuse and neglect.* Newbury Park, CA: Sage.

Runyon, D., Everson, M., Edelsohn, G., Hunter, W., & Coulter, M. (1988). Impact of legal intervention on sexually abused children. *Journal of Pediatrics, 113*(4), 647–653.

Russell, D.E.H. (1986). *The secret trauma: Sexual abuse of girls and women.* New York: Basic Books.

Salter, A. (1988). *Treating child sex offenders and victims: A practical guide.* Newbury Park, CA: Sage.

Saunders, B., Kilpatrick, D., Lipovsky, J., Resnick, H., Best, C., & Sturgis, E. (1991, March). *Prevalence, case characteristics, and long-term psychological effects of sexual assault: A national survey.* Paper presented at the Annual Meeting of the American Orthopsychiatric Association, Toronto.

Saunders, B., Villeponteaux, L., Lipovsky, J., Kilpatrick, D., & Veronen, L. (1992). Child sexual abuse as a risk factor for mental disorders among women: A community survey. *Journal of Interpersonal Violence, 7*(2), 189–204.

Saywitz, K., Goodman, G., Nicholas, E., & Moan, S. (1989). *Children's memories of genital examinations: Implications for cases of child sexual assault.* Paper presented at the Biennial Meeting of the Society for Research on Child Development, Kansas City.

Sgroi, S. (1982). *Handbook of clinical intervention in child sexual abuse.* Lexington, MA: Lexington Books.

Sivan, A., Schor, D., Koeppl, G., & Nobel, L. (1988). Interaction of normal children with anatomical dolls. *Child Abuse and Neglect, 12,* 295–304.

Sorenson, T., & Snow, B. (1991). How children tell: The process of disclosure of child sexual abuse. *Child Welfare, 70*(1), 3–15.

Summit, R. (1983). The child sexual abuse accommodation syndrome. *Child Abuse and Neglect, 7,* 177–188.

White, S., Strom, G., Santilli, G., & Halpin, B. (1986). Interviewing young sexual abuse victims with anatomically correct dolls. *Child Abuse and Neglect, 10,* 519–529.

Whitcomb, D., Runyon, D., De Vos, E., Cross, T., Everson, M., Peeler, N., Porter, C., Toth, P., & Cropper, C. (1992, Spring). New research: The impact of testifying on child sexual abuse victims. *APSAC Advisor,* pp. 2, 20.

11

Treatment Interventions for Child Sexual Abuse

Steven P. Cuffe
Sandra B. Frick-Helms

The treatment of sexually abused children is a complex undertaking that intimidates many therapists. As the previous chapters illustrate, there are many variables which mediate the effects of sexual abuse in children and many ways in which these children respond to the abuse. There is no "child sexual abuse syndrome" (Kendall-Tackett, Meyer Williams, & Finkelhor, 1993; Green, 1993). Each child responds to sexual abuse based on the complex biological–psychological–social matrix in which he or she lives. Thus, treatment must be appropriate for the child's developmental level and individual history. Diagnostic considerations run the gamut of psychiatric disorders and are further complicated by the fact that the child may look very different in varying settings or time periods (Terr, 1991).

There is remarkably little treatment outcome research on the efficacy of sexual abuse treatment (Green, 1993; Kolko, 1987; Mrazek, 1983; O'Donohue & Elliott, 1992). Most studies are uncontrolled and provide little scientific evidence on which to base interventions. The most recent review found only 11 treatment outcome studies of sexually abused children (O'Donohue & Elliott, 1992) and most of these included older children in their samples. Four of these utilized single-subject (case study) designs and employed cognitive and behavioral interventions and social skills training. Therapeutic gains were made by subjects in all four studies, suggesting that behavioral interventions (token economy, social skills training, operant differential reinforcement procedures) can be useful in treating sexually abused children. However, questions concerning the generalizability of the results arise due to the single-subject design. Another generalizability issue that arises is the age of subject groups in studies. Children under the age of 5 years tend to be underrepresented. It is not yet known if results would be similar or different if studies were more representative of the age distribution of the population of sexually abused children. One of the methodological problems in researching outcomes of sexual abuse treatment for preschool-age children is the lack of available outcome measures appropriate for use in this age group.

Two studies evaluated individual treatment programs on larger numbers of children. In the most carefully designed study, Deblinger, McLeer, and Henry (1990) studied cognitive–behavioral and social skills training therapy for 19 sexually abused girls aged 3 to 16 who met the criteria for post-traumatic stress disorder (PTSD). None of the subjects met PTSD criteria after treatment in the 12-session program. This was a well-controlled study, whose only major experimental flaw was the failure to use interviewers who were blind to the treatment protocol.

Group therapy was evaluated in four studies. One study conducted a six-session treatment group that included 25 girls aged 8 to 13. Treatment involved education, progressive muscle relaxation, response-contingent positive reinforcement, and role-playing to teach ways to prevent revictimization. Improvements in anxiety and depressive symptoms were noted. Another study achieved significant decreases in fearfulness and depression in 3 boys and 15 girls aged 5–15 using group treatment emphasizing behavioral rehearsal and cognitive reframing techniques. Verleur, Hughes, and de Rios (1986) used "homogenous group therapy" with a sex education component. They included a nontreatment control group, and found statistically significant improvements for both groups, but no statistically significant differences between groups. Corder, Haizlip, and DeBoer (1990) conducted a 20-session group using multiple techniques, including cognitive relabeling, role plays designed to increase self-esteem, games, and art work. Self-reports of subjects, parents, and therapists suggested the children improved.

Although O'Donohue and Elliott (1992) conclude that there is no evidence that definitively demonstrates the efficacy of any treatment method, the children studied all showed improvements in symptoms and behaviors after treatment. Behavioral and cognitive interventions, in particular, are fairly well supported; however, some studies include psychodynamic interventions which also appear successful. The clinical significance of the improvements were sometimes unclear, and the long-term benefits are not known at this time.

Obstacles to Treatment

There is great need for research into the service utilization patterns of sexually abused children and their families. Many obstacles to treatment are evident. Fear and denial serve as internal barriers to proper treatment of the child and family (Stavrakaki, Ellis, & Williams, 1988). These can be strong even in the face of court-ordered treatment. Studies show that approximately 45 percent of families referred for treatment failed to comply with the referral (Byrne & Valdiserri, 1982; Krener, 1985). Once in treatment, nonattendance is a frequent problem, and usually is seen during the intermittent crises these families face (Furniss, Bingley-Miller, & Van Elburg, 1988). Some families respond to the crisis of disclosure by moving and are lost to follow-up (Byrne & Valdiserri, 1982).

External barriers can also impede treatment. Multiple agencies, and therefore complex systems, are involved with sexual abuse cases. Social service agencies, law enforcement departments, courts, mental health agencies, solicitors, and guardian ad litems all have some role or responsibility. Who has responsibility for overall case management and the mandate to refer these children for treatment? All too often children fall between the cracks due to poor communication (Meddin & Hansen, 1985), a lack of consensus between agencies (Finkelhor, 1984), or underreferral for mental health treatment by social service agencies (Adams-Tucker, 1984). Coordination and communication between agencies is vital. This is probably best accomplished by the formation of multidisciplinary teams from the different agencies for tracking the process.

Once the referral is made, it is important to engage the family quickly and to be very clear about the extent and limits of the confidentiality of the treatment. Frequently multiple contacts are required before the family is engaged in treatment. Trust and security issues are paramount during this time. Home visits can sometimes facilitate this process by engaging the family where it is most comfortable and secure.

Phases of Treatment

Treatment should occur as soon as possible and should be conceived in three phases: (1) Crisis intervention, (2) trauma-specific treatment, and (3) long-term treatment. The crisis-intervention phase is generally the shortest and consists of stabilizing the child and family, evaluating their psychological needs, and supporting them through the process of evaluations, medical exams, and court appearances.

This immediate postdisclosure phase of treatment is an extremely important, even critical, time for the child. His or her emotional response to the trauma may be shaped at this time. The child's view of the abuse, of himself or herself, and of the world is vulnerable. Some authors report that children who were asymptomatic prior to disclosure are made symptomatic or dramatically worsened by the events that occur afterward (Lipovsky, 1992). It is imperative that the interventions made in the investigations and evaluations that follow disclosure are sensitive to the needs of the child. This means that, first and foremost, the child should be protected from continuing abuse. The number of interviews should be minimized and the child should be reassured that he or she is not responsible for the abuse or the events ensuing after disclosure.

The child's living situation should be stabilized as soon as possible. Removing children from the home is traumatizing. Whenever possible, the child should remain within the family or with nonabusing family members. These family members, however, must be supportive of the child. The research to date is clear about the consequences of an unsupportive environment: the child suffers greatly (Everson, Hunter, Runyon, Edelsohn, & Coulter, 1989; Green, 1993). Green (1993) goes so far as to recommend that children should be removed from the care of a nonoffending parent who denies the abuse.

The needs of the family, however, should not be overlooked in the aftermath of abuse disclosure. This is an extremely traumatic period for the entire family unit, whether or not the abuse was perpetrated by a family member (Newberger, Gremy, Waternaux, & Newberger, 1993; Terr, 1989). When there is potential for the breakup of the family, the anxiety levels can be overwhelming. Fear, suspicion, and anxiety, in addition to denial, can make these families extremely difficult to reach.

If the child's parent(s) or guardian(s) are sufficiently supportive and the child is asymptomatic, crisis treatment may be all that is required, at least for the time being. Although prospective studies are lacking, studies of adults who were molested as children show serious long-term effects (Briere & Runtz, 1988; Wyatt & Powell, 1988). Parents should be educated concerning the typical problems seen in survivors, so they can observe for symptom development over time. The asymptomatic child may well require treatment at a later date. Parent education should also include instruction about how to talk to their child about the abuse. One set of guidelines for such education was presented by Dumas (1992).

Trauma-specific treatment of up to six months is required for most children. However, in our experience, many parents will not see the need for ongoing treatment even if the child is clearly symptomatic and everyone from the teacher to the daycare worker is concerned about the child's symptoms. Utilizing multiple informants is essential if one is to gain an accurate picture of the child. This information can be used to gently convince reluctant parents that treatment is required.

The trauma-specific phase of treatment should focus on the traumatic aspects of the abuse, allowing expression of affects and working through of traumatic memories. Symptomatic children with relatively stable and supportive homes, and who were not multiply traumatized over a longer period of time (or, victims of type 1 trauma as defined by Terr, 1991) may be effectively treated with short-term therapy.

Children who have been multiply traumatized over longer time periods (victims of the type 2 traumas Terr, 1991, describes) will most often require long-term treatment. This group will also include many children who may have been sexually abused only once, or a small number of times, but who continue to experience significant traumas after disclosure, such as removal from the home, unsupportive parental responses, or otherwise chaotic and punitive reactions to the abuse. These children require long-term treatment to deal with major characterologic problems.

Specific Treatment Issues

Biological

Evaluating genetic and biological components of psychopathology is an important part of any assessment, but is typically not addressed in evaluations of sexually abused children. This is undoubtedly due to the obvious environmental cause of the problem. However, this oversight could have significant consequences. Children are born with inherited vulnerabilities to physical and emotional illnesses that can become manifest under stress. Sexual abuse is a serious but relatively nonspecific stressor to which the child responds in keeping with his or her own vulnerability. Major depressive episodes, anxiety disorders, conduct disorders, attention deficit disorders, and even psychotic disorders can all be precipitated or exacerbated by sexual abuse. Evaluation for a family history of psychiatric illness and for symptoms of major psychiatric illnesses in the child is thus important. A treatable illness should not be overlooked. Biological treatments, such as medications for depression, can be an important piece of the treatment plan for these children.

Evidence is also accruing that severe traumas can cause long-term biochemical changes in those who experience them (Bourne, 1970; Kosten, Mason, Giller, Ostroff, & Podd, 1987; Mason, Giller, Kosten, Ostroff, & Podd, 1986; Ornitz & Pynoos, 1989). The changes generally involve the noradrenergic neurotransmitters and cortico-steroids, which have been implicated in the formation of post-traumatic stress symptoms. Medications, such as imipramine and clonidine, can be helpful in controlling the intrusive recollections, anxiety, and hyperarousal in these patients. It is generally best to use medications sparingly and with clear target symptoms in this population. As always, medications should be a part of a comprehensive treatment plan.

Psychological

Sexual abuse can have a devastating psychological impact. Several authors have written extensively about the psychological issues involved in treating sexually abused children (Browne & Finkelhor, 1984; Finkelhor, 1986; Kendall-Tackett, Meyer Williams, & Finkelhor, 1993; MacFarlane et al.,

1986; Sgroi, 1982). We have coalesced these issues into five main symptom areas. Conveying to the family and child (when developmentally appropriate) that these are typical and expected responses allows for normalization of the child's reaction, an important part of the crisis intervention phase. The major areas to be addressed are:

1. **Guilt.** There are many factors that induce sexually abused children to feel guilty and develop low self-esteem. Children are often blamed by both the perpetrator and other family members for causing the abuse and also for causing the breakup of the family following disclosure. The child may infer responsibility from the lack of consequences to the abuser, as is most often the case. These guilty feelings often result in a child with low self-esteem who feels damaged and depressed. The feeling of being damaged and "dirty" is often part of the abusive relationship, as was the case with a young adolescent patient whose abusive father called her a "whore" and continually accused her of having sex with boys. This can set the stage for revictimization, with the child fulfilling the prophesy of the abuser and confirming in the child his or her sense of guilt, badness, and low self-esteem.

2. **Betrayal.** Sexually abused children have been betrayed, usually by someone the child and family knows and trusts. This results in the child's inability to trust in other relationships. In addition, these children are frequently betrayed by others in the aftermath of disclosure. Parents and other trusted adults may question the veracity of the report or deny it altogether. Wyatt and Powell (1988) found that when sexual abuse is reported, a majority of the time the child is disbelieved, punished, and not supported by nonabusing adults and professionals. The therapeutic relationship is a vehicle through which trust can be repaired. It is essential that the therapist is consistent, dependable, and able to deal with issues of trust in the therapeutic relationship which inevitably develop. The therapist must also work with the parent(s) to repair any loss of trust in the child's relationship with them. Rebonding between mother and daughter in an incest case is vital (Long, 1986).

3. **Pseudomaturity and Boundary Confusion.** The developmentally inappropriate sexualization of a relationship and the role boundaries that are transgressed serve to prompt sexualized behavior and role confusion in the child. These children often take on more responsibility than they should and behave and dress in very mature, often sexually provocative ways. Frequently the nonabusing parent is drawn into the confused role boundaries created by the father–child incest. In one such case, the first author was seeing a 13-year-old girl who was abused by her father from age 8 to age 11. She dressed in a very mature manner and wore makeup like an older teenager. In a session with her mother, the mother painfully acknowledged that "Sometimes I can't help thinking she is the woman who slept with my hus-

band." The inappropriately sexualized behavior is also often continued into the adolescent years, as evidenced by another patient who had sexual relations with multiple boys. When this sexual activity was discussed in therapy, she stated, "I know they'll like me if I have sex with them." She was cognitively able to realize this was not reality since she did not maintain relationships with them; however, the ingrained feeling that sexuality was part of establishing relationships proved very difficult to resolve.

4. **Self-Mastery.** Sexually abused children feel caught in a powerful web by the perpetrator during the abuse. They are unable to control the violation of their bodies, and then, following disclosure, they are swept into the chaotic period of investigations. During this process they are stigmatized by the abuser, and frequently by the family and society. It is from within this cauldron of affect and events that children feel overwhelmed and often recant the allegations of abuse. Summit (1983) described this process as the "child sexual abuse accommodation syndrome." As a result of these experiences, sexually abused children have problems with self-mastery, control, and feelings of powerlessness. They may be overly passive and compliant, showing little initiative or assertiveness. They tend to repress feelings of anger and hostility, although these will be expressed in tantrums, fights with peers, and often in the playroom in younger children. Older children and adolescents may become oppositional and defiant.

5. **Fear and Symptoms of Post-Traumatic Stress.** Thirty to fifty percent of sexually abused children can be diagnosed with post-traumatic stress disorder (PTSD) (Kiser et al., 1988; McLeer, Deblinger, Atkins, Foa, & Ralphe, 1988), and even more exhibit some of the symptoms. This disorder is characterized by high levels of fear and anxiety. These children often fear the abuse will be repeated and are constantly on the lookout for signs of impending danger. Fear of retribution by their abusers after disclosure is also common. Frequently, the abuser has threatened the child in order to preempt disclosure. One young adolescent patient was raped by a gang member who threatened to rape her mother and sister if she reported him. After she did (weeks after the event), the family received numerous phone calls from the rapist threatening the entire family. Other symptoms of PTSD include recurrent memories or nightmares of the abuse, behavioral reenactments of the abuse in play or with peers, emotional numbing and detached interpersonal relationships, poor sleep and concentration, and an exaggerated startle response. These trauma-specific symptoms must be dealt with by working with memories of the trauma. The therapist should not collude with the child (and frequently the family) by suggesting that the trauma is too upsetting or frightening to deal with. The child will take cues from the therapist as to whether it is safe to work on the memories of the abuse. The traumatic nature of the abuse will not be resolved by ignoring it. Good clinical judgment is required in order to know that the child is ready to confront the abuse. Trust generally needs to be established in the

therapeutic relationship before children are willing to undertake this task. The clinician must titrate work on the abuse so that it does not become overwhelming to the child and precipitate a worsening of intrusive and hyperarousal symptoms such as nightmares, repeatedly perceived memories, poor sleep, reduced concentration, and aggression. Younger children are frequently more accessible than older children, since they naturally express themselves through posttraumatic play.

Family

The importance of the family cannot be overemphasized. The support of family members, particularly the mother, is vital for successful treatment. Authors have noted that parents have their own sequelae from the abuse of their child, including anxiety, depression, guilt, and sometimes symptoms of post-traumatic stress (Deblinger et al., 1990; James, 1989; Newberger et al., 1993; O'Donohue & Elliott, 1992; Terr, 1989). Additionally, since one hour of therapy per week is often not sufficient for the treatment of many sexually abused children, involving the families in their treatment can "significantly enhance clinical case work" (James, 1989, p. 9). Therefore, families should be included in the treatment whether the perpetrator was a family member or not. In the case of incest, family dynamics may be extremely complex and difficult. Many treatment programs recommend a multimodality approach utilizing individual therapy for the child and both parents, parent–child dyads (first with the mother and then with the father), and finally family therapy when treatment has reached the point where reintegration seems possible (Giarretto, 1989; Kolko, 1987; Orenchuk-Tomiuk, Matthey, & Christensen, 1990; Sgroi, 1982). Orenchuk-Tomiuk, Matthey, and Christensen (1990) conceptualize families as falling along a continuum of three stages of acceptance or denial of the abuse. The authors utilize this assessment to coordinate several treatment modalities, which they feel are crucial for effective treatment. The three stages consist of (1) the noncommittal or oppositional stage, (2) the middle stage, and (3) the resolution stage. Characteristically, each family member moves along this continuum independently, and at times fluidly. Issues involve conflict resolution, roles, boundaries, and the awareness and management of perceived responsibility for the abuse.

Treatment Modalities

Multiple modalities have been utilized in the treatment of sexually abused children and their families. Preliminary evidence indicates that individual, group, family, and self-help group settings have been helpful in treating these families. Unfortunately, evidence is mostly subjective and anecdotal

(Kolko, 1987; O'Donohue & Elliott, 1992). Although we would wish it were not so, the cost, the availability of therapists, the support and involvement of parents, and the reaction of the child and family to the abuse all influence the type and length of treatment received.

Orenchuk-Tomiuk, Matthey, and Christensen (1990) base their interventions on a systems approach modeled after programs developed by Giarretto (1982) and Sgroi (1982). The suppositions that form the basis for their treatment are as follows: (1) the child is not responsible for the abuse and treatment of the child must support this truth; (2) the perpetrator is responsible and must actively assume this responsibility; (3) the nonoffending parent has an important role and may be supportive of the child, or deny that the abuse occurred; and (4) treatment processes of the child, nonoffending parent, and perpetrator are interdependent.

In the Orenchuk-Tomiuk, Matthey, and Christensen model, the noncommittal stage is the first stage of treatment. The child may feel totally responsible for the abuse and for resolving the stress caused by disclosure. The child may retract allegations, deny problems, and attempt to protect family members at his or her own expense. Treatment should occur in an individual or group setting. Frequently groups are preferred for the peer validation that develops and helps the child gain insight into her or his victimization (Steward, Farquar, Dicharry, Glick, & Martin, 1986). Some authorities believe that group treatment of sexually abused children is not advisable before age 6. Guerney (1993, p. 277) states that "therapists do not believe that group therapy is useful for young children or for children whose ego is so fragile or underdeveloped that they can not deal with a group." Some children are too fearful of group therapy and must first be treated individually. The noncommittal stage may be too early for treating the child with the parents or families. Without an ally in the family, the child could be further victimized by the treatment process.

The nonoffending parent in the noncommittal or oppositional stage may deny the abuse and reject the child. She or he may be unable to protect the child from further abuse or to support the treatment. Treatment needs of this parent include admitting that abuse has occurred, learning to support and protect the child, understanding and accepting the feelings of the child, and setting appropriate limits and role boundaries for the child. Treatment may be in individual or group settings; however, group may be the more effective modality to break the denial. It is important to note that many nonoffending parents skip this stage and are supportive from the onset.

The perpetrator in the noncommittal or oppositional stage denies the abuse and blames the child. Abusive relationships (verbal, physical, or sexual) may continue if the perpetrators have contact with the child. They must accept responsibility for the abuse and acknowledge the need for treatment. Frequently, treating the offender requires legal backing.

The middle stage of treatment is characterized by the awareness of who is responsible for the abuse, the need to ally with the child, and the need for treatment. The child typically has conflicted and ambivalent feelings, making this a particularly affect-laden stage. Post-traumatic stress symptoms are frequently seen. This is the first time it is appropriate to combine the treatment of parents and child. Usually the nonoffending parent reaches this stage first and parent–child dyad treatment can occur. The nonoffending parent is now able to support the child and deal more appropriately with feelings and boundaries. Individual or group treatment should continue to allow processing of the feelings raised by the family work. The offender in the middle stage can now verbalize responsibility for the abuse to the child and family. Anger toward the victim and family may still be expressed, but the abusiveness of the relationships has stopped. Expression of their responsibility and remorse, by the offender and the nonoffending parent, to the child is important in this stage.

The resolution stage resolves the remaining conflicts in the individuals and the family system. The child mourns the loss of idealized relationships with parents and no longer feels responsible for the abuse or its aftermath. Coping skills have been learned to deal with the trauma and feelings in productive rather than self-destructive ways. The nonoffending parent has worked through feelings of anger and blame toward the child, and is dealing with anger and betrayal feelings with the offender. Guilt over past failings in protecting the child is also dealt with in this stage. It is also during this stage when the choice of whether to rebuild or terminate the relationship with the perpetrator is made. The offending parent can now accept total responsibility and can establish more appropriate boundaries in relationships. Treatment issues for offenders are complex and often require very long-term treatment.

The comprehensive treatment program just described is very labor-intensive, and is usually not available outside major cities. In addition, many children and families may not require such elaborate treatment, especially in the case of extrafamilial abuse, or abuse that has not caused a symptomatic response. Specialized group therapy programs (Corder, Haizlip, & DeBoer, 1990; Damon & Waterman, 1986; Hazzard, King, & Webb, 1986) can meet the needs of these families, and can be effectively utilized in a comprehensive treatment program.

Group therapy offers certain opportunities that individual therapy does not (Hazzard, King, & Webb, 1986). The child's experience can be normalized and his or her isolation reduced. Social skills can be enhanced and the group can provide social validation for the child. Fearful children are able to discuss another person's problem rather than their own, until they feel more comfortable. In fact, some authors have described group therapy as the treatment of choice for sexually abused children (Steward et al., 1986).

Sometimes group therapy is inappropriate because of the child's age and developmental stage. Children 5 years of age and younger often do not possess the cognitive skills necessary to process information in group therapy.

The main problem with relying on group therapy as the primary modality is how to involve the family. Our experience with parallel groups for children and their nonoffending parents suggests this is a viable way to engage the families. The program is very similar to that described by Damon and Waterman (1986). The children's and parent's groups are time-limited, run in parallel, and are structured to deal with similar issues. Since the mothers of the abused children frequently have been abused themselves, they must often deal with their own abuse in addition to their reactions to their child's abuse. The program combines education and social skills training (trust building, communication skills, assertiveness training, prevention of revictimization, and sex education), cognitive–behavioral interventions (such as self-talk and cognitive reframing), and psychotherapy (utilizing art and talk therapies). This model is particularly useful where resources are limited or short-term intervention is needed (Damon & Waterman, 1986).

Filial therapy is a frequently used group therapy technique for younger children. Filial therapy is a technique in which parents are trained in groups to deliver client-centered play therapy to their child (Glass, 1986; Guerney, 1964, 1976, 1993). Training and supervision methods have been developed that allow parents to function effectively in this role (Stover & Guerney, 1967). With child sexual abuse, this technique may be used with nonabusing parents who acknowledge that abuse has occurred and are motivated to help their child. Group sessions continue after the parents begin filial therapy with their child. These sessions provide therapist feedback and the opportunity for sharing of experiences by participants. One obvious advantage of filial therapy is the involvement of the child's family in the therapy process. Additionally, filial therapy assists the parent to respond to his or her child's concerns in a therapeutic (empathic) manner. Another method that can be used to involve the family of a young child directly in the child's therapy is family play therapy. Ariel (1992), the originator of family play therapy, points out that using the child's natural medium of expression and communication in the process of family therapy allows accessibility to young children who otherwise might not be reached in family therapy.

Treatment Techniques

As in the model just described, the needs of the sexually abused child require the integration of multiple techniques and interventions. They may be used in any treatment modality effectively. These include education, coping skills training, social skills training, prevention of revictimization, role-playing and storytelling, cognitive–behavioral techniques, play therapy, art therapy, and psychotherapy.

Treatment planning must be based on the developmental level of the child. Thus, certain techniques must be modified based on the child's cognitive development. This is particularly true when dealing with the child's affective response to the trauma. Detailing the trauma and encouraging affective expression is an important aspect of any treatment program. Young children have neither the cognitive skills nor the fund of life experiences necessary for verbal expression of difficult feelings. Play is the most important avenue for affective expression in children. It allows the child to adapt to new (and sometimes traumatic) realities.

Pretend play is usually based on common events in children's lives; therefore it supports perspective taking (Rubin, 1988; Matthews, Beebe, & Bopp, 1980) and enhances problem solving by encouraging flexibility in thinking and by providing children with symbolic ways of coping with the anxiety and fear generated by new or problematic situations. The anxiety-decreasing function of play operates in much the same way that talking or thinking through a problem does for adults (Vygotsky, 1967; Curry & Arnaud, 1974). Play allows children to experiment with and experience feelings, fears, and conflicts in a relatively safe and socially acceptable manner. Traumatic life events can be reenacted in play, allowing the child to remember the event and express feelings about it that may have been too painful or frightening to handle at the time of the experience. Play also allows children to reverse the roles of actors in a remembered situation. Through play, a child can become the perpetrator, while the perpetrator becomes the victim. This role reversal empowers the child by giving him or her a sense of mastery and control that was not present in the original situation.

For these reasons, play therapy is a highly effective and developmentally appropriate way of treating sexually abused children. Play therapy is most commonly used with children who have serious emotional/psychological problems, as is most often true with severely traumatized children, and consists of a wide variety of treatment modalities with varying theoretical orientations and technical strategies (O'Connor, 1991). According to Bettleheim (1987, p. 35), "So valuable is play in this connection that play therapy has become the main avenue for helping young children with emotional difficulties."

When using play therapy as a treatment modality with sexually abused children, the therapist should remember that following the child's play and "staying within the metaphor" (or, not connecting the play themes with reality too soon) will encourage the child to express feelings regarding the abuse. Connecting play themes too directly (and/or too soon) with the child's abusive experiences may result in an interruption of the play and a setback in the therapy. It is important, however, that the actual trauma and associated feelings not be avoided by the therapist. Many children will not be able to bring up their experience or the feelings accompanying it even in play. If the child is to be afforded the cathartic value of play (Ginsberg, 1993), he or she must be assisted to confront it. Johnson (1989) recommends that the therapist begin with nondirective play therapy and carefully establish a close, trusting relationship with the child. Then the therapist can assist the child to gradually confront his or her abuse by carefully planned and structured play sequences. James (1989) describes the recommended approach as direct, open, straightforward, and with an intense, fun style. James (1989) and Gil (1991) describe many unique play techniques to accomplish the aim of assisting the child to confront and work through feelings about the abuse. In one situation, a 6-year old who had been sexually abused 2½ years earlier had two years of therapy that had never directly addressed her abuse. When brought to one of the authors, the child was told that they would play and work and the work would be about the "bad people who touched her where they shouldn't and put things inside of her, and made her put her mouth on little boys' pee pees." The therapy process following this was marked by a gradual production by the child of fantasy material directly related to the molestation.

Children have a natural tendency to repeat their trauma in play. Terr (1983) described a repetitive, compulsive, unsatisfying reiteration of play involving traumatic themes, called "post-traumatic play," as a particular characteristic of PTSD in children. Unfortunately, children often become stuck in these highly negative play themes, with no chance of resolving the traumatic situation. Terr (1981) warns that play, in and of itself, may not resolve the child's dilemma of powerlessness. Therapists may need to interrupt such repetitions with possible solutions for the child. This caution is echoed by James (1989) who suggests that the child be shown (in play) how to "restructure the traumatizing event as a victorious survivor." For example, one 5-year-old girl named Anna constantly reenacted her trauma by having "the bad man" come out of nowhere to abduct the girl doll. No one was ever there to help her. She was asked who might be able to help the poor little girl, and she said "the police, but they aren't here." After multiple reenactments over weeks of therapy, her cue was taken and the police car was taken out of the cabinet in an effort to help the little girl doll. Anna resisted at first and would not allow the police to find the "bad man" and the girl. However, over time she did allow the police to help, and eventually the little girl doll was able to deal with the "bad man" by herself.

There are many directive but highly useful play techniques that encourage the expression of feelings. Children can be taught to write, to say, or to sing affirmations such as "I am a loveable child and I can be happy." "Clay bombs" is a powerful exercise that involves the child and the therapist throwing bombs at a paper outline of the perpetrator while calling him names (James, 1989). Wet paper towels can be used where clay is inappropriate. Children can choose colors to represent different feelings, then draw an appropriate face, for example, smiley or frowney, on a strip of that color. Feelings can be "gotten rid of" by tearing them up in tiny pieces and throwing them in the trash or flushing them down the toilet. Gil (1991) recommends the use of toys that facilitate communication, such as telephones and walkie-talkies. She notes that sunglasses have a "magical" effect on children, in that the children think they are invisible when they put them on. This invisibility promotes freer communication by the child.

Art therapy is another highly effective technique for affective expression. It has been used with success with sexually abused children (Johnson, 1989; Kelley, 1985). Allan (1988) and James (1989) have described unique uses of art materials and art therapy for abused children. Oaklander (1988) uses a variety of art materials in a child-focused approach to Gestalt therapy. We have integrated art into our group therapy program with excellent results. Art can be used to explore the details of the abuse, feelings about the abuse and the perpetrator, and the child's self-esteem (through the use of self-portraits). Indeed, art can be helpful with any age group; we also employ it with the nonoffending parents group.

Older children and adolescents may be much more verbal, and therefore amenable to more traditional psychotherapy. The typical sexually abused child, however, is generally reluctant to discuss the trauma, and often unable to tolerate the intensity of the therapeutic process. Time may be required to allow feelings of safety and security in the relationship to develop before these themes can be approached successfully. In our experience, it is sometimes easier to engage children in this task in a group setting.

Success with cognitive–behavioral therapy has been discussed earlier in this chapter. Lipovsky (1992) describes the range of cognitive–behavioral interventions appropriate for use with sexually abused children. Generally, this treatment approach combines coping skills training with behavioral and cognitive techniques.

Coping skills can help sexually abused children cope with the intrusive thoughts and secondary serious anxiety they frequently experience. It is particularly important that the children have these skills to use after therapy sessions detailing the abuse or dealing with affective expression regarding the abuse. Relaxation training can be very useful to reduce tension and anxiety. Many techniques are available, including deep muscle relaxation, deep breathing, and guided imagery. We find guided imagery to be especially helpful for children. They are taught to imagine their personal safe place where they are free from any possible harm and can let the tension drain from them. Combining this technique with deep breathing exercises can be very successful, if the child feels safe with the therapist or group. Creating a safe therapeutic environment is thus a prerequisite to teaching relaxation techniques, or the children will be unable to let their guard down to complete the exercises. The techniques should be utilized in the therapy when the child shows evidence of becoming overwhelmed by the memories and affect he or she is working on. This will not only titrate the level of affect the child experiences in the treatment process, but will also reinforce the utility of the relaxation techniques he or she has been taught. This kind of practice will allow the child to transfer the skill outside the treatment setting.

Self-talk is another useful technique that can be used with children old enough to comprehend the instructions and the significance of this technique. Abused children feel overwhelmed and helpless in dealing with the abuse and with their feelings. After assuring the child's safety and teaching some coping skills for dealing with feelings, children can reinforce themselves through self-talk. For instance, Stacey was a 9-year-old girl who felt afraid whenever she entered a strange bathroom. She had been abused in a bathroom, and anxiety frequently prevented her from using available facilities when she was away from home. She was instructed to talk to herself each time she felt afraid in this way, saying: "I am safe, nothing will happen; I can remain calm." By focusing on this self-dialogue and using deep-breathing techniques, Stacey gradually improved in her ability to use bathrooms away from home. Stacey's therapist also employed another useful cognitive technique in treating this symptom, desensitization.

Desensitization is a core cognitive technique that has been highly effective in treating anxiety symptoms. Patients are generally asked to make a list of all the situations that produce anxiety in them, and prioritize them from the least frightening to the most frightening. Therapists then systematically treat each in turn, beginning with the mildest situation. The patient is first instructed in relaxation, and is totally relaxed at the onset of the desensitization therapy. The patient is then instructed to imagine themselves in the frightening situation, until they become unable to tolerate the feelings and anxiety is felt. This routine is repeated until the patient is able to tolerate the imagined experience without anxiety. Next, the patient begins to confront the actual situation, again beginning totally relaxed and proceeding until anxiety is felt. Each fearful situation is handled similarly in turn, until the most frightening situation is encountered without anxiety. Play reenactment and drawings can be used for desensitization of younger children (Gil, 1991).

A process similar to desensitization can be used with sexually abused children, although generally it is much less structured and occurs within the framework of psychotherapy that focuses on the abusive experiences. When the child details these experiences, the therapist can observe which elements are most upsetting to the child and which may be more easily discussed. The therapist should focus initially on the areas that the child can tolerate, moving gradually to areas that are especially anxiety-provoking for the child. When the child begins to experience anxiety, the therapist should intervene and instruct the child to utilize her or his relaxation skills to feel calm again before restarting the process. This allows a graded exposure to the child's frightening memories and prevents the child from dropping out of treatment because of overwhelming feelings. This technique can also be used with younger children.

Finally, treatment of sexually abused children can make use of education, prevention, and social skills training. Educating the child about sexual abuse and the development of symptoms can help "normalize" her or his feelings and decrease her or his feelings of isolation. Sex education is also important since most of these children have very little knowledge about sex and procreation.

Communication and problem-solving skills can be taught well in groups, in addition to assertiveness training which deals with preventing further abuse. The ability to say "No," and to know when to say it, is vital with sexually abused children. Games, stories, and role-playing can be used to teach these skills. Board games, such as "Communicate" and "Communicate, Jr." (Mayo & Gajewski, 1991) are fun for the children and set up various situations to role-play. Group activities such as "Lighthouse," where a blindfolded child is verbally led through a room full of other group members by the child playing the "lighthouse," can teach both communication skills and the ability to trust other people. Therapists should use their imaginations and their knowledge of the children to develop ideas for skits, stories, and dramas to encourage communication, social interaction, and processing of traumatic elements. One group program is designed to have the children in the group produce a drama about sexual abuse (Powell & Faherty, 1990). The children then act out the drama, including roles of the perpetrator, victim, family, judges, and so on. This is similar to the reenactment typically seen in the play of preschool-age sexual abuse survivors. In addition, videotapes concerning prevention of revictimization, such as *No Easy Answers* (Anderson, Morris, & Robins, 1987), are available for use in groups.

A final note concerns the treatment needs of sexually abused males. There is consensus that sexual abuse of boys is underreported even more than that of females, and that the incidence may be as high as 1 in 6 males victimized in childhood. There has been a good bit of speculation that boys may differ from girls in their reaction to abuse and in their treatment needs. These assumptions do not appear to be corroborated by the current research, which shows no consistent differences in the reaction of boys and girls to sexual abuse (Kendall-Tackett, Meyer Williams, & Finkelhor, 1993). Thus, for the most part, treatment recommendations will not differ significantly for boys, at least until further research develops that proves they have different needs.

There is, however, one area where males may differ from females. Although female–boy sexual abuse does occur more commonly than was previously suspected, the majority of sexual perpetrators of boys are males (Shrier & Johnson, 1988), and males are more often subjected to anal abuse (Watkins & Bentovim, 1992). A high rate of homosexual orientation has been found in victimized adolescent boys (Shrier & Johnson, 1988). It has recently been postulated that sexual abuse of boys in this manner may encourage homoerotic development (Friedrich, 1990, p. 54). It is also possible, however, that male perpetrators seek out victims with homosexual traits, who later develop homosexual orientation. Treatment recommendations must await further research on this issue.

References

Adams-Tucker, C. (1984). The unmet psychiatric needs of sexually abused youths: Referrals from a child protection agency and clinical evaluations. *Journal of the American Academy of Child and Adolescent Psychiatry, 23,* 659–667.

Allan, J. (1988). *Inscapes of the child's world.* Dallas, TX: Spring.

Anderson, C., Morris, B., & Robins, M. (1987). *No easy answers.* Minneapolis, MN: Illusion Theater.

Ariel, S. (1992). *Strategic family play therapy.* New York: John Wiley and Sons.

Bettleheim, B. (1987, March). The importance of play. *Atlantic Monthly,* pp. 35–46.

Bourne, P. G. (1970). Military psychiatry and the Vietnam experience. *American Journal of Psychiatry, 27,* 123–130.

Briere, J., & Runtz, M. (1988). Symptomatology associated with childhood sexual victimization in a non-clinical adult sample. *Child Abuse and Neglect, 12,* 51 59,

Browne, A., & Finkelhor, D. (1984). The traumatic impact of child sexual abuse: A conceptualization. *American Journal of Orthopsychiatry, 55,* 530–541.

Byrne, J. P., & Valdiserri, E. V. (1982). Victims of childhood sexual abuse: A follow-up study of a noncompliant population. *Hospital and Community Psychiatry, 33,* 938–940.

Corder, B. F., Haizlip, T., & DeBoer, P. (1990). A pilot study for a structured, time-limited therapy group for sexually abused pre-adolescent children. *Child Abuse and Neglect, 14,* 243–251.

Curry, N., & Arnaud, S. H. (1974). Cognitive implications in children's spontaneous role play. *Theory and Practice, 13,* 273–277.

Damon, L., & Waterman, J. (1986). Parallel group treatment of children and their mothers. In K. MacFarlane, J. Waterman, S. Conerly, L. Damon, M. Durfee, & S. Long (Eds.), *Sexual abuse of young children* (pp. 244–298). New York: Guilford Press.

Deblinger, E., McLeer, S. V., & Henry, D. (1990). Cognitive behavioral treatment for sexually abused children suffering from post-traumatic stress: Preliminary findings. *Journal of the American Academy of Child and Adolescent Psychiatry, 29,* 747–752.

Dumas, L. S. (1992). "Mommy, I know a bad secret!": Talking with your child about sexual abuse. In L. S. Dumas, *Talking with your child about a troubled world.* New York: Fawcett Columbine.

Everson, M. D., Hunter, W. M., Runyon, D. K., Edelsohn, G. A., & Coulter, M. L.

(1989). Maternal support following disclosure of incest. *American Journal of Orthopsychiatry, 59,* 197–207.

Finkelhor, D. (1984). *Child sexual abuse: New theory and research.* New York: Free Press.

Finkelhor, D. (Ed.). (1986). *A sourcebook on child sexual abuse.* Newbury Park, CA: Sage.

Friedrich, W. N. (1990). *Psychotherapy of sexually abused children and their families.* New York: W. W. Norton and Company.

Furniss, T., Bingley-Miller, L., & Van Elburg, A. (1988). Goal-oriented group treatment for sexually abused adolescent girls. *British Journal of Psychiatry, 152,* 97–106.

Giarretto, H. (1989). Community-based treatment of the incest family. *Pediatric Clinics of North America, 12,* 351–361.

Gil, E. (1991). *The healing power of play.* New York: Guilford Press.

Ginsberg, B. G. (1993). Catharsis. In C. E. Schaefer (Ed.), *The therapeutic powers of play* (pp. 107–141). Northvale, NJ: Jason Aronson.

Glass, N. (1986). *Parents as therapeutic agents: A study of the effects of filial therapy.* Unpublished Ph.D. diss., North Texas State University, Denton, TX.

Green, A. H. (1993). Child sexual abuse: Immediate and long-term effects and intervention. *Journal of the American Academy of Child and Adolescent Psychiatry, 32,* 890–902.

Guerney, B. (1964). Filial therapy: Description and rationale. *Journal of Consulting Psychology, 28,* 303–310.

Guerney, B. (1976). Filial therapy as a method for disturbed children. *Evaluation, 3,* 34–35.

Guerney, L. F. (1993). Relationship enhancement. In C. E. Schaefer (Ed.), *The therapeutic powers of play* (pp. 267–290). Northvale, NJ: Jason Aronson.

Hazzard, A., King, H. E., & Webb, C. (1986). Group therapy with sexually abused adolescent girls. *American Journal of Psychotherapy, 40,* 213–223.

James, B. (1989). *Treating traumatized children.* Lexington, MA: Lexington Books.

Johnson, K. (1989). *Trauma in the lives of children.* Claremont, CA: Hunter House.

Kelley, S. J. (1985). Drawings: Critical communications for sexually abused children. *Pediatric Nursing, 11,* 421–426.

Kendall-Tackett, K. A., Meyer Williams, L., & Finkelhor, D. (1993). Impact of sexual abuse on children: A review and synthesis of recent empirical studies. *Psychological Bulletin, 113,* 164–180.

Kiser, L. J., Ackerman, B. J., Brown, E., Edwards, N. B., McColgan, E., Pugh, R., & Pruitt, D. B. (1988). Post-traumatic stress disorder in young children: A reaction to purported sexual abuse. *Journal of the American Academy of Child and Adolescent Psychiatry, 27,* 645–649.

Kolko, D. J. (1987). Treatment of child sexual abuse: Programs, progress, and prospects. *Journal of Family Violence, 2,* 303–318.

Kosten, T. R., Mason, J. W., Giller, E. L., Ostroff, R. B., & Podd, L. (1987). Sustained urinary norepinephrine and epinephrine elevation in post-traumatic stress disorder. *Psychoneuroendocrinology, 12,* 13–20.

Krener, P. (1985). After incest: Secondary prevention? *Journal of the American Academy of Child and Adolescent Psychiatry, 24,* 231–234.

Lipovsky, J. A. (1992). Assessment and treatment of post-traumatic stress disorder in child survivors of sexual assault. In D. F. Foy (Ed.), *Treating PTSD: Cognitive–behavioral strategies* (pp. 127–164). New York: Guilford Press.

Long, S. (1986). Guidelines for treating young children. In K. MacFarlene, J. Waterman, S. Conerly, L. Damon, M. Durfee, & S. Long, *Sexual abuse of young children* (pp. 220–243). New York: Guilford Press.

MacFarlene, K., Waterman, J., Conerly, S., Damon, L., Durfee, M., & Long, S. (1986). *Sexual abuse of young children.* New York: Guilford Press.

Mason, J. W., Giller, E. L., Kosten, T. R., Ostroff, R. B., & Podd, L. (1986). Urinary free-cortisol levels of post-traumatic stress disorder patients. *Journal of Nervous and Mental Disease, 174,* 145–149.

Matthews, W. S., Beebe, S., & Bopp, M. (1980). Spatial perspective taking and pretend play. *Perceptual and Motor Skills, 5,* 49–50.

Mayo, P., & Gajewski, N. (1991). *Communicate, Jr.* Eau Claire, WI: Thinking Publications.

McLeer, S. V., Deblinger, E., Atkins, M. S., Foa, E. B., & Ralphe, D. L. (1988). Post-traumatic stress disorder in sexually abused children. *Journal of the American Academy of Child and Adolescent Psychiatry, 27,* 650–654.

Meddin, B. J., & Hansen, I. (1985). The services provided during child abuse and\or neglect case investigation and the barriers that exist to service provision. *Child Abuse and Neglect, 9,* 175–182.

Mrazek, P. B. (1983). Sexual abuse of children. In B. B. Lahey & A. E. Kazdin (Eds.), *Advances in clinical child psychology* (Vol. 6, pp. 199–215). New York: Plenum.

Newberger, C. M., Gremy, I. M., Waternaux, C. M., & Newberger, E. H. (1993). Mothers of sexually abused children: Trauma and repair in longitudinal perspective. *American Journal of Orthopsychiatry, 63,* 92–102.

Oaklander, V. (1988). *Windows to our children.* Highland, NY: Center for Gestalt Development.

O'Connor, K. J. (1991). *The play therapy primer.* New York: John Wiley and Sons.

O'Donohue, W. T., & Elliott, A. N. (1992). Treatment of sexually abused children: A review. *Journal of Clinical Child Psychology, 21,* 218–228.

Orenchuk-Tomiuk, N., Matthey, G., & Christensen, C. P. (1990). The resolution model: A comprehensive treatment framework in sexual abuse. *Child Welfare, 69,* 417–431.

Ornitz, E. M., & Pynoos, R. S. (1989). Startle modulation in children with post-traumatic stress disorder. *American Journal of Psychiatry, 146,* 866–870.

Powell, L., & Faherty, S. L. (1990). Treating sexually abused latency age girls. *Arts in Psychotherapy, 17,* 35–47.

Rubin, K. H. (1988). Some "good news" and some "not-so-good" news about dramatic play. In D. Bergen (Ed.), *Play as a medium for learning and development* (pp. 67–71). Portsmouth, NH: Heinemann.

Sgroi, S. M. (Ed.). (1982). *Handbook of clinical intervention in child sexual abuse.* Lexington, MA: Lexington Books.

Shrier, D., & Johnson, R. L. (1988). Sexual victimization of boys: An ongoing study of an adolescent medicine clinic population. *Journal of the National Medical Association, 80,* 1189–1193.

Stavrakaki, V. C., Ellis, J., & Williams, E. (1988). Child sexual abuse: Its impact and treatment. *Canadian Journal of Psychiatry, 33,* 468–473.

Steward, M. S., Farquhar, L. C., Dicharry, D. C., Glick, D. R., & Martin, P. W. (1986). Group therapy: A treatment of choice for young victims of child abuse. *International Journal of Group Psychotherapy, 36,* 261–277.

Stover, L., & Guerney, B. (1967). The efficacy of training procedures for mothers in filial therapy. *Psychotherapy: Theory, Research, and Practice, 4,* 110–115.

Summit, R. (1983). The child sexual abuse accommodation syndrome. *Child Abuse and Neglect, 7,* 177–193.

Terr, L. C. (1981). Forbidden games: Post-traumatic child's play. *Journal of the American Academy of Child Psychiatry, 20,* 741–760.

Terr, L. (1983). Time sense following psychic trauma: A clinical study of ten adults and twenty children. *American Journal of Orthopsychiatry, 53,* 244–261.

Terr, L. C. (1989). Family anxiety after traumatic events. *Journal of Clinical Psychiatry, 50*(11, Suppl.), 15–19.

Terr, L. C. (1991). Childhood traumas: An outline and overview. *American Journal of Psychiatry, 148,* 10–20.

Verleur, D., Hughes, R. E., & de Rios, M. D. (1986). Enhancement of self-esteem among female adolescent incest victims: A controlled comparison. *Adolescence, 21,* 843–854.

Vygotsky, L. (1962). *Thought and language.* Cambridge, MA: MIT Press.

Watkins, W. G., & Bentovim, A. (1992). The sexual abuse of male children and adolescents. *Journal of Child Psychology and Psychiatry and Allied Disciplines, 33,* 197–248.

Wyatt, G. E., & Powell, G. J. (1988). Identifying the lasting effects of child sexual abuse: An overview. In G. E. Wyatt & G. J. Powell (Eds.), *Lasting effects of child sexual abuse* (pp. 11–17). Newbury Park, CA: Sage.

Part 4

Problems of Gender Development and Sexual Orientation

12

Differential Diagnosis and Rationale for Treatment of Gender Identity Disorders and Transvestism

George A. Rekers
Mark D. Kilgus

C ross-sex behavior in children and adolescence may merely represent the normal exploration of masculine and feminine sex role behaviors while the individual is in the process of learning the distinctions between masculine and feminine sex-typed roles and the expectations of his or her social environment (Rekers, 1977a, 1987; Rekers, Bentler, Rosen, & Lovaas, 1977; Rekers, Rosen, Lovaas, & Bentler, 1978; Rekers & Yates, 1976). "Tomboyish" behavior in girls is far more prevalent and much more likely to be merely a transient phase than is "sissyish" or "effeminate" behavior in boys (Rekers & Mead, 1980). Normal girls who prefer masculine activities during their childhood years are typically secure in their basic female identity, and developmentally they usually follow a course of adopting increasingly larger numbers of feminine interests during the course of the adolescent years (Brown, 1956; Saghir & Robins, 1973).

In contrast to normal girls, the "tomboyism" of gender-disturbed girls typically persists into and throughout the adolescent years and is more likely to result in the conditions of adulthood transsexualism or homosexuality (Green, 1975; Saghir & Robins, 1973). Stoller (1975) pointed out that the adult female transsexual is typically masculine in her behavior and interests which are pervasively present from a very early age, perhaps 3 or 4 years old, whereas the "tomboyish" females demonstrate an earlier period of typically feminine development in younger childhood followed by a secondary development of interests in masculine activities. Similarly, cross-sex behavior in boys can become a persistent and compulsively stereotyped pattern indicative of the development of a transvestic disorder or a "gender identity disorder of childhood" (American Psychiatric Association, 1994; Rekers, 1988b; Zucker & Green, 1993).

Gender Disturbance in Childhood and Adolescence

Parents or teachers may become concerned that the behavior of a child or adolescent is atypical compared to same-aged peers. The clinician who is consulted must be able to distinguish normal adjustment problems in sexual development from potential gender-related psychological disturbances that require specific interventions (Rekers & Milner, 1978).

As of 1994, official criteria (American Psychiatric Association, 1994) for "gender identity disorder" include a "strong and persistent cross-gender identification (not merely a desire for any perceived cultural advantages of being the other sex), manifested by four (or more) of the following:

1. Repeatedly stated desire to be, or insistence that he or she is, the other sex

2. In boys, preference for cross-dressing or simulating female attire; in girls, insistence on wearing only stereotypical masculine clothing

3. Strong and persistent preferences for cross-sex roles in make-believe play or persistent fantasies of being the other sex

4. Intense desire to participate in the stereotypical games and pastimes of the other sex

5. Strong preference for playmates of the other sex" (p. 537).

In adolescents and adults the disorder "is manifested by symptoms such as a stated desire to be the other sex, frequent passing as the other sex, desire to live or be treated as the other sex, or the conviction that he or she has the typical feelings and reactions of the other sex" (p. 537).

Another essential criterion is a "persistent discomfort with his or her sex or sense of inappropriateness in the gender role of that sex" (p. 537). This is manifested in children "by any of the following: in boys, assertion that his penis or testes are disgusting or will disappear or assertion that it would be better not to have a penis, or aversion toward rough-and-tumble play and rejection of male stereotypical toys, games, and activities; in girls, rejection of urinating in a sitting position, assertion that she has or will grow a penis, or assertion that she does not want to grow breasts or menstruate, or marked aversion toward normative feminine clothing" (p. 537). In adolescents and adults, manifested symptoms include "preoccupation with getting rid of primary and secondary sex characteristics (e.g., request for hormones, surgery, or other procedures to physically alter sexual characteristics to simulate the other sex) or belief that he or she was born the wrong sex" (p. 538).

"Gender identity disorder" may not be "concurrent with a physical intersex condition" (p. 538).

Additionally, "the disturbance causes clinically significant distress or impairment in social, occupational, or other important areas of functioning" (p. 538).

Case Examples of Disorders in Boys

Gender Identity Disorder in Young Boys

Craig was referred for an evaluation at the age of 4 years and 11 months. He lived in an intact family that included a psychologically normal brother 8 years of age and a sister 9 months of age. The referring physician had found Craig to be physically normal as assessed by currently available methods of biomedical testing (see Rekers, Crandall, Rosen, & Bentler, 1979). He had been cross-dressing in female garments from the age of 2 years and had also begun to play with cosmetic items belonging to his mother and grandmother at about the same time. When girls' clothing was unavailable to him, Craig very frequently improvised his cross-dressing by using a mop or towel over his head for "long hair" or a long shirt for a "dress." Craig also displayed high rates of very pronounced feminine mannerisms, gestures, and gait, he had an exaggerated feminine voice inflection, and the content of his speech was dominated by feminine topics. Others would remark that he had a keen ability to imitate many of the subtle feminine behaviors of an adult woman. At the same time, he avoided boyish play, being both unable and unwilling to participate in the rough-and-tumble games of other boys his age in the immediate neighborhood. He also regularly avoided playing with his brother; he declined to defend himself when with his peers; and he expressed fears of getting hurt. He clearly preferred to play with girls, and with one neighborhood girl in particular; he invariably insisted on playing the part of the "mother" when he played "house" with the girls, and he rigidly assigned the part of "father" to one of the girls in the group. For his age, Craig was overly dependent upon his mother and repeatedly demanded her attention. Observations of his interactions with his mother indicated that he was developing skills at manipulating his mother to satisfy his feminine interests—for example, he would offer to "help Mommy" by carrying her purse when she had other packages to carry. It was noted that he was almost compulsive or rigid in the extent to which he would refuse contact with typical boy activities and to the extent upon which he insisted on being a girl (Rekers & Lovaas, 1974). Craig satisfied the diagnostic criteria for a "gender identity disorder of childhood" that first became an official diagnosis in 1980 (American Psychiatric Association, 1980). Such boys exhibit many cross-gender behaviors in conjunction with a cross-gender identity evidenced by persistent repudiation of their male anatomic status. (See pages 284–286 for a case of gender identity disorder in an adolescent boy.)

Gender Behavior Disturbance in Young Boys

In the absence of a gender identity disorder, the cross-dressing of a gender-behavior-disturbed boy would more typically involve the use of undergarments such as panties and nylons. The term "juvenile unmasculinity" has been used to describe such boys who have a persistent and profound sense of masculine inadequacy which typically leads to a negative self-evaluation (Friedman, 1988).

Eight-year-old Paul was such a boy who had been living with foster parents for four years together with his 5-year-old and 9-year-old brothers. Paul would frequently dress in feminine sex-typed clothing whenever given an opportunity. He often played with baby dolls and he played with girls more frequently than with boys. His hand, wrist, and arm movements, as well as his gait, gave him an effeminate appearance. Furthermore, he frequently spoke with a "feminine speech inflection" and between 36 and 58 percent of his recorded speech (at observation periods) contained feminine topics. He denied being a girl and also denied having any wish to be a female. He specifically wanted to learn which of his actions were being labeled "girlish" by his peer group because he was concerned about the ostracism that he was experiencing (Rekers, Willis, Yates, Rosen, & Low, 1977).

Transvestic Behavior in Adolescent Boys

By age 16, Tom had developed a general heterosexual orientation but his own sexual activity involved female clothing. He would completely disrobe and then dress in female undergarments and a dress. Although he rarely masturbated, when he did masturbate, he did not employ manual manipulation but instead rolled on the bed while wearing the feminine clothes. During masturbation he would focus on a transvestic fantasy (Bentler, 1968).

Case Examples of Disorders in Girls

Gender Identity Disorder in Young Girls

A true cross-gender identity in a girl is rarely reported; however, this disorder is sometimes clinically seen and can be differentiated from a normal "tomboy" phase in childhood (Rekers & Mead, 1980).

Becky was referred for psychological treatment at the age of 7 years 11 months by a psychiatric nurse specialist who had assessed her at the request of the girl's mother. Becky had two younger sisters aged 2 and 6 years old. The girls' father was absent from the home due to divorce. For as long as the mother could remember, Becky had been dressing exclusively in boys' pants and she also often wore cowboy boots. At the same time she consistently rejected any feminine clothing such as dresses and she had no interest in female jewelry. Becky's only use of female cosmetic articles that her mother could recall involved drawing a mustache and/or a beard on her face several times. Becky appeared "masculine" in her gestures, mannerisms, and gait. It was reported that she would occasionally masturbate in public and rub her body up against other girls in her peer group. She frequently projected her voice very low so she would sound like a "man." She repeatedly expressed her desire to be a boy, and she adopted male roles in her play. She definitely preferred the company of boy playmates and did not interact very well with other girls. Her behavior was described as excessively aggressive. She had a very poor relationship with her 6-year-old sister who displayed a typical preference for feminine play activities (Rekers & Mead, 1979).

Gender Identity Disorder in Adolescent Girls

Deviant cross-gender behavior or transvestic behavior are rarely reported in adolescent girls in the absence of a gender identity disorder, essentially because of the low incidence of such phenomena and because "tomboy behavior" in girls is socially more acceptable than "sissy" behavior in boys.

Joan was a 14-year-old adolescent girl who lived in a rural area. Her mother had experienced two divorces in Joan's lifetime, and had initiated 15 moves during Joan's past six years. As a result, Joan had experienced very little affection from any adult male figure. When Joan first appeared in the clinic, she was wearing a distinctly masculine shirt, a black leather jacket, faded blue jeans, and cowboy boots. She exclaimed that no one could ever get her to wear a dress. She reported that she had felt like and wanted to be a boy all of her life. When presenting at the university teaching hospital, she requested a transplant of male sexual organs; in the past, she had made repeated requests for sex-reassignment surgery. Her voice inflection and the content of her speech were both quite masculine in appearance, as were her gestures and mannerisms. She openly stated that she had a strong sexual interest in other females, but not as a "homosexual" but as a "male" wanting a girlfriend. Her social interactions were largely limited to males in her peer group, and she indicated her own cross-gender identification in her numerous references to this male peer group and herself as "we." She had repeatedly received failing grades in her physical education class because she refused to participate in the girls' class and the coach would not allow her to play on the boys' teams and to use the boys' locker room. She preferred to be called "Paul" and strongly identified with Paul Stanley, a male rock star with the group called Kiss. She deliberately and frequently would cross-dress so she would resemble Paul Stanley, with white shoe polish on her face, a black star on her right eye, and red lipstick on her lips. Joan was disgusted by her physical maturation as a woman; she would wear a jacket or an overshirt to hide her developing breasts and she refused to ever wear a bra. Further, Joan would not even tell her mother when she would need feminine hygiene articles. As a result of her cross-gender behavior, Joan was rejected by the vast majority of her peers. Reportedly, her very small circle of friends consisted of males noted for their social maladjustment and tendency to act out behaviorally. Joan suffered frequent depressive episodes accompanied by suicide ideation, and she would state that she felt she would rather be dead than remain a female.

Descriptive Characteristics Associated with the Dimensions of Sex and Gender

In the diagnostic assessment of a particular child, it is more helpful to describe the individual across the several dimensions of sex and gender (see Table 12–1; Rosen & Rekers, 1980) rather than to immediately attempt to assign the child to one of the currently limited diagnostic categories of disorder (Rekers, 1988b; Rosen & Rekers, 1980; Rosen, Rekers, & Friar, 1977).

Physical Sex Status

The individual child or adolescent can be medically categorized as male, female, or intersex (hermaphroditic) with regard to the congruity or incongruity across the five physical variables of genetic constitution, gonads, external sex organ anatomy, internal accessory genital structures, and sex endocrinology. A further refinement of sex status would be to provide a rating on the Tanner Scale in terms of the stage of the individual's prepubertal, pubertal, or postpubertal development (Marshall & Tanner, 1969, 1970; Tanner, 1955).

Social Assignment

The infant's assignment as "boy" or "girl" is typically announced to the parents at birth by the attending physician. However, in rare cases, a psychologically disturbed mother will assign a gender that is opposite to the child's anatomy. One such case was reported by the Stanford University Gender Dysphoria Clinic in the 1970s (Gebhard, 1973). A disturbed mother announced to her relatives that she had had a baby girl, although the infant was male. The mother never allowed others to change the baby's diapers. The infant grew to assume a female identity as a result of social assignment as female by the mother. It was only when the little "girl" attended kindergarten that she discovered in the girls' room that her geni-

Table 12–1
Dimensions for Psychosexual Assessment

Level of Assessment	Dimension	Major Categories
Sexual status	Physical sex	Male, female, or intersexed; Tanner's stages for prepubertal, pubertal, or postpubertal development
	Social assignment	Male, female, or intersexed; child, adolescent, or adult
Intrapersonal behavior	Gender identity	Normal, undifferentiated, cross-gender, or conflicted
	Sexual identity	Heterosexual, bisexual, homosexual, transsexual, transvestite, "queen," "fag," "drag queen," "gay," etc.
	Sexual arousal	Human object choice (male, female, both); animal orientation object choice; magnitude and frequency; fantasies
Interpersonal behavior	Gender role	Masculine, feminine, undifferentiated, androgynous behavior
	Sexual behavior	Human partner (male, female, both); animal partner; inanimate object; intrusive vs. receptive roles; group vs. individual partner, etc.

tals were different from the genitals of other girls. "She" could stand up to urinate, while the other girls could not.

In cases of intersexed children, physicians typically postpone social assignment as male or female at birth, informing the parents that the child's sexual development is incomplete and that further medical evaluation is necessary to establish the sex and to begin medical intervention to "complete" the child's sexual development (see Chapter 6).

Gender Identity

A child's gender identity is considered normal when the self-concept is strongly male or female and matches the child's physical and sex status. *Ambiguous or undifferentiated identity* is a normal developmental phase of infancy or the later abnormal condition in which a firm and consistent self-concept as male or female is lacking. A *conflicted gender identity* is the result of having strong feelings of both masculine and feminine identity coexisting or alternating in an individual's personality. *Cross-gender identity* involves the strong sense that one is a member of the physical sex opposite to one's actual physical sex status.

Sexual Identity

Another aspect of identity is the kind of self-label a person assumes in describing himself or herself to others. These self-assumed labels represent the individual's own expectations for his or her sexual behavior. Most individuals consider themselves as "heterosexual." However, there are a variety of other self-labels that people assume, such as "bisexual," "homosexual," "transsexual," "transvestite," or some more colloquial terms such as "queen," "fag," "drag queen," "gay," "dyke," and so on. It is essential to assess this sexual identity of a patient, and to get the patient to describe what that self-label means to him or her because such terms are used in varying ways. For example, a child may think of himself as "homosexual" even though he has never engaged in sexual behavior with another male, or just because an adult male has sexually abused him. Other children make fine idiosyncratic distinctions between such terms as "gay," "fag," "queer," or "homosexual," and assign themselves one of the labels. Many adolescent male prostitutes who engage in sexual behavior with adult male customers do not regard themselves as "homosexual" because they decline to participate in receptive sexual roles and restrict themselves to insertive sexual behaviors, orally or anally.

Sexual Arousal Orientation

An individual's magnitude and frequency of sexual arousal patterns can contribute to his or her sexual orientation.

Gender Role

Behaviors, attitudes, and personality characteristics have been sex-typed as masculine (high on masculine and low on feminine), feminine (low on masculine and high on feminine), undifferentiated (low on both masculine and feminine), or androgynous (high on both masculine and feminine) (Bem, 1974).

Sexual Behavior

One's history of sexual activity with males, females, and/or with animals or with inanimate objects constitutes the individual's sexual behavior pattern.

In the developmental stages of childhood and adolescence, any incongruity across any two of the above seven psychosexual dimensions could constitute a source of psychological conflict in the present and also may be predictive of future sexual maladjustment.

Differential Diagnosis

It is necessary to assess not only the episodic presence of certain behaviors but also the ratio of masculine to feminine sex-typed behaviors together with their duration.

Gender behavior disturbance in boys can include any cluster of the following behaviors: dressing in feminine clothing, using female cosmetics, predominant preoccupation with girls' activities together with avoidance of male playmates and rough-and-tumble play, taking female roles in play, preferring female playmates, projecting the voice into a high femalelike voice inflection, predominantly talking about female topics as compared with male topics, and displaying effeminant gait and body movements or feminine-appearing gestures.

In the case of gender identity disorder in boys, there is typically a pattern of the presence of some or all of the above cross-gender behaviors together with a persistent repudiation of the boy's male anatomy by repeatedly saying that (1) he will become a woman, (2) that it would be better not to have male sex organs, (3) that his penis or testes will disappear or are disgusting.

Cross-gender behavior, transvestic behavior, and gender identity disorder in childhood has been differentiated from the kind of episodic and flexible exploration of sex-typed behaviors that is found during the course of normal psychosexual development of many boys and girls (Rekers, 1985b), and also has been distinguished from androgyny (Rekers, 1977b; Rekers, Rosen, Lovaas, & Bentler, 1978; Rosen & Rekers, 1980; Rosen, Rekers, & Friar, 1977; Rosen, Rekers, & Brigham, 1982). Children and adolescents evidence a psychosexual disorder when they develop a persistent, compulsive, and rigidly stereotyped pattern of sex-typed behavior, one that is often so extremely different from their same-aged peers as to be a caricature of a cultural sex role. Hyperfemininity in boys is a rigid and compulsive pattern that is quite different from the adaptive flexibility of psychological androgyny (Bem, 1974) and goes well beyond the normal curiosity-induced exploration of feminine stereotypic play found in some normal boys (Green, 1974, 1976; Rekers & Yates, 1976).

Etiological Factors and Associated Aspects of Cross-Gender Syndromes

The specific interactions of the potential variables involved in the etiology of deviant psychosexual development are not fully understood at the present time, although some suggestive data and a variety of theories have been advanced (Green, 1987; Mead & Rekers, 1979; Meyer-Bahlburg, 1993; Money, Hampson, & Hampson, 1955; Rekers, 1988a; Rekers, Mead, Rosen, & Brigham, 1983; Rekers & Swihart, 1989; also see discussion by Rekers, 1988a, 1988b, and Zuger, 1970). Zucker and Green (1993) have provided a recent review of the psychological and familial variables associated with gender identity disorder, including IQ; temperament; behavior problems such as separation, anxiety, creativity, and physical attractiveness; and sexual orientation in fantasy and behavior at follow-up.

Evidence for biological factors influencing psychosexual development comes from a variety of sources. The administration of testosterone to laboratory animals at critical times during the perinatal period can significantly change affect, conduct, and neuroanatomy. However, in humans, sexual dimorphic behavior seems to be less dependent on hormonal influences. Perhaps subtle variations in prenatal hormone levels could predispose an individual to intrasex differences in behavior. Yet, except for those individuals with anomalies of sexual differentiation such as ambiguous genitalia resulting from congenital adrenal hyperplasia or 5-alpha reductase deficiency (Zucker, Bradley, & Hughes, 1987), there is little support for brain androgenization ("testosterone imprinting") or other biological phenomena as major factors in establishing gender identity or sexual orientation (Byne & Parsons, 1993). Researchers have *not* discovered differences in sex steroids or gonadotropin secretion between transsexual and heterosexual females (Spinder, Spijkstra, Gooren, & Burger, 1986) or males (Hendricks, Graber, & Rodriguez-Sierra, 1989). There have been a couple of reports of transsexuals with an abnormal karyotype, for example, a fertile male with 47XYY chromosomes (Taneja, Ammini, Mohapatra, Saxena, & Kucheria, 1992). Nonetheless, the vast majority of those with gender identity disorder have normal chromosome numbers, external genitals, and hormone levels. Given the present state of our knowledge, we must tentatively conclude that the main source of gender deviance is found in psychological development variables and social learning within the family environment, including the processes of identification with parental figures and peers of the same sex, the development of complementation toward members of the opposite sex, the development of differential expectations for gender role behaviors influenced by parenting practices, and the child's recognition and degree of acceptance of his or her sexual anatomy with its reproductive function.

Clinical Rationale for Diagnosis and Treatment of Gender-Related Disorders in Childhood and Adolescence

Parents, teachers, and other professionals often refer the child or adolescent with a potential gender disturbance for both diagnosis and treatment. The rationale for such clinical intervention has been comprehensively and extensively elaborated in a number of publications (Bates, Skilbeck, Smith,

& Bentler, 1975; Bentler, 1968; Green, 1974, 1987; Marlowe, 1979; Myrick, 1970; Rekers, 1972, 1977b, 1982a, 1982b, 1984, 1985a, 1985b, 1985c, 1986, 1988a; Rekers, Bentler, Rosen, & Lovaas, 1977; Rekers & Mead, 1980; Rekers, Rosen, Lovaas, & Bentler, 1978; Rosen, Rekers, & Bentler, 1978; Rosen, Rekers, & Friar, 1977; Stoller, 1968, 1970; Zucker, 1990). Earlier critics of therapeutic intervention for gender-related disorders doubted that these childhood conditions were significantly associated with later gender dysphoria or sexual deviance, but such critics generally had little, if any, clinical experience with such youngsters (e.g., Nordyke, Baer, Etzel, & LeBlanc, 1977; Serbin, 1980; Winkler, 1977; Wolfe, 1979). Other early critics, such as Morin and Schultz (1978), had political agendas in mind. However, as the connection between childhood cross-gender behavior and adulthood sexual deviance became more apparent (e.g., see Blanchard & Steiner, 1990; Green, 1987; Zucker & Green, 1993), the ethically appropriate strategy of early identification and prevention of gender dysphoria, sexual deviance, and the associated emotional suffering became quite apparent (Zucker, 1990). Although a small minority continued to raise questions about the appropriateness of clinical intervention for cross-gender behavior and cross-gender development (such as Coleman, 1986, and Whitam, 1989), their objections tend to be more on the basis of their own personal preferences and political philosophy rather than upon the standard considerations used by clinicians for interventions for childhood and adolescent disorders.

Clinical Intervention to Detect Psychological Maladjustment

It would be an error for the young boy to suppose that it is inappropriate for him to nurture a baby, and therefore this incorrect and negative sex-role stereotype should be avoided. However, on the other hand, it is an appropriate diagnostic objective to assess whether a compulsive, inflexible, and chronic pattern of cross-gender behavior may be present in a boy, such as a cluster of behavior in which masculine play and activity is actively avoided in a way that makes the child's behavior pattern atypical among same-aged peers. Further, if a boy or girl is found to be chronically uncomfortable with or rejecting of his or her anatomic sexual status, it is reasonable for clinicians to intervene to help the child feel more comfortable in accepting his or her biological sexuality and associated gender (Zucker, 1985). An important sex education lesson to be learned by boys, for example, is that they will neither develop the biological possibility of becoming pregnant through intercourse with a man and deliver a baby, nor be able to breast-feed an infant.

The astute clinician will differentiate crippling sex-role stereotypes from gender role disturbance in a child. For example, the sensitive clinician would not impose negative sanctions against the expression of soft, tender emotions and crying by boys or men. Nor should a clinician impose unnecessary stereotypic limitations on individuals (e.g., "Doctors are male and nurses are female"), thereby hampering the optimal personal development of the patient or client or others. However, such sensitivity does not necessitate the conclusion that there exists no legitimate distinctions between masculine and feminine roles (see discussion in Rekers, 1986, 1988b). For example, it is not inappropriate for a given society, such as American society, to teach girls to clothe their upper torso in public and to prohibit males from regularly wearing skirts and dresses in public; this form of arbitrary assignment of sex-typed clothing does not, in fact, necessarily impose any unfair restriction upon individual development (Rekers et al., 1978). Therefore, a boy who prefers wearing dresses, lipstick, and eyeliner, or the boy who puts on his mother's apron to wash the dishes while fantasizing that he is a woman, is exhibiting problematic behavior in need of intervention for the child's own adjustment. Similarly, the girl who rigidly refuses to wear a dress under any circumstances is not evidencing the adaptive qualities of androgyny that are promoted by the American culture for girls. Careful assessment needs to be made whether or not such a rejection symbolizes a gender identity disorder in a girl.

A boy who steals his mother's or sister's undergarments as obligatory masturbation devices or for stress reduction is also moving outside the normal range of sexual development and is at risk for developing a paraphilia in adulthood (see Goodwin & Peterson, 1990). In both children and adolescents, there are cases of gender-disturbed girls who reject their sexual anatomy and develop desires to have their genitals medically and hormonally transformed to resemble a male. Similarly, a boy who frequently and chronically cross-dresses; who states that he wants to grow up to become a mother, to deliver children, and to breast-feed infants; and who repeatedly states that his penis and testes should be surgically removed, manifests a clear case of deviant rejection of his male sexuality.

Clinical Intervention to Eliminate Peer Ostracism

Cross-gender behavior, particularly in boys, typically elicits ostracism by the same-age peer group which can result in social isolation and alienation. Older cross-gender-identified boys have been found, for example, to be described by their mothers in terms of general psychopathology (Zucker, 1985, 1990) and the negative labeling and peer rejection experienced by the cross-gender-identified boy can be a major factor in his unhappiness and discontent (Rekers et al., 1977). For these and related reasons, Zucker (1990) has argued that the treatment of a child's cross-gender identity might not only alleviate the individual's short-term social distress but also may help the child to more readily socialize with same-sex peers as other youngsters normally do, and also prevent the development of psychopathological sequelae (Zucker, 1990). Furthermore, some gender-disturbed boys specifically request help from a clinician because other children are calling them "sissy," "fag," "queer," or "girlie."

Clinical Intervention to Prevent Adulthood Gender Dysphoria and Sexual Deviation

The various prospective and retrospective studies tracing the relationship between childhood gender-related behaviors to adulthood gender dysphoria and/or sexual deviation have been reviewed elsewhere (Green, 1987; Rekers, 1988a, 1988b; Zucker & Green, 1993). A detailed review of this literature is beyond the scope of this chapter; however, it can be concluded that there is a significant association between childhood cross-gender behavior and various adulthood outcomes such as transvestism, transsexualism, ego-dystonic homosexuality, or other adult gender dysphoria. At the present time, given the current scientific data, it is not possible to differentially predict transsexualism versus transvestism versus homosexual orientation from specific clusters of childhood cross-gender behaviors. However, there is little debate that transsexualism, transvestism, and many forms of homosexuality result in considerable emotional distress, marital conflicts, and, in some cases, other forms of psychopathology in adulthood. This provides an added rationale for clinical intervention in childhood and adolescent years (Rekers 1988a, 1988b; Zucker, 1990). In addition to preventing gender dysphoria or sexual deviation in adulthood, the clinician should also be concerned about the prevention of serious maladjustment problems in adulthood that are usually secondary to adulthood sexual deviations and gender dysphorias (see discussion in Rekers 1988a, 1988b).

Clinical Intervention as a Response to Parental Requests

It has been argued elsewhere (Rekers, 1977b) that it is appropriate to intervene for a child with cross-gender behavior upon the request of concerned parents who possess the legal rights to grant informed consent for clinical interventions for their children. Green (1987) has expressed this same rationale for intervening in the lives of children:

> Should parents have the prerogative of choosing therapy for their gender-atypical son? Suppose the boys who play with dolls rather than trucks, who role-play as mother rather than as father, and who play only with girls tend disproportionately to evolve as homosexual men. Suppose the parents notice, or suspect this. The rights of parents to oversee the development of their children is a long-established principle. Who is to dictate that parents may not try to raise their children in a manner that maximizes the possibility of a heterosexual outcome? If that prerogative is denied, should parents also be denied the right to raise their children as atheists? or as priests? (p. 260)

Conclusion Regarding Rationale

There is adequate standard clinical rationale for the intervention in the lives of children and adolescents with cross-gender or transvestic behavior and the interested clinician can consult the extensive reviews of this issue in the articles cited here.

References

American Psychiatric Association. (1980). *Diagnostic and statistical manual of mental disorders* (3rd ed.). Washington, DC: Author.

American Psychiatric Association. (1994). *Diagnostic and statistical manual of mental disorders* (4th ed.). Washington, DC: Author.

Barlow, D. H., Reynolds, E. J., & Agras, W. S. (1973). Gender identity change in a transsexual. *Archives of General Psychiatry, 28,* 569–576.

Bates, J. E., Skilbeck, W. M., Smith, K.V.R., & Bentler, P. M. (1975). Intervention with families of gender-disturbed boys. *American Journal of Orthopsychiatry, 45,* 150–157.

Bem, S. L. (1974). The measurement of psychological androgyny. *Journal of Consulting and Clinical Psychology, 42,* 155–162.

Bentler, P. M. (1968). A note on the treatment of adolescent sex problems. *Journal of Child Psychology and Psychiatry, 9,* 125–129.

Blanchard, R., & Steiner, B. W. (Eds.). (1990). *Clinical management of gender identity disorders in childhood and adults.* Washington, DC: American Psychiatric Press.

Brown, D. G. (1956). Sex-role preferences in young children. *Psychological Monographs, 70*(14), whole number 421, 1–19.

Byne, W., & Parsons, B. (1993). Human sexual orientation: The biologic theories reappraised. *Archives of General Psychiatry, 50,* 228–239.

Coleman, M. (1986). Nontraditional boys: A minority in need of reassessment. *Child Welfare, 65,* 252–269.

Friedman, R. C. (1988). *Male homosexuality: Contemporary psychoanalytic perspectives.* New Haven, CN.: Yale University Press.

Gebhard, P. H. (July 9, 1973). Human sexuality and sex education. Continuing education course at the Institute for Sex Research, Indiana University, Bloomington, Indiana

Goodwin, L. J., & Peterson, R. G. (1990). Psychological impact of abuse as it relates to transvestism. *Journal of Applied Rehabilitation in Counseling, 21,* 45–48.

Green, R. (1974). *Sexual identity conflict in children and adults.* New York: Basic Books.

Green, R. (1975). Sexual identity: Research strategies. *Archives of Sexual Behavior, 4,* 337–352.

Green, R. (1976). One-hundred-ten feminine and masculine boys: Behavioral contrasts and demographic similarities. *Archives of Sexual Behavior, 5,* 425–446.

Green, R. (1987). *The "sissy boy syndrome" and the development of homosexuality.* New Haven; CN: Yale University Press.

Hendricks, S. E., Graber, B., & Rodriguez-Sierra, J. F. (1989). Neuroendocrine responses to exogenous estrogen: No differences between heterosexual and homosexual men. *Psychoneuroendocrinology, 14*(3), 177–185.

Marlowe, M. (1979). The assessment and treatment of gender-disturbed boys by guidance counselors. *Personnel and Guidance Journal, 58*(2) 128–131.

Marshall, W., & Tanner, J.M. (1969). Variations in the pattern of pubertal changes in girls. *Archives of Disease in Childhood, 44,* 291–303.

Marshall, W., & Tanner, J. M. (1970). Variations in the pattern of pubertal changes in boys. *Archives of Disease in Childhood, 45,* 13–23.

Mead, S. L., & Rekers, G. A. (1979). The role of the father in normal psycho–sexual development. *Psychological Reports, 45,* 923–931.

Meyer-Bahlburg, H.F.L. (1993). Psychobiologic research on homosexuality. *Psychiatric Clinics of North America, 2*(3), 489–500.

Money, J., Hampson, J. G., & Hampson, J. L. (1955). Hermaphroditism: Recommendations concerning assignment of sex, change of sex, and psychologic management. *Bulletin of the Johns Hopkins Hospital, 97,* 284–300.

Morin, S., & Schultz, P. (1978). The gay movement and the rights of children. *Journal of Social Issues, 34,* 137–148.

Myrick, R. D. (1970). The counselor-consultant and the effeminant boy. *Personnel and Guidance Journal, 48,* 355–361.

Nordyke, N. S., Baer, D. M., Etzel, B. C., & LeBlanc, J. M. (1977). Implications of the stereotyping and modification of sex role. *Journal of Applied Behavioral Analysis, 10,* 553–557.

Rekers, G. A. (1972). *Pathological sex-role development in boys: Behavioral treatment and assessment.* Unpublished Ph.D. diss., in psychology, University of California, Los Angeles (Ann Arbor, MI: University Microfilms No. 72–33, 978).

Rekers, G. A. (1977a). Assessment and treatment of childhood gender problems. In B. B. Lahey & A. E. Kazdin (Eds.), *Advances in clinical child psychology* (Vol. 1, pp. 267–306). New York: Plenum.

Rekers, G. A. (1977b). Atypical gender development and psychosocial adjustment. *Journal of Applied Behavior Analysis, 10,* 559–571.

Rekers, G. A. (1982a). *Growing up straight.* Chicago: Moody Press.

Rekers, G. A. (1982b). *Shaping your child's sexual identity.* Grand Rapids, MI: Baker Book House.

Rekers, G. A. (1984). Ethical issues in child assessment. In T. H. Ollendick & M. Hersen (Eds.), *Child behavioral assessment: Principles and procedures* (pp. 244–262). New York: Pergamon Press.

Rekers, G. A. (1985a). Gender identity disorder of childhood. In D. G. Brenner (Ed.), *Baker's encyclopedia of psychology* (pp. 446–448). Grand Rapids, MI: Baker Book House.

Rekers, G. A. (1985b). Gender identity problems. In P. H. Borstein & A. E. Kazdin (Eds.), *Handbook of clinical behavior therapy with children* (pp. 658–699). Homewood, IL: Dorsey Press.

Rekers, G. A. (1985c). Transvestim. In D. G. Benner (Ed.), *Baker's encyclopedia of psychology* (pp. 1179–1181). Grand Rapids, MI: Baker Book House.

Rekers, G. A. (1986). Inadequate sex role differentiation in childhood: The family and gender identity disorders. *Journal of Family and Culture, 2*(3), 8–37.

Rekers, G. A. (1987). Cross-sex behavior. In R. A. Hoekelman, S. Blatman, S. B. Friedman, N. M. Nelson, & H. M. Seidel (Eds.), *Primary pediatric care.* (pp. 719–721). St. Louis, MO: C. V. Mosby.

Rekers, G. A. (1988a). The formation of a homosexual orientation. In P. F. Fagan (Ed.), *Hope for homosexuality* (pp. 1–27). Washington, DC: Center for Child and Family Policy.

Rekers, G. A. (1988b). Psychosexual assessment of gender identity disorders. In R. J. Prinz (Ed.), *Advances in behavioral assessment of children and families* (Vol. 4, pp. 33–71). Greenwich, CN: JAI Press.

Rekers, G. A., Bentler, P. M., Rosen, A. C., & Lovaas, O. I. (1977). Child gender disturbances: A clinical rationale for intervention. *Psychotherapy: Theory, research and practice, 14,* 1–11.

Rekers, G. A., Crandall, B. F., Rosen, A. C., & Bentler, P. M. (1979). Genetic and physical studies of male children with psychological gender disturbances. *Psychological Medicine, 9,* 373–375.

Rekers, G. A., & Lovaas, O. I. (1974). Behavioral treatment of deviant sex-role behaviors in a male child. *Journal of Applied Behavior Analysis, 7,* 173–190.

Rekers, G. A., & Mead, S. (1979). Early intervention for female sexual identity disturbance: Self-monitoring of play behavior. *Journal of Abnormal Child Psychology, 7*(4), 405–423.

Rekers, G. A., & Mead, S. (1980). Female sex-role deviance: Early identification and developmental intervention. *Journal of Clinical Child Psychology, 9*(3), 199–203.

Rekers, G. A., Mead, S. L., Rosen, A. C., & Brigham, S. L. (1983). Family correlates of male childhood gender disturbance. *Journal of Genetic Psychology,* 142, 31–42.

Rekers, G. A., & Milner, G. C. (1978). Sexual identity disorders in childhood and adolescence. *Journal of the Florida Medical Association, 65,* 962–964.

Rekers, G. A., Rosen, A. C., Lovaas, O. I., & Bentler, P. M. (1978). Sex-role stereotypy and professional intervention for childhood gender disturbances. *Professional Psychology, 9,* 127–136.

Rekers, G. A., & Swihart, J. J. (1989). The association of parental separation with gender disturbance in male children. *Psychological Reports, 65,* 1272–1274.

Rekers, G. A., Willis, T. J., Yates, C. E., Rosen, A. C., & Low, B. P. (1977). Assessment of childhood gender behavior change. *Journal of Child Psychology and Psychiatry, 18,* 53–65.

Rekers, G. A., & Yates, C. E. (1976). Sex-typed play in feminoid boys vs. normal boys and girls. *Journal of Abnormal Child Psychology, 4,* 1–8.

Rosen, A. C., & Rekers, G. A. (1980). Toward a taxonomic framework for variables of sex and gender. *Genetic Psychology Monographs, 102,* 191–218.

Rosen, A. C., Rekers, G. A., & Bentler, P. M. (1978). Ethical issues in the treatment of children. *Journal of Social Issues, 34*(2), 122–136.

Rosen, A. C., Rekers, G. A., & Brigham, S. L. (1982). Gender stereotypy in gender-dysphoric young boys. *Psychological Reports, 51,* 371–374.

Rosen, A. C., Rekers, G. A., & Friar, L. R. (1977). Theoretical and diagnostic issues in child gender disturbances. *Journal of Sex Research, 13*(2), 89–103.

Saghir, M. T., & Robins, E. (1973). *Male and female homosexuality: A comprehensive investigation.* Baltimore: Williams and Wilkins.

Serbin, L. A. (1980). Sex-role socialization: A field in transition. In B. B. Lahey & A. E. Kazdin (Eds.), *Advances in clinical child psychology* (Vol. 3, pp. 41–96). New York: Plenum.

Spinder, T., Spijkstra, J. J., Gooren, L. J., & Burger, C. W. (1989). Pulsatile luteinizing hormone release and ovarian steroid levels in female-to-male transsexuals compared to heterosexual women. *Psychoneuroendocrinology, 14*(1–2), 97–102.

Stoller, R. J. (1968). Male childhood transsxualism. *Journal of American Academy of Child Psychiatry, 7*, 193–209.

Stoller, R. J. (1970). The transsexual boy: Mother's feminized phallus. *British Journal of Medical Psychology, 43*, 117–129.

Stoller, R. J. (1975). *Sex and gender: The transsexual experience.* New York: Jason Aronson.

Taneja, N., Ammini, A. C., Mohapatra, I., Saxena, S., & Kucheria, K. (1992). A transsexual male with 47,XYY karyotype. *British Journal of Psychiatry, 161*, 698–699.

Tanner, J. M. (1955). *Growth at adolescence* (2nd ed.). Oxford: Blackwell Scientific Publications.

Whitam, F. L. (1989). *Cross-cultural aspects of cross-gendering in male and female homosexuals.* Paper presented at the Annual Meeting of the Society for Sex Therapy and Research, Tucson, AZ.

Winkler, R. C. (1977). What types of sex-role behavior should behavior modifiers promote? *Journal of Applied Behavioral Analysis, 10*, 549–552.

Wolfe, B. E. (1979). Behavioral treatment of childhood gender disorders: A conceptual and impirical critique. *Behavior Modification, 3*, 550–575.

Zucker, K. J. (1985). Cross-gender identified children. In B. W. Steiner (Ed.), *Gender dysphoria* (pp. 75–174) New York: Plenum.

Zucker, K. J. (1990). Treatment of gender identity disorder in children. In R. Blanchard & B. W. Steiner (Eds.), *Clinical management of gender identity disorders in children and adolescents* pp. 27–45. Washington, DC: American Psychiatric Press.

Zucker, K. J., Bradley, S. J., & Hughes, H. E. (1987). Gender dysphoria in a child with true hermaphroditism. *Canadian Journal of Psychiatry, 32*(7), 602–609.

Zucker, K. J., & Green, R. (1993). Psychological and familial aspects of gender identity disorder. *Child and Adolescent Psychiatric Clinics of North America, 2*(3), 513–542.

Zuger, B. (1970). The role of familial factors in persistent effeminate behavior in boys. *American Journal of Psychiatry, 126*, 1167–1170.

13
Assessment and Treatment Methods for Gender Identity Disorders and Transvestism

George A. Rekers

Transvestic behavior in adolescence, cross-gender behavior disturbances in childhood, and gender identity disorder in childhood and
adolescence can all be conceptualized as conditions that vary in individuals in degree of severity. Each of these conditions can range from the
most severe case through varying degrees to normal. A five-point clinical
rating scale has been used that ranges from (1) profound, through (2)
severe, to (3) moderate, to (4) mild, and to (5) no disorder (Bentler, Rekers,
& Rosen, 1979; Rosen, Rekers, & Friar, 1977; Rosen & Rekers, 1980).

Clinical Methods of Assessment

Accurate assessment of transvestic behavior, gender behavior disturbance,
and gender identity disorder requires the collection of data from several
sources such as parental report, parent and child interviews, behavioral
observations, psychological studies, and in some cases home and school
observations (Rekers, 1988b).

Interviewing the Parents or Caretakers

In separate clinical interviews with the mother and the father, or the male
and female caretakers, the clinician can gather information regarding the
current status of the child or adolescent in the past six months as well as a
behavioral history that can assist in diagnosis (Rekers, 1987). Evidence
should be sought regarding the presence or absence of compulsive cross-
sex behavior patterns from the parents' retrospective reports of the child's
history and with regard to the child's current behavior patterns.

272

The parents or caretakers can be asked individually the following questions:

1. What do you include as a masculine behavior in a child? What are the frequencies of these masculine behaviors in your child?
2. What do you include as a feminine behavior in a child? What are the frequencies of these feminine behaviors in your child?
3. Does your child identify with the father, a father figure, a brother, and/or male peers?
4. Does your child identify with the mother, a mother figure, a sister, and/or female peers?
5. To what extent does your child interact with boys?
6. What are the ages of the boys whom your child relates to?
7. To what extent does your child relate to girls?
8. What are the ages of the girls whom your child relates to?
9. To what degree does your child feel comfortable and identify with his or her sexual anatomy?
10. To what extent does your child understand the future reproductive functions of his or her sexual anatomy?
11. To what extent does your child understand the future reproductive functions of a member of the other sex?
12. What is the history and frequency of each of the following behaviors?
    Cross-dressing
    Masculine gestures and mannerisms
    Feminine gestures and mannerisms
    Play with girls' toys and activities
    Play with boys' toys and activities
    Avoidance of play with peers of the same sex
    Avoidance of play with members of the opposite sex
    Play with cosmetic items, real or imagined
    Masculine voice inflection
    Feminine voice inflection
    Desire to be called by a name of the other sex
    Deviant sexual behaviors (describe them)
    Masturbation with cross-dressing articles
    (name the cross-dressing articles)
13. Does your child insist on being or pretending to be a member of the other sex?

14. Has your child ever asked for a sex-change operation, and if so, how often?

15. What is your attitude and response toward your child's masculine behaviors and activities?

16. What is your attitude and response toward your child's feminine behaviors and activities?

It is also important to ask the parents to report their early acceptance, nonacceptance, or ambivalence toward the child's sex at the time of birth and also with regard to the child's performance of masculine or feminine behaviors since that time. Each parent or caretaker should be directly asked about father–child relationships, mother–child relationships, husband–wife relationships during the child's lifetime, and other significant relationships of the child. Further, the clinician should ask the parents to report on their own sex-typed behaviors.

The clinician interviews of the parents should also inquire about any potential sexual abuse of the child by male or female perpetrators, and if necessary determine the ages of the perpetrators and the extent of the sexual abuse (see Chapter 10).

The clinician should both directly and indirectly ask interview questions designed to ascertain parental or caretaker attitudes toward sex-typed behaviors, that is, whether cross-sex-typed behaviors are viewed with amusement or with seriousness or with punitiveness. It can be helpful to assess the parents' beliefs regarding sex-typed behaviors in terms of whether or not they are innate, learned, or modifiable (Rekers, 1987; Rekers & Milner, 1979).

Parent Report Inventories for Preadolescent Children

Several parent report measures have been validated with normal children and are useful for diagnostic screening for gender identity disorder of childhood. The Games Inventory is a 64-item questionnaire (Bates & Bentler, 1973) that has been demonstrated to differentiate between the play patterns of normal boys and girls. It has also been found to significantly differentiate gender-disturbed boys from a nonclinical reference group on its scales for Feminine Preschool Games, Masculine Nonathletic Games, and Masculine Athletic Games, as well as on its composite index for Feminine Play Preference; however, only the composite index (and none of the three subscales) was correlated significantly ($r = .34$) with degree of severity of gender disturbance (Rekers & Morey, 1990).

The Gender Behavior Inventory (Bates, Bentler, & Thompson, 1973) for boys is a fixed-choice parent report questionnaire that differentiates gender-disturbed boys from normal boys on three factors: Feminine Behavior, Extraversion, and Behavior Disturbance. The Feminine Behavior subscale consists of statements describing cross-dressing, effeminate gestures, and feminine play patterns. The Extraversion subscale contains items focusing on friendliness and physical activity. The Behavior Disturbance subscale includes items dealing with negativism, irritability, emotional upset, and disobedience. In separate studies it has been found that the gender-disturbed boys scored significantly above the mean of the standardized normal boys on the Feminine Behavior subscale and below the mean on the Extraversion subscale (Bates, Bentler, & Thompson, 1973; Rekers & Morey, 1989b). While Bates, Bentler, and Thompson (1973) found that boyhood gender disturbance is positively related to general Behavior Disturbance, Rekers and Morey (1989b) did not find a significant difference between normal boys and gender-disturbed boys on the Behavior Disturbance subscale. The Gender Identity Questionnaire was originally developed by Elizabeth and Green (1984) and has been demonstrated to show reasonable psychometric properties in subsequent studies (Elizabeth, Meyer-Bahlburg, Janal, Ehrhardt, & Green, 1984; Zucker & Torkos, 1987).

Rekers and Morey (1989b) have also reported on the use of the Parents' Evaluation of Child Behavior, a behaviorally oriented open-ended questionnaire requiring the parent to list the child's behavioral excesses, deficits, and assets. The questionnaire was modified by Rekers to include specific gender-related behavioral excesses, deficits, and assets in addition to nongender behaviors. Rekers and Morey (1989b) reported the following findings for the Parents' Evaluation of Child Behavior for a sample of gender-disturbed boys: cross-dressing or improvised cross-dressing was reported for 57 percent of the boys with gender disturbance, a preference for play with girls along with an avoidance of play with boys was found in 43 percent, effeminate gestures and mannerisms were listed by 37 percent, and feminine voice inflection was listed by 31 percent of the parents of gender-disturbed boys. Other reported behaviors included aversions toward sports (29 percent), play with dolls (26 percent), frequent adoption of female role in play (23 percent), cross-gender identity statements (23 percent), wearing of feminine jewelry (17 percent), wearing feminine cosmetic articles (17 percent), and excessive dependence on mother (14 percent).

For children without a reliable parental figure available, a schoolteacher or a relative may be able to fill in similar kinds of inventories regarding the child.

Clinical Diagnostic Interview with the Child or Adolescent

Important diagnostic data may be obtained by interviewing the child or adolescent directly. Clinical experience indicates that younger children tend to be more open and transparent in making statements regarding their desire to be a member of the opposite sex, whereas older children and adolescents who perceive their cross-gender behavior to be socially disapproved will typically be reluctant to directly acknowledge their cross-gender identification (Rekers, 1988b). A young or very undefensive boy may directly tell a clinician, "I am a girl" or "I want to grow up to be a mommy and have babies." The older or more defensive child or adolescent may be quite reluctant to be so straightforward.

Thus the clinical interview may need to be devised to elicit indicators of cross-gender identification, cross-gender role behaviors, or transvestic practices in a rather indirect manner. For example, it is useful to ask the child or adolescent to name his or her friends at school and in the neighborhood, in order to determine the ratio of male to female names of playmates. Such data can be indicative of either the child's peer preferences, opportunity, and/or social acceptance by male or female peers. A number of questions can be asked about the child's friendships; relationships with other children of the same, younger, and older ages; and favorite activities and games (noting sex-typing and the ratio of masculine to feminine play). The clinician should carefully note the nonverbal behavior of the child such as degree of enthusiasm and voice animation when talking about feminine activities as compared to masculine activities.

Clinicians can ask the child or adolescent to name his or her favorite people, places, activities, and things in order to gauge the amount of time spent with each. Rekers, Sanders, Strauss, Rasbury, and Morey (1989) reported on activities that have clear sex differences in reported participation in 11–18 year-old-males and females in a nonclinical population. Normal boys report higher rates of having romantic thoughts about girls, dating girls, working with engines and electronics, playing football, thinking about becoming a car mechanic, hunting, watching football on TV, building models, thinking about a military career, and being a member of a sports team. Females were found to have higher rates of having romantic thoughts about boys; dating boys; participating in sewing and knitting; doing needlepoint, embroidery, and macrame; reading glamor and fashion magazines; reading romantic novels; cleaning house; doing dishes, dusting, and laundry; playing with makeup; going to slumber parties; thinking about becoming a secretary or typist; and collecting dolls.

The interview should also focus on the child's knowledge of physical differences between males and females and the child's level of knowledge regarding reproductive anatomy and sexual behavior patterns. Very young children need to be assessed with regard to their concept of "gender constancy," that is, whether it is possible for them to grow up to be like the opposite-sex parent or will they necessarily be like the same-sex parent (see Slaby & Frey, 1975; Thompson & Bentler, 1973).

Rekers, Lovaas, and Low (1974) developed a clinical interview procedure whereby a clinician spends the initial 20 minutes of the interview in a "baseline condition" where the child is essentially allowed to talk spontaneously while the clinician limits verbal responses to short, nonleading, and direct answers to the child's questions. This portion of the interview is tape-recorded and later scored for sex-typed verbal content and verbal inflection, categorizing each phrase by the child as masculine, feminine, or neutral (see also Rekers & Mead, 1979a, for a similar procedure with gender-disturbed girls).

In the context of the clinical interview described above, the following are examples of specific questions that have been found to be useful in the diagnosis of a child during an interview (Rekers, 1981a, 1987; Rekers & Milner, 1979, 1981):

1. What are the first names of your friends and playmates at home and school? (Note and compare the number of male and female friends.)
2. How often do you feel like a boy?
3. How often do you feel like a girl?
4. When you have free time, what are your favorite things to do?
5. Most kids are called names at some time or another. What names do other kids call you?
6. If you could have three wishes, what would you wish for?
7. What are your favorite subjects and activities at school?
8. Are you more like your mom or like your dad? How?
9. How often do you wear dresses? Female undergarments?
10. How often do you wear male underwear?
11. How often do you play with cosmetic articles?
12. How often do you play with girls?
13. How often do you play with boys?
14. How often do you pretend to be a woman?
15. How often do you pretend to be a man?

Clinical Observation of Sex-Typed Play Behavior in Children

Play is a primary mode of expression, particularly with young children in regard to their developing personal and social attitudes and skills; consequently, the behavioral assessment of sex-typed play is a central task in assessing a potentially gender-disturbed boy or girl.

Rekers (1972, 1975; Rekers & Yates, 1976) developed and validated a behavioral play assessment procedure in which two specific sets of masculine and feminine toys are made available for the child to play with in five different social stimulus conditions: while the child is alone in the playroom (but knowingly observed from behind a one-way mirror); while the child plays with the mother present and observing; while the child plays with the father present and observing; while the child is playing with a male clinician present; and while the child is playing with a female clinician present. This procedure has been demonstrated to have diagnostic utility in a replication and validation study by Zucker, Doering, Bradley, and Finegan (1982; see also Doering, Zucker, Bradley, & MacIntyre, 1989). It has been reported that the child's free play in the "alone" condition while being observed from behind a one-way mirror is most highly correlated with the degree of gender disturbance (Rekers, 1975; Rekers & Morey, 1990).

This play behavior procedure is appropriate for administration to boys or girls ages 3 to 8 years (Rekers & Lovaas, 1971; Rekers & Yates, 1976). Two sets of masculine and feminine sex-typed toys are placed in a room on two child-size tables. On one table there are dress-up articles such as girls' cosmetics and apparel, toy jewelry sets, and boys' apparel, football and army helmets with the accessories, and a battery-operated play electric razor. On the other table there are baby dolls and accessories dart guns, and set of plastic cowboys and Indians. The clinician can use two stopwatches to record cumulative seconds of masculine play and cumulative seconds of contact with feminine toys in the free-play situation in which the child is told he or she can play with any of the toys. If one uses a standard of 70 percent cross-sex play to 30 percent same-sex play (excluding time in which the child is not in contact with any toy) before considering a pattern to be gender deviant, the finding of "false positives" would be rare, although the assessment task may be more vulnerable to instances of "false negatives" (Rekers & Yates, 1976; Zucker et al., 1982).

This procedure has also been useful for establishing a pretreatment baseline to monitor therapy progress and for posttreatment and follow-up assessments of boys who have been treated for gender disturbances (Rekers, 1983).

Observation of Sex-Typed Gestures and Mannerisms

The family, the child's peers, and clinicians will describe the gender-disturbed boy as having "feminine" appearance due to their cross-sex-typed gestures and mannerisms. Rekers, Lovaas, and Low (1974) provided operational definitions of a number of these expressive effeminate gestures that were observed in a gender-disturbed boy, and subsequently normative studies were conducted providing base rates of these gestures in normal boys and girls at various age groups between 4 and 18 years of age (Rekers, Amaro-Plotkin, & Low, 1977; Rekers & Mead, 1979b; Rekers & Rudy, 1978; Rekers, Sanders, & Strauss, 1981). The same specific sex-typed body movements and gestures were recorded in gender-disturbed boys ages 7 to 17 years (Rekers & Morey, 1989c) in which it was found that the gender-disturbed boys have higher frequencies of the following gestures:

1. "Limp wrist"—operationally defined as flexing the wrist toward the palmar surface of the forearm or upper arm while the elbow is either flexed or extended;

2. "Hand clasp"—defined as touching the hands together in front of the body;

3. "Hyperextension"—defined as moving the hand(s) in the direction of the posterior surface of the forearm while the elbow is either flexed or extended.

Whereas gender-disturbed children can suppress their cross-sex play in the presence of a clinician (Rekers, 1975), this has not been found true with regard to sex-typed mannerisms and behavioral gestures. The gender-disturbed boy is typically unable to discriminate his own effeminate gestures adequately enough to inhibit them even under conditions of severe peer criticism on the school playground (Rekers, 1977; Rekers, Willis, Yates, Rosen, & Low, 1977). These behavioral gestures can best be observed while the child is playing a game requiring body movements such as the "toss across" game in which the child tosses a bean bag to a large plastic "tic-tac-toe" type of play device.

Clinical Psychological Testing and Clinical Ratings

Several conventional, clinical psychological tests have been found to be useful in conjunction with behavioral assessment data, including the Schneidman Make-a-Picture-Story Test; the Bene–Anthony Family Relations Test (Rosen, Rekers, & Friar, 1977; Rosen, Rekers, & Morey, 1990), and the Brown IT Scale for Children (Green, 1974; Rosen, Rekers, & Friar, 1977), Human Figure Drawings (Green, 1974; Skilbeck, Bates, & Bentler, 1975; Rosen, Rekers, & Morey, 1990; Zucker, Finegan, Doering, & Bradley, 1983). The Feminine Gender Identity Scale for Males (Freund, Langevin, Satteerberg, & Steiner, 1977) is particularly useful for older adolescent patients being evaluated for transsexual, transvestism, or homosexual conditions. The Rorschach protocols of cross-gender-identified children have been compared to the protocols of their siblings, psychiatric controls, and normal controls by Lozinski (1988). This study found that the cross-gender-identified boy had significantly more cross-sex responses than same-sex responses in comparison with normal controls who produced more same-sex-typed responses than cross-sexed responses (see also Zucker, Lozinski, & Bradley, 1992).

Assessment of Athletic Game Skills

As a result of avoiding play with other boys for many months and years, gender-disturbed boys typically develop a deficit in athletic game skills such as "over hand ball throw" and other skills that require specific practice for therapeutic remediation (see discussion in Rekers, 1988b). Behavioral observations have been made of the gender-disturbed child's skill level in comparison with his same-aged peers in such skills as distance in throwing the football, distance in socking a playground ball, distance and accuracy in kicking a kickball, percentages of baskets made from the free throw line, and accuracy and distance in throwing a softball (Rekers, 1972, 1979; Rekers, Lovaas, & Low, 1974; Rekers et al., 1977).

Assessment in the Home Setting

Behavioral checklists can be individually designed for a child or adolescent which a parent or caretaker can use with a time-sampling procedure to make daily observations on such sex-typed behaviors as "play with girls," "play with boys," "play with dolls," "cross-dressing," "taking feminine roles in play," "taking masculine roles in play," and specifically naming particular feminine or masculine gestures manifested by the individual (Rekers & Lovaas, 1974; Rekers, Lovaas, & Low, 1974; Rekers, Amaro-Plotkin, & Low, 1977). Parents can be instructed to observe the child's behavior for 10 minutes at a time, at two or three specified times per day.

Assessment in the School Setting

The parent can be asked to confer with the child's teacher on the status of her or his peer relations. If the teacher comments on cross-sex-typed behavior, then the parent might ask the schoolteacher to make similar behavioral observations on a checklist form in the school setting (Rekers, 1984, 1988b; Rekers, Lovaas, & Low, 1974; Rekers & Varni, 1977b).

Medical Examination

The majority of children with gender identity problems have not been found to have any detectable physical abnormalities as revealed in a study of their medical history; a physical examination, including examination of external genitalia; chromosome analysis, including two cells karyotyped and 15 counted; and sex chromatin studies (Rekers, 1991; Rekers, Crandall, Rosen, & Bentler, 1979).

Psychotherapeutic Treatment

Treatment for Gender Identity Disorder and Gender Behavior Disturbance in Children

There are both general therapeutic management strategies (Rekers & Milner, 1979, 1981) and specific behavior therapy and family therapy techniques that have been demonstrated to be effective in the successful treatment of childhood gender identity disorders and gender behavior disturbance (Rekers, Kilgus, & Rosen, 1990; Rosen, Rekers & Brigham, 1982; see also Haber, 1991).

General Management Strategies.
1. Encourage the same-sex parent to invest time and positive play and interaction with the child while scrupulously avoiding criticism of the child. In cases where the same-sex parent is unavailable, recommend finding a substitute same-sex adult who can be a positive role model, such as an uncle, grandfather, or "big brother" for a boy.
2. Recommend ignoring the cross-sex-typed behavior whenever possible and redirecting the child to more appropriate gender-related behavior as a substitute activity, and avoid excessive verbal reprimands for cross-sex behavior.
3. Advise parents to praise the child and provide various rewarding activities in response to appropriate sex-typed play and behavior mannerisms.
4. Equip the parent to provide appropriate sex education to the child, or the clinician can provide sex education to the child upon parental request (Rekers, 1992).
5. Schedule regular clinic office visits for the child and parent figures to assess the progress of the child in developing more appropriate ratios of sex-typed behavior.
6. Ask the parents to periodically confer with the schoolteacher to inquire about the child's relationship with other boys and girls. Parents should be advised not to label the child as a "gender problem" to school personnel. In some cases it is helpful to have the teacher "team up" the problem child with a more appropriate partner in school activities to encourage and help the patient to develop normal friendship patterns.
7. Encourage the parent of a boy to consider the "Big Brother" program, or the parent of a girl to consider the "Big Sister" program in the community, or provide the child with another appropriate same-sex role model.
8. In the case of boys, have the parent provide for the child some nonthreatening and nonpunitive training experiences in developing athletic skills. Ideally this should be done by the father or father figure for the gender-disturbed boy.

Specific Behavior Therapy Techniques. The first systematic experimental investigation of the treatment of boys and girls with gender disturbances and gender identity disorders was initiated by Rekers (1972) who published a number of intrasubject replication studies as well as group outcome studies on the effect of a combination of behavioral treatment techniques (Rekers, 1972, 1978, 1979, 1980, 1981a, 1981b, 1983, 1985a, 1985b; Rekers, Kilgus, & Rosen, 1990; Rekers & Lovaas, 1971, 1974;

Rekers, Lovaas, & Low, 1974; Rekers & Mead, 1979a; Rekers & Milner, 1979; Rekers & Varni, 1977a, 1977b; Rekers, Willis, Yates, Rosen, & Low, 1977; Rekers, Yates, Willis, Rosen, & Taubman, 1976; Rosen, Rekers, & Brigham, 1982).

For preschool- and early-elementary-aged children, the clinician can demonstrate to the parents (preferably behind a one-way mirror) how to socially reinforce appropriate sex-typed play by giving verbal praise and attention, as well as how to decrease inappropriate and maladaptive cross-gender play by ignoring it (putting it on "extinction"). Then the therapist can closely observe and supervise the parents' learning of behavior-shaping skills in the playroom by inviting the parent in to join the therapy session in the clinic. This procedure requires a playroom supplied with a variety of masculine and feminine sex-typed toys. When it is available, it has been demonstrated that a "bug-in-ear" receiver worn by the parent can help therapists communicate with the parents while they are with their child in the room, while the therapist observes and supervises from behind a one-way mirror.

Children who are somewhat older, as well as more intelligent younger children, can be taught to monitor their own gender-role behavior using a wrist counter (commonly used to keep golf scores). The child can be instructed to press the wrist counter only when playing with gender-appropriate toys. These points can be exchanged for some kind of privilege or reward. In the clinic setting, the "bug-in-ear" device has also been used to verbally reinforce the child for correct observance of these self-monitoring instructions and to prompt the child to press the wrist counter at the appropriate time (Rekers & Varni, 1977a, 1977b; Rekers & Mead, 1979a).

The therapist can also differentially reinforce appropriate gender-related speech content by withdrawing all social attention from cross-gender verbal content (e.g., when a boy talks excessively about dresses, mascara, lipstick, or delivering babies), and by providing positive interest for any kind of neutral or gender-appropriate speech content as well as appropriate voice inflection (Rekers, Lovaas, & Low, 1974).

Normalizing gestures and mannerisms in order to eliminate one source of peer rejection and ridicule has required much more intensive behavior therapy procedures. Beginning with obtaining a baseline of various feminine gestures, the therapist can next clearly explain one of the gestures to the boy or use a videotape feedback approach to help the child label feminine gestures in his repertoire (Rekers et al., 1977). During play sessions the therapist can give the child a set number of tokens at the beginning of the session, and subtract one token for each instance of observing one specific feminine gesture. After the first specific feminine gesture has been successfully treated this way, the second gesture, a third gesture, a fourth, and so on, can be successfully treated in the same manner (Rekers et al., 1976). In some cases this treatment which is begun in the clinic needs to be extended to *in vivo* environments of the home (Rekers, 1988a) and school settings (Rekers, Lovaas, & Low, 1974).

Skill deficits in athletic games in gender-disturbed boys can be remediated by the use of positive reinforcement beginning with very easy tasks for the boy and then gradually shaping the skills such as throwing footballs, socking a playground ball, kicking a kickball, or shooting baskets by increasing the distance and the like. The particular skills required for that child in his own physical education class or playground should be observed, for example, in terms of distances the normal children can throw or kick a ball. Then in therapy sessions to desensitize the boy's fear and to help him enjoy success the skill development, positive reinforcement procedures have been found to be quite effective (Rekers, Lovaas, & Low, 1974; Rekers et al., 1977; Rekers, 1979). Wherever possible, the father should be included in such training.

To overcome the setting-specificity of behavior therapy effects, the treatment should be extended to the home environment by training the parents to serve as the child's therapists first in the clinic setting and then in the home setting (e.g., Rekers & Lovaas, 1974).

Throughout all the specific behavior therapy treatment approaches, a pretreatment baseline consisting of data on behavioral observations of the specific masculine and feminine behaviors should be obtained. Then during treatment, time sampling methods can be used to monitor the frequency rates of gender-related behaviors to monitor the progress of treatment.

In a follow-up study with a mean of 4 years 3 months after the completion of behavioral treatment, behavioral treatment approaches were found to be durable, with the younger patients who received more severe initial diagnoses showing the greatest improvement (Rekers, Kilgus, & Rosen, 1990).

Treatment of Adolescent Transvestism

Bentler (1968) presented a treatment approach for adolescent boys with a fetishistic sexual involvement with women's clothes, whose sexual fantasies were clearly heterosexual in nature. These boys rarely masturbated, but when they did masturbate they did so by rolling on the bed while wearing feminine clothes. In the psychotherapeutic sessions, the therapists socially reinforced any statements by the boys about heterosexual dating, conducted behavior rehearsals of heterosocial interaction, and encouraged frequency of masturbation with heterosexual fantasy rather than with transvestic fantasy. Bentler reported that within 7 to 12 months of weekly therapy sessions, the cross-dressing in these boys ceased, the masturbation with heterosexual fantasy increased, and social dating behavior reportedly increased. No follow-up evaluation, however, was reported. Similar assessment and treatment approaches have been reported by other investigators (e.g., Blanchard & Hunker, 1991; Deutsch, 1954; Haydn-Smith, Marks, Buchaya, & Repper, 1987; Money, 1986).

Treatment of Adolescent Gender Identity Disorder

There appear to be only a few successful attempts to change gender identity in diagnosed adolescent transsexuals (see review by Bradley & Zucker, 1990). A 17-year-old boy was systematically treated with behavioral procedures by Barlow, Reynolds, and Agras (1973). This published report was a significant contribution to the literature in light of the fact that all other prior treatment approaches for transsexualism had failed, and because, unlike many other reports of psychotherapeutic interventions for adolescent sex problems, specific procedures were experimentally demonstrated to be responsible for the therapeutic changes (Rekers, 1978).

This adolescent patient had every major component previously described as contributing to the diagnosis of transsexualism: (1) a validated history of spontaneous cross-dressing before age 5 persisting into adolescence; (2) early development and continuity of feminine interests, coupled with avoidance of masculine activities; (3) reports of early cross-gender fantasies and identification that persisted into adolescence; (4) extremely effeminate behavior from childhood into adolescence; (5) gender-inappropriate vocational interests; (6) reported cross-gender sexual fantasies from age 12 to time of referral; and (7) requests for physical change of sex.

During pretreatment baseline, three measures were administered: (1) a score of 32 out of a possible 40 was obtained on a "transsexual attitude scale" based on a card-sort procedure using statements such as "I want to have female genitals"; (2) daily records in a notebook revealed the patient to have an average of seven homosexual and no heterosexual urges and fantasies each day; (3) daily measures of penile circumference found sexual arousal to male nude slides to average around 50 percent of a full erection, but virtually no arousal to female nude slides.

Barlow and coworkers attempted to alter the deviant patterns of sexual arousal, first by increasing heterosexual arousal through techniques of "fading," and second by decreasing arousal to transsexual fantasies and to male stimuli by electric shock aversion therapy. Although treatment was administered daily for two months, no changes were found in the patterns of sexual arousal, reports of sexual urges and fantasies, or the transsexual attitude scale scores.

This failure to change sexual arousal patterns led the investigators to attempt direct modification of sex-role behaviors. Modeling, videotape feedback, and social reinforcement were used to alter gender-specific motor behaviors (sitting, standing, and walking) from predominantly feminine to predominantly masculine. A multiple baseline design across behaviors demonstrated that the treatment procedures resulted in a change to masculine motor behaviors, as reliably recorded by trained behind-the-scene observers. This treatment phase extended over a two-month period and also included modeling and reinforced practice in male role behavior, for example, discussing sports and dates with other males and rehearsing dating behavior. Daily voice retraining for three weeks, with the use of prompting and feedback methods, successfully eliminated his high pitch and feminine voice inflections. The boy reported liking these newly acquired masculine behaviors, but all other aspects of gender identity and sexual arousal remained at baseline levels at this point.

A direct attempt to modify transsexual thoughts and fantasies was then initiated by developing competing gender-appropriate fantasies in which the patient visualized himself as a boy having intercourse with a girl. Successively longer and more detailed heterosexual fantasies were prompted and socially reinforced by the female therapist. An *ABA* reversal design demonstrated that the praise (rather than the practice alone, or expectancy effects) was responsible for the increasing ability to fantasize in the gender-appropriate manner. Transsexual attitudes as measured by the card-sort procedure also decreased dramatically with this therapy. The boy's continuing notebook recordings indicated a transfer of these newly developed heterosexual fantasies to the natural environment. At the end of this two-month phase of 34 sessions, the patient behaved, thought, and felt like a boy, but his sexual arousal patterns remained deviant.

The boy was now diagnostically a homosexual after nearly one year of treatment. A classical conditioning procedure was administered to increase heterosexual arousal. Slides of nude females were used as the conditioned stimuli followed by slides of nude males (the unconditioned stimuli). *ABA* reversal replication demonstrated that the classical conditioning procedure was responsible for the increased sexual arousal to females as measured by penile circumference changes. Reports of sexual attraction to girls in the natural environment increased at this time. Since homosexual attraction was still present, the investigators applied a combined aversion therapy procedure, incorporating electrical aversion and covert sensitization techniques. Unlike the first attempt, the 20 aversion therapy sessions administered over a two-month period resulted in a gradual reduction of homosexual arousal. Masculine components of sitting, standing, and walking showed sharp increases at this point in time, although no direct therapeutic attempts had been made to alter them.

After treatment, the boy's parents reported overall improvement in his social, academic, and emotional adjustment. He was seen in supportive, individual sessions over the next year at weekly, then monthly, and finally three-month intervals. The transsexual card sort remained at zero, masculine behavior continued stable at high levels, heterosexual arousal continued to predominate, heterosexual fantasies continued to increase, and the boy began appropriately dating a steady girlfriend. Gender-relevant motor behaviors, sex-typed social behavior, vocal characteristics, sexual fantasies and attitudes, and patterns of sexual arousal had been changed one by one, resulting in a total change from transsexual to normal adjustment.

In most instances, procedures were experimentally demonstrated to be responsible for the therapeutic changes in intrasubject replication designs. The adolescent boy's gender identity and total sexual adjustment was changed through behavior modification procedures, and he no longer requested that his body be changed through medical and surgical sex-reassignment procedures.

References

Barlow, D. H., Reynolds, E. J., & Agras, W. S. (1973). Gender identity change in a transsexual. *Archives of General Psychiatry, 28*, 569–576.

Bates, J. E., & Bentler, P. M. (1973). Play activities of normal and effeminate boys. *Developmental Psychology, 9*, 20–27.

Bates, J. E., Bentler, P. M., & Thompson, S. K. (1973). Measurement of deviant gender development in boys. *Child Development, 44*, 591–598.

Bentler, P. M. (1968). A note on the treatment of adolescent sex problems. *Journal of Child Psychology and Psychiatry, 9*, 125–129.

Bentler, P. M., Rekers, G. A., & Rosen, A. C. (1979). Congruence of childhood sex-role identity and behaviour disturbances. *Child: Care, Health and Development, 5*(4), 267–284.

Blanchard, R., & Hunter, S. J. (1991). Age, transvestism, bondage, and concurrent paraphilic activities in 117 fatal cases of autoerotic asphyxia. *British Journal of Psychiatry, 159*, 371–377.

Bradley, S. J., & Zucker, K. J. (1990). Gender identity disorder and psychosexual problems in children and adolescents. *Canadian Journal of Psychiatry, 35*, 477–486.

Deutsch, D. (1954). A case of transvestism. *American Journal of Psychotherapy, 8*, 239–242.

Doering, R. W., Zucker, K. J., Bradley, S. J., & MacIntyre, R. B. (1989). Effects of neutral toys on sex-typed play in children with gender identity disorder. *Journal of Abnormal Child Psychology, 17*(5), 563–574.

Elizabeth, E. H., & Green, R. (1984). Childhood sex-role behaviors: Similarities and differences in twins. *Acta Geneticae Medicae et Gemellologiae, 33*, 173–179.

Elizabeth, P. M., Meyer-Bahlburg, H.F.L., Janal, M. N., Ehrhardt, A., & Green, R. (1984). *Do human twins show a "free-martin" like phenomenon?* Paper presented at the Annual Meeting of the International Academy of Sex Research, Cambridge, England.

Freund, K., Langevin, R., Satteerberg, J., & Steiner B. (1977). Extension of the gender identity scale for males. *Archives of Sexual Behavior, 6*, 507–514.

Green, R. (1974). *Sexual identity conflict in children and adults.* New York: Basic Books.

Haber, C. H. (1991). The psychoanalytic treatment of a preschool boy with a gender identity disorder. *Journal of the American Psychoanalytic Association, 39*, 107–129.

Haydn-Smith, P., Marks, I., Buchaya, H., & Repper, D. (1987). Behavior treatment of life-threatening masochistic asphyxiation. *British Journal of Psychiatry, 150*, 518–519.

Lozinski, J. A. (1988). *Sex-typed responses in the Rorschach protocols of cross-gender-identified children*. Unpublished master's thesis, University of Toronto, Canada.

Money, J. (1986). *Love maps*. Buffalo, NY: Prometheus Books.

Rekers, G. A. (1972). *Pathological sex-role development in boys: Behavioral treatment and assessment*. Ph.D. diss., University of California, Los Angeles (Ann Arbor, MI: University Microfilms No. 72–33, 978).

Rekers, G. A. (1975). Stimulus control over sex-typed play in cross-gender identified boys. *Journal of Experimental Child Psychology, 20*, 136–148.

Rekers, G. A. (1977). Assessment and treatment of childhood gender problems. In B. B. Lahey & A. E. Kazdin (Eds.), *Advances in clinical child psychology* (Vol. 1, pp. 267–306). New York: Plenum.

Rekers, G. A. (1978). Sexual problems: Behavior modification. In B. B. Wolman (Ed.), *Handbook of treatment of mental disorders in childhood and adolescence* (pp. 268–296). Englewood Cliffs, NJ: Prentice-Hall.

Rekers, G. A. (1979). Sex-role behavior change: Intrasubject studies of boyhood gender disturbance. *Journal of Psychology, 103*, 255–269.

Rekers, G. A. (1980). Therapies dealing with the child's sexual difficulties. In Jean-Marc Samson (Ed.), *Enfance et sexualité* (pp. 525–538). Montreal: Les Editions Etudes Vivantes.

Rekers, G. A. (1981a). Childhood sexual identity disorders. *Medical Aspects of Human Sexuality, 15*(3), 141–142.

Rekers, G. A. (1981b). Psychosexual and gender problems. In E. J. Mash & L. G. Terdal (Eds.), *Behavioral assessment of childhood disorders* (pp. 483–526). New York: Guilford Press.

Rekers, G. A. (1983). Play therapy with cross-gender-identified children. In C. E. Schaefer & K. J. O'Connor (Eds.), *Handbook of play therapy* (pp. 369–385). New York: John Wiley and Sons.

Rekers, G. A. (1984). Ethical issues in child assessment. In T. H. Ollendick & M. Hersen (Eds.), *Child behavioral assessment: Principles and procedures* (pp. 244–262). New York: Pergamon Press.

Rekers, G. A. (1985a). Gender identity disorder of childhood. In D. G. Brenner (Ed.), *Baker's encyclopedia of psychology* (pp. 446–448). Grand Rapids, MI: Baker Book House.

Rekers, G. A. (1985b). Gender identity problems. In P. H. Borstein & A. E. Kazdin (Eds.), *Handbook of clinical behavior therapy with children* (pp. 658–699). Homewood, IL: Dorsey Press.

Rekers, G. A. (1987). Cross-sex behavior. In R. A. Hoekelman, S. Blatman, S. B. Friedman, N. M. Nelson, & H. M. Seidel (Eds.), *Primary pediatric care* (pp. 719–721). St. Louis, MO: C. V. Mosby.

Rekers, G. A. (1988a). *Counseling families*. Waco, TX: Word Books.

Rekers, G. A. (1988b). Psychosexual assessment of gender identity disorders. In R. J. Prinz (Ed.), *Advances in behavioral assessment of children and families* (Vol. 4, pp. 33–71). Greenwich, CN: JAI Press.

Rekers, G. A. (1991). Cross-sex behavior problems. In R. A. Hoekelman, S. Blatman, S. B. Friedman, N. M. Nelson & H. M. Seidel (Eds.), *Primary pediatric care* (2nd ed., pp. 691–693). St. Louis, MO: C. V. Mosby.

Rekers, G. A. (1992). Development of problems in puberty and sex roles in adolescence. In C. E. Walker & M. C. Roberts (Eds.), *Handbook of clinical child psychology* (2nd ed., pp. 606–622). New York: John Wiley and Sons.

Rekers, G. A., Amaro-Plotkin, H., & Low, B. P. (1977). Sex-typed mannerisms in normal boys and girls as a function of sex and age. *Child Development, 48,* 275–278.

Rekers, G. A., Crandall, B. F., Rosen, A. C., & Bentler, P. M. (1979). Genetic and physical studies of male children with psychological gender disturbances. *Psychological Medicine, 9,* 373–375.

Rekers, G. A., Kilgus, M., & Rosen, A. C. (1990). Long-term effects of treatment for childhood gender disturbance. *Journal of Psychology and Human Sexuality,* 3(2), 121–153.

Rekers, G. A., & Lovaas, O. I. (1971). Experimental analysis of cross-sex behavior in male children. *Research Relating to Children, 28,* 68.

Rekers, G. A., & Lovaas, O. I. (1974). Behavioral treatment of deviant sex-role behaviors in a male child. *Journal of Applied Behavior Analysis, 7,* 173–190.

Rekers, G. A., & Lovaas, O. I., & Low, B. P. (1974). The behavioral treatment of a "transsexual" preadolescent boy. *Journal of Abnormal Child Psychology, 2,* 99–116.

Rekers, G. A., & Mead, S. (1979a). Early intervention for female sexual identity disturbance: Self-monitoring of play behavior. *Journal of Abnormal Child Psychology,* 7(4), 405–423.

Rekers, G. A., & Mead, S. (1979b). Human sex differences in carrying behaviors. A replication and extension. *Perceptual and Motor Skills, 48,* 625–626.

Rekers, G. A., & Milner, G. C. (1979). How to diagnose and manage childhood sexual disorders. *Behavioral Medicine,* 6(4), 18–21.

Rekers, G. A., & Milner, G. C. (1981). Early detection of sexual identity disorders. *Medical Aspects of Human Sexuality,* 15(11), 32EE–32FF.

Rekers, G. A., & Morey, S. M. (1989a). Personality problems associated with childhood gender disturbance. *Italian Journal of Clinical and Cultural Psychology,* 1, 85–90.

Rekers, G. A., & Morey, S. M. (1989b). Relationship of maternal report of feminine behavior and extraversion to the severity of gender disturbance. *Perceptual and Motor Skills, 69,* 387–394.

Rekers, G. A., & Morey, S. M. (1989c). Sex-typed body movements as a function of severity of gender disturbance in boys. *Journal of Psychology and Human Sexuality, 2,* 183–196.

Rekers, G. A., & Morey, S. M. (1990). The relationship of sex-typed play with clinician ratings on degree of gender disturbance. *Journal of Clinical Psychology, 46,* 28–34.

Rekers, G. A., & Rudy, J. P. (1978). Differentiation of childhood body gestures. *Perceptual and Motor Skills, 46,* 839–845.

Rekers, G. A., Sanders, J. A., & Strauss, C. C. (1981). Developmental differentiation of adolescent body gestures. *Journal of Genetic Psychology,* 138(1), 123–131.

Rekers, G. A., Sanders, J. A., Strauss, C. C., Rasbury, W. C., & Morey, S. M. (1989). Differentiation of adolescent activity participation. *Journal of Genetic Psychology, 150*(3), 323–335.

Rekers, G. A., & Varni, J. W. (1977a). Self-monitoring and self-reinforcement processes in a pre-transsexual boy. *Behavior Research and Therapy, 15,* 177–180.

Rekers, G. A., & Varni, J. W. (1977b). Self-regulation and gender-role behaviors: A case study. *Journal of Behavior Therapy and Experimental Psychiatry, 8,* 427–432.

Rekers, G. A., Willis, T. J., Yates, C. E., Rosen, A. C., & Low, B. P. (1977). Assessment of childhood gender behavior change. *Journal of Child Psychology and Psychiatry, 18,* 53–65.

Rekers, G. A., & Yates, C. E. (1976). Sex-typed play in feminoid boys vs. normal boys and girls. *Journal of Abnormal Child Psychology, 4,* 1–8.

Rekers, G. A., Yates, C. E., Willis, T. J., Rosen, A. C., & Taubman, M. (1976). Childhood gender identity change: Operant control over sex-typed play and mannerisms. *Journal of Behavior Theory and Experimental Psychology, 7,* 51–57.

Rosen, A. C., & Rekers, G. A. (1980). Toward a taxonomic framework for variables of sex and gender. *Genetic Psychology Monographs, 102,* 191–218.

Rosen, A. C., Rekers, G. A., & Brigham, S. L. (1982). Gender stereotypy in gender-dysphoric young boys. *Psychological Reports, 51,* 371–374.

Rosen, A. C., Rekers, G. A., & Friar, L. R. (1977). Theoretical and diagnostic issues in child gender disturbances. *Journal of Sex Research, 13*(2), 89–103.

Rosen, A. C., Rekers, G. A., & Morey, S. M. (1990). Projective test findings for boys with gender disturbance: D-A-P Test, IT Scale, and M-A-P-S Test. *Perceptual and Motor Skills, 71,* 771–779.

Skilbeck, W. M., Bates, J. E., & Bentler, P. M. (1975). Human figure drawings of gender-problem and school-problem boys. *Journal of Abnormal Child Psychology, 3,* 191–199.

Slaby, R. G., & Frey, K. S. (1975). Development of gender constancy and selective attention to same-sex models. *Child Development, 46,* 849–856.

Thompson, S. K., & Bentler, P. M. (1973). A developmental study of gender constancy and parent preference. *Archives of Sexual Behavior, 2,* 379–385.

Zucker, K. J., Doering, R. W., Bradley, S. J., & Finegan, J. K. (1982). Sex-typed play in gender-disturbed children: A comparison to sibling and psychiatric controls. *Archives of Sexual Behavior, 11,* 309–321.

Zucker, K. J., Finegan, J. K., Doering, R. W., & Bradley, S. J. (1983). Human figure drawings of gender-problem children: A comparison to sibling, psychiatric, and normal controls. *Journal of Abnormal Child Psychology, 11,* 287–298.

Zucker, K. J., Lozinski, & Bradley, S. J. (1992). Sex-typed responses in the Rorschach protocols of children with gender identity disorder. *Journal of Personality Assessment, 58,* 295–310.

Zucker, K. J., & Torkos, H. (1987). *Measurement of androgyny in children.* Paper presented at the Annual Meeting of the Society for Research and Child Development, Baltimore.

14

Homosexuality: Development, Risks, Parental Values, and Controversies

Michael S. Lundy
George A. Rekers

Adolescence is a time of exploration and opportunity. It is also a period during which a relatively small number of critical choices will actually be made. Such decisions, while rooted in a mixture of past experiences, parental expectations, emerging personal beliefs, and social pressure, will either greatly limit or greatly expand the nature and quantity of future choices. Parents, educators, youth leaders, and clinicians will need to offer guidance of a sort that will lead to the expansion, rather than the constriction, of future freedom. The *postponing of choices that require wisdom until some degree of wisdom is achieved* is critical to the expansion of both the quantity and quality of choices. The consequences of choices made with the advantage of developmental maturity are preferable to those consequences resulting from decisions made impulsively, in the absence of adequate knowledge, or without the moderating benefit of maturity. The latter choices will, of course, be imperfect, but the former regularly result in personal and social consequences that are painful, destructive, and not fully reversible.

Homosexuality is not a new phenomenon. Those who interpret the increased publicity evident in recent decades on issues such as gay and lesbian rights, life-style diversity, and sexual freedom as evidence to the contrary fail to understand that what is new is the presence of *controversy*. According to Meyer-Bahlburg (1993, p. 489), "Despite its gradual depathologicalization by the American Psychiatric Association since 1974, homosexuality continues to be a topic of clinical relevance in child and adolescent psychiatry. The reason is that homosexuality has remained a difficult issue for parents and their children." In spite of a major shift toward social legitimization of homosexuality, parents do remain concerned about the sexual orientation of their children. The relatively recent paradigm shift represents a radical departure from commonly held views of homosexuality which "despite periods of greater tolerance, had been considered an abomination in the West for much of the past two thousand years" (Bayer, 1981, p. 15). In fact, homosexuality is well documented by ancient historical texts, notably the Old Testament, and much later, the New Testament. However, for the most part, there was little discussion about it, not because homosexuality did not exist or because it was considered acceptable, but because it was not a controversial issue. Controversy arises when conventional standards are called into question. Silence, on the other hand, cannot be interpreted as ignorance on the part of the ancients regarding homosexuality. Rather, such silence, punctuated by occasional negative references, is reflective of a *heteronormative* worldview. According to Rueda (1982, p. 2), "America's traditional religious beliefs have always condemned the practice of homosexuality, and social convention has systematically reduced even the mention of the subject to a minimum, and then in roundabout ways." It is the recent and effective challenge to this worldview that has sparked heated controversy.

Parents, educators, youth leaders, and clinicians cannot wistfully long for days of simplicity past, when such matters "weren't talked about." Similarly, they cannot and should not assume that mere open discussion of sexuality in general and of homosexuality in particular will somehow render an exceedingly complex set of issues amenable to "easy answers." As has been noted by persons of widely divergent opinion, the current publicity is not a solution in and of itself. According to William Bennett (1972),

> The gay rights movement will foster resentment; many citizens will not unfairly consider it to be a form of indecent exposure. More important, those who insist on making a deviant sexual preference a matter of public knowledge and discussion may get attention, but the public reaction will not be kind. By making overheated, active, public avowals, many leaders of the gay rights movement will bring about an equally overheated condemnation. If pushed, most people will, not unreasonably, refuse to ratify and approve homosexuality. (p. 24)

Similarly, those supportive of liberalization and destigmatization of homosexuality have expressed pessimism. Bayer (1981, p. 194), for example, notes that "there is every indication that the necessary social transformation [for the acceptance of homosexuality] will not occur. Whatever small prospect there had been in the recent past for the full integration of homosexuals into American social life seems to have all but vanished." Bayer wrote just as Ronald Reagan, a social conservative, assumed the office of president of the United States. The president's appointment of William Bennett as secretary of Education appeared to support Bayer's pessimism (Bayer, 1981). Currently, however, in 1995, a politician clearly committed to the advancement of homosexual rights occupies the White House, and the debate continues.

Diversity or Deviance?

A sexual revolution began in the 1960s, and has not yet run its course. While social, legal, moral, ethical, and religious debates are destined to continue, and perhaps reach some degree of closure, those who are maturing during revolutions must, to put it simply, get on with life. For adolescents, this means reaching closure on identity formation, including but not limited to sexuality. Those who offer guidance to children and adolescents must be prepared to assist in the navigation of an increasingly complex set of choices.

Leading professional associations have only recently formally rejected the notion that homosexuality is a medical or psychological disorder and is an inherently undesirable life-style (Bayer, 1981). Individual advocates have been even more explicit in pressing for broader acceptance of the homosexual life-style, and of the intrinsic worth of homosexual persons. Fikar (1992, p. 519) remarks: "Gay teens have to hear clearly a message from pediatricians and all care providers that Gay teens are every bit as wholesome and important as their non-Gay peers and that their sexuality is totally acceptable to us." Theoretical formulations, particularly within the psychoanalytic community, have generated more heated debates. Typically, more-traditional elements within that subsegment of psychiatry have insisted that homosexuality be viewed as a developmental anomaly or distortion, though not necessarily one that should be a focus of intervention. Rosen (1988, p. 28), for example, argues that "psychoanalysis seeks to understand the process in homosexuality. It does not infer that all homosexuals should be treated." And, while the official positions of organizations such as the American Psychiatric Association and the American Psychological Association are clearly in sympathy with the extension of full legitimacy to the sexual practices associated with all sexual orientations, "significant numbers of psychiatrists and psychologists continue to view homosexuality as a pathological condition, and are able to lend professional and scientific weight to the powerful social resistance to the legitimation of the homosexual orientation" (Bayer, 1981, p. 192). Rosen (1988, pp. 28–29) a psychoanalyst, complains that "problems of diagnosis and treatment have now been made redundant . . . because . . . homosexuality is no longer a disorder, and any individual's worries about homosexuality can now be rapidly dealt with by a short homily on acceptance or referral to a 'gay' agency."

As one moves from a clinical perspective, expressed opinions take on the language of values, tradition, and duty. Harvey (1988, p. 65), for example, points out that "church teaching assumes also that men and women can live a life of complete sexual abstinence, or celibacy whenever the moral law requires them to do so. It most certainly does require the homosexual person to live this way, all dissenting opinion to the contrary not withstanding." Similarly, Jewish tradition maintains that one reason for "the Torah's prohibition of homosexuality . . . must be that in the Order of Creation the sexual 'nature' and 'structure' of the human male and female—including what we refer to as their anatomy, physiology, and psyche—call for mutual complementation, completion, and fulfillment through a heterosexual relationship" (Matt, 1978, p. 15). Protestant interpretation of the Decalogue is consistent with traditional Jewish thoughts about sexuality. The proscribed attitudes and behaviors related to the sin of adultery (forbidden by the Seventh Commandment) are multiple. As the *Westminster Confession of Faith* (1985, p. 223) points out, "The sins forbidden in the seventh commandment, besides the neglect of the duties required, are adultery, fornication, rape, incest, sodomy, and all unnatural lusts." Advocates for gay and lesbian rights might classify such logic as antiquated (Fikar, 1992) or very prejudicial. Utribe and Harbeck (1991, p. 9) complain, "Negative attitudes toward homosexuals are primarily the result of homophobia, a prejudice similar in nature and dynamic to all other prejudices including anti-Semitism, racism, and sexism." Persons all along the continuum of the controversy surrounding homosexuality have appealed to reason, science, religion, and other tactics (some less than noble) to support particular views. The traditions that have endured the centuries at least are deserving of a closer examination which places them in historical context.

Ultimately, those who advocate for the broadening of homosexual acceptance may find themselves increasingly using the language of politics rather than of science. The decision of the American Psychiatric Association to revise the diagnostic status of homosexuality was "not a conclusion based on an approximation of the scientific truth as dictated by reason, but was instead an action demanded by the ideological temper of the times" (Bayer, 1981, p. 3–4). Because politics represents the process of contention for conflicting ideas and values, it is less than surprising that "the role of values in psychiatry has become a matter of increasing attention and concern" (Bayer, 1981, p. 179). It is critical to understand that the contention for dominance of one set of beliefs and values over other conflicting ones is a healthy and vital part of a republican form of government. Compromise would be unnecessary if there were no conflict, or if the absolute victory of one position over another were possible. Rarely have such conditions prevailed, and even more rarely have they proved to be a desirable state of affairs.

Many advocates for a more open integration of gays and lesbians into mainstream culture insist that a homosexual life-style, in and of itself, is in no way inherently different in quality, healthiness, or the potential for psychological adjustment. Fikar and Koslap-Petraco (1992, p. 901) argue that "there exists no intrinsic link between persons' sexual orientation and the number of sexual partners with whom he or she ultimately will connect. The link between gayness and promiscuity is a vicious myth perpetrated by homophobic and ignorant individuals who, hopefully, will find the time to better educate themselves." While the preceding statement is a useful reminder that sweeping generalizations are not useful, it ignores well-acknowledged worries within the homosexual community, particular with respect to the spread of AIDS among gay males. However, life-threatening individual behaviors that place millions of lives at risk cannot be easily explained on the basis of "a vicious myth" (Fikar & Koslap-Petraco, 1992).

Shilts (1988, p. 96), remarking on the early spread of AIDS in San Francisco, noted the role of homosexual promiscuity in its spread: "It seemed that just about every friend of a patient was also somebody the patient had once made love to, usually as a prelude to a platonic relationship. That was simply how you tended to meet other gay men in San Francisco and New York." He also noted that, initially, the "only factors that seemed to distinguish cases [of AIDS in male homosexuals] from controls was the number of sexual partners . . . [and] . . . the behavior that made possible large numbers of sexual partners" (Shilts, 1988, pp. 96–97). Similarly, with respect to *adolescent* homosexual behavior, Remafedi (1987) found that partners located "in gay bars or public places (e. g., parks, beaches, on the streets) accounted for the majority of encounters (50/79, 63%). In nearly one third of cases (24/79, 30%), subjects reported that 'we didn't know each other' before initiating sex." Over a period of one year, the average number of male partners for adolescents in this study was seven. Remafedi's (1987) findings are consistent with Seidman and Rieder's (1994, p. 338) observation that, in males, "homosexual behavior is associated with acquisition of sexually transmitted disease. Moreover, choosing high-risk partners (i. e., men who have sex with men) and engaging in receptive anal intercourse are both behaviors associated with risk for HIV transmission."

The level of diversity that has been documented between male and female homosexuals is well accepted. Bell and Weinberg (1978, p. 257) report, "Unlike homosexual men, whose cruising interests may lead them to make a large number of contacts with others standing around the bar, lesbians often sit at a table or in a booth with others or with groups standing around the bar, seemingly not interested in a new face and sometimes anxious to keep their partners from entering conversations with persons they do not know." Similar differences *among* gays and *among* lesbians are acknowledged, and point out the need for an open-minded, but not naive, assessment of individuals and their unique situations. With respect to adolescents in general, and teenagers who engage in homosexual behavior, a significant level of concern about the prevalence of high-risk behaviors is justified. Such behavior includes, but is not limited to, promiscuity, which epidemiological survey has shown to have disproportionate representation among male homosexuals (Cameron, Cameron, & Proctor, 1989). Cwayna, Remafedi, and Treadway (1991, p. 52) argue that "the increased risk of medical and psychosocial problems sometimes associated with homosexuality are presumably caused not by the sexual orientation itself but by the isolation and discrimination it generates." Nevertheless, few informed individuals, whether advocates for or opponents of homosexual rights, would argue that this "increased risk of medical and psychosocial problems" (Cwayna, Remafedi, & Treadway, 1991) is artifactual, or that some of this risk is mediated by individual behavior. Such behavioral components, while not necessarily intrinsic to a homosexual life-style, appear to be sufficiently prevalent to preclude their trivialization. The need for special concern for homosexual youth is acknowledged (Cwayna, Remafedi, & Treadway, 1991), though it is difficult to attribute the need for special concern primarily to a difference in *orientation* as opposed to or distinct from *behavior*.

Meyer (1985, p. 1056) correctly notes that understanding "homosexuality—as a lifestyle, a preference, an illness, a sociopolitical movement, a biological predisposition—is marked by a fundamental lack of consensus." Nevertheless, with respect to adolescents, persons from very divergent theoretical persuasions have expressed concerns about the likelihood of such a life-style to be associated with a great deal of misery. For example, in response to the question, "If a teenager who was just starting homosexual activity came to you and asked your advice, what would you tell them?," 80 percent of adult homosexuals said they would suggest that the adolescent stop such activity (Gebhard & Johnson, 1979). Prejudice and open hostility against homosexual persons is, correctly, cited as a major impediment to healthy adjustment, particularly among adolescents. Although some attribute the homosexual life-style itself for certain negative factors associated with it (Cameron, Playfair, & Wellum, 1993), others tend to view the high risk of suicide, substance abuse, and school problems in young homosexual adolescents to be based, at least in part, on "emotional and physical immaturity, unfilled developmental needs for identification with a peer group, lack of experience, and their dependence upon parents who may be unwilling or unable to provide emotional support around the issue of homosexuality" (Remafedi, 1987, p. 336). "In our present culture, the homosexual, transsexual, and transvestite are socially handicapped individuals. Therefore they have developed their own subcultures. It would be psychologically helpful for these people if society were more tolerant," write Rekers, Bentler, Rosen, and Lovaas (1977, p. 8). Similarly, Bell, Weinberg, and Hammersmith (1981, p. 222) note that "as long as parents are unable to accept gender nonconformity in their children, and as long as institutional policies of various kinds reflect unkind preoccupations with stereotypical notions of what males and females are required to be, nonconformists will continue to suffer painful consequences both as they grow up and throughout adulthood." A developing or incipient homosexual life-style in a teenager thus appears likely to be viewed with more concern by adults of both heterosexual and homosexual orientation, with some exceptions. On the one hand, concern is expressed by those who are opposed to homosexuality on religious or other grounds, but anxiety is also evident in those adults who have unambiguously embraced such a life-style them-selves. While there is evidence, not surprisingly, that homosexual parents may be more accepting of such a life-style in their own children, "no study found lesbian mothers who hoped their children would be homosexual" (Kirkpatrick, 1987, p. 207). Another documented discussion revealed a similar impression that "none of the lesbian mothers wanted their children to be homosexuals. They hoped that they would be heterosexual 'because it's an easier life' or that they would be strong enough to decide for them-selves. Like the heterosexual mothers, they were more concerned about feminine behavior in boys than about tomboy behavior in girls" (Wolfson, 1987, p. 168). This seems to be consistent with those who argue that, in situations where developing sexual orientation may be affected as a result of the individual's autonomous choices, that choices which decrease the probability of a conflictual outcome should be encouraged. Socarides (1988, p. 59–60), a vocal critic of the American Psychiatric Association's revised stance on homosexuality, says, "Nowhere do parents say: 'It's all the same to me if my child is heterosexual or homosexual.'"

True compassion for children crosses all ideological barriers. The expression of that compassion by one group may well be seen as being other than compassionate by another. Nevertheless, there appears to be some common ground. Adolescents who exhibit homosexual behavior, ori-entation, or identity are at risk for prejudicial treatment by peers, society, and family members; for serious health consequences; and for considerable social isolation, among other things. It is highly appropriate that clinicians of all persuasions work to develop rational approaches to help these young people develop in as healthy a manner as possible.

Developmental Issues

The degree of speculation about the etiology of the homosexualities is matched only by the tenacity with which some proponents hold to their own favored theories. The scope of this chapter precludes an exhaustive review of these theories, most of which are not without considerable merit, but which, taken in isolation, offer inadequate etiological explanations. It is somewhat ironic that, while homosexuality is known to be multifaceted, those who seek to explain it often use two-dimensional models, which may appear pro-crustean to those more comfortable with greater degrees of uncertainty.

Bell, Weinberg, and Hammersmith (1981, p. 6) expressed concern that "some gay activists may object to *any* study of the origins of sexual prefer-ence," which they "may view . . . as simply the continuation of heterosexu-als' attempts to understand how homosexuals 'get that way' in order to reduce, through preventive measures, the incidence of homosexuality among the population." Conversely, those who hold to an unexamined rejection of the homosexual life-style may be suspicious of the identical research efforts, and dismiss the findings as "pro-gay" in the same manner that others reject the studies as "pro-heterosexual."

Currently, a great deal of attention has been paid to so-called biological factors in the development of homosexuality (Bailey & Pillard, 1991; LaVay, 1991; Byne & Parsons, 1993). However, *biological* approaches are often either reductionistic models of causality or statistical inferences based upon theories that are themselves naive in their simplicity. There is a great deal of rich and complex data about the development of homosexual orientations, yet the careless misapplication or misappropriation of such information for the sake of expediency does little to advance understanding.

The political aspects of an issue are the underpinnings that shape the nature of discussion of the ideas central to important controversies. As Bayer (1981, pp. 4–5) points out, the "political analysis of the psychiatric battle over homosexuality . . . is not, however, external to the 'real issue.' . . . To assume that there is an answer to this question that is not ultimately political is to assume that it is possible to determine, with the appropriate scientific methodology, whether homosexuality is a disease given in nature." While Bayer was referring to whether or not homosexuality was to remain classified as a medical disorder, his comments remain perfectly relevant.

The current questions are still about etiology and classification, and are framed, variously, to either "prove" that homosexuality is biological in origin, and therefore natural and acceptable, or that, if proven biological, may provide through the "societal acceptance of the notion of a biological basis for homosexuality . . . the possibility of biology's being used as a tool for even more vigorous efforts to eradicate homosexuality" (Bell, Weinberg, & Hammersmith, 1981, p. 219). Recent trends in medicine have raised frightening concerns within the homosexual community that genetic research will be used to advance a heteronormative policy of eugenics. Headlines such as "Researcher Promises Gene Won't Be Used against Gays" (1994) may not prove to be reassuring to anyone familiar with the present abuses of the "healing arts." Sex-selection abortion is already practiced; the specter of a concerted in-utero "prevention" program directed at homosexuals is alarming, and should be of great concern to all persons who value the life of individual persons. The history of genocide in the twentieth century continues to unfold. Those who imagine that it would not be employed against an unaccepted segment of the population greatly underestimate the capacity of humans to be inhumane.

It may be helpful to temper the enthusiasm for reductionistic biological formulations while retaining skepticism for monolithic explanations from other theoretical perspectives. Byne and Parsons (1993) point to the weakness of biological theories:

Recent studies postulate biological factors as the primary basis for sexual orientation. However, there is no evidence at present to substantiate a biologic theory, just as there is no compelling evidence to support any singular psychosocial explanation. While all behavior must have an ultimate biological substrate, the appeal of current biologic explanations for sexual orientation may derive more from dissatisfaction with the present status of psychosocial explanations than from a substantiating body of experimental data. (p. 228)

Bell, Weinstein, and Hammersmith (1981, p. 213) cite Masters and Johnson as holding to a belief "that homosexuality is entirely a learned phenomenon, without any physiological basis. They propose that persons are born with no particular predisposition toward either homosexuality of heterosexuality." There is a great deal of complementary as well as conflicting opinion between the supposed extremes of biology and learning.

The separate developmental theories of sexual orientation—biological, genetic, social learning, behavioral, and psychodynamic, to name only some—are both too numerous and too complex to permit their comparative discussion in this chapter. Even those few relatively conclusive statements that can be presented are not without controversy. Because there is a significant degree of diversity among homosexuals, it is logical to expect that different combinations of causal factors give rise to homosexuality in particular individuals (Rekers, 1988). Thus, the question of how homosexual orientation develops is highly complex. Those motivated to further inform themselves of the various theories and opinions associated with etiological concepts of homosexuality are referred to existing works (Bell & Weinberg, 1978; Byne & Parsons, 1993; du Mas, 1979; Green, 1987; Masters & Johnson, 1979; Rekers, 1988; Weinberg & Bell, 1972). Ironically, in spite of the earlier publication dates of some of these suggested readings, they remain useful references. Some readers may find that the *volume* of opinion published in the intervening years is greater than the *content* of the actual scientific contributions upon which those opinions are based.

Broadening Perspectives

For the most part, sexual orientation *is* determined by genetics: sex chromosome patterns usually determine eventual sexual behavior, orientation, and identity, and phenotype seems to be even more critical than genotype. Gender phenotype is associated with very high levels of predictive power, both positive and negative. Those children who are, or at least appear to be, one particular gender, and are raised as such, will, in the great majority of cases, settle into a preferentially heterosexual orientation. That there is often considerable experimentation along that pathway is well known.

Nevertheless, it appears that "growing up straight" is, for most individuals, exactly that: straightforward. What is much more difficult to explain is why some persons, apparently from a very early age, develop differently.

Sexual curiosity and episodic sex play with same-sex and other-sex peers is not uncommon in early and later childhood in the general population. However, a pattern of overtly expressed sexuality, homosexual or heterosexual, is not typically evident until adolescence. However, the sexuality that manifests in adolescence is, for the most part, an extension of patterns of attraction and behavior that have been in development since early childhood. Bell, Weinstein, and Hammersmith (1981, p. 186) argue that "by the time boys and girls reach adolescence, their sexual preference is likely to be already determined, even though they may not yet have become sexually very active." But the period of development *preceding* adolescence that is so critically important in the development of sexual orientation is the one of which we know so little. As Martin (1991, p. 161) notes, "[One] reason for the limited data on homosexuality is that the coming-out process is largely an aspect of adult development; the data on homosexuals' development as children are limited exclusively to retrospective self-reports." Nevertheless, the consistency of certain aspects of retrospective reports of many adult homosexuals appears to confirm some level of "innate" predisposition to a specific sexual orientation. Memory is not always entirely reliable, but it is a useful tool. *The wholesale dismissal of retrospective self-report data cannot be justified any more than the uncritical acceptance of theories based upon the evidence presented by such data.*

It should be noted, however, that sexual orientation may be much more fluid and subject to change than is typically reported. Kirkpatrick (1987) reported the onset of stable lesbian (not bisexual) orientations and life-styles following relatively successful heterosexual marriage. Of note is the fact that such heterosexual marriages did not appear to be marriages of convenience or attempts to "prove heterosexuality," but seemed to have been characterized by a rather typical love relationship in which competing homosexual interests were conspicuously absent. Kirkpatrick (1987, p. 202) argues: "The presence of a durable heterosexual relationship in the life of a woman who later has a durable homosexual relationship requires us to consider that sexual orientation may not be, as we once believed, the fixed compass that directs all intrinsic and extrinsic aspects of personality formation." Late lifestyle changes have been assumed to always represent a late "coming out" after a period of struggle with homosexuality. Those who recognize this evident fluidity in a change from conventional heterosexuality to homosexuality without a bisexual "transition" may be open to the contention, advanced by several "Ex-gay" associations, that true conversion from homosexuality to heterosexuality is possible (Harvey, 1988; see Exodus International and related organizations listed together in the References).

Childhood variables cited as often associated with some forms of adult homosexuality include an unavailable distant/hostile father, the presence of cross-gender behavior (Green, 1987), and an enduring sense of "being different"—all of which may well predate adolescence or overt sexual experience. Older literature focused on blaming parents, with both mother and father receiving credit for a homosexual outcome in a child. More recent studies suggest that the relationship of the child to the father may be more a more critical predictive of outcome than any aspects of relationship with the mother (Bell, Weinstein, & Hammersmith, 1981; Rekers, 1988).

It should be kept in mind, however, that statistically significant associations only point out trends, but do not explain the preponderance of the variance in outcome. There are essentially no variables that are, by themselves, totally predictive. For example, Bell, Weinstein, and Hammersmith (1981) reported that 72 percent of homosexual males recalled felling "very little" or "not at all" like their fathers during childhood. However, while a significantly greater percentage of heterosexuals identified with their fathers during youth, a significant number *did not* (34 percent). Similarly, fully 34 percent of homosexual men *did* identify with their fathers while growing up. The pendulum may have swung too far away from psychosocial explanations, however. Byne and Parsons (1993) advocate the psychosocial model:

> The inadequacies of psychosocial explanations do not justify turning to biology by default—especially when, at present, the biologic alternatives seem to have no greater explanatory value. In fact, the current trend may be to underrate the explanatory power of extant psychosocial models. . . . Perhaps a majority of homosexual men report family constellations similar to those suggested . . . to be causally associated with the development of homosexuality (e.g., overly involved, anxiously over-controlling mothers, poor father–son relationships). This association has been observed in nonclinical as well as clinical samples. (p. 236)

A more useful discriminant is gender conformity. Gender nonconformity in childhood may be the single most common *observable* factor associated with homosexuality. Bell, Weinstein, and Hammersmith (1981, p. 81) found such nonconformity among homosexual males to be "directly related to experiencing both homosexual activities and homosexual arousal before age 19, a sense of an explicitly sexual or at least gender-related difference from other boys, and a delay in feelings of sexual attraction to girls, as well as an adult homosexual preference."

The retrospective sense of having been different from other children is reported very commonly by adult homosexuals. An awareness of same-sex feelings, which is separate from a sense of being different, may not occur until much later. McDonald (1982) found that an awareness of same-sex attraction was reported, on average, as having begun at age 13. Bell, Weinstein, and Hammersmith (1981) further note that very few individuals reporting predominantly homosexual feelings during childhood and adolescence considered themselves to be heterosexual as adults.

If gender nonconformity is so highly associated with a sense of being different from others of the same gender, and with eventual sexual attraction to those of one's own gender, what is behind this nonconformity? Once again, the data are not clear. The relationship of a child to his or her parents had long been postulated as critical in the development of homosexuality. Bell, Weinstein, and Hammersmith (1981, p. 62), for example, note that "unfavorable relationships with fathers do seem to be connected with gender nonconformity and early homosexual experiences," although they did not find in their own analysis that this correlation was particularly robust. Nevertheless, this association is consistent with that found by other investigators. It is emphasized particularly by those who have researched the nature of gender nonconformity that is so characteristic of gender identity disorders found in young children. Less weight has been given recently to the influence of mothers in the development of sexual orientation. Perhaps due to a frequently poor relationship with the father, fewer adult male homosexuals recall having been very masculine as young people.

A still prevalent popular conception of homosexuality is that it results from a seduction or recruitment by a homosexual adult or older adolescent. Bell, Weinstein, and Hammersmith (1981, p. 101) reported that they "found no evidence for the notion that homosexual males are likely to have been 'seduced' by older men, with few respondents (homosexual or heterosexual) describing the other persons involved in their first homosexual encounters as men much older than themselves." Other evidence suggests that sexual learning experiences appear to be important pathways to later heterosexual or homosexual preference (Van Wyk & Geist, 1984). Thus, somewhat intuitively, there seems to be some type of interaction between the nature and/or intensity of preadult homosexual experience and subsequent orientation.

Most adolescents achieve some degree of closure regarding their sexual orientation through experience, and although this experience is not necessarily through overt sexual acts, it appears more likely to be so with boys. With respect to the acquisition of data about the homosexual life-style, Utribe and Harbeck (1992) found that most males in their research sample used homosexual activity to explore their sexuality, thereby risking sexually-transmitted diseases. Similar patterns of high-risk behavior have been noted among the general adolescent population. Mellanby, Phelps, and Tripp (1993) report that individuals beginning sexual relations before 16 manifested a high degree of risk taking, including serial short-term sexual relationships and that young teenagers generally were found are to be more likely to take risks than older teenagers. Thus, if overt sexual activity begins during adolescence, it tends to be of a nature that will provide numerous experiences that will quickly and probably prematurely lead to an entrenched pattern of non-monogamous relationships. While these studies referred to *adolescent* sexuality, they beg the question of whether or not long-standing antecedent behaviors and affections lead to the initial experimentation, or in some way rendered the younger children sexually attractive to older adolescents or adults. Such antecedent behaviors, if present, must never be interpreted as indicative of a mature readiness on the part of a child to become sexually active. Certainly, behavior that may be expressive of childhood gender nonconformity in no way excuses sexual advances toward children by adults. On the contrary, such children and adolescents—who may indeed be rendered vulnerable by atypical behaviors or affections—place a greater burden upon adults to ensure that they are not exploited by those who espouse "intergenerational" sexual relationships (e.g., Thorstad, 1990).

Bell, Weinstein, and Hammersmith's (1981) major and respected study of sexual preference suggests that simple experimentation is usually *not* associated with antecedent homosexual attractions or other prehomosexual tendencies. They reviewed previous findings of the Kinsey studies (Kinsey, Pomeroy, & Martin, 1948) that showed that overt homosexual behavior leading to orgasm is common, at least among adolescent males. As many as 37 percent of young males may engage in such practices. Nevertheless, only a small fraction of those inclined toward explicit homosexual experimentation develop a homosexual orientation. It appears that it is not only the experiences themselves, but *the meaning of those experiences* that are formative in establishing sexual orientation. As Bell, Weinstein, and Hammersmith (1981, p. 124) conclude, "What differs markedly between the homosexual and heterosexual respondents, and what appears to be more important in signaling sexual preference, is the way respondents *felt* sexually, not what they *did* sexually."

Thus, it is quite possible (and perhaps even normative) for a homosexual orientation to develop in the absence of any explicit homosexual activity. This should surprise no one, as the majority of heterosexuals seek explicit sexual experience well after the awareness of opposite-sex attraction. Similarly, "probably an even smaller subset [of] adolescents may clearly identify themselves as homosexual, although *expression of same-sex orientation can be suppressed until early adulthood, or it can be delayed indefinitely* [emphasis added]" (Kokotailo & Stephenson, 1993, p. 285). On the other hand, it has been noted that early sexual experience may be more common among homosexual males, at least among those characterized as displaying effeminate behavior (Holeman & Winokur, 1965). Nevertheless, homosexual behavior among homosexuals (as opposed to phenomenologically similar homosexual behavior in heterosexuals) tends to *follow* the development of some degree of homosexual orientation. As McDonald (1982) notes that his research participants reported same-sex feelings at a mean age of 13, with first homosexual activity and comprehension of the term 'homosexual' occurring two years later." The degree to which very early sexual experimentation occurs among homosexuals as compared to hetero-sexuals is unclear. However, it would seem that certain high-risk behaviors, such as having multiple partners in short-term relationships, is related to an early age of first intercourse, for both homosexuals and heterosexuals (Mellanby, Phelps, & Tripp, 1993; Seidman & Rieder, 1994).

Sexual Abuse and Subsequent Homosexual Behaviors and Orientation

Shrier and Johnson (1988) reported that, in a clinical sample, forty male adolescents disclosed their experience of being sexually assaulted by a man before puberty. In comparison to a matched control group of 40 adoles-cents from the same clinic, Shrier and Johnson (1988) report finding that these homosexually-assaulted males identified themselves as subsequently homosexual nearly seven times as often and bisexual nearly six as often as the non-assaulted comparison control group. The magnitude of statistical difference for these measures between study and control groups was highly significant. A total of 23 (58 percent) of those adolescents who reported sexual abuse by a man prior to puberty revealed either homosexual or bisexual orientation. Of the control group, fully 90 percent reported a het-erosexual orientation.

An extension of the study found an additional 14 adolescent males who, as children, were molested my men. In half of these molestations, physical force or threats were employed. The mean age at which the molestation was reported was 18.2 years, with a range of 15 to 24 years. The age at molestation ranged from 4 to 16 years of age, with a mean of 10 years of age. Only rarely had the molestation been revealed prior to participation in the study interview. Of this group of 14, "one half of the victims currently identified themselves as homosexual and often linked their homosexuality to their sexual victimization experience(s)" (Shrier & Johnson, 1988). These same investigators (Shrier & Johnson, 1988) suggest that

> findings of the high rate of homosexuality in the study population are a confirmation of Finkelhor's 1979 college student survey, in which nearly half of the men who reported "a childhood experience with an older man were currently involved in homosexual activity." It was Finkelhor's impression that the boy who has been molested by a man may label the experience as homosexual and misperceive himself as homosexual based on his having been found sexually attractive by an older man. Once self-labeled, the boy may place himself in situations that leave him open to homosexual activity. (p. 1192)

Concerns about the sexual molestation of boys by men are further support-ed by a report noting that the sexual abuse of boys is greatly underreported. Such abuse has received much less attention than the sexual abuse of girls, perhaps because a substantial degree of the abuse to which boys are subjected is homosexual in nature. Such homosexual abuse of boys may be particularly likely to include acts involving anal penetration (Watkins & Bentovim, 1992).

A substantial yet unquantified number of boys *do* experience homosexual molestation (Watkins & Bentovim, 1992). The "prevalent misconception . . . that young male victims [of sexual abuse] are uncommon" has been seriously challenged (Shrier & Johnson, 1988, p. 1192). Young persons have themselves attributed subsequent homosexual behaviors and orientation to childhood homosexual victimization by adults (Shrier & Johnson, 1988).

Here again, caution may be in order about over- or underinterpreting the prevalence or long-term impact of homosexual contact between children and adults. Of the 40 boys who reported homosexual abuse as children, 17 (42 percent) displayed a heterosexual orientation at the time of evaluation. Of importance is that the retrospective reports were fully supported by an extension to that study in which more detailed data were gathered on an additional 14 boys. According to Shrier and Johnson (1988, p. 1189), nine of the 14 (64 percent) boys "experienced the molestation as having had an intense traumatic impact on their lives, both at the time of the experience and at the time of reporting several years later." Given that fully half of the male molesters used physical force or threats, the retrospective report of psychological trauma would appear to have substantial validity. The fact that the abuse was not reported until specific inquiry was made supports the notion that society still understands relatively little about the sexual experiences of children.

Cameron et al. (1986) in a multisite epidemiological survey of adults, found that 9 percent of males reported having had sexual contact with an adult before they themselves were 13 years old. However, if only contact with adult men during childhood was considered, only 3 percent of boys claimed molestation. According to Cameron et al. (1986, p. 327), "Considering only children's claims of sex with men, about a third were homosexual molestations." For some homosexually abused boys, such abuse may give rise to confusion about sexual orientation (Finkelhor, 1984). For other boys, it is postulated that *beliefs* about one's sexual orientation tend to *predate* actual *behavior*, rather than being caused by the behavior, which may nevertheless reinforce a preexisting conviction that one is homosexual, or heterosexual (McGuire & Carlisle, 1965). Bell, Weinstein, and Hammersmith (1981) had similar findings:

> Sexual experiences with members of the same sex were common among both the homosexual and heterosexual respondents; so were experiences with members of the opposite sex. What differs markedly between the

homosexual and heterosexual respondents, and what appears to be more important in signaling eventual sexual preference, is the way respondents felt sexually, not what they did sexually. A homosexual predisposition became evident, for the majority of our homosexual respondents, through their feelings of homosexual arousal or feeling sexually different, which in most cases occurred years before any advanced homosexual activities took place. And, among our respondents, virtually none of those who had predominantly homosexual feelings during childhood and adolescence identified themselves as heterosexual in adulthood. For such respondents, heterosexual contacts tended to be experienced superficially and were not especially gratifying. (p. 113)

Accordingly, while a substantial proportion of individuals who develop a homosexual orientation experience some form of sexual abuse or exploitation, such experiences, in some cases, may contribute to the development of homosexual orientation, but in other cases may only serve to *reinforce*, not cause, the initial feelings.

Sociological Factors and Homosexual Etiology

The abundance of thought and opinion on the role of society in the acceptance or rejection of homosexuality cannot be readily summarized. Readers are referred to independent readings which will guide their interests in acquiring a broad grasp of the issues at hand.

The role of society in the etiology of homosexuality, particularly male homosexuality, has been the focus of controversy. Guilder (1986) makes clear distinctions between gays and lesbians, and sees fundamentally different principles operating in the development of male and female homosexuality. While biological and psychological theories have tended to use parallel logic to explain the development of sexual orientation, Guilder argues that this is unnecessary:

> The facts of male homosexuality are also endlessly misrepresented and confused by the homosexual women who often speak for gay liberation. Female homosexuality *has nothing to do with male homosexuality* [emphasis added]. Just as male homosexuals, with their compulsive lust and promiscuous impulses, offer a kind of caricature of typical male sexuality, lesbians closely resemble other women in their desire for intimate and monogamous coupling. They most often explain their practice by denouncing the "meat market" of heterosexual single life and by proclaiming their own need for feminine tenderness and trust. (p. 73)

This observation is at least consistent with demographics compiled by researchers more sympathetic to the homosexual rights movement. It does appear that male sexuality (heterosexual or homosexual) seeks earlier overt expression than does female sexuality. Furthermore, the prevalence of female homosexuality, particularly in adolescence, is substantially lower than that of male homosexuality (Remafedi, Resnick, Blum, & Harris, 1992).

Guilder (1986) goes further, and postulates that male homosexuality is an artifact of the sexual liberation of heterosexuals. He sees the loosened bounds of marriage, and the ease with which competent men may acquire a series of young, attractive, women, as a contributing factor:

> Homosexuality remains chiefly a facet of polygyny. Polygyny reflects the natural desire of men of all ages for young women, the natural human tendency toward hierarchy, and the tendency of the powerful to use their power to take the nubile years of many young women, in a succession of wives and mistresses. Like female-headed families, homosexuality reflects the state of breakdown that occurs when the constraints of civilization succumb to the demands of male power. As the longer horizons of female sexuality give way to the short-term compulsions of masculinity, civilized societies break down into polygynous and homosexual formations, with related outbreaks of feminism and pornography.
>
> This process of moral decline is a liberation chiefly for established men who can take a series of young wives and for young women who can raid existing marriages. Homosexuals are just one of the groups who suffer from this trend of social decay and sexual revolution—and accommodate it. (pp. 77–78)

Religious and Moral Factors and Homosexuality

Finally, the oldest explanation for the development of sexual orientation is found in religious thought. Gallup polls have repeatedly documented, over a span of decades, that the vast majority of American parents endorse religious beliefs and values (Sheler, 1994). Homosexuality in particular has received attention in the predominant religions of the American people, the Judaic and Christian traditions. Both of these traditions share a common view of humanity that holds that things have gone greatly wrong with all individuals, and that the very nature of humanity has been corrupted. While historically maintaining that homosexual behavior is wrong and to be avoided, these traditions do not classify homosexuality as a unique form of sin (Dallas, 1992). Rather, heterosexuality is held to be appropriate within narrowly prescribed limits, and off-limits everywhere else. The National Conference of Catholic Bishops (1976) declared:

> Homosexuals, like everyone else, should not suffer from prejudice against their basic human rights. They have a right to respect, friendship and justice. They should have an active role in the Christian community. Homosexual activity, however, as distinguished from homosexual orientation, is morally

wrong. Like heterosexual persons, homosexuals are called to give witness to chastity, avoiding, with God's grace, behavior which is wrong for them, just as non-marital sexual relations are wrong for heterosexuals. (p. 18)

White, a psychiatrist and conservative Christian, (1977) argues:

Homosexual is a morally loaded term. It should be confined to those tho engage in homosexual acts. The people we label may have neither the wish nor even the impulse to engage in such acts, and we have no right to besmirch them. On the other hand, we must grasp that homosexual behavior is not in any sense inevitable in someone who engages in it. It may be understandable. But no homosexual (certainly no Christian homosexual) has the right to say, "I am not responsible for what I do because my homosexual nature *makes me* do it." (p. 111)

White (1977) goes on to note:

Now having said all this, let us make no mistake about what the Bible condemns. Nowhere is a man or woman condemned for having homosexual feelings. *It is the act, not the urge, that is condemned.* Let us lay aside, for the time being, the question of whether or not a homosexual can be delivered from all homosexual feelings and desires. Let us assume that many never will be.

In that case a homosexual is in exactly the same situation as a straight person whose circumstances demand chastity. Peter, an unmarried-twenty-three year-old teacher may feel very strong sexual urges. Provided he does not go out of his way to get turned on, no one may condemn him for that. His urges are the product of God-given instincts and the stimulation he cannot avoid in the world we live in. (p. 111–112)

Both male homosexual behavior and lesbian sexual activity are rejected by traditional Christianity, both in Rome, and by the churches arising from the Reformation. The appeal to Scripture is straightforward:

Therefore God gave them over in the sinful desires of their hearts to sexual impurity for the degrading of their bodies with one another. Because of this, God gave them over to shameful lusts. Even their women exchanged natural relations for unnatural ones. In the same way the men also abandoned natural relations with women and were inflamed with lust for one another. Men committed indecent acts with other men, and received in themselves the due penalty for their perversion. Furthermore, since they did not think it worthwhile to retain the knowledge of God, he gave them over to a depraved mind, to do what ought not to be done. (Romans 1:24, 26–28, The Holy Bible, New International Version)

In the stated context, "giving over" refers to the loss of God's promise of blessing and peace: "The Lord bless you and keep you; the Lord make his face shine upon you and be gracious to you; the Lord turn his face toward you and give you peace" (Numbers 6:24–26, The Holy Bible, New International Version). Thus, homosexuality is described both as an undesirable consequence of being rejected by God for having first rejected Him, and a sin in its own right. Thus, sin results in more sin, but the responsibility of individual behavior remains the burden of the individual (Bahnsen, 1978). The societal acceptance of behavior proscribed by the Ten Commandments can be interpreted as a corporate sin, with subsequent consequences (and responsibilities) both social and personal.

According to Dallas (1992, p. 23), "Adam and Eve's disobedience in the Garden brought consequences onto every aspect of our being, our genetic and biological structures included." According to this view, arguments about whether or not homosexuality is biological or inherited (Buhrich, Bailey, & Martin, 1991) are secondary to arguments about whether or not it is *moral*. Thus Dallas (1992, p. 23) declares that "even if it can be proven that genetic or biological influences predispose people toward homosexuality, that will never prove that homosexuality is in and of itself normal." Rekers (1977, p. 560) argues that "it is an epistemological error to base value decisions on empirical data alone. For example, parents may reject dishonesty or homosexual behavior on moral grounds, regardless of what percentage of the population happily engages in those behaviors."

At the same time, Christian writers acknowledge that the once almost unquestioning rejection of homosexuality on moral grounds is increasingly dismissed by influential segments of society as "archaic, irrelevant, and at times dangerous" (Dallas, 1992). Others agree that while "views on homosexuality have begun to change in the medical and psychological communities, religious organizations, particularly Christian denominations, are still debating the morality of homosexuality" (Brooke, 1993, p. 77). Bayer (1981, p. 5) concludes that the Christian "ethos has all but crumbled in the West," becoming "increasingly deserted by the populations over which its strictures once held sway."

Summary

Rekers (1988, p. 20) reviewed most of the factors cited above and concluded that "we may tentatively conclude that the main source for gender and sexual behavior deviance is found in social learning and psychological development variables." He suggested that the elements that comprise "social learning and psychological development variables" are very broad indeed, and include biological, psychological, social, familial, intrinsic, environmental, and religious factors. The confluences of these influences appear to determine, if indirectly, susceptibilities to particular predispositions and outcomes.

The various developmental theories about homosexuality are, in and of themselves, of little value to the clinician. So powerful are the underlying value judgments about sexuality in general, and about homosexuality in particular, that the applicability or acceptability of any theory or set of theories is usually viewed through the lenses of those judgments. Those who are advocates of increasingly liberal attitudes toward adolescent homosexuality will find things to embrace and reject, and in so doing, will tend to select those data that appear to support a particular philosophical outlook. Opponents of adolescent homosexuality are no less guilty of trying to bolster preexisting beliefs with data of convenience. As pointed out earlier, the struggle is political, though clinical and scientific language pervades the discussion of the issues. As Dallas (1992, p. 23) notes, "In this context, some are tempted to react with aggression and contempt toward anyone suggesting homosexuality is determined before birth," and therefore normal, or conversely, a genetic disorder. Others may be intimidated and fearful of expressing views that are not respected. Dallas (1992, p. 23) argues that "striking the proper balance of compassion and conviction" is the only truly rational option, and the only one likely to benefit the children for whom this chapter is written.

Professionals who serve children, adolescents, and their families need to remember that the locus of the contemporary controversy over the acceptance or rejection of traditional evaluations of homosexual behavior is between political factions at the societal level. There is virtually no controversy among parents, who nearly universally desire a heterosexual outcome for their own child or adolescent. Parents often turn to helping professionals to assist them in assuring a comfortable heterosexual potential for their child. In such cases, the ethical burden of proof is on helping professionals who would be tempted to impose their own political values regarding homosexuality on a child or adolescent against the explicit desires of that minor's legal guardian(s). Instead, attention should be paid to the following considerations: (1) there are life-threatening health risks associated with early onset of homosexual behavior; (2) there is a pervasive and emotionally charged controversy over the homosexual life-style (compared to the pervasive social support and lack of controversy for heterosexual marriage or a celibate life-style); and (3) there are significant psychological risks of premature sexual involvement. Given these considerations, the truly compassionate and most ethical course for the helping professional is to intervene promptly and effectively to expand the nature and quality of future choices of the minor. This is done by promoting the postponement of *all* forms of overt interpersonal sexual involvement by children and adolescents until the maturity of adulthood. In this way, clinicians, educators, and youth leaders can effectively collaborate with parents to offer the kind of guidance that will lead to the expansion, rather than the constriction, of future liberty and well-being.

References

Bahnsen, G. L. (1978). *Homosexuality*. Grand Rapids, MI: Baker Book House.

Bailey, J. M., Pillard R. C. (1991). A genetic study of male sexual orientation. *Archives of General Psychiatry, 48*, 1089–1096.

Bayer, R. (1981). *Homosexuality and American psychiatry: The politics of diagnosis*. New York: Basic Books.

Bell, A. P., & Weinberg, M. S. (1978). *Homosexualities: A study of diversity among men and women*. New York: Simon and Schuster.

Bell, A. P., Weinberg, M. S., & Hammersmith, S. K. (1981). *Sexual preference*. Bloomington: Indiana University Press.

Bennett, W. (1972, Fall). The homosexual teacher. *American Educator*, p. 24.

Brooke, S. L. (1993). The morality of homosexuality. *Journal of Homosexuality, 25*(4), 77–99.

Buhrich, N., Bailey, J. M., & Martin, N. G. (1991). Sexual orientation, sexual identity, and sex-dimorphic behaviors in male twins. *Behavioral Genetics, 21*, 75–96.

Byne, W., & Parsons, B. (1993). Human sexual orientation: The biologic theories reappraised. *Archives of General Psychiatry, 50*, 228–239.

Cameron, P., Cameron, K., & Proctor, K. (1989). Effect of homosexuality upon public health and social order. *Psychological Reports, 64*, 1167–1179.

Cameron, P., Playfair, W., & Wellum, S. (1993, April 17). *The homosexual lifespan*. Paper presented at Eastern Psychological Association Annual Meeting, Washington, D.C.

Cameron, P., Proctor, K., Coburn, W., Jr, Forde, N., Larson, H., & Cameron, K. (1986). Child molestation and homosexuality. *Psychological Reports, 58*, 327–337.

Cwayna, K., Remafedi, G., & Treadway, L. (1991, July). Caring for gay and lesbian youth. *Medical Aspects of Human Sexuality*, pp. 50–57.

Dallas, J. (1992, June 22). Born gay? *Christianity Today*, pp. 20–23.

du Mas, F. M. (1979). *Gay is not good*. Nashville, TN: Thomas Nelson.

Exodus International, P.O. Box 2121, San Rafael, CA 94912, 415–454-1017; Desert Stream, 12488 Venice Boulevard, Los Angeles, CA 90066–3804, 310–572-0140; His Heart Ministries, 12162 E. Mississippi Avenue, P.O. Box 12321, Aurora, CO 80011, 303–369-2961; Metanoia Ministries, P.O. Box, 33039, Seattle, WA 98133; Outpost, 1821 University Avenue S, #296, St. Paul, MN 55140; and Regeneration, P.O. Box 10574, Balto, MD 21285–0574. Support resources for parents of homosexuals are available from Spatula Ministries, P.O. Box 444, La Habra, CA 90631.

Fikar, C. R. (1992). Gay teens and suicide (letter). *Pediatrics, 89*, 519.

Fikar, C. R., & Koslap-Petraco, M. (1992). God, gays, and health care provision (letter of response). *American Journal of Diseases of Childhood, 146*, 901.

Finkelhor, D. (1984). *Child sexual abuse: New theory and research*. New York: Free Press.

Gebhard, P. H., & Johnson, A. B. (1979). *The Kinsey data*. Philadelphia: W. B. Saunders.

Green, R. (1987). *"The sissy boy syndrome" and the development of homosexuality*. New Haven, CT: Yale University Press.

Guilder, G. (1986). *Men and marriage*. Gretna, LA: Pelican.

Harvey, J. F. (1988). Homosexuality and hope: New thinking in pastoral care. In P. F. Fagan (Ed.), *Hope for homosexuality* (pp. 65–77). Washington, DC: Center for Child and Family Policy of the Free Congress Research and Education Foundation.

Healthy People 2000 (1990). *National health promotion and disease prevention objectives*. Washington, DC: Public Health Service, U. S. Department of Health and Human Services.

Holeman, E., & Winokur, G. (1965). Effeminate homosexuality: A disease of childhood. *American Journal of Orthopsychiatry, 35,* 48–56.

Kinsey, A. C., Pomeroy, W. B., & Martin, C. E. (1948). *Sexual behavior in the human male.* Philadelphia: W. B. Saunders.

Kirkpatrick, M. (1987). Clinical implications of lesbian mother studies. *Journal of Homosexuality, 14,* 201–211.

Kokotailo, P. K., & Stephenson, J. N. (1993). Sexuality and reproductive health behavior. In M. I. Singer, L. T. Singer, & T. M. Anglin (Eds.), *Handbook for screening adolescents at psychosocial risk* pp. 249–292. New York: Lexington Books.

LaVay, S. (1991). A difference in hypothalamic structure between heterosexual and homosexual men. *Science, 253,* 1034–1037.

Martin, H. P. (1991). The coming-out process for homosexuals. *Hospital and Community Psychiatry, 42*(2), 158–62.

Masters, W. H., & Johnson, V. E. (1979). *Homosexuality in perspective.* Boston: Little, Brown and Company.

Matt, H. J. (1978). Sin, crime, sickness, or alternative life style?: A jewish approach to homosexuality. *Judaism: A Quarterly Journal of Jewish Life and Thought, 24,* 15.

McDonald, G. J. (1982). Individual differences in the coming out process for gay men: Implications for theoretical models. *Journal of Homosexuality, 8*(1), 47–60.

McGuire, R. J., & Carlisle, J. M. (1965). Sexual deviations as conditioned behavior: A hypothesis. *Behavior Research and Therapy, 2,* 185–190.

Mellanby, A., Phelps, F. & Tripp, J. H. (1993). Teenagers, sex, and risk taking. *British Medical Journal, 307,* 25.

Meyer, J. K. (1985). Ego-dystonic homosexuality. In H. I. Kaplan & B. J. Saddock (Eds.), *Comprehensive textbook of psychiatry,* Williams & Wilkins, Baltimore, 1985, pp.1056–1065.

Meyer-Bahlburg, H. F. L. (1993). Psychobiologic research on homosexuality. *Child and Adolescent Psychiatric Clinics of North America, 2*(3), 489–500.

National Conference of Catholic Bishops. (1976). *To live in Christ Jesus: A pastoral reflection on the moral life.* (Washington, DC: United States Catholic Conference).

Researcher promises gene won't be used against gays. (1994, February 22). *State* Columbia, Sc), section 3A.

Rekers, G. A. (1977). Atypical gender development and psychological adjustment. *Journal of Applied Behavior Analysis, 10*(3), 559–571.

Rekers, G. A. (1988). The formation of a homosexual orientation. In P. F. Fagan (Ed.), *Hope for homosexuality* (pp. 1–27). Washington, DC. Center for Child and Family Policy of the Free Congress Research and Education Foundation.

Rekers, G. A., Bentler, P. M., Rosen, A. C., & Lovaas, O. I. (1977). Child gender disturbances: A clinical rationale for intervention. *Psychotherapy: Theory, Research, and Practice, 14*(1), 2–11.

Remafedi, G. (1987). Adolescent homosexuality: Psychological and medical implications. *Pediatrics, 79*(3), 331–337.

Remafedi, G., Resnick, M., Blum, R., & Harris, L. (1992). Demography of sexual orientation in adolescents. *Pediatrics, 89,* 714–721.

Report of the U. S. Preventive Services Task Force. (1989). *Guide to clinical preventive services: An assessment of the effectiveness of 169 interventions.* Baltimore: Williams and Wilkins.

Rosen, I. (1988). Psycho-analysis and homosexuality: A critical appraisal of helpful attitudes. In P. F. Fagan (Ed.), *Hope for homosexuality* (pp. 28–45). Washington, DC: Center for Child and Family Policy of the Free Congress Research and Education Foundation.

Rueda, E. (1982). *The homosexual network.* Old Greenwich, CT: Devin Adair.

Seidman, S. N., & Rieder, R. O. (1994). A review of sexual behavior in the United States. *American Journal of Psychiatry, 151,* 330–341.

Sheler, J. L. (1994). Spiritual America. *U.S. News & World Report, 116*(13), 48–59.

Shilts, R. (1988). *And the band played on: Politics, people, and the AIDS epidemic.* New York: Penguin Books.

Shrier, D., & Johnson, R. L. (1988). Sexual victimization of boys: An ongoing study of an adolescent medicine clinic population. *Journal of the National Medical Association, 80*(11), 1189–1193.

Socarides, C. (1988). Sexual politics and scientific logic: The issue of homosexuality. In P. F. Fagan (Ed.), *Hope for homosexuality* (pp. 46–64). Washington, DC: Center for Child and Family Policy of the Free Congress Research and Education Foundation.

Thorstad, D. (1990). Man/boy love and the American gay movement. *Journal of Homosexuality, 20,* 251–252.

Utribe, V., & Harbeck, K. M. (1991). Addressing the needs of lesbian, gay, and bisexual youth: The origins of PROJECT 10 and school-based intervention. *Journal of Homosexuality, 22*(3–4), 9–28.

Van Wyk, P. H., & Geist, C. S. (1984). Psychosocial development of heterosexual, bisexual, and homosexual behavior. *Archives of Sexual Behavior, 13,* 505–544.

Watkins, B., & Bentovim, A. (1992). The sexual abuse of male children and adolescents: A review of current research. *Journal of Child Psychology, Psychiatry and Allied Disciplines, 33*(1), 197–248.

Weinberg, M. S., & Bell, A. P. (1972). *Homosexuality: An annotated bibliography.* New York: Harper and Row.

Westminster Confession of Faith (The Confession of Faith, 1943). Glasgow, Scotland: Free Presbyterian Publications, 1985.

White, J. (1977). *Eros defiled.* Downer's Grove, IL: Intervarsity Press.

Wolfson, A. (1987). Toward the further understanding of homosexual women (panel). *Journal of the American Psychoanalytic Association, 35,* 165–173.

15
Homosexuality

Presentation, Evaluation, and
Clinical Decision Making

Michael S. Lundy
George A. Rekers

I observe the physician with the same diligence as he the disease.
John Donne, *Devotions on Emergent Occasions*, Number 6.

P resentation in the clinical setting must precede any sort of evaluation. As obvious as this logical sequence is, it must be kept in mind that adolescents, by and large, are not nearly as open about homosexual behavior as adults. Therefore, those teenagers with homosexual behaviors, orientation, or identity may not seek attention for sexual concerns or related matters. There are important and sometimes complex reasons for this reticence.

Clinicians treating children and adolescents are aware that much of the care given to young persons is initiated by parents. This is particularly true of behavioral or emotional concerns of any description. An all-too-typical scenario consists of a distraught, angry, or perplexed parent who brings a reluctant, perhaps overtly hostile, adolescent to the pediatrician, child psychiatrist, psychologist, or pastor. When the parental concern or vague suspicion touches a sensitive area for the teenager—a common situation—and when the clinical visit is at the parent's initiation, it is difficult for the adolescent not to see the adult clinician as an agent of the parent.

When the parental concern is about sexuality in general, or homosexuality in particular, the stage is set for tremendous tension. Opportunities for mistrust, mutual accusations, and other ill-considered words or actions abound. It is to be hoped that the very personal nature of sexual concerns, whether on the part of the parent, the teenager, or both, would lend itself to equally sensitive, dispassionate, and frank discussion. Only if an open, confidential relationship between parent and young person *already* exists is such discussion likely to occur. This is not the time for *building* relationships, but for drawing upon the intimacy which, hopefully, has been carefully tended, nurtured, and refined over many years.

Alarmist responses should be carefully suppressed by parents, if they are so blessed as to be the recipients of their adolescent's confidence, however partial. Equally to be avoided are glib, premature assurances of any sort. Adults may be surprised, however, to find themselves receiving the unsolicited confidence of someone else's teenager. While clinicians, teachers, and youth leaders are more accustomed to such situations, they can be exceptionally delicate. When disclosure of concerns or questions about homosexuality is directed by the adolescent to the parent of a friend, to an adult relative, to a church youth leader, to a teacher, or to a family physician, this is highly significant.

Nonanonymous disclosure, such as that described above, is particularly healthy, and to be encouraged and understood for what it is. In such circumstances, the adult to whom the adolescent confides is known directly or indirectly to the parents of the child. Accordingly, to the discerning teenager, the adult is seen as both an extension of parental authority and as someone who can also serve as an intermediary or advocate for the adolescent. The need for delicacy in such situations has much less to do with the content of any actual disclosures than with the unstated conditions under which disclosure is made.

Under conditions of *nonanonymous disclosure*, the adult or adults may be asked to give sweeping assurances of absolute confidentiality, but are simultaneously being tacitly asked to use discretion. Sweeping promises of confidentiality are quite inappropriate, and the extension of them may unintentionally set the stage for a great deal of mischief. If the relationship between the adolescent and his or her parents is basically sound, then in all probability the teenager is asking for some sort of advice. At the same time, there is an unstated expectation that the parents will "somehow" become aware of the issues according to a time table that will decrease the awkwardness between the young person and the parents. It is also possible that the approach to a nonparental adult is just what one might intuitively imagine it to be: a testing of the water. The reaction of the selected adult will be carefully studied by the adolescent, who will be looking for clues as to how to proceed, possibly with his or her own parents. The discerning adult will be faced with the difficult task of reading the situation correctly. If confidence is maintained too tightly, the adolescent's expectation that the issue will somehow come up "spontaneously" at home will not be realized. On the other hand, if an overly revealing and ill-timed disclosure to the adolescent's parents is made, the teenager's sense of betrayal and humiliation may be acute, and seriously hamper future discussion. Careful diplomacy, not abrupt or demanding directness, is in order.

Is it safe to confide such personal, and possibly troubling, information to *any* adult? If so, then it may be (so reasons the adolescent) possible to broach the subject with parents as well. Parents who have established and maintained good relationships and communications with their children may be approached more directly, that is, without the use of a mediator.

In either case, the directness of presentation or questioning may be minimal. Adolescents will ask first about "a friend" who thinks he might be gay, or who never dates, or who isn't sure she wants to ever get married, or the like. Responses to such inquiries may be best put in the form of open-ended questions where appropriate, so that premature closure is avoided. The young persons may wish to establish that the adult is willing to hear more, but according to a time table set by the adolescent, not the adult. Blunt, concrete answers or moralisms are almost certainly not called for at this stage.

Most parents, in spite of today's more liberal sexual attitudes, are hoping for a heterosexual adjustment of their own children (Kirkpatrick, 1987; Wolfson, 1987). No matter what they may say about tolerance, diversity, and the like, many parents find that when it comes to their *own* offspring, their open-mindedness is somehow shallower than expected. Under such pressures, parents and other adults may react with glibness, which may take several forms.

First, if the parent speaks prematurely, the "question" answered may not be the "real" one. Such an answer may prevent the more pressing and sensitive ones from emerging. Questions may also present themselves in the form of statements, some of which may be emphatic, provocative, and intended to elicit a response by the adult. The sensitive parent or other selected adult will be aware of this, and be circumspect. The use of denigrating descriptions may be a defensive way by which the adolescent obtains the parent's reaction to a hot issue. Some examples are in order.

The teenage boy who denounces a classmate (perhaps a close friend) with the statement "John is turning out to be a real *fairy!*" is certainly asking for his parents' opinions. Whether he is asking about "John" or himself is immaterial, in some respects. An opportunity is presented to the parent, and an appropriate response is required. There are a number of ways by which parents and other adults may show a callous attitude, and a few examples do not exhaust the possibilities. Fortunately, a well-considered response is equally possible. If the parent responds, "John? I'd never suspected *him* of being a faggot! What an idiot!," then one can see that the possibilities of continuing openness with the adolescent are immediately diminished.

Similarly, hasty assurances of heterosexuality are not in order. Example: "John? Oh, no. He's OK. Maybe he's a little confused. Lots of teenagers have that worry. It's silly, really. He just needs to date some. He'll figure things out quick enough." Such a reply may suddenly end the possibility of a more useful in-depth discussion. The nature of such a reply is such as to convince the adolescent who has questions about sexual orientation—his or her own, or related to a friend—that the adult is either unsympathetic to those concerns, or perhaps worse, unable to understand them. Such a response may reflect the parent's own anxieties and suspicions, and convey the clear message that the topic is off-limits. This empathic failure will effectively shut down communication and, if the young person is trying to express uncertainty about his or her *own* sexual orientation, may deliver an unintended message of rejection to the adolescent about their acceptance *as a person*. In fact, such a reply would be rather good evidence of the accuracy of one or both of the teenager's above-stated assumptions.

On the other hand, a less committal statement, such as "Oh, John. I haven't seen him around in a while. What's going on with him?," both expresses concern and opens the way for further disclosure or questions, either about John or someone else. It is probable that the young person raising the question is well aware of parental attitudes regarding homosexuality. If the parent–child relationship is fundamentally healthy, though, the adolescent will also have experienced a cumulative acceptance and affirmation as an individual that will make him or her willing to risk broaching such a difficult topic.

At this point, it will not be helpful for parents to be evasive, and it will similarly not be necessary for parents to disclose more than the situation will bear. It might be appropriate to acknowledge something on the order of "Many teenagers have sexual experiences with other young persons of the same or opposite sex. Such experiences are often very powerful, and can be difficult to understand."

The parent's own views about sexuality in general will determine the options available at this point. The parent who is upset *only because the sexual behavior is homosexual*, and not also because it is *premature* may be in a difficult position. Adolescents can detect hypocrisy intuitively. A casual or matter-of-fact parental attitude about adolescent *heterosexual* behavior coupled with an overt or covert hostility to adolescent (and/or adult) *homosexual* behavior will reek of inconsistency. On the other hand, a parent who wishes to protect her or his teenager from premature sexual choices may be either quite accepting of a homosexual life-style in adults or philosophically opposed to it. However, in these situations, the attitude presented to the adolescent can genuinely reflect a concern for the young person's true good. Fortunately, most parents will be advocates for delaying overt sexual involvement of *any* description. Few will be so unwise as to suggest that choices best left for maturity can be responsibly made in teenage years.

Questions or statements, direct or indirect, about homosexuality can be misinterpreted. The developing heterosexual adolescent may engage in homosexual behavior or experience same-sex attractions, and may be confused by these. The same initial statement, "John is turning out to be a real *fairy*!," may thus refer to a different underlying question. Just as it is possible to be glib or callous in reply, so it is possible to react with irritation at the adolescent's seeming or real prejudice. Taking a moralistic tone can be equally counter productive: "Well, each to his own" or "You really *shouldn't* call him that—you might hurt his feelings" or "It really doesn't matter whether or not someone is gay or straight," while superficially expressive of toleration, may nevertheless effectively shut down further communication. This will certainly be the case if the adult is insincere.

Sexual statements or questions by adolescents should be taken as invitations to engage in open dialogue. Keeping in mind that the concerns of the adolescent may be vague or poorly formulated will help the adult to avoid pressing for premature closure by offering information or opinion in a manner that takes the initiative away from the young person, or by cutting off further conversation by insensitive or inappropriate response. The desired response is one that extends the development of rapport at a pace with which the adolescent is comfortable. Attempts by the adult to reach quick closure may represent an attempt by adults to address their own needs and anxieties, rather than those of the young person. Setting aside one's own agenda in order to attend to the emerging agenda of one's child is in order. It is to be hoped that a gradual unfolding of the issues and open, candid, and useful dialogue between parent and child will result.

Establishing Rapport

If an adolescent, typically brought to a clinician by his or her parents, has a good relationship with the parents, any request for clinical evaluation and possible counseling may be uncomplicated. However, by the time the young person, with or without the parents, arrives in the consulting room, considerable tension may be present. The clinician must be prepared to assess the nature and temperature of the parent–child relationship, and to serve as effectively as possible as both the advocate for the adolescent and as a colleague of the parents. The potential trap for the clinician is to play either too much the advocate for the teenager *or* too much the agent of the parents. Either is potentially destructive.

Some clinicians have recommended absolute confidentiality: "Establishing the extent of a promise of confidentiality will also help create an atmosphere of trust: 'What you tell me about your feelings and behavior I will tell no one, not even your parents. The only situation in which I would tell someone what you have told me is if I thought you were in immediate danger of suicide or homicide, or if you report abuse" (Cwayna, Remafedi, & Treadway, 1991, p. 53).

While this approach may *appear* to be reassuring and empowering for the adolescent, there is a serious downside. Adults who place themselves, deliberately or inadvertently, between the adolescent and the parents run the risk not only of alienating the parents, but of furthering any existing mistrust between the young person and the parents. The implicit message in such an encompassing confidentiality as suggested by Cwayna, Remafedi, and Treadway (1991) is that the parents are not to be trusted, but that the clinician is good and on the side of the patient. Not only may confidentiality have to be breached for reasons *other* than abuse or potential self-harm, such an ill-considered promise by a professional may encourage pseudomaturity on the part of the patient. This pseudomaturity is facilitated by, among other things, either an unintended or overt usurpation of parental authority by the clinician.

An understanding of the complex, multifaceted, and changing nature of an adolescent's interface with the adult world is essential. Such knowledge will help the clinician to check the sometimes cavalier responses which adolescents can elicit from their caretakers. Countertransference reactions can be powerful. Sincere and ethical clinicians are scarcely immune to acting hastily upon rescue fantasies that arise from their own good and noble desires to do good. At the same time, negative reactions within the clinician can provoke untoward remarks or hasty referrals in an attempt to deal with a situation with which the clinician may be very uncomfortable. An example would be the unexamined dislike of homosexual *or* heterosexual persons simply because of their sexuality, orientation, or values. A considered and deliberate response, which *must* include an understanding of the parents' perspective as well as that of the adolescent, will go far toward protecting the interests of the teenager in the context of the family.

Nevertheless, the mention of abuse as one reason to breach confidentiality (Cwayna, Remafedi, & Treadway, 1991) emphasizes that the adolescent who presents with one *overt* consequence of sexual behavior (i.e., sexually transmitted disease) is quite likely to have another, *covert* problem (Remafedi, 1987; Rotheram-Borus & Gwadz, 1993; Utribe & Harbeck, 1991). This reiterates the need to consider abuse—physical and sexual—when evaluating an adolescent who presents with homosexual behavior (Watkins & Bentovim, 1992; Shrier & Johnson, 1988). Some adults, unfortunately, are not always to be trusted to act in the best interests of their children, or behave benignly toward the children of others.

Jason

Jason, a 15-year-old boy, had been forced to perform homosexual acts from the time he was 11 until he was 14. Homosexual actions that had initially been repulsive to him had become pleasurable after some time. He subsequently found himself repeatedly initiating homosexual activity with boys his own age. Jason requested assistance in resisting his homosexual urges, which were strong and entrenched. He ceased all homosexual behavior. Over the following several months, he experienced fewer and fewer homosexual desires.

Abuse may be subsequent to and a result of homosexual orientation, as when an adolescent is ridiculed and even beaten for displaying nonconventional behaviors and/or orientation. Clinicians must be aware that "it is grossly unjust for the peer group to label such . . . [an individual] . . . and to reject him [or her] for that behavior" (Rosen, Rekers, & Bentler, 1978, p. 130). Because such rejection is not uncommon, and may be associated with more serious hostilities, professionals must be prepared to investigate the possibility—or even probability—that actual abuse may have occurred. Such ridicule and abuse may not be limited to (or even within) a peer group, but may come from adults (Cwayna, Remafedi, & Treadway, 1991), and even from the teenager's own parents. This consideration must be explored carefully with both the adolescent and the parents.

While keeping the above in mind, clinicians must also consider the reality that sexual abuse often predates premature sexual behavior of *any* kind—homosexual, heterosexual, or bisexual (Becker & Skinner, 1985; Shrier & Johnson, 1988)—and that homosexual abuse of children is not uncommon, particularly that which is directed against boys (Watkins & Bentovim, 1993; Cameron et al. 1986).

Any evaluation of premature sexual behavior must also specifically consider the possibility of sexual abuse. The association of childhood sexual abuse with homosexuality, particularly in males, is not trivial (Shrier & Johnson, 1988; Watkins & Bentovim, 1992). In addition, homosexual orientation and behavior is itself associated with early (i.e., premature) and poorly modulated sexual activity (Mellanby, Phelps, & Tripp, 1993; Utribe & Harbeck, 1992; Cameron et al., 1986). The index of suspicion should be higher in the face of multiple factors associated with sexual abuse. Accordingly, careful inquiry must be made of both the adolescent and the parents, as well as of other involved and responsible adults.

Bill

Bill was a 16 year-old white male who was referred to the outpatient psychiatric clinic following a visit to the hospital emergency room (ER) a few nights previously. Bill presented with bright red bleeding from his rectum. He was evaluated by the surgical team, and was admitted for surgery. Because of the volume of bleeding, he was admitted for emergency surgery; a temporary colonostomy was planned. However, once in the operating room, an exam was preformed under anesthesia which allowed repair of minor lacerations and control of the bleeding. No major surgery was necessary.

Bill maintained, after surgery as before, that he had been alone in the woods, needed to defecate, and proceeded to do so. He stated that he fell onto a "stick" that was somehow positioned vertically in the ground directly beneath him. The stick, he insisted, penetrated his anus and caused the bleeding. The physical exam was consistent with anal penetration, but evidence was not noted which would suggest that the penetration occurred as Bill described it.

The surgical team considered that Bill might have been subjected to coerced sexual activity. They also noted in the E.R. record that this might equally be the result of consensual behavior. For unclear reasons, a psychiatric referral was made, presumably on the mistaken assumption that the psychiatrist could "get to the bottom of the matter!" Bill maintained that he had never had any sort of homosexual experience whatsoever, and that he had no such inclinations. He adamantly denied any coerced activity, and denied that any threats were pending against him to prevent disclosure. He maintained this posture, and refused to alter his implausible story. His family, who visited the clinic with him, expressed a desire to "know what's going on." However, the persistent denial of sexual activity or other concerns did not provide the basis for any actual evaluation. Neither the adolescent nor the parents had further contact with the clinic.

The taking of a thorough history will assist the clinician in untangling what may prove to be a complex set of circumstances. Children who have been abused are at greater risk for subsequent abuse, so the finding of abuse at one point in the adolescent's life should prompt an inquiry about previous (or subsequent) abuse. Because abuse is often not confined to one "category," the clinician should suspect sexual abuse if physical abuse in detected, and to consider physical abuse if sexual abuse is documented. Clinicians involved in such evaluations must be prepared to gather evidence of a forensic quality, or to refer promptly to someone who is qualified to collect and preserve such evidence. The implications of past or current sexual abuse in an adolescent who is also showing homosexual behavior and/or orientation cannot be concisely stated. The current state of knowledge about the relationship of abuse to the formation of sexual orientation is immature. It will be fully satisfactory neither to those wishing to establish sexual abuse as causal in a homosexual outcome nor to those who wish to redefine the sexual abuse of children as an acceptable means of introducing young boys and girls into the homosexual life-style. Those who take the latter position denounce efforts by "the women's movement and lesbian activists" to protect children from such abuse. Such appropriate concern for children is vilified as a cowardly selling-out of the gay and lesbian rights movement "to internalize straight society's stereotype of pederasty as inherently exploitative" (Thorstad, 1990, p. 254). That there is even controversy about the absolute inappropriateness of pedophilia—much less its active *promotion*—suggests that clinicians should remain vigilant in the area of concern. Fortunately, there is a broad consensus in our society among nearly *all* persons—heterosexual, homosexual, libertarians, religious and secularists—that supports the unilateral condemnation of sex between children and adults.

With the current emphasis on "children's rights" (held by some to be somehow independent of a family context), it is understandable that some clinicians might err by conducting an overly adolescent-centered (as opposed to *family*-based) evaluation. Even (or perhaps especially) in cases of overt sexual abuse—familial or otherwise—an adequate understanding of the teenager and his or her problems cannot be gained by an assessment of the adolescent that is conducted in isolation.

The other extreme to be avoided is acting as the agent of the parents to the neglect of the adolescent's legitimate privacy and confidentiality. The fact that a parent may be paying for clinical services does not automatically confer the right to be present for physical examination, for example, particularly if the adolescent is older and has an objection to such an intrusion. Similarly, explicit details of actual sexual activity that the patient reports may or may not be legitimately conveyed to parents. While uncommon, some parents may believe that a pediatric or psychiatric evaluation may reveal "proof" of homosexuality or reassurance that the child is heterosexual. Accordingly, parental requests for HIV testing or psychological testing of adolescents without the child's informed participation should be viewed with concern. Such overt requests for surreptitious evaluation may be atypical, but parents are quite as capable of being indirect and anxious about suspected or actual homosexual behavior or orientation as are their adolescent children.

The primary role of the clinician is to facilitate a *progressively* more direct pattern of communication between parent and child. This requires considerably more skill than sequestering the adolescent or than acting as a mere extension of the parents.

Once it is openly established that the topic of interest and concern is homosexuality, the clinician's task can at least begin to be defined. It will first be necessary to determine if any emergent issues are present, such as imminent physical danger to the adolescent. Specifically, the probable reaction of the adolescent's parents to the revelation of homosexual behavior or orientation needs assessment. A variety of reactions may be anticipated, some negative, some supportive, but a critical concern that must be addressed is the risk of violence directed at the adolescent by family members. Given the presence of one or more parents with their child at the clinician's office is an encouraging sign that violence may not be a concern. Most parents will have very mixed and strong emotions; most will *not* be aggressive or otherwise abusive toward their children. Nevertheless, the question needs to be asked, and in a way that neither minimizes the concern nor suggests that violence is likely or acceptable in any way. The level of concern is related less to the *likelihood* of such a grossly inappropriate response by parents (it may be very low in many cases), than to the *seriousness* of such a response *if and when present.*

In the situations where clinical contact is initiated by the parents, and particularly when actual contact with the parents precedes any meeting with the adolescent, it is useful to begin by demonstrating some degree of experience with the clinical concern. For example, it may be helpful to begin by noting that "Many parents don't know quite how to react to *any* sort of homosexual behavior or inclinations in their own child. It is almost certain, though, that you will have strong feelings." It is then appropriate to outline a broad range of emotions and thoughts which—it can be pointed out in a neutral and supportive manner—may or may not be experienced by the parents. Depending upon the individual parents, and the degree of preparation which they may have had before the disclosure, a mixture of reactions, affects, and thoughts may be anticipated. The following list is, of course, abbreviated, and not intended to be exhaustive.

Denial remains one of the more predictable and commonly occurring reactions to news that is unwanted and perceived as unpleasant. Such disbelief will probably be more likely if homosexual tendencies have been so carefully concealed that the parents are totally unprepared for their revelation. On the other hand, *relief* that the subject is finally out in the open may accompany the revelation in the case of long-standing parental suspicions or previous tacit acknowledgement of homosexual behavior or inclinations by the adolescent. *Confusion*, a *sense of deep failure* and *disappointment*, and *increased protectiveness* are all common reactions. Paradoxically, these may be admixed with *rage, disgust, contempt*, and open or barely concealed *ridicule. Emotional distancing* on the part of the parents from one another and from their child may be observed. It will be helpful to remind the parents at such junctures that issues of sexual orientation are not so matter-of-fact nor as simple as has sometimes been suggested by both advocates and opponents of the homosexual life-style.

Debby

Debby's mother had just discovered and read fifteen year-old Debby's diary, which included several detailed entries describing her affection for and homosexual experiences with a teenage friend, Sandy, six months earlier. Debby wrote about her sexual curiosity, which had led to sexual experimentation with her friend. Subsequently, another schoolmate introduced Debby to 20-year-old Karen. Karen was an outspoken member of the Gay Student Alliance at the nearby university. Debby's curiosity prompted her to secretly attend a few meetings of the Gay Student Alliance, where she would go to see Karen. Debby's diary also detailed her crush on Karen and her dilemma about whether to tell Karen how much she wanted to have an intimate relationship with her.

The poor communication and paradoxically poor boundaries between Debby and her mother were manifested in her mother's invasion of her privacy. Debby's mother was carried away by her sense of anger, guilt, panic, and disgust over what she had read in Debby's diary. She was not calm enough to discuss Debby's concern with her. Instead, when Debby arrived home from school, she confronted Debby with an onslaught of hostility and accusations. Debby countered by accusing her mother of violating her privacy. The conflict increased. "How could you do this to me?" was the charge leveled by both mother and daughter. Finally, in tears, Debby rushed out of the house and dashed straight to Karen's house for comfort and sympathy. Debby's mother had precipitated a crisis in her relationship with her daughter, and, by her snooping and distrust, in the face of existing poor communication, had encouraged her daughter to do what she may already have suspected her of doing (Aldrich, 1974).

The initial manifestations of support by caring parents may prove to be awkward and perhaps inept, but should be accepted at face value as genuine expressions of love and concern. Those parents who consider themselves to be less bound by traditional social conventions may be quick to offer "help" in the form of superficial affirmation. "It's OK. We don't care that you're lesbian [or gay]. You're still our child, and we accept you just as you are," can be such a response. More traditional parents may attempt to "help" by stating, perhaps, "You're just confused. We know you're not *really* gay [or lesbian]. We'll help you get this straightened out." Criticism of either parental approach by the clinician at this juncture is mistaken. Common ground between parent and child should be sought, and the previously cited expressions of concern, as divergent as they may appear, are probably intended as genuine and may be the best that the moment will allow. Note that each expression has, underlying it, a desire for quick closure and a return to some degree of status quo. Clinicians should be prepared to deal with their own countertransference when advising parents who may have viewpoints very different from those held by the clinician.

The physician (in many cases) or pastor or other professional should quickly ascertain the relative risk of *serious* rejection of the adolescent by the parents. A past history of abuse directed toward the child is a red flag, and must be explored in a straightforward and expedient manner. If the professional discovers current abuse, or has strong reason to suspect that it is imminent, immediate reporting to the appropriate governmental authority is mandatory.

It is critical that the clinician not try to "protect" the adolescent from harm directly by being secretive toward the parents. Rarely does the assumption of the responsibilities of child protective services by a clinician accomplish the desired goal; more often, the need for social intervention may be obscured and delayed. The result may be increased rather than decreased danger. At the same time, the clinician will be careful to respect certain confidences that may not be necessarily relevant to the immediate situation. Failure here may also increase risk to the adolescent, if not from abuse, by precipitating runaway behavior in response to a sense of betrayal.

Inquiry must be made at this point about past runaway behavior; its presence will be grounds for heightened concern. The absence of past runaway behavior should not, however, make one complacent about assessing acute risk. Direct questions, asked of both the adolescent in private, and of the parents in separate session, followed by a open review of the information with both the adolescent and parents is in order. Although it will need to be addressed further, inquiry must be made about possible suicidal ideation or intent; the clinician must be convinced that suicide is not an acute concern, or must take steps to ensure that the risk is adequately reduced (Pfeffer, 1986). Because the assessment and management of suicidal ideation, intent, and behavior is a psychiatric emergency that may require hospitalization, consultation and/or referral may well be indicated. The same pattern of questioning as used for assessing runaway risk may prove useful.

Clinical Assessment

Assessment should precede the making of recommendations. As obvious as this will be to clinicians, it needs to be considered deliberately. The pressure from the adolescent patient, his or her parents, one's own internal need for closure, and time demands must not be allowed to short-circuit the necessary process of evaluation.

Tragically, a typical, or at least not uncommon presentation, at least for male adolescents, may be related to the recent acquisition of a sexually transmitted disease (STD). Paradoxically, the presence of a homosexually acquired STD implies a very explicit "openness" on the part of the adolescent, who may have, at the same time, kept his or her sexual behaviors a closely guarded secret from friends and family members. Cwayna, Remafedi, and Treadway (1991, p. 50) describe a young male whose sexual orientation, as with "many other gay teenagers . . . first came to the attention of a physician due to a sexually transmitted disease." His sexual behaviors, at age 16, were "with men he met on telephone 'talk lines' and at public places such as shopping centers." Not surprisingly, "he had not informed his parents that he was gay. In fact, he had told no one about his feelings for sexual activities except the physician who diagnosed his gonorrhea." Such sexual exploration, due to its casual and anonymous nature, is consistent with studies such as one conducted by the New York City Gay/Lesbian Community Clinic which found that "most males in the [study] sample used sexual activity as a method of exploring homosexuality, thus placing themselves at extremely high risk for sexually-transmitted diseases" (Utribe & Harbeck, 1991, p. 16).

The manner in which the adolescent presents for consultation—whether alone or with parents, and whether voluntarily or under pressure—will determine the tone, and to some degree the direction, of the initial assessment. It is highly desirable to have the cooperation and participation of both the adolescent *and* his or her parent(s). The likelihood of such is highly variable. The clinician should not be surprised to see one or more parents, who, in the absence of the teenager (and probably without their child's knowledge) will wish for advice about what they may suspect is a sexual problem in their child. Nonclinical professionals, such as pastors, may be particularly likely to be recipients of such requests. The dilemma here is obvious, though the solution to it will vary.

Basically, it is critical to establish open channels of communication between the adolescent and the parents. And, it must be done, if at all possible, without further damaging parent–child relationships which are probably highly strained (van den Aardweg, 1984). This does *not* imply that a "smooth" process of parent–child involvement is possible, but that a solid clinical evaluation must respect the child's total social setting, a large portion of which is historically and contemporarily occupied with the parent–adolescent relationships. Refusal to hear the parents out is nearly always a mistake. Anxious and frightened parents will be quick to detect a nonempathic attitude, and will shop elsewhere. While concern has been expressed that with the offering of premature advice "a homophobic inquirer may break off the contact and shop around for a mental health professional who offers an antihomosexual stance" (Meyer-Bahlburg, 1993), other concerns exist.

Loving parents want an evaluation, not a sermon. Clinicians and other professionals must resist the urge to impose closure before the process of evaluation has been completed, and most certainly before it has begun! Owen (1986, p. 530) wisely notes, "If for religious or other personal reasons a physician cannot provide the kind of care these patients require, the medically sound, ethical way to handle this situation is for the physician to refer the homosexual to aware, competent, and understanding physicians or clinics who can provide comprehensive care."

This advice cannot be emphasized too strongly, but it needs to be tempered by an understanding of what defines medically sound and competent care. Those physicians and other professionals who are unable to evaluate their patients except through a focus of narrow anti-homosexual *or* pro-homosexual bias should indeed refer their patients to someone more interested in the welfare of the child than in advancing a particular social agenda. "Personal reasons" arguing for referral include an actual disdain for homosexuals or heterosexuals as individuals (as distinguished from a disapproval of a particular behavioral life-style). Those who cannot make such a distinction (whether themselves heterosexual or homosexual) are not in a position to perform an objective evaluation. This self-disqualification should also be applied by those clinicians who are uncritically hostile toward or rejecting of "religious or other personal" (Owen, 1986) parental objections to homosexual behavior, and should not be required only of those clinicians who are themselves openly rejecting of homosexual individuals.

Persons who are of such a pro-homosexuality persuasion (as contrasted to pro-person) may similarly be so "gay-affirming" (Fikar, 1992) as to impair their clinical judgment. It is, one must suggest, possible to make the mistake of equating homosexual *behavior* with homosexual *orientation*. Most parents—both heterosexual *and* homosexual—appear, in spite of a more liberal social atmosphere, to desire and expect their own children to achieve a heterosexual adjustment. Those who, philosophically, are in agreement with these parental expectations must, of course, be careful to avoid letting their biases unduly influence the assessment process. While a genuinely neutral attitude is neither possible nor desirable, one should seek to put aside prejudices directed against persons, of whatever form, that will interfere with the clinical process. Glibness has no place, and the use of it is almost guaranteed to alienate both parents and adolescents.

If one's interventions are "preselected" in accordance with a too narrowly defined perspective, then one will find that evaluation is shaped in a procrustean manner to accommodate the intervention. As those familiar with the tension between competing interventions for various conditions will attest, the professional opinions and resulting choices offered to an individual may be more reflective of the interests (personal, financial, theoretical) of the provider than of the recipient. An advocate for developmentally appropriate self-control may be in a better position to advance the interests of the adolescent than one whose agenda is less objective. The promotion of the deferrment of certain decisions, particularly those best reserved for maturity, is much more compatible with the true liberty of the adolescent than the explicit encouragement of developmentally premature decisions or of taking a supposedly "neutral" approach to matters of life and death.

It is recognized that many professionals, because of sound medical evidence, will be opposed to the expression of homosexual behavior per se. This position is supported by a significant volume of contemporary medical literature. The distinction to be made is between *behavior* that is demonstrably unhealthy from a medical perspective, and the *individuals* who practice such behavior. Surely the matter is as much one of *approach* as of *conviction*. A physician or other health care provider will, it is to be hoped, find difficulty in taking a stance of clinical "neutrality" with regard to matters that clearly involve life and death. Homosexual behavior in children and adolescents is *not* adiaphorous. The responsible and ethical approach to evaluating children and adolescents is one that properly recognizes life-threatening risks, and then recommends interventions that will result in the greatest risk reduction. Just as compassionate and competent clinicians may ethically refuse to offer second- or third-rate treatment if the patient refuses available, safer, and more cost-effective treatment of first choice, those working with children should resist societal or political pressures to prescribe less than the best available. For many and perhaps most children, the rationale for offering substandard care is weak indeed.

Just as not all heterosexual experimentation is indicative of heterosexual orientation, not all homosexual behavior stems from or conveys evidence of a homosexual orientation, either incipient or established. This would appear to be particularly true in adolescence. The professional must be prepared to assess the adolescent comprehensively, keeping in mind that behavior is only one component of sexual orientation. Many teenagers will have distinct attractions to members of the same sex, but will not have acted upon them. Similarly, for a fairly large number of boys, "the acknowledgement of heterosexual feelings in a . . . [homosexual] no more suggests a mistaken sexual identity than the acknowledgement of homosexual feelings in a heterosexual" (Kirkpatrick, 1987, p. 203). Therefore, premature closure of the evaluative process must be avoided.

Because of the developmental immaturity of adolescence (cognitive and emotional), young people may themselves be the most anxious to achieve such closure. It is *not* in the interest of the teenager for clinicians to collaborate with an uninformed and superficial acceptance of sexual orientation. Any number of factors—familial, social, and psychological—may be exerting pressures upon the adolescent to *act*, when what is needed is a reflective deferment of action. The direction from which such pressures come is not always intuitive. It is not unlikely that a young person may, in a counterphobic maneuver, "accept" a homosexual (or heterosexual) orientation without exploring underlying ideas and feelings. For example, while one may acknowledge that there "are many gay, lesbian, and bisexual youth and adults who . . . lead productive and well-adjusted lives [, at] the same time, the counselor should present a realistic picture of the challenges and struggles that may be faced [by those who enter a homosexual life-style] and offer supportive services as needed" (Kokotailo & Stephenson, 1993, p. 286).

Ken

Ken related, "Last Friday, when nobody else was home, I took Mom's sharpest knife out of the kitchen drawer, and I decided that this time I would do it. Really, there's no reason to go on living anymore. Nobody understands how frustrated and unhappy I am."

Ken was a good-looking teenager of medium athletic build, dressed in blue jeans and a T-shirt. He looked like the typical, all-American boy that might live down the street. But he related a profound despair over his homosexual involvements.

Ken had been depressed on other occasions, but this time what was dragging him down was his grief over losing his homosexual lover, who, in addition to physical attention, had lavished Ken with money and gifts.

Ken was more confused, more unhappy, and in much greater trouble than his mother realized when she brought him to the psychologist's office. She had no idea that Ken had begun seeking out homosexual bars in order to pick up casual sexual partners in the hopes that such sexual encounters would put him in a better mood. But his recent succession of anonymous homosexual encounters had left him feeling as empty and depressed as before.

Ken related that he had quickly learned that his youth and physical attractiveness placed him in high demand in the gay world. All the social and physical attention he received at the gay bars flattered his ego and boosted his low self-concept. His homosexual encounters did not cure his depression as he had hoped; instead, his loneliness and sense of inadequacy made him vulnerable to flattery and exploitation.

At a time when many of his peers were thinking about dating and day-dreaming about the possibility of college, future careers, and being married, Ken was preoccupied with finding an older homosexual male who would provide him easy spending money in exchange for sexual favors. He thought he had figured out the easiest way to get by. He felt uneasy about submitting to certain sexual practices, and he had no affection for these older men, but he was gradually overcoming what he described as his initial aversion to the sexual favors required, and he enjoyed the easy money.

During the course of evaluation, with which Ken was cooperative, he confided that he believed his sexual life-style was "violating the moral structure of the universe." Although he himself was not especially religious, he sensed that he needed spiritual as well as psychological solutions to his dilemmas. But in spite of his internal conflicts, he decided that the pleasures of the gay life-style were something that he did not want to pass up during his teenage years. Although he sensed the moral and personal costs of his decision, he was impressed by the material reward and physical pleasure that his attractiveness could bring him.

Ken elected to participate in individual psychotherapy sessions once a week for two months. These were primarily of an exploratory nature. He overcame much of his severe depression, and the intensity of his sexual identity confusion lessened. When Ken considered the option of directing his therapy toward the goal of altering his homosexual life-style, he took a rather naive approach.

He continued to insist that, perhaps in his late 20s, that he planned to fall in love with a woman, get married, and have a happy family with a few kids. By then, he reasoned, "I'll completely give up my homosexual affairs, because I'm sure my wife would want me to go to bed only with her."

"I just can't imagine continuing to live my whole life in the gay world. I really want to have kids, and I want to be a better dad to them than my dad was for me. The gay life just doesn't lead to anything. It just doesn't end up with a family," Ken confided. He also expressed concern that "when I get older, the gays won't pay as much attention to me anymore."

Subsequently, he stated, "I want to straighten up. But I know that when I'm young, my body is more appealing than it ever will be again. What I want is to experience the thrill of gay life for two years. Then when I'm almost eighteen, I'll straighten up in time to get married when I'm in my 20s. I just don't want to pass up the good times now. Besides, I'm not ready to get married, so I might as well live it up while I can." Ken was not pressured to adopt a heterosexual life-style, to which he showed no real commitment. His insistence, though, on being able to change his orientation, or at least behavior, at any time he chose, was unrealistic.

The acuity of the initial clinical consultation may or may not serve as a measure of the intensity and potential volatility of the family situation. Careful but efficient inquiry, if necessary, should be conducted to answer the question, "What prompted you to seek consultation *now*, rather than last month or next week?" The answer to this question will be revealing. Once issues of basic concern and safety have been established, a more detailed assessment can and should commence.

A desire to please parents or friends, or to distance one's self from homosexual urges, may lead a teenager with no strong heterosexual urges to take rash action to "escape" from emerging homosexual attractions. It has been suggested that a substantial proportion of teen suicides may result from struggles with an incipient or feared homosexual orientation (Fikar, 1992). Perhaps it is more balanced to postulate that an act as rash as suicide may be due to a more general struggle with sexual orientation, without assuming that it is only youth who are incipient homosexuals who are killing themselves because of such struggles. It is equally possible than an insecure heterosexual, who is afraid that he or she is *thought* to be homosexual by peers, or who *mistakenly interprets* same-sex platonic affections as internal evidence of emerging homosexuality, may react destructively.

Just as parents deserve an evaluation of their adolescent child, so the teenager deserves and must be provided the opportunity to be heard. Depending upon the relationship of the adolescent with the parents, providing this opportunity may be difficult or relatively easy to accomplish. Assimilation of the data, however, may be anything but simple. The role of the professional, as stated previously, must encompass both the identification and management of actual emergencies and acute medical treatment, as well as the more protracted and difficult assessment of the family.

When possible, and where urgent concerns do not prevent it, it is preferable to schedule a large block of time, or a series of closely spaced smaller time blocks. Those clinicians who have no intention of taking the requisite time, for whatever reason, must consider referral to someone who can. Primary care physicians, such as pediatricians and family practitioners, may find the use of physician extenders, including nurses and social workers, to be a practical way of providing the necessary assessment. Such an approach, if part of a true multidisciplinary team approach, has the distinct advantage of protecting against the idiosyncracies inherent in an evaluation performed by a single practitioner.

Matters of cost are important, as well. The vital nature of the visit will not be readily apparent to third-party payers, yet the time required for a proper assessment cannot be reduced. The hourly cost of a pediatrician's uninterrupted time would be prohibitive to most persons. Nevertheless, the information must be gathered accurately and systematically. Fortunately, innovative means of increasing efficiency are possible. Before suggesting such techniques, the substantive issues of the evaluation process need to be developed further.

The first and most obvious task is to establish the chief complaint, which may be gathered only from the chief complainer. As noted, this may be either the adolescent or one or more parents. Adolescents, as well as adults, "tend to come into treatment for one of several motivations: for someone else; for themselves, but not for their homosexuality; and for their homosexuality. These ostensible motivations to some extent determine the course of treatment. Either or both may have questions which touch more on possibilities than upon actual active encountered difficulties" (Meyer, 1985 p. 1063). It is possible that some overt sexual behavior, or consequence of it, or question about possible or definite homosexual orientation will represent the presenting picture in a substantial number of situations, but certainly not in all. As noted, the psychosocial morbidity among young homosexuals is high, so one may equally expect to be asked by a parent to evaluate a child for depression, substance abuse, or other concerns. "School problems related to sexuality, substance abuse, and/or emotional difficulties warranting mental health interventions" are very common among teenagers who display homosexual behavior (Remafedi, 1987, p. 331). Importantly, while "families and youths may directly consult health professionals about homosexuality, the issue more commonly surfaces as a result of other concerns such as sexually transmitted diseases, substance abuse, family conflict, academic underachievement, prostitution, and attempted suicide" (Remafedi, 1987, p. 336).

Accordingly, the taking of a detailed sexual history is indicated in the primary care setting whenever dealing with adolescents, whether they are known to be heterosexual or homosexual, or if sexual orientation is unknown or not yet established. The detail of data needed will vary with age, whether or not sexual activity has occurred yet, and whether or not there are identified concurrent medical or psychosocial problems. The experienced clinician will recognize that little can be established by inference, and will use a direct and systematic form of evaluation for all adolescents. Decision points can be built into the evaluation process so that completeness is ensured without asking questions that can be established as irrelevant. It is also indicated when other concerns, such as those known to be associated with homosexuality in adolescence are noted. Runaway behavior, physical and/or sexual abuse, drug usage, school failure (particularly following previously good school adjustment), depression, and any sort of suicidal behavior or ideation are but a few of the concerns that should prompt an immediate assessment of sexuality in the young person. Those who detect such concerns but who know themselves unqualified for further assessment should be prepared to make a referral to a care provider who has expertise in these areas. Such concerns require family involvement for thorough evaluation and effective intervention.

In the absence of particular concerns, it can be argued that the comprehensive and continuing medical care of the adolescent demands the taking of a systematic sexual history, which should be updated on a regular basis. At the very least, a screening instrument should be developed that will help to detect particular needs of the young person. The survey utilized in a adolescent medicine clinic is one example of such an instrument (Shrier & Johnson, 1988). Note that behavioral measures, while necessary, are not sufficient for a complete sexual history. Inquiry must also be made into fantasy life, sexual attractions, intentions, self-perceived orientation, and future hopes and fears about partner choice, to name a few. The acquisition of this information may make an open inquiry about overt behaviors easier for both the adolescent and the clinician. *It should not be assumed that the young person is (or is not) sexually active.* In spite of great shifts in the sexual behavior of adolescents, it remains true that "abstinence is the norm for that age-group" (Kokotailo & Stephenson, 1993, p. 260). However, if it is established that the adolescent *is* sexually active, inquiry must be made about sexual partners; the overall number, age(s), and social connections (i.e., strangers vs. well-known acquaintances) are important. Needless to say, the clinician should have already become educated with respect to patterns and types of sexual practices that may be more common in homosexuals than in heterosexuals. Ignorance of such aspects of homosexuality will render the clinician ineffective (Owen, 1986). Inquiry must always be made about coerced sexual activity, in that it is reported that "a quarter of self-identified gay and bisexual youths have been [sexually] abused" (Rotheram-Borus & Gwadz, 1993, p. 423).

Psychosocial assessment, while outside the expertise of most primary care physicians, is readily available through the consultative relationships that many pediatricians and family practitioners have established. Such an assessment is often labor-intensive, but a well-planned protocol can minimize the delays in this phase of evaluation. Structured behavioral assessments that rely upon both the adolescent and parents as informants are particularly valuable (Achenbach & Edelbrock, 1983). If the clinician is not trained in the interpretation of such instruments, they will nevertheless provide useful data if referral is needed, as they gather standardized information about depression, school and social functioning, anxiety, and a number of other relevant factors. Referral is indicated if significant depression, substance abuse, suicidal ideation or intent, or suspicion about emotional disturbance is present. A child psychiatrist who has working arrangements with a psychiatric social worker and qualified clinical child psychologist should be sought. Input from these three disciplines are all likely to be necessary, if referral is in fact indicated.

Once a sexual history has been obtained and reviewed for accuracy, the clinician must be prepared to interpret this history. The context for interpretation must account for *behavior, orientation*, and *identity*, but must furthermore account for the admittedly sparse information about the prevalence of homosexual orientation in adolescence. Meyer-Bahlburg (1993) notes:

> In research work on homosexuality, three aspects are distinguished. Homosexual *behavior* refers to overt sexual activities between two partners of the same gender. Such activities are not uncommon as part of the sexual interactions of children or adolescents. By contrast, *orientation* refers to the overall sexual responsiveness of a person to men or women. It is specified for limited life periods and assessed on the basis of (1) sexual imagery (e.g., daydreams, nighttime dreams, masturbation fantasies), (2) erotica use, (3) erotica attraction, and (4) actual sexual partner experience. . . . Sexual orientation is not usually assessed before puberty, and despite some anecdotal retrospective accounts, there is no well-established empiric basis to decide the question of whether and to what extent a sexual orientation can be defined for prepubertal children. The third concept of homosexuality, homosexual *identity*, e.g., labeling oneself as *gay, lesbian*, or *bisexual*, is the result of a gradual *coming out* process: the recognition of one's own homosexual orientation and its partial or complete disclosure to others.
>
> An adolescent's sexual orientation may contrast with his or her sexual identity as *straight*, or *gay*, or *lesbian*, especially at the developmental stage when the adolescent first starts noticing sexual feelings toward people of the same sex. Also, one's sexual orientation may not parallel actual sexual partner experience, for instance, when the adolescence is not yet sexually active, when he or she is experimenting with partners of both sexes, or when in an institutional situation where sexual partners of the other sex are not available. In fact, many more adolescents engage transiently and sporadically in overt homosexual behavior than ever become homosexually oriented. (pp. 489–490)

Actual prevalence of homosexuality in adolescence has not been studied in great detail. However, research data that do exist suggest homosexual orientation to be relatively uncommon, though hardly rare. In a major study of 34,000 junior and senior high students, only 0.4 percent were self-described as "mostly or totally homosexual." Homosexual attractions occurred at a rate of 4.5 percent, homosexual fantasies at a rate of 2.6 percent, and actual homosexual behavior at a rate of just under 1 percent. These percentages exclude the 11 percent of students who reported being "unsure" of their current sexual orientation. Heterosexual orientation was reported in 99 percent of the remaining total, with the balance being bisexual (Remafedi, Resnick, Blum, & Harris, 1992). A recent review of broad-based survey data found that less than 3 percent of men between ages 20 and 39 had engaged in homosexual activity during the preceding decade (which would, presumably, include such behaviors in children as young as 10 years old); slightly over 1 percent have engaged in such activity exclusively during that time frame (Seidman & Rieder, 1994).

The clinician, after establishing rapport and a nonthreatening environment in which to facilitate open discussion, must now begin to evaluate internal attitudes and the degree of conflict, if any, which may be present between behavior, orientation, and identity. The older use of ego-dystonic and ego-syntonic descriptors of homosexual behavior and orientation may not be applicable in adolescence due to developmental immaturity. The presence of homosexual *behavior* in the *absence* of homosexual orientation, and especially in the *presence* of convincing heterosexual orientation, is instructive. Similarly, self-reported distress about homosexual attractions, fantasies, or other anxieties needs careful consideration. On the other hand, a homosexual *orientation*, with or without overt homosexual *behavior*, may well be more disturbing to the parents than to the adolescent boy or girl. If it is determined that the adolescent is well advanced in the "coming out" process, and in fact expresses no particular conflict about having and maintaining a homosexual orientation and life-style, the direction of the consultation will be very different than when the adolescent experiences a great deal of internal distress and uncertainty.

The clinician's task is more complex than the mere documentation of sexual experiences (or the lack of them). It is more difficult than a simplistic determination of current sexual orientation and/or behavior, which is dynamic, not static. Because overt homosexual behavior in adolescents, particularly among males, is associated with such health risks, the compassionate clinician will wish to work with the young person and the parents in order to reduce those risks.

Risk Assessment

"Primum non nocere," Hippocrates advised physicans: "First, do no harm." Risk reduction can be done only if one properly determines the adverse outcomes for which an adolescent is actually at risk (Boyle & Offord, 1990; Lundy, Pfohl, & Kuperman, 1993). "Preventive" intervention, if applied to one not actually at high risk for the outcome for which the intervention is designed, will not only fail to help the recipient, but may cause overt harm. It is the naive who, with the best of intentions, make the mistaken assumption that intervention "can't possibly hurt." Since almost *all* interventions, whether medical, surgical, or psychosocial, carry some inherent risk in and of themselves, it is essential to focus interventions where they are both necessary and likely to be efficacious (Lundy & Pumariega, 1993). By inadvertently encouraging the very activity that one wishes to prevent (Aldrich, 1974), "preventive" efforts can have an effect precisely opposite that intended. The application of so-called preventive interventions across the board without an actual assessment of risk, is irresponsible, and betrays a fundamental misunderstanding of epidemiology (Kelsey, Thompson, & Evans, 1986; Schlesselman, 1982).

Boyle and Offord (1990, p. 227) wisely remark, "If we choose characteristics for modification that are not important risk factors for disorder, then our programs will fail. If we select a population at low risk for disorder, then enormous samples will be needed to demonstrate that our programs are effective." A possible scenario is that of a poorly designed intervention strategy, applied to a population that is not at high-risk. In such a case, enormous sample sizes and fiscal expenditures would be necessary merely to demonstrate the ineffectiveness of a prevention program. If the program is not actually evaluated rigorously, then a worse scenario is established in which a poor program, applied inappropriately, is assumed to be doing only good and not harm. The current state of prevention in the social area is sufficiently primitive as to argue strongly against the glib acceptance or promotion of such assumptions (Buckner, Trickett, & Corse, 1985; Shaffer, Philips, & Enzer, 1989).

The physical, technical, and laboratory aspects of a comprehensive evaluation are mentioned last. While these are critical components of care, they may be relatively useless in the absence of an established environment that will encourage continued evaluation and rapport. Those clinicians who begin, conceptually or actually, with the "nuts and bolts" of an adolescent medical assessment that is divorced from the psychosocial component (or which is added in a merely perfunctory manner for "completeness") will place their patient and the parents at a significant disadvantage.

With that caveat, the pediatric physician evaluating the adolescent who presents with homosexual behavior and/or orientation, should perform or arrange for a complete general physician examination. This, if done tactfully, may even provide a less threatening initial phase of evaluation. Because many adolescents will have already experienced many of the components of a complete physical exam (perhaps during previous visits for typical childhood illnesses), this aspect of the assessment may be useful for establishing rapport. For some adolescents, the directness of the exam may actually set them at ease, and make the subsequent discussion more relaxed. For others, the reverse will be true. The clinician should use his or her judgment and intuition in deciding how to proceed.

Gender will, of course, influence to some degree the nature of the physical exam. For example, a physical examination to detect STD's in females should include the mouth and anus in addition to the genitals. This is also an appropriate route of examination for males involved or suspected of being involved in homosexual behavior. This may not be intuitive, however, to clinicians not familiar with common gender-specific homosexual practices (Owen, 1986). However, the sexual history will be essential in ensuring that the exam is appropriate to the particular young person's needs. Because persons with homosexual behavior are also likely to have engaged in heterosexual behavior, the physical and laboratory assessment should not assume that any risks are solely based upon gender and sexual orientation. Lesbian sexuality is not generally thought to be associated with the spread of HIV. However, because a substantial number of teenage girls with homosexual experience may have also had heterosexual experiences, this should dictate decisions. For example, failure to consider the possibility of pregnancy in such a woman, or a similar failure to consider the possibility of HIV exposure, could be a serious oversight.

Similarly, substance abuse should always be considered, and a urine drug screen is an appropriate laboratory test. It is proper to inform the adolescent of the intended uses of a urine sample, so that even the *appearance* of deception is avoided. Those who admit to active substance abuse must be tested, if for no other reason than that the misidentification of "street drugs" is common. Screens for sexually transmitted diseases are indicated, though perhaps some latitude is possible if there is convincing evidence from the adolescent that sexual activity has not yet been entered.

Parent–Child Conference

A postevaluative planning meeting (Meeks & Martin, 1969) with the adolescents and parents is greatly to be desired. If such a meeting cannot be conducted, then the clinician will find that avenues for effective advocacy on behalf of the teenager are quite limited. What is the purpose of such a meeting, and what is to be "planned"? That will depend upon the information already gathered. In fact, a preliminary meeting at the onset can be useful to brief the parents and adolescent on the intended process of evaluation. If they know in advance that they will have an extended time for review, questions, and answers, their participation may be optimized. This will create an air of expectancy that will help to bring some degree of working unity among the family, who are likely to have been in considerable turmoil. The assignment of participatory tasks may establish a useful (if only temporary) respite for those who may feel alienated (one or both parents, or the adolescent). At this stage, the "tasks" should be mundane, such as the completion of self-report general or emotional health (Achenbach & Edelbrock, 1985) structured questionnaires.

In the parent–child conference, the clinician will probably sense that a balance must be sought between the parents' (probable) expectation or demand that "something" be done, and the adolescent's very real need for empathic understanding. In situations in which the family actually draws together (no matter how reluctantly) as part of the consultation process, the needs of the adolescent and parents will be seen to be fundamentally similar. Even in the absence of overt hostility or of a long-standing poor parent—child relationship, both young persons and parents will likely feel misunderstood, perhaps betrayed, and very uncertain about the future. If the clinician can elicit genuine expressions of determination on everyone's part to "sort some things out," so much the better. In the absence of such a possibility, a less ambitious initial offering is in order. It is ill-advised to ask for superficial or insincere expressions of support and acceptance if these are evidently lacking.

As Bell, Weinberg, and Hammersmith (1981, p. 222) point out, "As long as parents are unable to accept gender nonconformity in their children, and as long as institutional policies of various kinds reflect unkind preoccupations with stereotypical notions of what males and females are required to be, nonconformists will continue to suffer painful consequences both as they grow up and throughout adulthood." Because such unkind treatment of those who differ (or appear to differ) from expected norms, can be expected to continue for the foreseeable future, it is critical that the home be, as much as possible, a place where the person of the teenager is respected and valued. Parents will not relax their opposition to homosexual behaviors quickly, and most may not at all. Efforts to "shame" them into so doing will prove fruitless, or rather will bear poor fruit. Similarly, efforts to suggest that the adolescent somehow simply "drop" an established homosexual orientation and simultaneously and instantaneously embrace heterosexuality are quite out of line.

Efforts should first be toward reestablishing rapport between the adolescent and his or her parents. Agreeing to disagree is a useful place to begin. If the adolescent of concern is uncertain about his or her sexual orientation, or is experiencing a considerable degree of turmoil because of homosexual behaviors, inclinations, or fantasies, such rapport may be more readily developed than if a clear and unambiguous homosexual orientation is present or stated by the adolescent. However, it must be stressed that the initial stage of the process is not to change anyone, but rather to get them talking and establishing common ground. As with any healing process, the groundwork for forgiveness and reconciliation must be carefully laid. While it will be obvious by this point that the assumption of "heterosexuality when asking about partners may lead to an instant dead end with homosexual youth" (Kokotailo & Stephenson, p. 285), less directive questions such as "Is there one person to whom you're especially attracted? What is that person's name?" (Kokotailo & Stephenson, p. 285) can pave the way to an understanding of the adolescent's sexual and broader social relationships.

All teenagers face several basic sexual choices. Parents who become aware that their adolescent child has become involved in homosexuality should try to lovingly and with humility convey a message of support, hope, and responsibility to their child. Ideally, this expression of love will be an extension of the bridges of communication and caring that have been built and maintained through the previous years. Parents and adolescents alike are well advised to think, if possible, before speaking. The damage done through unkind words spoken in haste may be as difficult to undo as any real or imagined concerns about sexual orientation and behavior. It is useful to remember that "it is common for young homosexual men and women who have just 'come out' to be referred for treatment by their parents. It is a difficult time for both patients and parents" (Meyer, 1985, p. 1063). The burden of setting a tone of civility may thus fall primarily upon the parents, who are well advised to seek to set such a tone.

Some behavioral changes are needed immediately. Parents should be counseled that ridicule, name-calling, and open harassment may already be directed at their child. The only ridicule, name-calling, or harassment that parents will be able to directly control and stop is that in which they themselves may be prone to participate. It *should* stop, and sincere apologies should be extended by the parents to the child, where indicated, as they often will be. In the same vein, provocative, hostile, and otherwise disrespectful behavior on the part of the adolescent should be acknowledged, with appropriate apologies. At this stage, the healing power of a sincere apology, in the form of "I'm sorry. Will you please forgive me?," should not be underestimated.

To the degree that the adolescent has already expressed a desire for behavioral change (such as reducing or altogether avoiding high-risk sexual behavior), common ground will be immediately evident. No matter how pro- or anti-homosexual a stance they may take, reasonable parents will be concerned about the physical safety of their child, and the teenager can be encouraged to accept this concern as valid.

It is here that the clinician's mettle will be tested. Because adolescence often brings with it an illusion of invulnerability and of unlimited choices, the clinician's concerns are more likely to be in sync with those of the parents than those of the child, and certainly so if high-risk behavior is occurring or is imminent. Overt homosexual behavior, particularly in adolescent males, must be assumed dangerous, and even life-threatening. As Seidman and Rieder (1994, p. 339) note, "Recent data suggest an alarming reversal of this widespread adoption of safe sexual practices among homosexual men: the incidence of hepatitis A among homosexual men increased dramatically in five North American cities in 1991. This may reflect *unsafe sexual practices by younger cohorts* [emphasis added]." Approaches by the clinician that acknowledge this danger and present it to the adolescent and parents in a balanced way should be sought.

Experienced clinicians will resist the tendency to give sweeping assurances either to parents or to adolescents. Depending upon one's own opinion about homosexuality, it is possible to overidentify with parental concerns and desires, or, on the other hand, to overidentify with an activist social agenda. Parents, when faced with a perceived or real threat to their children's well-being, react from values that are both fairly traditional and focused on protecting their children. Such parents, no matter how tolerant of "diversity," will be anxious that their own children not be sacrificed at such a social alter. Most will also feel a moral and ethical obligation to express disapproval of premature sexuality in general, and of homosexuality in particular. Adolescents may be forced into a "pseudomature" posture if the response by the parents is not well modulated. This can lead to the youth taking a more rigid position than he or she is actually comfortable with. Just as parents are capable of demonstrating protection in a way that may be perceived as "smothering" by the adolescent, the young person can easily project a sense of independence that serves as a defense against the parents' well-intended concern.

Clinicians or parents who imagine that "doing everything possible" will guarantee an outcome acceptable to everyone need to be given assistance in achieving a less controlling stance. By the same token, adolescents who feel pressure to become, overnight, who they know they are not, may be equally frustrated. Paradoxically, it is often in focusing upon one's own contribution to disrupted relationships (rather than demanding or trying to orchestrate change in others) that reconciliation begins to emerge. Trying to run the universe is a sizeable job which some would argue is best left in more capable hands. Probably the most that should be hoped for in an initial consultation is for some level of parent–child reconciliation to occur. This will be evident in the establishment of parent–child boundaries that are neither overly rigid or overly diffuse. If the adolescent and parents can agree to respectfully discuss how to manage the future, this will be a definite measure of progress.

References

Achenbach, T. M. & Edelbrock, C. S. (1983). *Manual for the Child Behavior Checklist and Revised Child Behavior Profile*. Burlington, VT: University Associates in Psychiatry.

Aldrich, C. K. (1974). Youth's fulfillment of adult prophecies. *Australian New Zealand Journal of Psychiatry, 8*, 127–129.

Becker, J. V., & Skinner, L. J. (1985). Sexual abuse in childhood and adolescence. In D. Shaffer, A. A. Ehrhardt, & L. L. Greenhill (Eds.), *The clinical guide to child psychiatry* (pp. 336–352). New York: Free Press.

Bell, A. P., Weinberg, M. S., & Hammersmith, S. K. (1981). *Sexual preference*. Bloomington: Indiana University Press.

Boyle, M. H., & Offord, D. R. (1990). Primary prevention of conduct disorder: Issues and prospects. *Journal of the American Academy of Child and Adolescent Psychiatry, 29*(2), 227–233.

Buckner, J. C., Trickett, E. J., & Corse, S. J. (Eds.). (1985). *Primary prevention in mental health: An annotated bibliography*. National Institute Rockville, MD: of Mental Health. (DHHS Publication No. ADM 85–1405).

Cameron, P., Proctor, K., Coburn, W., Jr., Forde, N., Larson, H., & Cameron, K. (1986). Child molestation and homosexuality. *Psychological Reports, 58*, 327–337.

Cwayna, K., Remafedi, G., & Treadway, L. (1991). Caring for gay and lesbian youth. *Medical Aspects of Human Sexuality, 25*, 50–57.

Fikar, C. R. (1992). Gay teens and suicide (letter). Pediatrics, 89, 519.

Kelsey, J. L., Thompson, W. D., & Evans, A. S. (1986). *Methods in observational epidemiology*. New York: Oxford University Press.

Kirkpatrick, M. (1987). Clinical implications of lesbian mother studies. *Journal of Homosexuality, 14*, 201–211.

Kokotailo, P. K., & Stephenson, J. N. (1993). Sexuality and reproductive health behavior. In M. I. Singer, L. T. Singer & T. M. Anglin (Eds.), (pp. 249–292). *Handbook for screening adolescents at psychosocial risk*. New York: Lexington Books.

Lundy, M. S., Pfohl, B. M., & Kuperman, S. (1993). Adult criminality among formerly hospitalized child psychiatric patients. *Journal of the American Academy of Child Adolescent Psychiatry, 32*(3), 568–576.

Lundy, M. S., & Pumariega, A. J. (1993). Psychiatric hospitalization of children and adolescents: Treatment in search of a rationale. *Journal of Child and Family Studies, 2*(1), 1–4.

Meeks, J. E., & Martin, J. (1969). Teaching the techniques of the postdiagnostic family conference. *Journal of the American Academy of Child Psychiatry, 8*, 306–320.

Mellanby, A., Phelps, F., & Tripp, J. H. (1993). Teenagers, sex, and risk taking. *British Medical Journal, 307*, 25.

Meyer, J. K. (1985). Ego-dystonic homosexuality. In H. I. Kaplan & B. J. Saddock (Eds.), *Comprehensive textbook of psychiatry* (pp. 1056–1065). Baltimore: Williams & Wilkins.

Meyer-Bahlburg, H. F. L. (1993). Psychobiologic research on homosexuality. *Child and Adolescent Psychiatric Clinics of North America, 2*(3), 489–500.

Owen, W. F. (1986). The clinical approach to the male homosexual patient. *Medical Clinics of North America, 70*(3), 499–536.

Pfeffer, C. R. (1986). *The suicidal child*. New York: Guilford.

Remafedi, G. (1987). Adolescent homosexuality: Psychological and medical implications. *Pediatrics, 79*(3), 331–337.

Remafedi, G., Resnick, M., Blum, R., & Harris, L. (1992). Demography of sexual orientation in adolescents. *Pediatrics, 89*, 714–721.

Rosen, A. C., Rekers, G. A., & Bentler, P. M. (1978). Ethical issues in the treatment of children. *Journal of Social Issues, 34*(2), 122–136.

Rotheram-Borus, M. J., & Gwadz, M. (1993). Sexuality among youths at high risk. *Child and Adolescent Psychiatric Clinic of North America, 2*(3), 415–430.

Schlesselman, J. J. (1982). *Case-control studies: Design, conduct, analysis.* New York: Oxford University Press.

Seidman, S. N., & Rieder, R. O. (1994). A review of sexual behavior in the United States. *American Journal of Psychiatry, 151*, 330–341.

Shaffer, D., Philips, I., & Enzer, N. B. (Eds.). (1989). *Prevention of mental disorders, alcohol and other drug use in children and adolescents.* U.S. Department of Health and Human Services, Public Health Service, Alcohol, Drug Abuse, and Mental Health Administration, Publication No. (ADM) 89–1646. Office for Substance Abuse Prevention. (DHHS Publication No. ADM 89–1646).

Shrier, D., & Johnson, R. L. (1988). Sexual victimization of boys: An ongoing study of an adolescent medicine clinic population. *Journal of the National Medical Association, 80*(11), 1189–1193.

Thorstad, D. (1990). Man/boy love and the American gay movement. *Journal of Homosexuality, 20*, 251–252.

Utribe, V., & Harbeck, K. M. (1991). Addressing the needs of lesbian, gay, and bisexual youth: The origins of PROJECT 10 and school-based intervention. *Journal of Homosexuality, 22*(3–4), 9–28.

van den Aardweg, G. J. M. (1984). Parents of homosexuals—not guilty? *American Journal of Psychotherapy, 38*, 181–189.

Watkins, B., & Bentovim, A. (1992). The sexual abuse of male children and adolescents: A review of current research. *Journal of Child Psychology and Psychiatry, 33*(1), 197–248.

Wolfson, A. (1987). Toward the further understanding of homosexual women (panel). *Journal of the American Psychoanalytic Association, 35*, 165–173.

16

Homosexuality in Adolescence

Interventions and Ethical Considerations

Michael S. Lundy
George A. Rekers

> When a person has sex, they're not just having it with that partner, they're having it with everybody that partner has had it with for the past ten years.
>
> Otis Ray Bowen,
> Former secretary of the
> U.S. Department of Health and Human Services

Children should receive an accurate understanding of sexuality, and this understanding should begin at an early age. It should be developmentally appropriate, by which is meant that very young children should be presented with more "black and white" scenarios and with sufficient but not overwhelming detail. An understanding of homosexuality is more difficult to present in a balanced manner than is conventional heterosexual behavior. While the prevalence of homosexual behavior remains quite low—approximately 1 percent in adult men (Seidman & Rieder, 1994)—there are serious health risks that continue to be associated with the homosexual life-style. Despite the contention that this "increased risk of medical and psychosocial problems are [*sic*] presumably caused not by the sexual orientation itself but by the isolation and discrimination it generates" (Cwayna, Remafedi, & Treadway, 1991, p. 52), there is evidence that the homosexual life-style may be somehow intrinsically unhealthy (Cameron, Playfair, & Wellum, 1993). It is difficult to explain these risks on the basis of "isolation and discrimination" unless one subscribes to a purely social theory of dysfunction. Accordingly, children and adolescents need to be educated about "the challenges and struggles that may be faced" (Kokotailo & Stephenson, 1993), including life-threatening health risks, by those who are active participants in a homosexual life-style.

Education of adolescents about homosexuality must avoid the extremes

341

of fear or intimidation, on the one hand, and a libertarian social indoctrination, on the other. Both are distinct possibilities. Those who seek to advance homosexual rights and acceptance of gay and lesbian persons will, perhaps, express concern about unnecessary emphasis upon the disadvantages and health risks of the homosexual life-style; they suggest that an emphasis that increases fears about HIV may yield a "short-term benefit in reducing adolescent risk acts, with a long-term negative consequence of decreasing sexual adjustment as adults" (Rotheram-Borus & Gwadz, 1993, p. 425). On the other hand, those concerned about pro-homosexual indoctrination have argued that those "with vested interests today ransack literature for bits of fact and theory which can be pieced together into a pro-homosexual or bisexual concept of nature, man, and society" (Socarides, 1988, p. 59).

Presenting real and present dangers, without exaggerating them, is necessary. At the same time, our knowledge of adolescent sexuality suggests that, even with accurate knowledge, many teenagers will continue to engage in "high-risk sexual behavior in the face of a deadly epidemic, when . . . well-informed regarding risk . . . [due to] . . . a problem with sexual control" (Quadland & Shattls, 1987, p. 282). The hope that "rational people do not choose to put their lives in jeopardy simply to satisfy a genital urge" (Quadland & Shattls, 1987) ignores much of what is known about adolescence, particularly when the suggestibility of the teenage years is combined with conflicting societal and family expectations (Aldrich, 1974). It is possible that, in the absence of self-control, concerns of poor "sexual adjustment as adults" (Rotherman-Borus & Gwadz, 1993) might be obviated by premature death. No service is done to our children by offering them life-style options before they are properly able to evaluate those options and make informed choices about them.

Education is inadequate to change behavior. For knowledge to be effective in preventing high-risk sexual behaviors, adults must believe that the lives of young people are sufficiently worth preserving. If we are willing to present them with the whole story, or as much as is known, and courageously advise "14-year-olds to *suffer* [emphasis added] in abstinence" (Thorstad, 1990, p. 265), rather than give the irresponsible message that abstinence is too dear a price to pay (Thorstad, 1990), a good beginning will have been made. Recommendations that are based on what is already popular or trendy or (supposedly) pragmatic would seem to be inherently ineffective, as well as unnecessary. Nevertheless, the political power of what McHugh (1992) calls "fashionable convictions" and the associated inertia of what has become conventional wisdom are high. Those who advocate for the true interests of children and adolescents may find themselves at odds with much of the current dogma, both popular and official. As McHugh (1992) has observed, engagements in these matters on behalf of children are not for the fainthearted, but they may well prove necessary.

To Intervene or Not to Intervene: Rationales and Directions

It has been suggested that the previous clinical approach of offering psychotherapy for the cessation of homosexual behavior has been replaced by three options the therapist can offer at the client's request: 1) eradication of homosexual with enhancement of heterosexual capability, 2) enhancement of homosexual behavior, or 3) considering homosexual behavior irrelevant when it is thought to be functionally unrelated to other presenting symptoms" (Phillips, Fischer, Groves, & Singh, 1976). Unfortunately, this somewhat dated list of options (written before the discovery of AIDS) fails to distinguish between behavior and orientation. Homosexual *behavior* is vastly more common than homosexual *orientation*. The question of modifying a homosexual orientation is both more controversial and more difficult. Part of the controversy is related to the difficulty of change. Those who maintain that homosexuality is an acceptable life-style will cite the resistance to change as evidence that it should not even be considered, much less attempted.

Those who are concerned with the high-risk behaviors that are commonly associated with the homosexual life-style may chose to emphasize the wide discrepancy between behavior and orientation. Several observations may be offered. First, sexual orientation is usually consolidated during adolescence, but remains fluid until actually established. It may remain malleable long afterward, unlike what is popularly believed (Kirkpatrick, 1987; Pattison & Pattison, 1980). Second, the vast majority of individuals—roughly 99 percent—are destined to develop a conventional heterosexual orientation, including those adolescents who experiment with homosexual behaviors (Kinsey, Pomeroy, & Martin, 1948; Remafedi, Resnick, Blum, & Harris, 1992; Seidman & Rieder, 1994). Third, the homosexual life-style itself is associated with tremendous social and personal disadvantage in the form of moral condemnation (Bennett, 1972), adolescent emotional dysfunction, substance abuse, sexually transmitted diseases (STDs), school problems, high suicide risk and foreshortened life-span from other, nonspecific causes (Cameron, Playfair, & Wellum, 1993).

Given the statistical probability of a heterosexual outcome for overt teenage homosexual behavior in the absence of intervention, the possibility of either a heterosexual or nonhomosexual adjustment even in the face of some degree of homosexual orientation in adolescence would seem to be high. Opportunities for reducing high-risk behavior become apparent. With regard to parental influence, it has been suggested that clinicians should encourage attitudes and child-rearing practices of parents that support a conventional gender role and discourage gender nonconformity (van den Aardweg, 1984). However, there is much more to establishing healthy patterns of sexual behavior than childrearing designed to encourage gender conformity. Parents who concern themselves exclusively or even primarily with issues related to gender orientation to the neglect of more foundational issues related to self-control, may contribute to a pattern of irresponsible heterosexual behavior in adolescence. Attitudes that permit or encourage sexual irresponsibility of any sort are incompatible with the promotion of healthy life-styles.

With respect to behavioral changes, adult sexual orientation tends to be more fixed than that of youth, thus more resistant to change. But the developmental plasticity of childhood and youth present substantial possibilities for change, if desired (Rekers, 1978). The rationale for such intervention is *not* to be based upon mere statistical likelihood, but instead based upon the desire of the child and parents. Adolescents, similarly, who are in the process of exploring their sexuality may "reject" homosexual behavior *even while engaging in it*, on the basis of religious or moral reasons, which may reflect their parent's values. An uninformed overemphasis on "self-determination" that fails to present an adolescent with true and informed choices can lead to prematurely and inappropriately burdening an adolescent with the label of 'homosexual'—a process that tends to produce unfortunate 'self-fulfilling' results (Rekers, 1977). Even those who are advocates of an increased legitimacy of homosexual life-styles will find common ground with those more comfortable with mere "toleration." This commonality may be found in the desirability of guiding young people away from premature sexuality and from early choices that may greatly restrict and lower the quality of subsequent choices.

Changes in Behavior, Changes in Orientation

Any overt sexual behavior that is age-inappropriate may be viewed as simply premature, and discouraged on that basis alone, whether homosexual or heterosexual. This is an ancient human insight, expressed by Augustine of Hippo when he wrote of his youth, "I was in love with loving." The added twentieth-century risk factors associated with homosexual behavior and orientation would add to the concerns about premature sexuality (Remafedi, 1987). Given the previously discussed tendency of adolescent homosexual activity to consist of very high-risk behavior (Remafedi, 1987; Utribe & Harbeck, 1992) and the equally disconcerting evidence that adolescents who begin sexual activity early are likely to continue to engage in such activity in spite of educational intervention (Howard & McCabe, 1990), such cautions are well grounded. Seidman and Reider (1994, p. 334) note that "once they are sexually experienced, adolescents do not generally plan intercourse; they have multiple, serial sexual relationships. . . . Unlike adults, a much smaller proportion remain sexually exclusive for a year or more; most have had many sex partners and continue to have new partners. Yet, like both age groups, most do not use condoms at every sexual encounter." It is not necessary to be hostile to the homosexual *person* (or even unsympathetic to the acceptability of such a life-style) to be worried about probable health consequences, particularly those associated with male homosexual behavior.

Persons concerned with the physical safety of adolescents will note that it is, indeed, easier to delay the onset of a behavior than to later modify an established behavioral pattern (Rotheram-Borus & Gwadz, 1993). Intervention that stresses premature consolidation of sexual orientation through broadening actual sexual experiences, or which refuses (on philosophical or supposedly pragmatic grounds) to recommend programs designed to delay sexual activity, will reduce choices for the adolescent. Young persons will be left with the far more difficult task of changing established, maladaptive behaviors, rather than maintaining existing abstinence (primary or secondary) until maturity.

As Rutter (1971, p. 271) notes, "Increasing sexual activity may serve to whet the appetite rather than deplete the drive." While it is relatively without controversy that "behavioral change is the most effective preventive measure for sexually transmitted disease, and it is the only effective prevention for HIV" (Seidman & Rieder, 1994, p. 331) among persons already sexually active, it is less evident that, in order for "appropriate behavioral change to occur, individuals need both *knowledge* (i.e., of HIV status and modes of HIV transmission) and *judgment* [emphasis added]" (Seidman & Rieder, 1994, p. 331). The observed behavior of persons who become prematurely sexual active is demonstrably lacking in this essential combination of knowledge and judgment (Planned Parenthood, 1987). In spite of wide spread, school-based education about AIDS, "many adolescents who are sexually active have multiple, serial sexual relationships, and the vast majority do not consistently use condoms" (Seidman & Rieder, 1994, p. 333). While one might argue that "rational people do not choose to put their lives in jeopardy simply to satisfy a genital urge" (Quadland & Shattls, 1987, p. 282), this ignores the great capacity of every person, young and old alike, to act in ways that are highly destructive. It is perhaps the height of folly to believe that the young of our demonstrably irrational species would act contrary to their natural inclinations without clear expectations from less irrational adults that they do so. Such expectations should be conveyed over time, in a manner that imparts both the knowledge and the judgment necessary to avoid self-destructive behavior. It is to be hoped that the shift from a "traditional association between sexuality and life. . . . by a new and devastating association between sexuality and death" will effect a positive as well as a "profound influence on the sexual attitudes, values, and behaviors of homosexual men in particular, and all sexually active people in general" (Quadland & Shattls, 1987, p. 279). Such a positive influence can serve to restore the vital association between sexuality and life by reestablishing sexuality as something to be reserved for and enjoyed in lifelong committments rather than as a given in casual and short-term relationships. Adults can convey this expectation only if they also demonstrate their own personal commitments to achieving and maintaining well-adjusted sexuality within the boundaries of permanent, monogomous relationships.

Some consider it "wrong, cruel, and irrational to attempt to *force* [emphasis added] a person to change his or her sexual orientation" (Fikar & Koslap-Petraco, 1992, p. 12). Whether or not such persons would distinguish between transient homosexual *behavior* as commonly evidenced in adolescence and *orientation* is not clear. Those homosexual adults who have changed their sexual behavior (from homosexuality to abstinence) without attempting to change their orientation make a clear distinction. A member of Courage, a Roman Catholic support organization for gays and lesbians who wish to change their behavior, stated, "Celibacy is peaceful. I like it. I spent years in the gay scene—years full of turbulence. I pray. I have friends here. I do my work, and I find support here" (Harvey, 1988, p. 71).

Those who are persuaded that healthy sexuality is always essentially heterosexual in nature may have some conceptual difficulties in distinguishing between degrees of maladaptiveness that may cross conventional boundaries of classification. Thus, it is useful to see that there are categories of severity that are to be distinguished from one another. Promiscuity is unhealthy (Seidman & Rieder, 1994). While some might argue that male homosexual promiscuity is somehow "worse" (in the sense of being more risky) than heterosexual promiscuity, this is becoming progressively a less tenable argument with the rise of AIDS among non-drug-abusing heterosexuals. Traditional religious thought, though, *has* distinguished between "degrees of sin," but not necessarily along patterns with which twentieth-century Americans are familiar. As the 17*th* century reformers so precisely articulated at Westminster (Westminster Confession of Faith, 1985, p. 238): "All transgressions of the law . . . are not equally heinous; but some sins in themselves, and by reason of several aggravations, are more heinous . . . than others . . . if done deliberately, willfully, presumptuously, impudently, boastingly, maliciously, *frequently* [emphasis added], obstinately, with delight, continuance, or relapsing after repentance."

The linkage between sexual orientation and promiscuity is problematic. While there is evidence to support the perception of fairly widespread promiscuity among male homosexuals (Shilts, 1988; Seidman & Rieder, 1994), a condemnation of promiscuity because it is homosexual without an equally unambiguous condemnation of heterosexual promiscuity is morally and intellectually dishonest. Those who are opposed to homosexuality in principle must avoid a common error in logic by which a promiscuous heterosexual is somehow accorded a higher moral standing than an abstinent homosexual. On the other hand, those who are supportive of increasing acceptance of homosexuals must avoid a similar trap that assumes that a stance against promiscuity is to be dismissed as "heteronormative" and "arguments of the right wing" (Thorstad, 1990). The tendency of many sexually active adolescents to display little moderation in their appetites (Seidman & Rieder, 1994) is clear, and such immoderate behavior is particularly prominent at an early age among homosexual youth (Remafedi, 1987; Utribe & Harbeck, 1991). Accordingly, the burden of proof is upon those who believe premature sexual activity to be reliably or even regularly associated with the responsible sexuality of maturity. Except through a paradoxical injunction, it is difficult to imagine how attitudes that overtly or covertly promote behavior that is rarely practiced with good judgment during adolescence (Ayd, 1987) can be expected to produce sexually mature behavior in immature people.

Some, while acknowledging the very real risks associated with male homosexuality in particular, would nevertheless argue against attempts to change orientation. Meyer-Bahlburg (1993, p. 496), for example, argues that "the fact that homosexuality per se is not a psychiatric diagnosis implies that treatment with the goal of changing homosexual orientation is inappropriate . . . I give all families the explicit message that there are many opinions in our society about homosexuality, both negative and positive ones; that the mental health professionals do not consider homosexuality as a mental illness; and that we do not recommend any treatment for homosexuality itself." Such an opinion, however, would be contested by those who maintain that personal freedom and desire for such change is a higher criteria by which to judge the appropriateness of intervention than whether or not certain behaviors are listed as psychiatric diagnoses or not. Furthermore, even Meyer-Bahlburg (1993) recognizes a need to "present this message after good rapport has been established, or a homophobic inquirer may break off the contact and shop around for a mental health professional who offers an antihomosexual stance" (p. 497). Concern has been expressed as to whether intervention for boys known to be at risk for homosexual outcome is consistent with the preferred long-term interest of society (Winkler, 1977). Others insist that it "is important to realize that freedom of sexual expression is accomplished when individuals are not oppressed by their own, as well as society's, perceived needs, but when they are free to make choices about their sexual lives" (Quadland & Shattls, 1987, p. 293).

When adolescent homosexual behavior or orientation is causing distress or health risks, then some form of intervention is indicated. Since the very nature of homosexual experimentation in adolescence, particularly among males, is associated with very high risk, the need for intervention, or at least education, is assumed, due to the high likelihood of exposure to real life-threatening danger. *It is the very presence of such risk factors in the individual adolescent that gives some confidence that risk reduction is feasible.*

The delay of overt sexual behavior during adolescence—homosexual *or* heterosexual—is perhaps the most clear-cut means by which risk can be reduced. Alteration of patterns of behavior, or delaying their onset, while undoubtedly related to orientation, should not be equated with a change in orientation. However, the level of controversy surrounding even this approach—altering established or incipient behavioral patterns—is high. Nevertheless, the rationale for deferment of overt sexual activity among those who are not yet sexually active is compelling. As Seidman and Reider (1994, p. 332) point out, "[Premature] first sexual intercourse has been associated with risky behaviors such as using drugs, not using contraception at first intercourse, having more sex partners, and having more frequent intercourse. It may also be a marker for other sexual behaviors that place an individual at greater risk for sexually transmitted disease, such as lack of condom use, less discriminating recruitment of sex partners, and having multiple sex partners in a short period of time. Finally, early age at first intercourse is directly linked to sexually transmitted disease. . . . Its role in a constellation of high-risk behaviors . . . makes early first intercourse a natural target for research and public health intervention."

Abstinence-based prevention programs are gaining momentum. A school-based program in Atlanta, associated with a major medical university, was designed and implemented with the express goal of delaying the onset of sexual activity among school children. The program was based upon the goal

> of postponing sexual involvement for two reasons: First, minors below the age of 16 years are not capable of understanding the full implications of their actions. And secondly, minors younger than 16 typically are not sufficiently mature to anticipate and manage the consequences of sexual behavior. (Planned Parenthood Poll, 1987)

They offered evidence that for some young people, the program was effective, in that program participation resulted in increased delay of sexual involvement. They also found the program to be ineffective in influencing the sexual activity of students with sexual experience prior to participation in the program. This program was designed with the assumption that all teenagers are sexual beings, and thus given the peer pressure (Planned Parenthood Poll, 1987) and the strong physiological drives of teenage years, are "at risk" for premature sexual involvement. The choice of an age limit of 16 appears to have been arbitrary, but was perhaps based upon the knowledge that many more 16 year olds, as compared to 13 year olds, have *already* become sexually active. The study did *not* specifically state that persons older than 16 are necessarily "mature enough to deal with the consequences of their sexual actions." The failure of the program to effect the behavior of those already sexually active is not surprising. The relatively rare combination of the requisite knowledge and judgment (Seidman & Rieder, 1994) necessary for controlled sexual activity in adolescence is one reason. In addition, the program design had targeted those at risk for initiating premature sexual activity. It was not designed to influence those who, mature or immature, had become sexually active. It did not appear designed to target students of any particular sexual orientation.

"Safe sex" has become the buzzword of the 1990s. However, there is little to suggest that adolescents are capable of displaying the habits of sexual control that some advocates believe are necessary to reduce risk. The earlier that sexual activity begins, the more casual is the attitude adopted toward high-risk behavior. Again, it must be emphasized that "those starting sex under 16 exhibited a high degree of risk taking, including having sex . . . in short-term relationships" (Mellanby, Phelps, & Tripp, 1993, p. 25). Those who are truly concerned with safe sex should consider that, for most adolescents, the only truly safe sex is delayed sex—that is, sex that is delayed until maturity. The difficulty of delaying sexual activity until maturity should not be underestimated, particularly in an age where conventional morality has not only been challenged, but to a substantial degree discarded. As Bayer (1981, p. 6) notes, "Renunciation, restraint, and inhibition, so crucial to the periods of human history characterized by scarcity and to the era of early capitalist development, are now perceived as old-fashioned virtues."

Those who are themselves sexual libertarians may have some difficulty in recommending delaying sexual activities to adolescents. Thorstad (1990, p. 265), an open advocate for explicit and unlimited childhood sexual freedom, asks, rhetorically, "Is it appropriate for gay adults to advise gay 14-year-olds to suffer in abstinence? Does this differ from the arguments of the right wing in favor of abstinence and against contraception?" His point is well taken. Practically, there would appear to be little difference. Those who are concerned with the well-being of young people, however, cannot afford to allow their own sexual orientation (homosexual or heterosexual) or their own political conservatism or libertarianism to blind them to effective strategies of intervention for risk reduction. Thorstad (1990, p. 252), however, emphasizes that "sex is fun, homosexuality is fun, boy-love is fun, gay liberation is a movement for everyone's sexual liberation." He laments that "the gay movement limits its concerns to what consenting adults do in private. In the era of AIDS, it has de-emphasized sex, and seeks to sanitize the image of homosexuality to facilitate its entrance into the social mainstream. The sexual needs of young people have been devalued in favor of an upwardly mobile adult gay middle class. . . . In short, the gay movement's agenda is being determined increasingly by straight society, rather than by homosexuals themselves" (p. 252).

Perhaps it is possible that society, both heterosexual and homosexual (excluding certain extremists), is beginning to agree upon certain issues and standards of conduct that affect all of society. Adult homosexual males—much less adolescents—have not practiced the "safe sex" that is being so widely promoted (Seidman & Rieder, 1994). Condoms, in particular, touted as potentially able to slow or even prevent the spread of AIDS, have been found to be both mechanically unreliable and generally unacceptable to adult homosexual men. Adolescents appear even less likely to employ them; in fact, according to Seidman and Reiter (1994, p. 333), *"the vast majority do not consistently use condoms"* [emphasis added]. Even were they used religiously, there is little reason to be cavalier about their likely impact. A 26 percent condom failure rate was recently documented in a research setting. The investigators concluded that they had "not answered the question of whether condoms offer complete protection. Since this can never be guaranteed, they should be used with restraint. *Changes in sexual behavior remain the main goal* [emphasis added]" (Wigersma & Oud, 1987, p. 94). Even those who are, on principle, opposed to the practice of homosexuality, should agree that the adoption of such a life-style, as evidenced by both behavior and orientation, is a choice best deferred until maturity is reached. Hopefully, those who are outspoken advocates for legitimization of homosexuality will acknowledge that the potential decimation (by AIDS) of younger generations through early and promiscuous homosexual behavior is undesirable, and avoidable.

Those who, with good intentions, offer options to young people which are beyond their maturity may adversely affect the future choices available to these adolescents. Aldrich (1974) explains the problem:

> Thus the expectations of society in general or of the community in particular as expressed in the media, through police, teachers and other caregivers, or through ordinary social interaction appear to have a sanctioning effect on the control systems of young people that is analogous to that of parental expectations. The expectations from the two sources may be in phase or out of phase: thus, parental expectation of delinquent behavior appears to be balanced against the community expectation of conforming behavior, with the balance tipped in one or the other direction according to the strengths of the respective expectation. Parental expectation of socially acceptable behavior may or may not be strong enough to counteract the contrary expectations of the delinquent subculture. When the two kinds of expectations are in phase, the outcome is more predictable. (p. 128)

Aldrich (1974, p. 129) cautions that "educational procedures . . . education aimed at . . . prevention . . . can result in a greater rather than a reduced incidence if the educational emphasis communicates an expectation that the target group will" engage in the behavior, such as premature sexual activity. Today, with official government programs promoting "safe sex" preferentially over traditional abstinence, it would appear that the natural proclivity of adolescents to indulge themselves has been placed in phase with powerful societal expectations that they practice such short-sighted self-indulgence.

The expectation of careful, mature sexual self-control *and* overt sexual activity in adolescence is inconsistent with an informed understanding of the cognitive and emotional development of adolescents. Those young people who become sexually active at an early age are likely to develop a pattern of continued premature, frequent, and unprotected sexual activity, and are likely to be sexually abused, display emotional disturbance, and have substance abuse problems (Cwayna, Remafedi, & Treadway, 1991; Seidman & Reider, 1994). Those adolescents who identify themselves as gay are at particular risk, as are those who are incarcerated, mentally ill, or who live in inner city areas (Remafedi, 1987). Rotheram-Borus and Gwadz (1993, p. 417) claim that "the onset of early sexual activity is problematic because young adolescents may be limited in their ability to anticipate realistically the consequences of their actions or assess risk situations." Further, they (1993, p. 426) state that "sexual risk behaviors do not occur in isolation and are typically associated with other high-risk acts, such as substance abuse, delinquency, emotional distress, and trouble at school."

Curiously, these very authors essentially minimize abstinence-based prevention programs as unworkable on the grounds that "almost all adolescents become sexually active *at some point during their lives*" (p. 425). Presumably adulthood represents a point on this continuum, yet they further argue that increased fears about HIV may yield only a "short-term benefit in reducing adolescent risk acts, with a long-term negative consequence of decreasing sexual adjustment as adults" (Rotheram-Borus & Gwadz, 1993, p. 425). Evidence for such a point of view is lacking. In fact, evidence to the contrary reveals that adult sexual adjustment is actually enhanced by delaying sexual involvement. Hypoactive sexual desire disorder, or HSDD (American Psychiatric Association, 1987) has been linked not "to a lack of experience during adolescence," but rather it was noted that "HSDD patients were significantly more likely than controls to have engaged in premarital intercourse" (Yates, 1993, p. 453). While acknowledging that if "a primary prevention approach is to be adopted, the first target is to delay and to reduce sexual behaviors among adolescents (p. 425)" because "it is far easier to delay the onset of a risk than it is to change a behavior that has already been acquired or experienced (p. 425), Rotheram-Borus and Gwatz (1993, p. 425) concede that "political issues immediately emerge" when discussing prevention programs for teenagers. It is to be hoped that conscientious professionals will put the life and health of those young persons under their care before the whims of political correctness. A certain reserve is in order in considering the pronouncements of those who maintain that "everyone is doing it," and that we must therefore base our educational and preventive efforts upon this "eventuality." As George Santayana observed, "Skepticism is the chastity of the intellect, and it is shameful to surrender it too soon or to the first comer."

Intervention

Because sexually active "young teenagers are more likely to expose themselves to risks and less likely to use contraception [i.e., condoms] than their older counterparts" (Mellanby, Phelps, & Tripp, 1993, p. 25), and because modification of acquired high-risk behavior is exceedingly difficult, and not likely to result in a stable set of healthy behaviors (Seidman & Rieder, 1994), the intervention of first choice is primary prevention. Unless clinicians, educators, and parents embrace this possibility with conviction, and convey it to young people, the language of "safe sex" may be spoken, but to little practical avail. Secondary prevention should be just that, and while it does have a place, choosing it first or as if it were equivalent to and as effective as primary prevention is a mistaken strategy. It is unfortunate that an approach that is both effective and possible to maintain, abstinence, has been challenged in favor of one that is both much more difficult to achieve and to maintain in adolescence, sexual moderation. Those who advocate for moderation without first establishing and supporting a developmentally necessary period of self-control may find that adolescents who do not learn the practice of self-denial may be unable and unwilling to practice moderation. These adolescents become like Augustine of Hippo, who in his self-indulgent youth, said, "Give me chastity and continence, but not just now." Greater wisdom was voiced by Samuel Johnson when he observed, "Abstinence is as easy to me as temperance would be difficult."

Those who insist that it is a ready possibility for adolescents to exercise moderation (as opposed to chastity) should consider whether parents, teenagers, and society would be better off dealing with the consequences of the practice of this so-called moderation (not to mention the inevitable failures to maintain it), or better served by efforts that manage the failures of a nonambivalent commitment to delayed sexual involvement. It is difficult to postulate any harmful consequences to the practice of abstinence throughout the immature period that characterizes adolescence. Overt sexual experimentation and regular sexual activity have, do, and will continue to occur in adolescence. Current school and government efforts notwithstanding, these authors will not endorse the encouragement of premature sexual activity, and do not wish to propagate the fallacious notion that "mature premature" sexual activity is possible. Many may disagree with this stance, and those who are uncomfortable with it will find plenty of sex education programs that are prepackaged to present opinions that are more agreeable to them. The burden of proof, however, rests upon those who claim that "safe sex" in adolescence is a viable option for our young people. In an era of AIDS and other painful long-term consequences of irresponsible sexual behavior, is it too much to recommend what is *really* safe, even if unpopular in some quarters?

The modification of sexual behavior has already been distinguished from modification of sexual orientation. It has been argued that the modification of high-risk behavior—an urgent priority—is a secondary defense. The primary prevention of high-risk sexual behaviors should be pursued by encouraging young people to delay sexual activity until they reach maturity. Such advice, while currently unpopular, is gaining favor with those who are concerned about increasing rates of STDs, teenage pregnancies, and the spread of AIDS by both heterosexual and homosexual activity.

Abstinence is not a pipe dream. Kokotailo and Stephenson (1993) argue that abstinence is a method that can work:

> With the extensive media coverage of the problem of premature sexual activity and the ensuing problems . . . counsellors and health professionals may feel that they have little influence on a teenager's decision to remain sexually abstinent. Although the United States has witnessed a trend of earlier and more frequent sexual activity by adolescents, many teenagers remain abstinent. The majority of early and middle adolescents are not sexually active. . . . Abstinence should be seen as a viable option for young people. Delay of sexual activity allows an adolescent to mature cognitively, prior to assuming the responsibility of expressing sexuality through intercourse. (pp. 257–259)

Unless professionals consider the viability of healthy options, they may be inclined to neglect them or recommend them with little enthusiasm. Kokotailo and Stephenson (1993, p. 259) observe that "health care providers and counsellors who deal with children and adolescents are often reluctant to offer education and counselling about abstinence and sexuality. They frequently feel uncomfortable in their own counselling skills." This discomfort in skill level may also reflect discomfort with the directive nature of counseling, which is value-laden and which recommends a specific strategy to the adolescent for maintaining abstinence (primary or secondary). Those who are inclined to overly identify with the young person should consider whether or not they may be having trouble setting appropriate adult–child boundaries. It will be helpful for professionals to remember that the establishment of emotional intimacy among peers is a much more arduous task than that of engaging in overt sexual acts. Not only is physical intimacy not essential to the development of a more general sexual intimacy (Kokotailo & Stephenson, 1993, p. 260), its premature or casual expression may serve to hinder the development of a stable and rewarding intimacy (Mosher & Cross, 1971; Schumm & Rekers, 1984).

Adolescents should be presented with *real* information about their sexuality, and not merely a set of "equivalent" behaviors that are presented without any intrinsic value. Kokotailo and Stephenson (1993, 260) argue that younger adolescents need to be taught that *abstinence is normal* for their age-group. It will be useful to point out to those adolescents struggling (or *not* struggling) with homosexual desires, that abstinence is not a "heterosexual" concept, and that the overt "expression of same-sex orientation can be suppressed until early adulthood, or it can be delayed indefinitely" (Kokotailo & Stephenson, 1993, (p. 285).

The following guidelines were proposed by then U.S. Secretary of Education William Bennett for guiding children and adolescents into healthy patterns of sexual behavior:

1. Help children develop clear standards of right and wrong
   • Teach restraint as a virtue.
   • Present sex education within a moral context.
   • Speak up for the institution of the family.
   • Set clear and specific rules regarding behavior.
2. Set a good example
   • Demonstrate moral standards through personal example.
   • Follow the principles of good health.
   • Demonstrate responsibility for others in personal relationships.
3. Help children resist social pressures to engage in dangerous activities
   • Help students identify negative pressures.
   • Be attentive to children's behavior inside and outside of school.
   • Encourage students to provide a good example to their peers.
   • Be able to discuss drugs knowledgeably.
4. Instruct children about AIDS
   • Provide facts about AIDS.
   • Talk to children about their fears.
   • Teach sex in a way that emphasizes the reasons for abstinence, restraint, and responsibility.
   • Get the community involved in AIDS education.
   • Teach drug prevention to children.
   • Find appropriate opportunities to discuss AIDS. (*Aids and the Education of Our Children*, 1987).

The overall tone and intent of this guideline remains useful in formulating approaches for all children and adolescents.

Such an approach of informed responsibility is to be encouraged whether or not any change in sexual orientation is desired or deemed likely. Given the particular high-risk status of male homosexuals, delayed sexual activity in this group would be particularly beneficial. Those who dismiss it as impractical or who criticize it as outdated should consider the degree to which they are exhibiting a particularly pernicious form of homophobia, one that encourages sexual activity under conditions most likely to increase the prevalence of HIV sero positivity in the homosexual community.

Clinicians will be presented with increasing opportunities to put aside seeming moral and philosophical differences and work toward developing and evaluating abstinence-based sex education programs. Only if such programs are developed, honestly implemented, and rigorously compared to programs that have a very different emphasis will it be possible to determine their relative effectiveness. Abstinence-based programs, if carefully constructed and implemented, offer considerable advantages over combined abstinence and "safe sex" programs versus "safe sex"–only approaches. The presentation of delaying sexual involvement through primary or secondary abstinence must establish abstinence as an unequivocal priority. On the other hand, presenting abstinence as only one of several "neutral" approaches to teenage sexuality is not likely to be effective. Advocacy for age-appropriate adolescent sexual responsibility through abstinence must arise from clinicians and educators who, for the sake of the young people whose lives are at stake, are able to put aside any narrow heterosexual or homosexual agendas. It may encourage some professionals to know that teenagers themselves appear to be leading a movement to promote abstinence (Brown, 1993). This is ironic in the face of some adult expectations which argue that such an approach is "idealistic" or "naive" or otherwise doomed to failure. It is to be hoped that this attitude on the part of adults—who may have some justification for their cynicism—will not pluck defeat from the jaws of victory.

An example of the degree to which homosexual orientation is tolerated, homosexual behavior repudiated, and the worth of the homosexual person is respected is evident in the numerous "ex-gay" programs that have developed nationwide. These efforts tend to be religiously affiliated and staffed by persons who classify themselves as "ex-gay" or "ex-lesbian." Initial emphasis is, appropriately, on establishing sexual behavioral control (Quadland & Shattls, 1987). The actual goals of the various groups differ. Some maintain that only a complete change in orientation is adequate (Pattison & Pattison, 1980). Others maintain that celibacy is an appropriate goal for most homosexuals, given that a change in orientation is a much more difficult goal to achieve, and one that may not even be indicated (Harvey, 1988). Still other groups express differing philosophies, but all begin with behavioral changes. Currently, these organizations are directed toward adults wishing to leave the homosexual life-style, but local chapters may have services available for adolescents and their families (see Exodus International in the References for a list of these organizations).

While these organizations primarily serve adults who wish to change their sexual life-style, some principles from their approaches transfer to the care of adolescents. Their emphasis on peer support, mutual accountability, and self-discipline are approaches that apply whether the goal is to effect behavioral change or actual change in orientation. Specifically, successful change in sexual orientation in adults appears to be related to the presence of a robust and vital religious life. Of note, the presence or absence of a strong religious orientation in young persons determines, in part, whether or not homosexuality develops in adolescence. A large survey of high school students revealed that "religiosity was negatively associated with all dimensions of homosexuality," though this association was, for unclear reasons, limited to boys (Remafedi et al., 1992).

Motivation for change is apparently crucial. Furthermore, it is highly correlated with personal beliefs. Behavioral change typically follows a change in values, which is itself commonly induced by a religious conversion (Pattison & Pattison, 1980). Others have noted that value absolutes are necessary for motivation and actual change, and find that "there is no adequate substitute for a spiritual support system for homosexual persons" (Harvey, 1988 p. 67). On the other hand, a change in values in another direction may follow increasing involvement with a homosexual life-style that is not compatible with conservative Christian religion.

Case Study 1: Larry

Sixteen year old Larry's father called to schedule a psychotherapy session for his teenaged son. He explained that he had recently discovered that Larry had been engaged in a homosexual relationship with a man in his mid-20s, and that the relationship had been going on for nearly a year. The family was active in the Roman Catholic church, and Larry's father explained that he would not schedule an appointment for Larry to see a doctor unless the doctor agreed with him that his son's homosexual behavior was not in his best interest.

In the initial session, Larry was guarded, but embarrassingly acknowledged that he had engaged in mutual manual genital stimulation, oral receptive, oral insertive, and anal receptive homosexual behavior several times weekly with his adult partner. He stated that this was his first and only homosexual partner, and that the adult male had initiated the sexual relationship, which he agreed to hesitatingly at first. This man was a source of many gifts, including cash, an expensive stereo, and transportation. Larry had decided that he "must be a homosexual" because the man had initiated sexual behavior with him and because he became sexually aroused (to the point of orgasm) with the man. Further, he gradually began to enjoy their sexual relationship more and more over the 11 months of their relationship. However, he expressed considerable anguish and conflict over his sexual behavior, describing his strong Roman Catholic beliefs and his inner desire to confess the homosexual behavior to his priest. However, he had been too embarrassed to mention his sexual behavior with the priest, and he began to feel added guilt for failing to confess his sexual sin over the past 11 months. His homosexual behavior also led him to experience major conflicts over his male identity. He felt that in some senses, he was serving like a "wife" to his sexual partner who preferred that Larry serve in the receptive sexual role.

Although psychotherapy was his father's idea, Larry quickly established an open therapeutic relationship, being relieved that there was someone whom he could talk to about his otherwise secret conflicts. The initial therapy sessions centered on clarifying what Larry's goals would be for psychotherapy. He vacillated between wanting to resolve his guilt over sexual behavior condemned by his church and disapproved by of his parents versus wanting to continue the homosexual relationship for its monetary and sexual gratifications. For the initial three months of psychotherapy, he displayed ego-dystonic homosexual conflicts, and he expressed a preference to work toward the goal of ceasing his homosexual behavior and attempting to reshape his sexual orientation to being heterosexual.

However, Larry experienced increasing conflict with his parents, and his father angrily "threw him out of the house," so Larry moved in with his homosexual partner. Now Larry was even more dependent upon the material support available from his sexual partner. From the time that he moved in with his sexual partner, he began to dismiss his previously stated strong spiritual commitment, and he began to strongly pursue the possibility of permanently living a homosexual life-style. Thus, in the fifth month of therapy, he firmly abandoned his prior goal to reorient as a heterosexual, and he declined therapeutic consideration of ceasing his high risk anal-receptive homosexual behavior.

At age 17, Larry dropped out of psychotherapy, deciding that he was no longer motivated to cease living in a homosexual lifestyle. Since he was no longer living in his father's house, his father decided that he no longer had influence over Larry to persuade him to continue in therapy, although the father expressed willingness to continue paying for psychotherapy for his son if his son should decide he needed future sessions.

In the above situation, the adolescent's motivation for entering "treatment" was based upon a hope to please his father. Given the poor quality of that relationship, and the father's seeming lack of interest in his son as a person, the outcome was perhaps predictable.

Case Study 2: Debby

"I'm coming to talk with you for my parents' sake only," Tammy stated, as she kept the office visit that had obviously been arranged for her. Tammy was 17, and her parents had insisted that she seek psychological help.

Tammy spoke honestly about herself, but she was not at all sure that she wanted to end her homosexual relationship with Laura, a college sophomore. Although Tammy and Laura both claimed to be Christians, and that homosexual practices were wrong, they had been involved in a homosexual relationship for seven months. Neither wanted to end it, even though they felt guilty.

Tammy experienced several conflicts related to her homosexual behavior. At home, tension increased after her brother and parents had learned about her affair with Laura. Sometimes the conflict was open. For example, her father often told her, "Sexual sin is just like smoking—all you have to do is decide to quit, and then quit, cold turkey." Tammy would complain that he did not understand. At times the conflict was indirect, as when her brother would look at her disapprovingly and shake his head.

Tammy had made an apparently solid commitment to the Christian faith several years previous. She noted, "Usually, I try to put my beliefs about sex completely out of my mind, but I can't avoid thinking about how my beliefs and my life are going in opposite directions. I feel stuck. I can't give up my Christian beliefs, but I can't give up Laura, either." Tammy's guilt over her homosexual experiences had caused her to increasingly avoid attending the youth meetings and worship services at her church over the preceding year.

Tammy was upset about having to continuously be on guard so that people wouldn't discover her homosexuality. In group settings with Laura, Tammy felt inhibited and unnatural; she couldn't be her "real self." She and Laura also sneaked about and lied in order to arrange times together alone. Tammy was more and more uncomfortable about deceiving her friends and family, and she disliked herself for living a double life.

Tammy's identity conflict intensified. "I've always thought of myself eventually getting married and having children. I really want to be a mother someday." But to continue her relationship with Laura, she avoided dating boys. Laura's jealousy of the attention boys showed Tammy was distressing. At the same time, while Tammy did not dislike boys, she wondered if she could ever feel the same intense love for a man that she felt for Laura.

Tammy was able to openly explore her options in therapy. She could not tolerate the idea of giving up Laura, nor could she stand the idea of remaining in conflict with her family, her religion, her social contacts, and herself. Between the sixth and seventh therapy session, Tammy broke up with Laura. She had told her that the relationship could not continue because it was wrong. "What a relief! It's like a heavy load of guilt has been taken off my back. I never thought it would make that kind of difference. Oh, it still hurts to think I won't see her much anymore, but this is what I have to do."

Tammy elected to move away from a developing homosexual life-style and toward a more conventional, heterosexual adjustment. She remained in psychotherapy for months to help her in the various transitions, and also resumed active involvement in a church near her college, where she found both moral and spiritual support.

A study of a nonclinical "folk treatment" of homosexual orientation is instructive. Pattison & Pattison (1980) documented that those adult homosexuals who made a successful transition to heterosexuality were active in church and they believed that homosexual activity is wrong. "All regretted having been homosexual, and all had considered giving it up. They wanted to change to heterosexuality as a religious responsibility" (p. 1558). Significantly, the desire to change came only after the religious conversion of the ex-gays. Because the church with which the subjects affiliated was very accepting of homosexual persons yet intolerant of sexual activity outside of heterosexual marriage, and because there was no coercive effort to make the homosexual men "change their homosexuality" (Pattison & Pattison, 1980), the possibility of change was promoted by personal acceptance into an alternative community.

Similar principles apply in helping to establish a supportive environment within the home of the adolescent. Parents and siblings need to demonstrate acceptance of the adolescent who is showing homosexual orientation and/or behavior. A demand that orientation change is only likely to result in alienation. On the other hand, the rejection of premature overt sexual behavior (homosexual or heterosexual) along with the expectation that all adolescents within the home will conform to a specific moral code (Aldrich, 1974) will create an atmosphere in which mutual acceptance and mutual change are possible. If the parents and adolescent can agree upon certain common goals, which should be deliberately simple and pragmatic, there is reason to believe that progress toward those goals can be achieved.

As noted previously, the delay of overt sexual behavior is sought. For this to be possible, there must be adequate and age-appropriate substitutes for overt sexuality. The degree to which orientation change is desired, or simple behavioral control is sought, will determine the nature of substitutive behaviors that may be introduced. It is critical to note that isolation of the adolescent must be reduced, both within and outside the family. As Harvey (1988, p. 71) wisely advises, "While one can do without sexual–genital relationships, one cannot develop fully as a human person without a measure of human friendship." Similarly, seeking merely to prevent expression of sexuality is not useful. Mattox (1994) states the case succinctly:

> It is unrealistic to expect a fear-based message to be enough. Teens, after all, tend to be poor risk assessors and magnificent risk ignorers. They tend to have a mistaken belief in their own immortality. They often lack the maturity to appreciate just how risky certain behaviors can be. That's part of the reason many drive fast and experiment with drugs and engage in dangerous or irresponsible sex.
>
> Yet even if an entirely negative message were to succeed in deterring unwanted sexual behavior, it would be a mistake to rely solely on such an appeal. Sex is very different from smoking or using drugs. Whereas the latter are bad ideas at any time and under any circumstances—hence, the legitimacy of a "just say no" message—sex is a very beautiful and wonderful thing when it is entered into at the right time and under the right circumstances. (p. 5–6)

Specific suggestions that may assist the adolescent and the parents are simple in concept. The clinician should not let the mundane quality of the interventions mislead about either their potential efficacy or about the difficulty inherent in the consistent implementation of them. Kokotailo and Stephenson (1993, p. 261) advise, "For example, if a teenager has decided to remain abstinent, the provider can help the adolescent to identify potentially high-pressure sexual situations that should be avoided, such as an empty house or the backseat of an automobile. Leaving the scene or double-dating may be an alternative." Of course, the adolescent's commitment to abstinence will often be dependent upon support from both family members, and peers.

Parents and the adolescent can sometimes discuss the situations and conditions under which intimacy is more likely. These can be generally viewed as situations in which two ingredients are present: *privacy* and *time*. Adolescents need a certain amount of privacy, but the level of absolute privacy afforded by a house empty of adults or other adolescents may present, to some adolescents, under easily imagined circumstances, an opportunity that may be difficult to refuse. Parents need to discuss openly their expectations with their children, including their concern that adolescents not be burdened beyond their ability to resist a universal temptation. In this way, parental expectations are clear yet framed in a positive manner that need not convey an expectation of misbehavior (Aldrich, 1974). With older adolescents, loyalty to a peer group that is committed to maintaining chastity can be particularly useful. The increasing presence of such groups suggests that many adolescents are, as they are wont to do, rebelling against the perceived adult convention that expects them to be sexually active. Such peer-group influence may serve to counter not only negative expectations within society in general, but within families who have not established appropriate guidelines for these youth (Brown, 1993).

Specific techniques to recommend in assisting the adolescent who wishes to actually change from a homosexual to a heterosexual orientation are relatively few, but straightforward. While some have advocated the use of behavioral modification programs for ego-dystonic or other homosexualities, such programs have not been widely used, despite their possibility for success.

There are empirical reasons to expect a positive outcome in the treatment of childhood and many adolescent homosexual behaviors (Rekers, 1978). Unlike the relatively more fixed sexual orientation of adults which is more resistant to change, the inherent plasticity of childhood and youth present possibilities for change. The concurrent shaping of dating skills and the enhancement of heterosexual responsiveness appears to be as important as the elimination of homosexual patterns of behavior and arousal. Homosexual behaviors must be extinguished and replaced with heterosexual arousal, otherwise, there is the risk of an adjustment which is bisexual.

Before beginning any course of intervention intended to modify sexual orientation, the clinician will, of course, want to determine *if* intervention is indicated. While this is particularly true if the adolescent expresses a desire to change orientation, it applies substantially to changing behavior with no attempt to alter orientation (Harvey, 1988). Some of the relevant factors that have been cited (Fagan, 1988) as prognostic of successful intervention include:

1. True and high motivation for reorientation
2. Young age
3. Presence of orientation, or only homosexual fantasies, without actual sexual experience
4. Environmental and family support for change.

Relevant factors that suggest that intervention may not be successful, and hence possibly contraindicated, include:

1. Lack of motivation for change
2. A high level of passivity
3. A stable homosexual identity
4. Severe "characterological" problems.

In considering interventions, either to alter behavior without having an impact on orientation, or in attempting to affect both, it must be remembered that reinforcement of patterns of behavior and thinking arises from multiple sources. Family interactions, opportunity, established sexual patterns of behavior, social and environmental cues, and the opportunity for privacy and anonymity are only a few. Environmental planning deserves some consideration, as it is one area where the parent and adolescent who is committed to behavioral and/or orientation change can cooperate in a complementary fashion. It is the agreement in spite of differences that is to be sought in the adolescent–parent relationship. Such agreement can add much needed direction to the process of maturation.

Environmental planning encompasses those strategies that an individual can use to change his or her environment which, in turn, will exert a definite influence on behavior. For example, a deliberate decision to *not* frequent a gay bar would remove both social cues and reduce the relative opportunity for taking a sexual partner. Similarly, discarding any homosexual pornography will help to control fantasy life by reducing the opportunity for viewing pornography that would have an activating effect on homosexual fantasies. In other cases, a person may plan to avoid being alone with anyone who is already known to be attractive in a homosexual sense.

Sexual fantasies may be much more difficult to control than overt behaviors, but they are the substance of eventual sexual expression, in some form or another. Young people who are consciously trying to suppress premature sexual behavior may find that fantasies associated with masturbation are especially reinforcing of patterns of thought and arousal that they are seeking to set aside. For the determined young person, alterations in the frequency of masturbation may be useful in bringing unwanted imagery under control. While masturbation *may* serve as an outlet for sexual energies, its tendency to reinforce established fantasy patterns may prove problematic for some young people, in that frequent "sexual activity may serve to whet the appetite rather than deplete the drive" (Rutter, 1971, p. 280).

Case Study 3: John

John, a 16 year old, had been aware of homosexual interests since age 9. He was afraid to tell his parents for fear that they might kick him out of the house. A boy of religious background, John wanted to tell his own pastor about his sexual problem, but didn't because he had a crush on his pastor's son. Nevertheless, John sought out another pastor, and related a desperate desire to cease his homosexual behaviors.

John was a good-looking blond boy of medium build. He had been involved in homosexual relations with other teenagers about three times per month for the past year. Following review of his experiences, John confessed: "For a long time, I've felt guilty about either being this way or for having done these things. I realize what I have done was wrong." He stated that other boys seduced him into sexual activity as a child. "I feel like I got taken advantage of, but it's not their fault that I kept doing this after I knew it was wrong. It's like with Ted now. I wouldn't mind going to bed with him, but I would also like not to want to. Ted doesn't seem to be bothered by how I feel about him, but maybe it's because he's just affectionate toward everyone."

John had many questions about whether or not he could or should overcome his homosexual tendencies. He wished to know if he could expect to marry successfully and to have his emotional needs cared for so that he would not be constantly seeking attention and sexual favors from other males. Then John finally blurted out his biggest question: "Am I—is this mentally ill, or what? Am I sick, or what?" He wanted his doctors to support his goal to overcome his homosexual behaviors and orientation. He expressed a real fear that he would be told that he was gay, and that there was nothing that could or should be done about it.

For personal, moral, and social reasons, John was highly motivated to change his homosexual orientation as well as his behavior. During the following year, in which he attended psychotherapy, John gradually stopped sexual relations with males and ceased visiting gay bars. He stopped his possible counterphobic and open talk about his homosexual escapades that had labeled him among his peers. He disciplined himself to stop flirting with males, and he dressed and acted in a more masculine manner. This improved his self-image and acceptance with both male and female peers. He began to date girls, to enjoy them as girlfriends, and to be became comfortable dating.

He quit reading homosexual pornography, and participated in conditioning therapy that helped reduce the strength of his homosexual urges while strengthening his already existent heterosexual drives (McConaghy, 1975). He achieved more self-control over his homosexual fantasies. John had hoped for an "instant cure" for his homosexuality, but change was gradual. He learned first how to control his sexual actions, even though he still experienced homosexual attractions. Then, with guidance from his psychologist, he began to apply self-control strategies to his fantasy life. The process of change demanded hard work and discipline from John. But as he refrained from homosexual fantasies, his homosexual urges decreased and he experienced fewer and less intense homosexual attractions.

At the end of the school year, John moved to another town. A year later, he phoned to give a progress report. He had found new friendships with people who knew nothing of his prior homosexual involvements. He found that had made it easier to develop a new, heterosexual male role. As his outward role became normal, his self-concept as a male was also strengthened.

To reiterate, the basic strategy of establishing abstinence is applicable in preventing premature sexual behavior, reestablishing sexual controls after premature sexual behavior has occurred, and in those situations where change in sexual orientation is deemed to be clinically feasible. It is not to be hoped that a task as admittedly difficult as changing orientation will be possible without an initial cessation in overt sexual behaviors that are part of the expression of that orientation. By the same token, it is preferable, when possible, to delay sexual involvement (Howard & McCabe, 1990) when the possibility of sexual reorientation is being considered. The alteration of entrenched patterns of fantasy and/or overt behavior may require clinical intervention. For those adolescents who are appropriately motivated for such intervention, the basic behavioral techniques used to alter pathological sexual behavior may be used, with modification, to suppress subjectively bothersome fantasy as well as undesired behavior.

The motivation for change will determine whether or not even behavioral change (in terms of abstinence) is likely during adolescence. It will be even more influential as to whether or not the adolescent chooses a life as a celibate nonheterosexual. If an actual transition to a heterosexual is to be attempted, the clinician will wish to assure that this is actually the best approach to take with the adolescent at this time. The precautions about premature closure should not be taken as merely injunctions against the internalization of a premature homosexual orientation. For the young person who has not matured along typical heterosexual lines of development, pressure to adopt an overtly heterosexual pattern of behavior and orientation will not be useful. The professional must be vigilant to guard against encouraging such a reaction in the adolescent, while respecting a genuine desire to move from an overtly homosexual pattern of behavior or fantasy life.

Marriage has been used as an attempt to "convert" to heterosexuality, with little or no success. In adolescence, overt heterosexual experimentation is often entered into for similar reasons, with as little success. In both cases, it can be argued that a premature attempt is made to promote transition from one sexual orientation to another. When such a transition is attempted without knowing whether it is even feasible (and if so, under what conditions?) or not (and if not, why not?), the likelihood for increasing confusion and guilt is high. Others may be exploited as part of the effort to gain certainty about one's own orientation, as married homosexuals can affirm. White (1977, p. 143) reports that "marriage [and by analogy, adolescent heterosexual involvement] in and of itself, never 'cures' homosexuality. Experience has shown that it may even deepen the frustration of the homosexual partners and bewilder and humiliate the ones they marry" or do not marry, in the case of sexually active adolescents. White (1977, p. 143) suggests that marriage (and, presumably serious adolescent dating) should not be dismissed as a possible option, but should be "considered very seriously and carefully, and with a full awareness of the problems it may involve. It should never be contemplated as an easy escape from homosexual feelings."

Parents, similarly, should openly cooperate with the adolescent who is seeking change. Such cooperation may involve a deliberate synchronization of schedules within a family so that unwanted or potentially dangerous privacy is avoided or minimized. If an open approach like this is taken, there is the chance of reducing anxiety-driven and deceitful "checking up" behavior, in which parents and friends may try to covertly monitor the adolescent's behavior. Such monitoring can inadvertently create the expectation of failure (Aldrich, 1974).

Companionship that is both loving and nonsexual (male or female) can be maintained more readily in group settings than in couples settings. Such settings need to be chosen carefully so that the interests of the young person are met. Group members should demonstrate (and require of others) acceptance of the individual person while also establishing and preserving a mutual accountability on matters pertaining to behaviors that are either premature (such as overt sexuality) or always to be proscribed (use of drugs and violence). Entry into such a group will not be easy for an adolescent who may already perceive himself or herself as "different." Any degree of existing social isolation should be addressed in a direct manner with the young person and the parents. It is possible that acceptance into a structured coed group that is *not* primarily therapeutic in orientation is desirable. Such groups can be found in many synagogues and churches. Care will need to be taken, however, that such groups do not have as a covert agenda the "sexual conversion" of the young person. Ideally, such a group would be social in nature, but with a significant opportunity for the formation of real and intimate friendships of a nonsexual nature. Any pressure, overt or covert, that demands a change in orientation as a prerequisite for membership needs to be avoided. A personal relationship between the professional and a skilled youth worker at a church or synagogue will facilitate more confident referrals. Youth-initiated groups that advocate chastity are also valuable options worth exploring (Brown, 1993). It is to be kept in mind that acceptance of the individual and proscription of premature behaviors are necessary for such a group to be effective in breaking down the social isolation that may affect the young person of concern. Groups that focus only on a "negative" message of proscription will not be able to offer the supportive environment so necessary for the delaying of sexual choices until maturity. By the same token, those groups that offer only a "positive" message of acceptance will not provide the expectations of self-control (Aldrich, 1974) that are necessary for healthy adolescent development. The need to provide socially supported values within the context of a peer group cannot be overemphasized. Paradoxically, such peer groups often look to respected adults to reinforce their choices and to provide a less-than-parental concern and approval which, for many adolescents, is much easier to accept than the same advice or direction coming from parents.

Concurrent family and individual therapy are indicated, assuming that both parents and adolescent are in agreement that an exploration of mutual concerns is desirable. Rarely is individual therapy alone indicated in younger adolescents, and it is often the case that family therapy is necessary to provide a supportive foundation for conducting subsequent individual work.

Many theoretical issues related to therapy styles will emerge, but these are beyond the scope of this chapter to address. It will be noted that therapy with adolescents and their families is demanding, and often avoided in favor of individual therapy, which offers a superficial sense of "completeness" to those therapists whose training restricts them to one model of intervention. A skilled family therapist will be able to "juggle" between family issues, and those that need to be addressed with the adolescent in private, or with the parents in the absence of the adolescent. In particular situations, the intermittent or permanent inclusion of a cotherapist of the opposite gender (from that of the therapist) will be indicated. Gender of the primary therapist may well be an issue; extreme discomfort on the part of the adolescent with one gender or another should influence decision making when the selection of a therapist is in order. It is not simple enough to state that the adolescent's initial comfort should determine the choice of therapist gender. It is a clinical decision that should take into consideration a variety of factors in the adolescent's background and in the young person's current level of functioning. Some teenagers will do best with a therapist of the same sex; others will need one of the opposite gender. While for still others the choice may be initially indifferent.

Case Study 4: Martha

Martha was utterly surprised upon learning that her 20-year-old-daughter was a lesbian. Her ongoing fear to that point, like that of the parents of many adolescent girls in those days, was that her daughter might become pregnant. A tumultuous period in their relationship ensued. Her efforts to convince her daughter to abandon her lesbian relationship were met by promises by her daughter to break off the relationship, but they were inevitably broken. Her daughter, she recalls, was terribly hurt and upset by her unsupportive and unloving reaction. Martha reflected that she did many things that she now regrets, and that her own attitude and words damaged her relationship with her daughter.

Martha has become more reflective over the ensuing years. Her advice to parents of homosexuals is to "Let their child know that they were *not* born that way [homosexual]. While they may not have *chosen* to be homosexual, they can *choose to change*." When her second daughter announced, several years later, that she too was a lesbian, the shock was not as great, nor was the level of turmoil as intense. Her daughter already knew that she was philosophically and unalterably opposed to the homosexual life-style. Martha chose not to bring up the issue of sexual orientation with the agenda of attempting to change her daughter. She began to focus on learning to be a more loving mother.

Martha became socially acquainted with one of her older daughter's lovers, but this relationship ended when the lover moved. Both of her daughters visit her irregularly. Because they respect Martha's wish that they no longer bring their companions home with them, their vacations and important events are spent elsewhere. Martha related that this decision has made her own life less complicated. She feels, however, that her daughters "judge my sanity by whether or not I accept homosexuality." Because of the great gulf between her daughters' beliefs and her own, conversations tend to be stilted, and carefully avoid mention not only of overt sexuality, but of things and people that confirm that they have very different life-styles. Martha wistfully observed that this gives a shallow and two-dimensional aspect to her relationships with her daughters. It is a compromise, she confesses, which is uneasy but better than it has been. There is no more confrontation by Martha, though there are still some accusations of intolerance leveled at her, to which she tries not to react.

It has not been easy, this middle-aged mother relates, to adjust to an outcome that she had neither anticipated nor desired. She suggests that parents keep in the forefront of everything the need to love their children, which she emphatically says does not mean accepting everything they believe or practice. "We *don't* have to hold the Bible in their face," she notes. To use a self-righteous attitude, she reflects, is "the *worst* thing to do."

Martha has become deeply introspective, and still tends to blame herself in part for her daughters' life-styles. She knows her daughters are themselves not uncomfortable with their lesbian orientation, and though she *wishes* they were, she no longer feels it her prerogative to try to *make* them so. Martha has become active in a local support group for ex-gays, most of whom are men. She admits that she makes herself particularly available to those women trying to leave the lesbian life-style. Her rationale seems to be that since her own daughters are quite resistant to change, that she should offer help to those women who have themselves initiated efforts to leave a homosexual life-style. She has a particularly strong sense of empathy for other parents who have had similar experiences, and wishes them to respond to their children in a more informed manner than she did, and with adequate support.

It is unreasonable to believe that parental opposition to homosexuality, coupled with love for the child, will invariably or inevitably "straighten them out." Such an attitude on the part of parents may prove to be deeply disappointing. Motivated as it may be by an underlying effort to control and to change another's behavior, rather than one's own, it may be interpreted as self-serving, whether actually so or not. There will be many parents and professionals who will be faced with homosexual orientation that appears to be "nonnegotiable," and parental insistence upon change in such circumstances is likely to be unhelpful. Parents will be faced with the difficult task of balancing true love for their children with not compromising their own moral principles.

Whether or not the establishment of such a fixed homosexual orientation is probable during the relatively fluid years of adolescence is not clear. On the other hand, an undesirable restriction of available life-style choices is certainly not inevitable. It is known that the behavioral expression of even a fixed and unequivocal sexual orientation (homosexual or heterosexual) is by no means obligatory or inevitable. Some choose to delay the behavioral expression of their sexual orientation indefinitely, as demonstrated by those who live a life-style that is primarily or secondarily celibate. This does suggest that *during childhood and adolescence, a deliberate discontinuity between orientation and the expression of overt sexual behavior is not only desirable, but entirely feasible* (Kokotailo & Stephenson, 1993, p. 285).

Ethical Issues

Ethical standards should govern the offering or denying of any intervention. Those who hold to a rigidly and inflexible social agenda may find themselves struggling with tendencies to advance those agendas at the expense of individual adolescents. The desire to advance homosexual rights, and to eliminate abuses to which homosexuals have been unfairly subjected, may lead to a trivialization of risks inherent in specific sexual conduct.

Continued focus on an early and libertarian sexuality is counterproductive, and is also detrimental to the health of young people. The freewheeling sexual experimentation that has been particularly characteristic of significant segments of the male homosexual community (Shilts, 1988, pp. 88, 96–97) is dysfunctional. As Quadland and Shattls (1987, p. 282) argue, "In the face of the mortal danger which the AIDS epidemic represents . . . formerly idiopathic behavior may be viewed as a psychological or psychosocial problem. Continued high-risk sexual behavior in the face of a deadly epidemic, when individuals are well-informed regarding risk, may be an indication of a problem with sexual control. . . . Most rational people do not choose to put their lives in jeopardy simply to satisfy a genital urge."

The insistence that homosexual behavior and/or orientation in adolescence are somehow incompatible with a healthy heterosexual adjustment denies valid options to young people. On the other hand, those who insist that nothing short of a change in sexual orientation from homosexual to heterosexual are similarly restricting the options for free and informed choice. The ethical clinician will seek to advance that adjustment which promotes the individual's best overall and age-appropriate adjustment. If, in the considered opinion of the clinician, a change in sexual orientation is indicated, it should be pursued, if this is reflective of the desire of the adolescent and the parents, and if such a change seems to be clinically feasible.

Such efforts should not be an "attempt to *force* [emphasis added] a person to change his or her sexual orientation" (Fikar & Koslap-Petraco, 1992, p. 12). Similarly, efforts by a professional to orchestrate an unwanted or ambivalent "coming out," or otherwise "force" premature closure is wrong. Reassurance and referral of those who are *becoming aware of their sexual orientation* to gay organizations (as Owen, 1986 advocates), could, inadvertently, precipitate premature closure, or at the very least, confusion.

Furthermore, therapeutic efforts should be terminated if no further help is possible (Rekers & Rosen, 1978). Protracted or coercive efforts by the clinician to bring about goals that are clearly not supported, but which are resisted unambivalently, cannot be sanctioned. It may be that the expressed goal of intervention is to effect a shift to a heterosexual orientation, but evidence that such a goal is obtainable may be absent. In such cases, no therapy—or a very brief intervention—may be the appropriate intervention. The possibility of a negative or untoward response to treatment must always be kept in mind (Frances & Clarkin, 1981). Those whose training and practice is outside of the medical field may be less likely to appreciate the range and severity of treatment sideeffects; it is not necessary to prescribe a powerful medication to create unwanted results. Those who fail to consider such possibilities may be most at risk for contributing to negative reactions (Lundy & Pumariega, 1993). The timing of a specific intervention may be wrong. For example, while it may be quite appropriate to facilitate the delay of sexual activity, or to establish a means of maintaining secondary abstinence, it may be premature to explore issues of sexual orientation with a younger adolescent. The therapist should not press his or her time table here. It is possible that the creation of socially reinforced behavioral changes will permit the younger adolescent to "get on with life" in other areas that may be more important to him or her.

Insistence that the young person "work through" such important issues prematurely is unconscionable. Efforts by young people, professionals, or parents to force consolidation of sexual identify, especially through overt sexual experimentation, is neither necessary or prudent. As Kokotailo and Stephenson (1993, p. 259) wisely advise, "Delay of sexual activity allows an adolescents to mature cognitively, prior to assuming the responsibility of expressing sexuality through intercourse." As previously noted, the ability to defer sexual involvement is not an issue of homosexuality *or* heterosexuality; but, clearly, any actual "expression of same-sex orientation can be suppressed until early adulthood, or it can be delayed indefinitely" (Kokotailo & Stephenson, 1993, p. 285). An adolescent's decision to delay the expression of overt sexuality should be emphatically and unambiguously supported. Attempts to provoke a heterosexual reorientation through the encouragement of explicit heterosexual experiences are no more to be condoned than suggestions that an adolescent confirm (or deny) incipient homosexual orientation through experimentation.

The degree to which change in behavior and/or orientation are possible will vary. Parental expectation for a change in sexual orientation in an adolescent may, unfortunately, be based upon other than genuine concern for the well-being of the young person. Under such unfavorable conditions, change is less likely. When a change in sexual orientation is to be attempted, it should be attempted as early as possible. Later intervention renders success less likely and intervention becomes more ineffective. Nevertheless, as noted in the preceding paragraph, early intervention may be limited to the establishment of sexual controls intended to allow the adolescent time to develop the cognitive and emotional maturity necessary for making free choices.

In adolescents who have been experimentally (as opposed to persistently) active sexually, the establishment and reinforcement of secondary abstinence would still be a requisite for a therapeutic exploration of the choices open to the young person. The comparison of sex to drugs or alcohol is problematic (Mattox, 1994), but a limited analogy is useful. Responsible, adult alcohol consumption is an appropriate option for many adults; for some, it clearly is not. For those who have a familial or biological tendency toward alcoholism, or an actual drinking problem, a therapeutic and objective review of the pros and cons of alcohol would be best conducted in a state of sobriety rather than at the neighborhood tavern, or the day after overindulgence. Few clinicians would consider working with a person with an alcohol problem in the absence of a commitment to establishing abstinence. It is similarly unlikely that an exploration of sexual options with an adolescent is going to be profitable while the young person is actively exploring those very options. A little distance is necessary for objectivity.

When one observes the substitutes for abstinence advocated by some child and adolescent clinicians, one must agree with Voltaire, "Common sense is not so common."

It is possible for an inexperienced professional to inappropriately support an adolescent's resistance or supposed enthusiasm to change. The clinician may be drawn into "treating" with the expectation of heterosexual adjustment, or, alternately, of recommending homosexual adjustment, when in reality the presenting "symptoms" are evidence of a much deeper family pathology, which may or may not be related to sexual problems per se. This is especially likely if recommendations are made without adequate understanding of underlying family dynamics. Offering to help an adolescent "change" sexual orientation when the real motivation is to give an appearance of change in order to avoid being disinherited by parents is not wise. Similarly, if it is determined that the parents are merely interested in superficial appearances, and are primarily embarrassed by the prospect of a homosexual son or daughter, this will affect both the intention of the professional and the attitude of the young person about the relative merit of potential change. Encouragement of duplicity on the part of parents or adolescents is to be avoided. We should make every attempt to guarantee that a child is not manipulated contrary to his or her own best interests (Rekers & Rosen, 1978).

Objection, in principle, to an attempted change in sexual orientation may be anticipated from certain segments within the broader society that are sympathetic to goals of the gay/lesbian rights movement. Similarly, refusal of treatment on ethical grounds may be faulted by those who are advocates for "more vigorous efforts to eradicate homosexuality" (Bell, Weinberg, & Hammersmith, 1981, p. 219). The decision to treat or not to treat will not be without controversy, and so should be made on grounds that can be justified clinically. As McHugh (1992) observed, major psychiatric misdirections typically mix a medical mistake to a trendy idea. A successful challenge to such a misdirection must neutralize both the authority of the professional proponents and the power of politically fashionable values.

The goals of individuals and family-based treatment should be balanced between breaking down inappropriate gender stereotypes which impose unfair expectations and limitations on the person (Rekers & Rosen, 1978), and the promotion of behaviors and attitudes that can be legitimately held as pro-social. As examples, childhood interest in occupations once held to be "reserved" for the opposite gender, such as doctor/male and nurse/female may still generate unnecessary and harmful sanctions within the family, if less so in society at large. Similarly, it is injust and unkind for child peers to call such a boy a 'sissy,' or 'fag,' or to reject him for atypical behavior (Rekers & Rosen, 1978). Encouraging or even allowing social ostracizing of girls who show either gender atypical behavior or overt homosexual orientation must be actively resisted and spoken against.

Professional judgment must be used in considering if intervention is indicated, and consists of: (1) the accurate assessment of what is deviant, (2) an estimation of the child's prognosis with and without treatment intervention, and (3) the development of specific intervention goals (Rekers & Rosen, 1978).

Treatment from any theoretical perspective involves "an explicit value assumption" (Rekers & Rosen, 1978) that one outcome is more desirable than others. The goals of treatment will be monolithic if the formulation is monolithic. The establishment of an exaggerated male [or female] stereotype is not an appropriate intervention goal. Instead, clinicians should expand the behavioral repertoire of the child or adolescent to increase his [or her] choices (Rekers & Rosen, 1978). An increase in choices, paradoxically, means not exercising certain options. When there is genuine ambivalence between a heterosexual and a homosexual adjustment, the delaying of particular choices can be conceptualized as allowing time for the process of maturation to at least allow a more considered choice later. Maturity holds the potential of informing young persons about the impact of major choices. Orientation may not be a choice, but life-style certainly is.

This ability to effect an increase in choices with respect to sexual orientation is acknowledged to be highly dependent upon previous and subsequent sexual experiences (Howard & McCabe, 1990). Those with strong biases will find it nonintuitive to pose certain critical questions, such as "Is this boy, who displays serious anxiety about possibly being homosexual, an emerging homosexual or is he in need of help in making a transition to healthy heterosexual adjustment?" Similarly, "Is this late adolescent female, who displays long-standing ego-syntonic homosexual orientation and behavior, asking to change her sexual orientation because she will be economically disenfranchised by her family if she refuses their pressure to seek treatment?"

Should persons who are potentially capable of heterosexual adjustment be encouraged not to change because a society that is less capable *should* change? Should persons who are highly unlikely to make a successful adjustment from homosexual to heterosexual orientation nevertheless be encouraged to make the attempt? Or should attempts at changes in orientation be secondary to efforts to establish behavioral controls that are compatible with good health (Quadland & Shattls, 1987) and/or social conformity, even if this means "complete sexual abstinence, or celibacy?" (Harvey, 1988). Because each clinician adheres to certain values, "no therapy is value free. Whether the therapist's beliefs are political, educational, philosophical, or spiritual; they obviously, or not so obviously, may have effects upon therapist decision making. This does not reduce the responsibility of every therapist to be in touch with how his or her beliefs or bias's may affect therapy outcome and to *make sure the client is aware of this as well* [emphasis added]" (Younggren, 1993, p. 1).

Clinicians should be as open and as candid about their own biases and values as they would wish others to be with them. The use of deceit, false advertising, or covert agendas is simply unacceptable. This will mean that different values will be espoused by different clinicians, and that different outcomes will be viewed as relatively favorable or undesired. The process of self-selection inherent in an open referral process will, to some degree, assuage the fear, by homosexuals and heterosexuals alike, that only one perspective will be encountered.

Conclusion

Those who seek to increase the possibility of young persons to make considered and healthy choices will find that these choices are not routinely accepted. However, it is better to offer the *real* choices that delayed sexual activity offers than to settle for the easier short-term "solution" of allowing or even encouraging a level of autonomy that is beyond the capacity of the adolescent to successfully manage.

It is acknowledged that a persistent behavioral expression of sexuality will take place in a substantial number of young persons. There will, additionally, be many situations where opportunities to prevent such involvement will not present themselves. Similarly, the possibility of establishing secondary abstinence will be a less viable option, for a variety of reasons, in many such situations. Established patterns of behavior are to some degree self-perpetuating. In the absence of a fundamental change in one's values and worldview, the general trend is for individuals to do tomorrow pretty much as they have done today. For example, a well-established pattern of active sexual involvement is more difficult to change; it is much less complex to return to a previously established pattern of abstinence following a single indiscretion or even a brief series of sexual encounters. In such circumstances, it is certainly necessary to try to provide influence and guidelines that will offer the "least detrimental" alternatives to such young people. The "best interests of the child" (Goldstein, Freud, & Solnit, 1979a, 1979b) are, unfortunately, all too often rendered out of reach due to previous choices and/or circumstances well beyond the control of the young person and/or the professional. Noncondescending empathy in such situations in vital. There are less destructive ways by which premature sexuality may be expressed. Ironically, the "safe sex" message that is inappropriately targeted at the general child and adolescent population (Bull, 1994) rather than preferentially at high-risk subgroups (Bolye & Offord, 1990) may have real potential for saving lives. Its overly broad application, however, may so dilute its impact that, where there is a real prospect for secondary prevention, lives that could be saved will be lost (F. Brown, 1993). Research is indicated that will help to discriminate those youth who are "beyond" a pure abstinence approach from those who have simply never been given adequate exposure to its message. Fortunately, there is now some evidence of an incipient bipartisan political support to make federal aid to schools contingent upon the promotion of abstinence "as the only effective protection against unwanted pregnancy and AIDS" ("Rep. Kennedy Fights Stereotypes," 1994). It is probable that many and probably most children can benefit from such an approach to sexual education. It will, nevertheless, be important to identify characteristics of those many who can benefit from a consistent message explaining the advantages of delaying sexual involvement. Then the rigorous design and evaluation of such approaches will be possible (Boyle & Offord, 1990).

The broad promotion of "safe sex" as clinically, morally, or socially equivalent to the true "best interests of the child" (Goldstein, Freud, & Solnit, 1979a, 1979b) is intellectually dishonest, as well as technically problematic to implement and evaluate. Encouraging deferment of sexual involvement will offer the adolescent the greatest freedom for making choices that are both powerfully important and intensely personal. As Griffin (1993, p. 38) notes, "Someone needs to tell them. And kids need to know that they shouldn't be having sex when they are kids. And even though it may not be very popular these days, I think kids need to know that the only really safe sex is between two faithful marriage partners who are free of sexually transmitted diseases. I would add that the 'no-risk sex' is worth waiting for." United States representative (D-Mass) Joseph P. Kennedy II appears to agree, and openly stated that people should begin to support "basic values and be proud of it and not be embarrassed by it or try to hide from it" ("Rep. Kennedy Fights Stereotypes," 1994). Such commonsense advocacy for true sexual freedom is to be emulated by professionals working with young persons.

References

Aids and the education of our children: A guide for parents and teachers. (1987). Washington, DC: U.S. Department of Education.

Aldrich, C. K. (1974). Youth's fulfillment of adult prophecies. Australian New Zealand Journal of Psychiatry, 8, 127–129.

American Psychiatric Association. (1987). Diagnostic and statistical manual of mental disorders (3rd ed., rev.). Washington, DC: Author.

Ayd, F. J. (1987, February). Teenage sexuality. Psychiatric Times, p. 18.

Bayer, R. (1981). Homosexuality and American psychiatry: The politics of diagnosis. New York: Basic Books.

Bell, A. P., Weinberg, M. S., & Hammersmith, S. K. (1981). Sexual preference. Bloomington: Indiana University Press.

Bennett, W. (1972, Fall). The homosexual teacher. American Educator, p. 24.

Boyle, M. H., & Offord, D. R. (1990). Primary prevention of conduct disorder:

Issues and prospects. *Journal of the American Academy of Child and Adolescent Psychiatry, 29*(2), 227–133.

Brown, D. L. (1993, November 21). Virginity is new counterculture among teens. *Washington Post*, p. 3.

Brown, F. G. (1993, April 26). Meet your Surgeon General: Life and death in Arkansas. *National Review*, p. 38.

Bull, C. (1994, March 22). The condom queen reigns: Surgeon General Joycelyn Elders speaks out where the President fears to tread. *Advocate*, pp. 32–38.

Cameron, P., Playfair, W., & Wellum, S. (1993, April 17). *The homosexual lifespan*. Paper presented at the Annual Meeting of the Eastern Psychological Association, Washington, D.C.

Cwayna, K., Remafedi, G., & Treadway, L. (1991, July). Caring for gay and lesbian youth. *Medical Aspects of Human Sexuality*, pp. 50–57.

Exodus International, P.O. Box 2121, San Rafael, CA 94912, 415–454-1017; Desert Stream, 12488 Venice Boulevard, Los Angeles, CA 90066–3804, 310–572-0140; His Heart Ministries, 12162 E. Mississippi Avenue, P.O. Box 12321, Aurora, CO 80011, 303–369-2961; Metanoia Ministries, P.O. Box 33039, Seattle, WA 98133; Outpost, 1821 University Avenue S, #296, St. Paul, MN 55140; and Regeneration, P.O. Box 10574, Balto, MD 21285–0574. Support resources for parents of homosexuals are available from Spatula Ministries, P.O. Box 444, La Habra, CA 90631.

Fagan, P. F. (1988). *Hope for homosexuality*. Washington, D.C.: The Center for Child and Family Policy.

Fikar, C. R., & Koslap-Petraco, M. (1992). God, gays, and health care provision (letter of response). *American Journal of Diseases of Childhood, 146*, 12.

Frances, A., & Clarkin, J. F. (1981). No treatment as the prescription of choice. *Archives of General Psychiatry, 38*, 542–545.

Goldstein, J., Freud, A., & Solnit, A. J. (1979a). *Beyond the best interests of the child*. New York: Free Press.

Goldstein, J., Freud, A., & Solnit, A. J. (1979b). *Before the best interests of the child*. New York: Free Press.

Griffin, G. C. (1993). Condoms and contraceptives in junior high and high school clinics. *Postgraduate Medicine, 93*(5), 1–6.

Harvey, J. F. (1988). Homosexuality and hope: New thinking in pastoral care. In P. F. Fagan (Ed.), *Hope for homosexuality* (pp. 65–77). Washington, DC: Center for Child and Family Policy of the Free Congress Research and Education Foundation.

Howard, M., & McCabe, J. B. (1990). Helping teenagers postpone sexual involvement. *Family Planning Perspectives, 22*(1), 21–26.

Kinsey, A. C., Pomeroy, W. B., & Martin, C. E. (1948). *Sexual behavior in the human male*. Philadelphia: W. B. Saunders.

Kirkpatrick, M. (1987). Clinical implications of lesbian mother studies. *Journal of Homosexuality, 14*, 201–211.

Kokotailo, P. K., & Stephenson, J. N. (1993). Sexuality and reproductive health behavior. In, M. I. Singer, L. T. Singer, & T. M. Anglin (Eds.), *Handbook for screening adolescents at psychosocial risk* (pp. 249–292). New York: Lexington Books.

Lundy, M. S., & Pumariega, A. J. (1993). Psychiatric hospitalization of children and adolescents: Treatment in search of a rationale. *Journal of Child and Family Studies, 2*(1), 1–4.

Mattox, W. R. (1994). What's marriage got to do with it? Good sex comes to those who wait. *Family Policy, 6*(6), 1–8.

McConaghy, N. (1975). Aversive and positive conditioning treatments of homosexuality. *Behavioral Research and Therapy, 13*, 309–319.

McHugh, P. R. (1992). Psychiatric misadventures. *American Scholar, 61*(4), 497–570.

Mellanby, A., Phelps, F., & Tripp, J. H. (1993). Teenagers, sex, and risk taking. *British Medical Journal, 307*, 25.

Meyer-Bahlburg, H. F. L. (1993). Psychobiologic research on homosexuality. *Child and Adolescent Psychiatric Clinics of North America, 2*(3), 489–500.

Mosher, D. L., & Cross, H. J. (1971). Sex guilt and premarital sexual experiences of college students. *Journal of Consulting and Clinical Psychology, 36*(1), 27–32.

Owen, W. F. (1986). The clinical approach to the male homosexual patient. *Medical Clinics of North America, 70*(3), 499–536.

Pattison, E. M., & Pattison, M. L. (1980). "Ex-gays": Religiously mediated change in homosexuals. *American Journal of Psychiatry, 137*(12), 1553–1562.

Phillips, D., Fischer, S. C., Groves, G. A., & Singh, R. (1976). Alternative behavioral approaches to the treatment of homosexuality. *Archives of Sexual Behavior, 5*(3), 223–228.

Planned Parenthood. (1987). American teens speak: sex, myths, TV, and birth control. New York: Lou Harris and Associates. (Poll)

Quadland, M. C., & Shattls, W. D. (1987). AIDS, sexuality, and sexual control. *Journal of Homosexuality, 14, 277–298.*

Rekers, G. A. (1977). Atypical gender development and psychological adjustment. *Journal of Applied Behavior Analysis, 10*(3), 559–571.

Rekers, G. A. (1978). Sexual Problems: Behavior modification. In B. B. Wolman, J. Egon, & A. O. Ross, (Eds.), *Handbook of treatment of mental disorders in childhood and adolescence* (pp. 268–296). Englewood Cliffs, NJ: Prentice-Hall.

Rekers, G. A., & Rosen, A. C. (1978). Ethical issues in the treatment of children. *Journal of Social Issues, 34*(2), 122–136.

Remafedi, G. (1987). Adolescent homosexuality: Psychological and medical implications. *Pediatrics, 79*(3), 331–337.

Remafedi, G., Resnick, M., Blum, R., & Harris, L. (1992). Demography of sexual orientation in adolescents. *Pediatrics, 89*, 714–721.

Rep. Kennedy fights stereotype. (1994, April 2). *State* (Columbia, SC), p. A5.

Rotheram-Borus, M. J., & Gwadz, M. (1993). Sexuality among youths at high risk. *Child and Adolescent Psychiatric Clinic of North America, 2*(3), 415–430.

Rutter, M. (1971). Normal psychosexual development. *Journal of Child Psychiatry and Psychology, 11*, 259–283.

Seidman, S. N., & Rieder, R. O. (1994). A review of sexual behavior in the United States. *American Journal of Psychiatry, 151*, 330–341.

Schumm, W. R., & Rekers, G. A. (1984). Sex should occur only within marriage. In H. Feldman & A. Parrot (Eds.), *Human sexuality: Contemporary controversies* (pp. 105–124). Beverly Hills, CA: Sage.

Shilts, R. (1988). *And the band played on: Politics, people, and the AIDS epidemic.* New York: Penguin Books.

Socarides, C. (1988). Sexual politics and scientific logic: The issue of homosexuality. In P. F. Fagan (Ed.), *Hope for homosexuality* (pp. 46–64). Washington, DC: Center for Child and Family Policy of the Free Congress Research and Education Foundation.

Thorstad, D. (1990). Man/boy love and the American gay movement. *Journal of Homosexuality, 20,* 251–274.

Utribe, V., & Harbeck, K. M. (1991). Addressing the needs of lesbian, gay, and bisexual youth: The origins of PROJECT 10 and school-based intervention. *Journal of Homosexuality, 22*(3–4), 9–28.

van den Aardweg, G. J. M. (1984). Parents of homosexuals—not guilty? *American Journal of Psychotherapy, 38,* 181–189.

Westminster Confession of Faith (The Confession of Faith, 1643). Glasgow, Scotland: Free Presbyterian Publications, 1985

White, J. (1977). *Eros defiled.* Downer's Grove, IL: InterVarsity Press.

Wigersma, L., & Oud, R. (1987). Safety and acceptability of condoms for use by homosexual men as a prophylactic against transmission of HIV during anogenital intercourse. *British Medical Journal, 295,* 94.

Winkler, R. C. (1977). What types of sex-role behavior should behavior modifiers promote? *Journal of Applied Behavior Analysis, 10,* 549–552.

Yates, A. (1993). Sexually inhibited children. *Child and Adolescent Psychiatric Clinic of North America, 2*(3), 451–461.

Younggren, J. N. (1993). Ethical issues in religious psychotherapy. *Register Report, 19*(4), 1.

Part 5

Problems of Sexual Behavior

17
Nonmarital Sexual Behavior

Walter R. Schumm

R esearch on nonmarital sexual behavior has become plentiful since the Kinsey studies were published in the late 1940s and early 1950s (Kinsey, Pomeroy, & Martin, 1948; Kinsey, Pomeroy, Martin, & Gebhard, 1953). However, it continues to be fraught with methodological and political hazards. My observations of the research problems are many. Many studies focus on quantitative aspects of sexual behavior while ignoring qualitative aspects; from a symbolic interaction perspective, that omission is almost unforgivable (LaRossa & Reitzes, 1993). For example, a woman who has been raped may be a nonvirginal statistic, but is surely in a different position than a woman who has voluntarily entered into a sexual relationship; however, strictly quantitative statistics will not catch the difference. Nonresponse to sensitive sexual issues is a troublesome problem; for example, there are indications that as many as 50 percent of women who have had an abortion will not readily admit their experience in surveys (Jones & Forrest, 1992; Koop, 1989). If a scholar compares those who have aborted with those who haven't—except that aborters and nonaborters are often confounded in the supposedly "nonabort" group—it will be difficult to generate accurate contrasts between the two actual groups. Another interesting methodological issue, tied to abortion, involves estimating the actual age of the fetus, as the traditional method, from first day of last menstrual cycle, overestimates the age of the fetus since fertilization or implantation by one to two weeks or more (Santee & Henshaw, 1992).

Many studies use race as an independent variable but fail to control for socioeconomic variables, possibly misleading some readers into citing race rather than socioeconomic disadvantages as causal factors. Furthermore, it is common for researchers to look at race and gender but not at gender by race interaction effects. Relationship status is another variable that is often confounded. Some studies combine cohabiting and married couples to contrast against never-marrieds; other studies will combine cohabiting and never-marrieds to contrast against married individuals. Other studies do not distinguish marital status at all, looking at virginal status strictly as a function of age. A final observation is the continued reliance on volunteer samples of college students, samples that cannot be said to provide any degree of representiveness, even of the college student population; however, larger, more representative national samples are finally being conducted. In a review of abortion effects literature, Speckhard and Rue (1992) cited 20 major methodological flaws, noting that the average study was affected by nearly 7 such shortcomings.

Turning to the political issues, some recent, large government research projects have been canceled because of political opposition generated by Congress (Gardner & Wilcox, 1992; Udry, 1993) against sex-related research. Researchers who come from more conservative (Udry, 1993), middle-of-the-road (Baumrind, 1982), or more liberal (Ellis, 1990; Reiss, 1993) viewpoints may interpret the same objective research evidence quite differently (e.g., Mould, 1990). Given the probability that any one study will have some limitations, it is easy for opponents to find something flawed in almost any study and then use that as the basis for discrediting it, even if the opponents are motivated largely by their value biases rather than by a neutral desire to see research improved. Conservatives may see research on sex as a threat to a natural moral order, while feminists may see it as a way of maintaining a status quo whereby white males continue their domination of women and minorities (Udry, 1993). Udry (1993) and Baumrind (1982) have argued that most sex research has been conducted by researchers whose values often at least appeared to favor more permissive sexual attitudes or behavior. Both Baumrind (1982) and Reiss (1993) agree that scholars should try to be value-aware rather than supposedly value-free. Reiss (1993, p. 7) states his values outright:

> That sexuality in all its freely chosen forms can and usually is pleasurable and good.

> That people can and should learn to avoid, for themselves and their partners, the unwanted outcomes of sexuality such as disease, pregnancy, and psychological distress.

> That the basis for judging sexual morality should be the amount of honesty, equality, and responsibility in a relationship and not the number of such relationships that a person has.

However, alternative value positions are possible. Although I have many disagreements with structural–functional theory (Kingsbury & Scanzoni, 1993), one assumption of that theory that seems plausible to me is that an important function for adult members of any society must be to help socialize the next generation so as to preserve and even improve the quality of life of that next generation. It would be possible to think otherwise and to devote adult resources to enhancing only the way of life of the present generation. Sexuality could be used in either manner, too. Sexuality could be used to promote the quality of life of the next generation or to enhance merely the pleasures of the present generation. I assume that sexuality is indeed pleasurable, so pleasurable in fact that it ranks at or near the top of human pleasures. At the same time, over time, it might be observed that the moist, warm environments of sex organs and their proximity to vascular entrances to the body create a dangerous potential for many diseases to spread from one person to another, with extremely discomforting, if not fatal, results for huge portions of any society. In this context, societies might well consider how best to regulate sexuality so as to take best advantage of such a powerful human incentive for promoting the welfare of subsequent generations without sacrificing the health of significant portions of the adult population in the process. Many societies appear to have arrived at the conclusion that promiscuous sexual behavior did not meet such objectives, whereas normatively restricting at least intercourse to relationships in which both partners were committed to each other for the duration of their childbearing stages of the life cycle might reduce the risk of disease and enhance the incentives of such adults to work together for the sake of their offspring. From an exchange theory perspective (Sabatelli & Shehan, 1993), sex was a reward to adults who accepted the costs and investments involved in rearing offspring and staying together during stages of the family life cycle that are often difficult (Anderson, Russell, & Schumm, 1983); furthermore, the alternative of leaving the partner and/or the children might not seem as profitable if doing so meant losing, at least temporarily, any legitimate opportunity for sexual fulfillment. In contrast, if sex was equally available to all adults, there might be less incentive for adults to pair together to raise offspring or to work on improving a relationship if it proved to be more difficult than expected, situations that might impact on the quality of childrearing. With the advent in this century of new technological means to avert some of the negative outcomes of sexuality mentioned by Reiss (1993), it seemed to many that the traditional rules could be changed to create a new formula for maximizing one's sexual profit. It is inevitable that a review chapter such as this one will continually touch on some of the consequences possibly associated with that new formula, just as other areas of human sciences are struggling with value and religious issues (Bergin, 1991; Kurtines, Alvarez, & Azmitia, 1990.)

This chapter will focus on nonmarital heterosexual behavior and will not consider either marital heterosexual behavior (including extramarital sex) or homosexual behavior; hence, the focus will generally be on adolescent/young adult heterosexual behavior. The specific topics to be reviewed include:

Premarital sexual standards
Onset of premarital sexual activity
Premarital sexual activity
Sexually transmitted diseases
Acquaintance rape
Unplanned pregnancies
Abortion
Postabortion syndrome
Cohabitation

The order of topics reflects, in part, a chronological order of the development of nonmarital sexual behavior, starting with attitudes held about it, to onset of the behaviors and their frequencies, along with some consequences, including cohabitation, which often precedes marriage in today's society.

Premarital Sexual Standards

Jurich and Jurich (1974) added a fifth premarital sexual standard to the four previously proposed by Reiss (1967), nonexploitive permissiveness without affection in which partners could engage in sex either for love or for physical pleasure as long as both agreed clearly on their intentions. The other standards included the double standard (bad girls do, good girls don't, whatever boys do is OK); the permissiveness-with-affection standard (sex is OK if you love each other)—the standard that appears to be most popular among university students at the current time (Sprecher, 1989); the permissiveness-without-affection standard (sex is OK between consenting adults even without love); and the traditional standard (usually presented as the "no sex before marriage" standard). The more permissive standards appear to be gaining in popularity, with more "friendly sex" (Gecas & Libby, 1976) occurring. Support for the double standard appears to have declined over the past two decades with few respondents, at least of college age, willing to endorse different levels of permissiveness as a function of gender (Sprecher, 1989). Weis, Rabinowitz, and Ruckstuhl (1992) found the following percentages of college students (male/female) approving of various sexual standards for their own gender: premarital sex is OK if engaged (86 percent/90 percent), if in love (89 percent/88 percent), if feeling affection (73 percent/62 percent), if feeling no affection (37 percent/14 percent).

Wyatt, Peters, and Guthrie (1988a, 1988b) have presented data suggesting that the traditional standards in which one's first sexual partner would be one's fiancée or spouse have declined in popularity since the beginning of the century. They used Kinsey data and their own data with women aged 18 to 26 and 27 to 36 to capture an old Kinsey cohort, a young Kinsey cohort, an old Wyatt cohort, and a young Wyatt cohort; the percentage of white females who first had sex with their fiancée or husband declined in each cohort, respectively, from 62 to 48 to 23 to 5 percent. In other words, in the Wyatt cohort of women aged 18 to 26, 95 percent had first had sex with an acquaintance or boyfriend rather than with a fiancée or spouse. The parallel data for black females changed from 22 to 25 to 10 to 4 percent—that is, in Wyatt's latest cohort, black and white standards appeared to be converging.

Sexual standards are important as possible predictors of sexual activity, though they may change in response to changes in sexual activity (Weis, Slosnerick, Cate, & Sollie, 1986). Sexual permissiveness appears to increase with age, especially between the ages of 14 and 18 (Sprecher, 1989; Earle & Perricone 1986; Jemmott & Jemmott, 1990; Miller & Olson, 1988) and is greater for males than for females (Earle & Perricone, 1986; Wilson & Medora, 1990; Miller & Olson, 1988; Whitley, 1988; Sprecher, 1989; Oliver & Hyde, 1993). However between 1975 and 1981, Earle and Perricone (1986) found in their surveys of undergraduates at a small southern university that approval for casual sex declined for both men and women, but increased for dating regularly for men (56 to 64 percent) while declining for women (39 to 30 percent). Earle and Perricone (1986) found that only 12 percent of freshmen were totally opposed to premarital coitus but the percentage of coeds so disapproving declined from 50 percent for freshmen to only 9 percent for seniors. It has also been found to be correlated with nonintact family status, low socioeconomic status background (Miller & Olson, 1988; Earle & Perricone, 1986; Rosenbaum & Kandel, 1990; Flewelling & Bauman, 1990), and use of drugs (Rosenbaum & Kandel, 1990). Some research has indicated that while both men and women often want affection before sex, women are more likely to want a greater level of commitment as well (McCabe, 1987). Sexual permissiveness is usually found, not surprisingly, to be negatively related to religiosity (Brown, 1985; Weis, Slosnerick, Cate, & Sollie, 1986; Simpson & Gangestad, 1991; Miller, Christensen, & Olson, 1987; Earle & Perricone, 1986; Miller & Olson, 1988), as well as to school grades and various measures of expected educational attainment (Miller & Sneesby, 1988), though it is positively related to educational attainment (Simpson & Gangestad, 1991). Simpson and Gangestad (1991) found that permissiveness as measured by their inventory was negatively related to relationship love, investment, commitment, and dependency among a student sample of 144 couples. Miller et al. (1987) found unusual effects for self-esteem, depending on religiosity: for religious youth, self-esteem was negatively related to permissiveness, but for nonreligious youths, it was positively related to permissiveness, though both effects were weak. Others have found simply a positive relationship between permissiveness (Tanfer & Schoorl, 1992) and number of sexual partners and self-esteem (Walsh, 1991). Since high self-esteem has been related to having a steady boyfriend and more dates (Long, 1989), it is possible that the advantages of having a "steady" may outweigh any guilt experienced over violations of sexual standards, even for some highly religious individuals.

It is possible to redefine the five major premarital sexual standards into three major categories: permissive standards, conditional standards, and commitment-oriented standards (Schumm & Rekers, 1984). As Table 17–1 demonstrates, each standard is associated with an increasing set of requirements. For example, the double standard requires physical presence, consent, and a consideration of the reputation and gender of the partners; in addition, the modified traditional standard requires affection, communication, personal commitment, and engagement as a form of public commitment. Defined accordingly, the commitment-oriented standards are the most cognitively complex in contrast to the usual simplistic and negatively-oriented definition along "no sex before marriage" lines. It is the author's view that the failure of religious and traditional groups to educate youth in such depth about premarital standards may account for the dim view taken of the "traditional standard" by many youth. Nevertheless, it is likely that even negative, overly simplistic religious training may foster self-restraint in terms of sexual permissiveness given the consistent negative relationships found between religiosity and sexual permissiveness.

A variety of conflicts may present themselves clinically. Most basic may be a conflict between male and female partners as to the appropriate sexual standard for their relationship, especially when each person has a different view. The rapid change in standards with age may lead to conflicts between adolescents whose views may be out of synchrony with their peers, at a time when peer acceptance is very critical to their sense of self-esteem. Such conflicts can lead to broken relationships, even unrequited love, a problem for both the rejected and the rejecter (Baumeister, Wotman, & Stillwell, 1993). Differences in ways men and women are aroused sexually can also add to the potential conflict; for example, when a woman caresses a man sexually, it is perceived as much more stimulating by the man than to the woman (Geer & Broussard, 1990), which could create misunderstandings over how far a couple intended to go sexually in their relatiaonship.

Conflicts are also possible between traditional institutions (parents, church) and adolescents since adolescents are apt to move from similar nonpermissive standards to much more permissive standards, if not behavior, within a fairly rapid period of time. Attempts by traditional institutions to enforce nonpermissive norms with platitudes and slogans may only further convince intelligent adolescents of the irrelevance of such institutions.

Table 17–1
Prerequisites for Sexual Intercourse/Activity Versus Different Sexual Standards

	Permissive Standards		Permissiveness with Affection	Conditional Standards		Commitment-Oriented Standards	
	Permissiveness without Affection	Double Standard		Nonexploitative Permissiveness without Affection	Semitraditional	Traditional (Modified)	Traditional (Ideal)
Religious commitment/ covenant							?
Legal commitment/ contract							X
Public commitment/ engagement						X	X
Personal commitment/ cohabitation					X	X	X
Nonexploitiveness/ communication				X	X	X	X
Perceived love/ affection			X	?	X	X	X
Consideration of reputation		X	X	X	X	X	X
Physical consent	X	X	X	X	X	X	X
Physical presence	X	X	X	X	X	X	X

Even more sophisticated approaches to educating adolescents about sexuality will be difficult given the tendency for many adolescents to see themselves as invulnerable or to weigh short-term inconvenience far more heavily than long-term risks to themselves or their partner(s) (Loewenstein & Furstenberg, 1991).

Onset of Premarital Sexual Activity

In their review of adolescent sexual behavior research during the 1980s Miller and Moore (1990, p. 1026) report that "by age 15, approximately one-quarter of females have had sex; by age 19, four out of five females have had sex," and that "a third of teen males have had sex by age 15, as have 86 percent by age 19." However, it is most common for teenage girls to begin sexual activity with a somewhat older male, on average about 3 years older, with perhaps 9 percent being 23 or older (Miller & Moore, 1990). Miller and Moore (1990) also note that between 0.4 and 6.3 percent of youth aged 18 to 22 interviewed in the 1987 National Survey of Children said they had been forced to have sex by age 15. Likewise, between one third and two-thirds of the sex experienced by females before age 14 was not voluntary.

As mentioned under sexual standards, Wyatt et al. (1988a) also looked at onset of sexual activity as a function of Kinsey versus Wyatt cohorts. For white females, the percentage having had sex before age 16 increased from 3–5 to 18–32, with the more recent cohorts being much more experienced sexually at young ages. In Wyatt's most recent cohort of white females, only 9 percent had not experienced sexual intercourse by age 19 compared to 80 percent of Kinsey's older cohort. In a survey in San Francisco area, Trocki (1992) found that 27 percent of females and 42 percent of males had had sex by age 16 with average age of onset of 17.2 for males and 18.6 for females. Forrest and Singh (1990) used National Survey of Family Growth data for never married, noncohabiting women to determine that even between 1982 and 1988 the percentage of women aged 15–19 who had experienced sexual intercourse increased from 42.1 percent to 49.5 percent. For never married males, Sonenstein, Pleck, and Ku (1991) found that the percent having experienced sexual intercourse increased with age as follows: 13 (5.4 percent), 14 (11.0 percent), 15 (21.1 percent), 16 (37.8 percent), 17 (57.5 percent), 18 (67.4 percent), and 19 (79.0 percent).

While evidence has been available for some time on the timing of onset, much less has been reported on the correlates of the transition (Miller and Moore, 1990). Research generally reported since Miller and Moore's (1990) review has indicated that age (Scott-Jones & White, 1990; Dorius, Heaton, & Steffen, 1993; Koyle, Jensen, Olsen, & Cundick, 1989; Whitbeck, Hoyt, Miller, & Kao, 1992), male gender (Elliott & Moore, 1989), drug use (Dorius, Heaton, & Steffen, 1993), low religiosity (Murry, 1992), dissatisfaction with school and/or low educational aspirations (Scott-Jones & White, 1990; Murry, 1992), low socioeconomic status (Scott-Jones & White, 1990; Murry, 1992; Handler, 1990), possibly delinquency (Ketterlinus, Lamb, Nitz, & Elster, 1992), early pubertal development (Miller & Moore, 1990), early dating (Dorius, Heaton, & Steffen, 1993), dissatisfaction with family life (Whitbeck, Hoyt, Miller, & Kao, 1992), higher self-esteem (for males only) (Rosenberg, Schooler, & Schoenbach, 1989), runaway status (Rotheram-Borus et al., 1992), permissiveness (Miller, Christensen, & Olson, 1987), peer pressure (Miller & Moore, 1990), and parental divorce during the adolescent years (Dorius, Heaton, & Steffan, 1993) are correlated with early onset.

Clinicians should not be surprised to discover very early onset of sexual behavior by many adolescents; at the same time, a minority of adolescents are successful at delaying onset until their 20s. Delaying onset appears to be a reasonable clinical goal, since more mature adolescents appear to be better able to deal with most aspects of sexuality, romantic relationships, and the possible negative consequences of nonmarital sexual behavior. This author's interpretation of the literature suggests that it is particularly important to delay onset until age 16 or 17. At the same time, another goal might be to help adolescents meet their emotional needs and resolve their questions about sexuality without using "trial and error" approaches to their sexual life. Ideally, abstinence should be encouraged over sexual experimentation.

Premarital Sexual Activity

Once adolescents have engaged in intercourse, they are likely to do so again within a few months; even if their first intercourse was forced, they are likely to initiate it voluntarily while they are still teenagers (Miller & Moore, 1990). Earle & Perricone (1986) did not find much change in college students who had more than five sexual partners between 1970 and 1981 (18 percent for men vs. 7.5 percent for women in 1981) but the percentage with two to five partners increased from 44 percent (men) and 19 percent (women) in 1970 to 56 percent (men) and 49 percent (women) in 1981. Elliott & Morse (1989), in the National Youth Survey panels from 1976 to 1980, found annual frequency of intercourse increasing from 18 to 40 for males and from 29 to 41 for females. Rates were as high as 54 and 56 for 17-year-old males and females, respectively, but for serious juvenile offenders using several types of drugs the rates reached 90 for females and 100 for males.

High rates of premarital sexual activity have been associated with permissive attitudes (Whitley, 1988; Jemmott & Jemmott, 1990; Gibson &

Kempf, 1990; Tanfer & Schoorl, 1992; Loewenstein & Furstenberg, 1991; Earle & Perricone, 1986; Keith, McCreary, Collins, Smith, & Bernstein, 1991; Whitbeck, Conger, & Kao, 1993), having sexually permissive or active friends (Chilman, 1989; DiBlasio & Benda, 1990; Gibson & Kempf, 1990; Loewenstein & Furstenberg, 1991; Whitbeck, Conger, & Kao, 1993), dating frequency at age 15 (Tanfer & Schoorl, 1992) (however, this became insignificant when controlling for age at first sex), lower religiosity (Miller & Moore, 1990; Miller & Olson, 1988; Chilman, 1989; Tanfer & Schoorl, 1992; Tanfer & Cubbins, 1992; Ketterlinus et al., 1992; Loewenstein & Furstenberg, 1991; DiBlasio & Benda, 1990), a lower age at first intercourse (Tanfer & Cubbins, 1992; Tanfer & Schoorl, 1992), urban residence (Elliott & Morse, 1989; Tanfer & Schoorl, 1992), being out of school or having lower educational success or aspirations (Tanfer & Schoorl, 1992; Chilman, 1989; DiBlasio & Benda, 1990; Ketterlinus et al., 1992; Keith, McCreary, Collins, Smith, & Bernstein, 1991; Gibson & Kempf, 1990; Loewenstein & Furstenberg, 1991), male gender (Whitley, 1988; Trocki, 1992; Elliott and Morse, 1989 didn't find any difference), lower social class (Tanfer & Schoorl, 1992; Elliott & Morse, 1989; Ketterlinus et al., 1992), lower levels of parental support (Chilman, 1989; Walsh, 1992; DiBlasio & Benda, 1990), nonintact family structure (Tanfer & Schoorl, 1992; Keith et al., 1991), early drug use (Chilman, 1989; Walsh, 1992; DiBlasio & Benda, 1990; Elliott & Morse, 1989), age (Walsh, 1991; Chilman, 1989; DiBlasio & Benda, 1990; Miller & Olson, 1988; Tanfer & Schoorl, 1992; Ketterlinus et al., 1992; Elliott & Morse, 1989; Keith et al., 1991), perceptions that the risks are worth the immediate rewards (DiBlasio & Benda, 1990), not living in a middle-class, family-focused neighborhood (Chilman, 1989), being involved in a deeper romantic relationship (Chilman, 1989), high unemployment in the community (Chilman, 1989), and delinquency (Elliott and Morse, 1989).

Age may moderate the relative importance of some factors related to premarital sexual activity; Gibson & Kempf (1990) found that peer influence was most important for younger (ages 12–15) Hispanics but personal values were most important for older (ages 16–18) adolescents. Elliott and Morse (1989) using longitudinal data from the National Youth Survey found that the most typical sequence of behaviors was from delinquency to drug use to sexual onset.

Clearly, high rates of premarital sexual behavior don't just happen. The factors that consistently predict premarital sexual behavior include individual variables that might be amenable to preventive education or to counseling, family variables that may not be easily changed but whose effects might be ameliorated clinically, and community variables that might be ameliorated through appropriate social work interventions (Chilman, 1989). As Chilman (1989) notes, it is important for clinicians to work through their own perspectives on healthy adolescent sexuality, to be able to evaluate each client individually rather than on the basis of stereotypes. The confounding nature of the relationship between self-esteem and sexual behavior illustrates the difficulty of working in the area clinically, as some unhealthy behaviors may in the short run at least appear to be correlated with better mental health, as measured by self-esteem and an internal locus of control. Certainly, it seems likely that a behavior defined as right by a client will not impact as negatively on that client as it might for a client who defines the same behavior as wrong. While some client behaviors may be acceptable to some clinicians, others may be deemed exploitive, illegal, or harmful regardless of the client's interpretation of their merits. The gender effects consistently observed for attitudes and behavior leave open the need for clinical interventions to reduce the gender-related conflict that is bound to occur regarding mutually satisfying and appropriate sexual behaviors at various stages of relationship development. Sprecher, McKinney, and Orbuch (1991) found that for both male and female college students high levels of sexual activity were valued in dates, less in friends, and least in prospective mates. Thus, it can be recommended that students guard their choices carefully since high levels of activity are not typically valued by prospective marriage partners, even if those levels gain short-term dates or friends.

Sexually Transmitted Diseases

Over the past 20 years, the level of sexual activity of teenagers and concomitant infections with STDs have continued to increase (Cates, 1991). At present, nearly 300,000 individuals have been diagnosed with AIDS, with AIDS being "the second leading cause of death among American men between the ages of 18 and 44 and the sixth leading cause of death among women in that same age group" (Kelly, Murphy, Sikkema, and Kalichman, 1993, p. 1023). Among homeless youths, HIV positive test rates are running as high as more than 5 percent (Rotheram-Borus, Koopman, & Ehrhardt, 1991). Each year as many as 2.5 million adolescents, up to one in seven, are affected by STDs in the United States (Olsen, Weed, Ritz, & Jensen, 1991; Quadrel, Fischhoff, & Davis, 1993). Gillmore, Butler, Lohr, & Gilchrist (1992) found that 39 percent of their sample of pregnant adolescents had already contracted an STD. At least one-third of all American adults have engaged in sexually risky behavior during their lifetime, with at least 7 percent at high risk of contracting AIDS (Smith, 1991). The danger of STDs is complicated by at least two factors—they are often asymptomatic, so that (1) those infected are not aware of it and (2) those who do know they are infected often choose to not tell their potential sexual partners that they are infected (Lindemann, 1988). Therefore, it has become potentially fatal to engage in unsafe sex with an unknown partner. In addition to the well-known threat of AIDS, less dangerous STDs such as chlamydia, herpes, genital warts, genital ulcer disease, pelvic inflammatory disease, gonorrhea, syphilis, and many others pose a threat to personal well-being and fertility. Even herpes, which is not fatal, can lead to severe depression in its victims (Mirotznik, Shapiro, Steinhart, & Gillespie, 1987).

Being infected with an STD has been correlated with drug use, especially crack cocaine[1] (Chirgwin, DeHovitz, Dillon, & McCormack, 1991; Chiasson, Stoneburner, Hildebrandt, & Ewing, 1991; Bowser, Fullilove, & Fullilove, 1990), problem drinking (Ericksen & Trocki, 1992; Romanowski & Piper, 1988), multiple sex partners (Ericksen & Trocki, 1992; O'Gorman, Bownes, & Dinsmore, 1989; Romanowski & Piper, 1988), early age at first intercourse (Ericksen & Trocki, 1992), prostitution (Chiasson et al., 1991), lower success in school (Holmbeck, Waters, & Brookman, 1990; lower socioeconomic status (Holmbeck, Waters, & Brookman, 1990), and coming from a more permissive home (Holmbeck, Waters, & Brookman, 1990). HIV infection has been correlated with having genital ulcer disease (Chirgwin et al., 1991), as well as factors associated with STDs in general. Safer sex practices have been correlated with assertiveness (Yesmont, 1992) and being female (Bustamante, 1992; Yesmont, 1992).

In spite of the risks being well documented, it has proven difficult to educate or persuade clients to change their sexual activity so as to reduce their risk of becoming infected with STDs (Baldwin & Baldwin, 1988; Crane & Carswell, 1992; Bownes, O'Gorman, & Dinsmore, 1990; Kelly, Murphy, Sikkema, & Kalichman, 1993; Rotheram-Borus et al., 1991; Klepinger, Bill, Tanfer, & Grady, 1993; Maticka-Tyndale, 1991; Kirby, Waszak, & Ziegler, 1991). Condom use appears to be relatively low in many research reports (Baldwin, Whiteley, & Baldwin, 1992; Bowser, Fullilove, & Fullilove, 1990; McCoy, McKay, Hermanns, & Lai, 1990; Kost & Forrest, 1992), sometimes even among those with an STD (Chang, Murphy, Diferdinando, & Morse, 1990), but has been improving over the past 15 years (Sonenstein, Pleck, & Ku, 1989). Indeed, less than one-third of heterosexuals with multiple partners always use condoms (Dolcini et al., 1993; Kost & Forrest, 1992). Condom use is higher if males do not think use is much of a hassle, if their girlfriend supports their use, if the male is confident in how to use them, and if he is older (Pendergrast, DuRant, & Gaillard, 1992) or if the person thinks they are at risk for getting or have already been infected with an STD (Bruce & Moineau, 1991). The effectiveness of condoms is limited by ineffective use, among other factors

---

[1]However, correlational evidence does not prove causation as discussed recently with respect to substance use and HIV exposure (Leigh and Stall, 1993). A plausible hypothesis would be that some third factor causes both drug abuse and risky sexual behavior, which then both lead to exposure to STD infections. When Gillmore, Butler, Lohr, and Gilchrist (1992) controlled for other factors, the relationship they had observed between drug abuse and risky sexual behavior disappeared.

(Grady & Tanfer, 1994; Steiner, Piedrahita, Glover, & Joanis, 1993; Trussell, Warner, & Hatcher, 1992). Relatively few well-designed prevention programs have been applied to STD prevention, compared to other areas of health, such as smoking cessation, nutrition, or weight control (Simons-Morton, Mullen, Mains, & Tabak, 1992; Price, Cowen, Lorion, & Ramos-McKay, 1989). Even when sex education is mandated for public schools, program implementation and quality are often quite variable (Calamidas, 1990), in spite of the availability of information on how to design and present effective instruction on STDs (Moore, 1988; Kelly et al., 1993) and condom use (Grieco, 1987; Ku, Sonenstein, & Pleck, 1992) and evidence that STD programs in the schools can at least improve awareness of the facts about STDs (Yarber, 1988).

For now, preventive education is the key to reducing the spread of STDs (Millstein, 1990). Unfortunately, people who appear to be committed to a sexually active life-style outside of a monogamous relationship find it difficult to accept programs that encourage abstinence or monogamy, while people who are committed to sex within marriage fear that teaching safe sex will encourage people to adopt values that encourage just about any type of consensual sex as long as one is using protection (e.g., a condom with spermicide). This author views the dilemma as one of adopting a short- versus a long-term perspective. From a long-term perspective, ignoring the short-term losses of not having a certain number of orgasms right away with a partner, it is clearly better to wait to have sex within marriage. From a short-term perspective, one has to weigh the advantages of having more orgasms sooner with a possibly interesting variety of partners against the risks of possibly becoming infected with an STD or causing an unwanted pregnancy. Unfortunately, no single contraceptive method may protect adequately against both risks simultaneously. As Cates and Stone (1992) have concluded from their review of the literature, "No currently available method [of contraception,] however, is highly effective in protecting simultaneously against pregnancy and infection. Thus, couples who place high priority on minimizing both risks may have to use two methods (p. 75)."

Saying that students or clients should engage in safe sex may be demeaning to their integrity because it assumes that they will not choose to live in accordance with a long-term perspective that is clearly less risky, both to themselves and their partners, from a variety of viewpoints. I believe that is analogous to telling someone who is getting drunk frequently that it's OK as long as he stays home and doesn't drive, when in fact, having to get drunk frequently is probably a symptom of deeper problems with self-esteem, job loss, relationship problems, or other factors that require assistance. From a long-term perspective, it would be better to learn to live without a dependence upon alcohol rather than merely engaging in damage control. Hajcak & Garwood (1988) have argued that much adolescent sex is an attempt to meet other unmet needs, for affection, self-esteem, a less boring life; two adolescents can end up having sex, which neither really wants, because both want to make up for a lack of affection at home. To me it seems that there are individuals who are solidly in favor of monogamous sex, individuals who are solidly in favor of having risky, unsafe sex with multiple partners, and individuals somewhere in between. The challenge is to determine what mix of programs, with the inherent treatment by subject interactions, will yield the least number of STD infections, unwanted pregnancies, and other problem behaviors that ultimately cost the public in time, money, quality of life, and lives. Unfortunately, I think we are a long way from finding that out empirically; indeed more concerted research might prove useful (Kelly et al., 1993). However, some preliminary research suggests that abstinence-based programs can be successful at changing attitudes (Olsen et al., 1991), but more research is needed (Hofferth, 1991; White & White, 1991). One flaw with the long-term approach is that youth who do not believe that they have much of a future may be difficult to persuade to adopt a long-term perspective when making sexual decisions; that may not be a new aspect of the human condition, though "without vision, the people perish."

Acquaintance or "Date" Rape

Parrot (1989) has reviewed the literature on acquaintance or "date" rape[2] and indicates that it usually happens between the ages of 15 and 25; more importantly, she observed that between a third and a half of college males surveyed in several studies reported that it would be OK to force a coed to have sex under at least some conditions (e.g., after having spent a lot of money on a date, if the man becomes so turned on he thinks he cannot stop, if they have been dating more than six months, etc.).[3] Sadly, similar percentages of female students agreed with the male viewpoints, feeling they had no right to deny a man sex under such conditions. In fact, nearly half of college women who have legally been raped may not realize that they have been victimized (Koss, 1985). In one of the better incidence studies to date, data from the 1987 National Survey of Children found that rates of nonvoluntary intercouse varied by race and gender (Moore, Nord, & Peterson, 1989): for black females, from 2.4 percent at age 14 or less to 8.0 percent at age 20; for white females, from 5.8 percent at age 14 or less to 12.7 percent at age 20; for black males, from 1.4 percent at age 15 to 6.1 percent at age 18; and for white males, from 0.3 percent at age 14 to 1.9 percent at age 19. Six risk factors were identified: parental heavy

---

[2]Some have discussed date rape under the rubric of courtship violence (Thompson, 1987).

[3]Porter and Critelli (1992) have done an excellent review of methodologies used in assessing sexual aggression by college men.

drinking, parental drug use, parental smoking as a teenager, having physical/emotional/mental limitations, living in poverty, and living apart from both parents prior to age 16. The percentage of white females who had ever experienced nonvoluntary sexual intercourse increased from 5.7 percent for no risk factors, to 9.4 percent for one risk factor, to 25.5 percent for two risk factors, and to 67.8 percent for three or more risk factors (Moore, Nord, & Peterson, 1989). In a Canadian study, DeKeseredy, Schwartz, & Tait (1993) found that nearly a third of the undergraduate female students surveyed had been victims of sexual coercion, usually forced intercourse. Other research has shown that acquaintance rape is either more likely to be perpetrated or seen as justifiable when the partners have been drinking alcohol (Corcoran & Thomas, 1991; Leigh, Aramburu, & Norris, 1992; Craig, Kalichman, & Follingstad, 1989), when the perpetrator is male (Feltey, Ainslie, & Geib, 1991; Lane & Gwartney-Gibbs, 1985; Muehlenhard & Cook, 1988), when the female has voluntarily gone to either his or her residence alone (Feltey, Ainslie, & Geib, 1991), when there is an established relationship (Feltey, Ainslie, & Geib, 1991; DeKeseredy, Schwartz, & Tait, 1993; Murnen, Perot, & Byrne, 1989), when the male holds traditional gender role attitudes or values male sexual dominance (Muehlenhard & Falcon, 1990), when the male thinks that weak resistance or participation in some sexual activity grants permission for any sexual activity (Hull, Forrester, Hull, & Gaines, 1992), when the male is a substance abuser (Hull et al., 1992), when the male frequently uses pornography (Hull et al., 1992), when the male exhibits hostility toward women (Hull et al., 1992), when the female has low self-esteem or an external locus of control (Parrot, 1989), and when the female believes the male is so aroused that it is "useless to stop him" (DeKeseredy, Schwartz, & Tait, 1993). While males are occasionally victims of sexual assault (Muehlenhard & Cook, 1988), it appears that women are usually less successful at completing the sexual aggression if the man resists (O'Sullivan & Byers, 1993) and the incident results in less trauma to the man than it might if done to a woman (Struckman-Johnson, 1988).

Strategies that appear to work in preventing date rape include screaming, running away, reasoning, and crying (Hull et al., 1992). It is important that women understand that they are not responsible for providing sexual relief for men and have the right to stop a sexual encounter at any point, even if they indicated previously that they wanted to complete it. If the victim is asleep or passed out, forced sex is still rape. Self-defense skills can help compensate for the typically greater male strength. It is also useful for women to help other women avoid date rape by offering rides home, advice, support, and the like. Women and men should understand "that sexual behavior is not an appropriate expectation as a return on one's financial or time investment" (Hull et al., 1992, p. 195). It is important to educate both men and women about date rape; to educate only women implies that women "are ultimately being held responsible for their own victimization, . . . [and] given the responsibility of stopping rape. We are too often unwilling to hold men accountable for rape" (Feltey, Ainslie, & Geib, 1991, pp. 246–247). Acquaintance rape may not be acknowledged by its victims, who often feel they are to blame for what happened; their symptoms may include withdrawal, acting out sexually, and sudden changes in relationships with family or friends (Parrot, 1989). Some victims may feel that having lost their virginity or their integrity as a result of the rape, they no longer have any right to refuse sex to anyone and may engage in "non-discriminating sexual behavior patterns," having sex with many partners (Parrot, 1989, p. 55). Counselors should either believe the victim or act as if they do; otherwise, they should refer the client elsewhere. Counsels should then learn the facts of the case, in the context of local and state rape laws (Parrot, 1989). Helping the victim regain a sense of self-control and self-esteem is critical; an important avenue is to help the victim learn methods to avoid future victimization (Parrot, 1989). Reporting rape and going to court is a complex decision because of the difficulties involved in maintaining one's reputation and winning such cases in either civil or criminal court (Parrot, 1989).

Unplanned Pregnancies

Although few U.S. adolescents report that they want to become pregnant, the United States leads the industrialized democracies in pregnancy rates among adolescents, even though rates of sexual activity are similar to those in other nations (Baumeister, Kupstas, & Klindworth, 1991); in 1985, 11 percent of females aged 15 to 19 became pregnant, with 4.4 percent having an abortion and 5.1 percent giving birth (Miller & Moore, 1990). The birthrate for adolescent women declined between 1970 and 1984, primarily due to the availability of abortion services (Chilman, 1989), but the percentage of births to unwed teenage mothers increased from one-third to over one-half. In 1987, 64 percent of the births to women under age 20 were to unwed mothers (Miller & Moore, 1990). For a variety of reasons, U. S. youths appear to use contraception less effectively than youths in other nations. While religious youths are less likely to engage in intercourse, they are also less likely to use contraception if they do engage in sex, presumably because of guilt reactions about planning ahead for sex (Miller & Moore, 1990). Surprisingly, the male partners of teenage girls who become pregnant or infected with an STD are not usually other teenagers, but are most often between 20 and 25 years of age (Males, 1992). The popular notion of "children having children" may be true for teenage girls but is not normally true for the fathers involved! Other facts may be surprising. Births and rate of births to adolescents have declined, largely due to the availability of abortion, since 1970, but the percentage of adolescents who do give birth and keep their babies increased to 93 percent in 1979 (Miller & Jorgensen, 1989). Pregnancy rates for all females aged 15 to 19 in the United States increased from 9 percent in 1971 to 16 percent in 1979 (Zelnik & Kantner, 1980), with 36 percent of sexually active such females becoming pregnant in 1979 (Koenig & Zelnik, 1982). Adolescents from single-parent families of origin and those who are in less committed dyadic relationships are less likely to use effective contraception and more likely to become pregnant (Miller & Jorgensen, 1989; O'Campo, Faden, Gielen, Kass, & Anderson, 1993). Using data from the National Longitudinal Survey of Youth, Plotnick (1992) found that premarital pregnancy was negatively related to strong internal locus of control, more traditional sex role attitudes, positive attitudes toward school, high educational aspirations, and frequent church attendance among Catholics. Casper (1990) found that older adolescents and Protestants were more likely to use contraception as were adolescents whose parents communicated with them about contraceptive use. Horwitz, Klerman, Kuo, and Jekel's (1991, p. 168) research indicated that "emotional deprivation, particularly at an early age, may predispose adolescents to seek emotional closeness through sexual activity and early parenthood." Some adolescents delay using contraception from fear of parental discovery or fear of allegedly dangerous aspects of using contraception (Zabin, Stark, & Emerson, 1991). Sexual abuse during childhood may be related to less effective use of contraception by adolescents (Boyer & Fine, 1992). Contraceptives fail at varying rates: 25 for spermicides, 26 percent for periodic abstinence, 15 percent for condoms, and 8 percent for the pill (Jones & Forrest, 1992). Community-level variables (restrictions on contraceptive advertisement, proportion of counties with family planning clinics, use of family planning services, and the proportion of Medicaid-eligible women did not predict much of the variance in premarital pregnancies in Lundberg and Plotnick's (1990) study. Lamb (1991) notes that the causal link between educational attainment and adolescent pregnancy is not clear; it may be that educational failure leads to situations where such adolescents risk unplanned pregnancies rather than the pregnancy or birth leading to academic failure (though it could reinforce such failure). Upchurch and McCarthy's (1989, 1990) research suggested that having a baby did not hinder high school graduation for those students enrolled but reduced the chances of ever graduating for those who dropped out of high school; however, since the 1950s, graduation rates for mothers have increased from 19 percent to over 50 percent.

Some programs have achieved success in increasing the use of contraception in order to prevent unplanned pregnancies (Barth, Fetro, Leland, & Volkan, 1992; Hofferth, 1991). Several programs have proven to increase the chances of an adolescent mother staying in school and delaying subsequent pregnancies (Warrick, Christianson, Walruff, & Cook,

1993; Ruch-Ross, Jones, & Musick, 1992). Some doubts about the ability of school-based clinics to reduce birthrates have been raised by the evaluation of Kirby et al. (1993). On some occasions, adolescent pregnancy is a symptom of deeper family problems, as when an adolescent becomes pregnant as a way of preserving family harmony (Romig & Thompson, 1988; Atwood & Kasindorf, 1992).

Pregnancies are more likely to be resolved by abortion if the female has high self-esteem, is a Catholic who attends church occasionally, and reports an external locus of control; females with high educational expectations are less likely to give birth out of wedlock, but are evenly split between abortion and marriage (Plotnick, 1992). Community factors that promote abortion decisions are higher availability, less restrictive laws, and less restrictive funding of abortions (Lundberg & Plotnick, 1990). Adolescents from suburban residences, of higher socioeconomic status, who are older, who have higher self-esteem, who have had less labor-force experience, and with higher educational aspirations may be more likely to give up unwanted children for adoption (Resnick, Blum, Bose, Smith, & Toogood, 1990; Stern & Alvarez, 1992; Bachrach, Stolley, & London, 1992). An important concern is delayed pregnancy testing for those adolescents who may choose to abort, since the longer the time since conception, the more risky the abortion. One recent study found that denial, a psychological barrier, was more important than demographic information in predicting delay (Bluestein & Rutledge, 1992).

Adolescent motherhood is of concern because it has been associated with increased medical complications, lower occupational and educational attainment, greater marital instability, a greater chance of child abuse, and generally poorer mothering (de Anda, Darroch, Davidson, Gilly, Javidi, Jefford, Komorowski, & Morejon-Schrobsdorf, 1992; Grogger & Bronars, 1993; Zuravin, 1991; Scott-Jones & Turner, 1990), although some adolescent mothers do exceptionally well in spite of their youth (Miller & Moore, 1990). In fact, in physiological terms at least, adolescents are perhaps "optimally suited for childbearing" (Lamb, 1988). At least one study of low income adolescents found that mothering adolescents (and those adolescents who were not sexually active) appeared to be experiencing fewer mental health problems than those adolescents who were sexually active, whether or not they had ever been pregnant; in other words, early mothering may not always seem to be a bad option, given a low-income context (Stiffman, Powell, Earls, & Robins, 1990).

Abortion

Abortion is a worldwide practice, though the United States and China share the uncommon distinction of being the two largest nations that allow

abortions up to viability (Henshaw, 1990).[4] In 1987, there were as many as
31 million legal and 22 million clandestine abortions worldwide (Henshaw, 1990). In the United States, where abortion is now the most common surgical procedure (Speckhard & Rue, 1992), just over a quarter
(26.2 percent) of abortions are performed for teenagers; only 1.1 percent
are performed for females under 15 years of age, with about 10.4 percent
for females 15 to 17 years old. The largest percentage of abortions are performed for women of college age, 20–24 years (34.5 percent), with smaller
percentages for older women: 21.2 percent (25–29 years old), 11.4 percent
(30–34 years old), 5.4 percent (35–39 years old), and 1.3 percent (40 years
and older) (Henshaw, 1990). However, the highest rate of abortions, 63
per 1,000 women, occurs for 18–19 year olds, followed by the rate for
women aged 20 to 24, at 52.3 per 1,000 (Henshaw, 1990). Henshaw and
Kost (1992) reported that in 1988 about 41 percent of pregnant women
under the age of 18 had abortions (of those who did not miscarry). The
rate of abortions for women under 15 years of age is very low, at 4.8 per
1,000 (Henshaw, 1990). The United States has the highest percentage of
abortions that occur in clinics outside hospitals of any nation in the world
(86.9 percent). In the United States, most abortions (51.5 percent) occur at
less than eight weeks gestation, with most of the rest between 9 and 12
weeks (39.6 percent), although 3.7 percent occur after 17 weeks gestation
(Henshaw, 1990). The average cost for a nonhospital first-trimester abortion in the United States was $251 in 1989 (Henshaw, 1991, p. 246);
despite the low cost, as many as 20 percent of poor women will defer abortions when not funded by Medicaid (Henshaw, 1991). Some evidence suggests that abortion rates have declined slightly in recent years in the United
States, though still remaining at about 1.5 million a year (Henshaw & Van
Vort, 1994).

Pregnant adolescents are more likely to choose abortion as a way of
resolving their crisis pregnancy if they intend to complete their schooling,
if they are less religious (and not Catholic), if they have more liberal attitudes regarding abortion, if their boyfriends want them to have an abortion
or do not want to marry them, if they are ambivalent themselves about
having the abortion, if their relatives support their getting an abortion, or if
they are using illegal drugs (Miller & Moore, 1990; Miller, 1992). However, one national study of over 1,500 adolescents who had had abortions
(Henshaw & Kost, 1992) found that 17 percent reported being evangelical
or "born-again" Christians and 27 percent attended church about once a
week; 31 percent reported that their mother attended church once a week.
Thirty percent of the respondents were Catholics. In another major abortion study (Major et al., 1990) involving 283 women who had abortions at

---

[4]Interestingly, the other nation cited by Henshaw (1990) is the Netherlands which has one of
the lowest abortion rates in the world at 5 per year per 1,000 women of reproductive age.

a private clinic, 58 percent were Catholic.[5] A national survey of over 1,800 adolescent males found that positive attitudes toward abortion were significantly related to higher parental education, sexual permissiveness, not wanting many children, not being of fundamentalist religious affiliation, not citing religion as personally important, and not wanting to become a father at the present time (Marsiglio & Shehan, 1993). Notably, 61 percent of the respondents did not think it was good for a woman to have an abortion if her partner objected. Much of the time, boyfriends are willing to pay for at least part of the cost of an abortion (Henshaw & Kost, 1992).

Women's decision making about abortion choice has been successfully modeled using the Fishbein and Ajzen model of reasoned action (Rosen, 1992; Brazzell & Acock, 1988), suggesting that adolescents are making rational decisions, given their perceptions of the anticipated consequences of abortion versus childrearing or adoption.

Postabortion Syndrome

There have been several reviews of the literature on possible psychological consequences of abortion, relative to other outcomes (Adler, 1979; Rogers, Stoms, & Phifer, 1989; Posavac & Miller, 1990; Adler et al., 1990, 1992; Cates, Schulze, & Grimes, 1983; Olson, 1980; Zabin, Hirsch, & Emerson, 1989; Wilmoth, 1992; Adler, 1992; Major & Cozarelli, 1992; Speckhard & Rue, 1992; Miller, 1992; Wilmoth, de Alteriis, & Bussell, 1992; Pliner & Yates, 1992; David, 1992; Rutherford Institute, 1988).[6] Adolescents appear to be concerned about possible negative consequences of abortion, overestimating the dangers because of allegedly inaccurate pro-life rhetoric, according to Stone and Waszak (1992). Adolescents appear to receive pressure both to have and to not have an abortion from their parents, boyfriends, or other friends.

Ascertaining the truth about possible postabortion syndrome is difficult since a large percentage, as high as 50 percent, either deny ever having had an abortion (Wilmoth, 1992) or any negative effects of it (Reardon, 1987) or otherwise rationalize their decision to abort (Brennan, 1974) or refuse

---

[5]Over 91 percent of the women who had abortions during the time frame of the study participated in the project, so attrition did not seriously affect the percentages of the women who were Catholic.

[6]Mortality rates for legal abortions in the United States have been reported per 100,000 to be: 0.2 at eight or fewer weeks, 0.3 at 9–10 weeks, 0.6 at 11–12 weeks, 3.7 at 16–20 weeks, and 12.7 at 21 weeks or more since last menstruation, compared to 6.6 deaths per 100,000 live births (Henshaw, 1990). While Henshaw (1990) says the mortality rate for live births is 11 times the rate for legal abortions, his own data actually show a rate twice as great as live births for the later abortions. Since it is not clear that all deaths resulting from abortion complications are reported, the rates cited by Henshaw (1990) may be underestimated more than the rates for live births.

to participate in abortion research. Medical complications, very rarely maternal death, can occur after abortions, as discussed in detail (Rutherford Institute, 1988). Most meta-analyses of abortion effects provide data to support either position (Wilmoth, 1992); for example, the classic Denmark study found higher psychiatric hospitalization rates for women who had had abortions, but that finding held only for women who were divorced, separated, or widowed (David, Rasmussen, & Holst, 1981).[7] Such women may have wanted their child but may have been forced by the loss of their husband to have the abortion; and they may have more often had second-trimester abortions, if they were conflicted about having the child (Adler, 1992). Wilmoth (1992) concedes that the best evidence supports some form of postabortion negative psychological reactions but leaves in dispute the frequency, severity, and cause of those reactions. Wilmoth (1992, p. 7) notes that "Catholics and those with strong religious beliefs, those without social support, those who have abortions after the first trimester, those who have saline or dilation and evacuation abortions, those who have been pressured or coerced to have an abortion, those with pre-pregnancy physical or psychological conditions, and those with particular psychological dispositions have more negative psychological consequences." Adler (1982) cites a preponderance of evidence that younger women are at greater risk for adverse effects, possibly because they are at greater risk for having been forced to have an abortion they did not really want, for having a second-trimester abortion, and for lacking social support. Major and Cozarelli (1992, p. 139) argue that most women "did not immediately experience their abortions as particularly traumatic," but they cite risk factors that are associated with greater trauma: low levels of social support, higher levels of self-blame, and having expectations of being less able to cope well with the abortion. However, Major and Cozarelli (1992) admit that little evidence is available on the possible long-term effects of abortion. Miller's (1992) research cited by Wilmoth, Alteriis, and Russell (1992) as being the best probability sampling of any published U.S. study (though done entirely in the San Francisco area) found 22 percent of those who had had an abortion feeling worse about their sexuality, 6 percent saying it had made their relationship with their boyfriend worse, 18 percent saying that they felt distress only for the first week or two after the abortion, and 13 percent saying that they would not have the abortion again even under the same circumstances (6 percent more were not sure). With reference to experiencing any significant emotional upset or disturbance after the first few postabortion weeks, some women reported a little dis-

---

[7]Psychiatric admission rates within three months of either an abortion or a live birth were similar, about 12 per 10,000 compared to 7 per 10,000 for all women of childbearing age. However, among for the formerly married women the rates were 64 (post abortion) versus 17 (post birth) per 10,000 (Adler, 1992).

tress (4 percent), some distress (8 percent), and some much distress (10 percent) (Miller, 1992). Since the negative responses probably did not overlap exactly, it is likely that approximately a quarter to a third of the Miller (1992) subjects reported some noticeable psychological distress after their abortions. Even Major et al. (1990), in a study involving 91 percent participation by private abortion clinic clients, found that immediately after the abortion 4 percent were experiencing severe depression, 11 percent were experiencing moderate depression, and 21 percent were experiencing mild depression, for a total of over a third of the clients feeling troubled.

Speckhard and Rue (1992) suggest that a constellation of dysfunctional behaviors and emotional reactions similar to post-traumatic stress disorder (PTSD) should be labeled "postabortion syndrome" or PAS; they are also recommending use of the terms "postabortion distress (PAD)" and "postabortion psychosis (PAP)." However, the effect sizes suggested by Speckhard and Rue (1992) of 0.01 to 0.04 percent are relatively small, smaller than the effect sizes associated with the extent to which researchers (Fowers, 1991) have found women to be less satisfied with marriage than their husbands (0.1 to 0.2 percent), with the latter effects too small to be detected as significant in samples of less than 200 subjects (Schumm, Bollman, Jurich, & Bugaighis, 1985).

Anecdotal evidence suggests that some women experience a range of debilitating phenomena, including nightmares, anniversary reactions, intrusive thoughts, flashbacks, survivor guilt, denial, replacement pregnancies, depression, intimacy avoidance, and relationship difficulties (Caltenberger, 1982; Speckhard & Rue, 1992). In this author's own experience, one acquaintance reported anger lasting nearly 15 years over the alleged comments by an Ohio Planned Parenthood Clinic staff member who had reassured her about having an abortion on the basis that her baby's soul was sure to go to heaven, implying perhaps that its eternal security was more likely through an abortion than if it were to be carried to term. Another friend, a man, commented with sadness after seeing a movie in which the 18-year-old hero was about the same age as his child (he and his wife decided to abort in 1973) would have been. Guilt can be experienced even after unintentional abortions. Another friend tried to help her husband load a canoe onto their truck and felt something snap inside herself, followed immediately by a miscarriage; she still feels guilty about harming her child, though unintentionally. Perhaps the most tragic case I have encountered was an army reservist who was activated and scheduled to fly to Desert Storm with her unit, until she found out she was pregnant the Friday before the Saturday that her unit was to leave the United States. A military civilian employee told her that if she had an abortion at her own expense, they would fly her out to Saudi Arabia on Sunday so she could join her comrades. Flush with desire to serve her country and to be loyal to her fellow soldiers, she immediately drove 200 miles home, had the abortion on Saturday, and returned on Sunday only to be told that there were no more flights out and she would have to remain stateside; thus, instead of a soldier fighting to protect her children, we had a soldier destroying, at least potentially, her child, in order to fight, a bizarre role reversal. Worse yet, when the unit returned, her commanding officer effectively ostracized her for having gotten pregnant and having avoided service with the unit overseas! When her subsequent commander commented briefly on his appreciation of the magnitude of her sacrifice, her face visibly relaxed as if a large burden were being removed.

There are risks associated with carrying a pregnancy to term (Pliner & Yates, 1992; Zabin, Hirsch, & Emerson, 1989) for the mother and for her unwanted children (David, 1992; Russo, 1992). In one of the apparently better, recent studies comparing the effects of having an abortion versus having an unwanted child, it appeared that women who had only one abortion were slightly better off in terms of self-esteem than women who had children or repeat abortions (Russo & Zierk, 1992). In another major research project (Zabin, Hirsch, & Emerson, 1989), having a baby was shown to delay educational attainment relative to having an abortion. However, in a recent Israeli study, abortion patients were found to be more distressed than relevant comparison groups (Teichman, Shenhar, & Segal, 1993); the legal restrictions on abortion in Israel may, however, keep such results from generalizing accurately to the United States. While it is possible that unwanted children may contribute less on average than wanted children to society, this author has not yet seen evidence to confirm the hypothesis that their total contribution is so minimal or so negative that it would have been better had they not been born.

Clearly, many women undergo abortions and experience relatively little distress, while a significant minority of other women are greatly distressed. It appears that the social support a woman receives and her own values are critical factors in determining how she is most likely to respond after an abortion. Counselors must be extremely sensitive to clients who are considering abortion or other options. As Minden and Notman (1991, p. 131) wisely note, "A woman who is considering terminating a pregnancy for any reason is experiencing a crisis in her life." There are many issues that might merit clinical exploration, as the woman's feelings can run deep and be connected to both past experiences and future expectations and goals. All options should be explored (Gold, 1991). Regardless of one's own values, it would seem best to try to ensure that the woman makes a truly free choice, as opposed to having been pressured into making a certain type of decision. If a client is primarily considering an abortion for lack of money to pay for her medical expenses and would otherwise want to continue her pregnancy, it might be appropriate to refer her to local physicians who are often willing to reduce fees or help make arrangements for fee payment through charitable or governmental sources. Countertransference is possible and should be controlled, as it may adversely affect the counselor's ability to empathize with the client and help her make the best decision (Minden & Notman, 1991). However, as noted by Lemkau (1991, p. 100), "In a political environment in which a woman's right to choose abortion is constantly challenged, it is easy to forget the importance of the right to choose *not* to abort. Health care professionals need to be alert to possible coercion around decisions to abort and should support women in making decisions that are as free as possible from pressures by others."

From my own perspective, I would hope that women might not be pressured into having abortions on the basis of what the Army calls risk-management issues. For example, a couple might be told, as we were with respect to our most recent child, that certain fetal measurements (head width to height) were not "right." But our baby girl was born perfectly normal. In another case, a woman conceived unexpectedly at the age of 42 and drank alcohol and smoked a pack of cigarettes a day during her pregnancy, resulting in a two month premature infant that contracted jaundice and was diagnosed by the pediatrician as having a 100 percent chance of dying (not to mention a 25 percent chance of total blindness and a lesser chance of permanent mental retardation), but the infant ate like crazy and turned out well.[8]

Yet that situation today would seem like an excellent situation for a preemptive abortion, knowing what we know about the effects of older age, cigarettes, and alcohol during pregnancy. A woman may be told that having a baby will cost her a lot of money she can't afford (but there are many willing doctors who will accept reduced fees so a client can avoid an abortion); she may be told that children born to single mothers can't make it in life (but President Clinton did all right!); she may feel that her boyfriend will abandon her if she doesn't have an abortion (but maybe such a fellow isn't worth keeping!)—my point being that one can always paint a gloomy picture if one insists on it but the odds may not be as bad as one thinks they are.[9]

---

[8]The infant in question was myself, born in 1951 when a three pound infant was in much more serious trouble than today.

[9]In the Army, an officer is taught that there is always risk; no course of action entails no risk at all. Therefore, the best decision rule is to select the course of action that offers the most benefits, provided that common sense is used to minimize the known risks. In the case of abortion, adoption, and single parenthood, two options seem to offer the priceless benefit of bringing a human person into the world who will in all probability make an overall positive contribution to the world, whereas the other option offers only freedom from childcare responsibilities, a risk avoided in fact by two options, not just one. Hence, from a risk-taking perspective, adoption would seem to minimize risk compared to at least one course of action but maximize opportunity for the unborn child. No matter what option is chosen, some risk will be entailed in ending the pregnancy, which will occur one way or another, whether by birth, miscarriage, or abortion. Often one may hear the slogan "If you can't trust me with a decision, how can you trust me with a child?" Actually, I think that women, as well as military commanders, can be trusted with decisions and make good decisions *if* they have good information and adequate resources; in the military, a commander with inadequate information and few resources

Cohabitation

Surra (1990) has provided a concise review of the recent literature on cohabitation. Cohabitation rates appear to have increased substantially since 1970—up as much as 117 percent between 1970 and 1978 and another 63 percent between 1980 and 1988, to a total of 2.6 million households in 1988.[10] From an analysis of couple data from the 1987 National Survey of Families and Households, DeMaris and MacDonald (1993) found that 23 percent of the couples had cohabited with their current spouse (only) before marriage while another 10 percent had cohabited with multiple partners before marriage. Gwartney-Gibbs (1986) found that in two Oregon samples of newlyweds' marriage license applications from 1970 and 1980 cohabitation rates had increased from 13 to 53 percent. Stump and Knudsen (1988) found that nearly half of the 573 marriage licenses they examined featured similar addresses for each spouse prior to marriage, which seemed to be a valid indication of prior cohabitation. While only a small percentage of the population is cohabiting at any point in time—about 4 percent—the percentage that have ever cohabited may

---

can be trusted to make bad decisions—therefore, I am not ashamed to expect women to do the same thing in the same circumstances. Therefore, I think it is critical to do all we can to provide women with crisis pregnancies with both complete information and adequate resources so they can make the best decisions.

A neutral illustration of this problem of risk management comes from my last annual training period in which my unit went from Nebraska to Virginia for two weeks. While the senior commander discouraged it, I decided to take a calculated risk and allow my soldiers off for one day a week. Sure, if they had had a wreck while off duty, my career might have been over, I might have lost 25 percent of my maximum retirement, and been forced out of the U.S. Army Reserve in disgrace. But some of my soldiers got to see an ocean for the only time in their lives, something they will remember forever. Some got to visit Washington, DC, and see the Holocaust Museum (this was a training event because the unit's mission was to prevent mistreatment of prisoners and civilian internees) and the Vietnam War Memorial and touch the names of friends killed in that war, which they would never have been able to do otherwise. One female soldier got to visit a friend from Desert Storm that she hadn't seen in two years; sadly, he was killed three months later in an accident, meaning that my willingness to take a risk allowed her one last chance to see him. In fact, the chance that they would have had a wreck was probably quite small and the chance of getting something precious quite high, making it a good call on my part. But all it would have taken would have been an attitude of ignoring the precious possibilities and focusing on the slight risks to lead to a decision that would have entailed more opportunity costs than anyone could have imagined, even though it would have been more convenient for me. As far as reducing the risks, I allowed the soldiers to use my own car (if there was a wreck, the army wouldn't sue me for damage to government equipment and my insurance would cover their medical expenses), sent them out with a senior officer to discourage any foolishness, stayed back at the base myself to handle any flak that might arise there, and carefully advised all about safety and calling in on a 1–800 number to my home office so I could determine if they were overdue at their destinations and to remind them to stay on schedule. I believe that if women felt freer to envision the possibilities of their unborn and to manage the risks involved in an unplanned pregnancy that far fewer abortions would occur, even if their availability remained unchanged.

[10]The U.S. Census data on cohabitation includes a variety of nonmarital relationships and may overestimate the number of romantic attachments, according to Surra (1990).

approach 50 percent, as cohabitation appears to be becoming a more normative stage in the courtship process (Bumpass & Sweet, 1989; Thornton, 1988; Tanfer, 1987; Gwartney-Gibbs, 1986; Spanier, 1983; Larson, 1991) that may be partly responsible for the trend for young adults to delay formal marriage (Bumpass, Sweet, & Cherlin, 1991).

Cohabiters are generally young adults, often have children, are more often never-married singles than divorcées, have earlier and greater sexual experience, and usually hold more liberal attitudes about family life, religion, and drug use (Surra, 1990), factors confirmed since 1990 by Thornton, Axinn, and Hill (1992), Wu and Balakrishnan (1992), Axinn and Thornton (1992, 1993), and Thomson and Colella (1992). Cohabiting couples may initiate more sexual interactions with each other than married couples (Byers & Heinlein, 1989), although other research has found no differences (Samson, Levy, Dupras, & Tessier, 1991). Parental marital instability appears to predict their children's chances of cohabitation (DeMaris & MacDonald, 1993; Thornton, 1991; Black & Sprenkle, 1991).

Although Macklin (1983) and Newcomb (1979) concluded that marital quality was unrelated to prior cohabitation, Surra (1990) and White (1990) concluded from their more recent reviews of the literature that cohabitation was negatively correlated with marital quality and marital stability (Balakrishnan, Rao, Lapierre-Adamcyk, & Krotki, 1987; Booth & Johnson, 1988; Watson, 1983; Bumpass & Sweet, 1989; DeMaris, 1984[11]; DeMaris & Leslie, 1984; Kurdek & Schmitt, 1986; Newcomb, 1986, 1987; Bennett, Blanc, & Bloom, 1988),[12] although at least one study involving over 10,000 Canadians had found a positive relationship with marital stability (White, 1987), while other studies found no relationship (Watson & Demeo, 1987; Yelsma, 1986). Since 1990 Shachar (1991) found no association with marital satisfaction but Bumpass, Martin, and Sweet (1991), Axinn and Thornton (1992), Stets (1993), Teachman, Thomas, and Paasch (1991), Thomson and Colella (1992), DeMaris and Rao (1992), and Teachman and Polonko (1990) found a negative relationship between cohabitation and marital outcomes. A positive relationship has been observed in recent research between cohabitation (as compared to marriage) and more frequent abuse of one's female partner by the male partner (Ellis, 1989; Stets & Straus, 1989). However, Teachman and Polonko (1990), DeMaris and MacDonald (1993), and Stets (1993) found that the negative relationship between cohabitation and marital success was nullified for couples who married the only person they had ever cohabited with. Furthermore, any adverse effects

---

[11]However, the results were not significant for remarried couples.

[12]Bennett, Blanc, and Bloom (1988) found that Swedish wives who had cohabited premaritally had almost an 80 percent higher marital dissolution rate; those wives who had cohabited for over three years had a 50 percent higher dissolution rate than those who had cohabited for shorter periods.

of cohabitation do not appear to carry over into marriage for more than 10 years (DeMaris & MacDonald, 1993).

However, Tucker and Grady (1991), in an analysis of data from 128 college undergraduates, found that their subjects did not project that cohabitation would reduce a person's chances for marital happiness; Hobart and Grigel (1992), in a study of nearly 1800 Canadian young adults, found widespread support for cohabitation. Moore and Stief (1991) with data from the 1987 National Survey of Children found that half of the respondents held favorable attitudes toward cohabitation. Brooks and Kennedy (1989), in a study of American and British students, found greater support for cohabitation among the British students. Cohabitation does appear to be a transitional, if not unstable (Sarantakos, 1991), phenomenon, with a median duration of only 1.3 years (Bumpass & Sweet, 1989). Thornton (1988) found an interesting gender reversal in endings for cohabitation: 23 percent for men and 37 percent for women ending in marriage with 40 percent for men and 23 percent for women ending altogether within two years. Axinn and Thornton (1992) express concern, based on their multiwave panel study of 867 Detroit area families from 1962 to 1985, that high divorce rates may encourage cohabitation, with cohabitation leading to higher divorce rates. Cohabitation appears to be associated with higher rates of courtship violence than other types of relationships (Lane & Gwartney-Gibbs, 1985).

In summary, current research suggests that individuals who are willing to cohabit generally are less committed to their partner, an attitude that probably is responsible for subsequent marital instability.[13] However, cohabitation that leads to marriage may escape the negative effects observed overall for cohabitation and marital success; at the same time, cohabitation with multiple partners or for longer periods of time (i.e., several years) may bode very poorly for subsequent marital success. Any negative effects of cohabitation are probably overtaken by other events after several years of marriage. In any event, it does not appear—contrary to popular opinion—that cohabitation is, on average, a viable method for improving subsequent marital adjustment, as its effects are usually neutral under the best of conditions.

There have been few clinical discussions of cohabitation (Cole, 1988; Macklin, 1988). Nevertheless, cohabitation should not necessarily be considered a pathological development in courtship progress, unless its participants find their actions in clear contrast to their own ethical value system. For example, if conservative Christians were to cohabit before marriage, they might well be setting themselves up for a marriage in which at least one partner feels that the marriage was formalized out of guilt over cohabi-

---

[13]DeMaris and MacDonald (1993) represent one study whose results do not support this assertion.

tation or premarital sex rather than out of free personal choice. On the other hand, couples who cohabit in order to improve their marriage may find the results disappointing in the long run. Furthermore, those who cohabit for reasons of convenience rather than relationship development may be setting themselves up for failure in subsequent relationships. Clearly, any clinical assessment of the merits of cohabitation for any couple must take into account the meaning of cohabitation for each partner, especially with respect to their commitment to each other and their honesty with each other about that commitment. Feelings of betrayal and exploitation may well occur if one partner discovers late in the game that his or her sense of commitment to the relationship is not, in fact, being reciprocated. Because cohabitation creates two new transitions—"moving day" and an informal to a formal, legal commitment day—couples might experience stress at either or both transitions. Living together under the legal restrictions of marriage may seem oppressive to individuals accustomed to the relative freedoms of cohabitation, raising serious issues of personal autonomy and independence that may require therapeutic assistance for satisfactory resolution. Since a substantial percentage of cohabitations end without marriage but may feel like a divorce to the participants, counselors may find it useful to apply some divorce counseling procedures when dealing with such former cohabitants; it is also likely that some prospective newlyweds may be struggling with divorcelike feelings that reflect unfinished business from previous cohabiting relationships. While formal guidelines may not be available for dealing with current or former cohabitants, issues of separation, loss, and transition stress are likely to be similar to those experienced by married or divorcing couples and responsive to similar clinical interventions.

Conclusions

Several independent variables appear to be common correlates, if not antecedents, to most if not all of the nonmarital sexual variables considered in this chapter. With the possible exception of contraceptive use and hence unplanned pregnancy, religiosity seems to correlate negatively with most instances of nonmarital sexuality. With the exception of abortion, males seem to be more involved in or interested in nonmarital sexual behavior; however, with respect to abortion, there is relatively little empirical data on males with which to form much of a judgment anyways. Having lower educational aspirations appears to correlate positively with nonmarital sexuality with the exception of abortion, which is used in essence to preserve at least perceived educational opportunity for women. Drug use, lower socioeconomic resources, and permissive attitudes appear to correlate positively with most nonmarital sexuality. Early age at first intercourse and or early dating appear to predict earlier or more frequent involvement later in nonmarital sexuality. Finally, coming from a nonintact family of origin seems to correlate with higher rates of nonmarital sexuality. It is not clear empirically what themes may underlie these common predictors. To me, it appears plausible that a short-term orientation compared to a long-term orientation may be one factor. "Eat, drink, and be merry" would seem to be a good decision rule if indeed there is no future, or no hope for one's future. For some clients there may be no future, but hopefully one role of family life educators and/or family clinicians may be to remind the majority of our clientele that there is hope, and that there may be more viable alternatives out there than there may appear to be at the height of one's distress. At the same time, referrals should be used to ensure that all available social support is at least offered to clients so their personal decisions can be based from strength rather than weakness. Given the empirical support for the effectiveness of religiosity in reducing nonmarital sexuality, it would be foolish to not enlist the aid of healthy sorts of religion for those clients who are interested in it.

As far as the consequences of nonmarital sexuality are concerned, some are negative almost by definition—acquaintance rape, for example. Sexually transmitted diseases can be cured in some cases, not in others, but a cure does not usually leave one in better health than one would have had before infection. Few see unplanned pregnancies as a positive event; all options involve stress that would not have occurred without the pregnancy. Abortion may be a relief of stress to a majority of women, but it only returns a woman to a previous condition: it does not improve her previous condition, unless fortuitously. Cohabitation may have no negative effects if engaged in by individuals who later marry each other, but otherwise it appears to have negative results. While premarital sexual activity entails some short-term pleasures, perhaps, it remains a necessary if not sufficient prerequisite for infection by STDs and unplanned pregnancies; there is no evidence that it normally helps people make better decisions about whom to marry or to cohabit with. While premarital sexual permissiveness and early onset of sexual activity may seem innocuous, those variables are important predictors of later sexual activity and its concomitant problems. While nonmarital sexual behavior may increase immediate gratifications, my interpretation of the evidence suggests that it provides little, if any positive, long-term benefits and puts individuals at risk for many long-term negative experiences.

References

Adler, N. E. (1979). Abortion: A social–psychological perspective. *Journal of Social Issues, 35*, 100–119.

Adler, N. E. (1982). The abortion experience: Social and psychological influence and aftereffects. In H. S. Friedman & M. R. DeMatteo (Eds.), *Interpersonal issues in health care* (pp. 119–139). San Diego, CA.: Academic Press.

Adler, N. E. (1992). Unwanted pregnancy and abortion: Definitional and research issues. *Journal of Social Issues, 48,* 19–35.

Adler, N. E., David, H. P., Major, B. N., Roth, S. H., Russo, N. F., & Wyatt, G. E. (1990). Psychological responses after abortion. *Science, 248,* 41–44.

Adler, N. E., David, H. P., Major, B. N., Roth, S. H., Russo, N. F., & Wyatt, G. E. (1992). Psychological factors in abortion: A review. *American Psychologist, 47,* 1194–1204.

Anderson, S. A., Russell, C. S., & Schumm, W. R. (1983). Perceived marital quality and family life-cycle categories: A further analysis. *Journal of Marriage and the Family, 45,* 127–139.

Atwood, J. D., & Kasindorf, S. (1992). A multisystemic approach to adolescent pregnancy. *American Journal of Family Therapy, 20,* 341–360.

Axinn, W. G., & Thornton, A. (1992). The relationship between cohabitation and divorce: Selectivity or causal influence? *Demography, 29,* 357–374.

Axinn, W. G., & Thornton, A. (1993). Mothers, children, and cohabitation: The intergenerational effects of attitudes and behavior. *American Sociological Review, 58,* 233–246.

Bachrach, C. A., Stolley, K. S., & London, K. A. (1992). Relinquishment of premarital births: Evidence from a national survey. *Family Planning Perspectives, 24,* 27–32, 48.

Balakrishnan, T. R., Rao, K. V., & Lapierre-Adamcyk, E. (1987). A hazard model analysis of the covariates of marriage dissolution in Canada. *Demography, 24,* 395–406.

Baldwin, J. D., & Baldwin, J. I. (1988). Factors affecting AIDS-related sexual risk taking behavior among college students. *Journal of Sex Research, 25,* 181–196.

Baldwin, J. I., Whiteley, S., & Baldwin, J. D. (1992). Changing AIDS- and fertility-related behavior: The effectiveness of sex education. *Journal of Sex Research, 27,* 245–262.

Barth, R. P., Fetro, J. V., Leland, N., & Volkan, K. (1992). Preventing adolescent pregnancy with social and cognitive skills. *Journal of Adolescent Research, 7,* 208–232.

Baumeister, A. A., Kupstas, F. D, & Klindworth, L. M. (1991). The new morbidity: A national plan of action. *American Behavioral Scientist, 34,* 468–500.

Baumeister, R. F., Wotman, S. R., & Stillwell, A. M. (1993). Unrequited love: On heartbreak, anger, guilt, scriptlessness, and humiliation. *Journal of Personality and Social Psychology, 64,* 377–394.

Baumrind, D. (1982). Adolescent sexuality: Comment on Williams' and Silka's comments on Baumrind. *American Psychologist, 37,* 1402–1403.

Bennett, N. G., Blanc, A. K., & Bloom, D. E. (1988). Commitment and the modern union: Assessing the link between premarital cohabitation and subsequent marital stability. *American Sociological Review, 53,* 127–138.

Bergin, A. E. (1991). Values and religious issues in psychotherapy and mental health. *American Psychologist, 46,* 394–403.

Black, L. E., & Sprenkle, D. H. (1991). Gender differences in college students' attitudes toward divorce and their willingness to marry. *Journal of Divorce and Remarriage, 14*(3–4), 47–60.

Bluestein, D., & Rutledge, C. M. (1992). Determinants of delayed pregnancy testing among adolescents. *Journal of Family Practice, 35,* 406–410.

Booth, A., & Johnson, D. (1988). Premarital cohabitation and marital success. *Journal of Family Issues, 9,* 255–272.

Bownes, I. T., O'Gorman, E. C., & Dinsmore, W. W. (1990). Factors influencing perception of risk of HIV acquisition among male heterosexual STD clinic attenders. *Irish Journal of Psychological Medicine, 7*(2), 94–100.

Bowser, B. P., Fullilove, M. T., & Fullilove, R. E. (1990). African-American youth and AIDS high-risk behavior. *Youth and Society, 22,* 54–66.

Boyer, D., & Fine, D. (1992). Sexual abuse as a factor in adolescent pregnancy and child maltreatment. *Family Planning Perspectives, 24,* 4–11, 19.

Brazzell, J. F., & Acock, A. A. (1988). Influence of attitudes, significant others, and aspirations on how adolescents intend to resolve a premarital pregnancy. *Journal of Marriage and the Family, 50,* 413–425.

Brennan, W. C. (1974). Abortion and the techniques of neutralization. *Journal of Health and Social Behavior, 15,* 358.

Brooks, D. M., & Kennedy, G. E. (1989). British and American attitudes toward family relationships. *Psychological Reports, 64,* 815–818.

Brown, S. V. (1985). Premarital sexual permissiveness among black adolescent females. *Social Psychology Quarterly, 48,* 381–387.

Bruce, K. E., & Moineau, S. (1991). A comparison of STD clinic patients and undergraduates: Implications for AIDS prevention. *Health Values: Journal of Health Behavior, Education, and Prevention, 15*(6), 5–12.

Bumpass, L. L., Martin, T. C., & Sweet, J. A. (1991). The impact of family background and early marital factors on marital disruption. *Journal of Family Issues, 12,* 22–42.

Bumpass, L. L., & Sweet, J. A. (1989). National estimates of cohabitation. *Demography, 26,* 615–625.

Bumpass, L. L., Sweet, J. A., & Cherlin, A. (1991). The role of cohabitation in declining rates of marriage. *Journal of Marriage and the Family, 53,* 913–927.

Bustamante, A. M. (1992). College student sexual knowledge and behavior in the AIDS era. *Journal of College Student Development, 33,* 376–378.

Byers, E. S., & Heinlein, L. (1989). Predicting initiations and refusals of sexual activities in married and cohabiting heterosexual couples. *Journal of Sex Research, 26,* 210–231.

Calamidas, E. G. (1990). AIDS and STD education: What's really happening in our schools? *Journal of Sex Education and Therapy, 16*(1), 54–63.

Casper, L. M. (1990). Does family interaction prevent adolescent pregnancy? *Family Planning Perspectives, 22,* 109–114.

Cates, W., Jr. (1991). Teenagers and sexual risk taking: The best of times and the worst of times. *Journal of Adolescent Health, 12*(2), 84–94.

Cates, W., Jr., Schulze, K. F., & Grimes, D. A. (1983). The risks associated with teenage abortion. *New England Journal of Medicine, 309,* 621–624.

Cates, W., Jr., & Stone, K. M. (1992). Family planning, sexually transmitted diseases and contraceptive choice: a literature update, Part 1. *Family Planning Perspectives, 24,* 75–84.

Chang, H. H., Murphy, D., Diferdinando, G. T., & Morse, D. L. (1990). Assessment of AIDS knowledge in selected New York State sexually transmitted disease clinics. *New York State Journal of Medicine, 90*(3), 126–128.

Chiasson, M. A., Stoneburner, R. L., Hildebrandt, D. S., & Ewing, W. E. (1991). Heterosexual transmission of HIV-1 associated with the use of smokable freebase cocaine (crack). *AIDS, 5,* 1121–1126.

Chilman, C. S. (1989). Some major issues regarding adolescent sexuality and childbearing in the United States. In P. Allen-Meares & C. H. Shapiro (Eds.), *Adolescent sexuality: New challenges for social work* (pp. 3–25). New York: Haworth Press.

Chirgwin, K., DeHovitz, J. A., Dillon, S., & McCormack, W. M. (1991). HIV infection, genital ulcer disease, and crack cocaine use among patients attending a clinic for sexually transmitted diseases. *American Journal of Public Health, 81,* 1576–1579.

Cole, C. L. (1988). Family and couples therapy with nonmarital cohabiting couples: Treatment issues and case studies. In C. S. Chilman, E. W. Nunnally, & F. M. Cox (Eds.), *Variant family forms* (pp. 73–95). Newbury Park, CA.: Sage.

Corcoran, K. J., & Thomas, L. R. (1991). The influence of observed alcohol consumption on perceptions of initiation of sexual activity in a college dating situation. *Journal of Applied Social Psychology, 21,* 500–507.

Craig, M. E., Kalichman, S. C., & Follingstad, D. R. (1989). Verbal coercive sexual behavior among college students. *Archives of Sexual Behavior, 18,* 421–434.

Crane, S. F., & Carswell, J. W. (1992). A review and assessment of non-governmental organization-based STD/AIDS education and prevention projects for marginalized groups. *Health Education Research, 7*(2), 175–193.

David, H. P. (1992). Born unwanted: Long term developmental effects of denied abortion. *Journal of Social Issues, 48,* 163–181.

David, H. P., Rasmussen, N., & Holst, E. (1981). Postpartum and postabortion psychotic reactions. *Family Planning Perspectives, 13,* 88–93.

de Anda, D., Darroch, P., Davidson, M., Gilly, J., Javidi, M., Jefford, S., Komorowski, R., & Morejon-Schrobsdorf, A. (1992). Stress and coping among pregnant adolescents. *Journal of Adolescent Research, 7,* 94–109.

DeKeseredy, W. S., Schwartz, M. D., & Tait, K. (1993). Sexual assault and stranger aggression on a Canadian university campus. *Sex Roles, 28,* 263–277.

DeMaris, A. (1984). A comparison of remarriages with first marriages on satisfaction in marriage and its relationship to prior cohabitation. *Family Relations, 33,* 443–449.

DeMaris, A., & Leslie, G. R. (1984). Cohabitation with the future spouse: Its influence upon marital satisfaction and communication. *Journal of Marriage and the Family, 46,* 77–84.

DeMaris, A., & MacDonald, W. (1993). Premarital cohabitation and marital instability: A test of the unconventionality hypothesis. *Journal of Marriage and the Family, 55,* 399–407.

DeMaris, A., & Rao, K. V. (1992). Premarital cohabitation and subsequent marital stability in the United States: A reassessment. *Journal of Marriage and the Family, 54,* 178–190.

DiBlasio, F. A., & Benda, B. B. (1990). Adolescent sexual behavior: Multivariate analysis of a social learning model. *Journal of Adolescent Research, 5,* 449–466.

Dolcini, M. M., Catania, J. A., Coates, T. J., Stall, R., Hudes, E. S., Gagnon, J. H., & Pollack, L. M. (1993). Demographic characteristics of heterosexuals with multiple partners: The national AIDS behavioral surveys. *Family Planning Perspectives, 25,* 208–214.

Dorius, G. L., Heaton, T. B., & Steffen, P. (1993). Adolescent life events and their association with the onset of sexual intercourse. *Youth and Society, 25,* 3–23.

Earle, J. R., & Perricone, P. J. (1986). Premarital sexuality: A ten-year study of attitudes and behavior on a small university campus. *Journal of Sex Research, 22,* 304–310.

Elliott, D. S., & Morse, B. J. (1989). Delinquency and drug use as risk factors in teenage sexual activity. *Youth and Society, 21,* 32–60.

Ellis, A. (1990). Commentary on the status of sex research: An assessment of the sexual revolution. *Journal of Psychology and Human Sexuality, 3*(1), 5–18.

Ellis, D. (1989). Male abuse of a married or cohabiting female partner: The application of sociological theory to research findings. *Violence and Victims, 4*(4), 235–255.

Ericksen, K. P., & Trocki, K. F. (1992). Behavioral risk factors for sexually transmitted diseases in American households. *Social Science and Medicine, 34,* 843–853.

Feltey, K. M., Ainslie, J. J., & Geib, A. (1991). Sexual coercion attitudes among high school students: The influence of gender and rape education. *Youth and Society, 23,* 229–250.

Flewelling, R. L., & Bauman, K. E. (1990). Family structure as a predictor of initial substance use and sexual intercourse in early adolescence. *Journal of Marriage and the Family, 52,* 171–181.

Forrest, J. D., & Singh, S. (1990). The sexual and reproductive behavior of American women, 1982–1988. *Family Planning Perspectives, 22,* 206–214.

Fowers, B. J. (1991). His and her marriage: A multivariate study of gender and marital satisfaction. *Sex Roles, 24,* 209–221.

Gardner, W., & Wilcox, B. L. (1992). Political intervention in scientific peer review. *American Psychologist, 48,* 972–983.

Gecas, V., & Libby, R. (1976). Sexual behavior as symbolic interaction. *Journal of Sex Research, 12,* 33–49.

Geer, J. H., & Broussard, D. B. (1990). Scaling heterosexual behavior and arousal: Consistency and sex differences. *Journal of Personality and Social Psychology, 58,* 664–671.

Gibson, J. W., & Kempf, J. (1990). Attitudinal predictors of sexual activity in Hispanic adolescent females. *Journal of Adolescent Research, 5,* 414–430.

Gillmore, M. R., Butler, S. S., Lohr, M. J., & Gilchrist, L. (1992). Substance use and other factors associated with risky sexual behavior among pregnant adolescents. *Family Planning Perspectives, 24,* 255–261, 268.

Gold, J. H. (1991). Adolescents and abortion. In N. L. Stotland (Ed.), *Psychiatric aspects of abortion* (pp. 187–195). Washington, DC: American Psychiatric Press.

Grady, W. R., & Tanfer, K. (1994). Condom breakage and slippage among men in the United States. *Family Planning Perspectives, 26,* 107–112.

Grieco, A. (1987). Cutting the risks for STDs. *Medical Aspects of Human Sexuality, 21*(3), 70–84.

Grogger, J., & Bronars, S. (1993). The socioeconomic consequences of teenage childbearing: Findings from a natural experiment. *Family Planning Perspectives, 25*, 156–161, 174.

Gwartney-Gibbs, P. A. (1986). The institutionalization of premarital cohabitation: Estimates from marriage license applications, 1970 and 1980. *Journal of Marriage and the Family, 48*, 423–434.

Hajcak, F., & Garwood, P. (1988). Quick-fix sex: Pseudosexuality in adolescents. *Adolescence, 23*, 755–760.

Handler, A. (1990). The correlates of the initiation of sexual intercourse among young urban black females. *Journal of Youth and Adolescence, 19*, 159–170.

Henshaw, S. K. (1990). Induced abortion: A world review, 1990. *Family Planning Perspectives, 22*, 76–89.

Henshaw, S. K. (1991). The accessibility of abortion services in the United States. *Family Planning Perspectives, 23*, 246–252, 263.

Henshaw, S. K. (1992). Abortion trends in 1987 and 1988: Age and race. *Family Planning Perspectives, 24*, 85–86, 96.

Henshaw, S. K., & Kost, K. (1992). Parental involvement in minors' abortion decisions. *Family Planning Perspectives, 24*, 196–207, 213.

Henshaw, S. K., & Van Vort, J. (1994). Abortion services in the United States, 1991 and 1992. *Family Planning Perspectives, 26*, 100–106, 112.

Hobart, C., & Griger, F. (1992). Cohabitation among Canadian students at the end of the eighties. *Journal of Comparative Family Studies, 23*, 311–337.

Hofferth, S. L. (1991). Programs for high-risk adolescents: What works? *Evaluation and Program Planning, 14, 3–16.*

Holmbeck, G. N., Waters, K. A., & Brookman, R. R. (1990). Psychosocial correlates of sexually transmitted diseases and sexual activity in black adolescent males. *Journal of Adolescent Research, 5*, 431–448.

Horwitz, S. M., Klerman, L. V., Kuo, H. S., & Jekel, J. F. (1991). Intergenerational transmission of school-age parenthood. *Family Planning Perspectives, 23*, 168–172, 177.

Hull, D. B., Forrester, L., Hull, J. H., & Gaines, M. (1992). In J. C. Chrisler & D. Howard (Eds.), *New directions in feminist psychology: Practice, theory, and research* (pp. 188–189). New York: Springer.

Jemmott, L. S., & Jemmott, J. B., III. (1990). Sexual knowledge, attitudes, and risky sexual behavior among inner-city black male adolescents. *Journal of Adolescent Research, 5*, 346–369.

Jones, E. F., & Forrest, J. D. (1992). Contraceptive failure rates based on the 1988 NSFG. *Family Planning Perspectives, 24*, 12–19.

Jurich, A. P., & Jurich, J. A. (1974). The effect of cognitive moral development upon the selection of premarital sexual standards. *Journal of Marriage and the Family, 36*, 736–741.

Keith, J. B., McCreary, C., Collins, K., Smith, C. P., & Bernstein, I. (1991). Sexual activity and contraceptive use among low-income urban black adolescent females. *Adolescence, 26*, 769–785.

Kelly, J. A., Murphy, D. A., Sikkema, K. J., Kalichman, S. C. (1993). Psychological interventions to prevent HIV infection are urgently needed: New priorities for behavioral research in the second decade of AIDS. *American Psychologist, 48,* 1023–1034.

Ketterlinus, R. D., Lamb, M. E., Nitz, K., & Elster, A. B. (1992). Adolescent nonsexual and sex-related problem behaviors. *Journal of Adolescent Research, 7,* 431–456.

Kingsbury, N., & Scanzoni, J. (1993). In P. G. Boss, W. J. Doherty, R. LaRossa, W. R. Schumm, & S. K. Steinmetz (Eds.), *Sourcebook of family theories and methods: A contextual approach* (pp. 195–217). New York: Plenum.

Kinsey, A. C., Pomeroy, W. B., & Martin, C. E. (1948). *Sexual behavior in the human male.* Philadelphia: W.S. Saunders.

Kinsey, A. C., Pomeroy, W. B., Martin, C. E., & Gebhard, P. A. (1953). *Sexual behavior in the human female.* Philadelphia: W.S. Saunders.

Kirby, D., Resnick, M. D., Downes, B., Kocher, T., Gunderson, P., Potthoff, S., Zelterman, D., Blum, R. W. (1993). The effects of school-based health clinics in St. Paul on school-wide birthrates. *Family Planning Perspectives, 25,* 12–16.

Kirby, D., Waszak, C., & Ziegler, J. (1991). Six school-based clinics: their reproductive health services and impact on sexual behavior. *Family Planning Perspectives, 23,* 1, 6–16.

Klepinger, D. H., Billy, J.O.G., Tanfer, K., & Grady, W. R. (1993). Perceptions of AIDS risk and severity and their association with risk-related behavior among U. S. men. *Family Planning Perspectives, 25,* 74–82.

Koenig, M. A., & Zelnik, M. (1982). The risk of premarital first pregnancy among metropolitan-area teenagers: 1976–1979. *Family Planning Perspectives, 14,* 239–247.

Koop, C. E. (1989, March 21). Surgeon General's report on abortion. *Congressional Record,* pp. E906—E909. Also available in J. D. Butler & D. F. Walbert (Eds.), *Abortion, medicine, and the law* (4th ed., Appendix 1, pp. 731–744). New York: Facts on File.

Koss, M. P. (1985). The hidden rape victim: Personality, attitudinal, and situational characteristics. *Psychology of Women Quarterly, 9,* 193–212.

Kost, K., & Forrest, J. D. (1992). American women's sexual behavior and exposure to risk of sexually transmitted diseases. *Family Planning Perspectives, 24,* 244–254.

Koyle, P.F.C., Jensen, L. C., Olsen, J., & Cundick, B. (1989). Comparisons of sexual behaviors among adolescents having an early, middle, and late first intercourse experience. *Youth and Society, 20,* 461–476.

Ku, L. C., Sonenstein, F. L., & Pleck, J. H. (1992). The association of AIDS education and sex education with sexual behavior and condom use among teenage men. *Family Planning Perspectives, 24,* 100–105.

Kurdek, L. A., & Schmitt, J. P. (1986). Relationship quality of partners in heterosexual married, heterosexual cohabiting, and gay and lesbian relationships. *Journal of Personality and Social Psychology, 51,* 711–720.

Kurtines, W. M., Alvarez, M., & Azmitia, M. (1990). Science and morality: The role of values in science and the scientific study of moral phenomena. *Psychological Bulletin, 107,* 283–295.

Lamb, M. E. (1988). The ecology of adolescent pregnancy and parenthood. In A. R. Pence (Ed.), *Ecological research with children and families: From concepts to methodology* (pp. 99–121). New York: Teachers College Press of Columbia University.

Lane, K. E., & Gwaltney-Gibbs, P. A. (1985). Violence in the context of dating and sex. *Journal of Family Issues, 6*, 45–59.

LaRossa, R., & Reitzes, D. C. (1993). In P. G. Boss, W. J. Doherty, R. LaRossa, W. R. Schumm, & S. K. Steinmetz (Eds.), *Sourcebook of family theories and methods: A contextual approach* (pp. 135–163). New York: Plenum.

Larson, J. (1991). Cohabitation is a premarital step. *American Demographics, 13*, 20–21.

Leigh, B. C., Aramburu, B., & Norris, J. (1992). The morning after: Gender differences in attributions about alcohol-related sexual encounters. *Journal of Applied Social Psychology, 22*, 343–357.

Lemkau, J. P. (1991). Post-abortion adjustment of health care professionals in training. *American Journal of Orthopsychiatry, 61*, 92–102. (citation from page 100).

Lindemann, C. (1988). Counselling issues in disclosure of sexually transmitted disease. *Journal of Social Work and Human Sexuality, 6*(2), 55–69.

Loewenstein, G., & Furstenberg, F. (1991). Is teenage sexual behavior rational? *Journal of Applied Social Psychology, 21*, 957–986.

Long, B. H. (1989). Heterosexual involvement of unmarried undergraduate females in relation to self-evaluations. *Journal of Youth and Adolescence, 18*, 489–500.

Lundberg, S., & Plotnick, R. D. (1990). Effects of state welfare, abortion and family planning policies on premarital childbearing among white adolescents. *Family Planning Perspectives, 22, 246–251, 275.*

Macklin, E. D. (1983). Nonmarital heterosexual cohabitation: An overview. In E. D. Macklin & R. H. Rubin (Eds.), *Contemporary families and alternative lifestyles* (pp. 49–74). Beverly Hills, CA.: Sage.

Macklin, E. D. (1988). Heterosexual couples who cohabit nonmaritally: Some common problems and issues. In C. S. Chilman, E. W. Nunnally, & F. M. Cox (Eds.), *Variant family forms* (pp. 56–72). Newbury Park, CA.: Sage.

Major, B., & Cozarelli, C. (1992). Psychosocial predictors of adjustment to abortion. *Journal of Social Issues, 48*, 121–142.

Major, B., Cozarelli, C., Sciacchitano, A. M., Cooper, M. L., Testa, M., & Mueller, P. M. (1990). Perceived social support, self-efficacy, and adjustment to abortion. *Journal of Personality and Social Psychology, 59*, 452–463.

Males, M. (1992). Adult liaison in the "epidemic" of "teenage" birth, pregnancy, and venereal disease. *Journal of Sex Research, 29*, 525–545.

Marsiglio, W., & Shehan, C. L. (1993). Adolescent males' abortion attitudes: Data from a national survey. *Family Planning Perspectives, 25*, 162–169.

Maticka-Tyndale, E. (1991). Modification of sexual activities in the era of AIDS: A trend analysis of adolescent sexual activities. *Youth and Society, 23*, 31–49.

McCabe, M. P. (1987). Desired and experienced levels of premarital affection and sexual intercourse during dating. *Journal of Sex Research, 23*, 23–33.

McCoy, H. V., McKay, C. Y., Hermanns, L., & Lai, S. (1990). Sexual behavior and the risk of HIV infection. *American Behavioral Scientist, 33*, 432–450.

Miller, B. C., Christensen, R. B., & Olson, T. D. (1987). Adolescent self-esteem in relation to sexual attitudes and behavior. *Youth and Society, 19,* 93–111.

Miller, B. C., & Jorgensen, S. R. (1989). In D. M. Klein & J. Aldous (Eds.), *Social stress and family development* (pp. 210–233). New York: Guilford Press.

Miller, B. C., & Moore, K. A. (1990). Adolescent sexual behavior, pregnancy, and parenting: Research through the 1980s. *Journal of Marriage and the Family, 52,* 1025–1044.

Miller, B. C., & Olson, T. D. (1988). Sexual attitudes and behavior of high school students in relation to background and contextual factors. *Journal of Sex Research, 24,* 194–200.

Miller, B. C., & Sneesby, K. R. (1988). Educational correlates of adolescents' sexual attitudes and behavior. *Journal of Youth and Adolescence, 17,* 521–530.

Miller, W. B. (1992). An empirical study of the psychological antecedents and consequences of induced abortion. *Journal of Social Issues, 48,* 67–93.

Millstein, S. G. (1990). Risk factors for AIDS among adolescents. *New Directions for Child Development, 50,* 3–15.

Minden, S. L., & Notman, M. T. (1991). Psychotherapeutic issues related to abortion. In N. L. Stotland (Ed.), *Psychiatric aspects of abortion* (pp. 119–133). Washington, DC: American Psychiatric Press.

Mirotznik, J., Shapiro, R. D., Steinhart, J. E., & Gillespie, O. (1987). Genital herpes: An investigation of its attitudinal and behavioral correlates. *Journal of Sex Research, 23,* 266–272.

Moore, J. R. (1988). Learning about the psychosocial impact of sexually transmitted diseases: Teaching strategies. *Journal of Social Work and Human Sexuality, 6*(2), 121–133.

Moore, K. A., Nord, C. W., & Peterson, J. I.. (1989). Nonvoluntary Sexual activity among adolescents. *Family Planning Perspectives, 21,* 110–114.

Moore, K. A., & Stief, T. M. (1991). Changes in marriage and fertility behavior: Behavior versus attitudes of young adults. *Youth and Society, 22,* 362–386.

Mould, D. E. (1990). A reply to Page: Fraud, pornography, and the Meese Commission. *American Psychologist, 45,* 777–778.

Muehlenhard, C. L., & Cook, S. W. (1988). Men's self-reports of unwanted sexual activity. *Journal of Sex Research, 24,* 58–72.

Muehlenhard, C. L., & Falcon, P. L. (1990). Men's heterosocial skill and attitudes toward women as predictors of verbal sexual coercion and forceful rape. *Sex Roles, 23,* 241–259.

Murnen, S. K., Perot, A., & Byrne, D. (1989). Coping with unwanted sexual activity: Normative responses, situational determinants, and individual differences. *Journal of Sex Research, 26,* 85–106.

Murry, V. M. (1992). Incidence of first pregnancy among black adolescent females over three decades. *Youth and Society, 23,* 478–506.

Newcomb, M. D. (1986). Cohabitation, marriage and divorce among adolescents and young adults. *Journal of Personal and Social Relationships, 3,* 473–494.

Newcomb, M. D. (1987). Cohabitation and marriage: A quest for independence and relatedness. *Applied Social Psychology Annual, 7,* 128–156.

Newcomb, P. R. (1979). Cohabitation in America: An Assessment of consequences. *Journal of Marriage and the Family, 41,* 597–603.

O'Campo, P., Faden, R. R., Gielen, A. C., Kass, N., & Anderson, J. (1993). *Family Planning Perspectives, 25*, 215–219.

O'Gorman, E. C., Bownes, I. T., & Dinsmore, W. (1989). An alternative approach to AIDS prevention in heterosexuals. *Medical Science Research, 17*, 811–812.

Oliver, M. B., & Hyde, J. S. (1993). Gender differences in sexuality: A meta-analysis. *Psychological Bulletin, 114*, 29–51.

Olsen, J. A., Weed, S. E., Ritz, G. M., & Jensen, L. C. (1991). The effects of three abstinence sex education programs on student attitudes toward sexual activity. *Adolescence, 26*, 631–641.

Olson, L. (1980). Social and psychological correlates of pregnancy resolutions among adolescent women. *American Journal of Orthopsychiatry, 50*, 432–445.

O'Sullivan, L. F., & Byers, E. S. (1993). Eroding stereotypes: College women's attempts to influence reluctant male sexual partners. *Journal of Sex Research, 30*, 270–282.

Parrot, A. (1989). Acquaintance rape among adolescents: Identifying risk groups and intervention strategies. In P. Allen-Meares & C. H. Shapiro (Eds.), *Adolescent sexuality: New challenges for social work* (pp. 47–61). New York: Haworth.

Pendergast, R. A., DuRant, R. H., & Gaillard, G. L. (1992). Attitudinal and behavioral correlates of condom use in urban adolescent males. *Journal of Adolescent Health, 13*(2), 133–139.

Pliner, A. J., & Yates, S. (1992). Psychological and legal issues in minors' rights to abortion. *Journal of Social Issues, 48*, 203–216.

Plotnick, R. D. (1992). The effect of attitudes on teenage premarital pregnancy and its resolution. *American Sociological Review, 57*, 800–811.

Plotnick, R. D., & Butler, S. S. (1991). Attitudes and adolescent nonmarital childbearing: Evidence from the National Longitudinal Survey of Youth. *Journal of Adolescent Research, 6*, 470–492.

Posavac, E. J., & Miller, T. Q. (1990). Some problems caused by not having a conceptual foundation for health research: an illustration from studies of the psychological effects of abortion. *Psychology and Health, 5*(1), 13–23.

Price, R. H., Cowen, E. L., Lorion, R. P., & Ramos-McKay, J. (1989). The search for effective prevention programs: What we learned along the way. *American Journal of Orthopsychiatry, 59*(1), 49–58.

Quadrel, M. J., Fischoff, B., & Davis, W. (1993). Adolescent (in)vulnerability. *American Psychologist, 48*, 102–116.

Reardon, D. (1987). *Aborted women: Silent no more.* Chicago: Loyola University Press.

Reiss, I. L. (1967). *The social context of premarital permissiveness.* New York: Holt, Rinehart, and Winston.

Reiss, I. L. (1993). The future of sex research and the meaning of science. *Journal of Sex Research, 30*, 3–11.

Resnick, M. D., Blum, R. W., Bose, J., Smith, M., & Toogood, R. (1990). Characteristics of unmarried adolescent mothers: Determinants of child rearing versus adoption. *American Journal of Orthopsychiatry, 60*(4), 577–584.

Rogers, J., Stoms, G., & Phifer, J. (1989). Psychological impact of abortion. *Health Care for Women International, 10*, 347–376.

Romanowski, B., & Piper, G. (1988). Sexually transmitted diseases: An overview. *Journal of Social Work and Human Sexuality, 6*(2), 7–20.

Romig, C. A., & Thompson, J. G. (1988). Teenage pregnancy: A family systems approach. *American Journal of Family Therapy, 16*, 133–143.

Rosen, A. (1992). Beliefs, attitudes, and intention in the context of abortion. *Journal of Applied Social Psychology, 22*, 1464–1480.

Rosenbaum, E., & Kandel, D. B. (1990). Early onset of adolescent sexual behavior and drug involvement. *Journal of Marriage and the Family, 52*, 783–798.

Rosenberg, M., Schooler, C., & Schoenbach, C. (1989). Self-esteem and adolescent problems: Modeling reciprocal effects. *American Sociological Review, 54*, 1004–1018.

Rotheram-Borus, M. J., Koopman, C., & Ehrhardt, A. A. (1991). Homeless youth and HIV infection. *American Psychologist, 46*, 1188–1197.

Rotheram-Borus, M. J., Meyer-Bahlburg, H.F.L., Koopman, C., Rosario, M., Exner, T. M., Henderson, R., Matthieu, M., & Gruen, R. S. (1992). Lifetime sexual behavior among runaway males and females. *Journal of Sex Research, 29*, 15–29.

Ruch-Ross, H. S., Jones, E. D., & Musick, J. S. (1992). Comparing outcomes in a statewide program for adolescent mothers with outcomes in a national sample. *Family Planning Perspectives, 24*, 66–71, 96.

Russo, N. F. (1992). Psychological aspects of unwanted pregnancy and its resolution. In J. D. Butler & D. F. Walbert (Eds.), *Abortion, medicine, and the law*. (4th ed., pp. 593–626). New York: Facts on File.

Russo, N. F., & Zierk, K. L. (1992). Abortion, childbearing, and women's well-being. *Professional Psychology: Research and Practice, 23*, 269–280.

Rutherford Institute. (1988). *Major articles and books concerning the detrimental effects of abortion*. Manassas, VA.: Rutherford Institute.

Sabatelli, R. M., & Shehan, C. L. (1993). In P. G. Boss, W. J. Doherty, R. LaRossa, W. R. Schumm, & S. K. Steinmetz (Eds.), *Sourcebook of family theories and methods: A contextual approach* (pp. 385–411). New York: Plenum.

Saltenberger, A. (1982). *Every woman has a right to know the dangers of legal abortion*. Glassboro, NJ.: Air-Plus Enterprises.

Samson, J. M., Levy, J. J., Dupras, A., & Tessier, D. (1991). Coitus frequency among married or cohabiting heterosexual adults: A survey in French Canada. *Australian Journal of Marriage and Family, 12*(2), 103–109.

Santee, B., & Henshaw, S. K. (1992). The abortion debate: Measuring gestational age. *Family Planning Perspectives, 24*, 172–173.

Sarantakos, S. (1991). Cohabitation revisited: Paths of change among cohabiting and non-cohabiting couples. *Australian Journal of Marriage and Family, 12*(3), 144–155.

Schumm, W. R., Jurich, A. P., Bollman, S. R., & Bugaighis, M. A. (1985). His and her marriage revisited. *Journal of Family Issues, 6*, 221–227.

Schumm, W. R., & Rekers, G. A. (1984). Sex should occur only within marriage. In H. Feldman & A. Parrot (Eds.), *Human sexuality: Contemporary controversies* (pp. 105–124). Beverly Hills, CA: Sage.

Scott-Jones, D., & Turner, S. L. (1990). The impact of adolescent childbearing on educational attainment and income of black families. *Youth and Society, 22*, 35–53.

Scott-Jones, D., & White, A. B. (1990). Correlates of sexual activity in early adolescence. *Journal of Early Adolescence, 10*, 221–238.

Shachar, R. (1991). His and her marital satisfaction: The double standard. *Sex Roles, 25*, 451–467.

Simons-Morton, D. G., Mullen, P. D., Mains, D. A., & Tabak, E. R. (1992). Characteristics of controlled studies of patient education and counseling for preventive health behaviors. *Patient Education and Counseling, 19*, 175–204.

Simpson, J. A., & Gangestad, S. W. (1991). Individual differences in sociosexuality: Evidence for convergent and discriminant validity. *Journal of Personality and Social Psychology, 60*, 870–883.

Smith, T. W. (1991). Adult sexual behavior in 1989: Number of partners, frequency of intercourse and risk of AIDS. *Family Planning Perspectives, 23*, 102–107.

Sonenstein, F. L., Pleck, J. H., & Ku, L. C. (1989). Sexual activity, condom use, and AIDS awareness among adolescent males. *Family Planning Perspectives, 21*, 152–158.

Sonenstein, F. L., Pleck, J. H., & Ku, L. C. (1991). Levels of sexual activity among adolescent males in the United States. *Family Planning Perspectives, 23*, 162–167.

Spanier, G. B. (1983). Married and unmarried cohabitation in the United States. *Journal of Marriage and the Family, 45*, 277–288.

Speckhard, A. C., & Rue, V. M. (1992). Postabortion syndrome: An emerging public health concern. *Journal of Social Issues, 48*, 95–119.

Sprecher, S. (1989). Premarital sexual standards for different categories of individuals. *Journal of Sex Research, 26*, 232–248.

Sprecher, S., McKinney, K., & Orbuch, T. L. (1991). The effect of current sexual behavior on friendship, dating, and marriage desirability. *Journal of Sex Research, 28*, 387–408.

Steiner, M., Piedrahita, C., Glover, L., & Joanis, C. (1993). Can condom users likely to experience condom failure be identified? *Family Planning Perspectives, 26*, 220–223, 226.

Stern, M., & Alvarez, A. (1992). Pregnant and parenting adolescents: A comparative analysis of coping response and psychological adjustment. *Journal of Adolescent Research, 7*, 469–493.

Stets, J. E. (1993). The link between past and present intimate relationships. *Journal of Family Issues, 14*, 236–260.

Stets, J. E., & Straus, M. A. (1989). The marriage license as a hitting license: A comparison of assaults in dating, cohabiting, and married couples. *Journal of Family Violence, 4*(2), 161–180.

Stiffman, A. R., Powell, J., Earls, F., & Robins, L. N. (1990). Pregnancies, childrearing, and mental health problems in adolescents. *Youth and Society, 21*, 483–495.

Stone, R., & Waszak, C. (1992). Adolescent knowledge and attitudes about abortion. *Family Planning Perspectives, 24*, 52–57.

Struckman-Johnson, C. (1988). Forced sex on dates: it happens to men, too. *The Journal of Sex Research, 24*, 234–241.

Stump, L., & Knudsen, D. (1988). Cohabitation and marriage licenses: a research note. *Psychological Reports, 63*, 969–970.

Surra, C. A. (1990). Research and theory on mate selection and premarital relationships in the 1980s. *Journal of Marriage and the Family, 52,* 844–865.

Tanfer, K. (1987). Patterns of premarital cohabitation among never-married women in the United States. *Journal of Marriage and the Family, 49,* 483–495.

Tanfer, K., & Cubbins, L. A. (1992). Coital frequency among single women: normative constraints and situational opportunities. *The Journal of Sex Research, 29,* 221–250.

Tanfer, K., & Hyle, P. D. (1992). Determinants and effects of waiting time to coitus. *Social Biology, 39,* 183–202.

Tanfer, K., & Schoorl, J. (1992). Premarital sexual careers and partner change. *Archives of Sexual Behavior, 21,* 45–68.

Teachman, J. D., & Polonko, K. A. (1990). Cohabitation and marital stability in the United States. *Social Forces, 69,* 207–220.

Teachman, J. D., Thomas, J., & Paasch, K. (1991). Legal status and the stability of coresidential unions. *Demography, 28,* 571–586.

Teichman, Y., Shenhar, S., & Segal, S. (1993). Emotional distress in Israeli women before and after abortion. *American Journal of Orthopsychiatry, 63*(2), 277–288.

Thompson, W. E. (1986). Courtship violence: Toward a conceptual understanding. *Youth and Society, 18,* 162–176.

Thomson, E., & Colella, U. (1992). Cohabitation and marital stability: Quality or commitment? *Journal of Marriage and the Family, 54,* 281–284.

Thornton, A. (1988). Cohabitation and marriage in the 1980s. *Demography, 25,* 497–508.

Thornton, A., Axinn, W. G., & Hill, D. H. (1992). Reciprocal effects of religiosity, cohabitation, and marriage. *American Journal of Sociology, 98,* 628–651.

Trocki, K. F. (1992). Patterns of sexuality and risky sexuality in the general population of a California county. *The Journal of Sex Research, 29,* 85–94.

Trussell, J., Warner, D. L., & Hatcher, R. A. (1992). Condom slippage and breakage rates. *Family Planning Perspectives, 24,* 20–23.

Tucker, M. W., & O'Grady, K. E. (1991). Effects of physical attractiveness, intelligence, age at marriage, and cohabitation on the perceptions of marital satisfaction. *Journal of Social Psychology, 131,* 253–269.

Udry, J. R. (1993). The politics of sex research. *The Journal of Sex Research, 30,* 103–110.

Upchurch, D. M., & McCarthy, J. (1989). Adolescent childbearing and high school completion in the 1980s: have things changed? *Family Planning Perspectives, 21,* 199–202.

Upchurch, D. M., & McCarthy, J. (1990). The timing of a first birth and high school completion. *American Sociological Review, 55,* 224–234.

Walsh, A. (1991). Self-esteem and sexual behavior: exploring gender differences. *Sex Roles, 25,* 441–450.

Warrick, L., Christianson, J. B., Walruff, J., & Cook, P. C. (1993). Educational outcomes in teenage pregnancy and parenting programs: results from a demonstration. *Family Planning Perspectives, 25,* 148–155.

Watson, R.E.L., & DeMeo, P. W. (1987). Premarital cohabitation vs. traditional courtship and subsequent marital adjustment: A replication and follow-up. *Family Relations, 36,* 193–197.

Weis, D. L., Rabinowitz, B., & Ruckstuhl, M. F. (1992). Individual changes in sexual attitudes and behavior within college-level human sexuality classes. *Journal of Sex Research, 29,* 43–59.

Weis, D. L., Slosnerick, M., Cate, R., & Sollie, D. L. (1986). A survey instrument for assessing the cognitive association of sex, love, and marriage. *Journal of Sex Research, 22,* 206–220.

Whitbeck, L. B., Conger, R. D., & Kao, M. (1993). The influence of parental support, depressed affect, and peers on the sexual behaviors of adolescent girls. *Journal of Family Issues, 14,* 261–278.

Whitbeck, L. B., Hoyt, D. R., Miller, M., & Kao, M. (1992). Parental support, distressed affect, and sexual experience among adolescents. *Youth and Society, 24,* 16–177.

White, J. M. (1987). Premarital cohabitation and marital stability in Canada. *Journal of Marriage and the Family, 49,* 641–647.

White, L. K. (1990). Determinants of divorce: a review of research in the eighties. *Journal of Marriage and the Family, 52,* 904–912.

White, C. P., & White, M. B. (1991). The Adolescent Family Life Act: content, findings, and policy recommendations for pregnancy prevention programs. *Journal of Clinical Child Psychology, 20,* 58–70.

Whitley, B. E., Jr. (1988). The relation of gender-role orientation to sexual experience among college students. *Sex Roles, 19,* 619–638.

Wilmoth, G. H. (1992). Abortion, public health policy, and informed consent legislation. *Journal of Social Issues, 48,* 1–17.

Wilmoth, G. H., de Alteriss, M., & Bussell, D. (1992). Prevalence of psychological risks following legal abortion in the U.S.: limits of the evidence. *Journal of Social Issues, 48,* 37–66.

Wilson, S. M., & Medora, N. P. (1990). Gender comparisons of college students' attitudes toward sexual behavior. *Adolescence, 25,* 615–627.

Wu, Z., & Balakrishnan, T. R. (1992). Attitudes towards cohabitation and marriage in Canada. *Journal of Comparative Family Studies, 23,* 1–12.

Wyatt, G. E., Peters, S. D., & Guthrie, D. (1988a). Kinsey revisited, part 1: Comparisons of the sexual socialization and sexual behavior of white women over 33 years. *Archives of Sexual Behavior, 17,* 201–239.

Wyatt, G. E., Peters, S. D., & Guthrie, D. (1988b). Kinsey revisited, part 2: Comparisons of the sexual socialization and sexual behavior of black women over 33 years. *Archives of Sexual Behavior, 17,* 289–332.

Yarber, W. L. (1988). Evaluation of the health behavior approach to school STD education. *Journal of Sex Education and Therapy, 14*(1), 33–38.

Yelsma, P. (1986). Marriage versus cohabitation: couples' communication practices and satisfaction. *Journal of Communication, 36,* 94–107.

Yesmont, G. A. (1992). The relationship of assertiveness to college students' safer sex behaviors. *Adolescence, 27,* 253–272.

Zabin, L. S., Hirsh, M. B., & Emerson, M. R. (1989). When urban adolescents choose abortion: effects on education, psychological status, and subsequent pregnancy. *Family Planning Perspectives, 24,* 248–255.

Zabin, L. S., Stark, H. A., & Emerson, M. R. (1991). Reasons for delay in contraceptive clinic utilization: adolescent clinic and nonclinic populations compared. *Journal of Adolescent Health, 12,* 225–232.

Zelnik, M. & Kantner, J. (1980). Sexual activity, contraceptive use, and pregnancy among metropolitan area teenagers: 1971–1979. *Family Planning Perspectives, 12,* 230–237.

Zuravin, S. J. (1991). Unplanned childbearing and family size: their relationship to child neglect and abuse. *Family Planning Perspectives, 23,* 155–161.

18

Deviant Sexual Behavior in Children and Adolescents

William B. Arndt, Jr.

There are two cogent reasons why we should study children and adolescents who engage in deviant sexual behaviors. First, such study is important in its own right, since sexually deviant behaviors are not uncommon in this age group. This is especially true of illegal acts such as child sexual molestation. Out of 1,600 alleged sexual perpetrators seen at one child protection center, almost half (47 percent) were juveniles (Thomas, 1982). Retrospectively, more than half of adult voyeurs, pedophiles, fetishists and transvestites recall a paraphilic interest prior to age 17 (Abel, Osborn & Twigg, 1993). Hopefully, early detection and adequate treatment will prevent serious adult paraphilias. Second, such study will enable us to gain insight into the development of adult paraphilics and sexual offenders.

The template that describes the individual's preferred sexual objects and ways of relating to those objects is called the lovemap (Money, 1986). For some, their lovemaps have become distorted so that either the object and/or the mode of relating to it is deviant. Even though this deviant behavior usually manifests itself first in late childhood or early adolescence, the roots of the vandalized lovemap go back to before birth.

There is some evidence that the predilection for particular sexual behaviors may be, in part, genetically determined. An even stronger case can be made for the importance of prenatal hormones influencing later sexual life. The impact of these hormones is particularly important during the sensitive period of hypothalamic differentiation (Arndt, 1991).

The processes of psychological separation and individuation begin sometime after the physical separation of neonate from mother. During this time, the individual's stance toward other people, especially women, forms, since it is from the mother that one separates yet remains bonded. Secure attachment to the mother seems to inoculate the child against sexually deviant behaviors, whereas anxious, ambivalent, and avoidant attachment establishes a predisposition to nonintimate, nonconsensual, deviant sexual behaviors (Marshall & Eccles, 1993).

Many adult paraphilics recall childhood events that appear to be related to their adult condition. These childhood experiences are often reported to be nonsexual, but nevertheless exciting. Childhood peeping may be an expression of curiosity about sex. By the same token, a child may expose himself for the pleasure of shocking onlookers. Only later do these behaviors become sexually arousing. For example, an adult transvestite recalled walking with his mother, wearing her fur collar, and meeting another woman. The two women smiled at him and he "felt a pleasant sensation from the soft fur and from the approval" (Deutsch, 1954, p. 240).

One of the major tasks of adolescence is the attainment of a stable, integrated self-identity. This is accomplished by combining childhood identifications and role-related experiences. An individual's evolving self-identity is practiced in social interactions with others. A major component of self-identity for the developing male is his concept of what it means to be masculine and how well he matches these expectations. It takes years for many adolescents to attain a cohesive self-identity; they persist in a state of identity diffusion.

Similarly, late childhood and early adolescence signals the beginning of the emergence of sexual identity, that is, the emergence of an integrated lovemap. This is accomplished by resolving conflicting attitudes and feelings toward potential love objects and by integrating various sexually stimulating situations and behaviors. Just as an adolescent may be in a state of self-identity confusion, so he may persist in attempting to relate sexually to others with a disjointed lovemap. This is similar to Freud's (1905/1955) description of the young child's sexuality as being "polymorphous perverse," that is, undifferentiated and unintegrated, motivated by "partial instincts" such as sexualized mouthing, looking, exposing, dominating, and being dominated.

There is compelling evidence for the idea that the adolescent paraphilic lovemap is underdeveloped and unintegrated rather than simply distorted. That is, the sexually deviant adolescent is not operating from a unified distorted lovemap, but from a lovemap with several unintegrated, deviant scenarios. Intensive interviews with adult paraphilics reveal that most of them had a history of multiply deviant behaviors. Pedophiles had an average of 3.5 paraphilias including incest, rape, exhibitionism, voyeurism, and frottage. Adult voyeurs reported an average of 4.8 paraphilias (Abel, Becker, Cunningham-Rathner, Mittleman, & Rouleau, 1988).

Usually the first indication of distortion in sexual life is manifested in dreams and in masturbation fantasies at puberty (Wolf, 1988). Almost all boys (80 percent) aged 13 to 19 fantasize during masturbation most of the time, and about half (45 percent) experience anxiety or guilt sometimes or often (Sorensen, 1972). This emerging lovemap lacks clarity and it is through masturbation fantasies that the young person samples various sexual themes for their goodness of fit. Some of the ideation accompanying masturbation may be as shocking as it is provocative. One of the reasons for this disturbance is that the erotic imagery provokes guilt and fear. For example, if the fantasy is one of watching an unknown woman undress, the boy may be dimly aware that the "unknown" woman is actually a disguised representation of his mother, sister, or another relative (Noshpitz, 1982).

Masturbation fantasies are powerful enablers of deviant sexual behavior, serving several functions. First, if there is any repugnance concerning the deviant thought, the fantasy operates as in systematic desensitization by pairing the negative affect with the incompatible positive feelings of sexual arousal in a safe setting. Second, pairing the deviant idea with pleasure reinforces the activeness of deviant image. Third, to alleviate after-masturbation embarrassment and/or guilt, the fantasy incorporates permission-giving clauses such as, "She is really enjoying this" (Wolf, 1988).

In a group of sadistic assaulters, fantasies compensated for their lack of sexual experience. At puberty they had nonaggressive heterosexual masturbation fantasies, but by about 16 years of age their sadistic fantasy syndrome began. Accompanying these fantasies were behavioral rehearsals. In one case the syndrome started at age 14 when the individual began to imagine girls who took the initiative in sex. A year later he fantasized about stealing girls' purses so that he could lend them money. By age 16 he was fantasizing about kidnapping and torturing girls. At this time he was already following girls and snatching their handbags. Prior to murdering a woman, his only conviction was for the theft of house keys (MacCulloch, Snowden, Wood, & Mills, 1983).

It has been proposed that the pairing of deviant fantasies with masturbation-induced arousal forms the basis for later deviant behavior. With repeated pairings, the deviant aspects of the fantasy becomes more and more prominent (McGuire, Carlisle, & Young, 1965). While this hypothesis might explain the maintenance and strengthening of the deviant arousal, it is questionable whether it accounts for the initial emergence of the deviancy. For a critique of this and other respondent learning models, see Marshall and Eccles (1993).

Deviant child and adolescent sexuality will be considered in two general sections. The first focuses on solo activities such as arousal by objects (fetishism) and sexual asphyxia. The second centers on activities involving another person. Activities involving another person can be further divided into those in which there is no touching, as in peeping and exhibitionism (hands-off), and acts with body contact, including the legal categories of indecent liberties, rape, and incest (hands-on). Separate consideration is given to incest and also to female offenders. Sections on assessment and treatment follow.

Caution will be exercised in using *Diagnostic and Statistical Manual of*

Mental Disorders, fourth edition (DSM-IV; American Psychiatric Association, 1994), diagnostic labels, especially with children. This is because it is not clear from much of the literature whether the cases reported meet the criteria of repeated and intense sexual urges and sexually arousing fantasies (Saunders & Awad, 1988). Furthermore, it has not been established that these young people have a preference for their deviant sexual behavior (Marshall & Eccles, 1993) or that their deviant behavior stems from specific deviant arousal. Perhaps they are no different in arousal patterns from the non deviants, and merely have weaker inhibitions toward acting out (Davis & Leitenberg, 1987). Consequently, the terms used here will refer to behaviors rather than to diagnostic categories.

There is a distinct difference in the sampling of cases and the type of literature available between reports of solo activities and those involving another person. Solo activities are reported by clinicians as case studies, whereas those involving others, being criminal offenses, are usually court or family services referrals. The later tend to be statistical, group studies. Clearly, the sampling in both types is severely biased. Unfortunately, some of these group studies report data on "youthful sexual offenders" without designating the characteristics of the various offenses.

Solo Deviant Activities

Arousal by Objects (Fetishism)

Fetishism in the adult is fairly easily diagnosed when sexual arousal is repeatedly brought about by means of an inanimate object or by a part of the body not usually associated with sexuality. There is a high probability that the adult male who collects, licks, and kisses high-heeled shoes deserves the diagnosis of fetishist. However, this label cannot be given unequivocally to a young child who talks to, hugs, and mouths a pillow. Anna Freud (1965) maintains that the diagnosis of fetishism and related transvestism should not be used before adolescence. While many adult fetishists place the onset of their particular attraction between their eighth year and puberty (Gosselin & Wilson, 1980; Sargent, 1988), this does not mean that the childhood behavior in itself was sexual (Gagnon & Simon, 1970; Moll, 1924).

There has been a rather lively debate concerning the relation of childhood fetishism to the transitional object (TO). According to Winnicott (1953) having a TO is healthy. Babies of both sexes begin using TOs between 4 and 12 months. The special blanket or soft toy is the first "not-me" possession. It is important to the infant at sleep time and during anxiety-arousing situations. If washed, the TO's value to the child is often destroyed, perhaps because this breaks the continuity with its past comforting properties and also because its important odor has been obliterated. As the child's interest widens, the TO becomes less important, but may be needed later if deprivation occurs. It is possible that for males the TO may develop into a fetish, that is, become sexualized.

Sperling (1963), however, maintains that the TO itself is a pathological manifestations of object relation disturbances, enabling mother and child to present a facade of normalcy. A compromise to this controversy is offered by Greenacre (1953), who views the child's use of a TO as the result of normal mother–child relations, whereas the TO fetish stems from an impaired relationship.

It is the quality of the child's relation with his mother that determines his relation to objects. In order to acquire a fetish, the child must learn that other people, particularly his mother, are unreliable comfort givers. Also, he must learn that an object he can control provides comfort and satisfaction. Later, comfort and satisfaction take on strong sexual tones.

The important role the mother plays in fetish acquisition is illustrated by the case of Harry for whom, at 1½ years, silk stockings provided more solace than did mother (Sperling, 1963). Harry's mother would lay with him while he nursed from the bottle and stroked her stockinged legs. To allow herself more freedom she later offered Harry a stocking along with his bottle. By age 6½ Harry was carrying a strip of silk stocking to school, rubbing his scrotum with it.

Fetishism is more than the use of a pacifying mother substitute existing in an otherwise healthy child. And the fetish itself is more than a comfort-giving object. Over the course of its development, the fetish acquires multiple meanings. The case of a tail-pipe fetishist illustrates the importance of extreme disturbance in interpersonal relations, coupled with fear for personal integrity and violent, antisocial impulses (Bergman, 1947). His father was brutal and his mother was a silent, passive person. A mild attraction to pipes with no sexual component preceded the fetish. Shunned by other children, he had close contact with a only few who, like himself, were interested in torturing animals. His early fears were of bodily harm, usually involving his mother; he worried in particular that she might step on his head, cracking his skull.

When he was 12 he had a night terror in which he approached a large conveyance that had oil pouring out of it and was shooting flames. His fetish started when he was 13 with a masturbation fantasy in which his mother was in the front seat of a car, and he was in the back seat watching exhaust from the tail pipe. He had a strong erection. Only in part did his deviant behaviors mirror his fantasies. For example, he never put his penis in a tail pipe, but occasionally he would put his finger in one. Other unrealized fantasies were of sucking the pipe, feeling the warm, moist fumes. Another was that the pipe was in a hole in his pants blowing on this buttocks. In his early teens even his tenuous social relations started to deteriorate. He began setting minor fires until a serious arson brought him to therapy.

Often, early trauma and fear of abandonment are precursors of childhood fetishism. The case of Mac, a stocking fetishist at 2½ half years, bridges the gap between pure fetishism and childhood transvestism. There was no trace of femininity in Mac's behavior, which ruled out a gender identity disorder. Not only did he have an intense fascination for hose, he was almost frantic to wear his mother's pantyhose. They became more comforting to him than his mother. After all, they were readily available and under his control. At 1 year, he suffered from a very painful, unhealing circumcision. Just prior to the onset of his fetishistic behavior, this shy child suffered separation panic when he became lost from his mother in a large restaurant. His attraction for wearing pantyhose subsided until he was 3½, when he again became lost, this time in a hospital. It is as if Mac were saying, "If mother leaves me when I need her to protect and comfort me, then I will become mother and be my own comforter." Some years later, after behavior modification therapy, there was no evidence of unusual attraction for pantyhose (Stoller, 1985).

The preceding case fits well with the trauma–triumph theory of paraphilic origins. Initially there is a frightening or humiliating experience that provokes a phobia. Later, other traumas and conflicts are condensed on this original complex. A counterphobic reaction develops that allows the individual to transform the original trauma and its trappings into a triumph. Fear and humiliation are transformed into that which is sexually stimulating and pleasurable (Bergman, 1947; Stoller, 1975).

There is speculation regarding a heredity component to fetishistic behavior (Epstein, 1969). This speculation is addressed to the questions of what is it that predisposes one to develop a fetish and also what is it about certain objects that make them popular fetish items. Epstein proposed that an anomaly of the temporal lobes produces an "organismic excitability." This accounts for the purported association between fetishism and abnormal EEG readings. A mechanism akin to Seligman's preparedness is invoked to explain why objects with certain properties are more easily associated with sexual arousal than others (Marks, 1972).

Sexual Asphyxia

Somewhat typical of erotic asphyxiation is the case of a 16-year-old male found hanging from the shower rail in a locked bathroom. He was naked and in front of a mirror. Semen was found in the shower. His mood before death was described as "happy" (Sheehan & Garfinkel, 1988).

It is next to impossible to estimate the prevalence of autoerotic asphyxia because it is such a private act. Estimates of accidental deaths resulting from this practice in the United States vary from 500 to 1,000 each year (Hazelwood, Dietz, & Burgess, 1983). One-third of these deaths involve individuals in their teens (Burgess, Dietz, & Hazelwood, 1983; Sheehan & Garfinkel, 1988). These young people, overwhelmingly males, learn about sexual asphyxia by chance, perhaps during an aborted suicide attempt by hanging; by being told by others; and from literature and the media.

The most common method of asphyxiating oneself is by hanging. Other techniques are using plastic bags, gags that lead to choking, and anesthetics. Hanging is effective in inducing lowered supply of oxygen to the brain (hypoxia) by compression of the jugular veins and also the carotid arteries. This results in giddiness, blurring of consciousness, and eventually total loss of consciousness. Orgasm may occur naturally or through masturbation. The ritualistic nature of the act and the risk involved add to the arousal level.

There were definite signs that the 16-year-old boy whose case opened this section died from sexual asphyxia rather than from suicide. In asphyxia, some of the clues are that the victim is found nude, positioned in front of a mirror, with neck protected by a towel, cross-dressed, hands and/ ankles in bondage, with the presence of pornography, dildos, and vibrators. Fewer of these accoutrements are found with adolescents than with adults (Blanchard & Hunker, 1991).

Anal Masturbation

A rarely reported self-arousing activity is anal masturbation. In two reported cases age of onset was 9 and 13. Both boys claimed that they first inserted their finger into the anus to relieve constipation and found both the insertion and subsequent evacuation of feces pleasurable. They denied any homosexual ideation, or having been sexually abused. Neither was psychotic or mentally retarded. The anal masturbation probably would never have come to light had it not been for the presence of feces on the sheet or in their underwear (Clark, Tayler, & Bhate, 1990).

Deviant Behavior Involving Others

Introduction

Sometimes there is a direct connection between adult and adolescent deviant acts. half of adult heterosexual pedophiles attempted or committed a sexual act with a child before they themselves were 16 years old (Groth, Hobson, & Gary, 1982). Three-quarters of homosexual pedophiles were aware of their attraction to boys before they were 20 years old (Bernard, 1975).

Where there is no direct connection, adult offenders may have engaged in other deviant sexual behaviors as children or adolescents. Work with adult aggressive sex offenders reveals this indirect connection. These early behaviors include such nuisance offenses as exhibiting, peeping, making obscene phone calls, and also victimless acts such as fetishism and cross-dressing. Over one-fifth of these adults report that they had exhibited themselves and had engaged in peeping as juveniles (Longo & Groth, 1983). This gives credence to the theory that there is a continuum from nuisance offenses in adolescence to hands-on offenses in adulthood.

Sexually aggressive behavior in the adult is most likely to occur when it is preceded by repetitive behaviors in the juvenile. Another example of the critical role played by fantasy is that adult rapists report that aggressive fantasies accompanied their youthful peeping (Longo & Groth, 1983).

In general, for all varieties of youthful offenders, the median age at the time they are seen professionally is about 15 years (Atcheson & Williams, 1954; Fehrenbach, Smith, Monastersky, & Deisher, 1986). Twenty percent are diagnosed with a psychiatric disorder compared to only 3 percent for non-sex-related juvenile offenders (Atcheson & Williams, 1954).

Estimates of level of cognitive functioning vary from poorer than non-sex offenders to findings of no impairment (Atcheson & Williams; Lewis, Shankok, & Pincus, 1981; Tarter, Hegedus, Alterman, & Katz-Garris, 1981). Still, only about half (55 percent) have an appropriate grade placement. And only about half (48 percent) have not manifested school behavior problems (Fehrenbach et al., 1986). These boys are described as withdrawn, passive, immature, and socially inept (Thomas, 1982).

Mentally retarded youth are proportionally represented in the sex offending group. Most (66 percent) of their victims are children and they are more likely to engage in nuisance offenses than those not retarded (Gilby, Wolf, & Goldberg, 1989).

The sexual offending behaviors of children and adolescents should not be dismissed as examples of typical boyish curiosity. Often such behaviors are not part of normal adolescent development, but rather are symptoms of "pan-immaturity."

Hands-Off Offenses

In a group of about 300 juvenile sexual offenders, about one-fifth (18 percent) had engaged in various hands-off or nuisance offenses such as exposing, peeping, making obscene phone calls, and frottage (Fehrenbach et al., 1986). These interrelated offenses are termed "courtship disorders" because they are exaggerations of the initial stages of the sexual encounter (Freund & Blanchard, 1986).

Peeping is one of the most common of all courtship disorders. Adult voyeurs walk alone at night seeking to view a female disrobing or engaged in sexual activity. The minor voyeur hopes to see the same scenes, but most often travels with a group of peers. The excitement surrounding the surreptitious nature of the act heightens the sexual arousal. Masturbation may occur while viewing, or later with the fantasy of what was seen.

Indecent exhibiting (exhibitionism) is one of the most often reported hands-off offenses. It consists of the deliberate exposure of the genitals to another person. "Mooning," exposure of the buttocks, while indecent, is not considered exhibitionism because it is usually done as a prank or as an expression of defiance, and is not sexually arousing.

Another frequent offense is making obscene phone calls. Juveniles account for the most common variety of such calls. Whereas calls placed by adults involve threats or ruses to get the recipient to talk sexy to them, adolescents employ crude language to shock the listener and provoke an angry reply (Mead, 1975). Making obscene phone calls represents a compromise solution between the desire for contact and high sexual interest joined with low social skills (Matek, 1988). These "unseen exhibitionists" are closely related to those given to indecent exposure.

Frottage, or rubbing the genitals against another person, takes place in sites such as crowded public conveyances, elevators, and escalators. This act is at the border between hands-on and hands-off activities.

Females are almost always the victims of courtship-disordered acts. About one-third are acquaintances of the perpetrator, and the rest are unknowns. Typically they are older than the perpetrator, with about one-third being peers (Saunders, Awad, & White, 1986; Fehrenbach et al., 1986).

Hands-off offenders are repeaters. Almost all (90 percent) of peepers and well over half (65 percent) of exposers have committed prior sexual offenses. Only a few (8 percent) report having been themselves sexually abused (Fehrenbach et al., 1986).

One of the salient characteristics of these boys is social isolation, with half or more having no close friends (Fehrenbach et al., 1986; Saunders, Awad, & White, 1986). But they are not as friendless as many hands-on offenders. They describe their acts as meaningless and impulsive, with the victim selected at random. Many report not being sexually aroused; do not label the behavior as sexual; and deny experiencing sexual release after the act. If this is an accurate description of the situation, it points strongly to serious repression of sexuality (Saunders, Awad, & White, 1986; Saunders & Awad, 1988). However, in a sample of "lower-class, adolescent" hands-off offenders, two-thirds had had heterosexual experiences prior to their first offense compared with only 3 percent of nonoffending peers (McCord, McCord, & Verden, 1962).

Compared to hands-on offenders, hands-off boys are from less disorganized families. They are better adjusted (Saunders, Awad, & White, 1986) and their personality test profiles are fairly normal (Smith, Monastersky, & Deisher, 1987).

Hands-On Offenses

In a group of almost 300 male adolescent sexual offenders, the majority (59 percent) had engaged in indecent liberties, that is, sexual touching and fondling without penetration. About one-fourth had committed an act involving penetration of mouth, anus, or vagina with the penis, a finger or an object (rape) (Fehrenbach et al., 1986).

Adolescent hands-on offenders are typically about 16 years old at conviction. Their first sexual assault occurred when they were 14, but did not result in any commitment. In most instances, victims were female with an age range from 3 to 69. In about one-third of the cases a weapon was involved. Half reported having been sexually abused during childhood and most (76 percent) had their first sexual experience before they were 12 years old. Consenting sexual relations were common. Over half (59 percent) had such a relation with another male, and three-fourths (76 percent) with a female. Their consenting partners were about 8 years older than themselves. However, half (47 percent) reported sexual dysfunction during these consenting relations (Longo, 1982).

Their acts varied in amount and variety of force involved in a continuum from what some described as "consenting," to the use of cajolery and bribery, to threat of force, and finally to force itself. Less violent offenders display no major psychiatric disorders, while rapists showed the most disturbance (Smith, Monastersky, & Deisher, 1987).

Insufficient attention has been given to sexual abuse occurring during baby-sitting (Kourany, Martin, & Armstrong, 1979). Nearly half of the cases of indecent liberties (47 percent) and rape (40 percent) were perpetrated while baby-sitting (Fehrenbach et al., 1986). Compared to adult nonparental caregivers, adolescents engage in more sexual abuse of the children they baby-sit, and such abuse is more likely to consist of intercourse and physical assault (Margolin & Craft, 1990).

As is the case with adult offenders, the specific act is related to the age of the victim. While only a quarter of child victims under 6 years old were penetrated, nearly half (46 percent) of the victims who were age peers or older than the perpetrator were penetrated (Fehrenbach et al., 1986). Also, the use of violence and threat of violence depends on the age of the victim. Where the victim is the same age or older than the perpetrator, 90 percent of the incidents involved threat or force, compared to 50 percent when the victim is younger (Saunders, Awad, & White, 1986).

Most of the victims are known to the perpetrator; this is especially true in child molestation (Awad & Saunders, 1991). For all hands-on offenses, the bulk of the victims are 12 and older (60 percent), with the next largest group being age 6 or less (Fehrenbach et al., 1986). The age difference between the victim and the perpetrator is an important consideration. However, the younger the perpetrator, the less meaningful is this distinction. Compared to those who offend against same-age or older victims, those who offend against younger victims have a younger mean age themselves (15 vs. 16 years). Also, a larger percentage of their victims tend to be males (31 vs. 14 percent), with an average age of 5 years. Offenders against younger victims molested fewer victims, fewer strangers were involved (38 vs. 54 percent), and there were fewer attempts at or achieved penetration (24 vs. 67 percent), but there were more mouth–genital contacts (Groth, 1977; Shoor, Speed, & Bartelt, 1966; Davis & Leitenberg, 1987).

Child Molestation. Adolescent child molesters are loners with virtually no peer group activity, preferring the company of younger children. While many have an IQ in the normal range, school achievement is low to fair, but most always below capacity. They are not as apt to present a history of crimes against persons—including hands-off sexual offenses—as are those who offend against peers and older victims. However, perhaps because of difficulties with impulse control, they were rated as having more problems with physical aggression. Baby-sitting is often the only job experience they have had. Their immaturity is not confined to sexual matters, but is also manifested in school misbehaviors and preference for playing with younger children. This immaturity extends to their lovemaps, which appear rather undifferentiated and amorphous with diffuse object choice. These young men display a notable social deficit and lack of social skills. Compared with those who offend against peer or older victims, fewer of these boys report consensual sexual experiences, and more were judged to be undersocialized. Also, more claim to have been sexually abused and there is a greater prevalence of family sexual abusers (Shoor, Speed, & Bartelt, 1966).

There appears to be two varieties of child molesters, the aggressive and the passive. Aggressive, even sadistic elements are illustrated in the case of 14-year-old Bob. He is of average intelligence, but not doing well in school. A loner in school, he is frequently bullied by other children. He accosted a 5-year-old girl in a bathroom, slapped her, forced her over the toilet seat, and penetrated her anally. He had twice before abused children, using duress. Testing revealed that Bob confused sexuality with aggression, and was concerned about his masculinity. His indulgent parents were defensive, showing little concern for the harm he had done to the little girl. Their primary interest was that no untoward consequences be visited on Bob. Bob's father had left childrearing to his wife and she, in turn, was overprotective and deeply attached to Bob. Because of the aggressive nature of his assault and his parents' attitudes, Bob was remanded to the youth authority (Shoor, Speed, & Bartelt, 1966).

There is another subset of offenders against children who are more at ease with those younger than themselves than they are with their peers. They tend to be passive, immature, and dependent (Groth, 1977). These passive molesters use cajolery or bribery and confine themselves to touching and caressing. For example, since birth Sam had lived with his mother and grandmother. He was the neighborhood baby-sitter. When he was 15 years old, he asked two little boys to fellate him. When they refused, Sam did not pursue the matter further. Described by his mother as a model child, Sam helped with the household tasks and had no interests outside the home. He was of a passive personality, sexually immature, and somewhat feminine. He was sent to a juvenile probation department ranch. During his first weeks there, his mother tried to undermine this placement. Later, however, Sam had considerably improved, felt more adequate, and learned to get along with his peers and the adult staff (Shoor, Speed, & Bartelt, 1966).

It is from the ranks of these adolescent child molesters that adult child abusers come. Twenty-year-old Scott was sexually attracted to boys aged 10 to 12 only. He realized this attraction when he was 13: "I would run around making every kid in sight—anyone younger than I was. I'd talk them into it. I'd . . . fondle him, play with his ass, kiss him, and blow him. I enjoyed being with younger kids" (Groth, Hobson, & Gary, 1982, p. 133).

Forcible Sexual Assault. Of those who admit to forcible sexual intercourse, about a fourth (27 percent) did so while committing another crime and about a third were accompanied by another assailant. These were probably "opportunistic" offenders in contrast to those for whom the act was premeditated. About three-fourths (72 percent) said they were under the influence of alcohol or some other substance (Vinogradov, Dishotsky, Doty, & Tinklenberg, 1988).

Like the adult offense, adolescent forcible assault is an expression of anger and/or power. Like child molesters, adolescent assaulters tend to be loners and underachievers. Their prevailing mood is one of emptiness. They are impulsive and have low frustration tolerance for the ordinary problems of daily living. A pervasive problem involves their masculine identity (Groth, 1977). Compared to youth who assault only, they are more paranoid, estranged from peers, and anxious (Blaske, Borduin, Henggeler, & Mann, 1989).

Some assaulters are extremely violent, for example, beating and stabbing their victims. Such individuals have the highest of all non-sex offense rates, with histories of a variety of aggressive, antisocial acts since early childhood (Kavoussi, Kaplan, & Becker, 1988). Psychiatric problems are common. They may suffer from clinical depression (75 percent) and some hallucinate (47 percent) (Lewis, Shankok, & Pincus, 1979). In a group of outpatients, three-quarters of those admitting to rape and attempted rape were diagnosed as characters disordered, whereas only just over a third (38 percent) of those admitting to inappropriate sexual behavior with others were so diagnosed (Kavoussi, Kaplan, & Becker, 1988). For these rapists, it may well be that their sexual offense was simply one of many ways of acting out, and therefore they should not be considered as primary sexual deviants (Davis & Leitenberg, 1987).

Sibling Incest

Estimates of the prevalence of brother–sister incest vary with the population sampled and the particular definition of incest used. These estimates range from 2–3 percent of adults sampled (Hunt, 1974; Russell, 1986) to as high as 15 percent (Finkelhor, 1980). While many of these encounters were considered by the recipient to be relatively innocuous, about a fourth recalled the experience as abusive. Almost three-fourths (72 percent) of the brothers were under 18 years old at the time of the offense (Russell, 1986). Age discrepancy is most predictive of the evaluation of the experience, with lesser differences resulting in less abusiveness. In most cases (67 percent) the sister is about four years younger than her brother (Finkelhor, 1980).

Incest offenders admit to many more incidences extending over a longer period of time than do child molesters. This greater involvement can be attributed to the easier availability of sisters and the greater secrecy surrounding the relationship. The number of sexual contacts ranges from 2 to 10, with the duration from one week to one year. Probably because of the relatively long duration, sexual acts are more intrusive (sexual intercourse in incest [46 percent] vs. sexual intercourse in child molestation [28 percent]).

Brothers are able to maintain their liaisons by implicating their sister as accomplices. Force and threat are as common in the incest situation (58 percent) as in child molestation (56 percent) (O'Brien, 1989; Russell, 1986). One quarter of adults who have been victims recollect that force was involved. Force is more common when there is an age difference between the siblings (Finkelhor, 1980). Even when threats or force are not used, coercion is present by virtue of the status of the brother in the family, especially if there is an age difference.

As is true of father–daughter incest, brothers often approach their sisters while they are in bed. "I would be asleep and my brother would sneak under my bed and his hand would reach up and feel my breasts. It happened several times" (Russell, 1986, p. 284). The particular sexual activity depends of the age of the participants, with exposure decreasing, and genital touching, fondling, and attempted or actual intercourse increasing with increasing age (Finkelhor, 1980).

More incest victims are female (70 percent) and they tend to be a little older than victims of child molesters; still they are rather young, with three-fourths being under 9 years old (O'Brien, 1989). Adult victims recollect their age at the time of the incest to be between 10 and 13 (Russell, 1986).

Severe family dysfunction is frequently implicated. Indeed, nuclear family incest (22 percent) and physical abuse (61 percent) are rather prevalent, more so than for child molesters. Case managers rate over half (52 percent) of the families severely disturbed with only 2 percent healthy, compared to under half (45 percent) of families of child molesters severely disturbed with an eighth (14 percent) healthy (O'Brien, 1989).

It is often said that incest is passed from one generation to the next. Indeed, one-fourth of mothers of sexually or physically abused children reported having themselves been victims of incest as children compared to only 3 percent of mothers of nonabused children (Goodwin, McCarthy, & DiVasto, 1981).

Adolescent incest offenders are not likely to commit crimes against persons, but are likely to exhibit such antisocial behaviors as physical aggression, lying, and stealing. In one group, one-half had nonsexual arrests and two-thirds (63 percent) were diagnosed as conduct-disordered (Becker, Kaplan, Cunningham-Rathner, & Kavoussi, 1986). School performance is poor, but no worse than other adolescent sex offenders. Definitely under-socialized, they have not experienced consensual sexual interaction (O'Brien, 1989).

Female Adolescent Sexual Offenders

There is little information about female sexual offenders in general, and even less about female adolescent offenders. Most of what follows is based on two studies, one of 28 females seen in an adolescent sexual offender treatment program (Fehrenbach & Monastersky, 1988), and another reporting on 219 incidences from several treatment centers (Knopp & Lackey, 1987).

Over a third (38 percent) of female sexual abusers being treated are under 18 years old, with a mean age of 13. Over two-thirds (68 percent) of the incidents occurred while the girl was baby-sitting. The two studies report widely different percentages of rape (involving penetration) (54 and 16 percent). The other type of offense reported is indecent liberties (no penetration). In contrast to male offenders, there was no history of the usual hands-off offenses. Unlike most adult female offenders, the girls acted alone.

Most of the victims were female (57 percent), and the mean age of all victims was 5. Over one-half (57 to 65 percent) of the victims were acquaintances and most of the rest were related, with 10 percent strangers.

There were no group differences between the girls convicted of rape rape versus girls convicted of indecent liberties. Half (50 percent) reported having experienced sexual abuse, and a fifth (21 percent) reported physical abuse.

Assessment Considerations

There is a plethora of hypotheses regarding deviant sexual behavior (Davis & Leitenberg, 1987), and these should all be explored in a complete assessment. Among these are that these male youths have an inadequate sense of masculinity, low self-esteem, fear of rejection, anger toward females, lack sexual information, and are socially inept. This outline for assessment pertains primarily to sex offenders, but many points are applicable to solo deviants.

An initial problem is presented by those who deny their offense, as about half of offenders do. Deniers tend to come from enmeshed families that support their denial. Compared to admitters, who come from disengaged families, deniers have higher self-esteem, are more dependable, and more often offend in their role as baby-sitters (Sefarbi, 1990). Those who do admit their offense and also show remorse are excellent candidates for treatment.

Another initial task in assessment is to distinguish between innocuous experimentation and antisocial, deviant behaviors. Late childhood and adolescence is a time of sexual experimentation, with many adolescents willing to try something at least once. Previous sexual misconduct was admitted to by 65 percent of a group of "normal" college males. A full 42 percent reported they had engaged in secretly looking for a female disrobing, 35 percent reported engaging in frottage, 8 percent reported making obscene phone calls, 3 percent reported having sex with a girl under 12 years of age, and 2 percent reported exhibiting themselves (Templeman & Stinnett, 1991).

The complete assessment will be particularly difficult if the accused plans to enter an innocent plea, since the clinician might be called upon the testify. In such cases, risk and management assessment is best left until after guilt has been established (Saunders & Awad, 1988). The following topics should be explored in making the complete assessment (Groth, Hobson, Lucey, & St. Pierre, 1981; Knopp, 1991).

1. *Relation between offender and victim.* The more the two differ in age, the more symptomatic the behavior. This is especially true when the activity involved a prepubertal child. Also, extremes of social closeness from near relative to total stranger indicate seriousness of behavior.

2. *Sexual activity.* Intervention is indicated when the sexual behavior is more age-inappropriate, is nonconsensual, is persistent, and when there are indications of progression from nuisance to more serious acts. For child molesters it is crucial to differentiate between the passive and aggressive

type. Use of assaultive or sadistic behavior is definitely a danger signal (Shoor, Speed, & Bartelt, 1966). These are not easy areas to explore since admitted perpetrators tend to minimize their deviant acts. A case in point is the boy who went to an acquaintance's apartment. Pushing her against the bathroom wall, he had intercourse with her. Yet he refused to acknowledge that the gun in his hand at the time of this act amounted to coercion since she did not struggle (Saunders & Awad, 1988).

3. *Examination of suspect himself.* The inner-determined, rather than situational, source of the behavior is indicated if the salient fantasy theme is related to the actual offense. Also indicative is the presence of aggressive/sadistic elements in fantasy life. Such a determination is a special problem when dealing with those accused of courtship disorders since they often deny any sexual component to their behaviors (Saunders & Awad, 1988).

A useful tool in assessing deviant arousal is physiological monitoring of penile erection to "normal" and "deviant" stimuli. This technique is used less often with adolescents than with adults. Phallometrics is yet in the experimental stage when used with adolescent offenders and should be employed with caution and in extreme cases only (Saunders & Awad, 1988).

A detailed sexual history is imperative. One generally accepted explanation of deviant sexual behavior is that it is an attempt to compensate for an early sexual trauma. In fact, as many as one-half of sex offenders report having been sexually abused (Kahn & Lafond, 1988). In an effort to compensate for this unresolved trauma, the individual reenacts the event, but with alterations that turn the trauma into triumph and the victim into a predator. The connection between having been sexually abused and later abusing has intuitive appeal, but it is one that must be established in each case. There is an interesting symmetry between the sex of the abuser and the sex of the abused. Of boys victimized by males, over two-thirds (68 percent) themselves abuse males. If victimized by females, almost all (94 percent) abuse females only (O'Brien, 1989).

Sexual experience, information, and attitudes should be explored. It has been suggested that the offending boys' felt lack of sexual knowledge and experience might lead them to efforts to make up for "lost ground." While one may find such a lack in some cases, the majority (59–86 percent) of offenders have had sexual intercourse or genital experience with consenting partners (Becker et al., 1986; Groth, 1977; Longo, 1982).

Level of intellectual functioning is an important consideration. Cerebral dysfunction has been implicated in the more violent sexual offenses. However, in one test of this, no differences were found on various tests of cognitive abilities among juvenile violent, sexual, and nonviolent offenders (Tarter, Hegedus, Alterman, & Katz-Garris, 1983).

The extent of nonsexual deviant behaviors should be determined. It is also important to identify defects in interpersonal relations such as poor social and communication skills, mismanagement of aggression, and lack of assertiveness. These social skill deficits are often cited as contributing to deviancy. However, it has not been firmly established that these inadequacies are peculiar to sexual offenders and do not pertain to other adolescents. Especially important is the degree to which the individual is threatened by intimate male–female relations. Consideration also must be given to the extent of current life stress, loneliness, depression, and low self-esteem, and to the seriousness of psychological disturbance (Katz, 1990).

Once the decision is made that the person needs judicial and/or professional attention, the next task is to assess the severity of the disorder. In doing this, attention must be paid to the safety of the community, the degree to which the person should experience the consequences of his behavior, and whether in- or outpatient treatment is indicated. The degree of risk is directly proportional to the frequency of past deviant behaviors, the use of force or violence, and the presence of acts that are bizarre, ritualistic, and predatory. Those who present serious psychopathology are at high risk. Signs of psychological disturbance are academic or behavioral problems in school, dearth of or disjunctive peer relations, and deviant or lack of outside interests (Groth & Loredo, 1981). At risk also are those who do not admit responsibility for their behavior and who lack motivation for change.

When dealing with incest situations, special attention must be given to the role of the parents. If parents are asked to support removal of the offender, they can be seen as abdicating their parental loyalty and obligations. However, if they do not support removal, they can be seen as insensitive to the feelings of the offended victim (Saunders & Awad, 1988).

Treatment

The goals of intervention are several. One of the first tasks is getting the youth to accept responsibility for his or her deviant behaviors and to acquire understanding of them. He or she must become self-aware concerning thoughts, feelings, and events that precede deviant behavior. Armed with this information, he or she can hopefully learn how to interrupt this sequence and develop sufficient self-control to stop or divert the harmful sequence of events.

Another goal is to aid the youth in exchanging antisocial, negative attitudes for prosocial ones. Along with this is the aim of encouraging the erection of positive self-concept and the acquisition of sexual self-control. Facilitation of social contact and skills will enable him to engage in mutually satisfying relationships with others (Henderson, English, & MacKenzie, 1988).

There has been a move away from psychodynamic therapies based on the assumption of intrapsychic conflicts toward treatments involving varying levels of personal and social systems. Popular behavioral approaches include covert or imaginal desensitization and aversion therapy. While most of the discussion to follow is geared to sex offenders, many techniques are also applicable to those who engage in solo deviant acts.

A wide range of treatment modalities are available for the adolescent deviant. These include psychotherapy, cognitive therapy, and behavioral therapy. If he is over 16 and the behavior is dangerous and combined with violence, the possibility of antiandrogens must be considered. Also, when the behavior has clear obsessive–compulsive and anxiety components, antianxiety and antidepressive medication may be indicated (Lockhart, Saunders, & Cleveland, 1988). Such medications may be useful in cases of severe fetishism (Lorefice, 1991). Medication, principally antiandrogens, which are used rather extensively with adults, is prescribed in less than 10 percent of facilities treating adolescent offenders (Knopp, 1991).

Since some of the sources of these deviant sexual activities occur in the context of the family unit, family therapy is one of the treatment choices. Peer group therapy is another treatment of choice. An effective supplemental technique is the writing of an autobiography. This stimulates self-observation and points up those gaps in his awareness of his life (Groth et al., 1981). Keeping a daily journal in which activities, thoughts, and feelings are entered is a useful adjunct.

Because lack of social competence and assertiveness are implicated in some cases, training focusing on these areas is indicated. Related to this is training in the management of aggression. And because some of these youths are ignorant about sexual, relationship, and intimacy issues, sex education should be considered. Where deviant arousal has been established, satiation therapy can be employed to reduce the power of the stimuli. To give the patient greater control over his sexual urges, covert sensitization may be used. Here images of untoward consequences are paired with thoughts that occur at the beginning of the deviant act sequence.

Since most often the adolescent offender does not willingly come into treatment, it is often necessary to have a court mandate for treatment. Family involvement is often necessary. However, if the family context is detrimental to the adolescent's progress, then he should be removed from the home.

Posttreatment maintenance programs are crucial. To nip the deviant behavioral sequence in the bud, the offender must be able to recognize those experiences that precede the deviant act, such as boredom, anger, rejection, increase in deviant fantasizing, and urge to use alcohol or other substances. In addition, the offender must learn that seemingly unimportant decisions place him in situations of ever increasing risk of offending— for example, the decision to skip school leads to going to the park, which leads to playing catch with a younger child, which leads to molesting the child (Gray & Pithers, 1993).

In one study comparing the effectiveness of behavioral treatments, it was found that imaginal desensitization was superior to covert sensitization. Compared to adults, adolescents had a poorer response to treatment, perhaps because adolescents' behavior is under more hormonal control (McConaghy, Blaszczynski, Armstrong, & Kidson, 1989). The good news is that reports from several adolescent offender treatment centers indicate that 90 percent of their clients are not known to have been recommitted (Knopp, 1991).

References

Abel, G. G., Becker, J. V., Cunningham-Rathner, J., Mittelman, M., & Rouleau, J-L. (1988). Multiple paraphilic diagnoses among sex offenders. *Bulletin of the American Academy of Psychiatry and the Law, 16*, 153–168.

Abel, G. G., Osborn, C. A., & Twigg, D. A. (1993). Sexual assault through the life span: Adult offenders with juvenile histories. In H. E. Barbaree, W. L. Marshall, & S. M. Hudson (Eds.), *The juvenile sex offender* (pp. 104–117). New York: Guilford Press.

American Psychiatric Association. (1994). *Diagnostic and statistical manual of mental disorders* (3rd ed., rev.). Washington, DC: Author.

Arndt, W. B. (1991). *Gender disorders and the paraphilias.* Madison, CT: International Universities Press.

Atcheson, J. D., & Williams, D. C. (1954). A study of juvenile sex offenders. *American Journal of Psychiatry, 111*, 366–370.

Awad, G. A., & Saunders, E. B. (1991). Male adolescent sexual assaulters: Clinical observations. *Journal of Interpersonal Violence, 6*, 446–460.

Becker, J. V., Kaplan, M. S., Cunningham-Rathner, J., & Kavoussi, R. (1986). Characteristics of adolescent incest sexual perpetrators: Preliminary finds. *Journal of Family Violence, 1*, 85–97.

Bergman, P. (1947). Analysis of an unusual case of fetishism. *Bulletin of the Menninger Foundation, 11*, 67–75.

Bernard, F. (1975). An inquiry among a group of pedophiles. *Journal of Sex Research, 11*, 242–255.

Blanchard, R., & Hunker, S. J. (1991). Age, transvestism, bondage, and concurrent paraphilic activities in 117 fatal cases of autoerotic asphyxia. *British Journal of Psychiatry, 159*, 371–377.

Blaske, D. M., Borduin, C. M., Henggeler, S. W., & Mann, B. J. (1989). Individual, family, and peer characteristics of adolescent sex offenders and assaultive offenders. *Developmental Psychology, 25*, 846–855.

Burgess, A. W., Dietz, P. E., & Hazelwood, R. R. (1983). Study design and sample characteristics. In R. R. Hazelwood, P. E. Dietz, & A. W. Burgess (Eds.), *Autoerotic fatalities* (pp. 45–53). Lexington, MA: Lextington Books.

Clark, A. F., Tayler, P. J., & Bhate, S. R. (1990). Nocturnal faecal soiling and anal masturbation. *Archives of Disease of Childhood, 65*, 1367–1368.

Davis, G. E., & Leitenberg, N. (1987). Adolescent sex offenders. *Psychological Bulletin, 101*, 417–427.

Deutsch, D. (1954). A case of transvestism. *American Journal of Psychotherapy, 8,* 239–242.

Epstein, A. W. (1969). Fetishism: A comprehensive view. *Science and Psychoanalysis, 15,* 81–87.

Fehrenbach, P. A., & Monastersky, C. (1988). Characteristics of female adolescent sexual offenders. *American Journal of Orthopsychiatry, 58*(1), 148–151.

Fehrenbach, P. A., Smith, W., Monastersky, C, & Deisher, R. W. (1986). Adolescent sexual offenders: Offender and offense characteristics. *American Journal of Orthopsychiatry, 56*(2), 225–233.

Finkelhor, D. (1980). Sex among siblings: A survey on prevalence, variety and effects. *Archives of Sexual Behavior, 9,* 171–194.

Freud, A. (1965). *Normality and pathology in childhood.* New York: International Universities Press.

Freud, S. (1955). Three essays on the theory of sex. In J. Strachey (Ed. and Trans.), *The standard edition of the complete psychological works of Sigmund Freud* (Vol. 7, pp. 125–145). London: Hogarth Press. (Original work published 1905)

Freund, K., & Blanchard, R. (1986). The concept of courtship disorder. *Journal of Sex and Marital Therapy, 12,* 79–92.

Gagnon, J. H., & Simon, W. (1970). Psychosexual development. In J. H. Gagnon & W. Simon (Eds.), *The sexual scene* (pp. 15–42). N. P.: Transaction Books.

Gilby, R., Wolf, L., & Goldberg, B. (1989). Mentally retarded adolescent sex offenders: A survey and pilot study. *Canadian Journal of Psychiatry, 34,* 542–548.

Goodwin, J., McCarthy, T., & Divasto, P. (1981). Prior incest in mothers of abused children. *Child Abuse and Neglect, 5,* 87–95.

Gosselin, C., & Wilson, G. (1980). *Sexual variations.* New York: Simon and Schuster.

Gray, A. S., & Pithers, W. D. (1993). Relapse prevention with sexually aggressive adolescents and children: Expanding treatment and supervision. In H. E. Barbaree, W. L. Marshall, & S. M. Hudson (Eds.), *The juvenile sex offender* (pp. 289–319). New York: Guilford Press.

Greenacre, P. (1953). Certain relationships between fetishism and faulty development of body image. In *The psychoanalytic study of the child* (Vol. 8, pp. 79–98). New York: International Universities Press.

Groth, A. N. (1977). The adolescent sexual offender and his prey. *International Journal of Offender Therapy and Comparative Criminology, 21*(3), 249–254.

Groth, A. N., Hobson, W. F., & Gary, T. S. (1982). The child molester: Clinical observations. *Journal of Social Work and Human Sexuality, 1,* 129–144.

Groth, A. N., Hobson, W. F., Lucey, K. P., & St. Pierre, J. (1981). Juvenile sexual offenders: Guidelines for treatment. *International Journal of Offender Therapy and Comparative Criminology, 25,* 265–271.

Groth, A. N., & Loredo, C. M. (1981). Juvenile sexual offenders: Guidelines for assessment. *International Journal of Offender Therapy and Comparative Criminology, 25,* 31–39.

Hazelwood, R. R., Dietz, P. E., & Burgess, A. W. (1983). Asphyxial autoerotic fatalities. In R. R. Hazelwood, P. E. Dietz, & A. W. Burgess (Eds.), *Autoerotic fatalities* pp. 55–76. Lexington, MA: Lexington Books.

Henderson, J. E., English, D. J., & MacKenzie, W. R. (1988). Family centered casework practice with sexually aggressive children. *Journal of Social Work and Human Sexuality, 7*(2), 89–108.

Hunt, M. (1974). *Sexual behavior in the 1970s*. Chicago: Playboy Press.

Kahn, T. J., & Lafond, M. A. (1988). Treatment of the adolescent sexual offender. *Child and Adolescent Social Work, 5*, 135–148.

Katz, R. C. (1990). Psychosocial adjustment in adolescent child molesters. *Child Abuse and Neglect, 14*, 567–575.

Kavoussi, R. J., Kaplan, M., & Becker, J. V. (1988). Psychiatric diagnosis in adolescent sex offenders. *Journal of the American Academy of Child and Adolescent Psychiatry, 27*, 2241–2243.

Knopp, F. H. (1991). *The youthful sex offender: The rationale and goals of early intervention and treatment*. Orwell, VT: Safer Society Press.

Knopp, F. H., & Lackey, L. B. (1987). *Female sexual abusers: A summary of data from 44 treatment providers*. Orwell, VT: Safer Society Press.

Kourany, R. F., Martin, J. E., & Armstrong, S. H. (1979). Sexual experimentation by adolescents while baby sitting. *Adolescence, 14*, 283–288.

Lewis, D. O., Shankok, S. S., & Pincus, J. H. (1979). Juvenile male sexual assaulters. *American Journal of Psychiatry, 136*, 1194–1196.

Lockhart, L. L., Saunders, B. E., & Cleveland, P. (1988). Treatment of sex offenders in social and mental health settings. *Journal of Social Work and Human Sexuality, 7*, 1–32.

Longo, R. E. (1982). Sexual learning and experience among adolescent sexual offenders. *International Journal of Offender Therapy and Comparative Criminology, 26*, 235–241.

Longo, R. E., & Groth, A. N. (1983). Juvenile sexual offenses in the histories of adult rapists and child molesters. *International Journal of Offender Therapy and Comparative Criminology, 27*, 150–155.

Lorefice, L. S. (1991). Fluoxetine treatment of a fetish (letter). *Journal of Clinical Psychiatry, 52*(1), 41.

MacCulloch, M. J., Snowden, P. R., Wood, P. J., & Mills, H. E. (1983). On the genesis of sadistic behavior: The sadistic fantasy syndrome. *British Journal of Psychiatry, 143*, 20–29.

Margolin, L., & Craft, J. L. (1990). Child abuse by adolescent caregivers. *Child Abuse and Neglect, 14*, 365–373.

Marks, I. M. (1972). Phylogenetic and learning in the acquisition of fetishism. *Danish Medical Bulletin, 19*, 307–310.

Marshall, W. L., & Eccles, A. (1993). Pavlovian conditioning processes in adolescent sex offenders. In H. E. Barbaree, W. L. Marshall, & S. M. Hudson (Eds.), *The juvenile sex offender* (pp. 118–142). New York: Guilford Press.

Matek, O. (1988). Obscene phone callers. *Journal of Social Work and Human Sexuality, 7*(1), 113–130.

McConaghy, N., Blaszczynski, A. P., Armstrong, M. S., & Kidson, W. (1989). Resistance to treatment of adolescent sex offenders *Archives of Sexual Behavior, 18*, 97–107.

McCord, W., McCord, J., & Verden, P. (1962). Family relationships and sexual deviance in lower-class adolescents. *International Journal of Social Psychiatry, 8*, 165–179.

McGuire, R. J., Carlisle, J. M., & Young, B. G. (1965). Sexual deviations as conditioned behaviors. *Behavior Research and Therapy, 2*, 185–190.

Mead, B. T. (1975). Coping with obscene phone calls. *Medical Aspects of Human Sexuality, 9,* 127–128.

Moll, A. (1924). *The sexual life of the child.* New York: Macmillan.

Money, J. (1986). *Lovemaps.* Buffalo, NY: Prometheus Books.

Noshpitz, J. (1982). On masturbation. *Pediatric Annals, 11,* 747–749.

O'Brien, M. J. (1989). *Characteristics of male adolescent sibling incest offenders.* Orwell, VT: Safer Society Program.

Russell, D.E.H. (1986). *The secret trauma: Incest in the lives of girls and women.* New York: Basic Books.

Sargent, T. O. (1988). Fetishism. *Journal of Social Work and Human Sexuality, 7*(1), 27–42.

Saunders, E. B., & Awad, G. A. (1988). Assessment, management, and treatment planning for male adolescent sexual offenders. *American Journal of Orthopsychiatry, 58,* 571–579.

Saunders, E. B., Awad, G. A., & White, G. (1986). Male adolescent sexual offenders: The offender and the offense. *Canadian Journal of Psychiatry, 31,* 542–549.

Sefarbi, R. (1990). Admitters and deniers among adolescent sex offenders and their families: A preliminary study. *American Journal of Orthopsychiatry, 60,* 460–465.

Sheehan, W., & Garfinkel, B. D. (1988). Case study: Adolescent autoerotic deaths. *Journal of American Academy of Child and Adolescent Psychiatry, 27,* 367–370.

Shoor, M., Speed, M. H., & Bartelt, C. B. (1966). Syndrome of the adolescent child molester. *American Journal of Psychiatry, 122,* 783–789.

Smith, W. R., Monastersky, C., & Deisher, R. M. (1987). MMPI based personality types among juvenile sex offenders. *Journal of Clinical Psychology, 43,* 422–430.

Sorenson, R. C. (1972). *Adolescent sexuality in contemporary America.* New York: World Publishing.

Sperling, M. (1963). Fetishism in children. *Psychoanalytic Quarterly, 32,* 374–392.

Stoller, R. (1975). *Perversion: The erotic form of hatred.* New York: Delta.

Stoller, R. (1985). *Presentations of gender.* New Haven, CT: Yale University Press.

Tarter, R. E., Hegedus, A. M., Alterman, A. L., & Katz-Garris, L. (1983). Cognitive capacities of juvenile violent, nonviolent, and sexual offenders. *Journal of Mental and Nervous Disease, 171,* 564–567.

Templeman, T. L., & Stinnett, R. D. (1991). Patterns of sexual arousal and history in a "normal" sample of young men. *Archives of Sexual Behavior, 20,* 137–150.

Thomas, J. N. (1982). Juvenile sex offender: Physician and parent communication. *Pediatric Annals, 11,* 807–812.

Vinogradov, S., Dishotsky, N. I., Doty, A. K., & Tinklenberg, J. R. (1988). Patterns of behavior in adolescent rape. *American Journal of Orthopsychiatry, 58,* 179–187.

Winnicott, D. W. (1953). Transitional objects and transitional phenomena: A study of the first not-me possession. *International Journal of Psychoanalysis, 34,* 89–97.

Wolf, S. C. (1988). A model of sexual aggression/addition. *Journal of Social Work and Human Sexuality, 7*(1), 131–148.

19
Child and Adolescent Sexual Offenders

John M. W. Bradford
Gregory Motayne
Thomas Gratzer
Anne Pawlak

O ver the past 10 years, there has been an increased awareness by society concerning the serious nature of sexual abuse and assault. There is a growing body of scientific literature that deals with *adult* sexual offenders, their characteristics, and psychopathology (Marshall, Laws, & Barbaree, 1990). By contrast, the information pertaining to *adolescent* and *child* sexual offenders is scanty. A child sexual offender is someone 13 years of age or less. An adolescent sexual offender is someone between puberty and 18 years of age. As prepubertal deviant sexual behavior is rare, child sexual offenders would therefore constitute a small minority of all sexual offenders. This chapter will therefore principally address adolescent sexual offenders, some of whom could be defined as child sexual offenders. Another term relevant to child sexual offenders is "prepubertal perpetrators." Although the exact nature and prevalence of sexually aggressive behavior committed by prepubescent males or females is not known, the data that is available causes considerable concern.

Studies suggest that contrary to general perceptions, adolescent sexual offending behavior is very common. According to the uniform crime reports published during the late 1970s, at least 30 percent of rapes were committed by adolescents (U.S. Department of Justice, 1980). Further, such behavior was not the result of naive, awkward, indiscretions but instead was indicative of serious underlying psychopathology (Schoor, Speed, & Bartelt, 1966). There are a number of reasons why sexual offenses committed by adolescents have been underreported. Knopp (1982), which reviewing the literature, reported on an earlier published study by Doshay (1943). Doshay reported on 259 adolescent sexual offenders ranging in age from 7 to 16 years of age evaluated in the court clinics of New York City between 1928 and 1934. He was studying recidivism in the adult versions of this group of adolescent sexual offenders. He found that shame and guilt associated with the disclosure of the offender's activities was probably the main factor in preventing recidivism as adults. Prepubescent perpetrators who were treated also had a better prognosis than older adolescents, leading Doshay to conclude that the earlier the intervention, the less the risk of a future problem. Atcheson and Williams (1954) completed a similar study of male and female sexual offenders at the Juvenile and Family Court Clinic in Toronto and also recommended early intervention. Schoor, Speed, and Bartelt (1966) studied 80 adolescent sexual offenders and reported that those adolescents who had molested children less than 10 years of age were schizoid and sexually immature. The first large study of adolescents (N = 1,726) was completed by Ageton in 1983. The study consisted of a national probability sample of individuals between the ages of 11 and 17, and from 15 to 21 years of age. The study was fundamental in that it provided a reliable estimate of the prevalence of sexually aggressive behavior by adolescents. The sample consisted of 2 percent of the national youth population who committed sexual assault in 1976, and 1 percent of the youths who committed sexual assault in 1977 and 1978. Studies of adult sexual offenders report that a number of them give a history of starting the offenses as adolescents or even as children (Groth, Longo, & McFadan, 1982; Longo & McFadan, 1981; Longo & Groth, 1983). Some of these subjects reported first offenses as early as 9 years of age. Other estimates by experienced clinicians reported that approximately 30 percent of all child molestation and up to 20 percent of all rapes are the result of adolescent perpetrators (Becker et al., 1980).

Fehrenbach, Smith, and Monastersky (1986) reported that 44 percent of all victims in their sample of juvenile sexual offenders were less than 6 years of age and 62 percent less than 12 years of age. Similar findings were reported by other researchers (Deisher, Wenet, Paperny, Lark, & Fehrenbach, 1982; Wassermann & Kappel, 1985).

Offense, Victim, and Offender Characteristics

Offenses

Adolescent sexual offending behavior can be classified according to DSM-IV criteria used for adult sexual offending behavior. There are three main groups. The first group consists of individuals who commit sexual assaults and rapes. While this is a heterogenous group, it includes sexual sadists who find "psychological or physical suffering of the victims sexually exciting." The second group consists of those who commit "courtship disorders" or "hands-off" disorders. This group includes individuals with strong sexual fantasies involving voyeurism (seeking out or observing people who are naked), frotteurism (rubbing the penis against a fully clothed woman), exhibitionism (exposing the genitals to a stranger or an unsuspecting person), and telephone scatologia (obscene phone calls). The third group consists of individuals with pedophilia and fantasies involving sexual activity with prepubescent children generally 13 years of age or younger (Kaplan & Sadock, 1991).

A few studies have examined the relative frequency of the various offense behaviors in the adolescent population (Fehrenbach et al., 1986; Saunders & Watt, 1986). In general, about one-third of the offenders were found to have courtship disorders, one-third committed sexual assaults, and one-third were pedophilic offenders. While the literature on adolescent sexual offenders regards these categories as separate entities, there may well be considerable overlap among these subgroups. Abel and Rouleau (1990) observed multiple paraphilic diagnoses among a group of 561 adolescents and adult sexual offenders and found that some offenders had as many as 10 different paraphilias. Furthermore, among the group of sexual offenders, they noted that the typical history began in adolescence, with 53 percent of the offenders having at least one paraphilia prior to the age of 18, the average was two paraphilias and 380.2 sexual offenses.

Victims

In the "hands-off" offenses, the victim was generally not known to the offender. By contrast, sexual assaults usually involved someone known to the offender, either an acquaintance or a family member. In many cases, these offenses occurred when the offender was baby-sitting. The relative frequency of intrafamilial sexual assault would suggest that family dynamics play an important role in this behavior.

"Hands-off" offenses were directed against both children and adults. The victims were almost exclusively females. By contrast, adolescent sexual assaults were generally directed against children. The victims were predominantly, but not exclusively, females (Fehrenbach et al., 1986; Saunders & Watts, 1986).

Offenders

The study by Fehrenbach et al. (1986) examined the characteristics of the offenders. Many of the offenders had significant social impairment. In 57.6 percent of the offenders, the offender was involved in at least one sexual offense prior to the index offense. Sixty-five percent of the offenders were significantly socially isolated, and 33 percent of the offenders were behind in school or had dropped out of school.

The offenders were also examined in terms of a history of physical or sexual abuse. Eleven percent of the offenders had a history of being sexually abused, and 16 percent had a history of being physically abused. A history of sexual abuse was more common in those who committed sexual assaults than in those who committed "hands-off" offenses.

Saunders and Watt (1986) examined the offender subgroups in terms of these characteristics. Among the offenders who committed sexual assaults, there was a high rate of delinquency and violent behavior. These individuals tended to come from disturbed family backgrounds characterized by long-term parent–child separations. There was also a higher frequency of borderline intelligence in this subgroup compared to the other two subgroups. These individuals tended to know their victim and there was no doubt that the assault was sexually motivated.

By contrast, the "hands-off" offenders were better adjusted in school, less likely to be delinquent, and less disturbed. Their family background was less disorganized, with fewer divorces among the parents and fewer parent trial separations. They tended to choose their victim randomly. They described the offense as impulsive and did not experience the offense as sexual.

Finally, among the pedophilic offenders, there was a high incidence of violence in the family background and a high incidence of poor bonding with the parents. In addition to having a more disorganized family background, pedophilic offenders also exhibited a high rate of delinquency.

These studies provide interesting information about the typology of juvenile sexual offenders. However, this data is based on relatively small sample sizes, and it is unclear how representative these samples are of the general population. More extensive studies are needed to better delineate the characteristics of juvenile sex offenders and the differences between the various subgroups of these offenders.

Psychological Factors. It appears that adolescent sexual offenders have a number of associated psychological difficulties. They tend to be socially isolated; they have disruptive social, school, and family environments; and they do not have many friends. They have problems with their self-esteem and their sense of identity. Schoor et al. (1966) characterized these findings as "pan-immaturity" in adolescent sexual offenders. Other researchers have reported similar findings.

Biological Factors. Although psychological factors are associated with the development of adolescent offending behavior, there is increasing evidence of biological factors that might also be important. As already noted, Abel and Rouleau (1990) found a multiplicity of paraphilic behaviors among the sexual offenders they studied. The wide range of offending behaviors exhibited by the sexual offenders would suggest that instead of being related to specific emotional conflicts, this behavior may be biologically mediated. Additional support for this theory can be found in successful treatment of a number of paraphilic disorders with biological treatments including antiandrogens and hormonal treatment (discussed later in this chapter).

Assessment of Juvenile Sexual Offenders

Faced with the social and ethical issues of exposing minors to erotic and sexually deviant material, researchers have found it impossible to establish standards for adolescent physiological responses. However, given the findings that a significant proportion of sexual offenses are perpetrated by individuals less than age 18 (Fehrenbach et al., 1986) and that sexual offending in adults was initiated during adolescence (Groth et al., 1982; Abel, Mittelman, & Becker, 1985), the need to establish reliable and valid means of assessing adolescent sexual offenders is unquestionable. Without benefit of adolescent standards of physiological responses, adolescent phallometric responses have been interpreted using adult standards with the usual caveats proposed about interpreting the results (Hall, Proctor, & Nelson, 1988).

In attempting to assess an adolescent alleged to have committed a sexual offense, clinicians use the same data-gathering process used in assessing the adult sexual offender. It is important to be aware of the fact that a high degree of denial is used by offenders, both adults and adolescents, in the information-gathering process, particularly with respect to their sexual history and sexual offense (Sefrabi, 1990; Awad, Saunders, & Levene, 1984). Comprehensive assessment of an adolescent sexual offender would involve the same process as is used with any emotionally or behaviorally disordered adolescent. This would include birth and developmental histories; educational history supported by collateral information from schools or other educators, behavioral and social history, history of criminal activities supported by collateral information from the police, judicial system, child protection or other agencies; past medical and psychiatric history, including any previous neurological assessments; substance abuse history; and a comprehensive family history. Peculiar to the adolescent who has been accused of a sexual offense would be a comprehensive sexual history and a history of the circumstances surrounding the alleged offense. For purposes of the discussion involved herein, only the latter two subjects will be addressed, though it must be emphasized that a comprehensive history is essential to the complete understanding of the issues and to the subsequent management of the offending individual. In addition, a psychometric evaluation paying particular attention to intellectual capacity, personality profile, and adaptive behavior would contribute to the overall understanding of the adolescent and thus would be invaluable in formulating recommendations for treatment.

In our experience, none of the adolescents who have been involved in deviant sexual activity has voluntarily attended our Sexual Behaviours Clinic for assessment and/or treatment, but instead have been referred by the courts, probation officers, defense council, family physicians, or child protection agencies. In addition, these adolescents have either minimized or completely denied involvement in the incidents. This reality is not inconsistent with the information contained in the literature about sex offenders in general and juvenile sexual offenders in particular (Sefrabi, 1990; Grossman & Cavanaugh, 1990). The task of ascertaining the details of the circumstances surrounding the alleged sexual offense could be monumental and will be heavily influenced by the level at which the individual is involved in the judicial system, for example, pretrial, presentence, incarceration, or probation. Nonetheless, it is important to be able to clearly establish the details of the offense in order to understand the sexual offender's motivation (Saunders, Awad & White, 1986; Saunders & Awad, 1988), and thus his future treatment. In order to facilitate the flow of information, establishing a rapport with the adolescent is critical. For adolescents in particular, the interview conducted over at least two sessions has been used in our clinic in order to establish a rapport and free flow of information, with the first session being used to address less-threatening issues such as personal and family history, educational history, leisure time activities, and special interests. The second session is used to address issues surrounding the alleged offense, sexual history, and a mental status examination.

Most individuals who work with adolescent sexual offenders have developed a format for eliciting a sexual history and the details of the circumstances surrounding the offense. Groth and Loredo (1981) have outlined eight areas that need to be investigated and are important in establishing the details of the offense. These are as follows:

1. The age difference between the victim and the offender
2. The relationship of the victim to the offender
3. The type of sexual activity
4. The extent of persuasion, enticement, or coercion used to achieve sexual contact
5. The persistence of sexual activity, for example, frequency, compulsive or driven qualities
6. The evidence of progression in the nature and frequency of the sexual activity
7. The nature of the fantasies that proceed or accompany the behavior
8. The vulnerability of the victim due to a particular handicap or disadvantage.

Saunders and colleagues (Saunders Awad & White, 1986; Saunders & Awad, 1988) have noted that it is also important to fully explore all of the dynamics involved in the adolescent's behaviour pre-, post-, and during the offense, including the planning, the efforts to prevent discovery, and his perceptions of others' reaction to his behavior.

Like most individuals who engage in paraphilic activities, adolescents endorse cognitive distortions that facilitate manifestation of their behaviors. The more pervasive the distortion, the more engrained the paraphilia and hence the poorer the prognosis. It is also important to understand the motivating factors behind the offense, including whether it was an exploitative act arising out of a pattern of antisocial conduct or one associated with disinhibition and poor judgment in the face of temptation (Groth, Hobson, Lucy, & St. Pierre, 1981).

A variety of sexual questionnaires have been devised to assess the level of sexual sophistication and the cognitive processes of individuals with sexual dysfunction or socially unacceptable sexual behaviors, including the Derogatis Sexual Functioning Inventory (Derogatis, 1975; 1978) and the Burt Scale (Burt, 1980). Cognitive distortions are frequently present in individuals who sexually offend, and these offer a means whereby such individuals could minimize or rationalize their behavior, avoid accepting responsibility for the offense, and blame the victims. A cognition score has been developed for adult offenders that has been found to discriminate between offenders and controls (Abel et al., 1989). The Adolescent Cognition Scale (Hunter, Becker, Kaplan, & Goodwin, 1991), an instrument consisting of 32 first-choice items describing sexual attitudes, values, or behaviors, both the deviant and the socially acceptable, was designed to assess the cognitive distortions endorsed by adolescents. However, it was found that this scale contained items that might lend themselves to a social desirability response, and thus the reliability of the instrument was deemed to be only marginal. The authors suggested that this instrument should be used only for research purposes and they encouraged research relevant to increasing the understanding of the thinking patterns of juvenile sexual offenders.

There has been considerable controversy in the literature about the validity of physiological measures of sexual arousal that classify sexual offenders. Some researchers have reported successful use of physiological measures for the classification and identification of sexual offenders (Abel et al., 1981; Avery-Clark & Laws, 1984; Marshall & Christie, 1981). However, others have advised caution in interpretation of such measures to assess sexual offenders (Hall, Proctor, & Nelson, 1988). Moreover, particularly in the case of adolescents, there are additional social and ethical problems surrounding informed consent, for example, exposing adolescents to erotic paraphilic material and determining the "normal" arousal responses of a control group. It could be argued that clinicians might engage the exposure to the various stimuli used in the phallometric assessment according to the age, sexual experience, and type of offense committed by the individual, but it has been our policy that adolescents under age 13 would not be exposed to violent or aggressive stimuli, auditory or visual, unless these were relevant to their particular circumstance.

Various techniques for measuring male physiological sexual response have been described in the literature (Abel et al., 1981; Freund, 1963). Several parameters including heart rate, pupillary response, and penile tumescence have been used to measure the male sexual response. Penile tumescence by and large has been the technique determined to be the most reliable. A number of techniques including volume, displacement devices, and strain-gauge techniques have also been used. The Indium and Gallium strain gauge utilized in our laboratory is placed just below the glans of the penis by the individual himself after careful instruction by the technician in charge. The adolescent is alone in a cubicle adjacent to the technician's office and communication between them is facilitated by an intercom system. The gauges are connected to a computer system by the appropriate connectors. All instruments are calibrated prior to exposure to the various stimuli to measure changes from baseline to full erection, with calibration for each individual done at the beginning of the assessment.

Each adolescent may be exposed to visual stimuli in the form of videotapes of heterosexual or homosexual erotic activity and slides of adults and children, as well as auditory stimuli using audiotapes depicting consenting and nonconsenting sexual situations such as incest, nonsexual and sexual assault, nonphysical and physical coercion, depending on their own experience and the type of sexual offense involved. Exposure to each stimulus is limited to 2 minutes and responses are allowed to return to baseline before exposure to a subsequent stimulus is introduced. An index of a particular paraphilic activity, such as the pedophile index (Abel et al., 1981) is calculated as a ratio of the deviant sexual arousal response to that of the adult consenting heterosexual response. Indices greater than 1 are considered significant in our laboratory. Interpretations of these responses are made in conjunction with the history and collateral information as well as the psychological evaluation, and are designed to be used as a focus of treatment.

Most adolescent sexual offenders in our experience and according to Fehrenbach, Smith, and Monastersky (1986) have been male, and research has tended to focus on the characteristics and profile of the male offender. Previously females were seen as male co-offenders and accomplices (Finkelhor & Russell, 1984). Fehrenbach and colleagues (Fehrenbach, Smith, & Monastersky, 1986; Fehrenbach & Monastersky, 1988) compared presenting characteristics of male and female adolescent sex offenders and found that female offenders tended to be younger than their male counterparts and more likely to report being sexually abused. They tended to victimize younger children and were less likely to present with the "hands-off" paraphilias such as voyeurism, exhibitionism, or telephone scatologia. While the males tended to commit a variety of paraphilias, female adolescent sexual offenders limited their offense to the "hands-on" victimization of younger children. These investigators warned, however, that societal interpretation of "hands-off" paraphilias, like exhibitionism, in girls as promiscuity, might contribute to the smaller number of females sighted for these offenses.

Concern has been raised about the risk of sexual offending, the level of dangerousness, and recidivism in the mentally retarded adolescent (Murphy, Coleman, & Abel, 1983; Bereiansky & Parker, 1977; Griffiths, Hingsburger, & Christian, 1985). Gilby, Wolf, and Goldberg (1989) found that mentally retarded adolescents were significantly more likely to show inappropriate nonassaultive sexual behavior, equally likely to engage in sexually assaultive behavior, and were more indiscriminate in their sexual play involving both heterosexual and homosexual activity. Comparisons of types of offenses committed by the mentally retarded and nonretarded sexual offenders show that although both groups were as likely to display offenses not involving an assault, the nonretarded offenders were significantly less likely to commit a sexual assault on peers or on adults. Differences between the groups were found in their selection of victims.

Special attention to the specific limitations of the mentally retarded would need to be addressed in the assessment of such an individual. Particular attention should be paid to eliciting the presence of organicity in addition to neurological and endocrinological deficits. Psychological evaluation could be helpful in determining intellectual capacity and personality profiles, but the use of sexual questionnaires and standard written tests would be limited by the level of intellectual functioning of the individuals. Questions have also been raised about the applicability of the results obtained from such testing and also the individuals' ability to give informed consent for phallometric testing.

A treatment/follow-up program for sexual offenders upon their release into the community is crucial for their social rehabilitation. Incarceration often does not pave the way to social and sexual adjustments in the community, and often it self-contributes to social difficulties. An effective treatment program should reduce the risk to the community by helping offenders adjust to society. Unfortunately, recidivism research to date does not justify many treatment programs currently in operation (Furby, Weinrott, & Blackshaw, 1989).

In the 8 years of operation of the Sexual Behaviours Clinic at the Royal Ottawa Hospital as a clinical research program we have assessed and treated over 1,800 paraphilic individuals, mostly males. We provided service for hundreds more in the 5 to 6 years prior to that, but without any systematic program and data collection at that time. A detailed outline of the standardized assessment can be summarized as follows.

Psychiatric Assessment

All referrals to the program have an extensive clinical examination with a psychiatrist in the Sexual Behaviours Clinic early in their admission. Besides the clinical interview, participants complete a computerized diagnosis using the program "Decisionbase" (with assistance where necessary). Decisionbase (Long, 1986) is a computerized diagnostic interview that allows the clinician, client, or informant to diagnose all DSM-III-R disorders. The system gives multiaxial diagnosis and differential diagnosis. The interview is based on Robert Spitzer's structured clinical interview (SCID). This program helps the psychiatrist in obtaining systematic and complete information on all patients. The diagnostic interview of Decisionbase requires approximately 1½ hours to complete. The importance of comorbidity of psychiatric disorders in adolescents is dealt with systematically by this approach.

Medical/Biochemistry Assessment

As part of their medical assessment, participants have several laboratory tests done, including blood work for routine biochemistry sex hormones, urine drug screening, and where clinically indicated EEG (with and without alcohol), SPECT, and CT scan (where suspicion of organic brain damage exists).

Some investigators have suggested that there may be an association between temporal lobe impairment and sexually anomalous behaviour (Langevin et al., 1990; Bradford, Reid, & Currie, 1994, in preparation). Other "organic" factors linked to sexual aggression include hormonal abnormalities (Bradford & Bourget, 1987)

Recognizing the possible association between organic brain damage, increased impulsivity, and sexual sadism and sexual violence, we utilize the extensive resources available to us for the detection of organic brain damage. This allows us to rule out or treat (when possible) the organic damage.

We also use the biochemical lab tests to monitor substance abuse, which is recognized as a common cause of relapse, as well as monitoring compliance with pharmacological treatment such as sex hormones in antiandrogen. More recently we are starting to monitor blood levels of other pharmacological agents we use.

Phallometric Assessment

Among assessment procedures used recently with adolescent sex offenders is the measurement of sexual arousal in response to sexually relevant stimuli. This assessment procedure involves presenting subjects with a standard series of sexual stimuli, either auditory, visual, or both, which vary with respect to the age and the gender of the sexual partner depicted and with respect to degree of coercion and violence depicted. Sexual arousal patterns are analyzed to help determine sexual preference, and deviant patterns can be investigated further and treated (Earls & Marshall, 1983; Abel & Blanchard, 1976).

The research is inconsistent regarding the degree to which various groups of sex offenders exhibit deviant arousal in the laboratory (Darke,

1990). Evidence that subjects can successfully manipulate their responses limits its efficacy for "identifying" deviants or for discriminating between them and nondeviants. The greatest utility of penile tumescence testing and arousal patterns is in treatment where the profile of an individual is tracked throughout treatment and can provide one (of many) measures for follow-up. Furthermore, whether the investigator is interested in comparing an individual to a "norm" or comparing responses across time for a given individual, a profile showing deviant arousal will almost be always be a reflection of deviant orientation. As Earls and Marshall (1983) have suggested, a person would hardly fake a deviant pattern. Profiles showing normal or appropriate arousal, on the other hand, are subject to many different interpretations. Therefore, we interpret the deviant arousal pattern as one indication of problems that should be investigated further and possibly treated. Barbaree (1990) provides an excellent overview of the role of stimulus control of sexual arousal in sexual assault.

Penile Tumescence Testing Procedure. We calibrate for at least a 30mm expansion over flaccid baseline measure, before every session. A CAT analog-to-digital conversion interface (Computer Assisted Therapy, Farrall Instruments) monitors the conductance changes of the Indium Gallium gage, corresponding to changes in penile circumference. The CAT is interfaced with an IBM/PC compatible computer for session control, monitoring, printout, and storage. We use in addition a Toshiba VHS video cassette recorder, a Hitachi 14" color television, a Kodak Ecktographic slide projector and a 40" × 40" screen, a Realistic portable cassette recorder, and stereo headphones.

Videotape. Because of a "warm-up" effect commonly observed during tests of sexual arousal (Baxter et al., 1986), stimuli presented first during a session often produce unreliable responses. To mitigate this order effect, we initially present an explicit videotape depicting sex between consenting adults. The videotape also eases the respondent's attainment of a full erection, which will be used as a measure of comparison for his responses to the relevant stimuli. The use of a powerful erotic stimulus for the warm-up also serves to "prime" the examinee for the relevant stimuli. Patients invariably arrive at the lab apprehensive about the penile tumescence testing. Immediate introduction of the test stimuli may result in no or low arousal measures that are uninterpretable. Viewing the videotape serves to relax the patient, or to distract him from his anxiety and to heighten his total arousability.

Audiotapes. Audiotapes are based on transcripts provided by Abel et al. (1978, 1981). They consist of 2-minute segments or vignettes, each describing sexual activity varying with respect to age, sex, and degree of coercion and violence involved in the scenario. The rape series includes six vignettes (two in each of three categories). Two scenarios describe a violent rape, two describe mutually consenting sex between a man and a woman, and two depict a nonsexual violent assault. Three scenarios (one from each category) are presented with standard instructions ("Allow yourself to become aroused if you feel it") and three are presented with instructions to suppress sexual arousal.

The heterosexual and homosexual pedophilic series include 16 and 18 vignettes, (two in each eight or nine categories), respectively. Penile tumescence as circumference changes are recorded throughout testing and responses expressed as a percentage of maximum erection.

Slides. A series of slides designed to assess gender and age preferences consists of pictures of nude males and females in four age categories (four per category) for a total of 32 relevant slides. An additional four neutral slides (landscape) and blank slides serve as baseline and detumescence stimuli. We may also include a series of 60 slides that depict a violent rape among the stimuli presented to males who have raped women.

Alcohol-Loaded Tumescence Testing. Penile tumescence testing is routinely done without alcohol. However, investigation of an offender's use of alcohol and its influence on his behavior, particularly his offending behavior, often includes a second alcohol-loaded penile tumescence assessment.

Social Work/Family Assessment

The social worker's investigation of the family/social history helps to establish potential supports and stresses for the adolescent or adult offender in the community. Social/family/economic stability will have an important impact on his adjustment in the community. With the participant's agreement, contact with significant others becomes an effective means of obtaining verification of the participant's account of his social history. This contact is valuable later during treatment and follow-up in simplifying relapse prevention.

General Clinical Psychological Evaluation

Assessment of Intelligence. Information about an offender's intellectual abilities is important for assessing his capacity to reintegrate into society and for making decisions about his treatment. There is some evidence at least among rapists that IQ is associated with ability to produce nondeviant profiles (i.e., faking). The WAIS-R (Wechsler, 1981) has been a standard component of the psychological evaluation (WAIS-III is now available).

Assessment of Personality, Attitudes, and Cognitions. A psychological evaluation will usually include the Minnesota Multiphasic Personality Inventory (MMPI; Hathaway & McKinley, 1982) as a global personality assessment. As Knight, Roseberg, and Schneider (1985) note in their review of the psychometric research of sex offenders, the MMPI is the self-report inventory most frequently used in sex offender research. While earlier MMPI research included heterogeneous samples of sex offenders and yielded inconsistent results, later studies have yielded a few 2-point codes prevalent in sex offender samples. For example, the 4–8 (Pd–Sc) code reported in some papers (Armentrout & Hauer, 1978; Rader, 1977; Erickson et al., 1987) may have important implications for the study of some sexual offenders because of "its association with sexual preoccupations and crimes that are extremely brutal, often bizarre and poorly planned" (Knight, Roseberg, & Schneider, 1985, p. 239).

Other objective (e.g., the Millon Clinical Multiaxial Inventory or Millon Adolescent Inventory) and projective (e.g., Rorschach) instruments are employed in the psychological evaluation, depending on the preferences and expertise of the clinician. However, the issues explored or the purposes of the assessment invariably boil down to evaluating the personal (i.e., the intellectual and emotional) resources and cognitive style available to the offender. Information about strengths and weaknesses in these areas, evidence of possible pathology, antisocial attitudes, and so on, is vital for making appropriate treatment recommendations.

Additional Specific Psychological Questionnaires

As well as the psychological evaluation conducted by an experienced psychometrist, participants will be administered a questionnaire package compiled to provide further self-report information about his attitudes, sexual history, and fantasies. Marshall, Abel, and Quinsey (1983) have noted several personality characteristics and attitudes that are prevalent among sexual offenders. Among these are social–sexual incompetence, stress, poor self-esteem, and sexist attitudes.

Several investigators have studied attitudes toward rape, toward women, and toward interpersonal violence among nonoffenders (e.g., Burt, 1980; Burt & Albin, 1981). Studies have shown that rape myths are accepted by most of the general population (Malamuth, 1981; Burt, 1980). Briere and Malamuth (1983), investigating hypothetical likelihood to rape in nonoffenders, concluded that attitudes (toward women and rape) were more predictive of rape tendencies than were sexual frustration or sexual maladjustment. Graff and Chartier (1988), in a study of 72 male nonoffenders, found a positive correlation between "hostility toward women" as measured by Check's scale (as reported by Graff & Chartier, 1988) and subjects' self-reported sexual arousal to coercive sexual depictions. They concluded that this negative attitude toward women is an important component in a constellation of cognitive attitudes and perceptions that lead to positive evaluation and acceptance of coercive sexuality. Scott and Tretreault (1987) examined attitudes among 20 incarcerated rapists, 20 non-sex-related violent offenders, and 20 male controls using the Attitudes Toward Women scale. They, too, supported the hypothesis that the rapists had more "conservative attitudes" toward women, particularly with respect to sexual behavior.

Recurrent attitude themes, particularly hostility and "puritanical attitudes" toward women, emerge from studies of men who are hypothetically likely to rape or who have raped.

The package of self-report questionnaires administered to all participants includes the Derogatis Sexual Functioning Inventory (DSFI) to assess general sexual functioning and specific aspects such as sexual attitudes, drive, and so on (Derogatis, 1978, 1980). The Buss-Durkee Hostility Inventory (BDHI) is included to provide an overall measure of hostility which is standardized on the normal population (Buss & Durkee, 1957).

Burt's (1980) "Rape-Myth Acceptance Scale" is administered to assess the individual's belief in cognitive distortions about rape. Two short scales also developed by Burt (1980) are included to assess "Acceptance of Interpersonal Violence" and "Adversarial Sexual Beliefs." Abel's Cognition Questionnaire (Abel et al., 1989) quantifies the individual's degree of acceptance of several common cognitive distortions or myths about children and sex. The Coercive Sexuality Scale (CSS) (Rapaport & Burkhart, 1984) is included as an additional indication of forced sexual activity (not labeled rape) perpetuated by the individual in his past.

Other salient information will be solicited through this package, including evidence of alcohol abuse. The Michigan Alcohol Screening Test (MAST), which is used in the general population to identify incidence or behaviors indicative of alcohol abuse (Selzer, Vinokur, & van Rooijan, 1975; Gibbs, 1983), will provide a quick screen for alcohol abuse.

A questionnaire developed in the Sexual Behaviours Clinic of the Royal Ottawa Hospital, the Bradford Sexual History Inventory (Bradford, 1987) is included to derive information about the participant's sexual history and current sexual behavior.

The Family Assessment Measure, also a self-report instrument, has been standardized on both normal and clinical populations (Steinhauer & Skinner, 1986). This is included in the package, where applicable, as a measure of the individual's perception of his functioning within the marital relationship and the family. It provides a quantitative assessment of the presence of marital and/or family dysfunction for initial assessment and for therapeutic evaluation and follow-up.

The Dissociative Experiences Scale (DES; Bernstein & Putnam, 1986) is a brief rating scale with good criterion-related validity for differentiating between individuals who have a clinical diagnosis of dissociative disorder and those who do not. This has been included in our sex offender package in response to the suggestion that there may be an association between sexual victimization as a child, sex offending as an adult, and dissociative disorders. This is part of a specific clinical research project at this time.

Fantasy Assessment

Definitions of paraphilias (e.g., in DSM-IV) typically ascribe importance to sexual fantasies. An individual's sexual fantasies, particularly recurring or "favorite" ones, reveal a wealth of information about his sexual preferences. Furthermore, we propose that individuals will more readily reveal information about fantasies than about behavior, particularly when the acts being reported are illegal. One is permitted by law to fantasize about whatever one wishes, so disclosing deviant fantasies will have no legal repercussions. Nonetheless, fantasy data are valuable to us as treatment targets and measures, as well as general risk markers during monitoring and follow-up. Sex offenders frequently report that they had fantasies of their sexual assault, sometimes recurring and obsessional, before they actually offended. Treatment intervention during the fantasy phase, if we can recognize it, may avert the offenses.

We employ the fantasy subscale of the DSFI and verbal reports to therapists to elicit information about fantasies. We also ask all participants to write an open-ended description of their favorite sexual fantasy and to complete a brief fantasy rating scale in a forced-choice format (Greenberg's Sexual Preference Visual Analogue Scale).

The Treatment of Juvenile Sex Offenders

The label "sex offender" applies to a highly heterogeneous group whether or not they are adolescents or adults. As already outlined, they differ in their level of social and intellectual functioning, motivation for treatment, offense history, family status, and in the circumstances that led to their offense(s). Therefore, a wide range of treatment options allowing for flexibility in the design and implementation of the individual adolescent's treatment program is essential. The specific treatment package offered to an individual should be based on background information (referral information such as offense history) and the assessment that was completed. There are individual as well as group treatments. The group treatments as we apply them are directed toward auxiliary treatments to normalize deficits in sexual education, social skills, anger management, and relapse prevention rather than being directed toward the reduction of deviant sexual interest, the fundamental goal of stopping the paraphiliac behavior. The treatments geared to reducing deviant sexual interest are individual cognitive-behavioral treatments and pharmacological interventions. The cognitive-behavioral treatment may be given in small-group formats, usually with fewer than five in a group. Small groups are more cost-effective, but advantage has to be balanced against the degree of resistance to group treatment that is often encountered in adolescence.

Group Treatments

Sexuality and Social Skills Training. Baxter, Marshall, Barbaree, Davidson, and Malcolm (1984) conducted extensive psychometric testing on sexual offenders including rapists, homosexual pedophiles, heterosexual pedophiles, and heterosexual hebephiles (preference for adolescents). They found overall that these sex offenders tended to be unassertive, had low self-esteem had high social anxiety, and displayed negative "puritanical attitudes" toward women and sex. The authors concluded that social–sexual inadequacy appears to be a factor in deviant sexual behavior, and it does not appear to be specific to type of sexual offense. Other studies yield similar results. For example, Overholser and Beck (1986) observed more heterosexual social skill deficits among rapists and child molesters than among non-sex-offender inmates, volunteers with low self-esteem, and college students who were infrequent daters (N = 12 for each group) in a role-play situation. Other investigators have suggested that social–sexual inadequacy characterizes some child molesters, but not rapists (Segal & Marshall, 1985b; Stermac & Quinsey, 1986). Perhaps the inconsistency is related to the discrete way in which these offenders tend to be classified (i.e., the mutually exclusive categories). Data presented by Abel, Mittelman, and Becker (1985) and Bradford et al. (1992) suggest that paraphiliacs rarely have only one paraphilia. For example, men who have raped are likely to have also committed other sexual offenses (such as sexual assault of children or exhibitionism). Therefore, all sex offenders, but particularly adolescents, are encouraged to complete the sexuality and social skills program. Who would benefit from this program is decided by evaluation of the individual rather than on a priori assumptions about the type of sex offender. In adolescence, enrollment in the program also carries the potential for a preventative role against future paraphiliac behavior, for the highest degree of paraphiliac incidents occur after adolescence.

The sexuality and social skills training combines what are often viewed as separate therapies into one program. The approach taken by the therapists is "sexuality in the context of relationships" (i.e., sex education is not taught in isolation from the social context). For example, information about birth control is provided with some discussion of its impact on a relationship.

The goal of this program is to facilitate the development of healthy, responsible, sexual relationships. This is achieved by:

1. Reexamining sexual attitudes, beliefs, and values
2. Improving sexual knowledge
3. Becoming more comfortable with human sexuality
4. Fostering responsible sexual decision making
5. Improving social skills, communication skills, and in general the quality of relationships
6. Dealing with difficult emotions
7. Fostering empathy for others.

Participants receive feedback from the rest of the group about their participation at the conclusion of every session.

Anger Management/Victim Empathy/Cognitive Restructuring. The sexuality/social skills groups do not address offense-specific issues but instead focus on more general skills and information necessary for prosocial behaviour. Another program has been designed to address problems more directly related to their offense(s). This program addresses anger management, victim sensitization or empathy, and cognitive restructuring because these skills are all essential to prosocial thinking. While anger management is often touched on in the social skills group, it receives more direct focus in this program from a cognitive perspective. The role of cognitions and attitudes in sexual offending is extensively documented (cf. Darke, (1990). This treatment component is essential to discourage some of the destructive thinking and rationalizations that allow the offender to continue abusing victims.

Relapse Prevention. After other appropriate time-limited treatment options both in individual and group treatment have been completed, particularly in the case of pedophiles (i.e., both adolescent and adults), continued support and monitoring is essential. There are various techniques for promoting relapse prevention but essentially the therapeutic gains in the previous treatments are reinforced, particularly victim empathy and cognitive restructuring. Although a self-help model may work in the case of adults, it is unlikely to be effective in the case of adolescents. Further, because probation and parole is often a requirement of attendance, staff supervision is necessary and this can be built into the relapse prevention groups.

Individual Treatments

Behavioral Treatments. The techniques we use most frequently are covert sensitization, which can be done individually or in groups, and orgasmic reconditioning in the form of masturbatory satiation. This is modified in adolescents to verbal satiation as adolescents typically refuse to participate in a treatment involving masturbation.

Covert sensitization uses noxious imagery as aversive stimuli in a classical conditioning paradigm. The patient is required to incorporate noxious or aversive images into his deviant sexual fantasies over many trials both with the therapist and alone at home.

The principle of orgasmic reconditioning is to increase appropriate sexual arousal by pairing appropriate stimuli with elicited sexual arousal. It is based on the assumption that stimuli acquire erotic properties by their association with orgasmic pleasure. The procedure requires the patient to masturbate using his deviant fantasies. When he feels close to orgasm, he must switch to an appropriate fantasy. Over several trials, the patient switches to the appropriate fantasy earlier and earlier in the sequence until he masturbates to orgasm to the appropriate fantasy only (Adams, Tollison, & Carson, 1981). Verbal satiation is a similar technique that does not involve masturbation. It requires the adolescent to develop scenes of his most erotic deviant fantasy; if he denies that he has any fantasy his account of his offense can be used. Often considerable therapeutic effort is necessary to establish rapport with the adolescent and to establish the erotic significance of what has occurred. Once the scene has been established, the adolescent is then required to draft a nondeviant scene that is loving, clearly prosocial, and noncoercive. This usually involves mutually consenting marital sexual activity with a similar-age partner. The adolescent working at home repeats the consenting sex scene into a tape recorder, and then spends 30 minutes repeating the deviant scene. The degree of satiation of the deviant scene is measured by self-reported ratings after each session.

Pharmacological Treatments. In the prepubertal years the plasma levels of the various sex hormones, particularly the gonadotropins and the androgens, are low. The physiological changes that occur at puberty are primarily produced by the gonadal steroids, particularly testosterone (Griffin, 1990). These hormonal changes generate sexual drive, through the development of sexual fantasies, increases in sexual arousal, and overall increased sexual interest. Puberty is generally regarded as being delayed if there is no onset before age 15. Puberty begins with an increase in testosterone production in the male at about age 12 years. Following this it rises rapidly through to late adolescence and into early adulthood (Bancroft, 1983, 1989). In females, the process starts earlier with menarche at about 12 years after a rise of estrogen levels since late childhood. This initiates the onset of the typical cyclical hormonal changes that occur in females as part the menstrual cycle. Although the hormonal influences are less well understood, the female's sexual awareness and interest also increases as in male adolescents. In males, sexual behavior is clearly androgen-dependant; mostly based on a variety of castration studies in subhuman primates. Castration leads to a decline in sexual interest, sexual fantasies, and decreased arousability (Bancroft, 1989). In females, the degree to which hormones influence sexual behavior is less clear and discussion of this topic is beyond the scope of this chapter. It is unlikely that a large number of female adolescent sexual offenders are going to be seen by any clinician. And if they are seen, it is extremely unlikely that any form of hormonal treatment would be considered. This would only occur if there was precocious puberty or some other preexisting medical condition that was aggravating the problem of sexually deviant behavior through increased sexual drive.

Most paraphilia begin in adolescence. If there was an effective biological treatment that could be implemented at this time the potential savings in health-care costs, legal costs, and human costs to the traumatized victims would be enormous (Abel, Mittelman, & Becker, 1985).

The pharmacological treatment of adolescent sex offenders involves the use of antiandrogens and hormonal agents, and the use of other pharmacological agents.

Antiandrogen and Hormonal Agents. Antiandrogens and hormonal agents diminish paraphiliac behavior by suppressing sexual drive. These agents would only be considered in the treatment of males. Sexual drive consists of sexual interest, sexual fantasies, and the degree of arousability. These pharmacological agents suppress all elements of sexual drive. There is some evidence that cyproterone acetate (CPA), an antiandrogen, can also affect the direction of sexual drive (Bradford & Pawlak 1987, 1993a, 1993b). The principal pharmacological agents used today are medroxyprogesterone acetate (MPA) and CPA, but estrogens were used in the past (Foote, 1944; Golla & Hodge, 1949; Heller, Laidlaw, Harvey, & Nelson, 1958; Whittaker, 1959). Recently other antiandrogens such as flutamide (FL) and luteinizing hormone releasing hormone agonists (LHRHA) and antagonists (LHRH ANT) have been used.

The use of antiandrogens in adolescents is limited. In the Sexual Behaviours Clinic in Ottawa, antiandrogens or hormonal agents are not used prior to age 16 (unless there are exceptional circumstances such as severe sexual sadism), the outside limit of expected development of puberty. The reason for the cautious use of CPA or other antiandrogens and MPA is that, to a degree, they may cause impediment of puberty, although without serious implications such as premature epiphyseal closure. The clinical indication for the use of antiandrogens in adolescence is hypersexuality and/or a serious paraphilia such as pedophilia and sexual sadism. Another indication is failure of other treatments; in such cases, the short-term use of an antiandrogen is indicated to gain immediate control of paraphiliac behavior while cognitive behavioral treatments are started.

CPA was the first commercially available antiandrogen and has antiandrogen, antigonadotropic, and progestational effects. It is a true antiandrogen, meaning that it blocks the intracellular androgen receptors. As a mode of action it has both antiandrogen and synandrogen effects. Other clinical indications in adult males are the treatment of carcinoma of the prostate. CPA has also been used for the treatment of precocious puberty in children and adolescents (Gupta, 1977). CPA has a variety of actions that affect sexual behavior (Chapman, 1982; Flanigni et al., 1977; Mahesh, 1977; Bradford, 1988). The action that is basic to treatment of the paraphilias is the blockade of the androgen receptors, decrease in plasma testosterone, and its related effects on sexual behavior, particularly sexual fantasies, sexual drive, and sexual arousal. Adverse side effects include fatigue, weight gain, decrease in physical activity, anemia (usually mild), and occasionally a major depression episode. Negative nitrogen balance occurs and is transient. Weight gain can easily be managed by diet and exercise and is dose-related. There is the possibility of some degree of feminization. Gynecomastia during puberty appears to increase the risk of gynecomastia. Animal research has been reported implicating CPA with liver damage in rats with high dose treatment. As CPA is a steroid, this is a general steroid effect rather than specific to CPA (Neumann, 1977). Also CPA has been reported to produce hepatomas in laboratory animals. We are not aware of any of these adverse consequences being reported in humans, although increase of liver enzymes on occasions has been documented. Suppression of adrenal function can occur with CPA, this has been reported in children treated for precocious puberty. This has not been a contraindication for CPA in the treatment of precocious puberty. This is a hypothetical risk in adults, with possibly an increased risk in children and adolescents. It appears to be a dose-related phenomenon and careful medical management can safeguard against it. Reductions in self-reported psychopathology also occur, usually a reduction in anxiety and irritability. Reduction in recidivism of sexual offenders has been reported in studies of up to 5 years of follow-up. The pretreatment recidivism rates were greater than 50 percent and the posttreatment rates were less than 5 percent when corrected for compliance (Bradford, 1985, 1988; Neumann, 1977; Bradford & Pawlak, 1987, 1993a, 1993b).

The usual dose of CPA is 50 mg, given orally, once daily or a depot injection of 300 mg every 10 days to 2 weeks.

MPA is available in both oral and depot forms, known as Depo-Provera, and has been used to treat the paraphilias in the United States. Its mode of action is principally as a progestational agent with antigonadotropic effects without action on the androgen receptors. It increases the metabolic clearance of testosterone (Bradford, 1985). The plasma testosterone level needs to be reduced to prepubertal levels for it to be effective. The reduction of paraphiliac behavior is through the affects on sexual behavior because of low testosterone levels.

MPA's mechanism of action works principally through the induction of testosterone-A reductase in the liver, increasing the metabolic clearance of testosterone. In addition there is an antigonadotropic effect. It also reduces the production of testosterone from its metabolic precursors.

MPA is administered in a depot injection, usually at dosage levels of 300 or 400 mg intramuscularly every 7 to 10 days. It can also be given in an oral format of 100–200 mg daily in divided dosages.

There are some potential adverse side effects of MPA. Weight gain occurs in nearly 50 percent of subjects; suppression of sperm production sometimes occurs temporarily; some individuals experience a hyperinsulinemic response to a glucose load; and others suffer gastrointestinal problems, including gall bladder dysfunction (Hawker & Mayer, 1981). Diabetes mellitus is also reported, as is fatigue, hot and cold flushes, phlebitis, nausea, vomiting, headaches, and sleep disturbances (Gagne, 1981). Moreover, nightmare, hypoglycemia, leg cramps, and some other side effects have been reported by some researchers (Berlin & Menicke, 1981). However, MPA reduces sexual functioning, sexual drive, sexual fantasies, and paraphiliac behavior as well as possibly reducing irritability and aggressiveness (Blumer & Migeon, 1975). The first clinical studies of MPA were made in 1968 (Money et al., 1975). MPA has been successfully used in the treatment of paraphiliac men, but infrequently in late adolescence (Gagne, 1981; Berlin & Menicke, 1981; Money, 1968, 1970; Money et al., 1975; Money, Weideking, Walker, and Gain, 1977).

The use of either CPA or MPA in the treatment of sexually violent adolescents is clinically appropriate in a limited way so long as significant medical precautions are taken, we think that this kind of therapy is best reserved for late adolescence. There is a lack of long-term outcome studies with MPA and to a lesser extent with CPA. Several clinical treatment issues remain unanswered; such as whether treatment should be continuous and long term and what are the potential long-terms effects of such a treatment strategy. If CPA or MPA is used intermittently, what is the risk of relapse? Is pharmacological treatment when combined with cognitive–behavioral treatment a superior treatment strategy as opposed to pharmacological treatment alone? The most important issue is clear, however: effective intervention in adolescence has the ability of being a primary intervention with the potential to save millions in health-care and legal costs. This relates not only to the health-care costs of treating the adolescent sexual offenders. More significantly, the treatment of "hands-on" paraphilias in adolescence is going to prevent the traumatization of thousands of victims and their consequent health-care needs. It is this issue that has driven us and many of our colleagues to look for effective pharmacological treatments that can be used with adolescent and child offenders. What is most promising at this time is accepting a model of "obsessive–compulsive spectrum disorders" that would include the paraphilias. Clomipramine and more recently specific serotonin reuptake inhibitors may be the pharmacological agents of choice in the treatment of child and adolescent sexual offenders. We are engaged in clinical research in pedophilia at this time, attempting to answer some of these questions.

The Use of Other Pharmacological Agents. This is likely to be a very important area of clinical research in the paraphilias in the future. When dealing with adolescents, the use of other pharmacological agents that may suppress the sexual drive may provide an acceptable alternative to antiandrogens. The problem is that the other agents that have been used to date are neuroleptics, which carry with them the risk of extrapyramidal side effects, including tardive dyskinesia. But thioridazine (Mellaril) has been used in adolescents for various therapeutic indications without any problems or difficulties.

In certain cases where there is an organic personality disorder syndrome, in addition to a paraphilia, carbamazepine (Tegretol) has also been used with some success. However, there are no systematic studies that would support this type of clinical intervention at this time.

The most exciting development in the treatment of adolescent sexual offenders is the potential of specific serotonin reuptake inhibitors in the treatment of adolescents and adults with paraphilias. These drugs affect serotonin levels in the brain. Serotonin has been identified in animal research as the neurotransmitter involved in sexual behavior. There have been reports of success in the treatment of a variety of paraphilias with these drugs (Stein, Hollander, & Anthony, 1992; Bianchi, 1990; Emmanuel, Lydiard, & Ballenger, 1991; Perilstein, Lipper, & Friedman, 1991; Kafka, 1991; Kafka & Prentky, 1992). Because these drugs are safe to use in adolescents, if they prove in systematic trials to be effective agents in the treatment of the paraphilias, the potential impacts on the treatment of adolescent sexual offenders is enormous. They have the potential of being a primary prevention, in that the onset of deviant sexual fantasies is during adolescence but the highest level of victimization occurs at a later date. This means that if you could stop adolescent pedophiles, for example, before they start to victimize at a high level, the potential savings in health-care costs and court costs would be enormous. Moreover primary prevention measures prevent large numbers of children from being abused. Each pedophile has a large number of victims, and most result after the pedophile reaches adulthood (Abel, Mittleman, & Becker, 1985; Bradford et al., 1992). We are engaged in research of the use of sertraline in the treatment of pedophilia at the time of writing this report. The results of this treatment look very promising, but systematic research studies are needed to ascertain the effectiveness of this intervention.

The pharmacological treatment of adolescent sex offenders is an area of clinical research sadly neglected by psychiatry despite its potential for primary intervention. There is much to be optimistic about, however, including the specific serotonin reuptake inhibitors which have a low side-effect profile and are therefore safe to use in adolescents. Studies to evaluate their effectiveness are necessary, as is a change in thinking to accept impulse control disorders and the paraphilias as part of an expanded spectrum of obsessive–compulsive disorders.

Other Treatment Options. Other individual treatments that facilitate relapse prevention include pharmacological interventions for alcoholism (with disulfiram [Antabuse] or calcium carbamide [Temposil]) and other substance abuse/dependency treatment options. The abuse of substances greatly magnifies the potential for violence (Swanson et al., 1990).

Measures to Monitor Treatment and Follow-Up

Several indices can be used to assist in making clinical judgements in terms of response to treatment. The following measures are a routine part of the initial assessment, are repeated during and after treatment, and may be readministered periodically as part of follow-up monitoring:

1. Hormone monitoring (This acts as a compliance check for antiandrogen treatment and is also essential for the monitoring of this treatment in any event)
2. Random urine screen for alcohol and nonprescription drugs (This is very important in the monitoring of sadistic offenders and nonsadistic sexually violent adolescents)
3. Penile tumescence assessment at 3 months posttreatment and at 12 months and as necessary thereafter
4. Fantasy ratings
5. Sexual activity and sexual interest scores
6. Computerized progress notes with continuous statistical tests of change in symptoms
7. Where possible, regular contact with significant others by social workers
8. As we move to use specific serotonin reuptake inhibitors, the plasma levels of these drugs will be randomly monitored as a compliance and also to establish the effectiveness of treatment.

Conclusion and Comment

Clearly, a crucial measure of the success of any treatment program is treatment outcome. In adolescent sexual offenders the recidivism or relapse rate is the outcome measure. Further research is necessary, as the risk of recidivism is uncertain at this time. In order to do valid outcome studies, it is necessary to first establish the baseline untreated recidivism risk for adolescents so that valid comparison studies can be completed for all the treatment modalities.

The future is full of enormous potential in terms of the primary prevention of sexual abuse of children by pedophiles by intervening in the treatment of pedophilia in adolescence.

References

Abel, G. G., Blanchard, E. B. (1976). The measurement and generation of sexual arousal in male sexual deviates. *Progress in Behaviour Modification, 2*, 99–135.

Abel, G. G., Becker, J. V., Blanchard, E. B., and Djenderedjian, A. (1978). Differentiating sexual aggressors with penile measures. *Criminal Justice and Behaviour, 5*, 315–332.

Abel G. G., Becker J. V., Murphy W. D., Flannagan D. (1981). Identifying dangerous child molesters. In R. B. Stewart (Ed). *Violent behaviour in New York*. Brunner Mazel (pp. 116–137).

Abel, G. G., Blanchard, E., Barlow, D. (1981). Measurement of sexual arousal and several paraphilias: the effect of stimulus modality, instructional set and stimulus content. *Behaviour Research and Therapy, 19*, 25–33.

Abel, G., Mittleman, M. S., Becker, J. V. (1985). Sexual offenders: Results of assessment and recommendations for treatment. In M. H. Ben-Aron, S. J. Hucker, C. D. Webster, (Eds.), *Clinical Criminology: The Assessment and Treatment of Criminal Behaviour* (pp. 195–196). Toronto: M and M Graphics Ltd.

Abel, G. G., Gore, D. K., Holland, C. L., Camp, N., Becker, J. V., Rathener, J. (1989). The measurement of cognitive distortions of child molesters. *Annals of Sex Research, 2*, 135–153.

Abel, G., Rouleau, J. L. (1990) The nature and extent of sexual assaults In Marshall W. L., Laws D. R., Barbaree, H. E., *Handbook of Sexual Assault: Issues, Theories and the Treatment of the offender*. New York: Plenum Press.

Adams, H. E., Tillison, C. D., and Carson, T. P. (1981). Behaviour therapy with sexual deviations. In (Eds.) S. M. Turner, K. S., Calhoun and H. E. Adams. *Handbook of Clinical Behavior Therapy* (pp. 318–346. John Wiley and Sons Inc., New York.

Ageton, S. (1983). *Sexual Assaults Among Adolescents*. Lexington, Massachusetts: Lexington Books.

Albin, J. et al. (1973). On the mechanism of the antiandrogenic effect of medroxyprogesterone acetate, *Endocrinology, 93*, 417–422.

American Psychiatric Association. *Diagnostic and Statistical Manual of Mental Disorders, Fourth Edition (DSM-IV)*. Washington, D.C.: American Psychiatric Association, 1994.

Armentrout, J. A. and Hauer, A. L. (1978). MMPI's of rapists of children and non rapist sex offenders. *Journal of Clinical Psychology, 34*, 330–332.

Atcheson, J. D., Williams, D. C. (1954). A study of juvenile sexual offenders. *American Journal of Psychiatry*, Volume 3, pg. 366–370.

Avery-Clark, C. A., Laws, D. R. (1984). Differential erection response patterns of sexual child abusers to stimuli describing activities with children. *Behaviour Therapy, 15*, 71–83.

Awad, G., Saunders, E. Levene, J. (1984). Clinical study of male adolescent sexual offenders. *International Journal of Offender Therapy and Comparative Criminology, 28*, 105–116.

Bancroft, J. (1983). *Human sexualities and its problems.* Edinburgh: Churchill Livingstone, p. 77.

Bancroft, J. (1983). The hormonal and biochemical basis of human sexuality. In Bancroft, J., (Ed) *Human Sexuality and its Problems*, Churchill Livingstone, Edinburgh.

Bancroft, J. (1989). *Human Sexuality and its Problems*, 2nd edition, Longman Group .

Barbaree, H. E. (1990). Stimulus control of sexual arousal: its role in sexual assault. In W. L. Marshall, D. R. Laws and H. E. Barbaree (Eds.). *Handbook of Sexual Assault: Issues, Theories and Treatment of the Offender* (pp.115–142). New York: Plenum Press.

Barbaree, H. E., Hudson, S. M., Seto, M. C. (1993). Sexual assault in society: the role of the juvenile offender. In Barbaree, H. E., Marshall, W. L., Hudon, S. M. (Eds.), *The Juvenile Sex Offender* (pp. 1–24). New York: Guilford Press.

Baxter, D. J., Marshall, W. L., Barbaree, H. E., Davidson, P. R., Malcolm, P. B. (1984). Deviant sexual behaviour: differentiating sex offenders by criminal and personal history, psychometric measures and sexual response. *Criminal Justice and Behaviour, 11*, 477–501.

Baxter, D. J., Barbaree, H. E., Marshall, W. L. (1986). Sexual response to consenting and forced sex in a large sample rapists and non rapists, *Behaviour Research and Therapy, 24*, 513–520.

Becker, J. V., Cunningham-Rathner, J., Kaplan, M. S. (1986). Adolescent sexual offenders: Demographics, criminal and sexual histories and recommendations for reducing future offences. Special issue: The prediction and control of violent behaviour. *Journal of Interpersonal Violence, 1*, 431–445.

Becker, J. V., Kaplan, M. S., Cunningham-Rathner, J., Kavoussi, R. J. (1986). Characteristics of adolescent incest sexual perpetrators; preliminary findings, *Journal of Family Violence, 1*, 85–97.

Berdiansky, H. A., Parker, R. (1977). Establishing a group home for adult mentally retarded in North Carolina. *Mental Retardation, 15*, 8–11.

Berlin, F. S., Menicke, C. F. (1981). The treatment of sex offenders with antiandrogen medication: conceptualization, review of treatment modalities and preliminary findings. *American Journal of Psychiatry, 138*(5), 601–607.

Bernstein, E. M., Putnam, F. W. (1986). Development, reliability, and validity of a dissociation scale. *Journal of Nervous and Mental Disease, 174*(12), 727–735.

Bianchi M. D. Fluoxetine in the treatment of exhibitionism. *American Journal of Psychiatry, 147*, 1089–1090, 1990.

Blumer, D., Migeon, C. (1975). Hormone and hormonal agents in the treatment of aggression. *Journal of Nervous and Mental Disorders, 160*, 127–137.

Bradford, J. M. W. (1987). The Bradford Sexual History Inventory. Unpublished.

Bradford, J. M. W. (1985). Organic treatments for the male sexual offender. *Behavioral Sciences & the Law, 3*(4), 355–375.

Bradford, J. M. W., Pawlak, A. (1987). Sadistic homosexual paedophilia, treatment with cyproterone acetate: a single case study. *Canadian Journal of Psychiatry,* 32(1), 22–30.

Bradford, J. M. W., Bourget, D. (1987). Sexual aggressive men. *Psychiatric Journal of the University of Ottawa, 12*(4), 169–175.

Bradford, J. M. W. (1988). Organic treatment for the male sexual offender: human sexual aggression. *Current Perspectives, 528, Annals of the New York Academy of Sciences,* 193–201.

Bradford, J. M. W., Blooberg, D., Bourget, D. (1988). The heterogeneity/homogeneity of pedophilia. *The Psychiatric Journal of the University of Ottawa, 13*(4), 217–226.

Bradford, J. M. W. (1990). The antiandrogen in hormonal treatment of sexual offenders In Marshall, W. L., Laws, D. R., Barbaree, H. *Handbook of Sexual Assault: Issues, Theories and Treatment of the Offender.* New York: Plenum Press.

Bradford, J. M. W., Boulet, J. R., Pawlak, A. F. (1992). The paraphilias: A multiplicity of sexual deviant behaviours. *Canadian Journal of Psychiatry, 37,* 104–108.

Bradford, J. M. W., Pawlak, A. (1993a). A double-blind placebo crossover study of cyproterone acetate in the treatment of the paraphilias. *Archives of Sexual Behavior, 22*(5), 383–402.

Bradford, J. M. W., Pawlak A. (1993b). Effects of cyproterone acetate on the sexual arousal patterns of pedophiles. *Archives of Sexual Behaviour, 22*(6), 629–641.

Burt, M. (1980). Cultural myths and supports for rape. *Journal of Personality and Social Psychology, 38,* 217–230.

Burt, M. R., Albin, R. S. (1981). Rape myths, rape definitions and probability of conviction. *Journal of Applied Social Psychology, 11*(3), 212–230.

Buss, A. H., Durkee, A. (1957). An inventory for assessing different kinds of hostility. *Journal of Consulting and Clinical Psychology, 21*(4), 343–349.

Chapman, M. G. (1982). Side effects of antiandrogen therapy. In Jeffcoat, E (Ed), *Androgen and Antiandrogen Therapy* (pp.169–178). New York: John Wiley & Sons.

Darke, J. L. Sexual aggression: Achieving power through humiliation. In W. L. Marshall, D. R. Laws and H. E. Barbaree (Eds.). *Handbook of Sexual Assault: Issues, Theories and Treatment of the Offender* (pp. 58–72). New York: Plenum Press.

Deisher, W., Wenet, G. A., Paperny, D. M., Lark, T. F., Fehrenbach, P. A. (1982). Adolescent sexual offence behaviour. The role of the physician. *Journal of Adolescent Health Care, 2,* 279–286.

Derogatis, L. (1975, 1978). *Derogatis Sexual Functioning Inventory (D.S.F.I.).*

Derogatis, L. (1980). Psychological assessment of psychosexual functioning. *Psychiatric Clinics of North America, 3*(1), 113–131.

Derogatis, L. (1980). Psychological assessment of psychosexual functioning. In Meyer, J. K. (Ed.), *The Psychiatric Clinics of North America, Symposium on Sexuality* (pp. 113–132). Philadelphia: W. B. Saunders & Co.

Doshay, L. J. (1969) (Oriental 1943). *The Boy Sex Offender and His Later Career* (pp. 168–173). Montclair, New Jersey.

Earls, C. M., Marshall, W. M. (1983). The current state of technology in the laboratory assessment of sexual arousal patterns. In J. G. Geer & J. R. Stuart

(Eds.). *Sexual Aggression, Current Perspectives on Treatment,* (pp. 336–362). New York: Van Nostrand Reinhold.

Emmanuel N. P., Lydiard R. B., Ballenger J. C. (1991). Fluoxetine in the treatment of voyeurism. *American Journal of Psychiatry, 148, 950.*

Erickson, W. D., Luxemberg, M. G., Walbeck, N. H., Seeley, R. K. (1987). Frequency of MMPI two-point code types among sex offenders. *Journal of Consulting and Clinical Psychology, 55*(4), 556–570.

Fehrenbach, P. A., Smith, W., Monastersky C. (1986). Adolescent sexual offenders: offender and offense characteristics. *American Journal of Orthopsychiatry, 56*(2): 225–233.

Fehrenbach, P. A., Monastersky, C. (1988). Characteristics of female adolescent sexual offenders. *American Journal of Orthopsychiatry, 58*(1), 148–151.

Field, L. H. (1973). Benperidol in the treatment of sex offenders. *Medicine Science and the Law, 13,* 195–196.

Finkelhor, D., Russell, D. (1984). Women as perpetrators. In D. Finkelhor, *Child Sexual Abuse, New Theory and Research* (pp. 171–187). New York: Free Press.

Flanigni, C., Venturoli, S., Lodi, S., Bolelli, G., Nardi, M., Di Leo, A. (1977). Role of Androgens in Clinical Disorders. In Martini, L., Motta, M. *Androgens and Antiandrogens* (pp. 201–229). New York: Raven Press.

Foote, I. M. (1944). Diethylstilbestrol in the management of psychopathological states in males. *Journal of Nervous and Mental Disease, 99,* 928–935.

Freund, K. (1963). A laboratory method for diagnosing predominance of homo or heteroerotic interest in the male. *Behaviour Research and Therapy, 1,* 85–93.

Freund, K. (1980). Therapeutic sex drive production. *Acta Psychiatrica Scandinavica,* Suppl, 62, 5–38).

Furby, I., Wiiniott, M., & Blackshaw, I. (1989). Sex offender recidivism. A review. *Psychological Bulletin, 105,* (1), 3–30.

Gagne, P. (1981). Treatment of sex offenders with medroxyprogesterone acetate. *American Journal of Psychiatry, 138*(5), 644–646).

Gibbs, L. (1983). Validity and reliability of the Michigan Alcoholism Screening Test. A Review. *Drug and Alcoholism Dependence, 12,* 279–285.

Gilby, R., Wolf, L., Goldberg, B. (1989). Mentally retarded adolescent offenders. A survey and private study. *Canadian Journal of Psychiatry, 34,* 442–548.

Golla, F. L., Hodge, S. R. (1944). Hormone treatment of sexual offenders. *Lancet, 1,* 1006–1007.

Gordon, G. et al. (1970). Effect of medroxyprogesterone acetate (Provera) on the Metabolism of biological activity of testosterone. *Journal of Clinical Endocrinology, 30,* 449–456.

Graff, L. A., Chartier, B. (1988). Hostility toward women and men's responses to sexual stimuli. Paper presented at the Annual Convention of the Canadian Psychological Association, Montreal, Canada.

Griffin, J. A. D. (1990). Disorders of the testes and male reproductive tract. In J. D. Wilson, D. W. Foster (Eds), *Textbook of Endocrinology* (7th Ed., pp. 273–276).

Griffiths, D., Hingsburger, D., Christian, R. (1985). Treating developmentally handicapped sexual offenders. The York Behaviour Management Series Treatment Program. *Psychological Aspects of Mental Retardation Review, 4* (12), 49–54.

Grossman, L. S., Cavanaugh, J. L. (1990). Psychopathology in denial in alleged sexual offenders. *Journal of Nervous and Mental Disease, 178* (12), 739–744.

Groth, A. N., Hobson, W. E., Lucy, K. P., St. Pierre, J. (1981). Juvenile sexual offenders: guidelines for treatment. *International Journal of Offender Therapy and Comparative Criminology, 25,* 265–272.

Groth, A. N., Loredo, C. N. (1981). Juvenile sexual offenders: guidelines for assessment. *Journal of Offender Therapy and Comparative Criminology, 25,* 31–39.

Groth, N. A., Longo R. E., McFadan, J. (1982). Recidivism amongst rapists and child molesters. *Crime and Delinquency, 28:* 450–458.

Gupta, D. (1977). Androgens and antiandrogens in relation to human sexual maturity. In Martini, L., Motta, M. (Eds). *Androgens and Antiandrogens* (pp. 295–309). New York: Raven Press.

Hall, J. C. N., Proctor, W. C., Nelson, G. M. (1988). Validity of physiological measures of pedophilic sexual arousal in a sexual offender population. *Journal of Consulting and Clinical Psychology, 56,* 1, 118–122.

Hathaway, S. R., McKinley, J. C. (1982). *Minnesota Multiphasic Personality Inventory.* Minneapolis: The University of Minnesota Press.

Hawker, P. A., Mayer, W. J. (1981). Medroxyprogesterone acetate treatment for paraphilic sex offenders. In J. R. Hayes, T. K. Roberts and K.S. Solway (Eds) *Violence and the Violent Individual* (pp. 353–373). New York: S P Medical and Scientific Books.

Heller, C. G., Laidlaw, M. W., Harvey, H. T. et al. (1958). Effects of progestational compounds on the reproductive processes of the human male. *Annals of the New York Academy of Sciences, 71,* 649–655).

Hudson, S. M., Seto, M. C. (1993). Sexual assault in society: The role of juvenile offenders. In H. E. Barbaree, W. M. Marshall, S.N. Hudon, (Eds.), *Juvenile Sexual Offenders* (pp. 1–24). New York: Guilford Press

Hunter, J. A., Becker, J. V., Kaplan, M., Goodwin, D. W. (1991). Reliability and discriminative utility of adolescent cognition scale for juvenile sexual offenders. *Annals of Sex Research, 4,* 281–286.

Kafka M. P. (1991). Successful antidepressant treatment of nonparaphilic sexual addictions and paraphilias in men. *Journal of Clinical Psychiatry, 52* (2), 60–65.

Kafka, M. P., Prentky R. (1992). A comparative study of nonparaphilic sexual addictions and paraphilias in men. *Journal of Clinical Psychiatry, 53,* 354–350.

Kaplan, H. I., Saddock, B. J. (1991). *Synopsis of Psychiatry: Behavioral Sciences and Clinical Psychiatry* (6th Ed., pp. 443–448). Baltimore: Williams and Wilkins.

Knight, R.A., Roseberg, R. and Schneider, B.A. (1985). Classification of sexual offenders. Perspectives, methods and validation. In A.W. Burgess (Ed). *Rape and Sexual Assault* (pp. 222–293). New York: Garland Publishing Inc.

Knopp, F.H. (1982). *Remedial Intervention in Adolescent Sex Offences: Nine Program Descriptions.* Orwell, Vermont: Fay Honey Knoff.

Langevin, R., Patich, D., Hucker, S., Newman, S., Ramsey, G., Pope, S., Geller, G., Anderson, C. (1979). Affect of assertive training: provera and sexual therapists in the treatment of genital exhibitionism. *Journal of Behavioral Therapy and Experimental Psychiatry, 10,* 275–282.

Langevin, R. (1990). Sexual anomalies and the brain. In. W.L. Marshall, D. R. Laws and H. E. Barbaree (Eds.). *Handbook of Sexual Assault: Issues, Theories and Treatment of the Offender* (pp.103–113). New York: Plenum Press.

Long, P. (1986). *Decisionbase.* Vancouver (Computer Software).

Longo, R. E., McFadin, B. (1981). Sexually inappropriate behaviour: Development of the sexual offender. *Law and Order, 29,* 21–23.

Longo, R. E., Groth, A. N., 1983. Juvenile sexual offences and histories of adult rapists and child molesters. *International Journal of Offender Therapy and Comparative Criminology*, 27, 150–155.

Mahesh, V. (1977). Excessive androgen secretion and the use of antiandrogens in endocrine therapy. In Martini, L., Motta, M., *Androgens and Antiandrogens* (pp. 321–327). New York: Raven Press.

Malamuth, N. M. (1981). Rape proclivity among males. *Journal of Social Issues*, 37(4), 138–157.

Marshall, W. L., Christie, M. M. (1981). Pedophilia and aggression. *Criminal Justice and Behaviour*, 8, 145–158.

Marshall, W.L., Abel, G.G., Quinsey, V.L. (1983). The assessment and treatment of sexual offenders. In *Sexual Aggression and the Law* (pp. 43–52).

Marshall, W. L., Laws, D. R., Barbaree, H. E., (1990). *Handbook of Sexual-Assault, Issues, Theories and Treatment of the Offender*. New York: Plenum Press.

Money, J. (1968) Discussion of the hormonal inhibition of libido in male sex offenders. In R. Michael (Ed), *Endocrinology and Human Behaviour* (p.169). London: Oxford University Press.

Money, J. (1970). Use of androgen depleting hormone in the treatment of male sex offenders, *Journal of Sex Research*, 6, 165–172; 29.

Money, J. (1972). The therapeutic use of androgen depleting hormone. *International Psychiatric Clinics*, 8, 165–174.

Money, J., Weideking, C., Walker, P., Migeon, C., Mayer, W., Borgaonkar, D (1975). 47 XYY and 46 XY males with antisocial and/or sex offending behaviour: antiandrogen therapy plus counselling, *Psychoneuroendocrinology*, 1, 165–178.

Money, J. M., Weideking, C., Walker, P. A., Gain, D. (1977). Combined antiandrogen and counselling program for treatment of 46 XY and 47 XYY sex offenders. In E. Sachar (Ed) *Hormones, Behaviour and Psychopathology* (pp. 105–120). New York: Raven Press.

Murphy, W. D., Coleman, E. M., Abel, G. G. (1983). Human sexuality in the mentally retarded. In Matsol, J. L., Andrask, F. (eds.). *Treatment Issues and Innovations in Mental Retardation*. New York: Plenum Publishing Corporation.

Neumann, F. (1977). Pharmacology and potential use of cyproterone acetate. *Hormone and Metabolic Research*, 9, 1–13.

Overholser, J. C., Beck, S. (1986). Multimethod assessment of rapists, child molesters, and three control groups on behavioural and psychological measures. *Journal of Consulting and Clinical Psychology*, 54(5), 682–687.

Perilstein R. D., Lipper S., Friedman L. J. (1991). Three cases of paraphilias responsive to fluoxetine treatment, *Journal of Clinical Psychiatry*, 52, 169–170, 1991.

Rader, C. M. (1977). MMPI profile types of exposers, rapists and assaulters in a court service population. *Journal of Consulting and Clinical Psychology*, 45, 61–69.

Rapaport, K., Burkhart, B.R. (1984). Personality and attitudinal characteristics of sexually coercive college males. *Journal of Abnormal Psychology*, 93(2), 216–221.

Saunders, E., Watt, G.A. (1986). Male adolescent sexual offenders: the offender and the offence. *Canadian Journal of Psychiatry*, 122, 52–549.

Saunders, E., Watt, G. A. (1988). Assessment, management and treatment planning for the male adolescent sexual offender. *American Journal of Orthopsychiatry*, 54(4): 571–579.

Scott, R. L. and Tretreault, L. A. (1987). Attitudes of rapists and other violent offenders toward women. *Journal of Social Psychology, 127*(4), 375–380.

Sefrabi, R. (1990). Admitters and deniers among adolescent sex offenders and their families: A Preliminary Study. *American Journal of Orthopsychiatry, 60*(3), 460–465.

Segal, Z. V., Marshall, W. L. (1985). A self-report and behavioural assertion in two groups of sexual offenders. *Journal of Behaviour Therapy and Experimental Psychiatry, 16*, 223–229.

Segal, Z. V., Marshall, W. L. (1985b). Heterosexual social skills in a population of rapists and child molesters. *Journal of Consulting and Clinical Psychology, 53*, 55–63.

Selzer, M., Vinokur, A., Van Rooijan, L. (1975). A self-administered short Michigan Alcoholism Screening Test (S.M.A.S.T.). *Journal of Studies on Alcohol, 36*(1), 117–126.

Shoor, M., Speed, M., Bartelt, T. C. (1966). Syndrome of the adolescent child molester. *American Journal of Psychiatry, 122*, 783–900.

Steckman, P., Geerts, F. Is Benperidol (RF504). A specific drug for the treatment of excessive and disinhibited sexual behaviour. *Acta Neurologica Psychiatrica Belgique, 66*, 1030–1040; 36.

Stein, D. J., Hollander, E., Anthony, D. T. et al. (1992). Serotonergic medications for sexual obsessions, sexual addictions and paraphilias. *Journal of Clinical Psychiatry, 53*, 267–271.

Steinhauer, H. A., Skinner, P. D. (1986). The Family Assessment Measure.

Stermac, L. E., Quincy, V. L. (1986). Social competence amongst rapists. *Behavioural Assessment, 8*, 171–185.

Tennent, G., Bancroft, J., Cass, J (1974). The control of deviant sexual behaviour by drugs: a double-blind control study of benperidol, chlorpromazine and placebo. *Archives of Sexual Behaviour, 3*, 261–271.

Wasserman, J., Kappel, S. (1985). *Adolescent Sexual Offenders in Vermont*. Burlington, Vermont: Department of Health.

Wawrose F.E., Sisto T. M. (1992). Clomipramine and a case of exhibitionism. *American Journal of Psychiatry, 149*, 843.

Wechsler, D. (1981). WAIS-R Manual: Wechsler Adult Intelligence Scale Revised. New York: Psychological Corporation.

Weideking, C., Money, J., Walker, P. A. (1979). Follow-up of 11 XYY males with impulsive and/or sex offending behaviour. *Psychological Medicine, 9*, 287–292.

White, G. (1986). Male adolescent sexual offenders: the offender and the offence. *Canadian Journal of Psychiatry, 31*, 542–549.

Whittaker, L. H. (1959). Estrogens and psychosexual disorders, *Medical Journal of Australia, 2*, 547–549.

Wormith, J. S. (1986). Assessing deviant sexual arousal: Physiological and cognitive aspects. *Advances in Behaviour Research and Therapy, 8*(3), 101–137.

Index

477

Mental retardation
  Klinefelter's syndrome and,
    105–6
  in sexual offenders, 454
  Turner's syndrome and, 102
Michigan Alcohol Screening Test
    (MAST), 459
Micropenis, 120–23
Minnesota Multiphasic Personali-
    ty Inventory (MMPI),
    457–58
Moderation, sexual, 352
Molestation by adolescents,
    434–35, 447. *See also* Sex-
    ual abuse
Monitoring, 180
Mooning, 432
Morality, homosexuality and,
    306–8
Motayne, G., 11
Mothers
  adolescent, 398
  role in fetish acquisition, 428
  sexual victimization and,
    155–56
Mullerian (female) structure, 112
Multiple-choice questions, 216
Multiple personality, 144–45

National Longitudinal Survey of
    Youth, 397
National Summit Conference on
    Diagnosing Child Sexual
    Abuse, 21
National Survey of Children, 388,
    394, 407
National Survey of Families and
    Households, 405
National Youth Survey, 389, 390
Needs, sexual expression and, 19
Neuroleptics, 467
Neurotransmitters, noradrenergic,
    236

Nocturnal emissions, 36
Nolten, Patrick W., 8
Nondirective model for family life
    education, 46–48
Nonexploitive permissiveness
    without affection standard,
    384, 387
Nonmarital sexual behavior,
    381–413
  abortion and, 381, 398–400,
    409
  acquaintance or "date" rape,
    394–96, 409
  cohabitation and, 405–8, 409
  onset of, 388–89
  postabortion syndrome,
    400–404
  premarital sexual standards,
    384–88
  rate of, 389–91
  religiosity and, 385, 386, 387,
    396, 398, 399–400, 408,
    409
  research on, problems with,
    381–82
  sexually transmitted diseases
    and, 391–94, 409
  unplanned pregnancies and,
    396–98, 409
Noradrenergic neurotransmitters,
    236
Nudity in the home, 34–35
Nuisance offenses (hands-off
    offenses), 431–33, 447–48

Objects, arousal by (fetishism),
    417–19
Obscene phone calls, 432, 448
Obsessive–compulsive spectrum
    disorders, model of, 466
Organic brain damage, sexual
    offenders and, 455
Orgasm, 36

About the Editor

George A. Rekers, Ph.D., FAClinP, is Professor of Neuropsychiatry and Behavioral Science at the University of South Carolina School of Medicine, where he was elected Chairman of the Medical School Faculty in Psychology and where he also serves as the Research Director for the Child and Adolescent Psychiatry Outpatient Service of the Hall Psychiatric Institute. His university hospital teaching, research, and clinical duties focus on his specialization in child and adolescent sexual disorders. He has published well over 100 academic journal articles and textbook chapters, as well as seven books, on various child and adolescent psychosexual disorders and family interventions. His other books include *Shaping Your Child's Sexual Identity*, *Making Up the Difference: Help for Single Parents with Teenagers*, *Family Building: Six Characteristics of a Strong Family*, and *Counseling Families*. His clinical and research expertise is regularly sought out both nationally and internationally, such that he has delivered numerous invited lectures and professional consultations at leading universities and academic academies in Europe, Africa and Asia, including recently the countries of Austria, the Czech Republic, the former Soviet Republic of Estonia, France, the former Soviet Republic of Georgia, Germany, the Netherlands, Poland, Russia, the Republic of Slovakia, the former Soviet Academy of Sciences, the Republic of South Africa, Spain, the Royal Kingdom of Swaziland, and the World Laboratory.

Because of his leading scholarship in child and adolescent sexuality, clinical psychology, and related family issues, Professor Rekers has often been invited to give expert testimony in the areas of child and adolescent sexual problems and clinical services to public policy makers, including the U.S. Senate Subcommittee on Family and Human Services, the U.S. House of Representatives Select Committee on Children, Youth, and Families, the U.S. Attorney General's Task Force on Family Violence, and various state legislative hearings. His invited professional consultation has been sought on such issues as sex education, adolescent pregnancy prevention, adolescent health, sexual transmission of AIDS, family policy, strengthening families, and treatment programs, by the White House Domestic Policy Council, the White House Office of Policy Analysis, the Secretary of the

U.S. Department of Health and Human Services, the National Institute of National Health, the Deputy Assistant Secretary for Population Affairs of the HHS Office of Adolescent Pregnancy Programs, the Director of the HHS Office for Families, the Assistant Secretary for Human Development Services, the Office of the U. S. Secretary of Education, the National Institute of Education, the Undersecretary of the U.S. Department of Education, the Family Policy Office of the U.S. Department of Defense, the U.S. Congressional Office of Technology Assessment, and the South Carolina Governor's Office Children's Case Resolution System and Continuum of Care for Mentally Ill Children.

The National Institute of Mental Health awarded Professor Rekers several major grant awards for his research on the assessment and treatment of childhood sexual identity or gender identity disorders. He has also received grants from the Administration for Children, Youth, and Families of the U. S. Department of Health and Human Services, and the National Institute on Alcoholism and Alcohol Abuse. His doctoral fellowship grant was received from the National Science Foundation, while his postdoctoral fellowship at Harvard University was competitively awarded by the Foundations' Fund for Research in Psychiatry.

Professor Rekers has served as Consulting Editor and on the Editorial Boards of the Journal of Genetic Psychology and *Genetic, Social, and General Psychology Monographs.* He has been an advisory editor or reviewer for the *Journal of Sex Research, Child Development,* the *Journal of Consulting and Clinical Psychology,* the *Journal of Abnormal Child Psychology,* the *Journal of Pediatric Psychology, Behavioral Assessment,* the *Journal of Applied Behavioral Analysis,* and the *Journal of Behavior Therapy and Experimental Psychiatry .*

His clinical research career in child and adolescent sexual problems began in 1970 at the University of California at Los Angeles, when the internationally-acclaimed clinical child psychologist, Dr. O. Ivar Lovaas, his major professor, assigned him a dissertation research topic on the assessment and treatment of childhood gender identity disturbances. Then after receiving his Ph.D. in developmental psychology and psychopathology from UCLA in 1972, George Rekers accepted a postdoctoral research fellowship in clinical psychology at Harvard University as a Visiting Scholar in the Center for the Behavioral Sciences. His postdoctoral clinical internship was completed in 1974 at the Division of Child and Adolescent Psychiatry at the Tufts University School of Medicine/New England Medical Center Hospital in conjunction with the Boston Veterans Administration Hospital.

Licensed as a clinical psychologist in 1974, Dr. Rekers returned to UCLA as an Assistant Research Psychologist, Staff Psychologist in the UCLA Psychology Clinic, and Adjunct Assistant Professor of Psychology. In 1977, Dr. Rekers became Associate Professor and Chief Psychologist of the Division of Child and Adolescent Psychiatry at the University of Florida College of Medicine. Immediately prior to his present position at the University of South Carolina, Dr. Rekers served as Department Head and Professor of Family and Child Development at Kansas State University from 1980 to 1985.

Dr. Rekers was previously the President of the nonprofit Logos Research Institute, Inc., from 1975 to 1985. He also served as the founding Chairman and Chief Executive Officer of the Family Research Council of America, Inc., in the 1980's.

A part-time practicing clinician since 1974, Dr. Rekers was awarded the Diplomate in Clinical Psychology in 1979 from the American Board of Professional Psychology. He became a Fellow and Diplomate in Medical Psychotherapy of the American Board of Medical Psychotherapists in 1987. In 1994, he was elected a Fellow of the Academy of Clinical Psychology (FAClinP).

Dr. Rekers has been married since 1972 to his wife, Sharon, and they have five sons, Steven, Andrew, Matthew, Timothy, and Mark.